Holistic Public Agency in Complex Environments

Mirko Pečarič
Faculty of Public Administration, University of Ljubljana, Slovenia

A volume in the Advances in Public Policy and
Administration (APPA) Book Series

Published in the United States of America by
IGI Global
Information Science Reference (an imprint of IGI Global)
701 E. Chocolate Avenue
Hershey PA, USA 17033
Tel: 717-533-8845
Fax: 717-533-8661
E-mail: cust@igi-global.com
Web site: http://www.igi-global.com

Copyright © 2024 by IGI Global. All rights reserved. No part of this publication may be reproduced, stored or distributed in any form or by any means, electronic or mechanical, including photocopying, without written permission from the publisher. Product or company names used in this set are for identification purposes only. Inclusion of the names of the products or companies does not indicate a claim of ownership by IGI Global of the trademark or registered trademark.
Library of Congress Cataloging-in-Publication Data

Names: Pečarič, Mirko, author.
Title: Holistic public agency in complex environments / Mirko Pečarič.
Description: Hershey, PA : Information Science Reference, [2024] | Includes
  bibliographical references and index. | Summary: "The topic of public
  agencies is an important and relevant issue in the world today because
  these organisations play a crucial role in providing essential services
  to citizens and promoting public welfare. As the world becomes more
  complex, diverse, and interconnected, the functions and responsibilities
  of public agencies continue to expand and evolve to meet new challenges
  and demands. In many countries, there is an ongoing debate about the
  appropriate role and scope of public agencies, with some advocating for
  greater privatisation and market-based approaches, while others argue
  for the need for stronger and more robust public institutions. Recent
  events such as the COVID-19 pandemic have highlighted the importance of
  well-functioning public agencies in addressing public health
  emergencies, providing critical services to vulnerable populations, and
  ensuring public safety"-- Provided by publisher.
Identifiers: LCCN 2023021227 (print) | LCCN 2023021228 (ebook) | ISBN
  9798369305072 (hardcover) | ISBN 9798369305089 (paperback) | ISBN
  9798369305096 (ebook)
Subjects: LCSH: Administrative agencies--Management. | Public welfare
  administration.
Classification: LCC JF1351 .P356 2024 (print) | LCC JF1351 (ebook) | DDC
  353.5--dc23/eng/20230606
LC record available at https://lccn.loc.gov/2023021227
LC ebook record available at https://lccn.loc.gov/2023021228

This book is published in the IGI Global book series Advances in Public Policy and Administration (APPA) (ISSN: 2475-6644; eISSN: 2475-6652)

British Cataloguing in Publication Data
A Cataloguing in Publication record for this book is available from the British Library.

All work contributed to this book is new, previously-unpublished material. The views expressed in this book are those of the authors, but not necessarily of the publisher.

For electronic access to this publication, please contact: eresources@igi-global.com.

Advances in Public Policy and Administration (APPA) Book Series

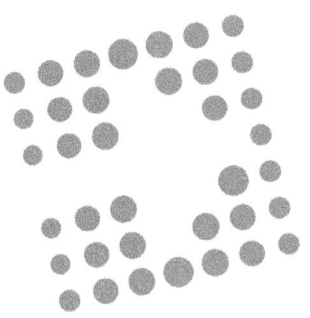

ISSN:2475-6644
EISSN:2475-6652

MISSION

Proper management of the public sphere is necessary in order to maintain order in modern society. Research developments in the field of public policy and administration can assist in uncovering the latest tools, practices, and methodologies for governing societies around the world.

The **Advances in Public Policy and Administration (APPA) Book Series** aims to publish scholarly publications focused on topics pertaining to the governance of the public domain. APPA's focus on timely topics relating to government, public funding, politics, public safety, policy, and law enforcement is particularly relevant to academicians, government officials, and upper-level students seeking the most up-to-date research in their field.

COVERAGE

- Government
- Law Enforcement
- Political Economy
- Politics
- Public Administration
- Public Funding
- Public Policy
- Resource allocation
- Urban Planning

IGI Global is currently accepting manuscripts for publication within this series. To submit a proposal for a volume in this series, please contact our Acquisition Editors at acquisitions@igi-global.com or visit: https://www.igi-global.com/publish/.

The Advances in Public Policy and Administration (APPA) Book Series (ISSN 2475-6644) is published by IGI Global, 701 E. Chocolate Avenue, Hershey, PA 17033-1240, USA, www.igi-global.com. This series is composed of titles available for purchase individually; each title is edited to be contextually exclusive from any other title within the series. For pricing and ordering information please visit https://www.igi-global.com/book-series/advances-public-policy-administration/97862. Postmaster: Send all address changes to above address. Copyright © 2024 IGI Global. All rights, including translation in other languages reserved by the publisher. No part of this series may be reproduced or used in any form or by any means – graphics, electronic, or mechanical, including photocopying, recording, taping, or information and retrieval systems – without written permission from the publisher, except for non commercial, educational use, including classroom teaching purposes. The views expressed in this series are those of the authors, but not necessarily of IGI Global.

Titles in this Series

For a list of additional titles in this series, please visit: https://www.igi-global.com/book-series/advances-public-policy-administration/97862

Global Trends in Governance and Policy Paradigms
Mahani Hamdan (Universiti Brunei Darussalam, Brunei) Muhammad Anshari (Universiti Brunei Darussalam, Brunei) Norainie Ahmad (Universiti Brunei Darussalam, Brunei) and Emil Ali (Universiti Brunei Darussalam, Brunei)
Information Science Publishing • copyright 2024 • 453pp • H/C (ISBN: 9798369317426) • US $240.00 (our price)

Soft Power and Diplomatic Strategies in Asia and the Middle East
Mohamad Zreik (School of International Studies, Sun Yat-sen University, China)
Information Science Reference • copyright 2024 • 386pp • H/C (ISBN: 9798369324448) • US $265.00 (our price)

Economic and Societal Impact of Organized Crime Policy and Law Enforcement Interventions
Alicia Danielsson (University of Bolton, UK & Hume Institute for Postgraduate Studies, Switzerland)
Information Science Reference • copyright 2024 • 350pp • H/C (ISBN: 9798369303276) • US $240.00 (our price)

The Convergence of Traditionalism and Populism in American Politics From Bannon to Trump
Adrian David Cheok (Nanjing University of Information Science and Technology, China)
Information Science Reference • copyright 2024 • 288pp • H/C (ISBN: 9781668492901) • US $235.00 (our price)

Regulating Fair Competition Toward Sustainable Development Goals
Siti Fazilah Abdul Shukor (University of Tunku Abdul Rahman, Malaysia) Farahdilah Ghazali (University of Malaysia Terengganu, Malaysia) Nur Yuhanis Ismon (University of Tun Hussien Onn, Malaysia) and Aerni Isa (Taylor's University, Malaysia)
Information Science Reference • copyright 2024 • 285pp • H/C (ISBN: 9798369303900) • US $275.00 (our price)

Analyzing Energy Crises and the Impact of Country Policies on the World
Merve Suna Özel Özcan (Kirikkale University, Turkey)
Engineering Science Reference • copyright 2024 • 283pp • H/C (ISBN: 9798369304402) • US $240.00 (our price)

Using Crises and Disasters as Opportunities for Innovation and Improvement
Saeed Siyal (School of Economics and Management, Beijing University of Chemical Technology, China)
Information Science Reference • copyright 2024 • 323pp • H/C (ISBN: 9781668495223) • US $240.00 (our price)

Cognitive Governance and the Historical Distortion of the Norm of Modern Development A Theory of Political Asymmetry
Renny Rueda (American University in the Emirates, UAE)

701 East Chocolate Avenue, Hershey, PA 17033, USA
Tel: 717-533-8845 x100 • Fax: 717-533-8661
E-Mail: cust@igi-global.com • www.igi-global.com

Table of Contents

Preface xiii

Introduction xxi

Chapter 1
Towards Holistic Agency 1

Chapter 2
Public Agencies: Dynamic Institutions With Social Meanings 22

Chapter 3
Predispositions on the Current State of Affairs 52

Chapter 4
Time and Context 78

Chapter 5
The Importance of Culture and Values in Public Reforms 82

Chapter 6
A Brief History of Public Agencies 104

Chapter 7
"Potemkin" Reason for Efficiency 115

Chapter 8
Dimensions of Public Agencies 127

Chapter 9
Agencies' Tasks 160

Chapter 10
Performance Management 165

Chapter 11
New Institutional Analysis 175

Chapter 12
Systems Theory and Agencies 193

Chapter 13
Complexity Theory and Agencies.. 211

Chapter 14
Strategies and Scenario Planning... 246

Chapter 15
Preconditions of Collective Wisdom Within Agencies and the Move From Experts to the People
and Databases 261

Chapter 16
Base-Rate Questions for Present Agencies 282

Chapter 17
Conclusion 287

Compilation of References 292

About the Author 320

Index 321

Detailed Table of Contents

Preface xiii

Introduction xxi

Chapter 1
Towards Holistic Agency 1

The holistic agency (HA) is based on the idea of system and complexity theory, which embraces action learning and organization development. HA is a planned change that takes a systems approach and makes extensive use of collaborative techniques to both solve the immediate problem and leave the organization in a more competent state to handle future challenges. The success of public agencies can be improved by implementing a systematic administration that demands the identification, monitoring, and analysis of areas and the need for flexibility due to institutional and contextual changes in real-time frames. Attention should also be paid to financial and security services and management activities, such as planning, organization, command and control, and coordination. The science of management, with its systemic component, is a system of knowledge that can be used to understand relationships, predict results, and influence results in all circumstances if individuals are organized to work together to achieve a common goal.

Chapter 2
Public Agencies: Dynamic Institutions With Social Meanings 22

The concept of social institutions, such as public agencies, is closely linked to human development, with early societies relying on group families. While organisations pursue economic goals, institutions also seek non-economic goals based on their members and position in society. Differences emerge between institutions in different legal systems despite the same competences and legal rules. Understanding social institutions goes beyond legal arrangements and is dependent on conversations and relationships between people in society. The development of professional ethics in organisations can help retain stability. Administrative capacity is critical for public agencies, as they employ most public servants and use vast resources. The efficient implementation of parliamentary-defined goals is vital for public agencies. The growth of work that focusses on the organisation, operation, and regulation of administrative agencies reflects their importance in modern society.

Chapter 3
Predispositions on the Current State of Affairs 52

This chapter discusses the creation and management of public agencies. It states that public agencies should retain their basic regulatory and supervisory functions, while other administrative tasks outside the core public administration should be transferred to public agencies for faster and more efficient performance. The chapter suggests that there is a need for similar, convergent approaches that consider the pros and cons of different combinations for the achievement of the desired goals based on different needs, contexts, and environments. The regulation of the operation of public agencies should answer at least four sets of questions relating to the establishment of public agencies, the provision of funds for their work and operations, the regulation of legal bases for the use of funds, and control over their work. Additionally, the chapter highlights the need for public agencies to be flexible and adaptable to the complex reality in which they work.

Chapter 4
Time and Context.. 78

This chapter discusses the historical ups and downs of regulatory cycles and their impact on public administration and governance. It emphasizes the importance of real-time and place in understanding and organizing public programs, and how governance adapts to changes in the environment. The chapter discusses the popularity of agencies during times of crisis and the rise of networked governance, social innovation, and citizen participation. The chapter also discusses the ongoing debate between private and public service provision and the appropriate market structure and regulation. Finally, the chapter predicts that after the Covid-19 crisis, there will be another regulatory reform that will emphasize the power of markets and the technological revolution based on advanced robotics and AI. The ownership-based perspective, citizen participation, performance, and human resource management will be critical in shaping the regulatory changes in agencies.

Chapter 5
The Importance of Culture and Values in Public Reforms 82

This chapter emphasizes the importance of culture and values in public reforms. The culture of public administration represents the pattern of values, norms, beliefs, attitudes, and assumptions that may shape the ways in which people behave and get things done. Although culture is a common word in agencies, it can still be seen as a secret coded approach to a subjective expression social glue of what is going on in an institution or how things are done. The author suggests that decision-makers should carefully analyse all relevant aspects, and different contexts in which actions are made and decisions are taken. The chapter emphasizes the importance of recognizing the complexity of modernization and the success or failure of reforms in the public sector because it shares a common denominator in cultural theory, which gives direction for public reforms. Finally, cultural theory can help describe the complexity of modernization in the public sector.

Chapter 6
A Brief History of Public Agencies... 104

The concept of agency refers to an individual's ability to act, not just their intentions to do something. Agency concerns events that an individual is responsible for, meaning that those events would not have occurred without their intervention. The concept of public agency is derived from human agency, with the latter being the ability of an individual to act. Public agencies are usually established to carry out specific functions on behalf of the state or society. Agency theory has emerged to address the challenges of principals ensuring that agents carry out their duties as intended. This theory proposes that monitoring and setting objectives for agents can ensure that objectives are achieved. Overall, agency is an essential element of human essence, and its theories have been used to explain the relationships between individuals and organizations, including public agencies.

Chapter 7
"Potemkin" Reason for Efficiency 115

Efficiency is one of the primary reasons for creating agencies, as this is thought to improve their effectiveness and efficiency. This belief was emphasized in literature and in the creation of agencies in the 1980s. However, there is little hard evidence to suggest that the agency form is more efficient than other forms of government operation. The German sociologist Max Weber believed that bureaucracy was the most efficient way to set up an organization, administration, and organizations, while Woodrow Wilson believed public administration should be geared toward maximization of effectiveness, efficiency, and economy. The criterion of efficiency is neutral as to what goals are to be attained, and this principle influences the decisions made by members of any administrative agency.

Chapter 8
Dimensions of Public Agencies 127

This chapter discusses various aspects of agency, autonomy, control, and decentralization in the context of different organizations and institutions, such as state bodies, semi-autonomous organizations, private law-based organizations, and commercial companies. The definition of an agency varies based on the type of organization, its legal status, and its relationship with other organizations. The chapter also explores different forms of decentralization, such as territorial decentralization and technical decentralization, and the challenges that arise with each. The concept of Latour's chain of translation is introduced to describe the transformation of ideas through intercessors. The passage concludes by discussing the importance of institutional arrangements, constitutional and legal demands, political culture, and public values in determining the meaning of agency and its relationship with other organizations.

Chapter 9
Agencies' Tasks 160

Governments may outsource executive tasks to agencies to improve service provision, increase efficiency, reduce conflicts of interest, and allow higher ministerial levels to focus on policy-making and strategic management. Administrative agencies are set up for various reasons, including to demonstrate independence, reduce the size and workload of departments, provide flexibility in human resources, ensure representativeness, and achieve coordination and uniformity. Agencies execute a wide range of tasks, such as providing guidance on delegated legislation, setting standards, regulating businesses and professions, administering the activities of other organizations, and providing goods and services. Delegating the day-to-day management of spending programs to specialized executive agencies has been a trend in public service reform over the last two decades. These tasks may include managing projects, adopting budget implementation instruments, and gathering and transmitting information to guide program implementation.

Chapter 10
Performance Management 165

Performance management is a strategic and integrated approach to improving the performance of people in organizations by developing the capabilities of teams and individual contributors. It involves continuous and flexible controlling and directing processes to accomplish tasks in future-focused work, with indicators used to measure success in terms of efficiency and effectiveness. Strategic performance management encompasses the clarification, assessment, implementation, and continuous improvement of organizational strategy and its execution. However, many organizations spend too little time clarifying and agreeing on their strategies and measuring everything that is easy to measure, without turning performance data into meaningful insights and learning. The main activities in performance management include role profiling, performance contract planning, personal development planning, managing performance throughout the year, and performance review. Finally, leveraging critical success factors and using key performance indicators can help organizations achieve their outcomes.

Chapter 11
New Institutional Analysis 175

New institutionalism emerged in the 1980s as an alternative to old functional institutionalism. It focuses on the importance of informal actions on the persistence of institutions through time, discovering institutional underlying patterns and processes. The new institutionalism tends to reduce variety, operating across organizations to override diversity in local environments. The mentioned elements derive legitimacy from more symbolic elements, sensible to cultural forms and cognitive models rather than from the discursive reason. The concept of agency emerged as the answer to the question of how to improve public institutions with the emphasis on larger autonomy, flexibility, performance, and more direct contact with the environment and citizen's needs. The agency's apparent hybrid nature based on private-sector methods could gain some advantage when formal goals would be not only quasi but de facto optimised with practice when the agency's autonomy and independence are balanced with control and accountability.

Chapter 12
Systems Theory and Agencies 193

A system is not just a collection of individual parts or ministries without any links or purpose between them. It is a set of elements that interact to achieve goals, and this requires a whole picture framework. Public administration must be effectively managed to change the pattern of results in a planned way. When classical rules cannot cope with complex environment, it not only creates a problem of efficiency, but also a major problem of legitimacy. Bureaucratic power is not only unelected, but its frameworks of public authority do not reflect the reality in which people live and are, therefore, mismanaged. A partial centralised approach can be more effective than a holistic one when a collective one must be used, and humans are complex adaptive systems, so diverse people should be involved in decision-making. The underlying structure of a system goes beyond individual political mandates, which they usually do not want to change.

Chapter 13
Complexity Theory and Agencies.. 211

Complex problems are characterized by uncertainty, complexity, exponentiality, divergent values, self-organization, emergence, interdependent processes, structures, and actors. To address such problems, a solution is to reflect real-life complexity using complex adaptive systems (CAS). Complexity theory emphasizes the benefits of CAS, which is attentive to the heterogeneity in the various subsystems, how parts at a sub-level in a complex system affect the emergent behaviour, and outcome of the system. The main aim of complexity theory is to explain counterintuitive order creation out of local simple rules, distant from the second law of thermodynamics that point at the increasing, irreversible entropy of the system and its surroundings. Public agencies can also be understood using the CAS model, with their levels of autonomy and independence from politics, the element of self-organization is roughly similar in CAS vis-à-vis public agencies.

Chapter 14
Strategies and Scenario Planning.. 246

The function of public agencies is to provide expectations, which are often unfulfilled in an increasingly complex environment. However, consistency and coherence usually presuppose a static environment, whereas the relationship between means and ends is dynamic, multi-layered, interdependent, and thus complex. The new approach aims to address and respond to a dynamic environment in relation to the content of rules and proposes solutions that can adapt to change in line with the principle of proportionality. The concept of emergence can be useful to describe the end of a decision-making process where the final decision is the result of many intertwined combinations that influence arguments and parts that were not included in the initial idea. To cope with this, legal norms should be more adapted to the elements of the future than is possible with classical law. This could be done with sunset clauses, legal experiments, flexible legal rules, decision-making algorithms, and simulations that could serve as inputs without legal force for the subsequent adoption of general legal rules.

Chapter 15
Preconditions of Collective Wisdom Within Agencies and the Move From Experts to the People and Databases 261

When people join groups, their personal biases and cognitive biases can lead to extreme herd behaviour, group polarization, and groupthink. Social systems can evolve to better adapt to environmental pressures by developing specialized organizations with legitimate authority. Traditional public deliberation may be less efficient as individuals tend to conform their interpretations to match those of others, rather than their actions, and they may not be aware of alternative possibilities. Evolutionary changes require diversity and independent thinking to adapt based on new information. Regulators need to consider diverse and unshared information to avoid unintended consequences. The degree of collective intelligence is linked to an individual's social sensitivity and ability to think about the mental states of other individuals. Superforecasters, who are open-minded, diverse, and analytical with developed social abilities, can beat individual experts and prediction markets.

Chapter 16
Base-Rate Questions for Present Agencies 282

The chapter discusses the concept of holistic agencies (HAs) and their potential role in public administration. Successful public agencies reflect some of the holistic elements, making them more adaptable and intelligent. HAs are seen as a part of overall institutional design and must be perceived as legitimate by society while also relating to norms, values, and culture. The demand for better institutions is necessary to achieve public goals optimally. The scholars or reformists should be pointing the way for future institutional development if there is a lack of demand from the people. Fukuyama's four aspects of stateness—organizational design and management, political system design, basis of legitimization, and cultural and structural factors—are essential for HA's success. The chapter concludes that establishing the reality on the ground is crucial to achieving HA's success, and while there may not be an optimal form of organization, HA is more about a manner of acting than a form.

Chapter 17
Conclusion 287

In the natural sciences, accurate testing of hypotheses using observed, collected, and comparable data can lead to new theories or guidelines for action. However, in social sciences, such as public agencies, recognizing patterns, forming categories, measuring, and comparing phenomena vis-a-vis the human will, make it difficult to reach similar levels of accuracy. Social science theory involves editing and studying factual material, where evidence is largely presented with definitions, concepts, and metaphors. The meaning of theories in social science is normative, explaining what should be, in addition to the actual sein or what is. However, the description of past events and inference on conclusions, causes, or events may be subject to cognitive biases such as confirmation bias or post hoc ergo propter hoc. Comparisons of past events and their placement on common denominators may not be a true description of the current state of affairs, as reasons, contingencies, and intentions behind similar occurrences may differ.

Compilation of References 292

About the Author 320

Index 321

Preface

We must also consider in which sense the nature of the universe contains the good or the supreme good; whether as something separate and independent, or as the orderly arrangement of its parts. Probably in both senses, as an army does; for the efficiency of an army consists partly in the order and partly in the general; but chiefly in the latter, because he does not depend upon the order, but the order depends upon him. All things, both fishes and birds and plants, are ordered together in some way but not in the same way; and the system is not such that there is no relation between one thing and another; there is a definite connection. Everything is ordered together to one end; but the arrangement is like that in a household, where the free persons have the least liberty to act at random and have all or most of their actions preordained for them, whereas the slaves and animals have little common responsibility and act for the most part at random. Aristotle, *Metaphysics*, Book 12, Section 1075a.

My intention is to present public agencies in a light of wholeness, in their similarity with us. Up to what point will I be successful at this, the readers will tell you, but the most important thing is how ideas from this book will be embraced and implemented by agencies themselves, that is, institutions. For Herbert Simon 'we are all expressionists part of the time. Sometimes we just want to scream loudly at injustice or to stand up and be counted. These are noble motives, but any serious revolutionist must often deprive himself of the pleasures of self-expression. He must judge his actions by their ultimate effects on *institutions* (Simon, 1996, p. 281).

Public agencies are organizations that are established by the government to perform specific functions and provide services to the public. Public agencies ensure the safety and welfare of citizens and uphold the laws and regulations of the government. These agencies are funded by taxes and are accountable to the government and the public they serve. Thus, it is of utmost importance to know how they word and how they can be managed. Public agencies are assembled – among other things – also with humans as complex adaptive beings, and thus also such agencies should be complex adaptive institutions that must manage the complexity of internal and external environment. This book presents a Holistic Agency as a new term in the field of public administration that is based on the fundamental interconnectedness. Holism starts with the basic characteristic and advantage of organizations, that is their ability to transform an individual act into a set of collective actions based on the relationships between individuals' acts and their combinations. The relations among these elements are called organizations. Therefore, the latter structure is a tool or, better, an integrated system, not an end in itself. The functions of public agencies are put in a wider context when public expectations are involved and public power is used. When taken as a whole, when the public agency is understood as one part in the net of other things, that nevertheless acts as a whole, the term holistic agency emerges. Nevertheless, this is a vast oversimplification; there is much more to it, which we will present in the following chapters. Proper, good, and efficient management does not depend on terminology and neither on the legal context, since such management can be achieved regardless of the different legal contexts. Successful organizations can be found all over the world; as their principles represent the elements of complex adaptive systems that are everywhere the same, their basic principles are somehow different from their specific legal arrangements. One of the strengths of this work is thus the presentation and linkage of the fundamental elements of complex systems, irrespective of the legal environment in which they operate. Although organizations are technical means to achieve goals, a kind of conscious, deliberate, and purposeful cooperation among people, they are infused with value beyond the technical requirements of the task at hand. Public agencies can thus be seen as organizations that can adapt, as their survival and growth depend upon the maintenance of an equilibrium of complex character in a continuously fluctuating environment of physical, biological, and social materials, elements, and forces, which calls for constant readjustments of processes internal to the organization. Public organizational types are effective when they are not only sustained in time but when they fulfil their tasks in a meaningful, effective, and efficient way. Their basic characteristic of an institution is public value, not profit. Public values and profit can be seen as the result of the evolutionary capacity to adapt mixed with past effective practices. Adaptiveness thus precedes value, but it is conditioned by the institutions' contexts that surround public values in a certain time and context.

The future directing of human behavior depends on an accumulated present value that an institution has and produces as its capital through each action when the public conforms to the mentioned directing; when successful, the institution gains or retains legitimacy. A predisposition is that an institution's ability to adapt its tasks to a certain context of relevant circumstances or facts – that frame the situation under question – makes institutions as the stable patterns in a flexible environment. Public agencies are presented in this work with the help of systems and complexity theory. Although public agencies act under certain common fundamental premises, they are always somehow different. Each agency has been designed to fulfil a particular need, and hence it is a challenge to determine how the common principles apply to that specific agency in a non-stop changing context. Given the variety of agencies and their practices, a one-size-fits-all approach will not fit everyone perfectly, but there are nevertheless some common perspectives by which each agency can show its unique level of adaptiveness systemic behavior, complexity, dynamism, flexibility, and agility. They can be seen as a composed behavior in which a dynamic system or the effective and efficient agency tends to evolve towards its growth and/or fulfilment of its tasks. This work will not deal with agency specifics, but with some preordained general elements with a focus on systems and adaptation.

To successfully manage the numerous connections, relationships, and processes of public agencies, they should be managed differently, due to their various elements. In the modern world of flexible, flexible and complex environments, public agencies should reflect even more and exhibit complex adaptable behavior. For the latter, public organizations usually lack the sensory organs, steering, and control systems to cope with the challenges of fundamental change. Communication and decision-making systems work much too slowly and with too great time lag, to permit correct decisions and quick adjustments. Before a deeper elaboration of public agencies and their increasing inability to manage and control their surroundings in a more dynamic and complex environment, a wider framework will be drawn to understand the context in which they work, and even then, understanding in detail all about public agencies in the face of complexity. They are subjected to many different influences so that only general inferences can be made.

Effective leadership of public agencies involves the attentive and integrative use of a variety of concepts rather than the hot pursuit of catchy phrases. It is easy to give a few simple solutions or

Preface

rules that in practice always turn out to be unsuccessful. Concepts could only be of a general nature and cannot be used in a specific campaign, but the general nature of public agencies could help leaders, citizens, and interest groups weigh the pros and cons of existing or potential situations to perform tasks more effectively. Public agencies depend on various social and other influences that are reflected in their work. Inductive and then deductive approaches, theories, and practices change our views along determinism and rationalistic elements; there are ways that unintentionally or unknowingly continuously affect behavior in different parts and particles. Causes and effects cannot be always directly linked or established, and a whole is more than a sum of its parts, new, unexpected, or emergent properties cannot be returned in previous states irreversibility. All this applies also to public agencies that were always but now also acknowledged that work in the multilayered TUNA conditions. If agreement is present on scientifically grounded statements and discoveries, in practice, the deterministic, Weberian, or mechanical idea of public agencies is still mostly present, seen through the static rigid law on which they operate. The vivid, livable, responsive, and flexible changes in natural science should also be reflected in public agencies to be able to address the former. Based on the presented predispositions, this book sees public agencies as dynamic institutions that have their social meanings. In the presence of enlarged complexity, there is no stable, classic principles of organization that are not constantly changed. There are many paradoxes of statically understood principles. Public agencies have power to manage the society as a system, and thus the first should also exhibit the basic elements of systems (systemic agency), where time and context, culture, and values are also important.

For someone who manages or works in a public agency, it is useful to know the grid and group cultural model, organizational strategy, structure and process, cultural dimensions, and different versions of public agencies (e.g. classic and dynamic public agency, complicated public agency, lean public agency, systemic or complex public agency) that fit in a different environment. To be acknowledged with public agencies, the book gives a brief history of public agencies, presents the notion of "agency" and its theory with reasons for the creation of agencies, their dimensions along with the deconcentration, decentralization, organizational division of autonomy, elements of independence, and policy making autonomy. Based on these, an ideal-agency model and its practical characteristics are presented along with different types of agencies. To be acquainted with systems theory and complexity theory is sine qua non for the management of agencies along with the notions of responsiveness, adaptability, agility, and robustness, strategies and scenario planning, collective wisdom. All of them are needed to better comprehend the notion of viable and holistic agency. The book gives some holistic recommendations for public agencies, also about the use of artificial intelligence, at the end with the base-rate questions for present agencies to be better adapted in the current world of complexity.

The topic of public agencies is an important and relevant issue in the world today because these organizations play a crucial role in providing essential services to citizens and promoting public welfare. As the world becomes more complex, diverse, and interconnected, the functions and responsibilities of public agencies continue to expand and evolve to meet new challenges and demands. In many countries, there is an ongoing debate about the appropriate role and scope of public agencies, with some advocating for greater privatization and market-based approaches, while others argue for the need for stronger and more robust public institutions. Recent events such as the COVID-19 pandemic have highlighted the importance of well-functioning public agencies in addressing public health emergencies, providing critical services to vulnerable populations, and ensuring public safety. Overall, the topic of public agencies is a crucial topic that touches on many aspects of society, including governance, policy, public service delivery, and citizen engagement. As such, it is a topic that will continue to be relevant and important in the world today and in the years to come.

The target audience for a book on public agencies are individuals who are interested in understanding how public agencies function and the role they play in society. This includes students who study public administration, political science, or other related fields, as well as public officials and policymakers who work in government agencies. Additionally, professionals in fields such as law, public policy, and social work may also find a book on public agencies of interest, as it can provide valuable insight into how government institutions operate and how they can be leveraged to promote positive social outcomes. Overall, a presented book on public agencies is relevant to anyone who wants to gain a deeper understanding of the complex and dynamic world of government institutions and the critical role they play in shaping nowadays societies.

In the Introduction, the book presents the concept of a Holistic Agency that has emerged as a new term in the field of public administration, reflecting the need for public agencies to manage complexity. A holistic agency is an integrated system that adapts to its environment and focusses on public value rather than profit. Enduring viability through adaptation is essential for both organizations and institutions. While each agency is designed to fulfil a specific need, they operate under certain common fundamental premises. A holistic agency operates based on the interconnectedness of all things, and systemic behavior, complexity, dynamism, flexibility, and agility are essential for its growth and fulfilment of its tasks. Proper management can be achieved regardless of the legal context, and the principles of complex adaptive systems are the same everywhere.

Today's administrative apparatus is still understood as a professional group of people who, as a spider web, increasingly intertwines all industrial, national, and transnational societies and who develops at least in the form of a policy of draught rules in the increasingly interconnected world. The understanding of a wider frame of institutions in the social construction of goals, tools, and purposes is conditioned on various alliances, cooperation, and co-optation with other stakeholders. This understanding is socially constructed; it depends on conversation, dialogue, and relations between people as members of a particular society and its groups, and on its meanings about words, actions, and managers. The individual meanings, desires, motives, and wishes would emerge from relations with other meanings and are further grouped and shaped by institutional forces and/or by common denominators that all involved respect and follow.

The first chapter is about the holistic agency (HA). HA is a planned change that takes a systems approach and makes extensive use of collaborative techniques to both solve the immediate problem and leave the organization in a more competent state to handle future challenges. The success of public agencies can be improved by implementing a systematic administration that requires the identification, monitoring, and analysis of areas and the need for flexibility due to institutional and contextual changes in real-time frames. Attention should also be paid to financial and security services and management activities, such as planning, organization, command and control, and coordination.

The 2nd chapter is about public agencies as dynamic institutions with social meanings. The concept of social institutions, such as public agencies, is closely linked to human development, and early societies rely on group families. While organizations pursue economic goals, institutions also seek non-economic goals based on their members and position in society. Differences emerge between institutions in different legal systems despite the same competences and legal rules. Understanding social institutions goes beyond legal arrangements and is dependent on conversations and relationships between people in

Preface

society. The development of professional ethics in organizations can help retain stability. Administrative capacity is critical for public agencies, as they employ most public servants and use vast resources. The efficient implementation of parliamentary-defined goals is vital for public agencies. The growth of work that focusses on the organization, operation, and regulation of administrative agencies reflects their importance in modern society.

The 3rd chapter is focused on predispositions that can serve as a starting point from which public agencies can perform their tasks. The creation of public agencies is supposed to represent an opportunity to reduce the scope of state administration, but to do this, they should emphasize, retain, and maintain its basic regulatory and supervisory functions from the view of complex adaptive systems, because they cybernetically and technically do not depend on legal norms. The management of such systems depends on elements that constitute the systems and complexity theory assembled in a way that, with the help of control, regulation, and steering, produces results. Therefore, the main findings of the CAS are applicable in different legal systems, as most of them have not prevented major financial or other crisis or wicked problems.

The fourth chapter explains the regulatory cycles that depend on time and political, economic, and social context. Regardless of all theories, there are always a system - man-made or natural - its underlying structure and people present in time and context. The importance of real-time is never emphasised enough; place and time are crucial to understanding and organisation of many public programmes. Theories have little importance apart from practices of real actions and results, because theories are only attempts to make sense of practices and guide actions by which we forge practices. This relation is also evident in the notion of governance, which is not a constant, but rather tends to change as needs, values, time, and context change.

The 5th chapter put the autonomy of public agencies in a relevant context. Promoting values only by their numbering and description as principles of good governance is not enough; values emerge in specific contexts in connection with specific actions and what can be good somewhere can be bad in other environments, or one man's poison is another man's cure. To manage public agencies, it should be known how values evolve, react and change their content in different surroundings and how they can be implemented in different countries. The culture of public administration is more known as an organizational culture that represents the pattern of values, norms, beliefs, attitudes, and assumptions that may not have been articulated, but shape the ways in which people behave and things get done.

The 6th chapter gives basic elements of public agencies. The successful and legitimate administration of agencies is more important when action, that is, the agency, is directly connected with power as the latter is created only in relations. Agency theory suggests that principles may have problems in ensuring that agents do what they are told. It is necessary to clarify ambiguities by setting objectives and monitoring performance to ensure that the objectives are met. The principal-agent relations should also recognize the importance of social, i.e., the institutional context in which such relations occur. One of the most important is the rule of law and control, which both prevent egocentric agents to seek only their benefits at the expense of the principal. Social mechanisms and/or institutional context impact the content, material, and formal agreements on the various roles people have, as well as how they interact with each other.

Efficiency is presented in the 7th chapter as one of the most prominent rational reasons for agencification. Agency performance seems to depend more on the quality of relations between the agency and its parent ministry than just on some formal performance criteria. Politics should be considered together with administration, while the first should be at the same time prevented from influencing centralized administration accompanied by a greater permanence in the tenure of administrative officers in its details. Highly structured bureaucratic forms provide a context in which individuals strive to act reasonably within all vagueness and restrictions, but a result – seen as the aggregate - still leads to similarities in the organizational structure, culture, and results on higher and lower levels.

Various aspects of agency, autonomy, control, and decentralization in the context of different organizations and institutions, such as state bodies, semi-autonomous organizations, private law-based organizations, and commercial companies are also discussed. The definition of an agency varies according to the type of organization, its legal status, and its relationship with other organizations. The chapter also explores different forms of decentralization, such as territorial decentralization and technical decentralization, and the challenges that arise with each. The importance of institutional arrangements, constitutional and legal demands, political culture, and public values in determining the meaning of the agency and its relationship with other organizations are aspects that should not be overlooked in the functioning of the agency.

The 9th chapter is focused on the tasks of agencies. Administrative agencies are established for various reasons, including to demonstrate independence, reduce the size and workload of departments, provide flexibility in human resources, ensure representativeness, and achieve coordination and uniformity. Agencies perform a wide range of tasks, such as providing guidance on delegated legislation, setting standards, regulating businesses and professions, administering the activities of other organizations, and providing goods and services. Delegating the day-to-day management of spending programs to specialized executive agencies has been a trend in public service reform over the past two decades. These tasks can include managing projects, adopting budget implementation instruments, and gathering and transmitting information to guide programe implementation.

The 10th chapter introduces performance management as a strategic and integrated approach to improving the performance of people in organizations by developing the capabilities of teams and individual contributors. It involves continuous and flexible control and direction processes to accomplish tasks in future-focused work, with indicators used to measure success in terms of efficiency and effectiveness. Strategic performance management encompasses the clarification, assessment, implementation and continuous improvement of organizational strategy and its execution. However, many organizations spend too little time clarifying and agreeing on their strategies and measuring everything that is easy to measure, without turning performance data into meaningful insights and learning.

The 11th chapter describes a new institutionalism that emerged in the 1980s as an alternative to the old functional institutionalism. It focusses on the importance of informal actions on the persistence of institutions over time, discovering the underlying institutional patterns and processes. The new institutionalism tends to reduce variety, operating across organizations to override diversity in local environments. The mentioned elements derive legitimacy from more symbolic elements, sensible to cultural forms and cognitive models, rather than from the discursive reason. The concept of agency emerged as the answer to the question of how to improve public institutions with an emphasis on greater autonomy, flexibility, performance, and more direct contact with the environment and the needs of the citizens.

The 12th chapter presents a system theory. The system is a set of elements that interact to achieve goals, and this requires a complete picture framework. Public administration must be effectively managed to change the pattern of results in a planned way. Bureaucratic power is not only unelected, but its frameworks of public authority do not reflect the reality in which people live and, therefore, are mismanaged. The underlying structure of a system goes beyond individual political mandates, which they usually do not want to change.

Preface

The 13th chapters elaborate complexity theory and complex problems that are characterized by uncertainty, complexity, exponentiality, divergent values, self-organization, emergence, interdependent processes, structures, and actors. To address such problems, a solution is to reflect the complexity in real life using complex adaptive systems (CAS). The main aim of complexity theory is to explain counterintuitive order creation out of local simple rules, distant from the second law of thermodynamics that point at the increasing, irreversible entropy of the system and its surroundings. Public agencies can also be understood using the CAS model; with their levels of autonomy and independence from politics, the element of self-organization is roughly similar in CAS vis-à-vis public agencies.

The 14th chapter is focused on strategies and scenario planning. Reality is neither deterministic, precise, nor certain. It is complex, made up of many parts and their relationships; it is rarely directly conditioned by a specific consequence and more often than not exponential. Strategic planning includes vision, mission, principles, key success indicators, while scenario planning includes the identification of the issue and the decisions to be taken, the key (mini, micro, macro) factors, their ranking in terms of importance and uncertainty, the logic of the scenario, the identification of the implications of the scenarios on the decisions, the identification of the key indicators, and the peripheral points/times of their verification.

The 15th chapter presents collective wisdom. When people join groups, their personal biases and cognitive biases can lead to extreme herd behavior, group polarization, and groupthink. Social systems can evolve to better adapt to environmental pressures by developing specialized organizations with legitimate authority. Classical public deliberation may be less effective because people tend to adapt their meanings to others' meanings rather than their actions, and they may not know about other possibilities. Evolutionary changes require diversity and independent thinking to adapt based on new information. Regulators should consider diverse and unshared information to avoid unintended consequences. Collective intelligence is correlated with social sensitivity and the ability to reason about the mental states of others.

The 16th chapter presents base-rate questions for agencies. Successful public agencies reflect some of the holistic elements, making them more adaptable and intelligent. The demand for better institutions is necessary to achieve public goals optimally. Scholars or reformists should point the way for future institutional development if there is a lack of demand from the people. Fukuyama's four aspects of stateness - organizational design and management, political system design, basis of legitimacy, and cultural and structural factors - are essential for HA's success. The chapter concludes that establishing the reality on the ground is crucial to achieving HA's success, and while there may not be an optimal form of organization, HA is more about a manner of acting than a form.

The 17th chapter concludes the book. In the natural sciences, accurate testing of hypotheses using observed, collected, and comparable data can lead to new theories or guidelines for action. However, in social sciences, such as public agencies, recognizing patterns, forming categories, measuring and comparing phenomena vis-a-vis the human will, make it difficult to reach similar levels of accuracy. Social science theory involves editing and studying factual material, where evidence is presented largely with definitions, concepts, and metaphors. Comparisons of past events and their placement on common denominators may not be a true description of the current situation, as the reasons, contingencies, and intentions behind similar events may differ. Despite this, the notion of HA can be useful for adaptability of complex systems, i.e. institution.

This book on holistic public agency can have a significant impact on the field by contributing new insights, perspectives, and approaches to the subject matter. Holistic public agency refers to an approach to public administration that emphasizes a more integrated, collaborative, and people-centered approach to service delivery. By exploring in-depth the principles and practices of holistic public agency, the book can help advance the understanding of this approach and its potential benefits for citizens and public officials alike. This can lead to new innovations and improvements in the way public agencies are designed, operated, and evaluated. Additionally, this book on holistic public agency can help to raise awareness of the importance of a more holistic approach to public service delivery and encourage greater collaboration and cooperation across different levels of government and between government and nongovernmental organizations.

Mirko Pecaric
University of Ljubljana, Slovenia

INTRODUCTION

We live in a society of organisations – more, larger, and more varied than ever before in history... all of them are centres of influence and power, of design and control.

(Malik, 2012).

Nowadays, public agencies are not only complex institutions per se but have to manage complexity. A hope is in a Holistic Agency as a new term in the field of public administration – except as far as can be taken into account *Dirk Gently's Holistic Detective Agency* as a humorous detective novel by English writer Douglas Adams, first published in 1987, focused in detective agency that operates based on the fundamental interconnectedness of all things, especially in missing cats and messy divorces... Despite the jocular nature of the mentioned novel, the notion of holism reflects the same meaning as is present in this work,[1] and for now, this definition of a holistic agency should suffice until an alternative is put forward. Holism starts with the basic characteristic and advantage of organizations, that is their ability to transform an individual act into a set of collective actions. A group of right people came together around a common cause, purpose, or type of value and tried to fulfil it through roles, resources, and actions based on continuous structural and procedural adaptiveness. Relations among these elements are called organisations. Therefore, the latter structure is a tool (or better: an integrated system), not an end in itself ("form follows function" or FFF). But there is much more – especially when public expectations are involved and public power is used. When taken as a whole, when the public agency is understood as one part in the net of other things, that nevertheless acts as a whole, the term holistic agency emerges. Nevertheless, this is a vast oversimplification; there is much more to it, which we will discuss below.

Proper, good and efficient management does not depend on the terminology of the different legal systems; in fact, it does not depend on the legal context since such management can be achieved regardless of the different legal contexts. Successful organisations can be found all over the world, so their basic principles must be somehow different from their legal arrangements. Their principles represent the elements of complex adaptive systems that are everywhere the same. One of the strengths of this work is in presenting and linking the fundamental elements of complex systems, regardless of the legal environment in which they operate. This work starts with Selznick's classic difference [1957] between an organisation and an institution; he based the latter on criteria that should distinguish it from an organisation: distinct identity and unique competence, strong reputation, high legitimacy, and *enduring viability through adaptation* (Selznick, 2011). While organisations are technical means to achieve goals, a kind of "conscious, deliberate, and purposeful cooperation between people" (Barnard, 1968) institutions are "infused with value beyond the technical requirements of the task at hand" (Selznick, 2011). The institution can thus be seen not only as an organization that can *adapt,* because 'survival of an organisation depends upon the maintenance of an equilibrium of complex character in a continuously fluctuating environment of physical, biological, and social materials, elements, and forces, which calls for readjustment of processes internal to the organization' (Barnard, 1968, p. 6), but as the adaptable institution that carries the weight of the environment and also of *value*. Both organisational types are effective when endure time, while the basic characteristic of an institution is in the *public value*, not profit. Enduring viability through adaptation is similar in long-lasting companies like Coca-Cola, Adidas, McDonald's, Nike, etc., as it is in long-lasting public agencies. Public values and profit can be seen as the result of the (evolutionary) capacity to *adapt* mixed with past effective practices. Adaptiveness thus precedes value, but it is conditioned with context: institutions are effective organisations that guard public value in a certain time and context (Boin, Fahy, & Hart, 2020).

The future "directing" of human behaviour depends on an accumulated present value that an institution has and produces as "its capital" through each action; when the public happily conforms to the mentioned directing, the institution gains/retains legitimacy. A predisposition is that an institution's ability to *adapt* itself and public tasks to a certain context (a whole set of relevant circumstances or facts that frame the situation under question) from which public values/results can be enhanced the most, makes institutions stable, valued, and recurring patterns of behaviour (Huntington, 1968), or persistent rules that shape, limit, and channel human behaviour (Fukuyama, 2014). Institutionalization can be seen as an evolutionary process (Boin et al., 2020; Goodsell, 2010; Selznick, 2011), which will be presented in this work with the help of systems and the complexity theory that will be applied on public agencies as a subgroup of (public) institutions (among which are the Ministries, Parliament, Courts, etc.). Public agencies are subordinate to their parent ministries, while they can sometimes even be at the forefront of a parent ministry (e.g., the US's CIA, NSA, FBI, NASA, the French *Grands Corps,* ENA, Louvre Museum, Israeli intelligence service Mossad or British MI6, BBC).

Although public agencies act under certain common fundamental premises, they are different. Not even two agencies are alike; each agency has been designed to fulfil a particular need, and it hence is a challenge to determine how the common principles apply to that specific agency. Given the variety of agencies and their practises, a 'one-size-fits-all' approach will not fit everyone perfectly, but there are still some common perspectives by which each agency can show its unique level of adaptiveness: systemic behaviour, complexity, dynamism, flexibility, and agility. They can be seen as a composed behaviour in which a dynamic system (or the effective and efficient agency) tends to evolve towards its growth and/or fulfilment of its tasks. This work will not deal with agencies' specifics, but with some preordained Aristotelian general elements (see the citation above) *general* elements present in all public agencies with a focus on *systems* and *adaptation*. The latter two characteristics could make the relationships between public agencies and their environment *with respect to* their purposes ("what" or a compelling public mission) and objectives ("how") more understandable, and thus also more effective ("right goals") and efficient ("right means") in practice. People are more and more dependent on various organisations in their life – we live in the culture of organisations, and when the latter collapse, we feel this directly. To avoid these numerous connections, relations, and processes must be handled differently due to the various crises in which today's societies live. 'Public and private sector organisations lack the sensory organs, steering and control systems to cope with the challenges of fundamental change. Communication and decision-making systems work much to slowly and with too great time lag, to permit correct decisions

Introduction

and quick adjustments' (Malik, 2016, p. 50). Before a deeper elaboration of public agencies and their increasing inability to manage and control their surroundings in a more dynamic and complex environment, a wider framework will be drawn to understand the context in which they work – and even then, understanding in detail all about public agencies in the face of complexity is 'no go'. They are subjected to many different influences so that only general inferences can be given. A parable of a recipe in a cookery book can be helpful: it is not a blueprint for a meal but only a set of instructions (Dawkins, 2006), or not a specific place, but its map. General perspectives are similarly nothing but instructions or navigations that, when obeyed in the right order, could result in something "edible" or arrive at the right place for various stakeholders, although with their own unique taste (of various interests). Effective leadership (also of public agencies) involves the attentive and integrative use of a variety of concepts rather than the hot pursuit of catchy phrases and glib advice (Rainey, 2009). It is easy to give a few simple solutions/rules that in practise always turn out to be unsuccessful. Concepts could only be of general nature and cannot be used in a specific campaign:[2] the general nature of public agencies could nevertheless help leaders, citizens, and interest groups to weigh the pros and cons of existing or potential situations to do tasks more effectively. Public agencies depend on various social and other influences that are reflected in their work. Inductive and then deductive approaches, theories, and practises change our views: along determinism and rationalistic elements, there are ways that unintentionally or unknowingly (continuously) affect behaviour in different parts and particles. Causes and effects cannot be always directly linked or established, and a whole is more than a sum of its parts; new, unexpected, or *emergent* properties cannot be returned in previous states (irreversibility). All this applies also to public agencies (that were always, but now also acknowledged) that work in the multi-layered, Volatile, Uncertain, Complex, and Ambiguous (VUCA) world and/or under TUNA conditions (Turbulence, Uncertainty, Novelty, and Ambiguity).

If the agreement is present on scientifically grounded statements and discoveries, how come there is still mostly present the deterministic, Weberian, or mechanical *idea* of public agencies, seen through the static (rigid) law on which they operate? The vivid, liveable, responsive, and flexible changes in natural science should be also reflected in public agencies to be able to address the former. If many of us could agree with this, how come books and papers on public agencies (despite of the comparative element) mostly explain (search for reasons of) their behaviours, correlations, and causal links *after* the event (and are thus close to the *ex post,* confirmation bias, where they rationally try to put reasons for results on the same denominators) without replications and predictions what could happen in the future, where relations and their combinations inevitably change and emerge in other forms? Public agencies are in legal science typically understood as certain, unchangeable or similar, but this is misleading. When they are rigid, they could conflict with the rule of law, where strict rules are paradoxically established for *pro futuro* cases/situations, where flexibility and dynamism are present and needed, where legal principles and indeterminant legal notions come to the fore. A valid enactment of rules could mean little for their future implementation, when things change. And they always change. In the implementation, penetrate also the nonlegal, informal, moral, emotional, psychological and other elements, due to the basic components of nature, human and their relations. As in law general legal principles are needed, the same holds for general perspectives on which public agencies work. If they are similar,[3] they only be such in the formal outer frames and principles, while each agency is its own world. Why then do we turn a blind eye (like a kind of blindfold over the eyes of the goddess of justice, but in a negative sense) and insist on a pre-defined framework for public agency action, when at the same time we know, as a kind of public secret, they have to intervene in the future that is largely indeterminate, dynamic and flexible? Is this some form of public secret that is to Eaglestone based on its elusive nature that cannot be described historically, but through literature?[4] Is there a contrast present between the idea of meaning (i.e. being, or how can an agency be logically and purposively meant regardless or beyond of what it only appears to be) and the idea of cognitive truth (how they experientially, *de facto* appear through our senses), mixed with complicity (due to silence on the presence of nonlegal elements in agencies) for which no one wants to be a 'hated messenger'?[5] How can the rule of law, understood as the expression of preordained rules, be aligned with public agencies, that is their inevitable flexible and changeable environment, or with even the basic mental activities of thinking and willing that are always present 'out of order', out of judgement as the third mental activity, which cannot be derived from the first two (Arendt, 1981) and *vice versa*? As complex entities, agencies do not depend only on past rules. A person and the public agency stand at the frontier between order and chaos, between stability and needed flexibility to correct flaws of the former. In theory, people know that, but in the (legal) practice they do not want to enact this. How can this form of public secrecy be revealed?

Peterson's *Beyond Order* (2021) can give us a path to consider how the dangers of too much security and control could be beneficially avoided. Peterson's Rule I ("Do not carelessly denigrate social institutions or creative achievement") describes the connection between stable and predictable social structures and the need for their update to retain vitality: 'a functional social institution—a hierarchy devoted to producing something of value, beyond the mere insurance of its own survival—can utilize the conservative types to carefully implement processes of tried-and-true value, and the creative, liberal types to determine how what is old and out of date might be replaced by something new and more valuable' (Peterson, 2021, p. 16).[6] Public agencies are often at the mentioned frontier, they are "the scissors and a canvas" of public policy, making them not only fall within the scope of administrative law,[7] but they (re)create it whenever it is decided that their presence benefits more to the society than the legislator, courts or private organisations. When this condition of necessary adaptation is fulfilled, they have significant effects on the national economy, welfare, growth, freedom, and justice. They are never only legal entities. They are various things; only when they are in the constant process of retelling, reunderstanding, when the past, present, and future are seen in a common net of fluctuating things, processes, and reactions, new results emerge – until the next iteration and turnaround.

Agencies are internally (legally) more similar than externally, that is, in how they appear to the public. A formal law (on public agencies) should hence anticipate along the basic deterministic, reductionist and rational elements (at the time of formal enactment and creation) also the uncertainty, probability, unexpected emergence of new rules and practices, their declines and rearrangements (at the time of implementation) – all that is present in the scientific path towards the Higgs boson (or simply, agencies should along order expect also [creative] chaos). People do not have only a tendency for (tangible) order, but also for (intangible) liberty, freedom, interconnectedness, and independence from the actual or even potential events, conditions, relations, and their combinations by which they co-create complex orders. This also applies to public agencies. But – if already an act of personal observation can confer shape and form reality that has been proved by the double-slit experiment (Feynman, Leighton, & Sands, 1965; Lanza & Berman, 2013) – what does this mean for the rule of law and its predictability in public agencies that must respect it along the complex environment, its contexts, and a whole mosaic of subjective behaviours of agents and/or public employees *vis-à-vis* customers or citizens? How can something be strictly legally prescribed when actions also depend on people, their thoughts, and observations? Examining formal legal instruments that determine legal paths and ways of doing things by agencies without knowing how they act *de facto* and iteratively nonstop and implement their tasks fails to capture the processes, interactions, and practices by which the public institutions of countries do their job. This is,

Introduction

of course, easier said (written/or even acknowledged) than done, but progress could already be made in a recognition of this. The formal law on agencies simply cannot embrace all the complexity present in public agencies, and the aim of this work is not only to present this but also to propose solutions. Along with the fact that processes, interactions, and practices change over time due to various more or less distant and more or less knowable causes and relations, things are also perceived or conditioned by the system's censoring/filtering criteria for 'relevant' data (what is relevant is conditioned on the criteria by which this relevancy is established), where this relevancy also depends on the (in)formal rules, education, lifestyle, values, experiences, the internal and external environment. Based on the already written lines, a reader should know that this book will not give some impenetrable or even half-truths to public agencies, as they are more flexible and unmanageable entities, as someone would think. According to George Bernard Shaw's saying that "the single biggest problem in communication is the illusion that it has happened", it could be said that the success of public agencies cannot be measured by the number of published books or articles, but by exposing an *underlying structure* in which they operate.

Over the last fifty years, countries have changed (based on various reasons that will be further elaborated) their governance structures by transferring the implementation of tasks to parastatal organisations known as public agencies, based on some version of ideal-type agency model; the latter was built on the claims of poor central performance, underpinned by ideas of much needed greater organisational and managerial autonomy and associated accountability that would apparently lead to greater performance. In the 1980s, governments were trapped between declining incomes and rising demands for better services; Gaebler and Osborne's idea of reinventing government emphasised one of the most common objections to government, that government agencies were incurably bureaucratic and resilient to change. They called on them to become more competitive, catalytic, community owned, mission driven, result-oriented, customer driven, enterprising, anticipatory, decentralised, and market-oriented (Osborne & Gaebler, 1993). In the UK, Australia, the US and New Zealand, this idea was/is known as neoliberalism or new public management (NPM) and was linked with four administrative 'megatrends', ie attempts to slow down or reverse government growth; the shift toward privatization and quasi-privatization, with renewed emphasis on 'subsidiarity' in service provision, the development of IT and the international agenda, focused on general issues of public management, all in addition to the older tradition of individual country specialisms in public administration (Hood, 1991). This idea was promoted in the EU with the introduction of market competition toward the creation of a single European market. The rise of agencies in the 1980s, known as 'agencification' (the creation or transfer of some governmental functions to subordinate or separated organisations from a ministry), marked the trend of relocation of many government activities into organisational forms that operated at an arms-length distance from policymakers. It was said that this 'will increase efficiency, encourage professional management, place services closer to citizens, reduce political interference, and enable ministers to focus on big policy issues (Pollitt, Talbot, Caulfield, & Smullen, 2004, p. 3). This trend follows the ideas of NPM (especially its emphasis on unit segregation in the public sector) also after the first (1973) and second (1979) world oil crisis, the 1991 global recession (due to the 1990-1991 Gulf War that heightened geopolitical uncertainty and another sharp increase in oil prices), the US credit crunch of 1990-1991, Scandinavian banking crises, the exchange rate mechanism of the European Monetary System, Japan's asset price bubble, and Central and Eastern Europe's transition to market economies that was accompanied by high inflation and output contractions (Kose, Sugawara & Terrones, 2000). The mentioned trends caused a decline of industrial production that was (and up to a large part still is) mainly oil-based driven. The consequences lead to the further decline of public resources through collected taxes, and 'the natural response of governments was to change their structures. One of them was the already mentioned agencification; it was believed that it would make governments more flexible, efficient, and effective if such bodies (agencies) were in arms'length from ministries and political influences. 'Such distribution of power to arm's length bodies has led to the ideas of increased managerial autonomy and the creation of new agencies. These arm-length bodies in central government now account for between 50% and 75% of public expenditure and public employment in OECD countries' (OECD, 2003, p. 5).

Most of the above-mentioned and other claims derived their ideas from the main idea of the *efficiency* of agencies as extensions of the organisational state that are at the same time (more or less) organisationally disjoint from the government, its ministerial departments, or its units. However, when efficiency is stretched too far, it breaks; this leads to the unmanageable and uncontrollable fragmentation, in this case, of autonomous units/agencies. Therefore, in the last decade, there has therefore been a reverse trend present to return tasks to the state or to merge smaller into larger agencies based on the ideas of greater transparency (and again of the "old") efficiency, control, and coordination.[8] The structural disaggregation and dispersion of delegated tasks were thus reversed due to concerns of horizontal coordination, known in the UK as 'joint-up government'', in Australia 'whole of government' in Canada 'horizontal management/government' and in New Zealand 'integrated government''. In all its versions, this reversal not only addresses the cross-boundary units, inter-departmental activity, and broader strategic and systemic initiatives of the government (Halligan, Buick, & O'Flynn, 2011), but also something deeper or more basic: *When similar ideas lead in opposite directions* (of centralization and deconcentration) *there is something more relevant behind them*, behind the motives on creation and functioning of agencies and state structures than only formally stated reasons. A discovery of this "something else" could be relevant if decision makers do not want to be endlessly trapped in pendulum swings. What is logical cannot necessarily also be real. Public agencies with their joint government initiative back to roots that brings the first within the parent ministries reflects a cyclic nature; a successive progress toward increasing structure and specialisation would lead them, due to their inflexibility and inadaptability, to their decay. This idea wrote Spencer in *The Principles of Sociology* (1898):[9] for him an increase of size in societies causes the increase of structure, division of labour, and specialisation. At first, hardly any mutual dependence among vital parts has dependent functions on one another, and injury on one hurts the other one also (this is an inevitable fact despite agencies being put under different parent ministries). Error facilitates adaptation with the help of 'the superior mind, aided by what we may figuratively call intellectual scent, passes by multitudes of unorganizable facts, but quickly detects facts full of significance, and takes them in as materials out of which cardinal truths may be elaborated' (Spencer, 1898 § 41).

A society and its institutions are living organisms undergoing continuing changes: parts, increase of mass leads to increase of structure, integration, coordination, clusters, growth, divisions, subdivisions, differentiations that lead to specialisations, reorganisations, maturity, and even decay, apply to all social structures as well as their functions. Their internal arrangements are nevertheless framed on the same principle: they relate with others through the incoming and outgoing channels of regulation and control on the primary (a person), secondary (family), and tertiary (and organisation) levels, where there is a contrast between the original mode of development and its later stages (Spencer, 1898 ch. IV-V). The relation between the lives of units and of the aggregate is conditioned by numerous factors where the first can exist without the second, while the latter usually exists longer than its units. They can be changed while the aggregate as an integrative whole continues. The same holds for agencies as units and their parent ministries as a whole – and as a unit at the same time of the government as

Introduction

a whole – and as a unit at the same time of the society as a whole. They will go through (in)sensible modifications and changes along the old, confirmed habits and practices. All are connected, and any kind of unnatural, gradual changes cause a disturbance: a cut of a blood vessel in a similar way to bad reorganisation without consent of units. This holds even more when the units are highly specialised and are thus hard to substitute without the risk of ill performance. It is better to exchange benefits between various units that are related to the aggregate – group, country, or society. Problems of adaptation to the environment (in the widest sense, to other persons, groups, organisations, their clusters and associations, the nature) usually occur due to lack of (intellectual, cooperative, connective) structure and functions (that are not seen as living organs).

This could be the reason why extensive agencification paths are the way to the uncontrolled fragmentation and back toward the unification of agencies under ministries; in such cases, there is probably a lack of needed control on the ingoing and outgoing relations (flows) *vis-a-vis* the main stocks, tasks, and purposes. Such binary relay on/off positions usually show an incompleteness of reforms that do not include or answer at least on the most relevant questions of management, control, and coordination of policy, its implementation, and their capability to see the whole (holistic vision, strategy, and tactics). In many cases, the best position is present somewhere in the middle between extremes; in cases of agencies *vis-à-vis* ministries, a middle ground could be in keeping the agencies but having a larger ministerial possibility of coordination and control. This is again only a logical statement but practically inflexible if public agencies would not be able to research their territories, extend their connections, select and convince each other in cooperative and integrative practices. An extensive presence of various types of agencies (agencification) present in many countries, and the reform based joined-up government and whole-of-government approaches towards the coordination of agencies, show not only that agencies are here to stay, but also, they are hard to coordinate[10] – with the present tools. This makes academic research particularly essential for all governance approaches (that do not address the flexibility and dynamism of the environment in which public agencies operate not only at the start of agency creation, but also continually *vis-a-vis* its main purposes and goals).

It can be said that the central authoritative functions are typically carried out by central departments, that agencies implement relatively comprehensible and quantifiable functions, that units which conduct more commercial functions operate closer to the private sector rules, while units that conduct more public functions are closer to public service rules. Instead of competition, here are units subordinated to more formally determined content and process compliance rules, to more ex ante input and (less ex-post) output-oriented administration than the private sector. The classification of authorities, agencies, and other public bodies can be done based on available data, but, as countries' differences show, a match between institutional forms, citizens' demands, government-agency functions, types of autonomy (managerial, policy, structural, financial, legal, and interventional autonomy), coordination, and control is hard to achieve. Even within ministerial units there is present information asymmetry that arises proportionately with the distance of the agency[11] (with "auto-pilot") from ministry, regardless of the range of controlling instruments that the ministry or some other institution has at its disposal. Among the key emerging issues regarding distributed public governance are the lack of clarity i) on differences between the various types of agencies, authorities, and other government bodies, their strengths and weaknesses, ii) on roles and accountability and lack of top governance capacity, iii) weak accountability mechanisms to ministers and ministries, Parliament, and civil society, and iv) weak coordination mechanisms (OECD, 2002). Despite the popularity of agencification from the 1980s onward, 'there is no universally accepted classification of arm's length bodies, which differ widely in terms of organisation, legal status, and degree of management autonomy or political independence' (OECD, 2003, p. 7). Almost two decades later, there are still no practical answers on these issues. Given such a blurred frame of distributed governance, it is no surprise that despite four decades of reinvention, which nevertheless has had some efficiency results, even in the author's home country, the US government is less trusted than ever before (from 1958's 73% in 1958 to 17%) (Pew Research Center, 2020) or that the European Values Survey saw a long-term decline in confidence in the British parliament, from 41% in 1981 to 23% in 2010 (Ipsos MORI, 2019). The enormous amount of new organizational forms, their various structures, practices, management, and reporting mechanisms have caused a distorted picture of how the public system is functioning as a whole. This new institutional environment has created new challenges for governments to maintain central direction and control, and for the public to maintain democratic control, the public needs accountability to trust in the actions of agencies. 'Most OECD countries have been creating non-commercial bodies outside the core public service on an ad hoc basis, resulting in administrative "zoos". This reduces the transparency of government for the citizen and may compromise oversight and accountability within government' (OECD, 2003, p. 9).

One reason for such a state of affairs could be to ignore the background elements of agencies that cannot be defined through agencification. The latter is nevertheless the worldwide spread phenomenon; one reason for this confluence or similarity among different countries could be isomorphism that describes a tendency of organisations to, over time, start to look and act more and more alike. DiMaggio and Powell (1991) attributed this mimicry to the need of organisations for legitimacy in order to survive (the need for legitimacy is even more important than the need for efficiency). By adopting legitimate standards (organisational formats and business techniques), organisations can be accepted by their environment and can thus continue to exist, but they also formally exist when they are not publicly taken as legitimate. The principle of transparency and openness (as the "late comers" of legitimacy elements) in the era of information technology could be achieved - some say – more easily and efficiently, but there is more than just 'appealing words'. Many people - not only Sir Thomas Moore, who coined the word "utopia" in 1516 – have tried to imagine a perfect world or here, a perfect agency. Such aspirations cannot be fully realised (as people argue already on what is perfect or ideal), but decision-makers can nevertheless alter the identification, estimation, determination, implementation, and evaluation of problems when they are attentive to the applied tools and processes. What is perceived and then recognised as (in)correct, what defines a person as a human being, or a public agency as efficient, is not a person's choice, but its prechosen and arranged frame of perspective (also by others) in which something emerges as a choice in the first place;[12] there is not only one public interest, and it is *contradictio in adiecto* when defined only by one person; its content contrasts in different relations send practises that are as icebergs understood/seen only by their visible *peeks*. Similarly, there is not only one public agency, and the latter cannot be defined only by one author.[13]

From Berkeley's point of view (*esse est percipi* – to be is to be perceived) there are many environments that people perceive; as there are some common effects, we all observe, the environment can be divided into the internal (subjective, system, a model) and the external (the outside world, things not present in our minds, systems, or models) one (already in such binary division there are four combinations possible, along the mentioned, also external-internal and internal-external). Attention is based on sense and perceptions; these latter people receive from the environment in which they act, interact, and react with each other; this is known as immaterialism. Berkeley in 1710 claimed that we know the laws of nature only by their effects that they have on our experi-

Introduction

ence that 'teaches us that such and such ideas are attended with such and such other ideas in the ordinary course of things ... [and] this gives us a sort of foresight which enables us to regulate our actions for the benefit of life ... All this we know not by discovering any necessary connection between our ideas, but only by the observation of the settled laws of nature' (Berkeley, 2003, p. 46). Although real things for him exist, we can know them not through the non-discoverable causality,[14] but through our senses and therefore 'exist in the mind, and in that sense they are alike ideas' (Berkeley, 2003, p. 48). From this point of view, a public agency can already mean different things for different people's senses and minds. Berkeley's immaterial essence with Sartre's existentialism (Sartre, 2001) where 'every choice reveals what I do' can be more tuned with the help of a *system*, where perceptions are changed and updated according to changes noticed in the environment by the system and its indicators that lead to system reactions. Flexibility and dynamism (of agencies) can be addressed through the system perspective, which can be upgraded to a complexity perspective. This is the main idea and the path of this work. Citizens have such public institutions as they and decision-makers *perceive (and tolerate)* through the 'good / bad' system that enables perceptions in the first place by paying attention to data. People should be attentive to numerous connections among structures, parts, relations and stakeholders – that form *patterns*[15] – in order to (know how to) achieve wanted goals. An assumption is that higher probability of success exists when all parts of the system in mutual relationships (at least slightly) change their primary or starting positions (recalibration). Working together to modify interactions or transactions (with collaborative effort) to remodify them, in the next step as the dynamic expression of effective adjustment, signifies not only efficiency and interdependency among parts, but also the basic expression of systems and systemic thinking. System theory, recognizing the final goals, seeks to identify the connections to adapt the system's operations to changes in the environment with the help of feedback loops. In multiple relations, multiple causations are present, and this further points to complexity. To be satisfied with an identification of one matter at a given moment is too static (for future cases). The same holds for the comparative analysis of various public agencies; the understanding of the same matter can be only partial (frozen in time) when its relations with other things are not incorporated in a real time-space sense. Despite its mainly functional orientation, system theory does not disregard organisational issues. The first is achieved through the second. A decision maker or an agent 'imagines' the system model based on the information he has from his previous experience and the environment. The identification of similarities among those two parts is condensed into a kind of 'schema' (Gell-Mann, 2002b) or a model of and from which he (re)acts on and in the real world. It thus matters how agencies, as the focus of this work, are perceived to be able to change their (from various sources recognised and assembled) schema. The advantage of system and complexity theory can thus go way above public agencies towards each complex adaptable system. Taking a system apart – and a human is also the complex adaptive system – does not reveal much about its processes because its *élan* is in *relations* among parts, while these relations are caused/recognised also by the free will, cognitive errors, and hidden, nonobservable subjective behaviour (the one exerted also by employees in public agencies). Relations among people are usually known as interactions or transactions, as acts of conduct (business, negotiations, activities, etc.) towards a goal (conclusion, settlement) or actions that in cooperation with others can lead to better solutions than the ones made in isolation. As action is an agent's predisposition, as in life itself, where events, actions, and relationships cannot be understood as isolated phenomena, agent actions can also be understood from their relationships.

The above-mentioned pro-NPM ideas on debureaucratization, decentralization, privatization, and managerialism, on the other hand, not only pose challenges to important public service values (Kearney & Hays, 2016) and public servants' minds or ideas, but they should also be embraced first in their *relations*. Despite the multifariousness, ubiquity, longevity, and endurance of agencies, there is still a lack of answers on their basic elements and goals because the *changeable* relations among them have not been adequately emphasised. Even the big proponents of "distributed public governance" (that per se points to different relations) like OECD acknowledge the existence of various problems: i) the use of ambiguous terminology and the absence of a coherent classification of the variety of organisational forms, ii) the creation of agencies on a case-by-case and ad hoc basis without systematic reflexion on the consequences for the government as a whole, iii) focus on organisations associated with New Public Management (NPM), although such bodies were created over a much longer period and for a wide variety of purposes, and iv) obtaining comparative data on the variety of very different government bodies functioning in different institutional contexts, and drawing general conclusions applicable to different countries (OECD, 2002). There is a lack not (only) of thresholds and indicators by which various activities could be compared despite their various frames *vis-à-vis* various organisational forms, but mainly of understanding the *complexity* in which public agencies operate. Complexity (being the upper step of systems) leads decision-makers towards different arrangements seen through flexible elements like self-organization, adaptation, bifurcation, or emergence. The need to elaborate a problem, to evaluate possible alternative solutions given their methodological, organisational, and other specifics, to put a possible solution under a test and/or experiment to measure its effects, could better address the structural changes, reasons, and conditions for creating new organisations, their possibility of coordination and control, and democratic transparency and accountability, but even this is not enough. If the most important goals are those that cannot be measured, there must be at least some general guiding principles.

Although increasing sums are being spent on organisational development, there is a significant gap in the practical understanding of how individual institutional transformations and development can best translate into a changed organization or systemic practice. This book focuses on the role of agencies in their widest possible meaning as public institutions and with governmental capacity to provide public services in a more successful manner, through agencies. This book consists of a collection of chapters on a range of themes that draw from across different agencies, including approaches to individual and common institutional development, with examples from both intra- and interagency contexts. In this way, it gives illustrations of internal organisation development and partnerships that work across the public service system. The book has three main aims, which are to:

– present the different ways in which agencification is currently being deployed in leadership and organization development in public service organizations;

– provide an evaluative critique of the outcomes, lessons, and issues in terms of capabilities developed, resources, opportunities, and constraints for institutional approaches;

– explore implications for future approaches to the development of public agencies and their leaders and organisations.

Fundamental to these issues are the questions of what is meant by 'agency' so that it can be developed, and what is systemic and adaptable agencification so that it attracts the hope of providing enhanced knowledge on agencies and their management. The topic of public agencies is complex enough per se but still beyond what is usually described in the literature, or what is sometimes even clearly stated but ignored; the aim here is not to build a consistent theory of agencies (as this is not possible due to the real-

Introduction

life time, space and context complexity and subjective practise of free-minded employees), but to present new perspectives by which agencies can be more clearly understood also in their (national) contexts in the real time-space frame. Their success depends on the nature of the broader political and administrative culture within which they are surrounded. The approach is built on the fact that complex problems cannot be comparatively analysed and solved, but must be elaborated as systems that are embedded in and implemented within higher and lower systems. This makes a difference between an organisational form *per se* and reasons (*e.g.*, managerial autonomy, efficiency, political independence, specialisation, public participation) for which decision-makers have created a particular agency and its *layers*. Given the variety of forms, competences, cadre, coordination, management and control of agencies in various countries and the continuous changes in the environment (natural, political, economic, and social contexts), this demands a similar variety of responses that work proportionally with the flexibility of changes. This procedural condition should be tested based on the material one, because *the real purpose of the system is what it (de facto) does* (Beer, 2002). The same or different organisational structures in one country can have different or similar results in another, while in the next cycle the results can be contrary even in the same country. Therefore, 'in assessing the agency model, one should pay less attention to motive and more to effect' (Shick, 2002, p. 35). Therefore, the essence is not to present an inexistent super agency", but the ways by which various agencies can address problems according to the rate of change in the continuous following, the best results could be with respect to systemic, structural, and complex elements.

The aim is to propose a model of an agency that could serve as a guide/recipe when, how, where, for whom, and why a specific form of an agency could be established, how or when different agencies could be changed/abolished/created or merged/divided. The main aim is to provide a tool by which each country can make its analysis of its agencies based on which conclusions can be drawn about their mergers, divisions, or transformations. It is not a universal tool, but only a helpful way to better understand public agencies. On the other hand, already from such aims, it can be inferred the claim that agencies are *institutions* with their specifics in time, place, context, and other elements and are hence not specified or taken for granted in the perspective of the systemic, institutional analysis of public administration and/or public institutions. Not only people but also organisations and countries go through structural transformations in time to change the environment. *Adaptability* thus becomes the legitimising rule needed to cope with changes, and national (organisational) structures (such as relations among parts) (also of agencies) are no exemption. Having this in mind, this work tries to emphasise some background, structural elements of complexity on which public agencies can be administrated differently than they are now. A fundamental challenge of organisations is that of integrating and coordinating the components and domains of the organisation (Rainey, 2009) and its entire context of the environment, decision making, values, culture, people and their behaviours in the widest sense, or can be named with the more popular notion of 'managing change.' No book, including this one, cannot produce direct effects on the ground, as implementation in a specific context is missing. There are too many (un)known elements present to be able to successfully predict what will a specific agency do in a specific context. There is no magic formula, no single way of doing things, in the way of Tolstoy's quote from Anna Karenina that "all happy families are alike; each unhappy family is unhappy in its own way". Some perspectives can nevertheless be presented, some frames could be given, based on system and complexity theory, to make the mentioned integration and coordination less stressful. When writing on complexity, applied here to public agencies, there is no way not to avoid complex statements, but it has been tried as much as possible to present everything as simple as possible, but not simpler, as Einstein would say.

REFERENCES

Adams, D. (2014). *Dirk Gently's Holistic Detective Agency*. Gallery Books.

Arendt, H. (1981). *The Life of the Mind*. Harcourt Brace Jovanovich.

Arnauld, A., & Nicole, P. (1996). *Logic Or the Art of Thinking* (J. V. Buroker, Trans.). Cambridge University Press. doi:10.1017/CBO9781139166768

Barnard, C. I. (1968). The Functions of the Executive. Cambirdge: Harvard University Press.

Beer, S. (2002). What is cybernetics? *Kybernetes, 31*(2), 209–219. doi:10.1108/03684920210417283

Berkeley, G. (2003). *A Treatise Concerning the Principles of Human Knowledge* (T. J. McCormack, Ed.). Dover Publications, Inc.

Boin, A., Fahy, L. A., & 't Hart, P. (Eds.). (2020). *Guardians of Public Value: How Public Organisations Become and Remain Institutions*. Springer Nature.

Bouckaert, G., Peters, B. G., & Verhoest, K. (2010). *The Coordination of Public Sector Organizations: Shifting Patterns of Public Management*. Palgrave MacMillan. doi:10.1057/9780230275256

Christensen, T., & Lægreid, P. (2007). The Whole-of-Government Approach to Public Sector Reform. *Public Administration Review, 67*(6), 1059–1066. doi:10.1111/j.1540-6210.2007.00797.x

Dawkins, R. (2006). *The Blind Watchmaker*. Penguin.

Descartes, R., de Spinoza, B., & Leibniz, G. W. V. (1974). *The Rationalists: Descartes: Discourse on Method & Meditations; Spinoza: Ethics; Leibniz: Monadolo gy & Discourse on Metaphysics*. Anchor Books.

Eaglestone, R. (2017). *The Broken Voice: Reading Post-Holocaust Literature*. Oxford University Press. doi:10.1093/oso/9780198778363.001.0001

Feynman, R. P., Leighton, R. B., & Sands, M. (1965). The Feynman Lectures on Physics, Vol. (Later Printing edition). Reading, Mass.: Addison Wesley. doi:10.1119/1.1972241

Fukuyama, F. (2014). *Political Order and Political Decay: From the Industrial Revolution to the Globalization of Democracy*. Farrar, Straus and Giroux.

Gell-Mann, M. (2002a). The Quark and the Jaguar (VIII edition). New York: W.H. Freeman & Company.

Goodsell, C. T. (2010). *Mission Mystique: Belief Systems in Public Agencies*. CQ Press.

Halligan, J., Buick, F., & O'Flynn, J. (2011). Experiments with joined-up, horizontal and whole-of-government in Anglophone countries. In A. Massey (Ed.), *International Handbook on Civil Service Systems* (pp. 74–102). Edward Elgar Publishing. doi:10.4337/9781781001080.00010

Introduction

Hood, C. (1991). A Public Management for All Seasons? *Public Administration*, *69*(1), 3–19. doi:10.1111/j.1467-9299.1991.tb00779.x

Huntington, S. P. (1968). *Political order in changing societies*. Yale University Press.

Ipsos MORI. (2019). *Trust the Truth?* IPSOS. https://www.ipsos.com/sites/default/files/ct/publication/documents/2019-09/ipsos-thinks-trust-the-truth.pdf

Kearney, R. C., & Hays, S. W. (2016). Reinventing Government, The New Public Management and Civil Service Systems in International Perspective: The Danger of Throwing the Baby Out with the Bathwater. *Review of Public Personnel Administration*. (Sage CA: Thousand Oaks, CA). doi:10.1177/0734371X9801800404

Kose, A. M., Sugawara, N., & Terrones, M. E. (2000). *Global Recessions: Policy Research Working Paper 9172*. World Bank Group. https://documents1.worldbank.org/curated/en/185391583249079464/pdf/Global-Recessions.pdf

Lanza, R., & Berman, B. (2013). *Biocentrism: How Life and Consciousness are the Keys to Understanding the True Nature of the Universe*. BenBella Books, Inc.

Leseure, M. (2010). *Key Concepts in Operations Management*. SAGE. doi:10.4135/9781446251720

Malik, F. (2012). *The Right Corporate Governance: Effective Top Management for Mastering Complexity*. Campus Verlag.

Malik, F. (2016). *Strategy: Navigating the Complexity of the New World*. Campus Verlag.

Newton. (1947). *Sir Isaac Newton's Mathematical Principles of Natural Philosophy and His System of the World* (A. Motte & F. Cajori, Eds.). Oakland: University of California Press.

OECD. (2002). *Distributed Public Governance Agencies, Authorities and other Government Bodies: Agencies, Authorities and other Government Bodies*. OECD Publishing.

OECD. (2003). *Public Sector Modernisation: Changing Organisations GOV/PUMA(2003)19*. OECD. http://www.oecd.org/officialdocuments/publicdisplaydocumentpdf/?cote=GOV/PUMA(2003)19&docLanguage=En

Osborne, D., & Gaebler, T. (1993). *Reinventing Government: How the Entrepreneurial Spirit is Transforming the Public Sector*. Plume.

Peterson, J. B. (2021). *Beyond Order: 12 More Rules for Life*. Penguin Publishing Group.

Pew Research Center. (2020). Public Trust in Government Remains Near Historic Lows as Partisan Attitudes Shift. Pew Research Center—U.S. Politics & Policy. https://www.pewresearch.org/politics/2017/05/03/public-trust-in-government-remains-near-historic-lows-as-partisan-attitudes-shift/

Pollitt, C., Talbot, C., Caulfield, J., & Smullen, A. (2004). *Agencies: How Governments Do Things Through Semi-Autonomous Organizations*. Palgrave MacMillan.

Powell, W. W., & DiMaggio, P. (Eds.). (1991). *The New institutionalism in organizational analysis*. The University of Chicago Press. doi:10.7208/chicago/9780226185941.001.0001

Rainey, H. G. (2009). *Understanding and Managing Public Organizations* (4th ed.). Jossey-Bass.

Sartre, J.-P. (2001). *Jean-Paul Sartre: Basic Writings* (S. Priest, Ed.). Psychology Press.

Selznick, P. (2011). *Leadership in Administration: A Sociological Interpretation*. Quid Pro Books.

Shick, A. (2002). Agencies* in Search of Principles. In OECD (Ed.), *Distributed Public Governance Agencies, Authorities and other Government Bodies: Agencies, Authorities and other Government Bodies* (pp. 33–52). OECD Publishing.

Spencer, H. (1898). *The Principles of Sociology* (Vol. 1). D. Appleton and Company.

Strauss, P. L., Rakoff, T. D., Metzger, G. E., Barron, D. J., & O'Connell, A. J. (2018). *Administrative Law, Cases and Comments* (12th ed.). Foundation Press.

von Clausewitz, C. (2007). *On War* (M. Howard & P. Paret, Trans.). Oxford University Press.

ENDNOTES

[1] "Holistic" refers to … the fundamental interconnectedness of all things … I see the solution to each problem as being detectable in the pattern and web of the whole. The connections between causes and effects are often much more subtle and complex than we with our rough and ready understanding of the physical world might naturally suppose (Adams, 2014, p. 127).

[2] Carl Von Clausewitz's in his classic treatise *On War* states that 'theory exists so that one need not start afresh each time sorting out the material and ploughing through it, but will find it ready to hand and in good order. It is meant to educate the mind of the future commander, or, more accurately, to guide him in his self-education, not to accompany him to the battlefield' (Clausewitz, 2007, p. 90).

[3] Administrative agencies are all of the authorities and operating units of the government, except for the constitutional established entities...except for Congress, the President and Vice president and the Supreme Court. They are sometimes called "agencies", but sometimes "departments", sometimes "boards", sometimes "commissions" – they are all still agencies. Just as agents, in the ordinary sense of the term, carry out tasks for their principals, so, too, do agencies carry out of the instructions of, and are responsible to, the three constitutionally established, institutional "principals". Because administrative agencies largely are not established or even mentioned by the Constitution, they have to be created by statute, or in some cases, by presidential order. … There are many commonalities among most administrative agencies. There is a head of agency, with a small cadre of advisors immediately responsible to that office, but the great bulk of agency personnel serve in "administrations", "services", "offices", or the like–subordinates units each with its own particular responsibilities and hierarchical organisation (Strauss, Rakoff, Metzger, Barron, & O'Connell, 2018, p. 22).

[4] When it is at its most socially and culturally powerful, it cannot be explicitly discussed, or only at great risk; when the secret no longer holds such power, people deny their knowledge of its content and their complicity with any concealment. One result of this is that both the subjective experience of the public secret and its wider meaning are beyond the limits of the discipline of history and both are better elucidated through a work of fiction (Eaglestone, 2017, p. 9).

Introduction

5   Arendt argues that 'the need of reason is not inspired by the quest for truth but by the quest for meaning. And truth and meaning are not the same. The basic fallacy…is to interpret meaning on the model of truth' (Arendt, 1981, p. 15). Thinking is focused on meaning and knowing on cognition. Agencies need both parts: to legally act in the present and to look into (or adapt for) the future.

6   Peterson's *Beyond Order* (2021) explores how the dangers of too much security and control might be beneficially avoided. As human understanding is insufficient one should keep one foot within order and the other in the beyond. People explore and find the deepest of meanings at the frontier, secure enough to keep fear under control but constantly learning, as they face something with what they have not been adapted yet.

7   See e.g. (Strauss et al., 2018).

8   Co-ordination is the alignment and synchronisation of people, processes, and information within operations systems in order to maximise productivity (Leseure, 2010, p. 44).

9   § 228. In societies, as in living bodies, increase of mass is habitually accompanied by increase of structure. Along with that integration … both exhibit in high degrees the secondary trait, differentiation. § 230 The advance of organization follows the advance of aggregation and … conforms to the same general law: differentiations proceed from the more general to the more special. § 268. Every organ of the one and institution of the other becomes, as maturity is neared, more coherent and definite, and offers a greater obstacle to alterations required either by increase of size or variation of conditions. … Then he might enlarge on the fact that, as in individual organisms so in social organisms, after the structures proper to the type have fully evolved there presently begins a slow decay. § 41 Progress is present where a higher ability to survive has a structure that has greater powers of selecting materials fit for assimilation.

10 Christensen and Lægreid warn on the fact that several strategies for whole-of-government (WG) can be competing, that WG is mainly about lower-level politics and getting people together on the ground to work together; that building a WG system is a long-term project that takes time to implement. Collaborate public management should consider that 'the division of labour and specialization are inevitable features of modern organizations, implying that WG initiatives will be difficult to implement. Working horizontally is a very time- and resource-consuming activity' (Christensen & Lægreid, 2007, p. 1063).

11 Information is power for organizations (public or private), and organizations are often reluctant to share information because they will lose their bargaining position with other organizations, or with political leaders (Bouckaert, Peters, & Verhoest, 2010, p. 30).

12 This can be shortened with the Latin phrase *Fortuna Eruditis Favet* ("fortune favours the prepared mind"). Duty to act in accordance with the law is never absolute – it must be primarily perceived as such in a person's mental system that is (re)assembled in a way that emotionally and physically corresponds to it. This does not mean only these emotional and physical elements also configure and hence co-define the mental ones, but also the second are based on intersecting processes and their combinations.

13 This work made by a single author, logically cannot present some "truth" to public agencies, but solely some general perspectives. The same stands for editorial monographs in which various authors put their views in their papers that are not merged with others to extrapolate common points, but present their individual views.

14 The connexion of ideas does not imply the relation of cause and effect, but only of a mark or sign with the thing signified. The fire which I see is not the cause of the pain I suffer upon my approach-

ing it, but the mark that forewarns me of it (Berkeley, 2003, p. 67). Similar thing was already stated in 1662 by Arnauld and Nicole: '[e]ven though people realized that the pain is not in the fire that burns the hand, they may well have been mistaken in thinking it is in the hand burned by the fire ... it is only in the mind, although occasioned by what happens in the hand, because bodily pain is nothing more than a feeling of aversion in the soul to some motion contrary to the natural constitution of its body' (Arnauld & Nicole, 1996, p. 50).

[15] All around us are facts that are related to one another. Of course, they can be regarded as separate entities and learned that way. But what a difference it makes when we see them as part of a pattern! Many facts then become more than just items to be memorized-their relationships permit us to use a compressed description, a kind of theory, a schema, to apprehend and remember them. They begin to make some sense. The world becomes a more comprehensible place. Pattern recognition comes naturally to us humans; we are, after all, complex adaptive systems ourselves. It is in our nature, by biological inheritance and also through the transmission of culture, to see patterns, to identify regularities, to construct schemata in our minds (Gell-Mann, 2002a, p. 89).

Chapter 1
Towards Holistic Agency

ABSTRACT

The holistic agency (HA) is based on the idea of system and complexity theory, which embraces action learning and organization development. HA is a planned change that takes a systems approach and makes extensive use of collaborative techniques to both solve the immediate problem and leave the organization in a more competent state to handle future challenges. The success of public agencies can be improved by implementing a systematic administration that demands the identification, monitoring, and analysis of areas and the need for flexibility due to institutional and contextual changes in real-time frames. Attention should also be paid to financial and security services and management activities, such as planning, organization, command and control, and coordination. The science of management, with its systemic component, is a system of knowledge that can be used to understand relationships, predict results, and influence results in all circumstances if individuals are organized to work together to achieve a common goal.

INTRODUCTION

My philosophy comes from a worldview that looks at the world as one. It's a holistic view that sees the world as interconnected and interdependent and integrated in so many different ways, which informs my politics.

– Dennis Kucinich

In the introduction of this work, it is stated that its aim is to propose a model of an agency that could serve as a guide/recipe when, how, where, for whom, and why a specific form of an agency could be established, how, or when different agencies could be changed/abolished/created or merged/divided. This tool by which each country can make its analysis on its agencies is here presented as the *holistic agency*. The latter could be something within or from which something else originates, develops, or takes form. With the help of a holistic agency (regardless of their level in the system of the EU), the right to good administration can also be further enhanced. Based on the Charter of Fundamental Rights of the

DOI: 10.4018/979-8-3693-0507-2.ch001

European Union, the right to good administration (Article 41) became one of the human rights. Although this right is written in the sense of an adjudicative administrative procedure, there are numerous other (informal) procedures by which agencies are getting their jobs done. The holistic agency is based on the viable one and does not refer to uniformity and stability between organizational units, activities, or programmes (such as joined government) in the classical sense of these words: *it exhibits uniformity and stability through the constant adjustment of differences and variables to establish a balance between various options* (i.e. be more effective with fewer resources), aligned with the pre-given formal purposes that are further balanced with mutually reinforced tools, actions, and outputs in the changing environment (as "a moving target") environment. The idea of holistic agency (HA) resembles the wholeness of human actions: *the achievement of main goals* (e.g. to prosper, grow, to be successful, happy, or without unwonted distractions) *based on dynamic approaches* that change or accommodate doings according to the given context, still in the light of main goals. The holistic agency is attentive to its structure and the power relationships that are present behind formal tasks and competences. The idea of holism and/or awareness of a wider frame in which one acts is similar in various levels, be it on the macro, meso, or micro, to the public or private sector. Holistic government was advocated first by Perri 6 in 1997; he argued that the government must become holistic, preventive, outcome-oriented and culture–changed, *i.e.,* concentrated around persuasion and information rather than coercion and command (Perri, 1997). Holistic governance is (more) attentive to the needs of the public (Perri, Leat, Seltzer, & Stoker, 2002), and transforms citizens into co-participants in public policy as co-designers, co-decision-makers, co-producers, and co-evaluators (Pollitt, Bouckaert, & Löffler, 2006). Three strategies could be adopted to realize such governance: online governance, integrated government organizations, and active civil service (Peng, 2005). The elements of holistic alternatives reflect what is already known as system theory that emerged in the 1940s by von Bertalanffy. He defined a system as 'consisting of parts "in interaction"' (1968, p. 19). A human *per se* is an evident example of such a system.

Seeing from this point of view, there was no large change in (still too rigid) regulatory techniques in decades, while at least in theory some steps towards higher flexibility were made: the UNDP is close to the effective and efficient public administration with its emphasis on the whole regulatory cycle (without using this specific phrase) with the notion of Resilience and/or ability to anticipate and prepare for future events (UNDP, 2011). The same stands for the OECD's notion of "regulatory governance" that reflects the need of governments to be actively engaged in assuring regulation through an integrated approach to the deployment of regulatory institutions tools and processes (OECD, 2011). Based on the OECD (2017) document, the European Commission claims approaches in public management need to shift to systems thinking (2017). Good administration (GA) and good governance (GG) could be more easily achieved with the help of the HA, provided that the perspectives of systemic and complex thinking are applied, when models and rules are seen as systems' parts, with the known goals and inputs, outputs, stocks, flows, positive and negative feedbacks through which reality is constantly monitored, and new conditions, states and patterns are detected, according to which the agency realigns its doings, without changing the main goals and legal obligations. There is no point to talk about administrative models if reality goes its own way. Administrative and legal science should work hand in hand. To reveal an underlying structure that causes events, there should be an effective model of HA; there should be present and connected elements of multiple inputs, outputs, environments, boundaries, flows and stocks, positive and negative, single and double feedbacks, adjustments, multiple (inter)connections, emergence (of new things), complexity, tensions, complexity, homeostasis, self-organisation, patterns and control. Decision-makers in HA do not apply them. The concepts of emergence, adaptation or self-organisation in the system represent by their flexibility a challenge to the classical legal principle of certainty and predictability, while the usual legal reactions are without tools to as quickly as possible address the unintended or unplanned actions, driven not by command and control but by chance, adaptation and emergence. Solutions exist, and they could be applied; one of them is HA, that is an agency based on system and complexity theory:

HA understands the need of planned or anticipated change; dynamism is here seen as the necessary element in the apparently stable environment, and has thus integrated the diagnostic process of relations, trends, and changes. It empowers employees and builds on interpersonal, group and intergroup communication, help and interventions (action learning and contrary, learning in action). Employees here learn how to solve real problems and take action on them in real time (because they can see the present patterns/effects from the preestablished indicators); they hence learn through questioning, reflection and action of their own proposals and solutions. The notion of HA based on system and complexity theory hence embraces action learning[1] and organization development that encompasses long-range efforts and programs intended to systemically improve an organization's ability to survive by changing its problem-solving and renewal processes; it 'involves moving toward an adaptive organization and achieving excellence by integrating the desires of individuals for growth and development with organizational goals' (D. R. Brown & Harvey, 2006, p. 3). Like organisation development, HA is about the planned the change, where change is the only stable constant. High performance and success are based on strategic changes that embrace people in systems and people as systems: 'managers can no longer function within the traditional organizational chart, but must integrate their department with the goals and strategy of the whole organization' (D. R. Brown & Harvey, 2006, p. 39). HA can be seen as an example or the result of organisational development, where the elements of such development, like action research as a change strategy, a systems approach, "the client knows best", the emphasis on processes (and not only on outcomes), working at multiple levels of analysis and the importance of values (Rothwell & Sulli-

Figure 1. Holistic agency

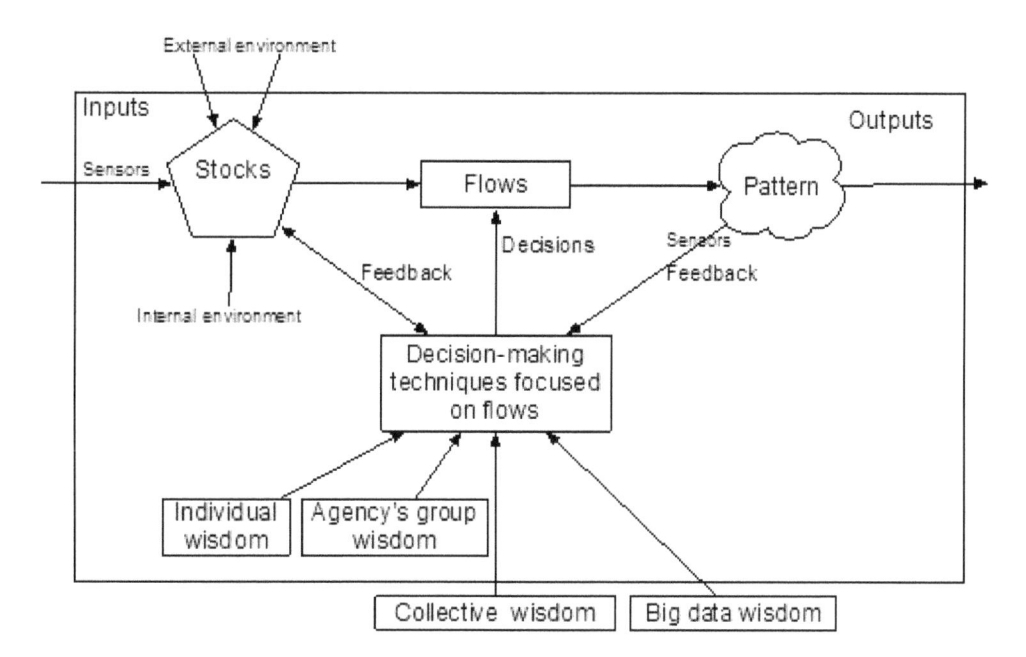

van, 2005) are all present. HA is about change management, about the constant practice of the agency's positioning/emplacement with its surroundings, similarly as a person's good, virtuous life, multiplied by many persons, it is about adaptation, evolution and growth.

In dynamic environments, a systemic and complexity approach is needed that will be based on the flexible management of policies and their implementation, rather than on the classical policy planning and mechanical implementation. HA as an expression of organisational development is 'planned change that takes a systems approach and makes extensive use of collaborative techniques to both solve the immediate problem and leave the organization in a more competent state to handle future challenges' (Rothwell & Sullivan, 2005, p. xxv). It is a system-based use of human deliberate actions with the designed plans, enhancement, and reinforcement of strategies, structures, relations, and processes on a path towards a successfulness of organization. For public agencies, there is not only an obvious developmental need to be flexible, not only due to various inputs or external forces (the government, unions, stockholders, customers, competitors, and suppliers), but due to inevitable flexibility itself, where change as said, is the only reliable element. The improbable is becoming probable, and the unthinkable is almost conventional. Agencies should continuously improve; this is the more important when compared with companies (that are changing or are going out of business) because agencies usually – due to tasks in the name of public interest – are not going out of business. Continuous change ("there is nothing permanent but change" – Heraclitus) is a way of life not to make a profit, but to fulfil goals in the public interest. A critical challenge for leaders is to inspire individuals to work as a team, to see themselves as an inevitable part of the agency's success. Due to the public interest task fulfilment, the importance of HA is the more important than as a successful company that does its doings only for their owners and stakeholders.

On the other side of flexibility, methods should be also certain, predictable, and accountable as this is not only the classical demand of the rule of law, but also of a human condition of being. System theory can be effective and accountable – HA and with it also public administration could be seen as the system, and careless is the one who does not assemble it as such. The HA, GA and GG can be closer to their goals when parts are seen as systems' parts. HA in the functional sense means aspirational decision-making for the maximisation of public interest. GG is also based on behaviour and focused on various stakeholders' present in different nets, while in holistic alternatives this is done with the integration of stakeholders in a co-productive manner. The holistic approach is nowadays at the front gate of the systemic approach. The HA, GA, GG, and/or all-encompassing holism (as a system) should address goals aligned with legal rules (when goals cannot be achieved otherwise). HA should act systemically to detect, act and resolve public problems. This kind of behaviour can be addressed with the notion of systematic administration that demands the identification, monitoring, and analysis of areas, and the need for flexibility due to institutional and contextual changes in real time frames. Systemic responses are needed to design and implement participation mechanisms, draft and implement best practices, develop information management systems, ensure evidence-based decision-making,[2] follow thresholds (that indicate a need to apply other rules or policies) and correct discrepancies in a never-ending regulatory cycle of our needs, goals and processes. Results and/or patterns that HA accomplishes represent nothing but its *culture*, its accepted or tolerated patterns of behaviour, its set of values, and behavioural norms. As these are only words, it is time to frame HA first here in theory and then "take it for a spin" in real practice. HA can be gradually achieved if the perspectives from system and complexity theory are not disregarded. Some of them are given in the next subsection.

HOLISTIC RECOMMENDATIONS FOR PUBLIC AGENCIES

Governments should have procedures to identify the potential to hive off some segments on lower levels and to consider the establishment or extension of agencies. The cost–benefit analysis should always be a starting factor of all changes; in this regard, the relevant and reliable data from various indicators related to the implementation of the delegated tasks, before and after separation should be at hand. A result of this should be further aligned with public value. The success and similar factors of programmes which continue to be managed in-house should be known, while the supervision of agencies can be done by setting results-oriented objectives, based on relevant performance indicators which form the basis for future changes. This approach can be more efficient when some systemic predispositions are considered. Science of management with its systemic component is a system of knowledge with which one can understand or explain relationships, predict results, and influence results in all circumstances if individuals are organized to work together to achieve a common goal. In diversified fields, the ability to manage is the more pronounced, and its weaknesses can be found in the lack of knowledge and management skills. If the division of labour is unavoidable, coordination becomes mandatory. The organizational problem thus refers to the implementation of coordination at with the centre, along the autonomous operation in individual parts and areas, mutual coordination, reporting and adjustment. The efficiency of work is thus reflected through the homogeneity of the management system. Just as human rights are important for an individual, similar is coordination essential for good organizations. In addition to technical operations that directly address goals, attention should be paid also to the area of financial and security services and management activities such as planning, organization, command and control, and especially coordination. In any case, the interministerial working groups for adaptation to common goals cannot represent an active coordination that responds to and adapts to changes in the dimension of real space and time i.e., here and now. To achieve this or be closer to this state of affairs, some obstacles are given below that should be properly addressed in the way towards HA.

STARTING POINT OF PLANNING: UNDERSTAND THE CONCEPTS

Planning starting points should be objective enough; individual parts of any system can be studied in three dimensions (philosophical,[3] strategic,[4] and tactical[5]) on the basis of which relevant findings and actions for the future can be made. Among (non) systemic operations and/or field management is not necessarily a direct link: management can be theoretically good, but practical reasons for poor results can be present elsewhere, just as management can be theoretically poor but results are still good due to good practice in the field. A link between the strategic management of management and practical results of implementers is always needed, but it should always be borne in mind, there are already at least four links between the two elements... A system capable of adapting (externally and internally) and learning from experience is crucial. Despite the use of the term "system/systemic", the management of public agencies through regulations in the light of what has been said is not already ex automata systemic. This type of management must understand concepts such as holism, system openness, goals, relationships, trends, patterns such as symptoms of internal structure, input, information flow, inventory-flow dynamics, transformation process, output, environment, feedback, control mechanisms, change perception and adaptations, system boundaries, structure-behaviour relationships, exponential out-of-sum results, and so on. Without understanding this, goals cannot be achieved. Consideration of the basic elements of the system and the organization as an open system allows a broader view of any organization or an individual area. If the system does not cover the relevant area under question well, it will not be able to address it effectively, which could lead to possible good results as a result of chance or luck. This also applies to all public policies, national programs and measures, regardless of their formal hierarchy. Systems are "cognitively open" (input) and "operationally closed" (determining meaning from the "own language" of the system).

PERCEPTION MECHANISMS

One of the biggest shortcomings of the documents under which agencies operate can be a noticeable lack of basic perception mechanisms, which would enable the identification and monitoring of the situation in real space and time. They, therefore, lack a systematic orientation. Interconnections and feedback in systems are essential, but they also mean that change can also lead to unwanted results that need to be prepared for and responded to in advance. The precondition is that they are detected as such with pre-determined thresholds and methods of measurement or determination. Understanding systemic change has an important impact on governance: the typical role of governments is changing dramatically, as these changes do not depend on formal decisions, but on the actual situation or the possibility to influence them. The role of governments as formal decision-makers here focuses on a role that encourages and facilitates innovation and transformation. Top-down planning still plays an important role here, but it is conditioned by the most objective determination of the actual situation. States need to find diverse ways to use the power of citizens, communities, and businesses here (e.g., the Climate Change Network). In order to achieve goals in a relevant field, it is necessary to intervene in all areas that affect them, from the micro-levels onwards. A wide range of measures, their integration, and experimentation will be needed to enable systemic change, which can allow the spread of new ideas and approaches. Due to the complexity and uncertainty of processes, it is necessary to find not only ways to coordinate and direct measures throughout society, but also to agree on how to measure/monitor them. Complex goals can usually only be achieved through more complex measures that are appropriate. Achieving full implementation will require funding and capacity building, better coordination between local, regional, and national authorities, and a stronger knowledge base. It is therefore essential to improve the implementation of policies, their interconnection, and coherence so that everyone can agree - but the problem remains in the way of solving it.

STATIC VS. DYNAMIC THINKING

The most important measures are usually political or normative documents adopted by the government or parliament, which are implemented through programs or action plans, but for their successful implementation, it is necessary to pay attention to the systemic characteristics of each system. In other words, if an activity or area is not systematically regulated, it will self-regulate regardless of formal documents. Since everything is embedded in one system and every system is part of another system, cybernetic theory (control mechanism theory based on the concepts of information and feedback as part of general systems theory) can give us an answer on the possibility of managing (any) state, i.e. systemic response and monitoring of the regulated environment. One of the preconditions for the quality provision of public

Towards Holistic Agency

services is the regulatory framework. This is most often a static thinking error that neglects the dynamic side of the problem; checking ("ticking" or "green light") of individual tasks performed (in the sense of a single set of measures) does not take into account their intertwining, exponential combinations and simultaneous, reciprocal changes in the processes of interaction. Classical (causal) thinking, in addition to the complex relationships of things, does not take into account the internal processes of living (adaptable) organisms, i.e. people (at all levels of regulation implementation) who control the aspects of the external environment through their own, conditioned structures. The information thus does not enter the system "from the outside", but its internal structure determines which data is recognized as information (input/output is replaced by non-causal, structural integration).

LACK OF PERCEIVED INTERCONNECTIONS AND EFFECTS

A major shortcoming of formal documents is the enumeration of individual measures without identifying their interrelationships or interactions. The strategy, action plan, plan or otherwise named documents, should set out - presumably - the most important objectives, indicators, target values, and their bearers. In addition to communicating something (un) consciously, every public document is also a power-driven (good/bad) structure of the mass, numerous connections or a system that, in a joint interaction of several elements tries to achieve strategic goals. If it is in fact a system, its parts must be interconnected in a way that achieves a new value that the parts themselves cannot achieve. This is the purpose of tactics such as the art of editing or (re) scheduling, which the implementation documents of the strategy (eg action plans) for the implementation of measures under individual strategic objectives, without coordinating, adapting, supplementing them according to a predetermined procedure and criteria - cannot be either become. Many objectives need to be generally guided in their interaction with each other, their scheduling, and redeployment according to their effects; if we set only goals and their indicators in the strategy - without the possibility of their management, coordination, supplementation, adjustment, correction, etc. - it would be similar to targeting only a victory, with the number of casualties, the number of destroyed buildings, vehicles, etc. as indicators. A system is a group of interconnected, interdependent devices, devices that make up a functional whole; a planned, rationally organized set of units, principles, procedures that determine an activity, especially regarding the achievement of a certain goal; a set of social units, components and relations based on interconnected principles, rules and regulates social events. A system can therefore be understood as a set of things, units, or people that connect with each other in certain ways, follow certain rules of interaction, and have a certain common purpose. The system should be any set of elements that interact with each other to influence the achievement of goals, provided that the "whole picture/frame" of the system is at all visible to the viewer. Repeated actions (or their phrases) thus increase only their number, but not their connections, or relations with others, which is crucial for the success of any strategy. Connections are those that create a common power to solve common problems.

REAL SITUATION REGARDLESS OF DOCUMENTS

A factual situation is always factual: it is always here, even if we do not direct it - the social situation will continue, regardless of the documents adopted, if measures do not actually affect the situation, the people. An action plan is not already an "action plan" if it is only so-called, if certain measures are just listed along with their (institutional) holders. An action plan can serve as a sign of an organization's responsibility as long as it is designed in a systemic way. An action plan is a detailed plan that describes the measures needed to achieve one or more (intermediate and final) goals and/or for the sequence of steps or activities that need to be carried out for the strategy to succeed. An action plan should contain a timetable for the tasks on the way to a goal and determines which persons or stakeholders will have to take certain steps/measures. Goal setting is the main element of the action plan; with appropriate motivation (which at the same time ensures the achievement of results), it also provides systemic possibilities for their realization through the most objective indicators possible. Goals must therefore be "as smart as possible" (SMART specific, measurable, attainable, realistic, time-based). When creating action plans, step-by-step (minor) steps within an integrated structure should be considered; it is necessary to describe what is to be achieved with the project, to assign specific roles and to provide a sufficient amount of training, resources and answers to questions to ensure that possible problems are solved. The next phase allows the analysis of progress by describing the milestones achieved, resolving any issues and making the necessary changes. During the project, the achievement of the goals must be checked, and at the end of the project, in the light of the new goals, the last phase must be checked/evaluated in the light of future actions.

The implementation of the action plan is conditional on the designation of a person responsible for monitoring progress, informing the group, ensuring timely action, and adapting the action; measures must be clear and feasible compared to vague ideas or thoughts; the responsibility of the person(s) must be present at each action's step, and for each step, it must be determined who will give/provide support to the responsible person. Keeping the right people in the communication loop for every action is crucial. In this way, it is possible to ensure that these people can understand the state of progress in their actions and at the same time see how they influence other actions and goals. Each measure must have a specific matrix and a budget that tells when the measure has been implemented or reached its limits. The plan must have a clear start and end date.

OBJECTIFICATION, THE OPENNESS OF CRITERIA

Different perspectives with different queries enable different data capture, through different approaches we can talk about a different "reality model". Greater objectification and transparency of criteria is needed, not only in terms of accessibility of data but also of the comprehensibility of individual tasks in relation to a specific institution (as a precondition for responsibility or transition from the classic form of responsibility to responsibility based on work/results/analysis of the situation - the greater emphasis should also be placed on annual work reports), training, education, ethical plus business approach ("Would I do what I do (now) in public administration also in my own private firm?") are the first preconditions for better governance in public administration. IT support is also needed for the public tasks in question, which enables direct insight into the status of the tasks, which provides information about the responsible person, how to contact him, etc. Especially in an area that has so many tasks, agility is needed, ie. not only responding to change but also pre-adapting of institutions to change in real-time and space, by responding quickly to deviations; at a higher, systemic level, political commitment from politicians, cooperation with open, structured participation, the participation of people in governance, decision-making in conjunction with strong institutions that enable transparency, open and free economy and protect, prevent unwanted activities (externalities) while maintaining legal frameworks (transparency, responsiveness and accountability); all this leads to greater equality, fair treatment and people's trust in public administration.

THE ROLE OF RESPONSIBLE PERSONS

The socio-administrative structure in which a document should be implemented should have a stable organizational pattern (clearly defined bodies, task responsibilities, and possibilities for changing them), a clear system of expert advice, and an evaluation system for achieving objectives. In this sense, the social structure should be made up of a network of positions held by individuals or groups; these positions can also be called roles. The social structure also consists of a network of roles. The structure and role are initially perceived by a specific individual as something external to him, so the individual only through the process of taking/internalizing the role or roles in this socio-administrative structure becomes an active member of this structure, which determines the formal relationships between roles; the role is thus never defined only as a set of work rights and duties and powers in a single job, but always represents a relationship between several people in different jobs. An individual's role thus always depends on the establishment of a relationship with another role or an individual who occupies it. The structure (informal and formal) always defines roles and their relationships; a pattern of roles and relationships between them creates an actual environment in which every day behaviour and conduct occur. Given the relationships between the structure, role, and roles, it is important to know who will be specifically responsible for the implementation of a document (or any other task), how it connects with other people's holding roles in other institutions and what impact they have on the actual performance of tasks. The appointment of guardians (of operations) to carry out the necessary activities to support progress towards the goals set is thus only a formal task within their (non/formal) role in relation to other roles in the body in which the guardian operates.

Certain patterns of behaviour (organizational culture as internal values between roles and people) prevail in each institution, which is reflected in the status (reputation, prestige) of an individual to whom it is attributed. The relevance of this status is in its possibility to change regardless of formal changes in the body, so it is an even more important the choice of people who will take care of the implementation of the strategy - by their colleagues (who will see the status in these people or not). The intertwining of structure, roles, relations between them in relation to the persons they occupy, their status in the organizational culture (internal values), which they have acquired/lost in relation to their personal characteristics, gives a specific "character" to the institution which pattern changes and develops according to the interaction of change in this interweaving of structure, culture, and personality. When planning changes, it is necessary to pay attention to the mentioned changes in the structure, to the probable changes in the culture and personal adjustments of individual public servants. Competence and power are thus not necessarily linked, and it is essential they are not too far apart from the point of view of achieving the body's objectives. The strength of key people in the success of the document will be based on technical, professional knowledge of the areas, their leadership skills, the efficiency of the communication chain and cohesiveness of the management group both within the document and within individual bodies. As these documents are not legal acts, it is the more important that they can be implemented on other grounds, without unnecessary legal coercion (at a higher level); all the more important therefore to understand the interconnectedness of the parts mentioned; if they do not work at least in a rough way, it matters will be resolved through (informal) power. It is due to the change in weight in power, the cohesiveness of leadership is so important, as it allows for continuous testing of situations through constructive dialogue rather than through individual powers that accompany tasks; the former was not agreed within or outside the body, and thus due to nonacceptance of tasks by others - lead to poorer results.

The implementor of a measure is thus never an agency (this is often designated as a responsible person; this will not even be an individual head of a service or department, because his subordinates - implementers are/will depend on other people. How they will fulfil their role is not only in their hands, but their "control over the situation" depends on the type (role) of other people. Of particular importance is the internal coherence of members and the ability of two-way communication to individual bodies (which increases in proportion to the fragmentation of tasks), which will give them information on the achievement of objectives. The primary activity of individual institutions (which are usually named in the documents after the name of the ministry) without a functioning operational group and/or networking that supposed to allow constant mutual communication between the primary activities and some liaison body (e.g. strategic council) that is supposed to evaluate the work (and promote cooperation between stakeholders), is mainly/too focused only on the already given content of documents, regardless of to new (future) circumstances. Usually, nothing determines in what ways, by what methods and why a document will be directed, what it will accelerate, what it will break when it will shift an emphasis from one goal to another.

In view of the above, the optimal approach to governance in this area requires not only the appointment of an individual head of service (no name and surname) or worse just the ministry as responsible for coordination between horizontal bodies, but also the establishment or of a government coordinating service.

COORDINATION: THE ROLE OF THE CENTRAL GOVERNMENTAL BODY

As said, in the system theory, there are *a la* Russian doll systems above and beyond systems. Above and beyond HA, there are also HAs. Above all, HAs on the level of public administration is the central governmental body. Hence, before stating specific proposals of an agency under question, it is necessary to have clear starting points and/or preconditions for the establishment of a theoretical framework that covers and manages the basic contents of good, system-oriented (smart), responsive and responsible management in this area; it is about placing the principles of system administration in the hierarchic management model on the level of government that prepares documents, establishes operational guidelines for the establishment of HAs, i.e. guidance, coordination, adaptation, verification, and correction (taking into account the whole structure of the field, which must be clearly known beforehand, otherwise it cannot be managed, parts and relations between them according to desired goals and various [empirical, data, participatory] inputs), for the implementation (behaviour and adaptation over time) of measures (with necessary feedback), i.e. to design an integrated, systemic approach. This can lead to a larger set of information, and thus to a better overview of the work and better coordination of institutions as HAs. In complex environments, more than a question of authority (i.e., which - preferably formally the highest possible document) is the more useful perspective that asks what works, in what way, how to achieve goals more easily, what leads to innovation, excellence, to the development of the individual and society, what leads to the satisfaction of us and others and how do we know that this is really the case.

The optimal approach to HA requires not only the appointment of an individual head of service or worse only a ministry responsible for coordination between horizontal bodies, but the establishment of a governmental coordinating organ or service that would itself work as HA. The latter would not only provide direct support and assistance to the Prime Minister, but would also bring together institutions, develop new procedures or approaches and systems for more effective coordination, effective consultation and communication within and beyond central government, improve policy-making i.e., write the most important documents in a relevant field and conduct an assessment of their effects. This service would perform the tasks of document preparation, coordination of development and planning of national documents and monitor the implementation of development policies and its programs in a given field; it would prepare and be responsible for the coordination of strategic documents with the EU and international organisations, coordinate, determine and monitor the activities of ministries, government services and other bodies and services involved in the implementation of the post-policy policy, and report to the government. It would provide conditions for the establishment, maintenance and operation of an information system in this field, would advise the government and ministries in adopting measures and acts relating to the implementation and monitoring of relevant policy development, would organize training, and inform the public about successful projects and perform other tasks in accordance with other regulations and government decisions.

Such tasks are mainly characterized by their informality, based mainly on the ability to coordinate, which must be clearly defined as the duty of other bodies to cooperate with the central body. The role of coordination without a formal background is not effective; without the possibility of setting the framework and the circumstances within which the authorities can choose, they cannot take the desired measures or actions. As with other things, when tasks are performed, things are always connected, co-effective. The existence of the presumption of connectedness indicates the existence of a higher level, which establishes diverse connections into a (meaningful) whole from the point of view of pursuing common goals. Gödel's logically indisputable theorem of imperfection states that any internally consistent and logical system must necessarily be based on assumptions that cannot be proved within that system (the system includes claims that cannot be resolved within it). Processes at the level of ministries or public administration can also be recognized as unsuccessful if they are not related to a higher (governmental) level, which stabilizes/unifies/makes sense of them on the basis of a hierarchy of values and common goals/denominators. The government, as the highest body of state administration, represents a common framework of thought; legitimacy is thus established through higher-level coordination, which focuses not only on the control of one institution but on all subordinate institutions that interact to influence society. Situations or the framework/conditions are the assumptions on the basis of which people act - the answer is in a (different) structure.

A government-level coordination centre would mean a new/old approach to "creating situations" or circumstances in which public institutions would be forced to participate not only in order to achieve their own but the common goals of the state.[6] At the national level, such a body can be described by the EU motto "united in diversity", which can be understand as a system. The latter is effective when the tasks of the centre are executed (better circulated) in a systematic way. If changes in the ways of doing things are needed, it is not only about replacing parts, but about changing and perceiving *relations* between them. The point is not to know that one or the other strategy "does not work" (so we will prepare a new one in a similar way), but to change the behaviour, parts of the system, its operation over time, the culture within the system, in short - the strategy should be written in a system-oriented manner. If all (previous or historic) action plans and strategies have not been successful, then the system does not work, or it is not even present as such (if new strategies are prepared in the same way, a similar result can be inferred already now). A reliable, responsive system requires responsive/adaptable actions that match the context of the environment, in accordance with objectives and rules that clearly define and implement the responsibility of actors through predetermined approaches and tools. A prerequisite for HA and/or the good performance of public services is, therefore, a similarly higher good systemic regulatory framework and its systemic functioning. Because the intrinsic consistency of a theory could have a "hypnotic effect on satisfaction," its value must always be verified in practice. Despite the value of uniform reporting, such an action cannot be successful if it focuses (only) on the implementation of actions in sectors, without (real, not just textual) systematic management of the whole framework. The more advanced role of the coordinating body is not only to promote but also to de facto coordinate (which is therefore never just a classical coordination but always has the possibility of direct action in the background) of strategic and sectoral policies based on a systemic view. The success and related implementation of key strategies depend as a precondition on the coordination centre, which achieves this general goal by coordinating all ministries and other public institutions. The main goal of such a centre is to ensure quality, system-oriented adoption, monitoring and correction of measures in all relevant areas and levels. Guidance, design, cooperation, coordination and similar concepts that indicate relations in the system of state functioning are unsuccessful in such a dialogue if there is no higher level that gives them the appropriate basis, support and support.

ONE, OVERALL, SINGLE PLATFORM

The need is hence expressed for a central institution, designed as HA that would take care of the preparation of professional bases as well as the formal regulation of more permanent cooperation with the research sphere. A particularly important area for this analysis are systemic-legal and other obstacles that could be spotted in agencies' operations: e.g. problems at the level of mental representations, the problem of the legal service, concept-level problems, a problem of dispersion of measures, a struggle between concepts and priorities, a lack of an overall integrated strategy, policy problem, communication problems, a problem of interdepartmental and structural integration, bureaucratic problems, weak institution structure, the problem of priorities at the state level, contradictions of measures, a problem of budget rigidity. In such a diverse field and the many measures, indicators, and other characteristics present in the work of public agencies, a single online, direct and publicly accessible platform in all areas, a set of all measures within them and their indicators, competent institutions and responsible persons are urgently needed, timeframes for action, response, reporting, monitoring and correction. In addition to a uniform overview of the field, the platform should be a space for the exchange of opinions, experiences and diverse proposals based on the principle of collective intelligence. A single overview of measures, areas, institutions, deadlines, (interim), reporting and other elements is a necessary element of good governance of any, and thus also the area of climate change, which is upgraded in a "live" information platform that would in real-time and enable the exchange of information, not only on potential negative forms of work but on all matters that would require the opinion of the general public. For such a system to operate as a platform, it is first necessary to determine its location and the service/person in charge of monitoring it (the operator of this platform could be the already mentioned government coordination centre), with the possibility of public (by citizens and others) stakeholders) insight into guiding (action) tasks regarding the established real situation (through pre-determined indicators).

HOLISTIC AGENCY AND ARTIFICIAL INTELLIGENCE

The availability of computing power, the availability of big data, the drive to innovate, the Digital Single Market, the Internet of Things (IoT), digitisation, artificial intelligence (AI) as mechanical data processing and online learning (the subfields are machine learning and deep learning), are presenting public administration and public agencies themselves with new organisational, ethical and regulatory challenges. The digitised, algorithm-driven operation of public agencies could lead not only to more rational use of budgets, more efficient data management, paperless operations, etc., but the use of systems theory and complexity theory as building blocks, transposed into the framework of algorithms, could ensure the necessary flexibility and responsiveness of public agency operations to the real situation (data-driven policies). Given the entry of algorithms into the sphere of (public) decision-making, it is essential to acquire the necessary knowledge about them to use them effectively, efficiently, legally, and ethically admissible.

Computations of large data are made by computing power and different software applications to make informed decisions based on algorithms. The latter is used in evidence-based management as 'the systematic, evidence-informed practice of management, incorporating scientific knowledge in the content and process of making decisions' (Rousseau, 2013, p. 3) and/or decision support systems (Burstein, Brézillon, & Zaslavsky, 2010) that 'simulate cognitive decision-making functions of humans based on artificial intelligence methodologies (including expert systems, data mining, machine learning, connectionism, logistical reasoning, etc.) to perform decision support functions' (Jao, 2012, p. 5). The practice of extracting information from data to determine patterns and predict future trends and for them relevant actions could be more algorithm-based. The use of algorithms can be divided into two broad areas, i.e., their search results as input for human decision-making, and direct decision-making or intervention in reality by algorithms. In the latter case, we can already speak of artificial intelligence (AI) as the ability of a machine to mimic human cognitive characteristics such as thinking, the ability to learn, plan and generate new results that cannot be deduced from basic databases alone (creativity). AI is the ability of technical systems to sense the environment, process what they sense and solve a problem according to a predefined goal. The detection is based on pre-prepared databases, or it collects the data itself using indicators or sensors, and then reacts appropriately once it has processed it.

The regulation of algorithms must navigate between the Scylla of too much uncontrolled interference in people's rights and the Charybdis of framing them too quickly and thus hindering their further development.[7] Without going into a deep discussion of the regulation of algorithms,[8] their credibility must be ensured above all. Only on this basis could we further talk about interference with citizens' rights and obligations. Experts at IBM Research have identified four pillars as the foundation for trustworthy AI systems: fairness, resilience, interpretability and provenance (Arya et al., 2019).[9] In early April 2019, the High Level Expert Group on AI, established by the European Commission, presented its Ethical Guidelines for Trustworthy Artificial Intelligence (Intelligence, 2019). In these guidelines, trustworthy AI has three elements that should be achieved in the life cycle of the system; it should be: (a) legal and respect all applicable laws and regulations, (b) ethical and ensure respect for ethical principles and values, and (c) robust from a technical and societal perspective, as AI systems can cause unintended harm even when used with good intentions. The Guidelines consist of three parts: I) the foundations of trustworthy AI include four ethical principles: respect for human autonomy, prevention of harm, fairness and explainability. II) The realisation of trustworthy AI contains seven key requirements: human agency and control, technical robustness and security, privacy and data management, transparency, diversity, non-discrimination and fairness, social and environmental well-being, and accountability. III) Assessing trustworthy AI ensures that the key requirements are met and adapted to the specific use of AI. The three "laws" of robotics developed by Asimov (Asimov, 1991), which could be paraphrased into the three laws of algorithms and/or the principles of nonharm (in the sense of a Hippocratic oath for data scientists who build algorithms, to administrative officials who use them): 1. An algorithm must not harm a human being without clearly and explicitly predefined legal conditions, or, by failing to act, cause harm to a human being without those conditions. 2. An algorithm must follow commands given by a human being, unless such commands would be in contravention of the first law. 3. The algorithm shall apply so long as such application is not contrary to the first or second law. As long as data on the various strata of modern society remain beyond the reach not only of scientific inquiry but also of practical action in the public administration, only those who are already in a subordinate position will be worse off.

Given these dilemmas, a first step is more likely to be the use of algorithms rather than just inputs for human behaviour and decision-making.

For the Nobel laureate, the two basic biases in human prediction are the neglect of base rates and insensitivity to the quality of the information: 'to maximise predictive accuracy, final decisions should be left to algorithms, especially in [complex] environments' (Kahneman, 2013, p. 225). Automation has great potential to eliminate common sense and cognitive errors in human reasoning; it enables consistent, uniform decisions to be made. Today's decision-making and operating systems of most public agencies do not exploit the full potential of algorithmic decision-making; this does not mean that this is also a reason for their elimination: childbirth problems do not mean abandonment, but even greater care for the child. The same applies to algorithms: automation is no longer on the march, it is here. It just needs to be properly integrated into the system to work. Use of intelligent algorithms should not be dimmed by fear: intelligent software learning is just like any other thing: useful when used appropriately by responsible human officials. It is like fire: it could be used to warm ourselves or to burn down someone's property. If a life-threatening human illness is evaluated by algorithms in medicine, where lives are put at stake, then also other human (healthy) conditions could be evaluated similarly. So, the plan of action could be to use algorithms, wait, see, trust and always verify. When the agency has no data, permanently or occasionally, when new databases would be consuming, and expensive *collective intelligence* can be used as it was previously proposed in this book. Functioning with more various, independent people and groups can similarly be a good way to obtain data. After this step, the computational power and algorithms can mimic human behaviour. The agency's management could in this way use public opinion instead of rough predictions or common sense.

This could be a new look at the public agency as a holistic one, as a form that could imitate and even enhance or improve human actions, implementation of public tasks, and in time, even proposing new regulatory frames. This way of doing things can be called "data-based agency" as the practice of finding action steps in data and using the latter to execute actions along the existing ways of doing things (similarly as legal engineering or academic research). A data-based public servant thus writes code in order to analyse an existing dataset to identify patterns and probabilities in that dataset, and as a result, he transfers patterns and probabilities in a form of codes into a computational model.

On the other hand, there are also limits too. A machine replicates the results and conditions that already exist in the world. It does not decide ethically but solely based on math and/or pregiven paths comes also from prejudices and biased common sense. About this Eubank talks in *Automating Inequality* that leads to digital poorhouses,[10] O'Neil in *Weapons of Math Destruction*,[11] or Noble in *Algorithms of Oppression*.[12] Machine learning models should thus use not only existing data, as they can be biased

Towards Holistic Agency

(in this way the difference between rich and poor can be only automated or enhanced, but not really addressed), but they must necessarily provide a better explanation than only "failure to cooperate in establishing eligibility" or "failure to cooperate in verifying income" to provide a really effective remedy.

All these algorithmic processes should be controlled and amended if needed to prevent bias. Otherwise, there will be no real progress, but only new means of repression. Algorithms should not be invisible "gatekeeper" that automatically (without knowing their human managers on their actions or step-by-step procedures) take decisions on human destinies, rights or possibilities based on data (algorithmic determinism); there should be also means to control algorithms themselves (algorithmic accountability) in the sense of *quis custodiet ipsos custodes* to uncover injustice and inequality encoded in algorithms or mathematical models. An algorithm could be designed that disregards race or gender entirely. The more challenging problem is that an algorithm could discriminate and turn out to be biased, even when it does not overtly use race and gender as predictors. Discrimination could also come from the source data. If an algorithm is trained on a data set that is biased, it will be biased, too (Kahneman, Sibony, & Sunstein, 2021). Cautious evaluation of algorithms is thus recommended to prevent inacceptable inputs and to test whether they discriminate when applied as outputs. Algorithms can (when designed appropriately) be superior than human decision-makers regarding precision, noise reduction (undesirable inconsistency of decisions), impartiality, objectivity, and equality.

In this regard, it should be mentioned that on 21 April 2021, the European Commission offered the first legal agenda on AI[13] to ensure and improve (among others) the governance and effective enforcement of existing law in relation to the fundamental rights and security requirements applicable to AI systems. The proposal for a Regulation on AI wants to ensure that AI systems placed on the EU market will be safe and that will respect the existing law on fundamental rights and Union values. Big data should increase equality and promote democracy. This is the crucial step towards algorithms that will not violate human rights, that will be (*a la* movie *Moneyball*) useful for humans, and with this also for the workings of HA. On this path, human elements and/or human decision making – although also many times imperfect – has additional elements that AI will not possess in the near future: imagination, virtues, morality, empathy, emotions, and other values[14] and data (inputs, processes and outputs) that specific AI does not have if they are not embedded in them by human programmers. AI, when used for decisions affecting our rights, should be tested similarly as today's written decisions in the form of individual legal acts. However, as people can develop and grow, also AI as the people's product can also learn and adjust. But human beings learn and adapt even more; based on combinations among various human and factual data people change differently than AI and can spot all discrepancies and biases that AI can exhibit. Only humans can solve this for the better future. Algorithms are series of known stages to progress towards a(n) (un)known goal, while heuristics is series of the less-known or more general rules-of-thumb stages to progress towards a known goal. Generally, you know how to reach it but not how it will look like. 'What boundaries (if any) will remain [in the New world, governed the laws of information, knowledge, insight, complexity and the dynamics of strongly interconnected systems] unchanged, and which of them will disappear entirely, is difficult to predict. That is why exploring is more important than analysing; testing is more important than planning; searching is more important than finding; heuristics are more important than algorithms' (Malik, 2016, p. 124).

Here, again, system and complexity theory can be helpful. Technology is not always the right answer, and even less the only answer. People should not mistakenly replace or equate popular with good. Nothing in excess the antient Greeks would say, but it is no unwarranted to take a step into the unknown with the help of some known systemic elements that include complexity to be able to adaptively react on a path that is created in parallel with our actions. HAs should incorporate all this in their doings along the established legal principles of transparency, accountability, legality, human rights, and other good achievements of human history. Probably the best way would be to comprise on what is possible to get from AI and synchronised with good and intelligent people. The latter know that AI is only one possible input that can offer possible solutions from the large amounts of data in the real time-space frame.

At the end of the road, it is time to define HA. This may be even presumptuous (as one definition cannot describe wholeness as such), but it can still be enough to at least get a sense of what such an agency is supposed to mean. Many terms are taken from Brown's *Dare to Lead* (2018) as HA also strives to lead (regardless that the cited work does not address public agencies, but human agency that is basically the same):

Holistic agency (HA) is not only interconnected with other things; in addition to being a complex system with all its characteristics, it is also a living thing that exhibits adaptability to its environment to be better. It exhibits feedback, dialogue, problem-solving, values, ethical decision-making, recognition of unity in diversity, flexibility, agility, resilience, robustness, childlike curiosity, empathy, care, integrity (courage over comfort) and other human skills that make HA – and us – alive. It exhibits openness to correction and courageous vulnerability in the acknowledgement that things can be different, where errors are possible and where efforts are needed to correct them to serve others (the public and each individual). The result of such an attitude is belongingness to the whole, where the one and the whole are united in their diversity.

If the above-mentioned elements of HA were used as criteria for agencies (Type 0 – Type 5) that could be scored, for example, on a scale from 1 to 10, it could give (dis)similar results on the different types of agencies in relation to their holistic perspective. This would mean that each formal agency type does not, or contrary, it does play an important role; this could lead to i) the grouping together similar agencies under the same formal umbrella type (or to the retain different types according to differences in scores) or at least, to ii) evaluation of new approaches that could improve an overall holistic result (and/or what should a specific agency do to be more holistic). The elements of HA are present regardless if HA is deconcentrated or decentralised, as the first level of government, or as the delegated power from a central authority to regional and local authorities: when seen as part of the larger whole, HA is not focused only on strict partial/local interests (as the latter were one of the essential conditions of feudal and not more global democratic era), but fulfils its goals within the continuous chain of connected elements.

This holistic perspective was – although with different words – expressed by Theodore Roosevelt, who gave – then already the ex-President of the United States – one of his best speeches at the Sorbonne in 1910, "Citizenship in the Republic". His speech later became known also as "The Man in the Arena" (1910) due to the following passage:

"It is not the critic who counts; not the man who points out how the strong man stumbles, or where the doer of deeds could have done them better. The credit belongs to the man who is actually in the arena, whose face is marred by dust and sweat and blood; who strives valiantly; who errs, who comes short again and again, because there is no effort without error and shortcoming; but who does actually strive to do the deeds; who knows great enthusiasms, the great devotions; who spends himself in a worthy cause; who at the best knows in the end the triumph of high achievement, and who at the worst, if he

fails, at least fails while daring greatly, so that his place shall never be with those cold and timid souls who neither know victory nor defeat."

HA exhibits all these characteristics; it may resemble also to Dworkin's Judge Hercules as an 'an imaginary judge of superhuman intellectual power and patience who accepts law as integrity' (Dworkin, 1986, p. 239), the latter being the set of moral principles that are in the best possible manner applied to the community as a whole. Although such an initialized version of a jurist with extraordinary legal skills or HA does not exist, in this place, we can recall on Plato's philosopher kings who never existed, but they can serve as an idea, as the unreachable star to which we nevertheless can to which we nevertheless can point our view. The same stands for HA: it is unreachable – as wholeness cannot be embraced – but we can always strive for it. This Plato's idea can be reconciled with Popper's criticism of such "universal laws" when these laws are composed by the open society, based on democracy, on the universal and equal suffrage of all citizens, while respecting fundamental human rights at the time, when the philosopher king becomes diverse society itself.

REFERENCES

AryaV.BellamyR. K. E.ChenP.-Y.DhurandharA.HindM.HoffmanS. C.ZhangY. (2019). One Explanation Does Not Fit All: A Toolkit and Taxonomy of AI Explainability Techniques. *ArXiv:1909.03012 [Cs, Stat]*. http://arxiv.org/abs/1909.03012

Broussard, M. (2019). Artificial Unintelligence: How Computers Misunderstand the World (Kindle). London: MIT Press.

Brown, B. (2018). *Dare to Lead: Brave Work. Tough Conversations. Whole Hearts.* Random House.

Brown, D. R., & Harvey, D. F. (2006). *An Experiential Approach to Organization Development.* Pearson Prentice Hall.

Burstein, F., Brézillon, P., & Zaslavsky, A. (2010). *Supporting Real Time Decision-Making.* Springer Science & Business Media.

Dworkin, R. (1986). *Law's Empire.* Belknap Press of Harvard University Press.

Eubanks, V. (2017). *Automating Inequality: How High-Tech Tools Profile, Police, and Punish the Poor.* St. Martin's Press.

European Commission. (2017). *European Semester: Thematic factsheet – Quality of public administration – 2017.* EC. https://ec.europa.eu/info/sites/info/files/file_import/european-semester_thematic-factsheet_quality-public-administration_en_0.pdf

Jao, C. (2012). *Decision Support Systems.* Olajnica: IntechOpen.

Kahneman, D., Sibony, O., & Sunstein, C. R. (2021). *Noise: A Flaw in Human Judgment.* Little, Brown.

Malik, F. (2016). *Navigating Into the Unknown: A New Way for Management, Governance and Leadership.* Campus Verlag.

Noble, S. U. (2018). *Algorithms of Oppression: How Search Engines Reinforce Racism*. NYU Press. doi:10.18574/nyu/9781479833641.001.0001

O'Neil, C. (2017). *Weapons of Math Destruction: How Big Data Increases Inequality and Threatens Democracy*. Penguin Books.

OECD. (2011). *Regulatory Policy and Governance: Supporting Economic Growth and Serving the Public Interest*. OECD Publishing.

OECD. (2012). *The Public Sector Salary System in Slovenia*. OECD Publishing.

OECD. (2017). *Systems Approaches to Public Sector Challenges: Working with Change*. OECD Publishing.

OMB. (2021). *About OMB*. OMB. https://www.whitehouse.gov/omb/freedom-of-information-act-foia/#q1

Peng, T. C. P. (2005). *Strategies to Build Up Holistic Governance*. EA. https://www.ea.sinica.edu.tw/file/Image/Strategies%20to%20Build%20Up%20Holistic%20Governance.pdf

Perri, 6. (1997). *Holistic Government*. London: Demos.

Perri, 6, Leat, D., Seltzer, K., & Stoker, G. (2002). *Towards Holistic Governance: The New Reform Agenda*. London: Macmillan Education UK.

Peters, B. G. (2020). The Politics of Bureaucracy: A Continuing Saga. *NISPAcee Journal of Public Administration and Policy*, *13*(2), 213–220. doi:10.2478/nispa-2020-0021

Pollitt, C., Bouckaert, G., & Löffler, E. (2006). *Making Quality Sustainable: Co-Design, Co-Decide, Co-Produce, and Co-Evaluate*. Report of The 4QC Conference, Tampere. https://circabc.europa.eu/webdav/CircaBC/eupan/dgadmintest/Library/6/1/2/meetings_presidency/meeting_26-27_october/4QCREPORT_final_version_October_2006.pdf

Rigg, C., & Richards, S. (2006). *Action Learning, Leadership and Organizational Development in Public Services*. Routledge. doi:10.4324/9780203966198

Roosevelt, T. (1910). *Man in the Arena Speech*. World Future Fund. http://www.worldfuturefund.org/Documents/maninarena.htm

Rothwell, W. J., & Sullivan, R. L. (Eds.). (2005). *Practicing Organization Development: A Guide for Consultants*. John Wiley & Sons.

Rousseau, D. M. (Ed.). (2013). *The Oxford Handbook of Evidence-Based Management*. Oxford University Press.

UNDP. (2011). *Governance Principles, Institutional Capacity and Quality*. UNDP. https://www.undp.org/content/dam/undp/library/Poverty%20Reduction/Inclusive%20development/Towards%20Human%20Resilience/Towards_SustainingMDGProgress_Ch8.pdf

von Bertalanffy, L. (1968). *General system theory: Foundations, development, applications*. George Braziller.

ENDNOTES

[1] Here employees who encounter difficulties, are stimulated to meet together in groups, and ask one another questions on an experienced problem in order to find solutions on their own, rather than to use experts to solve their problems for them (Rigg & Richards, 2006).

[2] Professor B. Guy Peters (2020) enumerates three paradoxes that are more or less present in nowadays public administration regarding evidence-based policymaking: despite the larger availability of more democratized expertise in the present time than in the past, there is less demand for its use, because political leaders mostly use their intuition, or to take advice that confirms their own ideological perspectives, rather than to attempt to use the already available advice. A second paradox is that political leaders (many of them with little experience in the public sector) attempt to exert control over their public bureaucracy, while the same political leaders are often intolerant of conflict and any questioning of their own ideas. A third one relates to mild reactions of individual countries and the world *vis-à-vis* a host of wicked problems that cannot be easily solved with the relative lack of preparation for governing of populist governments, and their unwillingness to use the expertise available within the civil service.

[3] Has the public agency a clear the picture of what it wants, how to find it and how it wants to/can achieve it, or does it just collect data according to a set of indicators without helping them to balance different views and interests? Is it only responds to the current situation, ie. is it shaping the future or the latter just "happens" to it? Does it work forward and explain itself backwards, as Kierkegaard once said for life itself? Before we can answer the question on the existence of a social consensus on objectives that the agency supposed to pursue, it is necessary to be clear about the way in which it is to be identified in the first place.

[4] The main features of strategic management are the analysis of the environment, stakeholders, control, planning and financing (re) allocation of funds, performance assessment, control of the organization, and information. The success of organizing is not about predicting and following trends; it is about anticipating threatening deviations from trends and taking timely action. In this dimension, we wonder how to connect the main ideas of the functioning of the agency with specific means, ie. programs and practices according to which they are implemented, ie. in what way how to link policies, priorities, resources, organization and procedures?

[5] In the tactical dimension, we ask about the ways in which ideas and strategies are translated into concrete programs, practices, and ways of doing things. When are the changes introduced in the organizational structure, management and control systems and in information collection and processing systems, and for what reasons? The tactical level should be based on (statistical and other "evidence-based") analyses, empirical research and randomly selected test environments with case studies.

[6] The OECD in the *Public Governance Review of Slovenia*, proposes the creation and empowerment of a professional central public employer's office that would operate at arm's length from the political level, responsible for strategic management and oversight of the overall human resource system. This is an essential pre-requisite for a coherent and efficient management of the public sector salary system. Such institutions can be found in many OECD member countries, for example Australia (Australian Public Service Commission), Belgium (*Service Public Federal Organisation et Personnel/Fédérale Overheidsdienst Personnel en Organisatie*), Denmark (*Personalestyrelsen*), Finland (*Valtion tyomarkkinalaitos/Statens Arbetsmarknadsverk*), France (*Direction générale de

l' administration et la fonction publique), New Zealand (*State Services Commission*), Sweden (*Arbetsgivarverket*) and the United States (*Office of Personnel Management*). The core responsibilities of the central HR institution may include strategic workforce planning across the whole of government; the design, promotion and enforcement of shared systems such as job classification, competence management, career management and performance assessments; the oversight and promotion of public service values and ethics; whole-of-service training; recruitment and retention; and management of senior civil service (OECD, 2012, p. 65). Such centres are mostly focused on HRM themes; as there are also other themes tightly connected with good administration, the US Office of Management and Budget (OMB) could be a good example of how to group fields that should operate more independently than ministries. OMB is an agency within the Executive Office of the President. It assists the President in the discharge of his budgetary, management, and other executive responsibilities. OMB assists the President in the preparation of the Federal budget and in managing its execution by the agencies. OMB works to assure that proposed legislation (as well as testimony, reports and policies) is consistent with Administration policies, including the President's Budget. OMB also has a central role in providing leadership in the development, oversight and coordination of the Federal government's policies in procurement, financial management, and information, statistical, and regulatory arenas as well as in the implementation of those policies. OMB promotes better program management, strengthens administrative management, develops agency performance measures, and improves coordination of the Executive Branch's various operations. OMB staff are divided into the following offices: the OMB Director's office; several small staff offices (General Counsel, Legislative Affairs, Strategic Planning and Communications, Management and Operations, and Economic Policy); the Budget Review Division (which provides support in the development and execution of the Federal budget); the Legislative Reference Division (which develops and supports the President's management and budget agenda by carrying out OMB's interagency legislative review function); five Resource Management Offices (which develop and support the President's budget); and four statutory offices (the Office of Information and Regulatory Affairs, the Office of Federal Financial Management, the Office of Federal Procurement Policy, and the Office of Electronic Government and Information Technology) (OMB, 2021).

[7] This is the so-called Collindridge dilemma of controlling a new technology: 'in the early stages, when it can be controlled, there is not enough information about its harmful consequences to control its development, but when the consequences are obvious, control becomes costly and slow' (Collingridge, 1980, p. 19).

[8] In addition to the open questions of traditional tort and contractual liability for acts and omissions by robots, their legal status, the relationship between adaptability and learning and human guidance (the degree of delegation or transfer of certain functions from humans to algorithms), there remain the issues of the use of algorithms for the purposes of decision-making or participation in governance, due process (the proportion of procedural rights of the parties in relation to the type of proceeding, the evaluation of the performance of the algorithms), non-discrimination and transparency.

[9] Fairness: AI systems must use unbiased data and learning models, as this is the only way to avoid unfair treatment of certain groups. Resilience: AI systems must be safe and secure and not vulnerable to tampering or compromise of the data on which they learn. Interpretability: AI systems must provide decisions or templates that can be understood by users and developers. Provenance:

[10] AI systems should include details of their development, deployment and maintenance to enable auditing throughout their lifecycle.

[10] Marginalized groups face higher levels of data collection when they access public benefits, walk through highly policed neighbourhoods, enter the health-care system, or cross-national borders. That data acts to reinforce their marginality when it is used to target them for suspicion and extra scrutiny. Those groups seen as undeserving are singled out for punitive public policy and more intense surveillance, and the cycle begins again. It is a kind of collective red-flagging, a feedback loop of injustice. ... The digital poorhouse kills people. The majority of them are women, children, the mentally ill, the disabled, and the elderly. Many are poor and working-class people of colour. Many others are poor and working-class whites. Addressing the digital poorhouse can help progressive social movements shift attention from "the police" to the processes of policing (Eubanks, 2017, pp. 7, 215).

[11] The math-powered applications powering the data economy were based on choices made by fallible human beings. Some of these choices were no doubt made with the best intentions. Nevertheless, many of these models encoded human prejudice, misunderstanding, and bias into the software systems that increasingly managed our lives. Like gods, these mathematical models were opaque, their workings invisible to all but the highest priests in their domain: mathematicians and computer scientists. Their verdicts, even when wrong or harmful, were beyond dispute or appeal. And they tended to punish the poor and the oppressed in our society, while making the rich richer (O'Neil, 2017, p. 3).

[12] While we often think of terms such as "big data" and "algorithms" as being benign, neutral, or objective, they are anything but. The people who make these decisions hold all types of values, many of which openly promote racism, sexism, and false notions of meritocracy ... Algorithmic oppression means 'algorithmically driven data failures that are specific to people of color and women' (Noble, 2018, pp. 1–2, 4).

[13] European Commission (2021) Proposal for a Regulation on Artificial Intelligence – Artificial Intelligence Act) and Amending Certain Union Legislative acts {SEC (2021) 167 final} - {SWD(2021) 84 final}). Available from: https://digital-strategy.ec.europa.eu/en/library/proposal-regulation-european-approach-artificial-intelligence [Accessed 21 April 2020].

[14] Because social decisions are about more than just calculations, problems will always ensue if we use data alone to make decisions that involve social and value judgments. Algorithms are designed by people, and people embed their unconscious biases in algorithms. It's rarely intentional—but this doesn't mean we should let data scientists off the hook ... We need to stop fetishizing tech. We need to audit algorithms, watch out for inequality, and reduce bias in computational systems, as well as in the tech industry. If code is law, as Lawrence Lessig writes, then we need to make sure the people who write code are doing so in accordance with the rule of law (Broussard, 2019).

Chapter 2
Public Agencies:
Dynamic Institutions With Social Meanings

ABSTRACT

The concept of social institutions, such as public agencies, is closely linked to human development, with early societies relying on group families. While organisations pursue economic goals, institutions also seek non-economic goals based on their members and position in society. Differences emerge between institutions in different legal systems despite the same competences and legal rules. Understanding social institutions goes beyond legal arrangements and is dependent on conversations and relationships between people in society. The development of professional ethics in organisations can help retain stability. Administrative capacity is critical for public agencies, as they employ most public servants and use vast resources. The efficient implementation of parliamentary-defined goals is vital for public agencies. The growth of work that focusses on the organisation, operation, and regulation of administrative agencies reflects their importance in modern society.

INTRODUCTION

Nothing is possible without men, but nothing lasts without institutions.

– Jean Monnet

Institutions and the (ancient) law are tightly connected with human development; as an early society, development begins with the group (family), not with the individual. Progressive societies have thus moved from status to contract (Maine, 1936). According to Selznick's distinction, public agencies are organisations and institutions. Organisations are technical and formal units that pursue economic goals, while institutions are also surrounded with values and informalities that pursue non-economic goals that arise from their members and their position in society. These two aspects of organizations are grouped in continual tension, so the essential task of management is to support technical imperatives as well as to protect and promote values at the same time.[1] Given the mix of (in)formal goals, means, values and

DOI: 10.4018/979-8-3693-0507-2.ch002

a variety of contexts, differences between institutions in different legal systems nevertheless emerge despite the same competences and legal rules. This applies also for agencies; this can be confirmed with differences between EU member states using the same EU regulations. 'Over the years, due to changes in society and growing demands on government, the relatively simple structure described above became more complex. To allow the government to carry out civil service functions with greater flexibility, efficiency, and expertise, special purpose agencies were established outside the traditional structure of the executive branch (Nastasi, Pressman, & Swaigen, 2020, p. 25).

When the same approach leads to different effects, it is rationally inferred that there are also other elements involved. The understanding of a wider frame of institutions in the social construction of goals, tools, and purposes is conditioned on various alliances, cooperation, and co-optation with other stakeholders. This understanding is socially constructed; it depends on conversation, dialogue, and *relations* between persons as members of a particular society and its groups, its meanings about words, actions, and gestions. The individual meanings, desires, motives and wishes emerge from relations with other meanings, and are further grouped and shaped by institutional forces and/or by common denominators that all involved respect and follow.[2] The understanding of public agencies goes hence much further than solely their legal arrangements, and due to their non-stop flexible relations, combinations and changes, it is also not very useful to study best practices.

Rationality and value also emerge in *relationships* (such as tools and manners or ways of doing things that should be somehow *related* to the goals); for Durkheim, the reason is the fundamental categories taken together, not how an individual thinks, but how 'collective representations... translate the states of the collectivity. They depend upon how the collectivity is organized upon its morphology, its religious, moral, and economic institutions, and so on' (Durkheim, 1995, p. 15). Durkheim is mentioned here not only because he equates rationality with collectivity, but because for him *sociology* as such is *synonymous* with *institutions*, their creation and operation: institutions are 'all the beliefs and modes of behaviour instituted by the collectivity; sociology can then be defined as the science of institutions, their genesis, and their functioning' (Durkheim, 1982, p. 45). Auguste Comte is known as the author of the term "sociology"; for him 'any system of society has as its final object to direct all individual powers towards a general goal' (1998, p. 66) he saw in the good of humanity or in the common good (2009). His saying 'savoir *pour prevoir, prevoir pour pouvoir*' (to know, predict, and predict to control) describes this and shows that he was 'frenzy for regulation.' He cannot bear that anything should be left unregulated: there ought to be no such thing as hesitation; nothing should remain arbitrary, for *l'arbitraire* is always favourable to egoism' (Mill, 1865, p. 58). For Comte 'the positive point of departure for the work of *the statesman* ... [is] to discover and institute practical forms to avoid ... crises which spontaneous development brings about when it has not been foreseen ... in this order of phenomena science leads to foresight, and foresight allows us to regulate action' (1998, p. 3).

Social institutions are therefore human configurations connected with other (cultural, economic, political, historical) systems in order to adapt their needs to the demands of their environments. Institutions are essential as structures that enable human populations to *adapt* to their environment (Turner, 2003). It is not superfluous to emphasise once again that social institutions are structures and with them the associated cultural (symbolic) and other systems that people create and use to adjust to the exigencies of their environment. Institutions are the 'extended arms' of people, with which they can achieve goals that would otherwise be impossible for them to reach as individuals. It is quite easy to replace the notion of 'social institution' with a 'public agency' and still have the same meaning, originally meant for the first: 'a complex of positions, roles, norms and values lodged in particular types of social structures and organising relatively stable patterns of human activity with respect to fundamental problems in producing life-sustaining resources, reproducing individuals, and sustaining viable societal structures within a given environment' (Turner, 1997, p. 6). For Turner, the core human social institutions are economy, kinship, religion, polity, law, and education; they are the outcome of macrolevel forces (population, production, reproduction, regulation, and distribution) that have generated selection pressures on human populations (2003). Social institutions arise as a result of forces of tension and compression[3] between different, for groups of people, the most important areas of activity and life. If one wants to understand how people and especially groups think about institutions and/or public agencies, it is important how they discuss, understand, and act on them. With the creation of new institutions, the society can, according to Durkheim, retain stability with a greater development of professional ethics in an organization of professional groups:[4]

This applies above all to those more or less directly connected with the State, that is, those having a public character…Each one of these groups of functions forms a clearly defined body having its own unity and its own particular regulations, special agencies being instructed to see these are enforced. These agencies are sometimes officials appointed to supervise the work of their subordinates (inspectors, directors, seniors of all kinds in the official hierarchy). Sometimes they are regular tribunals, nominated by election or otherwise, and charged with preventing any serious defections from professional duty (supreme councils of the law, of public education, disciplinary boards of all kinds) (Durkheim, 1992, p. 8).

Durkheim lived at the second half of the nineteenth century and in the beginning of the twentieth century, so it is not a surprise that his view on stability was connected with a greater development of professional ethics in an organisation of professional groups; this understanding has melted down in the frame of an enhanced later era of dynamism and complexity. Today's administrative apparatus is still understood as a professional group of people who, as a spider web, increasingly intertwines all industrial, national and transnational societies, and who develops (at least in the form of draft rules) policy in the increasingly interconnected world. This apparatus ensures that almost all pressing social needs, activities, and other public problems go through its 'administrative networks' filter, but the question remains whether the criteria or perspectives of the mentioned filter successfully address dynamism and complexity in a world increasingly connected and globalised. It should not be overlooked that all known cases of biological extinction have been caused by overspecialization, whose concentration of only selected genes sacrifices general adaptability (Fuller & Applewhite, 1997).

Administrative capacity with its economic and physical power, the means to control the information and other resources that administration has, sets the latter as the strongest state entity (relative to its level), so it is more important that this capacity is focused on the right goals with the right means and on the right ratio between specialisation and generalisation. People are increasingly dependent on the administration to improve welfare; this can become a negative tool to rule over people because of their greater dependence on public services and not on their personal capabilities. In addressing complex problems, people need a strong state, which in turn could iteratively bind to itself more and more dependent people. Administrative capacity as the strongest state entity is relevant to public agencies as they usually employ the majority of public servants and use large amounts of other means; it is relevant also in its dependence on the social, cultural, economic, regulatory, and political forces that which, as a malleable mixture, is formed into a certain model which is able to retain its shape for a certain period of time, but it can still accordingly change it later due to its flexible shape (clay can be used to make useful products, but it cannot be changed). New levels of understanding are conditioned by iteratively renewed views on the rearrangement of significant factors. Administrative capacity is tightly connected with efficient agencies that implement parliamentary-defined goals; hence, the rapid growth of work that deals with the administration agencies and their organisation, operation, and regulation. Public agencies not only reflect the beliefs instituted by collectivity as Durkheim thought, but the first also channels the beliefs of the second. In such a framework, it is no wonder that the public also strives to gain better control over the administrative system (transparency, sunshine laws, media, and legitimacy) that should be used as the operations of public agencies focused more on the *dynamics* between individuals, groups, and administrative institutions, on the ways in which decisions and actions occur.

Not only meaning and institutions, but also interests, as important elements of institutions, are composed and balanced on different societal levels and by unseen forces. When Charles Darwin had studied Adam Smith (Ridley, 2017) he could find Smith's idea of an invisible hand, that the individual's self-interest can benefit society more than direct actions intended to benefit society. From the institutional point of view, self-interest could not be at odds with the greater good when the latter is composed on a higher level, organised in a way (of the invisible hand and/or unseen forces that move the free market economy) that exhibits the public interest. Parsons used such an evolutionary approach in the idea that social systems may evolve to a state in which they can better deal with environmental pressures, where they can improve *adaptive* ability (Parsons, 1991), and where they further based on occupational differentiation cause the emergence of specialised organisations with 'legitimate authority' under a normative order system: '[f]or collective action in pursuit of such goals to be effective, there naturally has to be integration of the system concerning their acceptance and concerning the distribution of responsibilities and burdens that it entails; this is the 'consent' aspect of political organisation (Parsons, 1985, p. 182). Evolution led to the development of structures that control their behavioural processes within other similar structures based on a (structural) *hierarchy*. For Parsons (1985), the functions of any system of action (pattern-maintenance, integration, goal achievement, and adaptation) are links between the structural and dynamic aspects of the system (among which the latest function is the most important from the evolutionary point of view). Both aspects can be linked to processes: "the structure is nothing but the attention given to processes" (Beer, 1994) and / or the attention given to *relations*. From the evolutionary point of view, the latter define the structure (content – what), process (how), relationships (who), and cause (goal – where).

In this light, the question of how agencies can be best steered, or under what conditions do they perform best, seems easier to answer: agencies can be steered successfully when their relations are known and tasks applied in a relevant relational context. The same applies to the conditions under which agencies perform best. When the unseen forces can be recognised through the patterns that relations made, the public agency could be on a right path towards systemic management. Due to large variations in agency ways of doing things and their relations with parent ministries, Pollitt et al. (2004) similarly focused instead on organisational design rather than process and task outputs of the service; they named such an approach *the Task-Specific Path Dependency model*. Because an organisational change is neither driven solely by efficiency considerations nor by rational self-interest, Pollitt et al., due to many particularities, remain agnostic on the existence of a 'real reason' because of which the (general) agency form as such became popular; 'the particularities such as the local administrative culture, the operational characteristics of the function in question, and the strategies pursued by management often have far more influence on how a given organisation behaves than does the generality of its organisational form' (Pollitt et al., 2004, p. 24). The mentioned agnosticism fits in evolutionary unseen forces or intangible relations among various parts and stakeholders, with which the public agency deals on a daily matter. In this "camp" also fits the argument that 'autonomous agencies are often the result of political reactions and pressures, rather than of careful design' (Valdés, 2011), as this result points to the same hidden relations, hidden "by default" and not by a purposive human intention. When such relations are not even roughly understood and acknowledged, when one stops backward to see a larger picture, then based on evidence over 30 years on the application of NPM in the central and local government of the UK, conclusions like Hood and Dixon (2015) that an apparent government that 'worked better and cost less' really means 'higher costs and more complaints'.

Based on the (non)observability of outputs and outcomes even before the mentioned scholars already Wilson (1989) divided (US bureaucracy and/or public) agencies in *production* organisations (output or work and outcomes are here observable, so leaders [careerists have the best chance of being successful executives here] can design a compliance system to produce an efficient outcome, e.g. the Internal Revenue Service;[5] *procedural* organisations (managers can here observe subordinates' doings but not outcomes that result from those efforts; how officials do their jobs is more important than if their doings produce desired outcomes; e.g. a mental hospital or armed forces at peacetime), *craft* organisations (official activities are hard to observe but their outcomes are relatively easy to evaluate; e.g. armed forces during wartime, compliance inspectors, police detectives; here skills and group- or profession-induced ethos or *esprit de corps* is very important, and as in production agencies craft agencies also lend themselves to careerist leadership), and *coping* organisations (neither outputs nor outcomes cannot be measured; e.g. teachers, diplomats; focus could be given on good practises or citizens' trust).[6] Many times, the success of agencies is measured by the level of autonomy and resources the agency has or by infusing the vision of agency's importance on a wider environment, culture and policy; it could be that 'the greatest executives infuse their organisations with value and convince others that this value is not merely useful to the bureau but essential to the polity' (J. Q. Wilson, 1989, p. 217), but convincing others solely is just a method of good argumentation that maybe has nothing to do with objective facts. If an executive leader is good at rhetoric (this is, of course, not a bad thing) has nothing to do with real benefits. Wilson's division can be understood with the help of different relationships in different types of organisations mentioned. Transparent performance results are said to be a mechanism for public accountability, policy coordination, ministerial control, internal agency improvements, and with that connected responsiveness, but an additional step should be taken with the participation of *people* who could replace performance management with *democratic* performance management (Pollitt, 2000). However, again, the additional element of people points to additional relations that would be otherwise remain hidden in the net of hidden relations through which (as a parable of communication channels) communication occurs.[7]

The large variations on relations, particularities, processes and outcomes cannot lead to the state of the art in the field of agency organisational forms: There is no dominant agency type with similar processes, management, autonomy, performance, etc. that would be generally valid and equally effective in the contexts of various countries. Given all variations, the presence of the "one best approach" to manage and control an agency is dubious. Instead of general guidelines on how to run the agency or what form to apply, it could be more valuable to evaluate a particular agency's input, flows and stocks, outputs, feedbacks, performance and other indicators, patterns and decisions made regarding the relationship between inputs and output, or in one word: *relations,* in the broadest sense of meaning. This approach could be more valuable to answer not a general question, *for example,* about managerial or procedural autonomy, but rather a specific question on how much managerial autonomy should a manager have in an agency in the field of social security in country X given the constitution, legislation, public values, national strategy (ministerial and agency's) strategy and other criteria that seem important in this country.

This could be presented as an 'univergency' approach (Pečarič, 2020) that is built on the universal and ubiquitous general factors that transcend national borders (e.g., the science of public administration) and divergent practices (path dependencies of public administrations) that always emerge at the same time as similar ones.[8]

Today's organisations are faced with the complex environment and with related urging needs and forms for introducing continuously learning methods into organisational structures, with new knowledge to respond to the challenges of transforming environment, new technologies, and the like. Such needs reflect a basic condition for detecting the relations that had caused these needs. Peter Drucker has written somewhere that "the management is a major resource in developed countries and the most needed in underdeveloped ones"; yes, but the management that is aware of relations. Countries, groups, and individuals operate in different environments and situations; they are different. Given the differences in different situations, it should be understandable that there is no uniform organisational structure or leadership style that would be highly effective for all types of companies or institutions. Even the same team sometimes wins the game based on one strategy and sometimes on the other. Teams, companies, and states vary with organizational and situational variables and circumstances. The organisational structure and functional processes are determined by *the specific, but changeable situations* in which institutions operate; it is about situational or contingency variables that are recognised as such in the real time and space dimension. Due to constant adjustments to the actual and desired situation, which are shaped by different variables, the public agencies look like the proverbial Minerva (that takes only at dusk when a day has passed), because they too slowly adapt to the circumstances and yet, even when they begin to adapt to them, there are already new ones. Public agency is just a generic term; in reality, there is a crowd of institutions with that name and with even larger numbers of employees that should operate as smoothly, lawfully, and impartially as possible. A first deviation from the (theoretical, general[9]) concepts on which the public agency apparently operates, represents the reality itself from which the general ideas of abstraction (reflection) come now at the first place. Public agencies still work primarily as curative and too rarely as preventive or probabilistic. They are aware of a certain problem usually when it has already reached its peak; this could be the reason for the constant talk about reforms, where the word 'reform' is the wrong word for the description of *constant adjustment processes*. The sole word through the conclusion of the failure of previous reforms gives a bad connotation, which per se does not deserve. Agencies should not reform themselves (to discover 'the best structure for all times and problems'") but *adapt* to situations that make their content highly relevant in the context of public interest. It is not right to talk only about changing the words: they should be present in practise. There is often emphasised that public reforms depend on politics, but it is seldomly clearly stated that goals are practically defined mainly by agencies or their parent ministries (especially by conscious public servants).[10] The Ancient Egyptians, Babylonians, Aztecs, Greeks, and Romans managed to build large empires, without the theories of public administration. The very theory *before the mot* worked in practise, where rulers knew how to govern; they have moved the people like a puppet string. A bad connotation of administration that does not critically use the power of the human mind (and thus change relations if needed) can be seen in the old German saying *Wem Gott ein Amt gibt, dem gibt er dafür den Verstand* or 'whom God gives an office, he gives his mind to it' (an employee more or less uses an official understanding instead of his own). What is real, what is reasonable in each specific situation? Who establishes, defines reality reasonableness, relations? Most people depend on the presence of circumstances and other people, regardless of whether their presence is actual, implied, or even imaginary. In everyday life, social situations determine our behaviour and mental states and thus have a significant impact on our behaviour. A social situation in which people find themselves gives them a role to play and feedback information regarding the expected behaviour in each case,[11] while the more relevant conditions are hidden in relations. According to Robert Merton (1968), they form situational factors in terms of adaptation to the group and in the group. The main characteristics of bureaucratic organisations that were for Weber conceived as a means to an end (effectiveness) have become their own goal (displacement of goals). The instrumental value has changed into the final value (instrumental one in the terminal value). Discipline and conformity, which have been conceived as means, have become a value and an objective of their own. An organisation that changes means of goals becomes rigid, incapable of change and adaptation. It is natural for people with the same interests to be united by a common desire and with that related cooperation. In that way, officials also create their own *esprit de corps*, an informal organisation that leads them in defence of their interests. But sometimes this is done on behalf of the citizens and elected officials. In such a case, they regard their work with pride, which can lead to opposition to all changes that are opposite to the accepted routine. Crozier has provided an overview of Weber's ideal concept of effective bureaucracy, according to its actual development. 'Organizations represent the working people and the result of rival powers in the organization' (Crozier, 1964, p. 162). He opposed the rationalistic view and human relations because they ignore the role that rival battles play based on power in the shaping of organisation. However, still, and again all such states or conditions are based on relations (that further can cause new combinations). Organisational relationships are a series of strategic games, where the protagonists try to either take advantage of each area of discretion for their own goals or to prevent others to gain an advantage: 'each group is fighting to preserve and improve the areas in which it has some part of discretion, it tends to limit its dependence on other groups and adopt dependence only if there is no other choice' (Crozier, 1964, p. 156). This can be done when *relations* are known – this should not be overlooked, and it is not superfluous to repeat this many times throughout this monograph.

When the relations are not known, the possibility of manipulating the people opens. In the 1950s of the past century, Solomon Asch (1955) conducted a series of experimental studies in which he examined a strong tendency of people to adapt in accordance with the opinions and judgments of others. Asch confirmed Crozier's power of the group above the individuals to whom the individual unconsciously adapts. That argument also confirms the findings of Axelrod on the evolution of cooperation. Norms can be examined in terms of expectations, values, and behaviour. As a norm exists in a given social environment to the extent to which individuals behave in a certain way and are often punished if they do not behave similarly, he puts the argument that the norm is more about a stage than the proposition in the sense of 'all or nothing' (Axelrod, 1986). People tend to agree with others in the group, especially if others agree (Sunstein, 2009). This can be even more important when other people are leaders (Milgram, 2009; Zimbardo, 2008). Social psychology includes discoveries and theories, which are often foreign to the common view, oppose, intuition, and conviction of typical causes of personal cognition, emotion, and behaviour. Although the notions of completely rational actors have value for themselves, people usually in their daily lives behave more on tests and errors than on detailed calculations based on accurate future beliefs. Axelrod (2006) rejected the rationalistic approach and used an evolutionary one based on the principle that "what works well for a player will likely be reused and what is bad will probably be refuted".

Darwin believed in group selection instead of selfish individuals: '[w]hen two tribes of primeval man, living in the same country, came into competition, if (other circumstances being equal) the one tribe included a great number of courageous, sympathetic, and faithful members, who were always ready to warn each other of danger, to aid, and defend each other, this tribe would succeed better and conquer the other (Darwin, 1871, p. 162). The advantage of individually good, collective behaviour of persons in groups caused the emergence of morality, which was for Darwin the most advanced form of natural selection:

The primeval man, in a very remote period, was influenced by the praise and blame of his fellows. It is obvious, that the members of the same tribe would approve of conduct which appeared to them to be for the general good, and would reprobate that which appeared evil. To do good unto others, to do unto others as ye would they should do unto you, is the foundation stone of morality (Darwin, 1871, p. 165). An increase in the number of well-endowed men and an advancement in the standard of morality will certainly give an immense advantage to one tribe over another. A tribe including many members who, from possessing in a high degree the spirit of patriotism, fidelity, obedience, courage, and sympathy, were always ready to aid one another, and to sacrifice themselves for the common good, would be victorious over most other tribes; and this would be natural selection (Darwin, 1871, p. 166).

Harmonious kin group[12] and/or multilevel selection[13] offer not only 'complementary approaches to the study of social evolution: kin selection approaches usually focus on the identification of optimal phenotypes and thus on the end result of a selection process, whereas multilevel selection approaches focus on the ongoing selection process itself' (Kramer & Meunier, 2016), but also reflect the condition, known as *solidarity* or "one for all, all for one" (albeit sometimes to the detriment of the individual, but on average to the benefit of the group). Such a coherent and, at the same time, the most competitive and adaptable form of group has caused better chances of survival for a group as a whole. Morality and/or groupishness (the social counterpart of selfishness) is also for Haidt 'the key to understanding humanity' (2012). A human social element is present in groups, collectives, and / or relationships with other people. Human development is therefore closely connected with institutions that bring people and resources together with the same purpose of providing better results. When such an institution does not diminish the importance of other institution(s), a fertile ground for cooperation and trust among institutions (and by this also among their members and other people) can be put on a higher level. In the evolutionary approach, 'there is no need to provide rational calculations' (or at least they come after the instinctive and emotional ones) to determine the best strategy. This approach allows the introduction of new strategies in terms of random mutations of the old ones, if cooperation among elements is their common denominator. People observe each other, and those with poor reward imitate those who are doing better. There is no (necessary) need for the presumption that an individual is rational and that he understands the strategic impact of a given situation. He does not. This is happening also in agencies, when a mimic of other cases is represented in a form of good practise at the collective level, when, or if, relationships are (systemically) more relevant than individual parts, where new things emerge that parts do not possess. Good practice per se can be useful when relations (more or less) stay the same; under this condition, the evolutionary approach of mimicking is helpful, but when it is blindly followed, it leads towards negative results. The same holds for the 'rational' one, as it also relies on many more or less normal situational factors:

Theory of practical reasoning indicates that rationality is often less algorithmic than traditional views have suggested, in that it relies on situated judgments about what is appropriate in particular times, places, and contexts that are difficult to articulate using the instrumentalist framework... In particular, rationality relies on action and exploration as much as logical analysis—a feature that many traditional views of rationality overlook. This element of action and exploration... can be understood as a way of filling the gaps in the unfinished preferences of the policy actors. In this sense, commensurability at best results from the response to the conflict rather than guiding it (Thacher & Rein, 2004, p. 458).

To be closer to the reality of institutions (agencies), a focus should be given to *relations* among individuals and groups that subsume a factual position under a legal rule. The latter per se as much as clearly and reasonably stated cannot be a solution per se. Subsumption depends on logical comparison and other even non-logical elements. No rule is self-interpreting (Wittgenstein, 1986), no choice is clearly guided only by certain rules because 'the establishment of an acceptable proof, whether we are dealing with proofs in law, science, or technology, in fact presupposes that one can rely on resources that have already been subject to generalisation' (Boltanski & Thévenot, 2006, p. 12) and all social changes arise and are transformed by social *practices* ordered in space and time, which do not depend directly neither on the experience of individuals, nor on the existence of any form of societal totality (Giddens, 1984). Before giving precedence to agents or institutions, the practises, interactions, and/or relations between them should be conceptualised and then detected up to the highest possible way; an institutional formal design can rarely protect people from conflicts and to them relate substantial challenges. Conflicts (of values, rules) are always the problem that occurs in practice (where again, relations prevail).

Historical transitions (evolutionary jumps) into new arrangements have occurred when unstoppable social forces loosened a previous integration framework of established practises. These jumps agencies usually cannot prevent or soothe just because of their existence; hope remains on the sound analytical and holistic research, driven by anticipation and adaptions to new situations. Situational conditionality is closely connected with legality. An answer about a number of research units in the public administration (in ministries/agencies) could reveal a good/bad awareness of situations in which institutions have to adapt to avoid future unwanted consequences. Such units should give a focus on new outputs and changing events that go by or through established traditions; it is about a constant quest for evaluation of experiences in the light of changing contexts. A path towards discoveries usually begins with the help of hypotheses to confirm or refute initial assumptions (Einstein felt that the wording of the problem is often more important than its solution), but in the presence of numerous perspectives, one conclusion can conflict with another. Established practices and path dependence can lead to Veblen's "trained incapacity"[14] that prevents adaptation to new circumstances. The complex environment needs at least equal complex vision to be successful. Past practises are discarded by a different awareness of the situation (that is, of relations that produce it), so the question is how much agency present practises would fit the (more) complex environment. The answer can be given through the concept of *habitus*, as the central concept of Bourdieu's theory of practise.

It is about the system of fixed, deployable dispositions and structures, pre-disposed to act as a structurised structure … A correct one, without being the product of obedience to the rules adapted to its goals, without assuming a conscious end … Collectively orchestrated without being the product of orchestral activities by a conductor and of the permanently installed generative principle of regulated improvisation; it is a history changed in nature (Bourdieu, 1977, p. 72).

With the idea of habitus, Bourdieu criticises the objectivistic (that points to a society with a view of a distant observer) and subjectivist theories (the ones based on the idea that people choose what they will be), and structuralist objectivism (this approach makes an error of the rule that happens when the *ex post* descriptive generalisations are converted into 'causal' explanations of a described behaviour). The solution is to recognize the autonomy of practice in terms of rules and projects. The multitude of actions, stakeholders, institutions, etc. represent the complex (but unknowable) whole, a whole assembled in a net of relations. Agencies' practices fit into the complex environment when they as (other) social actors do not act like puppets on a string nor are free spirits; they are a kind of jazz musicians who are equipped at the beginning with a corpus of practical techniques to play on their instruments and with the agreed common format for improvisation on the theme, but they produce music that is not possible to foresee, as there would be a type of the realization of musical structure which existed before to the actual playing of notes and independent of them.[15]

Agencies operate in a complex system of the pre-dispositive formal, and informal rules and practises; they act based on rules, but also on modifications caused by the external and internal environment, human needs, and motives. The higher control above several agencies in their joint exercise of public tasks must allow an independent operation of each body and take care about its match with other agencies on similar tasks.[16] Habitus, the different but yet similar practices of many agencies (that strive to common goals in the frame of self-and-all-encompassing system), should be controlled by a higher authority based on the principle of subsidiarity, when a subordinate unit is "in trouble" (while otherwise leaves to it an autonomy of professional practice). This could represent the universal prescription of conduct in ensuring the internal and external legitimacy of public agencies, but it is still just a generalisation and abstraction. Agencies as parts of habitus combine the principles of social continuity and discontinuity: first, because through the *law in action,* form a society of otherwise individual organisms, and second, because it can modify an existing habitus of rules and forces through the acquisition of new information and alternatives that could lead to innovation. Like any science at the beginning claims more than it actually knows, new contours of action also come from a handful of items (hypotheses) on which a structure is iteratively (re)build. In this way, it represents itself as a complex structure that is capable of building new ideas for new or old problems. But this is just the beginning. An abstract rule can only mimic real behaviour (an error of rule), and the implementation of the rule can only mimic (it tries to be approximate to) a formally enacted rule (an error of conduct) leading to double error. Therefore, each repetition could be even more distant from real practices. These errors are also a problem in public administration; the agencies and employees in them, on the one hand, do not always look on the whole public system (but only on their work and their clients) and/or do not incorporate consequences of their actions in other areas, and, on the other, they cannot see a much larger picture from their point of view. It could be said that higher authorities must take care for the overall organisation of public administration, but also the awareness and participation of lower bodies/agencies not only replicate them or their practises on a higher level but also reflect their work on a general, wider scale. Parent ministries can never control daily matters of public agency, so without awareness of the latter, complex unity is doomed to fail. The awareness that each task, created with a repetition of simple actions, where each repetition slightly deviates from the previous, where any action goes to the potency of the previous until there is a new field should be present in all public institutions, in all public employees; only when a formal agency task encounters and 'brushes and polishes with' other tasks from other agencies, public interest can be truly promoted.

The above-mentioned perspectives on various things connected with agency on one way or another point at the impossibility of one or all-comprehensive work that could tell everything general and yet specific enough to agencies. Such multidisciplinary complexity is also present in agencies as part of wider and narrower systems. Agency elements could be generally presented but specific enough at the same time to be able to successfully manage and administer agencies in various contexts of tasks, environments, and countries. This could be done with the help of systems theory focused on relations. Cybernetics (as a branch of the system's theory that explores regulatory systems) emphasises (among others) that i) *the purpose of the system is what it really does* (Beer, 2002), not claims;[17] ii) *systems are always a part of larger and smaller systems,* and hence *no system cannot reflect its full meaning from within, but only from a higher system* from a 'metalanguage as a language of a higher order in which propositions written in lower-order language may be discussed' (Beer, 1981, p. 75).

No subsystem *per se* also does not have enough information to permit an accurate understanding of a wider system (society, nature), because the latter (from a meta-higher level), gives meaning to the former: there will always be true statements, but not deducible from them, but solely from other, higher systems (Beer, 1994; McCulloch, 1945). No agency or legal act thus itself neither provides its meaning nor can do so with wider systems (constitution, nature, society, and environment). The latter give meaning to it. An agency can (although roughly and more or less successfully) implement its tasks through its (more or less successful) functions, but its meaning can be obtained only from a higher metalevel as something that is 'situated behind or beyond', that is, more highly organised, or more comprehensive (Merriam-Webster, 2020b), something that could be in Aristotelian terms from *Metaphysics* (2015) named wisdom that deals with the first causes and principles of things. Along the importance of meta-level(s) there is also iii) *structural recursion,* derived from studying biological systems as the similar concept to *hierarchy*, but not understood in the managerial or administrative formal sense:

Living (viable) systems, from the most elementary cells to human beings, are self-organizing and self-regulatory. Evolution is responsible for their increasing complexification, where the functional differentiation and connectivity of cells may produce more complex living systems, without cells losing their self-organising and self-regulating characteristics. This produces viable systems within viable systems, at increasing levels of complexity. Each component maintains its autonomy *vis-à-vis* its environment, but contributes to the production of a larger, also autonomous viable system. It is like picturing Russian dolls within Russian dolls, only that there is not only one within each of the larger dolls but potentially many, which most importantly, for social organisations, can defect. All autonomous components amplify the complexity of their integrated wholes and share their structural and management requirements to remain viable. This is a recursive structure with huge complexity amplification capabilities, where the components are functionally differentiated but share an invariant structure (Espejo & Reyes, 2011, p. 93).

As Checkland résumés, hierarchy is 'the principle according to which entities meaningfully treated as wholes are made up of smaller entities that are themselves wholes...and so on. In a hierarchy, emergent properties denote the levels' (Checkland, 1981, p. 314). 'Hierarchy in the systems context does not refer to vertical relationships of organisational structure or power, but rather to the notion of nested subsystems' (Mitleton-Kelly, 2003, p. 44). Similarly, the embodiment of organisational complexity requires autonomous systems within autonomous systems, within autonomous systems, and so on. This is the idea of *recursive organisation* (Espejo, 2003). A higher metalevel (a denominator) is needed to understand the content of a subsystem, and the same holds for public agencies (and the same holds for parent ministries, governments, legislators, etc). What is preferable cannot be determined once and for all by any kind of formal organisation; the emergence of a decision depends on the concentration of relevant information that changes from moment to moment, and not by any kind of pre-established rigid structure, but by a time-and-place-dependent purpose. One set of rules cannot be addressed only with another set of rules because they have different denominators that could be compared or put together only on a higher meta- (systemic) level (of principles) that combines more general level mentality with rules and *vice versa*. And even here, the principles are again based also on their meta-elements that can be viewed as systems of gathering common points from various information, while also they depend on their higher meta-level that determines what is or can be included in this system.[18]

Turner made an interesting very similar multilevel connection (to the meta-levels and hierarchy of systems theory) at social institutions research by dividing the levels of social reality and/or sociocultural structures on the micro, meso, and macro levels of reality.[19] The macro level (symbolic) institutions give meaning to the meso level (formal) organisations are present (on micro level are interpersonal encounters are present) that further give meaning to the micro level interpersonal encounters and roles the people have here.

Typically, it is the organisational units from which institutions are constructed that receive the most attention. For example, sociologists study family rather than kinship systems, firms more than economies, churches more than religion, governmental organisations more than politics, medical professionals more than medicine, agents of law enforcement more than law. Even when the broader structural and cultural environments of organizational forms are examined, there is a tendency to conceptualize these in rather vague terms. Indeed, the 'new institutionalism' in organisational theory is more about organisations in their cultural environments than it is about the specific dynamics of institutional systems (Turner, 2003, p. 2).

For Turner, institutions of society are affected with five macrolevel active and viable forces (population, production, reproduction, regulation, and distribution), meso organisations with segmentation, differentiation, and integration, and micro encounters with emotions, transactional needs, status, roles, symbols, and demography/ecology. If macrolevel forces are used, the organisational arrangement of agencies at the meso level therefore depends on production (effectiveness and efficiency of agencies' services), population (the number, diversity and conditions under which people, *that is,* customers or citizens receive services from an agency's services), regulation (mechanisms of coordination and control, power dynamics between centralization, deconcentration and decentralisation), distribution (of information, resources and people based on the infrastructure or facilities to distribute information, resources, and people and exchange with other entities) and reproduction (a viable pass of cultural memes instead of DNA, based on the people's trust and legitimacy of agency). The mentioned forces affect each other in various and complex ways; when at least rough traces of their intertwined functioning can be traced, discovered, and predicted, we can talk about institutional order.

Some international institutions (IMF, WB, OECD) have wanted to 'skip the hard way' of determining an optimal agency's form for a specific country in development and thus proposed the 'ideal' type of agency. NPM's ideal-type agency (Verhoest, Roness, Verschuere, Rubecksen & MacCarthaigh, 2010) is made up of key dimensions such as *structural disaggregation* (large bureaucratic and monolithic departments are disaggregated into single-purpose and client-orientated organisations with a focus on service delivery focus), *managerial freedom* (a goal is to act more or less independently of their core government departments with the aim of increasing efficiency; let managers manage should encourage professionalism), results control (a shift of control from ex ante to results-based control, based on contractual instruments; a drop of input and process control for a firmer control on performance) and the split 'policy operations' (policy preparation as a 'political' task should be performed by democratically elected representatives [and their direct subordinate core departments], while policy operations as an 'administrative' task is to be performed by agencies arm, more or less free of ministerial interference). When leaders would follow this ideal-type model, agencies should probably have high levels of managerial freedom/autonomy and administrative implementation (that is, *ex post* controlled by results) and low levels of policy autonomy. The 'convergence-divergence' discussion is based on ex post emphasis on results, focused on practical similarities or differences between agencies, while it does not answer the reasons for these similarities or differences. An inference that agencies are (dis)similar does not tell anything about their context of doing things, about their dynamics among other higher- or lower-level organisations, about their relations with their higher authorities, stakeholders and other people, and about the ways they obtain the trust and legitimacy of people. A practical choice of an agency type, whether it is *ad hoc* or more text book (as a general draft or form) - although the first is more common due to various (political and other interests) - has in common that both choices disregard substantial relations and context in a specific country and its multiple levels (sic) that would be established with serious analysis and research.

"NO-LIMIT" A LA RUSSIAN DOLL PRINCIPLES OF ORGANISATION

There is no limit to the number of principles of management; every rule or managerial procedure which strengthens the body corporate or facilitates its functioning has a place among the principles so long, at least, as experience confirms its worthiness (Fayol, 1954, p. 19).

In the Aristotelian line of thought from the beginning of this work on the efficiency of an army *vis-à-vis* the order and in the general, the latter has priority as orders emanate from it and not contrary; similarly, for Barnard the nature of authority and/or legalism prevents the acceptance of essential facts of social organisations. The source authority cannot explain the fact that countries are also based on (formal) organisations as one of the systems within a *cooperative* system as 'a complex of physical, biological, personal, and social components which are in a specific systematic relationship by reason of the cooperation of two or more persons for at least one definite end' (Barnard, 1968, p. 65). The law is beside its formulation also something else, also the organisation of various kinds based on mutually more or less dependent functions. Before applying to agencies, there are some underlying basic principles at work in all organisations that deserve to be addressed.

For Barnard 'an organisation comes to being when (1) there are persons able to communicate with each other (2) who are willing to contribute action, (3) to accomplish a common purpose' [as the co-ordinating and unifying principle] ... The existence of an organisation depends on a combination of these elements appropriate [or adaptable] to the external conditions at the moment' (Barnard, 1968, p. 82). For him, 'this external equilibrium has two terms in it: first, the effectiveness of the organisation, which comprises the relevance of its purpose to the environmental situation; and second, its efficiency, which comprises the interchange between the organisation and individuals' (Barnard, 1968, p. 83). For Barnard, the functions of the executive are those of *control, management, supervision,* and *administration* in formal organizations, and are exercised by all those who are in positions of control of whatever degree (Barnard, 1968, p. 6). Thus, it matters how (personal) communication takes place on which a system of executive functions is based.

Communication, at first, depends on division of work, which reflects *reductionism;* the latter is one of the organizing principles of modern science that breaks the world into elementary building blocks.[20] On the other hand, the division of work needs its Janus-faced coordination and *vice versa*. This inference is already stated in the first paragraph of Gulick's *Notes on the theory of organisation* of 1937 (Gulick, 2003). Despite this, it seems that decision makers still chase efficiency "up and down" in various dimensions without a clear idea how to achieve it. That 'coordination is one of the oldest problems facing the public sector' (Bouckaert, Peters, & Verhoest, 2010, p. 13) is indisputable, and this is all with the more emphasis on the fact that 'organisational design varies systematically across issue areas and over time…[in which] autonomous agencies are not the result of a systematic design, but rather of a pluralistic chaos of political and bureaucratic forces' (Valdés, 2011, p. 3). Coordination can be (more) effective when clear goals are established, when "the left hand knows what the right hand is doing",[21] but already here – where only two parts/institutions are involved – problems occur. A stretch or limit of coordination is known as the span of control (a maximum number of subordinate persons who can be managed effectively and efficiently by superiors in an organisation). The traditional number is said to be between five and seven people, whereas there is no such number for subordinate organisational layers (a number of organizational levels have supervisory responsibilities). Spans and layers affect the way an organisation delegates tasks to specific functions, groups, and individuals. The span is conditioned on various contexts of a working environment (the nature of the job, the field, the organisation, the skills and competencies of the employees, the size, the manner of interaction, communication, and reporting). Mooney and Reiley, among the comparative principles of organisation, especially emphasise the importance of *coordination*:

This term expresses the principles of organisation *in toto*; nothing less. This does not mean that there are no subordinated principles; it simply means that the others are contained in this one of coordination. The others are simply the principles through which coordination' operates and thus becomes effective (Mooney & Reiley, 1931, p. 19).

Coordination as a 'harmonious combination or interaction, as a function or parts' (Merriam-Webster, 2020a) can be vertical (authoritative orders – hierarchy), horizontal (cooperation between peers / groups through division of work – market), vertical horizontal (instructions and directive - partnerships), and horizontal vertical (reporting – network). It can be *sensu lato* focused on purposes (planning and organization), processes (the transfers of methods of command and co-ordination, *stricto sensu*, among units, and external environment), goals (control) with the aim of a greater coherence,[22] but here basically means *viability*, the ability to live, operate and be sustained. For Mary Parker Follet, the nature of control is seen through coordination; for her four fundamental principles of organisation, start with coordination: '1. Coordination as reciprocal relating of the factors in a situation. 2. Coordination by direct contact with the responsible people concerned. 3. Coordination in the early stages. 4. Coordination as a continuing process' (Parker Follett, 2003, p. 172). Through these interweaving principles, control self-generates, where 'the degree of correlation is the measure of control: the more complete the reciprocal adjusting, the more complete the control' (Parker Follett, 2003, p. 177).

The manner in which coordination as a whole is seen externally is in the implementation of tasks and their results. The whole process can also be seen as a set of communicative actions. Fayol named them "administrative apparatus" or "administrative tools" as a system of recording or 'a vast documentation which includes the present, the past, and the future by which [the elements of management] planning, organization, command, coordination and control are carried out' (Fayol, 2003, p. 114). These contributions by members of the staff, together with information from outside sources, ensure that directors have the best possible means of appreciating the *probable* consequences of their decisions. For this aim, he used general surveys, plans of operations, reports or proceedings, minutes of conferences between heads of departments, and organisation charts. *Planning* as his first element of management (then follows organising, command, coordination and control) meant for him to foresee, *i.e.*, 'to assess the future and make provision for it' (Fayol, 1954, p. 48). Furthermore, in Gulick's well-known acronym POSDCORB, planning stands as the first task of the chief executive (*Planning*, Organizing, Staffing, Directing, Coordinating, Reporting and Budgeting) (Gulick, 2003).[23] Having this task in mind, Fayol also proposed what is now known as research units, or his "councils for improvements" (similar to the below-mentioned Beer System 4):

Administrative theory supposes that in every great enterprise there is a permanent council for improvements whose function it is to make research on all possible improvements in the enterprise and to carry them out under the auspices and authority of the director. An organism of this kind seems to me indispensable in order to study and carry out reforms in the enterprise of government, which perhaps, more than any other, is in constant need of them…the council for improvements should be composed of five members: the first would have charge of planning, organization, command, coordination and control, or in other words, of administration; the second of financial problems; the third of the organization of accounting and statistics; the fourth of legal matters; the fifth should be a business man. The council for improvements should be represented in each government department by a liaison officer subordinate to the Minister, and particularly charged with the duty of keeping him in touch with the studies being made in his department (Fayol, 2003, p. 120,121).

For Fayol, the essential condition for a successful public service operation is a good high command that demands good staff and good administrative tools. For him, there is nothing inflexible or absolute in management, and the same stands for general principles of management:[24] all is a question of *proportion*.

Seldom do we have to apply the same principle twice in identical conditions; allowance must be made for different changing circumstances, for men just as different and changing, and for many other variable elements. Therefore, principles are flexible and capable of adaptation to every need; it is a matter of knowing how to make use of them, which is a difficult art requiring intelligence, experience, decision, and proportion. Compounded of tact and experience, proportion is one of the foremost attributes of the manager (Fayol, 1954, p. 19).

The right proportion could be synonymous with efficiency, the latter with specialisation and division of work: they all fit in one another; such an approach could not only be an appropriate answer for the application of principles, but also to prevent their paradoxes (when stretched too far). The functions of the executive rest (are layered above) on the *division of work* (a general scenery), *functionalisation* (emphasis on a particular kind of work as a function within organisation), and *specialisation* (emphasis upon a person). Their opposite meanings (unification, generalisation, and grouping) could not reveal their functional Janus face perspectives of communication, coordination, and holism, while all these notions as a Russian doll in both examples fit in one another: the third occurs in the second and the latter within the first. Similarly, all other things fit into one another: the power of *exchange* of things/services gives occasion to the *division of labour*; the latter causes a proportionable increase of the productive powers of labour, which is *limited by the extent of that power* and/or by the extent of the market (Smith, 1977).[25] A good high command is thus revealed in a form of hierarchy as structural recursion, where each level knows of the existence of the higher and lower ones.

Another (along the division, new) perspective of 'hierarchy as a structure' that emerges (or is above) from coordination is *holism* (as coordination is done according to its goal) that not only connects interrelated parts into a larger whole, but also gives *meaning* (not as output, but in the meaning of outcome) to the former: they can be understood solely with a reference to the whole, which is *per se* greater than the sum of its parts. First, traces of holism can be seen in Gulick's four basic organizational systems (purpose, process, persons or things, and place) that are tightly *intertwined* and communicate with *an organization as a living and dynamic entity in the changing dimensions* of time, technological development, and size (the number of men at work and their geographical dispersion). He hoped that the right formula for 'administration measurement' will be found based on rapid machine statistics and new developments in communication, while on the other hand, the power of systemic coordination is limited by the lack of knowledge and the lack of administrative skills. The scalar process (a formal process by which the supreme coordination unit operates from the top through the lowest ranks), specialisation, the span of control, (vertical) line and (horizontal) staff, emphasis on the relationship between leaders and their subordinates, and other organisational principles came together under the principle of coordination as the fundamental principle of organization that encloses other principles, but stil connotes its human factor.[26]

These notions clearly denote the presence of relations between them, which point to 'systems of organization' that still do not lose importance to the present day: Scott and Davis (2016) use three major organisational perspectives (in a similar manner to which systems theory or complexity theory also have their own perspectives) developed over the course of the twentieth century to understand organizations. They are a *rational system* (that pursues relatively specific goals and exhibits relatively highly *formalised* social structures); a *natural system* (it pursues multiple, also nonrational *interests*, both disparate and common, but who recognise the value of perpetuating the collective or organisation as an important resource); an *open system* (it consists of interdependent flows and activities that link shifting coalitions of participants embedded in wider material-resource and institutional environments [such system exchanges energy, matter, and/or information with its environment]). The rational system can be challenged by the natural or 'reflective' one that stresses the effect of human subjectivity and by the open one that stresses the embeddedness (it could be seen as another notion of structural hierarchy) of institutions in the environment and pre-existing practices. A comparison of the systems mentioned above with each other helps to clarify the strengths and weaknesses of each. Formal rules with specific goals are present in the same framework as divergent interests, values, consensus/conflict, informal structure, and goal complexity along the external environment, where exchanges with the environment are a vital element of the sustainability of the system, composed cybernetically as a system. These systems can be used as organisational paradigms, but do not explain how they interrelate, self-organise, and change due to mutual interactions and how they collectively influence the overall performance of the organisation.

Due to various perspectives and changing contexts along different interests and motives, methodologically can be developed cumulative verifiable knowledge, but in such endeavours researchers along the formulation of conditional, context-specific generalities aspire to seek results under more universal, underlying laws (under which previous results could be different). Holism fits in this camp; it is expressed as *an emergence* that is not reducible to the properties of the elements and means 'the appearance of a level of complexity more advanced than the existing components of a system' (Feltz, Crommelinck, & Goujon, 2006, p. 341). All is not only more than the sum of its parts, but what is or could be 'all' cannot be known in advance; it emerges only *ex post* through interactions between parts (be it rational, natural and open systems or something else), and when these parts are again taken apart, an emergent connecting and unifying idea would be lost. The "beauty" of this (complex) behaviour is in its mostly unplanned emergence from simple rules. Emergence further reflects s*elf-organisation* that means 'the appearance of a structure or pattern without an external agent imposing it' (Heylighen, 1999, p. 253). It addresses the spontaneous emergence of an order (*e.g.*, the ice or the snowflake structure).

From the presented points of view (and Barnard's functions as executive), it matters how formal rules address not formal but the "no-limit principles of reality" or organisation (based on division of work, cooperation, communication, purpose, relations, coordination, hierarchy as structural embeddedness, holism, emergence and viable self-organisation) that clearly not only point at the importance of systems theory (parts, relations among them, structural hierarchy) and complexity theory (dynamism, combinations, iterations, emergence) theory, but also have elements from which the latter two are assembled; both theories will be further elaborated in the following chapters). Agencies and other types of public organisation should at least roughly address (be aware of) these elements as they will otherwise independently take over the organisation in a way of unpersonal, nonviolent, informal, and invisible *"coup d'etat"*, usually understood in negative terms of conflict, deterioration, corruption, illegality, etc. *When relations are left alone, they will (further) regulate themselves and others.* This could be the starting point for all talks on the management and administration of organisations. Agencies are also always embedded in other systems with their own rules (moral values, habits, and practises) that will determine first complex equilibria of various and multiple purposes, processes, persons, things, places, relations, and communications. There are always parallel arrangements present alongside the enacted, formal ones, within and outside of an agency. This is *the challenge of spontaneous self-organisation* that emerges from connections and combinations between those layers. This could be more in focus of the top-down hierarchy, within the principle of *coordination* that should address these interactions in the real-time and place dimensions, of course with the help of other findings arising from system, complexity, and other theories.

PARADOXES OF STATICALLY UNDERSTOOD PRINCIPLES: NOTHING IN EXCESS

The excessive enlargement of the government is probably caused proportionately with the growth of citizen demands. And unmanageable government in time leads to delays and inefficiency. A quest for efficient services unsurprisingly led to the spread of agencies and with this again also to the overstretched span of control, lack (asymmetry - adverse selection, and moral hazard) of information, weak coordination of interrelated activities, among ministries and agencies and the latter themselves, the way to the hollow government. Most countries responded to this state of affairs with the consolidation of separate agencies into integrated ministries, or towards tighter coordination backed by the ideas of 'joint-up government' and / or 'whole-of-government'. Thus, similar errors were repeated on different levels and times: the politics and public administration dichotomy of the early twentieth century was transferred or copied to the ministerial policy making and agency implementation of the late twentieth century. As later in the 20th century it was determined that the mentioned dichotomy lives only in theory and not in practice, it was similarly determined in the early 20th century that the full autonomy of the agency contradicts the need to coordinate and control. Some scholars also found that the split or merger of policy design and implementation is cyclical (Bouckaert et al., 2010). What are the reasons for such repetitions of errors and pendulum swings? When problems of slower performance, identification and determination of responsibility, accountability, transparency, functional control, and policy capacity reach a breaking point, a different approach is needed.[27] One could be in making necessary corrections of the existent arrangements and the other, in the public administration more common, is the creation of new institutions. This path was also followed with the 1980s agencies, with their emphasis on autonomy, structuration, specialization, and narrower policy implementation. Regardless of the various reasons for which agencies were created, some of them are the basic ones: a decision to create an agency should be based on a relevant analysis of needs and potential gains, benefits achieved *relative to* financial savings, citizens' rights, improved service, and other efficiency gains and of ways in which a parent ministry can carry out its supervisory role over agency activities. However, in practice these clear directions can turn on many sideways.[28] Conversely, these approaches and reasons result also in dependence, imbalance, and focus on the agency's (immediately seen) outputs rather on its (policy or wider) outcomes, higher costs and asymmetric information among too specialized focuses and missing the general point of view. And the cycle repeated: new reformistic ideas were focused on reinventing coordination by using old (classical, Weberian) or new, joint-up or whole-of-government hierarchical approaches, with a larger emphasis on market and network instruments. A key question is not whether, but when, these solutions will cause new problems.

When reforms are based just more or less on the leading management *ideas*, the latter could be analysed, due to their similarity or even evenness, in comparison with management principles. Principles enable new decisions and predict future behaviour.[29] Nozick gave one of the clearest statements about the connection between and future behaviour: 'a person's principles play a role in producing behavior … for him, the principles affect not (merely) estimates of the probabilities but these very probabilities themselves: the principles are not evidence of how he will behave but devices that help determine what he will (decide to) do' (Nozick, 1993, p. 12). When understood univocally, principles behave as standards, but in a changing environment, their meaning can change. Principles change with new information; this one is brought to an interested or sensible person through relations (or perspectives that reveal some of them) between different points. Principles were never the alpha and omega of doing things: they just frame and lead the way: 'the principle is the lighthouse fixing the bearings, but it can only serve those who already know the way to port' (Fayol, 1954, p. 42). Frederick Winslow Taylor should be emphasised as the father of task management (more commonly known as scientific management); in search of improving of national efficiency and workers efficiency, he has developed the principles of scientific management (Taylor, 1974),[30] but he did not consider that managing could be learned from books or taught in the classroom: it had to be learned in *practice,* where data is collected and scientifically evaluated by the management in the manner of "planning ahead". Taylorism wanted to ensure the values of efficiency and economy in a world view that promised to achieve harmony and affluence among mankind, where the essence of the managerial approach can be seen in a relation between the almost mathematical inputs and outputs. Simon has enumerated common principles that occur in the literature of administration[31] and subjected them to critical analysis. Each principle has exposed its incompatibilities, discrepancies, and controversies. 'The difficulty has arisen from treating as "principles of administration" what are really the only criteria for describing and diagnosing administrative situations' (Simon, 1997, p. 42).[32] It could be in a way of Simon's thought that the said principles are simply proverbs, because they can apparently contradict each other in different situations (e.g., transparency can contradict efficiency, less intensive political interference to more intensive direct political control [or indirect control by the higher number of government representatives on agencies boards], or contrary to the greater importance of agencies than their parent ministries, user-responsiveness to public interest, specialisation to generalisation, independence to coordination) – but they basically *should*. Their importance or *weights are always different proportionally with a degree of different context* changes, motives, and even meanings of the same terms (what can be for someone a highly needed autonomy can be for the other a possibility of high managerial earnings). Every kind of enumeration of principles always includes too much/little, and little can be done if circumstances change in which weights are given to different viewpoints.

After the scientific management movement at the beginning of the 20th century, some saw this movement as unsuccessful on the claim that principles cannot be used in practice and/or saw various controversies and paradoxes. But scholars of this movement have never claimed the absoluteness of principles: principles were seen only as Taylor's guidelines that can be applied to all classes of work and that secure better results than classic initiative and incentive, or as Fayol's lighthouses and evaluated in proportions *with* practice. Indeed, principles need facts to confirm and to re-establish them as they serve as boundaries that should not be crossed in new cases and could be usable when given as guidelines than as explicit statements. The content of the principles is different from that of the facts due to the heterarhic (interchangeable or ranked in a number of different ways) nature of the values they carry.

Apparently contrary to scientific management scholars, a public management reform, popular in many OECD countries during the 1980s and 1990s, known as 'New Public Management' (NPM), has de facto based its success not on principles or values, but on the ideas of effectiveness and efficiency (E&E) that were shown in practise as examples of under inclusiveness. E&E are still used today many times as two buzzwords, but in essence they represent the art of management, as Taylor would say, 'as knowing exactly what you want men to do, and then seeing that they do it in the best and cheapest way' (Taylor, 1974, p. 21). NPM included efforts to reinvent ("entrepreneurial") a government with assumed purposes (that were established as such only in theory and not as principles in practise, although the latter was the essence of Taylor's *Scientific Management*): the shift to privatisation, quasi-privatisation, contracting and public-private partnerships, away from core government institutions with independent executive agencies to slow or reverse government growth in public spending and staffing, with the introduction of performance measurement and results-orientated management systems, with more responsibility and accountability for public managers, more competition in the public sector, etc. (Cole & Eymeri-Douzans, 2010; Hood, 1991; Osborne & Gaebler, 1993; Pollitt & Bouckaert, 2011). Although NPM focused on *results,* the above-mentioned reforms are examples of efficiency, *not* of effectiveness: the mentioned reforms are for the most part just possible techniques by which better results can be achieved and not results *per se*. NPM has not addressed what is right or wrong (what values people have), but only how to be the best at doing the right or wrong things. Both parts should be addressed together. In this sense of non-inclusiveness of values, NPM has made the same mistake as Weber did before them; already Taylor has warned that when changes are not led by 'the true philosophy of management, the results are in many cases disastrous' (Taylor, 1974, p. 130). The *mental attitude* and *habits* of all of those engaged in the management, as well of the workmen should be changed 'only gradually and through the presentation of many object-lessons to the workman, which, together with the teaching which he receives, thoroughly convince him of the superiority of the new over the old way of doing the work' (Taylor, 1974, p. 131).

It is not accidental that, as an opposing answer to NPM, other doctrines in public administration have emerged and addressed what NPM left out: effectiveness (*i.e.*, the right things, values). This can be seen in the new public service (serving, not steering) (J. V. Denhardt & Denhardt, 2011; R. B. Denhardt, Denhardt, & Blanc, 2013) with a strong emphasis on ethics and the reaffirmation of democratic values, citizenship, and service in the public interest, in the principles of good administration (Parliamentary and Health Service Ombudsman, 2017; The Parliamentary and Health Service Ombudsman, 2009), in good administration through a better system of administrative procedures (OECD, 1999; SIGMA, 2012), in governance as a set of 'the involvement of society in the process of governing' (Pierre & Peters, 2000, p. 7), as governing processes that are 'hybrid and multijurisdictional, linking plural stakeholders in complex networks' (Bevir, 2010, p. 3) or as the 'participatory process of governing the social, economic, and political affairs of a country, state, or local community through structures and values that mirror the society [and] include the state as an enabling institution, the constitutional framework, the civil society, the private sector, and the international/global institutional structure within limits' (Farazmand, 2004, p. 11). Unescap is one of the rare examples among the principles of good governance parallel with participation,[33] consensus orientation, accountability, transparency, responsiveness, and rule of law, mentions also E&E, equity and inclusiveness (2009). Emphasising only one or the other side in different cycles always brings shortcuts, surprises, and paradoxes in both parts, in NPM (Dunleavy, Margetts, Bastow, & Tinkler, 2005; Hood & Peters, 2004; Slyke, 2003), in good governance (Dijkstra, 2013; Noore Alam & Mohd. Zin, 2007; Velluti, 2009; Wilén, 2007) or in any other reforms. Decision-makers should also not disregard a difference between theory and practice: along only mentioning all building elements,

Public Agencies

i.e., theory, there is also a practice that could have completely different results than the ones, stated as objectives. Theory and practise must be tightly connected, and the same holds for E&E, both in a theoretical and practical perspective.

The paradoxes (due to exaggerations) in the organisational principles of public administration could have roots in ancient Greece, where the temple of Apollo in Delphi apparently bore the inscriptions "*gnothi seauton* ("know thyself"), "*meden agan*" (nothing in excess) and also to Plutarch a large letter "E" (1936). While he enumerates seven likely explanations, it is possible to believe that it can represent five human senses, with which the human resonates if something can be done (in this manner, the letter 'E' could also stand for effectiveness, efficiency, and equity). It could be said that ancient Greek 'medicines' for unwanted effects were impartiality, moderation, and action in which a human uses all his senses and/or abilities to achieve goals. In all forms of complex adaptive systems (CAS), negative/positive (neutral) effects are present as a result of *the emergence* as the characteristic element of CAS. Hence, also two elements (*e.g.,* effectiveness and efficiency) give four combinations (like in any other combination of or 2^2), four parts causes sixteen combinations, etc. If this is not considered in the presence of numerous parts, no control span is adequate to successfully address them. If decision makers could agree with the idea of emergence on a general/organisational level, it brings a'surprise' for decision making: problems do not only preexist before their solutions/decisions, but also emerge spontaneously during multiple relations in the time of problem solving. This means that E&E relations and combinations must be *constantly re-evaluated* due to new differences/preferences that did not exist before. This insight in the theory of CAS along 'unmovable' rational, maximised utility decisions brings among them also the emergent ones that non-stop iteratively change through *interaction* – and with this also decisions and organisations.

The simplification of the organizational and procedural structures and processes, an increased use of IT technologies, better regulation tools, impact assessments, optimizations of information flow, etc. should be put in a new conceptual framework. This frame should have real-time-space data sensors, methods for data evaluation, the extraction of meaning, and for activating appropriate means towards planned goals, and this circle repeats in a never-ending story. This simply cannot be done within the classical command and control regulation. Despite all known indicators and indexes, they always measure something that is outside of them; there should be a real awareness present that an individual is always a part of the larger whole, that two individuals exponentially form a larger number of combinations, and that the relations spontaneously cause new relations and new characteristics. The classical rational decision-making is in an 'efficiency camp', while the values and principles are in the effective one, but they should always be intertwined, adapted to the context of their use (even in different wording), and evaluated through equity. Rationality per se is deaf, and values are blind; the first must always be counterbalanced in the second (specific in general and vice versa). Between science and the lives of people, there is some kind of irony present: Solutions are known many times, but not implemented, while implementation many times is implemented 'as long as it implements something'. The problem of rational decision tools (presented in the introduction) is in all three parts: in rationality, in the lack of a conceptual structure, and in insufficient attention on the ways through which privileges are retained (many times, this is done with the help of banal incorrect E&E wording). Despite advances in science, there are still hungry people in abundance of food, there are gas and oil pipelines in poor countries to no water line parallel to them, etc. The last sentence (almost sleazy) sentence was not meant to 'attack' the reader's conscience, but to demonstrate (along another paradox of immediate awareness *with* distant actions) that (natural) science without values is mere technicality, focused on efficiency, while effectiveness (social science) is weak without the right technical means. They should not only form deterministic unity in Heraclitus's change and flow, but *convince* us that they are the American *e pluribus unum* (out of many one) and the European *in varietate concordia* (united in diversity) at the same time. And the last paradox: if readers and regulators know all this, why does the situation not reflect it?

REFERENCES

Aristotle. (2015). *Metaphysics*. Aeterna Press.

Asch, S. E. (1955). Opinions and Social Pressure. *Scientific American*, *193*(5), 31–35. doi:10.1038/scientificamerican1155-31

Axelrod, R. (1986). An Evolutionary Approach to Norms. *The American Political Science Review*, *80*(4), 1095–1111. doi:10.2307/1960858

Axelrod, R. (2006). *The Evolution of Cooperation* (Revised edition). Basic Books.

Barnard, C. I. (1968). *The Functions of the Executive*. Harvard University Press.

Beer, S. (1994). *Beyond Dispute: The Invention of Team Syntegrity*. Wiley.

Bevir, M. (Ed.). (2010). *The SAGE Handbook of Governance*. SAGE.

Boltanski, L., & Thévenot, L. (2006). *On Justification*. Princeton and Oxford: Princeton University Press.

Bouckaert, G., Peters, B. G., & Verhoest, K. (2010). *The Coordination of Public Sector Organizations: Shifting Patterns of Public Management*. Palgrave MacMillan. doi:10.1057/9780230275256

Bourdieu, P. (1977). *Towards a Theory of Practice*. Cambridge University Press.

Cane, P. (2011). *Administrative Law*. Oxford University Press.

Checkland, P. (1981). *Systems Thinking, Systems Practice*. J. Wiley.

Cole, A., & Eymeri-Douzans, J.-M. (2010). Introduction: Administrative reforms and mergers in Europe - research questions and empirical challenges. *International Review of Administrative Sciences*, *76*(3), 395–406. doi:10.1177/0020852310373881

Comte, A. (1998). *Comte: Early Political Writings* (H. S. Jones, Ed.). Cambridge University Press. doi:10.1017/CBO9781139170833

Comte, A. (2009). *A General View of Positivism*. Cambridge University Press. doi:10.1017/CBO9780511692888

Crozier, M. (1964). Bureaucratic Phenomenon (y First edition edition). Chicago: University of Chicago Press.

Darwin, C. (1871). *The Descent of Man, and Selection in Relation to Sex*. J. Murray.

Denhardt, J. V., & Denhardt, R. B. (2011). *The New Public Service: Serving, Not Steering* (3rd ed.). Routledge.

Denhardt, R. B., Denhardt, J. V., & Blanc, T. A. (2013). *Public Administration* (7th ed.). Wadsworth Publishing.

Dijkstra, G. (2013). *Paradoxes around good governance, Inaugural Lecture*. University of Rotterdam. https://repub.eur.nl/pub/39219/metis_186511.pdf

Dunleavy, P., Margetts, H., Bastow, S., & Tinkler, J. (2005). New Public Management Is Dead—Long Live Digital-Era Governance. *Journal of Public Administration: Research and Theory, 16*(3), 467–494. doi:10.1093/jopart/mui057

Durkheim, E. (1982). *The Rules of Sociological Method* (W. D. Halls, Trans.). The Free Press. doi:10.1007/978-1-349-16939-9

Durkheim, E. (1992). *Professional Ethics and Civic Morals* (2nd ed.). Routledge.

Durkheim, E. (1995). *The Elementary Forms of Religious Life* (K. E. Fields, Trans.). The Free Press.

Espejo, R. (2003). Social Systems and the Embodiment of Organisational Learning. In E. Mitleton-Kelly (Ed.), *Complex Systems and Evolutionary Perspectives on Organisations* (pp. 53–70). Emerald Group Publishing Limited.

Espejo, R., & Reyes, A. (2011). *Organizational Systems: Managing Complexity with the Viable System Model* (2011 edition). Springer. doi:10.1007/978-3-642-19109-1

European Court of Auditors. (2009). *Delegating Implementing Tasks to Executive Agencies: A Successful Option?* ECA. https://www.eca.europa.eu/lists/ecadocuments/sr09_13/sr09_13_en.pdf

Farazmand, A. (2004). *Sound Governance: Policy and Administrative Innovations*. Praeger.

Fayol, H. (1954). *General and Industrial Management* (Reprinted edition). (C. Storrs, Trans.). Sir Isaac Pitman & Sons, Ltd.

Fayol, H. (2003). The Administrative Theory in the State. In L. Gulick & L. Urwick (Eds.), *Papers on the Science of Administration* (Vol. IV, pp. 109–124). Routlege.

Feltz, B., Crommelinck, M., & Goujon, P. (2006). *Self-organization and Emergence in Life Sciences*. Springer Science & Business Media. doi:10.1007/1-4020-3917-4

Fuller, R. B., & Applewhite, E. J. (1997). *Synergetics: Explorations in the Geometry of Thinking*. MacMillan.

Giddens, A. (1984). *The Constitution of Society: Outline of the Theory of Structuration*. Cambirdge: Policy Press.

Gulick, L. (2003). Notes On the Theory of Organisation. In K. Thompson (Ed.), *The Early Sociology of Management and Organizations: Papers on the Science of Administration* (Vol. IV, pp. 1–49). Routledge.

Haidt, J. (2012). *The Righteous Mind: Why Good People are Divided by Politics and Religion*. Pantheon Books.

Heylighen, F. (1999). The Science Of Self-Organization And Adaptivity. Knowledge Management, Organizational Intelligence and Learning, and Complexity, in: The Encyclopedia of Life Support Systems, EOLSS, 253–280. Publishers Co. Ltd.

Hood, C. (1991). A Public Management for All Seasons? *Public Administration, 69*(1), 3–19. doi:10.1111/j.1467-9299.1991.tb00779.x

Hood, C., & Dixon, R. (2015). *A Government that Worked Better and Cost Less?: Evaluating Three Decades of Reform and Change in UK Central Government*. OUP Oxford. doi:10.1093/acprof:oso/9780199687022.001.0001

Hood, C., & Peters, G. (2004). The Middle Aging of New Public Management: Into the Age of Paradox? *Journal of Public Administration: Research and Theory, 14*(3), 267–282. doi:10.1093/jopart/muh019

KramerJ.MeunierJ. (2016). Kin and multilevel selection in social evolution: A never-ending controversy? *F1000Research, 5*(776), F1000 Faculty Rev-776. doi:10.12688/f1000research.8018.1

Maine, H. S. (1936). *Ancient Law*. J. M. Dent & Sons Limited.

Merton, R. K. (1968). *Social Theory and Social Structure*. Free Press.

Milgram, S. (2009). Obedience to Authority: An Experimental View (Reprint edition). New York: Harper Perennial Modern Classics.

Mill, J. S. (1865). *Auguste Comte and Positivism*. N. Trübner & Co. Paternoster.

Mitleton-Kelly, E. (Ed.). (2003). *Complex Systems and Evolutionary Perspectives on Organisations*. Emerald Group Publishing Limited.

Mooney, J. D., & Reiley, A. C. (1931). *Onward Industry: The Principles of Organization and Their Significance to Modern Industry*. Harper & Brothers.

Nastasi, L., Pressman, D., & Swaigen, J. (2020). *Administrative Law: Principles and Advocacy* (Fourth). Torondo: Emond.

Noore Alam, S., & Mohd. Zin, M. (2007). Paradox of Public Sector Reforms in Malaysia: A Good Governance Perspective. *Public Administration Quarterly, 31*(3/4), 284–312.

Nozick, R. (1993). *The Nature of Rationality*. Princeton University Press. doi:10.1515/9781400820832

OECD. (1999). European Principles for Public Administration. *SIGMA Papers, No. 27*. https://www.oecd-ilibrary.org/docserver/download/5kml60zwdr7h.pdf?expires=1459602912&id=id&accname=guest&checksum=AD8421691668211416DB861810C0B737

Osborne, D., & Gaebler, T. (1993). *Reinventing Government: How the Entrepreneurial Spirit is Transforming the Public Sector*. Plume.

Parker Follett, M. (2003). The Process of Control. In L. Gulick & L. Urwick (Eds.), *Papers on the Science of Administration* (Vol. IV, pp. 170–180). Routlege.

Parliamentary and Health Service Ombudsman. (2017). *Principles of Good Administration*. Ombudsman. https://www.ombudsman.org.uk/about-us/our-principles/principles-good-administration

Parsons, T. (1985). *Talcott Parsons on Institutions and Social Evolution: Selected Writings*. University of Chicago Press.

Parsons, T. (1991). The Social System (New edition). London: Routledge.

Pečarič, M. (2020). Understanding Differences between Equal Public Governance Models. *Central European Public Administration Review*, *18*(1), 69–88. doi:10.17573/cepar.2020.1.04

Pierre, J., & Peters, B. G. (2000). *Governance, Politics and the State*. Palgrave Macmillan.

Plutarch. (1936). Plutarch: Moralia: Vol. V. *Isis and Osiris. The E at Delphi. The Oracles at Delphi No Longer Given in Verse. The Obsolescence of Oracles* (F. C. Babbitt, Trans.). Harvard University Press.

Pollitt, C. (2000). How do we know how good public services are? In G. Peters & D. J. Savoie (Eds.), *Governance in the Twenty-first Century: Revitalizing the Public Service* (pp. 119–154). McGill-Queen's Press - MQUP. doi:10.1515/9780773568884-006

Pollitt, C., & Bouckaert, G. (2011). *Public Management Reform: A Comparative Analysis - New Public Management, Governance, and the Neo-Weberian State* (3rd ed.). Oxford University Press.

Pollitt, C., Talbot, C., Caulfield, J., & Smullen, A. (2004). *Agencies: How Governments Do Things Through Semi-Autonomous Organizations*. Palgrave MacMillan.

Ridley, M. (2017). *What Charles Darwin owes Adam Smith*. Learn Liberty. https://www.learnliberty.org/blog/what-charles-darwin-owes-adam-smith/

Scott, W. R., & Davis, G. F. (2016). *Organizations and Organizing: Rational, Natural and Open Systems Perspectives*. Routledge.

Seidman, H. (1996). *Politics, position, and power: The dynamics of federal organisation*. Oxford University Press.

Selznick, P. (1949). *TVA and the Grass Roots: A Study in the Sociology of Formal Organization*. University of California Press.

SIGMA. (2012). *Good Administration through a Better System of Administrative Procedures*. SIGMA. https://www.sigmaweb.org/publications/Comments_LawAdminProceduresKosovo_JN_Oct2012_Eng%20%20.pdf

Simon, H. A. (1997). *Administrative Behavior* (4th ed.). Free Press.

Slyke, D. M. (2003). The Mythology of Privatization in Contracting for Social Services. *Public Administration Review*, *63*(3), 296–315. doi:10.1111/1540-6210.00291

Smith, A. (1977). *And Inquiry into the Nature and Causes of the Wealth of Nations*. University Of Chicago Press. doi:10.7208/chicago/9780226763750.001.0001

Sunstein, C. R. (2009). *Going to Extremes: How Like Minds Unite and Divide*. Oxford University Press. doi:10.1093/oso/9780195378016.001.0001

Taylor, F. W. (1974). *Scientific Management*. Greenwood Press.

Thacher, D., & Rein, M. (2004). Managing Value Conflict in Public Policy. *Governance: An International Journal of Policy, Administration and Institutions, 17*(4), 457–486. doi:10.1111/j.0952-1895.2004.00254.x

The Parliamentary and Health Service Ombudsman. (2009). *Principles of Good Administration*. The Parliamentary and Health Service Ombudsman.

Turner, J. H. (1997). *The Institutional Order: Economy, Kinship, Religion, Polity, Law, and Education in Evolutionary and Comparative Perspective*. Longman.

Turner, J. H. (2003). *Human Institutions: A Theory of Societal Evolution*. Rowman & Littlefield.

Unescap. (2009). *What is Good Governance?* Retrieved from https://www.unescap.org/resources/what-good-governance

Valdés, C. B. (2011). *Political Struggles and the Forging of Autonomous Government Agencies*. Palgrave MacMillan. doi:10.1057/9780230307957

Veblen, T. (1918). *The Instinct of Workmanship and the State of the Industrial Arts*. B. W. Huebsch.

Velluti, S. (2009). *Experimental Forms of New Governance and the Paradoxes of European Legal Integration*. University of Lincoln. Retrieved from https://cor.europa.eu/en/activities/governance/documents/7ad863ed-fb54-46b3-adf6-babcc0366c3e.pdf

Verhoest, K., Roness, P., Verschuere, B., Rubecksen, K., & MacCarthaigh, M. (2010). *Autonomy and Control of State Agencies: Comparing States and Agencies*. Palgrave MacMillan. doi:10.1057/9780230277274

Wilén, N. (2007). *Paradoxes or Strategies in International Governance? The Case of Kosovo*. Regimen Conference. Retrieved from https://repository.uantwerpen.be/docman/irua/cbf2d4/1a86b087.pdf

Wilson, J. Q. (1989). *Bureaucracy: What Government Agencies Do and why They Do it*. Basic Books.

Wittgenstein, L. (1986). *Philosophical Investigations* (G. E. M. Anscombe, Trans.). Basil Blackwell.

Zimbardo, P. G. (2008). *The Lucifer Effect: Understanding How Good People Turn Evil*. Random House Trade Paperbacks.

ENDNOTES

[1] All formal organizations are moulded by forces tangential to their rationally ordered structures and stated goals. Every formal organization...attempts to mobilize human and technical resources as means for the achievement of its ends. However, the individuals within the system tend to resist being treated as means. They interact as wholes, bringing to bear their own special problems and purposes; moreover, the organization is imbedded in an institutional matrix and is therefore subject to pressures upon it from its environment, to which some general adjustment must be made. As a result, the organization may be significantly viewed as an adaptive social structure, facing problems which arise simply because it exists as an organization in an institutional environment, independently of the special goals which called it into being. [...] Where significant, the adaptation is dynamic in the sense that the utilization of self-defensive mechanisms results in structural trans-

ormations of the organization itself. The needs in question are organizational, not individual, and include: the security of the organization as a whole in relation to social forces in its environment; the stability of the lines of authority and communication, the stability of informal relations within the organization; the continuity of policy and of the sources of its determination; a homogeneity of outlook with respect to the meaning and role of the organization (Selznick, 1949, pp. 251, 252).

2. An organisation is defined as a closed network of people in interaction creating, regulating and implementing its social meanings. If a collective achieves this closure it is producing a social system, regardless of whether it is a formal institution or not, or whether it is producing its intended meaning or not (Espejo, 2003, p. 59).

3. All structural systems are comprised of tension and compression components (Fuller & Applewhite, 1997). The geodesic dome of Buckminster Fuller represents this idea in reality.

4. A group's cohesion can be assured by its very organization, as agencies of various kinds take care for professional ethics that leads to the overall stability of a society. As the state is too far away from the life of an ordinary citizen, Durkheim required the reemergence of "secondary institutions" in the middle between the remote state's powers and the everyday world of the individual. Agencies can be in this manner seen as sui generis products of society that can effectively exist only as far as individuals incorporate them in their mental frames, beliefs, morality and language, when agency as the organisations of public cohesion can group people based on their professional ethics.

5. The problem here is that work that produces measurable outcomes tends to drive out work that produces unmeasurable outcomes, while officials can subvert of fudge numbers that show the final results.

6. In the coping and procedural organizations careerists executives can manage with difficulties as outsiders cannot easily observe and evaluate their outcomes; 'getting and holding that job depends less on their technical knowledge than on their ability to find political support, cope with critics, and negotiate a resolution of controversies' (Wilson, 1989, p. 202).

7. That could be the historic reason for the success of cities and countries that had/have many communication channels in the meaning of roads, rivers, harbours and easy access to water and see, ships that have enabled commerce, migrations, import and export... That could also be the reason why the majority of historic European cities are placed near rivers.

8. This approach along different fields also acknowledges their universal platform at the same time (like the EU's motto "united in diversity" or the concept of universal service in regulated industries). Such approach is present also in the practice of a public agency. The latter for the non-instrumentalists 'protects and promotes values by embodying and expressing them in its rules and principles [while to instrumentalists]… protects and promotes values chiefly by influencing and affecting the organization and practice of public administration' (Cane, 2011, p. 405). In both cases, values are their denominator.

9. More lives were lost due to abstract floccules then because of real reasons. Objective and subjective situations become in such situations blurred. On this basis, also elections are won many times.

10. It is highly relevant what agencies discover in their work and further propose to policymakers, because such proposals are usually taken as "professional" (many times regardless of arguments) and hence as an objective presentation of truth (despite the fact that this may not be so – this can be confirmed buying all new suggestions that run contrary to the previous ones).

11. A Weberian instrumental rationality that should, under the Prussian example, follow by means of selected targets, cannot provide clear guidance for activities where and when goals conflict with

each other. It can determine the path through which the decision-makers go as is generally accepted in the principle of proportionality, but it cannot resolve their mutual conflict in determining what is necessary, reasonable, appropriate, or proportionate to the benefits regarding the consequences.

12. Social behaviour correlates with relatedness (any genetic simfilarity, regardless of whether it arose by common descent or by other means such as green-beard effects) (Kramer & Meunier, 2016).

13. Selection not only acts on individuals but can act (simultaneously) on multiple levels of biological organization...even if behaviors that benefit other individuals are selectively disadvantageous at the level of the individual, they might still evolve if they are advantageous at—and hence selected for on—a higher level of the biological hierarchy (Kramer & Meunier, 2016).

14. The accustomed ways of doing and thinking not only become a habitual matter of course, easy and obvious, but they come likewise to be sanctioned by social convention, and so become right and proper and give rise to principles of conduct. By use and wont they are incorporated into the current scheme of common sense (Veblen, 1918, p. 6). Besides the obvious factors that influence personal attention, people should pay attention also to the relational satisfaction (a truth is not correlated with a degree of happiness) that affect the manner in which they perceive messages, a degree of involvement with other persons, past experiences, expectations, social roles, knowledge, self-conception, self-fulfilling prophecies, culture and habits in which they live. Despite the contrastive, repetitive and messages with intense stimuli messages with low stimuli, single or few repetitions and unexpected messages should not be disregarded. The union of things is composed of obvious (reasonable) and nonobvious (contra-intuitive) things.

15. Bourdieu invocates on Leibniz where he compares objective homogenization of habitus of a group or a class of beings with a simultaneous ticking of two hours that could be attributed to (1) mutual communication between hours, (2) activities of a craftsmen who cares that hours are ticking equally, or (3) the fact that they were made 'with such precision and skill that we can be sure that they will now match...following only to its own rules, but still matching each other' (Leibniz in Bourdieu, 1977, p. 80).

16. While formally ensuring an agency's independence, attention should be paid on the possibility of institutional or structural influence by the line ministry on the agency, where the legislation/regulations may hide the so-called *institutional bias* (various possibilities of the ministry to influence on the work of the agency through financing, the choice of members of agency councils, agency management, its director, its number of employees, work plans, etc.).

17. This systematic understanding of system functions is similar to a dynamic method of software evaluation: a program is started and the outputs assessed *vis-à-vis* inputs. In this line of thought, despite that an agency has a formal frame consistent of legal rules, it matters how they are implemented in practice.

18. E.g., the transparency principle is based on the principle of indifference, that is, based on a system that can differentiate what should (not) be transparent, which is again based on a system by which we can differentiate at all.

19. At the first encounters of face-to-face interactions are present, at the second, corporate [groups, organizations, and communities] and categoric [the distinctions that people make and use: gender, age, class, ethnicity/race, region, and the like] units are present, while at the third level, social institutions are the essential structures: 'the original core human social institutions–economy, kinship, religion, polity, law, and education–are the outcome of macrolevel forces that have generated selection pressures on human populations (Turner, 2003, p. xiii).

Public Agencies

[20] In this regard the creation of various types of smaller units, agencies (more or less) separated from ministries is similar to the break-up of monopoly companies and its split into separated, focused companies that continue to provide specialised services and further, within those companies, the creation of strategic business units.

[21] If in theory this can be simply put down, in practice is sometimes akin to search of a philosopher's stone: 'in ancient times alchemists believed implicitly in the existence of a philosopher's stone, which would provide the key to the universe and, in effect, solve all of the problems of mankind. The quest for coordination is in many respects the twentieth-century equivalent of the medieval search for the philosopher's stone. If only we can find the right formula for coordination, we can reconcile the irreconcilable, harmonize competing and wholly divergent interests, overcome irrationalities in our government structures, and make hard policy choices to which no one will dissent' (Seidman, 1996, p. 164).

[22] Coordination in a public sector interorganizational context is considered to be the instruments and mechanisms that aim to enhance the voluntary or forced alignment of tasks and efforts of organizations within the public sector. These mechanisms are used in order to create a greater coherence, and to reduce redundancy, lacunae and contradictions within and between policies, implementation or management (Bouckaert, Peters, & Verhoest, 2010, p. 16)

[23] With planning are connected the well-known terms of vision (a company's main purposes by focusing on the future), mission (vision expressed in practical terms), and strategy (ways to use the mission statement in order to achieve the vision statement through short- and long-term goals, timelines, indicators of success, action plans). In legal terms, the vision resembles to a constitution, mission to statutes and bylaws to strategies, but these legal terms are not close to planning (even when national programmes (strategies) are included), although the law with its anticipative, ex anti element should exhibit it.

[24] 1. Division of work; 2. Authority and responsibility; 3. Discipline; 4. Unity of command; 5. Unity of direction; 6. Subordination of individual interest to general interest; 7. Remuneration of personnel; 8. Centralization; 9. Scalar chain; 10. Order; 11. Equity; 12. Stability of tenure of personnel; 13. Initiative and 14. *Esprit de corps*.

[25] As the 40-year-old documentary *Powers of Ten* shows, smaller structures are reflected in the bigger ones and vice versa. The relation between the (general) legislator and the (implementing) executive is reflected on the lower level between the Ministry (policy) and the agencies (services), and still further between the agency's management board (strategic guidelines) and the president or director (signing contracts, individual decision-making). These are examples of the already mentioned *hierarchy as a structural recursion* (derived from studying biological systems, not from administrative systems).

[26] Care as a state of seeking good and right reason with serious attention, solicitude, heed, caution, and protection are the bases of principle's implementation. A purpose and process are interchangeably connected when we care for and evaluate certain things from the view of usefulness as individuals and community members.

[27] This is usually taken for granted, but the problem is not in a different approach but in a bad capacity that caused a breaking point in the first place, in a bad administration of affairs. A new "solution" would be similar to finding a new partner instead of keeping such relations (with the old one) that minimise a possibility for conflicts at the minimum level.

[28] The European Court of Auditors in the case of the EU executive agencies in 2009 found that the initiative of setting up executive agencies was mainly driven by constraints on employment than were based on the intrinsic features of the programmes themselves; the cost–benefit analyses required by the legislation to support the decision to create the agencies took little account of nonfinancial aspects and omitted some important factors on the side of costs; the lack of reliable information on the ex-ante situation at the Commission does not allow the extent of the savings to be verified; as a result of their specialisation in identifiable and specifically defined tasks, the agencies provide better service delivery in terms of reduced time for contracting, more rapid approval procedures for technical and financial reports and lower payment delays. Other qualitative improvements are the simplification of processes as well as increased external communication and dissemination of results, which contribute to enhance the visibility of the EU. On the other hand, the expected flexibility in hiring staff is not demonstrated; the commission's supervision of the agencies' work is quite limited: the annual work programmes (subject to the commission's approval) are scarcely used for setting targeted objectives; the monitoring is mainly focused on indicators related to how the tasks are carried out rather than to the results produced; the reports are usually confined to budgetary execution and omit to measure progress made on a multi-annual basis and identify corrective actions for the future (European Court of Auditors, 2009).

[29] Principles are transmission devices for probability or support, which flow from data or cases, via the principle, to judgments and predictions about new observations or cases whose status otherwise is unknown or less certain. Features that enable principles to transmit probability are lawlike statements; the latter do not contain terms for particular individual objects, dates, or temporal periods, but purely qualitative predicates. Lawlike statements have an unrestricted universality; they are not simply a finite conjunction that was established by examining all cases. Lawlike statements are supported not just by instances falling under them but also by a linkage of indirect evidence (Nozick, 1993, p. 5).

[30] First. They [managers] develop a science for each element of a man's work, which replaces the old rule-of-thumb method. Second. They scientifically select and then train, teach, and develop the workman, whereas in the past he chose his own work and trained himself as best he could. Third. They heartily cooperate with the men so as to insure all of the work being done in accordance with the principles of the science which has been developed. Fourth. There is an almost equal division of the work and the responsibility between the management and the workmen. The management take over all work for which they are better fitted than the workmen, while in the past almost all of the work and the greater part of the responsibility were thrown upon the men. It is this combination of the initiative of the workmen, coupled with the new types of work done by the management, that makes scientific management so much more efficient than the old plan (Taylor, 1974, pp. 36–37).

[31] 1. Administrative efficiency is increased by a specialization of the task among the group. 2. Administrative efficiency is increased by arranging the members of the group in a determinate hierarchy of authority. 3. Administrative efficiency is increased by limiting the span of control at any point in the hierarchy to a small number. 4. Administrative efficiency is increased by grouping the workers, for purposes of control, according to (a) purpose, (b) process, (c) clientele, or (d) place (Simon, 1997, p. 29).

[32] For Simon the so called principles of administration are only criteria for describing and diagnosing administrative situations [that]…must be balanced against each other…a valid approach to the study of administration requires that all the relevant diagnostic criteria be identified; that each adminis-

trative situation be analysed in terms of the entire set of criteria; and that research be instituted to determine how weights can be assigned to the several criteria when they are, as they usually will be, mutually incompatible (Simon, 1997, pp. 42–43).

[33] Although public participation is already a mantra of public administration, there are more citizens involved in the agencies' boards as their members then directly in the central administration.

Chapter 3
Predispositions on the Current State of Affairs

ABSTRACT

This chapter discusses the creation and management of public agencies. It states that public agencies should retain their basic regulatory and supervisory functions, while other administrative tasks outside the core public administration should be transferred to public agencies for faster and more efficient performance. The chapter suggests that there is a need for similar, convergent approaches that consider the pros and cons of different combinations for the achievement of the desired goals based on different needs, contexts, and environments. The regulation of the operation of public agencies should answer at least four sets of questions relating to the establishment of public agencies, the provision of funds for their work and operations, the regulation of legal bases for the use of funds, and control over their work. Additionally, the chapter highlights the need for public agencies to be flexible and adaptable to the complex reality in which they work.

INTRODUCTION

Every human behaviour is always sensible because with it an individual tries to satisfy his needs. Sensible but not always conscious and not always effective (Glasser, 1994).

Predispositions to the current situation can serve as a starting point from which public agencies (along with all other public but also private organisations) can do their tasks; the latter should be aligned with the increasingly complex reality in which agencies work. The creation of public agencies is supposed to represent *an opportunity to reduce the scope of state administration in the narrow sense*; it should emphasize, retain, and maintain its basic regulatory and supervisory functions from the view of complex adaptive systems, as they – cybernetically and technically – do not depend on legal norms. The management of such systems depends on elements that constitute the systems and complexity theory assembled in a way that with the help of control, regulation, and steering produces results. Therefore, the main findings of CAS are applicable in different legal systems, as the majority of them have not prevented

DOI: 10.4018/979-8-3693-0507-2.ch003

Predispositions on the Current State of Affairs

major financial or other (e.g. environmental) major crisis or wicked problems – many of them have not even broken legal demands by going towards disaster...

Even now, or without such elements, the majority of functions that do not belong to the core public administration in the narrower sense (atypical administrative tasks outside the participation in the formulation of policies, executive tasks, inspection, control, monitoring of conditions, development tasks and taking care that public services are provided) can be transferred to public agencies, as they[1] could apparently perform their tasks outside of the core public administration, faster, with less burden on public funds and better fulfilment of public interest. A public agency is a legal person under public law that is established to perform regulatory, developmental, or professional tasks in the public interest, unless otherwise provided by the law. When creating public agencies, there are differences in their names from country to country. The public agency can be established by the state, a local community, or an association of local communities. In performing its tasks, the public agency is more or less independent, and the supervision of its work and operations is performed by the competent ministries or local community administrations (public agencies can be, in terms of content, placed between the governmental exercise of public authority and provision of services and goods to users and/or public service tasks). On behalf of the state, the rights and obligations of the founder are exercised by the government, and control over work and operations is exercised by the competent ministry. For this reason, the regulation of the financing and operation of public agencies must also ensure an efficient system of financing and operation. Ministries must exercise control over public agencies, and the government, as the founder, must draw up guidelines with a view to uniform control (e.g., whether it is required a copy of all invoices, a list of invoices, or only a collection of expenditures by category). The regulation of the operation of public agencies should answer at least four sets of questions relating to the establishment of public agencies, the provision of funds for their work and operations, the regulation of legal bases for the use of funds, and control over their work. From the transparency, legality, and legal certainty point of view, it is desirable that tasks performed by each institution are defined in one place.

Control over the legality, purpose, and efficiency of the use of funds obtained from the budget, as well as over the management of assets owned or used by a public agency, over the implementation of regulations governing public finances, and regulations governing financial, material, and accounting operations of public agencies are performed by the finance ministry. Supervision over the implementation of regulations on administrative procedures, business hours, office hours, operations with clients, operations with documentary materials, and ensuring the publicity of operations should be performed by the ministry responsible for administration. According to the requirements of international organizations, some public agencies must have a special status that guarantees independence and their autonomy of work; this independence should be ensured primarily from the point of view of decision making and implementation of their policies and does not relate to business efficiency control. This is all the more important in cases where the founder of a public agency is subordinately liable for the obligations of the public agency if the public agency could not settle them from its assets, or if the settlement of obligations would seriously jeopardize the performance of public agency tasks.

The founder gives consent to the work program and financial plan, as well as to the annual report and other reports of the public agency. When public agencies receive funds from the state budget, the ministry may exercise control on the basis of the received documentation, which is reviewed by the contract administrator at the ministry before payment is made from the state budget. However, when public agencies do not receive funding from the state, budget control is mostly limited to the review of financial plans and annual reports. The roles of contract administrators in ministries are defined in the internal acts of individual ministries. The contract administrators must take care of the regularity and the correctness of expenditures from the state budget, but they cannot influence the economy by the use of funds, as the directors of public agencies are responsible for this. Ministries can also gain insight into the operation of public agencies and public funds through their representatives in the councils. They are supposed to represent and assert the interests of the founder, but in their work they must act with the care of a good businessman and are also liable for damages caused by their actions. This brief description of the current state of affairs regarding public agencies can provide a rough framework for the functioning of public institutions and at the same time gives a reassuring sense of the clarity of their functioning, but this is just a rough description of the so-called Type 2 agency. All types of agencies are described further in this work, but already here it can be said that all of them are faced with some common, below-enumerated denominators –

The environment is too complex to be fully managed. This recognition, which cannot be overturned through formal rules or models, relieves the negative mark on the public agencies up to a point. They, as a bureaucratic organization, struggle with the alleged difficulties of controlling its operations (Weber, 1978); In today's time, there are even more rules, coercion, and new regulatory authorities, while the bureaucratic apparatus is still firmly present (Christensen & Laegred, 2005; Cole & Eymeri-Douzans, 2010; Crawford, 2006; Vogel, 1998) with more arbitrary powers in the absence of accountability mechanisms (Aronson, 2009), and with people's overall opinion emphasising its wastefulness, irrationality, and other elements briefly described as bureaupathologies (Caiden, 1991). A strongly felt need to change bureaucracy (Frederickson, 1996) is still the dominant theme in the public sector and organisations within it, and the crisis of standards and measures of performance still demands that they "run better". 'Despite the salience of public administration reforms in Europe, there is surprisingly little systematic research identifying how and whether public-sector reforms have been implemented and with what outcomes' (Hammerschmid, Walle, Andrews, & Bezes, 2016, p. 4). There are 'several key concepts, including governance, networks, partnerships, "joining up", transparency, and trust and no dominant model' (Pollitt & Bouckaert, 2011, p. 11). As in the heydays of Taylor's Scientific Management, it seems that we are [still] dealing with a kind of 'measurement fever' (Diefenbach, 2009), and we hope to find *the* best model, be it management, public agency, law, or other fields. There is no one-size-fits-all model for public agencies; there is only a need for similar, convergent approaches that consider the pros and cons of different combinations for the achievement of the desired goals based on different needs, contexts, and environments.

A backlog of social vis-à-vis natural science. The search for flexibility and adaptability to complexity in social science lags natural science (for more than three decades[2]), which studies them within the laws of physics and biology, chaos theory, the theory of complexity etc. In social science, adaptation and flexibility are mainly present in informal processes (a rough approximation could be the open method of coordination as an intergovernmental means of governance in the EU), while they should also be built in the formal ones. The European Commission in its thematic factsheet on PA quality finds that 'institutions are rarely encouraged to nurture internal reflective capacity, learn from failure or innovate'. In many countries, prolonged and intensive formalistic restructuring has led to general reform fatigue' (European Commission, 2017, p. 2). Based on the OECD (2017) document, the Commission claims that approaches in public management need to shift to *systems thinking*. Aligned with the institutional structures and process,[3] the Commission proposes opportunities for policy development and implementation.[4] Systems thinking is a holistic attitude that simultaneously embraces the structure, its parts and relations, and reflects them through the light of *purpose*. There is no single or unique solution in the

Predispositions on the Current State of Affairs

complex world of many interacting, nonlinear elements with statistical long tails that produce disproportionately major consequences that are greater than the sum of their parts (emergence). There is no good practice that can be simply transferred to other countries, they all have their unique environments, people, processes, and relations.

Lack of adaptability to complexity with traditional approaches. A decision maker could, in such an environment, start from elements that can be *tested* in the form of factual (and formal or legal) experiments. Testing fits with the quality of public administration, because this is basically what it does (Fukuyama, 2014), and thus it also fits into the cybernetic idea that the (real) purpose of the system is what it does (Beer, 2002), but such a method is nevertheless too short: the results are only the final element that depends on the processes and relations that co-created them. Decision making in a complex environment is different from that in a stable one. Table 1 below presents the main differences between system thinking and traditional managerial thinking:

From these differences as comparable criteria, it can be already inferred that public agencies cannot adapt to complexity with their traditional approaches. If institutions want to absorb variety, they should be more like living organisms, needing to adapt to the surrounding environment to function and thrive. Even in the absence of bias, functionality, or legitimacy in statistical long-tail distributions – which today's flexible environment surely is – cannot be based solely on expert knowledge (trained primarily in classical environments) as the classical response to problems. Experts can be wrong (Landemore & Elster, 2012; Surowiecki, 2005; Taleb, 2010; P. Tetlock & Gardner, 2015; Žižek, 2010).

Experts can be wrong. There is a difference between "know-how" and "know-what". The ancient Greeks made a distinction between *techn (that is, 'craft')* and *episteme* (i.e., "knowledge," "science"); Taleb names this the expert problem and connects it with things that *move and, therefore,* require knowledge. Such things do not usually have experts, while static things seem to have some experts.[5] People who are confident about the quality of their own expertise and performance tend to see no need to change. Ironically, poor performers are more likely to overestimate their expertise. Their lack of ability makes recognizing their personal deficits difficult. And this also applies to experts in public agencies. Problems in society are also movable; experts with a classical point of view in a stable environment are not appropriate here. In such frames, lawmakers – despite of their apparent professionality – also cannot fully predict what will happen in the future as their decisions are neither (and cannot be statistically) representative, nor are they fully personal or impartial due to a party discipline. They simply do

Table 1. Command-and-control thinking vs. systems thinking (Seddon, 2005, p. 15)

Command-and-Control thinking	Perspective	Systems thinking
Top-down		Outside-in
Functional specialisation	Design	Demand value and flow
Separated from work	Decision-making	Integrated with work
Budget, targets, standards, activity and productivity	Measurement	Designed against purpose, demonstrate variation
Extrinsic	Motivation	Intrinsic
Manage budget and people	Management ethic	Act on the system
Contractual	Attitude to customers	What matters...?
Contractual	Attitude to suppliers	Partnering and cooperation
Change by project/ initiative	Approach to change	Adaptive, integral

not know how people will rearrange processes to have the greatest control over situations. Within such conditions, solely the idea that legislation should be more general than specific is taken for granted, but how general, which systemic ways can be applied, and how rules can be implemented is debatable. Especially in a flexible environment. This problem can also be a Turing-like solution for the division between the complex and complicated problems (see subsection "Complicated Public Administration").

Problems and solutions are derivatives of situations. Problems (and personal characters) change if the *situation* in which they are present changes, if an authority changes its demands, or even when people have the freedom to act (Beauvois, 2000; Milgram, 2009; Zimbardo, 2008). The emphasis on the (static) understanding of a situation can be wrong. Decision-makers should at first understand the ways in which situations and conditions arise and are driven towards a good or problematic outcome.[6] Creating situations that shape the situation/system (a contextual frame in which predispositions are already given and seen as unchangeable) is often in the hands of civil servants drafting legislation. They have power, at least if the latter is connected with Foucault and Schmitt: the first authority acts through the rule, and the second through decision-making.[7] Those who decide, have power, and given the total number of issued legal acts and prepared general draft rules, it is certainly the PA where power is present. Because of this, solutions should thus be searched within it.

The importance of information. It seems that nowadays information – which is also present in the result – is more important than how it was recognised or established as such. The organizational form under a single command should in the future be more a subject of intermediate stages, which should enable the feeding of information by those who are affected by the subject matter in any possible case (the various forms of governance or network organizations), but it will still be important how information is recognised as such. Just as a fisherman cannot catch a crab with a fishing rod, a data-recording system must also adapt to the environment in which it operates. There is the possibility of changing or 'catch' different data if the recording and evaluation system is changed. The detection of problems and their solutions thus also lie outside the established rules. The objectives go beyond the legal rules, although they are framed within them. New regulatory approaches will not be effective if they are viewed through the classical static focus. The effects are accomplished not through arguments, but through *actions*. These and similar shortcoming could be addressed through regulatory approaches, which can be more time- and effect-sensitive and adaptable.[8] This speaks for multiple oversights in the broad system of checks, and balances that can address the management of relations, context, dynamism, practice, effects, various views, sensitivities, feedbacks and adaptation. According to the mentioned notions (here and at the new *ius publicum europaeum*), systems theory can be helpful, because these concepts are among its basic elements. In the next chapter, the power as the *sine qua non* of legal rules and PAs will be compared with the properties of the system to see whether the latter were present in the former two even before our era of complexity.

POWER AND THE SYSTEM

Max Weber, as the founder of the bureaucratic model, knew the state 'is a relationship of rule by human beings over human beings that rests on the legitimate use of violence (that is, violence that is held to be legitimate)' (Weber, 1994, p. 311). C. Wright Mills, Weber's translator, similarly concluded that 'the power of decision makers is first limited by the level of technique, by the means of power and violence and organization that prevail in a given society' (Mills, 2000, p. 23). In a democracy [contrary to a mon-

Predispositions on the Current State of Affairs

archy], the area of power is *empty* (Foucault, 2001; Lefort, 1999). This place can only be shown through *effects* because the causes are not fully known. On the other side of emptiness, *human uncertainty and vulnerability* are the foundations of *power*. Uncertainty, the principal cause of insecurity, is by far the most decisive tool of power, it is of the same substance (Bauman, 2011; Crozier, 1964). The absence and potentiality of legitimate violence at the same time show power as the "uncertain emptiness of potential violence" – or in other words, 'power is based on the possibilities that a holder of power and his subordinate wish to *avoid*' (Luhmann, 2013);[9] therefore, power is greatest when not used, when subordinates voluntarily do what they are told to do. From these descriptions, it can be inferred that power is created only in *relations* (Arendt, 1972; Foucault, 1978, 1995, 2002, 2004; Luhmann, 2013). The location of real power is consequently – due to the dynamic element of relations – always during its reformation. It is empty, always during reformation towards a new will of the people (democracy *in statu nascendi*). An element, that is, with its element of absence, is like power. Also, democracy is (negative) liberty as the absence of coercion by an exterior social body.[10] Liberty and power can thus be seen as two sides of Janus's coin: both are seen at the same time, one passes into the other and *vice versa*. On the other hand, when power is considered, so is liberty.

One of the most discerning people who became immersed in power relations is Foucault. To him, power should not be 'examined on the basis of the original notion of relations, but on the basis of a relationship as such, because the relationship determines the elements to which it relates...it is necessary to investigate how subordination relationships can produce subjects' (Foucault, 2015, p. 285). To him, power relations must be seen in the first place in numerous specific, individual actions of institutions and their officials, not in the major constitutional and legal problems: '[i]t's about dispersed and peripheral phenomena [...] about the fact that some power is exercised and that it's an unbearable the bare fact that it is exercised [...] the power paradoxically individualizes more the more bureaucratic and etatistic it becomes' (Foucault, 2007, p. 44). For Arendt, *potestas populo* always means the empowerment of one person by a certain number of people to act in their name. 'Power corresponds to the human ability not just to act but to act in concert. Power is never the property of an individual; it belongs to a group and remains in existence only so long as the group keeps together' (Arendt, 1972, p. 143). Power means relationships among people, how they (do not) act, obey, or influence other people, and what tools/processes are used in these relations. For Foucault, the truth is overwhelmed by the relations of the authority acting through the *rule*: 'power acts by laying down the rule...It speaks, and that is the rule. The pure form of power resides in the function of the legislator and its mode of action' (Foucault, 1978, p. 83).[11] If these formal processes are not changed, an official version of the "truth" is fabricated as the most relevant one.

Countries (where public agencies have the most information and knowledge) group the institutional means of power and of communications into regulatory instruments or techniques that administrations use for the implementation of rules. Therefore, what does the government (as an authority) say to the people through rules? The repertoire of activities of most state authorities is a typical Foucauldian example of governmental power games that do not have a government emblem of formal authority *per se*, where most of the work is done informally in the phase of the preparation of general (draft) rules, but it is precisely this supposedly neutral, impartial, invisible power ("hidden in rules") that makes this phase potentially dangerous and important at the same time (even more than the goals themselves, because the means used to achieve the goals predetermine conditions of the latter[12]). Therefore, people in all their different roles should be interested in the formation of means, tools, or processes through which future rules are made and (constantly in practice) changed. If we want a clearer picture of the current involvement of the public and its power, we must accept all (in)formal agreements and relations and collect them within the formal decision-making. In the absence of different actions, nothing different will formally occur: 'predictions of the future are never anything more than projections of present automatic processes and procedures, that is, of occurrences that are likely to come to pass if men do not act and if nothing unexpected happens; every action, for better or worse, and every accident necessarily destroys the whole pattern in whose frame the prediction moves and where it finds its evidence' (Arendt, 1972, p. 109).

Due to the complexity and unpredictability of the future, it is relevant to how 'official truths' are established, managed, and changed. How can this set of powers and uncertainty be more clearly stated to determine liberty? How can power be vested in people? At the beginning of a new formal rule, there is an empty set of potential powers, democracy, and uncertainty. If we clearly knew what to do, we would have universal rules for action, but we do not – we only have universal principles. However, the future can be directed through the means we have now, through *processes* we know now. The constant changes, power relations, effects, and patterns in the frame of power indicate *systems theory* as a potential and appropriate means by which power can be addressed and administered. After the power has been established in public agencies, we should reflect on the ability of the latter to address problems given the predispositions to the current state of affairs.

ADMINISTRATION IS DYNAMIC DECISION-MAKING BETWEEN (IN)TANGIBLE

The theory of public administration (PA) focuses on questions of why, what, and *how* organisations could be constructed to accomplish their goals effectively and efficiently. This is done mainly through *decision making*, which is the lifeblood of every organisation and the central focus in the practice of the increasingly popular evidence-based management (OECD, 1996, 2011, 2012; Rousseau, 2013).[13] This is also done by transposing, implementing and enforcing the *acquis* according to the principle of "obligatory results" (*obligation de résultat*) (SIGMA, 2014). Nowadays, the executive prepares most of the draft laws and is more legislative than the legislator itself. It thus matters how decisions/rules are made, because the Courts[14] are increasingly active in their oversight of *rational (substantial)* (Breyer, Stewart, Sunstein, & Vermeule, 2006; Meßerschmidt & Oliver-Lalana, 2016) rather than solely procedural lawmaking. Deciding with the help of classical legal frames (majority of votes, case-law, legislative amendments) or even neoclassical ones (analysis of costs and effects, regulatory impact analysis, independent agencies) is hardly able to cope with the environmental and other complex changes and are a pale approximation of processes that constantly change, evolve, emerge and combine in dynamic reality.[15] In that manner, new interdisciplinary approaches were developed, like the mathematical Bayes theorem (Ayres & Nalebuff, 2015; Carrier, 2012; Finkelstein & Fairley, 1970; Hacking, 2001), statistical sampling (Dodge & Romig, 1959; Fiedler & Juslin, 2006; Schilling & Neubauer, 2009; Wetherill, 2013), decisional analysis (Edwards, 1999; Edwards, Jr, & Winterfeldt, 2007; Keeney & Raiffa, 1993; Raiffa, 1994) or risk analysis (Black, 2012; Franklin, 1998; Hood, Rothstein, & Baldwin, 2001; Molak, 1996; Slovic, 1996).

Countries can affect citizens in the context of power or regulation; since the first should be a relic of absolutist states, the preferred second is a symbol of legal state, so it is no wonder that 'everybody's [still] talking about…regulations' as in John Lennon's song *Give Peace a Chance* (1969). On the other hand, the conduct of citizens and organisations does not *ex automata* comply with the rules. Although 'regulation is back [and still] in fashion' (Moss & Cisternino, 2009, p. 7), it also has its (power-parental) shortcomings: egoism, cheating force, subtle forms of behaviour with regard to quasi-legal rules, human

Predispositions on the Current State of Affairs

errors, information asymmetry, and associated moral hazards. The quest to (again) have better (regulatory) results is, in this document, focused on the dynamicity of rules and their implementation, on executive and administrative practice, or on dynamics that can be briefly described as 'Yes Minister'. Many of us would agree that '[m]otives, ethics and values are all difficult things to pin down. They ... are psychological or philosophical constructs, not things that can easily be observed, weighed or counted' (Pollitt, 2003, p. 133). Personal characteristics play a role in these relationships but will not be elaborated on here. However, they can be better understood if management is focused on *better understanding the dynamism between the environment and the relations between stakeholders*. As systems or organizations depend on the context in which they operate, *an individual's mind also depends on the context in which it thinks*. Administrators should therefore focus on objective obstacles to implementation, while subjective ones should not be overlooked.[16] What that can be seen can be studied more easily, and this could probably be an answer to why organizational forms receive more attention than forces that affect these forms through intangibles. For Turner, this is the reason why 'sociologists study family rather than kinship systems, firms more than economies, churches more than religion, governmental organizations more than politics, medical professionals more than medicine, agents of law enforcement more than law' (Turner, 2003, p. 2).

History is filled with the efforts of rulers to control the entire system and its individual parts, but these efforts applied in a more or less static environment cannot cope with flexible and complex ones. Today, we are at the edge of a new era, where developments – such as Europeanization, globalisation, privatisation, deregulation, increasing complexity, territorial pluralism, independent agencies, and new forms of regulation – 'create the need for new intellectual tools that analyse and regulate the new forms of public intervention ... the most advanced research in this area relies on the theory of regulation ... that includes an economic, sociological and legal approach' (Auby, 2017, p. 624). On the general, introductory level of the new *ius publicum europaeum* (the new law that consists of the law of EU, the ECHR, and the laws of the European states), there are notions that clearly show this trend ("structural transformation, systemic deficiencies, increased legal complexity, horizontal networking, a normatively established constitution, global administrative law, engagements between legal orders, the existence of hybrid legal phenomena, interconnections and relations between parts in the spatial dimension") and 'the intuition that the connection deeply affects the exercise of authority under its different public laws (Bogdandy, Huber, & Cassese, 2017, p. 14). Europeanization as a study of complexity (Bobek, 2017) consists of many elements from *systems theory*, although it is not mentioned as such. Systems theory could be among the theories that gain their popularity in popular speech (*a la* 'this should be done systemically"), but it is still often not understood in practice.

Between official dogmas and our lives, there should be a place for *reflection*, for the reinterpretation of rules and rights, for maintaining vitality, humanity, and new ideas of social life adaptable to change. Reflection cannot base its action on answers given solely by the law but on a methodologically based question on *who has the right to make and present reality as such*. Therefore far, in the law this has been done mainly through case law, where judges decide what was rational (Meßerschmidt & Oliver-Lalana, 2016; Wintgens & Thion, 2007). In defining rationality, *administration* also has its place, being the "rationality applied to social control" (Lowi, 2009). Public agencies create, monitor, implement, and change themselves and other systems. Although there are many different actors in vertical and horizontal networks, public agencies can still be seen as one of the most powerful entities in the world. The assumption is that people's problems are not caused by a lack of technical equipment in public agencies or by a lack of knowledge of natural science, but by a lack of good, better, effective, wise, etc. administration that should apply insights from that science. All being said, systems theory should be aligned in practice with public agencies, *i.e.*, with the legal or administrative regulatory system that in the majority cases prepares draft laws. *Nomen est omen* already shows a connection between systems theory and the legal/administrative system; even fully supported by arguments, this connection can still only be or have a hypnotic effect (arguments – no matter how logical they are – without objective facts are nothing more than good stories or fairy tales). Even the duty to give reasons that attempt to explain the need for a new approach usually fails to solve a problem 'since explanation is barely synonymous with understanding, which comes from a far deeper and more hands-on engagement with the work itself' (Zokaei, 2010, p. 36). The main message is focused on finding a solution to the problem of complexity.

There is a lack of modus operandi that could on multiple levels gather, filter, process, act, test, and control the effectiveness of the desired goals in a never-ending loop of regathering, refiltering, reprocessing, reacting, re-testing and re-controlling information and actions.

The main path of research could be in *relations, i.e.,* in attention to various connections from which assumptions are then made. It is believed that when relations are discovered, also a fine line between the tangible and intangible parts can be exposed, and thus better addressed. The increased flexibility of rules (without endangering the principle of reliability, predictability, and legal certainty) should gain more importance in the legal and public institutional systems. These systems are only one aspect in the context of various contemporary things and processes. Reality depends on what *people* in their different roles recognise as important. Reality could be (and somewhere *is*) different. This paper claims that the first step towards a general meta-presentation of reality (that is, who gives predispositions in which reality is reflected as such) could be *a systematic public administration* based on the principle of *responsiveness*. The purpose is to demonstrate that 'there cannot be a right purpose' without a prior focus on structures, parts, actions, relations, feedback and environments. There are just different perspectives or predispositions from which the purposes are extracted. The next chapter enumerates and explains some of them.

LACK OF AND ELEMENTS OF SYSTEMIC AGENCY

The quality of public institutions is of the utmost importance for the well-being of its citizens (Holmberg & Rothstein, 2012; Kaufmann, Kraay & Mastruzzi, 2010), but such quality cannot be equated only with having impartial institutions. Impartiality in the exercise of public power is only a prerequisite of quality. Holmberg and Rothstein do not include in the quality of government *reasonableness* that is stipulated in the policy or the law as its material and legal element from which impartiality is derived in the first place.[17] Impartiality and reasonableness are elements of decision-making, be it in the form of formal decisions or of actions. Along with the already mentioned ones, other scholars also address legitimacy through reasonable decisions (Bell, Elliott, Varuhas, & Murray, 2016), through the examination of the variation of legal powers, procedures, and standards that bind regulators (Bignami & Zaring, 2016), the ways through which individuals and organizations test and challenge the legitimacy of the modern state outside of the electoral process (Rose-Ackerman & Lindseth, 2011), the search for satisfactory theories of the place of administrative agencies in a tripartite constitutional order (Cass, Diver, Beermann, & Freeman, 2011) or address techniques or tools for influencing human behaviour (Baldwin, Cave, & Lodge, 2012, 2013; Morgan & Yeung, 2007). In their specific ways and under their specific conditions, they all want to legitimise power in the hands of unelected officials. They have information and thus knowledge (Weber, 1978; Witte, 1942), which has not changed up to the present day (Guy-Ecabert, 2018) – despite the mentioned expert shortcomings in the dynamic environment); thus, it is of the highest importance how public agencies prepare drafts of primary and enact secondary legislation, not only from the viewpoint of numbers, but mainly of the *dysfunctions* they have.

Variations, adaptations (dis)functions, and tensions offer an analytical focus in the study of dynamics and operative changes during regulation and implementation and motivate us to find a way by which these elements could not disrupt adaptive stability within its normal limits. Merton's less known 'medicine' for these elements/consequences is *functional analysis*, based on the interpretation of data and their consequences (Merton, 1968),[18] and his focus on the evaluation of consequences (to see or understand an organization through a function it performs) puts him directly in the centre of our E&E debate. Each case or action has multiple (good, bad, semi-good/bad, neutral) consequences, present on different layers. These trigger an evaluation problem of the best, worst, and average consequences, which becomes more important in the *salus populi* domain. The mentioned notion of emergence could explain Merton's observation that 'activities oriented toward certain value release processes which so react is to change the very scale of use which precipitated them' (Merton, 1936, p. 903), or the very process of prediction affects the process predicted (the self-fulfilling prophecy). Therefore, it is highly relevant how predictions are made to (dis)enable adaptations of systems (or Merton's [dis]functions). Merton's unwanted consequences and/or social disorganisation describe difficulties that are not fully contrary to intended actions, but focus mainly on side effects: '[t]he composite of faults in the normative and relational structure of a social system described as social disorganization can be thought of as inadequacies in meeting one or more functional requirements of the system' (Merton, 1961, p. 720). This functionalistic focus could preempted or *satisfied* him to disregard other elements that could not only also have a stake in unintended effects, but amplify them: one is the more elaborated role of human agency,[19] the second is the role of control and communications in systems, the third is the role of the system's innate properties (adaptation, emergence, relations, exponential growth, other social systems) and the fourth that 'consensus is not society-wide; it is local...each separate social unit maintains not the whole society, but its own special needs...and these special interests often conflict' (Parrillo, 2005, p. 16). Sieber enumerates seven mechanisms that convert the intentions of the agent into *opposite* (not side) ones: 'functional disruption, exploitation, goal displacement, provocation, classification, commitment, and placation. These mechanisms should not be thought of as exhaustive nor...do I have any illusion that the last word has been uttered on the dynamics whereby each mechanism produces reverse effects' (Sieber, 1981, p. 56). Here is no place to describe all unintended consequences, but when one talks about emerging unintended consequences, self-precaution is needed: each intervention can be a cause for a new one or a change for the old ones. A recommendation can be a proposal/hypothesis that requires further experimentation and/or investigation. Despite the difficulties mentioned, one very general note can be given: all CASs are of *evolutionary nature* in which variation, differentiation, selection, and integration are their building elements; the latter should be built into all systems of (non-technical) human decision-making, because humans themselves are CAS.

There are many scholars who have addressed dysfunctions (Merton, 1936; Selznick, 1949; Sieber, 1981; Weber, 1978) that include also the systemic ones. Here, we will only mention three authors who have addressed dysfunctions connected with 'the system' and public administration (Drucker's six deadly sins in public administration, Caiden's bureaupathologies, and Chapman's system failure). For Drucker, sins include giving lofty, unspecified objectives without clear targets that could be measured, appraised, or judged; doing several things at once without establishing and sticking to priorities; believing that "fat is beautiful" and throwing more money and people at problems; being dogmatic rather than experimental where even successful an application still demands adaptation, cutting, fitting, trying and balancing; failing to learn from experience and systematic feedback; and the inability to abandon obsolete programs (Drucker, 1980, pp. 103–105). To him, 'perhaps even more important than cowardice as an explanation for the tendency of so much of public administration today to commit itself to policies that can only result in non-performance is the lack of concern with performance in public administration theory' (Drucker, 1980, p. 105). Caiden invented the notion of "bureaupathologies", which are 'not the individual failings of individuals who compose organizations but the systematic shortcomings of organizations that cause individuals within them to be guilty of malpractices' (Caiden, 1991, p. 490). Chapman enumerates his "bureaupathologies" that lead to system failure: a culture that is averse to failure; a desire for uniformity in public services that stifles innovation and variety; an adversarial political system, supported by the media, that uses failure as a way of scoring points; shared assumptions between politicians and civil servants that command and control is the correct way to exercise power; a lack of feedback on the results of policies; a lack of time to do anything other than cope; a tradition of secrecy that is used to stifle feedback and learning; a system that requires policies to be negotiated with competing power centres in government; turf wars between departments and individuals; loss of professional standards under the knife of efficiency (Chapman, 2004, p. 85). Within the concepts of systems theory, the current conditions of state activities frequently lack feedback in the real-time dimension, which means the established control on the basis of *actual* performance with sensors that perform the function of monitors and effectors, rather than expected performance (Wiener, 1989).

For Lipsky, to (re)gain popular trust (or confidence) in a government's fairness, the line should be drawn between exception and universalism by democratic *widespread approval*,[20] while Davis proposes rules – along with generalisations (as a form of popular approval) and adjudication – in the form of hypotheticals (or case-to-case rule-making).[21] While the first is not-operative (in a short period of time and within the established procedures of majority voting), the second cannot imagine all the potential cases that could happen. More promising is Ridder's idea that 'legal quality results from behaviour [as a derivation of the adaptability of living organisms]: from the choices of people, administrators, and politicians – the choices of actors, more generally speaking. In order to understand administrative behaviour, it is necessary to identify factors that influence such behaviour' (Ridder, 2007, p. 32). In the PA, behaviour as an element of adaptation can be found in the principle of *responsiveness*, which 'does not refer to an individual official's ability to comprehend the needs of a person and make an appropriate response, but rather an administration's ability to gather information from users in an organized manner, synthesising it and making sense of it so that a political or administrative response can be made when necessary' (Pasquier, 2018, p. 225). The attitude of the PA towards responsiveness could be enhanced by considering some basic insights from systems theory.

In 2018, legal science still talks about the classical design of legislative projects (with an internal working group, a joint working group, and a group of experts), of a preliminary draft and its explanatory report, of an external consultation on the preliminary draft and of finalizing the bill (Eskridge (Jr.), Frickey, Garrett, & Brudney, 2014; Guy-Ecabert, 2018; Karpen & Xanthaki, 2017), while Witte claimed as early as 1942 that administrative departments deserve more attention in law-making. Regarding the quality of decision-making in public law, '[t]here is no *systematic* overview of non-legal factors, nor do we know very much about the way in which quality factors – separately or in conjunction – exert their influence (Graaf, Jans, Marseille, & Ridder, 2007, p. 7 emphasis added). Based on these and other reasons related to the dynamic environment, which public agencies hardly follow, the systemic approach is shyly and slowly receiving more attention (European Commission, 2017; Morgan & Yeung, 2007;

OECD, 2017). Changing the dynamics of a well-established and complex system requires not only a new way of examining problems, but also bold decision making that fundamentally challenges public sector institutions. This entails (OECD, 2017) putting the desired outcomes first instead of institutional interests and resource control, promoting value-based decisions (instead of simply regulating) to allow individual organisations to set their own processes to achieve shared goals, and designing functions and organisations around users rather than the government. In flexible or dynamic surroundings, quality is not about the extent to which a certain concrete phenomenon corresponds to the ideal version of that phenomenon; in such an environment, quality "moves" and is unknowable from the present point of view. Dynamism and a system that could reflect all this are needed.

Information-communication. In complex environments, people are successful when they adapt, but 'in studying any complex adaptive system, we follow what happens to the information' (Gell-Mann, 2002, p. 23). From this, it can be inferred that the capacity of a regulator is equal to its ability to be a channel of communication in such an environment. People acquire information from their environment, from their own interaction with the latter and identify regularities in that information; people compress these regularities into a concise "schema" or model, and act in the real world on the basis of that schema (Gell-Mann, 2002). Thus, this schema is only one of the many possibilities related to mutation or substitution. Schemata in science compress something (a set of equations) into a brief law; in biology, schemata are genotypes, while in the case of societal evolution, schemata consist of laws, customs, myths, traditions and so forth (Gell-Mann, 2012).

Public power can reflect natural justice in administrative matters with the help of systems. The rule against bias, the right to a fair hearing, and error of law, has its common denominator in the duty to give reason, but this also has its metadenominator in a *system* that collects data, which is then transformed into information, i.e. reasons / legal arguments. System ideas are most appropriate when dealing with 'messes': problems that are unbounded in scope, time, and resources and have no clear agreement on what a solution would even look like, let alone how it could be achieved (Chapman, 2004). As in the case of all problems, a system approach also depends on how the system is defined and on what relations are known and elaborated as important.

Adaptation approaches. There are two adaptation approaches: filtering or reducing the complexity of incoming stimuli to minimise the internal complexity and amplifying the latter to be equal to or greater than the external complexity it faces. The OECD document (2017) in this regard speaks of *complexity reduction* (by creating theoretical models that make information more manageable or actionable), complexity absorption (by the proliferation of new internal agencies within departments or ministries) and *design processes* as the part of the system itself that can achieve a more "stable" position than the first two (the stable rule, in this case, can only be stable changes, tests, measurements, systemic thinking and increased learning).

Requisite variety. One of the basic cybernetic laws states that a complex or assembled problem can only be administered with the same or similar measure of complexity; this is known as Ashby's law of requisite variety ("only variety can manage variety").[22] Behaviour as an element of an adaptable system is steered by data from the environment; such a system controls its internal essential variables to be within their normal limits (homeostasis) and by the external administration of the environment (by blocking the flow of information to essential variables and by amplifying sources towards the desired goals) so that the environment acts on the variables in a desired manner. Ashby speaks of the principle of ultrastability.[23] According to Ashby's law, a system must be at least as complex as the other system it controls, otherwise a complexity gap (the gap between the problems faced by institutions and their capacity to tackle them) will arise from this discrepancy.

System design. Despite its importance, Ashby's law only holds within the variety perceived by agents and/or from their ontological assumptions (Boisot & McKelvey, 2011). People have trust in the government when public problems are at a minimum, but it should be emphasised that problems are not objects of direct experience and cannot be treated separately – they are interrelated.[24] How problems *interact* and how they are embedded in context are more important than what they are independently of each other. This is 'valuable' information, but it can be good or bad depending on the capacity of the information channel, which further determines the amount of regulation and control the regulator has over its environment.

The regulator as a model of the regulated system. Desired outcomes are achieved when the regulator has control over them, so regulation and control are intimately related (William Ross Ashby, 1957). The Conant-Ashby theorem claims that every good regulator of a system must be a model of that system (Conant & Ashby, 1970). Therefore, decisions are as good as decision makers. If they do not include most of the relationships in a given context, complexity arises because their 'systemic' decisions are not designed to counteract the challenges they face. Therefore, it is essential to match 'the right responses to their equivalent problems in the appropriate regulatory regimes'. In a complex environment, regulation must block the flow of information: 'an essential feature of the good regulator is that it blocks the flow of variety from disturbances to essential variables' (William Ross Ashby, 1957, p. 201). A homeostatic loop of a regulator's amplifiers (from a regulator to a system) and filters (from the system's environment to the regulator) is inserted to deal with an interested part of the environment. If this is not done, the system will self-regulate towards its own equilibrium (self-regulation of situations). The role of regulation is thus to shrink the flow of external variables and to amplify its processes, structures, and tools towards the desired outcomes.

Regularities. Gell-Mann distinguishes *simple* regularities in data based on scaling laws as the laws of distribution, and "frozen accident" (effective complexity) regularities that only produce substantial effects in a limited region of space and time. 'Once it happens and its outcome is determined, an accident no longer belongs in the realm of the random. Frozen accidents, significantly affecting things judged to be important, give rise to regularities' (Gell-Mann, 2012, p. 21). A third type of semi-regularity is crude complexity, which 'fails to correspond to what we usually understand by complexity because they refer to the length of a concise description of the whole system or the string – including all its random features – rather than the regularities alone' (Gell-Mann, 2002, p. 50). A fourth type of (ir)regularity is the phenomenon of indeterminant chaos from nonlinear dynamics, associated with fractals and power laws.

The challenge of choosing the appropriate types of distribution for a given problem. Simple regularities produce ordered routinised practices that belong among the causal, cause-event, static Gaussian-type distributions, while effective complex regularities produce only temporary-ordered, semi-routinised practices based on exponential and butterfly-type effects. Thus, it is of utmost importance that at least approximately the right tools or processes are used when faced with problems. One approach is the Cynefin framework (a Welsh word that means *habitat, acquainted, familiar*) framework (Snowden & Boone, 2007), which gives decision-makers a 'sense of place'. This framework sorts the issues facing leaders into five contexts defined by the nature of the relationship between cause and effect; four of these: simple (a realm of "known knowns"; sense-categorize-respond; domain of best practice), *complicated* (a realm of "known unknowns"; sense-analyse-respond; domain of experts), *complex* (a realm of "unknown unknowns"; probe-sense-respond; the domain of emergence), and *chaotic* (a realm of unknowables; act-sense-respond; the domain of rapid response)—require leaders to diagnose situations and act in contextually appropriate ways. The fifth, disorder, applies when it is unclear which of the other four contexts is predominant.

WAYS TO HANDLE DIFFERENT PROBLEMS

Legitimacy gap. The difference between the service requirements and its real performance shows a legitimacy gap. Despite the recognition that the system is more than just the total sum of its parts, still (pretty much) nothing changes in the so-called "systemic" part of public administrations. The notion of "public interest" is often changed to the "systemic" approach whenever the public administration wants to change something in a one-way manner. A variety of different information is *sine qua non* for effective systems; if public participation has so far been intuitively seen as good for democratic process, this is also confirmed from the systemic point of view – input information from variable sources is needed. The legitimacy gap can be narrowed if systemic thinking is used.

Reductionist and holistic methods. Reductionist methods, focused on command-and-control regulation, adjudication, and inspection, with predetermined goals and tools, are good for a classic PA (and a dynamic one in its more static aspects), while complicated and especially systemic PAs should be focused on holistic thinking, cooperation, a variety of information, and relations from which new, interconnected things emerge. A final goal, be it the purpose of a customer or a citizen in an interconnected world, cannot be given top-down: It is co-designed and co-implemented. As a general rule of thumb, where simplicity, certainty, uniformity, linearity, repeatability, and simplicity prevail, Gaussian averages can be applied. 'Applying Gaussian statistical methods to power law distributions and getting rid of outliers – a process called "Winsorizing" – can produce quite misleading results and is thus inappropriate and blatantly distorting' (Boisot & McKelvey, 2011, p. 126). Where complexity, uncertainty, diversity, nonlinearity, nonrepeatability, and ambiguity prevail, systemic thinking can be applied with a focus on flows and stacks, relations, structure, purpose, and Gell-Mann's 'frozen accident' regularities. The complex relationships between cause and effect are not linear or simple, so different analytical and synthetical tools are needed.

Different decision-making for different problems. In the "simplicity camp", deduction and induction prevail, while in the complexity camp, the appropriate inferential strategy can only be called *abductive*.[25] An abductive formation of new ideas, theories and then hypotheses based on different and substantial data can be advanced with Popper's falsifiability: 'I shall require that [the system's] logical form shall be such that it can be singled out, by means of empirical tests, in a negative sense: *it must be possible for an empirical scientific system to be refuted by experience*' (Popper, 2002, p. 18, italics in the original). There are many tools available to pursue adaptive strategies, but 'the binding agent between the heterogeneous events that such strategies draw on is likely to be narratives, stories, case studies, and histories, not just numbers. If Gaussian thinking focuses on *probability*, PL [power law] thinking focuses on plausibility' (Boisot & McKelvey, 2011, p. 129). The 'black swans' of logic or 'story' can be reconfirmed mainly by non-stop empirical tests, and until refuted, there can only be a temporary agreement or convention on certain things or processes.

OECD tactics. The OECD report (2017) identifies several tactics that act as important elements in system change: *people and place* are essential drivers of a change process (time and other resources are also needed to re-examine the purpose of public sector systems and the problems connected to them).

Usually, only high-level leaders within organisations can allocate these assets. Thus, the *stewardship* of system change is needed from the outset. Once they have internalised 'crises', organizations need to create space for *dwelling* – this process instigates a debate on how to define public values, understand and articulate both the problem and the objectives within the system; *framework - to* focus discussion on the required change, it is necessary to frame the debate – and *connecting* to different parts of the system is therefore essential. In situations of uncertainty, additional steps must be taken to test the solutions (prototyping). Meaningful measurement is key to complex problems, as causality is usually established in hindsight and the effects of interventions are very difficult to assess; *evaluating* system change is a continuous process, and it is essential to ensure feedback with regard to unintended consequences and unforeseen conditions during the implementation phase and beyond.

Affective feedback. One of the most important lessons of systems theory for PAs is that feedback only exists between two parts when each affects the other (William Ross Ashby, 1957). Only when the public can *affect* decision makers is there real feedback and an effective organisation, focused on the wishes or demands of the citizens, and aligned with the PA's duty to protect a collective public interest *from* an individual's wish. Both points of view are changed during the process and affect each other. In this process, mutual effectiveness (doing the right thing) emerges and, step by step, also changes its efficiency (doing things right). Citizens' views as co-demand and co-actions are possible within a larger framework, in which information or context is given and established in mutual relations, based on the dialogue and actions (repeated experimentation in practice) needed to achieve goals.

Stochastic indicators of success. Among the general criteria of success, Boston (2000) enumerates economic and financial, constitutional, accountability, ethical, institutional design, management, ownership interest, purchase interest, client/citizen responsiveness, information-related, and system-wide criteria. In each of them, there are specific criteria that range from three to ten. Despite his effort to answer how one should evaluate comprehensive and far-reaching systemic reforms, because he is still within an evaluator's viewpoint (be it the government or someone else), he can only conclude 'more discussion and debate is needed on the question of what criteria should be employed when seeking to evaluate the performance of an entire system (or competing models) of public management, and how these criteria might be applied in practice' (Boston, 2000, p. 46). To measure the results of internal and external processes, a set of randomly chosen indicators should be defined (or benchmarking, accreditation, certification, rating, and initiatives of evidence-based professional practice can be applied). As mentioned, the analysis of a system usually depends on its analyser, and it is no wonder that there are difficulties from this (personal) point of view. Indicators should be as objective as possible; this represents a problem in assessing the actual situation and/or an identification problem for evaluators. For this reason, the indicators could be stochastic, so the system could randomly choose them.

Various models. Complexity could be better confronted and/or administered with the same or a similar measure of complexity, also known as Ashby's *requisite variety* (William Ross Ashby, 1957). Similarly, Page, based on Aristotle's value of combining the excellences of many, proposes a many-model thinking approach by which the complexity of the modern world should be confronted with multiple models (Page, 2018).

Aspirations or ideas usually cannot be fully realized, but decision makers can nonetheless alter the identification, estimation, determination, implementation, and evaluation of problems when they are attentive to the tools and processes, they use. Systems theory is based on the idea that everything is interconnected. People and decision makers cannot be sure that an intentional action will bring a comprehensive or sustained result; many times, some things (bad or good) unintentionally emerge. Systems thinking can enable different voices or their indicators to be tested *vis-à-vis* the real purpose and performance of the PAs (remember, a real purpose of an organisation is what it *de facto* does). The PAs are as efficient as their *processes* are. Systems thinking is a way of framing, administering, and measuring a flow through a system given a stock, as opposed to measuring and managing the work in functional units. It is a way of managing the entire organization based on the structure, parts, relations, purposes, and/or processes as an iterative sequence of activities to generate added value for an output that, through feedback, changes the input in an iterative manner until a goal is reached. After the identification of the model, its management over time (to keep processes up to date) changes and develops new processes. However, in an unforeseeable future, action must be taken, and some risks will always be present. A balance must be struck between the risk of suboptimization and over-optimization; a pragmatic suggestion is thus to run tests and experiments and to control predefined variables for changes. And to do this again and again, the periodically evaluated predispositions and purposes change. Then the whole process is repeated. Of course, this occurs with the right type of simplicity or complexity in the modus operandi of the public administration.

REFERENCES

Ackoff, R. L. (1994). *The Democratic Corporation: A Radical Prescription for Recreating Corporate America and Rediscovering Success*. Oxford University Press. doi:10.1093/oso/9780195087277.001.0001

Arendt, H. (1972). *Crises of the Republic: Lying in Politics, Civil Disobedience on Violence, Thoughts on Politics, and Revolution*. Harcourt Brace Jovanovich.

Aronson, M. (2009). The Great Depression, this Depression, and Administrative Law—Federal Law Review—ANU. *Federal Law Review*, *37*(2), 165–203. doi:10.22145/flr.37.2.1

Ashby, W. R. (1957). *An Introduction to Cybernetics*. Chapman and Hall.

Ashby, W. R. (1960). *Design for a Brain: The Origin of Adaptive Behavior*. Chapman and Hall.

Auby, J.-B. (2017). The Transformation of the Administrative State and Administrative Law. In A. von Bogdandy, P. M. Huber, & S. Cassese (Eds.), *The Max Planck Handbooks in European Public Law: The Administrative State* (pp. 601–630). Oxford University Press.

Ayres, I., & Nalebuff, B. (2015). The rule of probabilities: A practical approach for applying Bayes' rule to the analysis of DNA evidence. *Stanford Law Review*, *67*(6), 1447–1503.

Baldwin, R., Cave, M., & Lodge, M. (2012). The Oxford Handbook of Regulation (Reprint edition). Oxford; New York: Oxford University Press.

Baldwin, R., Cave, M., & Lodge, M. (2013). *Understanding Regulation: Theory, Strategy, and Practice* (2nd ed.). Oxford University Press.

Bauman, Z. (2011). *Collateral Damage: Social Inequalities in a Global Age*. Polity.

Beauvois, J.-L. (2000). *Razprava o liberalni suženosti: Analiza podrejanja*. Ljubljana: Krt.

Beck, U. (1992). *Risk Society: Towards a New Modernity*. SAGE Publications Ltd.

Beer, S. (2002). What is cybernetics? *Kybernetes, 31*(2), 209–219. doi:10.1108/03684920210417283

Bell, J., Elliott, M., Varuhas, J. N., & Murray, P. (Eds.). (2016). *Public Law Adjudication in Common Law Systems: Process and Substance.* Hart Publishing.

Bignami, F., & Zaring, D. (Eds.). (2016). *Comparative Law and Regulation: Understanding the Global Regulatory Process.* Edward Elgar Publishing. doi:10.4337/9781782545613

Black, J. (2012). The Role of Risk in Regulatory Processes. In R. Baldwin, M. Cave, & M. Lodge (Eds.), The Oxford Handbook of Regulation (Reprint edition, pp. 302–348). Oxford; New York: Oxford University Press.

Bobek, M. (2017). Europeanization of Public Law. In A. von Bogdandy, P. M. Huber, & S. Cassese (Eds.), *The Max Planck Handbooks in European Public Law: The Administrative State* (pp. 631–674). Oxford University Press.

Boisot, M., & McKelvey, B. (2011). Connectivity, Extremes, and Adaptation: A Power-Law Perspective of Organizational Effectiveness. *Journal of Management Inquiry, 20*(2), 119–133. doi:10.1177/1056492610385564

Boston, J. (2000). The Challenge of Evaluating Systemic Change: The Case of Public Management Reform in New Zealand. *International Public Management Journal, 3*(3), 23–46. doi:10.1016/S1096-7494(00)00033-7

Breyer, S. G., Stewart, R. B., Sunstein, C. R., & Vermeule, A. (2006). *Administrative Law and Regulatory Policy: Problems, Text, and Cases* (6th ed.). Aspen Publishers.

Caiden, G. E. (1991). What Really is Public Maladministration? *Public Administration Review, 3751*(6), 486–493. doi:10.2307/976599

Carrier, R. (2012). *Proving History: Bayes's Theorem and the Quest for the Historical Jesus.* Prometheus Books.

Cass, R. A., Diver, C. S., Beermann, J. M., & Freeman, J. (2011). *Administrative Law: Cases and Materials* (6th ed.). Aspen Publishers.

Chapman, J. (2004). *System Failure: Why Governments Must Learn to Think Differently.* Demos.

Christensen, T., & Laegred, P. (2005). Regulatory Reforms and Agentification. *Unifob AS, Working Paper 6. Stein Rokkan Centre for Social Studies.*

Cole, A., & Eymeri-Douzans, J.-M. (2010). Introduction: Administrative reforms and mergers in Europe - research questions and empirical challenges. *International Review of Administrative Sciences, 76*(3), 395–406. doi:10.1177/0020852310373881

Conant, R. C., & Ashby, W. R. (1970). Every Good Regulator of a System Must be a Model of that System. *International Journal of Systems Science, 1*(2), 89–97. doi:10.1080/00207727008920220

Crawford, A. (2006). Networked governance and the post-regulatory state? Steering, rowing and anchoring the provision of policing and security. *Theoretical Criminology, 10*(4), 449–479. doi:10.1177/1362480606068874

Crowder, G. (2004). Isaiah Berlin: Liberty, Pluralism and Liberalism. *Polity*.

Crozier, M. (1964). Bureaucratic Phenomenon. Chicago: University of Chicago Press.

Davis, K. C. (1979). Discretionary Justice: A Preliminary Inquiry (Fifth printing). Urbana, Chicago, London: University of Illinois Press.

Diefenbach, T. (2009). New public management in public sector organisations: The dark sides of managerialistic 'enlightenment'. *Public Administration*, *87*(4), 892–909. doi:10.1111/j.1467-9299.2009.01766.x

Dodge, H. F., & Romig, H. G. (1959). *Sampling inspection tables: Single and double sampling*. Wiley.

Drucker, P. F. (1980). The Deadly Sins in Public Administration. *Public Administration Review*, *40*(2), 103–106. doi:10.2307/975619

Edwards, W. (1999). *Decision Science and Technology: Reflections on the Contributions of Ward Edwards*. Springer Science & Business Media.

Edwards, W., Jr. R. F. M., & Winterfeldt, D. (2007). Advances in Decision Analysis: From Foundations to Applications. New York: Cambridge University Press.

Eskridge, W. N. Jr, Frickey, P. P., Garrett, E., & Brudney, J. J. (2014). *Cases and Materials on Legislation and Regulation: Statutes and the Creation of Public*. West Academic Publishing.

European Commission. (2017). *European Semester: Thematic factsheet – Quality of public administration – 2017*. EC. https://ec.europa.eu/info/sites/info/files/file_import/european-semester_thematic-factsheet_quality-public-administration_en_0.pdf

Fiedler, K., & Juslin, P. (Eds.). (2006). *Information Sampling and Adaptive Cognition*. Cambridge University Press.

Finkelstein, M. O., & Fairley, W. B. (1970). A Bayesian Approach to Identification Evidence. *Harvard Law Review*, *83*(3), 489–517. doi:10.2307/1339656

Foucault, M. (1978). The History of Sexuality: Vol. 1. *An Introduction (Reissue edition)*. Vintage Books.

Foucault, M. (1995). *Discipline & Punish: The Birth of the Prison* (2nd ed.). (A. Sheridan, Trans.). Vintage Books.

Foucault, M. (2001). *Power (The Essential Works of Foucault, 1954-1984) (J. D. Faubion* (R. Hurley Ed. & Trans.). The New Press.

Foucault, M. (2002). *The Order of Things: Archaeology of the Human Sciences* (2nd ed.). Routledge.

Foucault, M. (2004). *Naissance de la biopolitique*. Seuil.

Foucault, M. (2007). *Življenje in prakse svobode*. Založba ZRC.

Foucault, M. (2015). *Družbo je treba braniti: Predavanja na College de France 1975-1976* (A. M. Habjan, Trans.). Studia Humanitatis.

Franklin, J. (Ed.). (1998). *The Politics of Risk Society*. Polity Press.

Frederickson, H. G. (1996). Comparing the Reinventing Government Movement with the New Public Administration. *Public Administration Review, 56*(3), 263–270. doi:10.2307/976450

Fukuyama, F. (2014). *Political Order and Political Decay: From the Industrial Revolution to the Globalization of Democracy*. Farrar, Straus and Giroux.

Gell-Mann, M. (2002). The Quark and the Jaguar (VIll edition). New York: W.H. Freeman & Company.

Gell-Mann, M. (2012). What Is Complexity? In A. Q. Curzio & M. Fortis (Eds.), *Complexity and Industrial Clusters: Dynamics and Models in Theory and Practice* (pp. 13–24). Springer Science & Business Media.

Gigerenzer, G. (2003). Reckoning with Risk: Learning to Live with Uncertainty (Kindle version). London: Penguin UK.

Glasser, W. (1994). *Kontrolna teorija*. Taxus.

Graaf, K. J., Jans, J. H., Marseille, A. T., & Ridder, J. (Eds.). (2007). *Quality of Decision-making in Public Law: Studies in Administrative Decision-making in the Netherlands*. Europa Law Publishing.

Guy-Ecabert, C. (2018). The Pre-parliamentary Phase in Lawmaking: The Power Issues at Stake. In A. Ladner, N. Soguel, Y. Emery, S. Weerts, & S. Nahrath (Eds.), *Swiss Public Administration—Making the State Work Successfully* (pp. 87–104). Palgrave Macmillan.

Hacking, I. (2001). *An Introduction to Probability and Inductive Logic*. Cambridge University Press. doi:10.1017/CBO9780511801297

Hammerschmid, G., de Walle, S. V., Andrews, R., & Bezes, P. (2016). *Public Administration Reforms in Europe: The View from the Top*. Edward Elgar Publishing. doi:10.4337/9781783475407

Holmberg, S., & Rothstein, B. (2012). *Good Government: The Relevance of Political Science*. Edward Elgar Publishing. doi:10.4337/9780857934932

Hood, C., Rothstein, H., & Baldwin, R. (2001). *The Government of Risk: Understanding Risk Regulation Regimes*. Oxford University Press. doi:10.1093/0199243638.001.0001

Hubbard, D. W. (2007). *How to Measure Anything: Finding the Value of 'Intangibles' in Business*. Wiley.

Hubbard, D. W. (2009). *The Failure of Risk Management: Why It's Broken and How to Fix It*. Wiley.

Kahneman, D. (2013). Thinking, Fast and Slow (Reprint edition). New York: Farrar, Straus and Giroux.

Karpen, U., & Xanthaki, H. (Eds.). (2017). *Legislation in Europe: A Comprehensive Guide For Scholars and Practitioners*. Bloomsbury Publishing.

Kaufmann, D., Kraay, A., & Mastruzzi, M. (2010). *The Worldwide Governance Indicators: Methodology and Analytical Issues*. SSRN. https://papers.ssrn.com/abstract=1682130

Keeney, R. L., & Raiffa, H. (1993). *Decisions with Multiple Objectives: Preferences and Value Trade-Offs*. Cambridge University Press. doi:10.1017/CBO9781139174084

Landemore, H., & Elster, J. (Eds.). (2012). *Collective Wisdom: Principles and Mechanisms*. Cambridge University Press. doi:10.1017/CBO9780511846427

Lefort, C. (1999). *Prigode demokracije*. Ljubljana: Liberalna akademija.

Lipsky, M. (2010). *Street-Level Bureaucracy: Dilemmas of the Individual in Public Service*. New York: Russell Sage Foundation.

Lowi, T. J. (2009). *The End of Liberalism: The Second Republic of the United States*. W. W. Norton, Incorporated.

Luhmann, N. (2013). *Oblast*. Krtina.

Lynch, G. S. (2009). *Single Point of Failure: The 10 Essential Laws of Supply Chain Risk Management*. John Wiley and Sons.

Merton, R. K. (1936). The Unanticipated Consequences of Purposive Social Action. *American Sociological Review*, *1*(6), 894–904. doi:10.2307/2084615

Merton, R. K. (1961). Social problems and sociological theory. In R. K. Merton & R. K. Merton (Eds.), *Contemporary Social Problems* (pp. 697–737). Harcourt, Brace & World.

Merton, R. K. (1968). *Social Theory and Social Structure*. Free Press.

Meßerschmidt, K., & Oliver-Lalana, A. D. (Eds.). (2016). *Rational Lawmaking under Review: Legisprudence According to the German Federal Constitutional Court*. Springer. doi:10.1007/978-3-319-33217-8

Milgram, S. (2009). Obedience to Authority: An Experimental View (Reprint edition). New York: Harper Perennial Modern Classics.

Mills, C. W. (2000). *The Power Elite: New Edition*. Oxford University Press.

Molak, V. (1996). *Fundamentals of Risk Analysis and Risk Management*. CRC-Press.

Morgan, B., & Yeung, K. (2007). *An Introduction to Law and Regulation: Text and Materials*. Cambridge University Press. doi:10.1017/CBO9780511801112

Moss, D. A., & Cisternino, J. (2009). *New Perspectives on Regulation*. The Tobin Project.

OECD. (1996). *Public Management Occasional Papers Pay Reform in the Public Service Initial Impact on Pay Dispersion in Australia, Sweden and the United Kingdom No. 10: Initial Impact on Pay Dispersion in Australia, Sweden and the United Kingdom*. OECD Publishing.

OECD. (2011). *Regulatory Policy and Governance: Supporting Economic Growth and Serving the Public Interest*. OECD Publishing.

OECD. (2012). *Recommendation of the Council on Regulatory Policy and Governance*. OECD.

OECD. (2017). *Systems Approaches to Public Sector Challenges: Working with Change*. OECD Publishing.

Page, S. E. (2018). *The Model Thinker: What You Need to Know to Make Data Work for You*. Basic Books.

Parrillo, V. N. (2005). *Contemporary Social Problems* (6th ed.). Pearson/Allyn and Bacon.

Pasquier, M. (2018). Communication and Transparency. In A. Ladner, N. Soguel, Y. Emery, S. Weerts, & S. Nahrath (Eds.), *Swiss Public Administration—Making the State Work Successfully* (pp. 221–240). Palgrave Macmillan.

Peirce, C. S. (1931). *The Collected Papers of Charles Sanders Peirce (electronic edition* (C. Hartshorne & P. Weiss, Eds.). Harvard University Press.

Pollitt, C. (2003). *The Essential Public Manager.* McGraw-Hill International.

Pollitt, C., & Bouckaert, G. (2011). *Public Management Reform: A Comparative Analysis - New Public Management, Governance, and the Neo-Weberian State* (3rd ed.). Oxford University Press.

Popper, K. (2002). *The Logic of Scientific Discovery.* Routledge.

Raiffa, H. (1994). The Prescriptive Orientation of Decision Making: A Synthesis of Decision Analysis, Behavioral Decision Making, and Game Theory. In S. Ríos (Ed.), *Decision Theory and Decision Analysis: Trends and Challenges* (pp. 3–13). Springer Science & Business Media. doi:10.1007/978-94-011-1372-4_1

Ridder, J. (2007). Factors for legal quality of administrative decision-making. In K. J. Graaf, J. H. Jans, A. T. Marseille, & J. Ridder (Eds.), *Quality of Decision-making in Public Law: Studies in Administrative Decision-making in the Netherlands* (pp. 31–51). Europa Law Publishing.

Rifkin, E., & Bouwer, E. (2007). *The Illusion of Certainty: Health Benefits and Risks* (2007 edition). Springer. doi:10.1007/978-0-387-48572-0

Rose-Ackerman, S., & Lindseth, P. L. (2011). *Comparative Administrative Law.* Edward Elgar Pub.

Rousseau, D. M. (Ed.). (2013). *The Oxford Handbook of Evidence-Based Management.* Oxford University Press.

Schilling, E. G., & Neubauer, D. V. (2009). *Acceptance Sampling in Quality Control* (2nd ed.). CRC Press. doi:10.1201/9781584889533

Schmitt, C. (1985). *Political Theology: Four Chapters on the Concept of Sovereignty* (1st ed.). (G. Schwab, Trans.). MIT Press.

Seddon, J. (2005). *Freedom from Command and Control: Rethinking Management for Lean Service.* Productivity Press.

Selznick, P. (1949). *TVA and the Grass Roots: A Study in the Sociology of Formal Organization.* University of California Press.

Sieber, S. (1981). *Fatal Remedies: The Ironies of Social Intervention.* Plenum Press. doi:10.1007/978-1-4684-7456-5

SIGMA. (2014). *Principles of Public Administration.* OECD Publishing.

Slovic, P. (1996). Risk Perception and Trust. In V. Molak (Ed.), Fundamentals of Risk Analysis and Risk Management (p. Chapter III.1). New York: CRC-Press. doi:10.1201/9781439821978.sec3

Snowden, D. J., & Boone, M. E. (2007, November 1). A Leader's Framework for Decision Making. *Harvard Business Review.* https://hbr.org/2007/11/a-leaders-framework-for-decision-making

Surowiecki, J. (2005). The Wisdom of Crowds. New York, NY: Anchor.

Taleb, N. N. (2010). The Black Swan: The Impact of the Highly Improbable Fragility. New York: Random House Publishing Group.

Terje, A. (2003). *Foundations of Risk Analysis: A Knowledge and Decision-Oriented Perspective*. John Wiley & Sons.

Tetlock, P., & Gardner, D. (2015). Superforecasting: The Art and Science of Prediction (Kindle edition). London: Random House.

Tetlock, P. E. (2006). Expert Political Judgment: How Good Is It? How Can We Know? New Yersey: Princeton University Press.

Trevisani, D. (2007). *Regie di cambiamento. Approcci integrati alle risorse umane, allo sviluppo personale e organizzativo e al coaghing*. Franco Angeli Publisher.

Turner, J. H. (2003). *Human Institutions: A Theory of Societal Evolution*. Rowman & Littlefield.

Tversky, A., & Kahneman, D. (1974). Judgment under Uncertainty: Heuristics and Biases. *Science*, *185*(4157), 1124–1131. doi:10.1126/science.185.4157.1124 PMID:17835457

Vogel, S. K. (1998). *Freer Markets, More Rules: Regulatory Reform in Advanced Industrial Countries*. Cornell University Press. doi:10.7591/9781501717307

von Bogdandy, A., Huber, P. M., & Cassese, S. (Eds.). (2017). *The Max Planck Handbooks in European Public Law: The Administrative State*. Oxford University Press.

Weber, M. (1978). Economy and Society: An Outline of Interpretive Sociology (New Ed edition; G. Roth & C. Wittich, Eds.). Berkeley, California: University of California Press.

Weber, M. (1994). *Weber: Political Writings*. Cambridge University Press. doi:10.1017/CBO9780511841095

Wetherill, G. B. (2013). Sampling Inspection and Quality Control. Verlag: Springer.

Wiener, N. (1989). *The Human Use of Human Beings: Cybernetics and Society*. Free Associations Books.

Wintgens, L., & Thion, P. (Eds.). (2007). *Legislation in Context: Essays in Legisprudence*. Ashgate Publishing, Ltd.

Witte, E. E. (1942). Administrative Agencies and Statute Lawmaking. *Public Administration Review*, *2*(2), 116–125. doi:10.2307/972284

Zimbardo, P. G. (2008). *The Lucifer Effect: Understanding How Good People Turn Evil*. Random House Trade Paperbacks.

Žižek, S. (2010). *Living in the End Times*. Verso.

ENDNOTES

1. Such tasks could be *regulatory* in which the agency issues general acts (regulations) regulating legal relations of wider significance and deciding on individual matters, if so, determined by a special law that gives an individual public agency a direct legal basis; *developmental* (they mainly include consulting, performing professional development tasks for the national bodies, local community and natural or legal persons, taking measures within their competence and allocating and allocating financial incentives and other resources); *analytical and professional* and supervisory tasks (they include supervising the suitability and professionalism of the work of legal or natural persons to whom it allocates financial resources or other forms of incentives, and other persons for whom the law so provides). If agencies can perform also inspections, authorized persons have the rights, duties and powers of inspectors. The public agency issues a report on its doings. Of course, the law or the founding act may stipulate that a public agency also performs other tasks if these tasks are inextricably linked to the purpose for which the public agency was established.
2. The Santa Fe Institute, founded in 1984, was the first research institute dedicated to the study of complex adaptive systems.
3. Opportunities that could contribute to improving the overall system: improve systemic productivity by improving the quality of relationships and collaboration; strengthen multi-level governance and ensure that powers/responsibilities are matched with resources at every administrative level; encourage intermunicipal cooperation; streamline and simplify processes; promote the use of holistically designed ICT solutions (European Commission, 2017, p. 9).
4. Opportunities for the policy-making process include: building analytical capacity and a better evidence base, and applying data analytics, design thinking and behavioural insights to policy-making; engaging civic society, research and professional organisations in co-creation and policy-making early on; establishing an effective centre of government to set standards, broker policy development across institutional boundaries and monitor implementation; moving to test/experiment and reflect, monitoring on an ongoing basis and adjusting in real time (adopt-and-adapt); increasing transparency and openness, thinking beyond legislation, gather data from an array of sources and viewpoints, and challenge preconceived ideas and current practices in the search for more effective policy solutions (European Commission, 2017, p. 11).
5. Experts who tend to be experts: livestock judges, astronomers, test pilots, soil judges, chess masters, physicists, mathematicians (when they deal with mathematical problems rather than empirical ones), accountants, grain inspectors, photo interpreters, insurance analysts (dealing with bell curve–style statistics). Experts who tend not to be experts: stockbrokers, clinical psychologists, psychiatrists, college admissions officers, court judges, councillors, personnel selectors, intelligence analysts, economists, financial forecasters, finance professors, political scientists, "risk experts"…and personal financial advisers (Taleb, 2010). Tetlock, based on more than 20 years of research, concluded that the average expert was roughly as accurate as a dart-throwing chimpanzee, *i.e.* s/he had done little better than guessing on many of the political and economic questions (2006; 2015).
6. According to American psychologist Zimbardo, the banality of evil is equally as likely as the banality of heroism. Both occur in special situations where the circumstances play the most important role for an individual, for his or her decision (not) to take measures or ac-

Predispositions on the Current State of Affairs

tion. From a value-based view on any system management, one needs to realise that there is 'greater power to make evil from good within the System [rather than in the behaviour of individuals] as a complex of powerful forces creating the Situation. Ample evidence from social psychology supports the concept that situational power prevails over individual power in the given circumstances' (Zimbardo, 2008, p. x).

7   See infra n 62.
8   E.g., a legal experiment in France based on constitutional Articles 72 and 37, the "free commune experiments" in Sweden, Denmark, Norway and Finland, the universal service in the EU, the power to amend primary legislation using the executive or Henry VIII clause, a sunset clause or a precautionary principle. The experiment is *per se* a scientific element that, unlike political ideas is based in observation, results, comparison, evaluation, and final assessment. Unlike other amendments to and performance targets concerning the regulations based on "public sector reform", the experiment is based on changes in the environment, to which it tries *in vivo* to be as close as possible in the most objective and scientific manner (although there are values present in choosing the field of experimentation and in its evaluation).
9   From the sociological point of view, public agencies gain *more* power (although this means a clear abuse of law) when their silence is passively allowed by the people, when the latter are uncertain, but still do not demand legal action.
10 What is the area within which the subject is or should be left to do or be what he is able to do or be, without interference by other persons (Crowder, 2004)?
11 As authority acts through the rule for Foucault, for Carl Schmitt, similarly, sovereignty is established through *decision-making*: 'the essence of the state's sovereignty ... [is not] the monopoly to coerce or to rule, but...the monopoly to decide. The exception reveals most clearly the essence of the state's authority. The decision parts here from the legal norm and (to formulate it paradoxically) authority proves that to produce law, it need not be based on law' (Schmitt, 1985, p. 13).
12 Since the end of human action, as distinct from the end products of fabrication, can never be reliably predicted, the means used to achieve political goals are more often than not of greater relevance to the future world than the intended goals (Arendt, 1972, p. 106).
13 Among other things, stronger regulatory governance for the OECD will require *evidence-based* impact assessments to promote effective regulation in support of policy coherence; more attention to the *voice of users* who need to be part of the policy process; a renewed emphasis on consultation, communication, co-operation and collaboration across all levels of government; reviewing the role of the regulatory agencies and the balance between private and public responsibilities for regulation, to secure accountability and avoid capture; and tools to evaluate and measure performance and progress and to communicate the costs and benefits of reform (2011, p. 15). Evidence-based management is a systematic, evidence-informed practice that incorporates scientific knowledge in the content and process of making decisions.
14 The Court of Justice of the European Union, the European Court of Human Rights, the US Supreme Court and the German Federal Constitutional Court.
15 19th-century institutions are currently being outmoded by 21st-century problems stemming from interconnectivity, cyber threats, climate change, changing demographic profiles and migration (OECD, 2017, p. 12).

16 Our decisions are often obfuscated by erroneous or incomplete analyses that e.g. use relative risks instead of absolute ones (Gigerenzer, 2003; Rifkin & Bouwer, 2007), heuristics and biases (Kahneman, 2013; Terje, 2003; Tversky & Kahneman, 1974), no real, scientific evidence that results in a measurable reduction in risk or improvement in decisions (Hubbard, 2007, 2009), and the lack of good communication and confrontation of risk management solutions with reliable partners (Beck, 1992; Lynch, 2009). This makes the human factor sometimes heavier than its tangible and technological counterpart (Trevisani, 2007).

17 A legal norm cannot only be abused when corruption, clientelism, favouritism, discrimination, patronage, nepotism or undue support to special interest groups occurs, it can also be abused when an unreasonable (even absurd) decision is implemented equally for everyone.

18 The descriptive protocol of this kind of analysis should, so far as possible, include: 1) location of participants in the pattern within the social structure—differential participation; 2) consideration of alternative modes of behaviour excluded by emphasis on the observed pattern (i.e. attention not only to what occurs but also to what is neglected by virtue of the existing pattern); 3) the emotive and cognitive meanings attached by participants to the pattern; 4) a distinction between the motivations for participating in the pattern and the objective behaviour involved in the pattern; 5) regularities of behaviour not recognized by participants but which are nonetheless associated with the central pattern of behaviour (Merton, 1968).

19 This variable includes rationalisation of conduct, self-monitoring, goal setting, and a host of private motives for action, the relationship of which the system requirements seem highly tenuous in the functionalist scheme (Sieber, 1981, p. 32).

20 Treating everyone alike is a requisite of building popular trust. But good rules allow for appropriate exceptions. How, then, can a society tolerate benign exceptions when universalism is so important? Exceptions that favour people because of their social ties or ethnic backgrounds are undermining. We cannot specify where the lines should be drawn, but we can acknowledge that responsiveness within a norm of universalist rule application can be consistent with fair and efficient public services, even if it requires a departure from strict mechanical accountability. The exceptions that mark a superior public agency must pass the test of deserving popular approval through facts and local values and not be tainted by implications of favouritism based on the identities of those favoured (Lipsky, 2010, p. 230).

21 An agency can often make rules through hypotheticals when it is unable to make rules through generalizations. An agency that uses three tools for making laws – adjudication, rules in the form of generalizations, and rules in the form of hypotheticals – is much better equipped to serve the public interest than an agency that limits itself to the first two of these tools (Davis, 1979, p. 61).

22 If the variety of the outcomes is to be reduced to some assigned number…variety must be increased to at least the appropriate minimum. Only variety…can force down the variety of the outcomes (William Ross Ashby, 1957, p. 206).

23 The organism that can adapt has a motor output to the environment and two feedback loops. The first gives the organism non-affective information about the world around it, and the second carries information about whether the essential variables are or are not driven outside the normal limits and it acts on the (external) parameters. The first feedback plays its part within each reaction; the second determines which reaction shall occur (W. Ross Ashby, 1960, pp. 82–84).

24 Ackoff warned about the damaging problem-related misconception that problems are objects of experience: '*problems are abstractions extracted from experience by analysis*…Managers are not

confronted with separate problems but with situations that consist of complex systems of strongly interacting problems. I call such situations messes (Ackoff, 1994, p. 211).

[25] Abduction is the process of forming an explanatory hypothesis. It is the only logical operation that introduces any new idea for induction does nothing but determine a value and deduction merely evolves the necessary consequences of a pure hypothesis (Peirce, 1931).

Chapter 4
Time and Context

ABSTRACT

This chapter discusses the historical ups and downs of regulatory cycles and their impact on public administration and governance. It emphasizes the importance of real-time and place in understanding and organizing public programs, and how governance adapts to changes in the environment. The chapter discusses the popularity of agencies during times of crisis and the rise of networked governance, social innovation, and citizen participation. The chapter also discusses the ongoing debate between private and public service provision and the appropriate market structure and regulation. Finally, the chapter predicts that after the Covid-19 crisis, there will be another regulatory reform that will emphasize the power of markets and the technological revolution based on advanced robotics and AI. The ownership-based perspective, citizen participation, performance, and human resource management will be critical in shaping the regulatory changes in agencies.

INTRODUCTION

For me, context is the key, and from that comes the understanding of everything.

–Kenneth Noland

Before we go deeper into the meaning of agencies, their historical ups and downs should be explained; one way is to use regulatory cycles that depend on time and (political, economic, social) context. Regardless of all theories, there are always a system - man-made or natural - (its underlying structure[1]) and people present in time and context. The importance of real-time is never emphasized enough; the 'place and time are crucial to understanding and organisation of many public programmes…as citizens live and work in place, not in policies' (Pollitt, 2012, p. vii). Theories have little importance apart from practices of real actions and results, because 'theories are [only] attempts to make sense of practices, and guide actions by which we forge practices' (Bevir, 2010, p. 7). This relation is also evident in the notion of governance, which 'is not a constant, but rather tends to change as needs and values change… The process of governing represents a continuing set of adaptations of political and administrative ac-

DOI: 10.4018/979-8-3693-0507-2.ch004

Time and Context

tivities to changes in the environment, not least of which are changes in the ideas of what constitutes appropriate modes of developing and implementing collective goals' (Peters, 2002, p. 1). The common ground between theory and practice is an adaptation which should also be present in regulation, and is the common goal by which coordination and control on the society are made. For the OECD 'the goal of regulatory reform is to improve national economies and improve their ability to adapt to change' (OECD, 2005, p. 1).

As life and nature go through changes and cycles, the same holds for the popularity of agencies that up to a point follow the Kondratiev cycle (Alexander, 2002). The latter refers to wavelike fluctuations in the modern world economy and can be used also for the anticipation of regulatory changes about agencies and other institutional forms, as they are based on the constant reevaluation and/or adaptation to changes. If we combine the mentioned cycle with the regulatory one, we can expect what regulatory stage will follow after the previous one ends. This lifelike regulatory cycle can tell us to which tool or process we should emphasize in different periods (Pečarič, 2016, p. 99):

Within a regulatory cycle, special attention should be given to systems that ensure laws are coherent and well managed, *i.e.,* that enable data in the *real-time* period. This is the core statement of regulatory quality and performance because it captures a dynamic environment for systematic assessment of the various impacts *of* and *on* regulations. Time is an important element in regulation, so both liberals and interventionists have their point – if they are placed in relevant time perspectives. From this predisposition, we can more easily understand why the hierarchical recession-based Weberian model of PA, characteristic for the New Deal and post–WWII development were present, and why the market-focused governments since the 1970s became in 1980s and 1990s less hierarchical, more decentralized, liberalised, and privatised: time and context have changed. These changes must also be reflected in the PA's models to be useful, as their content should echo the basic cybernetic rules in time and context-based practice: for a complex problem one can approach with the same (or very similar) amount of complexity. The popularity of agencies grows in the time of crisis, when the pressures on public finances are larger and the free market is hence emphasised that should act more efficiently: the 1980s rise of agencies could be put on the start line in Figure 1: Regulatory cycles, while the market failure in 2008 announced the higher government regulation in the times of recession and depression, agency mergers, or their incorporation back into governmental/ministerial bodies and new ideas how in the time of austerity efficiency (or "do more with less") can be improved.[2] There is a nonstop "battle" between the hierarchical, centrally controlled, one-way directed, but slow organisa-

Figure 1. Regulatory cycles

P: prosperity ≈ Market
R: recession ≈ Regulation
D: depression ≈ Failure
E: enhancement ≈ Reform

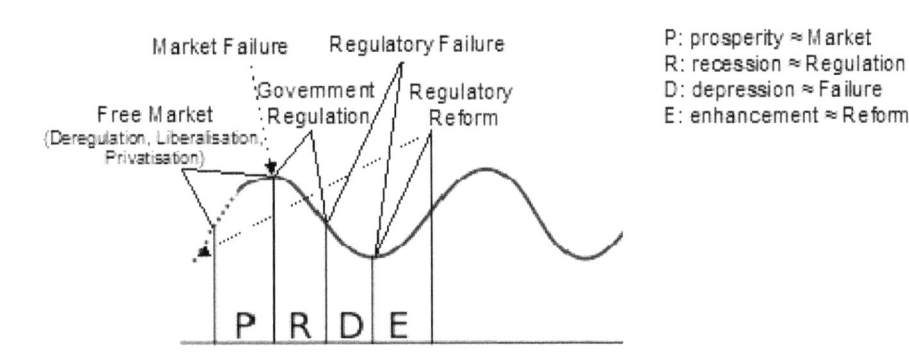

tions vs. decentralised, faster, horizontal, more innovative, adaptive and multipurpose organisations, where, in fact an underlying structure simply responds to changes in the environment. Both sides can be effective if they are used under proper conditions: centralised in the time of recession in depression and decentralised in the time of enhancement, development, and prosperity.

After the emphasis of NPM on people as customers, it was time for them to also be seen as active citizens that could help their country 'keep up the pace' and / or 'back in the saddle'. Governments should apply a holistic[3] approach to be able to respond to the needs of citizens and to be aligned with the citizens. The democratic approach was updated beyond the concept of citizenship and the ballot box to a variety of public activities based on transparency, and (digital) citizen participation or participation with elected and appointed officials. Dunleavy, Margetts and their co-authors at the beginning of the twentieth century displaced the concept of NPM in PA with the concept of digital era governance (DEG) (Dunleavy, Margetts, Tinkler, & Bastow, 2006). Some contra-NPM moves, such as decentralisation, networked governance, social innovation and social enterprise, transparency, and participation, found a natural match with the potential of digital technologies. This led to the emergence of the broadly defined Digital Era Government (DEG) paradigm' (Misuraca, 2020, p. 20). Recent decades show the shift from the model of the 'careful welfare state' (direct provision of public services) to the model of the 'enabling and ensuring state' (transfer of public services to institutions outside the core administration), predisposing the division to different levels of responsibility for service provision. This results in a complex network of public and private actors (described as principal–agent relationships), where institutional arrangements for services provision vary and where each option has its own specific advantages and disadvantages with no one-size-fits-all solution (Friedländer, Schaefer, & Röber, 2021). Discussions on private or public service provision, on functions, institutional frames, and structures are (still or always) open to discussion about the most suitable one. After the Covid-19 crisis, another regulatory reform is expected (also in the realm of agencies) that will again emphasise the power of markets (to regain the past levels of economic development, and recovering of countries' budgets), where the technological revolution, based on the benefits of advanced robotics and AI, is expected to be further promoted, emphasised and developed.[4] Ownership-based perspective (privatisation, corporatisation, outsourcing and re-municipalisation) will be behind the questions of appropriate market structure and its regulation along the citizen participation, performance and human resource management. The power of learning algorithms within big data and/or artificial intelligence will further redefine communications, while possession and the ability to administrate information will probably redefine also views on agencies.

REFERENCES

Dunleavy, P., Margetts, H., Tinkler, J., & Bastow, S. (2006). *Digital era governance: IT corporations, the state, and e-government*. Oxford University Press. doi:10.1093/acprof:oso/9780199296194.001.0001

Friedländer, B., Schaefer, C., & Röber, M. (2021). Institutional Differentiation of Public Service Provision in Germany: Corporatisation, Privatisation and Re-Municipalisation. In S. Kuhlmann, I. Proeller, D. Schimanke, & J. Ziekow (Eds.), *Public Administration in Germany* (pp. 291–310). IIAS, Palgrave MacMillan. doi:10.1007/978-3-030-53697-8_17

Gharajedaghi, J. (2007). *Systems Thinking, Third Edition: Managing Chaos and Complexity: A Platform for Designing Business Architecture* (3 edition). Burlington, MA: Morgan Kaufmann.

Misuraca, G. (Ed.). (2020). *Assessing the impacts of digital government transformation in the EU.* Luxemburg: Publications Office of the European Union.

Verhoest, K., Thiel, S. V., Bouckaert, G., & Lægreid, P. (Eds.). (2012). *Government Agencies: Practices and Lessons from 30 Countries.* Palgrave Macmillan. doi:10.1057/9780230359512

ENDNOTES

[1] Piketty has, based on the persistent structural links determined that on the eve of World War I that is, 125 years after the abolition of privileges the concentration of wealth in France was higher than it was at the time of the Revolution; the same links caused also that socioeconomic inequality has increased in all regions of the world since the 1980s. 'Modern inequality exhibits a range of discriminatory practices based on status, race, and religion, practices pursued with a violence that the meritocratic fairy tale utterly fails to acknowledge…Inequality is neither economic nor technological; it is ideological and political' (Piketty, 2020, pp. 2, 7).

[2] In the face of global crises (for example, security, environment and economic crises) and the increasing demand by citizens for integrated service delivery, a countertrend can be observed in many countries – labelled the post-NPM movement – in which politicians aim to restore central control and coordination through mergers and reshuffling of agencies (Verhoest, Thiel, Bouckaert, & Lægreid, 2012, p. 4).

[3] A holistic approach is "the Emperor new clothes" substitute of the 1970s systemic one: systems thinking is focused on 'design as a vehicle for enhancement of choice and holistic thinking' (Gharajedaghi, 2007, p. xx) that includes a choice regarding the whole.

[4] See the European Parliament resolution of 16 February 2017 with recommendations to the Commission on Civil Law Rules on Robotics (2015/2103(INL)) (2018/C 252/25).

Chapter 5
The Importance of Culture and Values in Public Reforms

ABSTRACT

This chapter emphasizes the importance of culture and values in public reforms. The culture of public administration represents the pattern of values, norms, beliefs, attitudes, and assumptions that may shape the ways in which people behave and get things done. Although culture is a common word in agencies, it can still be seen as a secret coded approach to a subjective expression social glue of what is going on in an institution or how things are done. The author suggests that decision-makers should carefully analyse all relevant aspects, and different contexts in which actions are made and decisions are taken. The chapter emphasizes the importance of recognizing the complexity of modernization and the success or failure of reforms in the public sector because it shares a common denominator in cultural theory, which gives direction for public reforms. Finally, cultural theory can help describe the complexity of modernization in the public sector.

INTRODUCTION

A culture is not the behavior of the people "living in it"; it is the "it" in which they live—contingencies of social reinforcement which generate and sustain their behavior (Skinner, 1969, p. 13).

Liberalism is the predominant political and moral philosophy in countries based on liberty and the rule of law. Although liberalism comes from the Latin *liber*, that is, 'free', this cannot mean absolute freedom to do anything one wants; there are values related with liberalism such as pluralism, toleration, autonomy, or integrity that are usually mentioned in this context, while there are also other values that are respected in countries. Autonomy is self-rule, self-administration, and independence. The level of autonomy could be seen as the achieved level of human/organisational morality when related not only to individual virtues (ethics), but to collective values (morality). If the types of organisational autonomy are put under the same denominator, autonomy could mean the level of organization's decision making role in (human, financial, and other) resources that overall lead to rationality in the frame of goodness

DOI: 10.4018/979-8-3693-0507-2.ch005

and justice in society. There are also different levels of autonomy found at the macro, meso, and microlocal level. Autonomy (or freedom) is not an 'isolated island' (this would be *contradictio in adiecto*, as autonomy is always autonomous to something else related to the former): along with time and context, there are also elements of culture and values important to better understand the framework in which something is done (economy, politics, agencies, people, etc.) is done, and the same applies to autonomy. Individuals and organizations are 'not free' to choose values/autonomy as they see fit – they can gradually change practices and indirectly affect values, but this is a long and ongoing process in which all relevant stakeholders or relevant entities should not be ignored.

Therefore, the autonomy of public agencies should be put in a relevant context. In the last decade of the 20th century, the OECD wanted (in the instrumental way) to bring the EU candidate countries closer with the EU member states with the notion of 'the European Administrative Space' (1999), which reflects the administrative capacity of candidate countries to successfully achieve the chosen EU policy outcomes, while the European Commission (in a semi-non-instrumentalist way) recognises all principles as values, while values are more important: 'distinguishing principles as durable values is less important than ensuring the set of values governing public behaviour is clear and widely shared' (2015, p. 17). A promotion of values only by their numbering and description as principles of good governance is not enough; values emerge in specific contexts in connection with specific actions (and what can be good somewhere can be bad in other environments or one man's poison is another man's cure[1]). The latter by repetition transform external motions into intrinsic desirability (they become embedded in culture). Values can emerge or are changed only in the same frame of practice, so the instrumental manner by which public bodies operate has precedence over the non-instrumental one. The European Commission acknowledges that 'there is very little rigorous research on how values become integrated and ingrained in the culture of public administrations' (European Commission, 2015, p. 23), so we must at first know how values evolve (re)act and change their content in different surroundings and how they can be implemented in different countries. The culture of public administration is more known as an organisational culture that represents 'the pattern of values, norms, beliefs, attitudes, and assumptions that may not have been articulated, but shape the ways in which people behave and things get done' (Armstrong, 2003, p. 263). Although culture is a common word in agencies or other institutions, it can still be seen as a secret coded approach to a subjective expression ('social glue') of what is going on in an institution or how things are really done. The employees of it in their personal attitudes exhibit not only values, beliefs, and unwritten rules of behaviour (ways of doing things, "the rules of the game"), but also elements of complex adaptive systems that cannot be easily managed up front. If the former is more focused on the institution in which culture is present, the latter is more focused on the external environment. Culture can be nevertheless guided when a current state of affairs is known, measured, corrected, or re-aligned in a direction of common purposes and goals. Here, (re)determination of the latter that should be checked on determined time periods is important, but it is even more important that these goals are based on the serious, objective and impartial research.

As the New Public Management (NPM) has strongly argued for the establishment of dependent agencies, it will be used also to point out the discrepancy between inner values and an outer formal law. Today, when the 'euphoria' of the NPM has subsided and resembles more and more other theories of public administration that wanted (or still want) to improve the effectiveness or efficiency of public administration, in Waldo's style, decision-makers should ask 'Efficiency for what' (1948)? If they want relevant answers, they should ask who, what, when, how, and what something should be done. Answers would probably be up to some point different for each agency, and the same has been spotted in NPM's reforms.[2] There are many specifics in each country, and any kind of "good" ideas should be handled with care: 'far from being new-minded in the 1980s, most of the basic ideas about how to manage in government have a history…[so] we need to be wary of taken-for-granted assumptions about who is to count as a manager of public services, what management means, what "best practice" amounts to and who or what to blame when things go wrong' (Hood, 1998, p. 22). A relevant agency or other institution must carefully and impartially analyse all relevant aspects; this is known also as the principle of care, which means 'a duty of the administration to carefully examine relevant factual and legal aspects of the individual case' (Nehl, 1999, p. 107).[3] There is neither time nor space to further enumerate all authors that have elaborated the positive and negative effects of the public administration's reforms (Crozier, 1964; Merton, 1968; Simon, 1997), but decision-makers should be aware of different contexts in which actions are made and decisions are taken. The results depend on elements that also include the unknown, uncertain, or probable (that might later undermine the desired results). Nature is more complex than people; there is always more variety in the world than can ever be built into the law. Despite numerous claims about the interdisciplinarity of public administration, there is a need for an even wider perspective from which to understand the evaluation, balance, and better explanation of the intended actions.

One among the appealing ways to explain considerable diversity and path-dependency[4] is the cultural one. For Parsons, 'social systems depend on cultural ones, which provide symbols, values and norms, and on personality systems, which provide motivations. Motivated attachment to cultural demands provides integration and stability for social systems' (Parsons, 1985, p. 13). An element of the social system are institutions: 'ideas and values only become strongly entrenched when they are embedded in institutions' (Douglas, 2012), while the latter are embedded in the culture of a nation. PA decisions could be more effective if they address common assumptions. In cultural theory, a boundary line between the (il)legal is not self-evident; it is socially constructed. This constructionism reflects different predispositions from which people (even unintentional, known as *social fact*[5]) construct this boundary, and its position is always in dispute that arises from social context. Classification is for social theory creation of culture: '[t]he culturally learned intuitions guide our judgment for any of our fields of competence, [and] teach us enough probabilistic principles, but they are heavily culture-bound' (Douglas, 1994, p. 57).

For Durkheim, as the author of the concept of (mechanical and organic) solidarity, social solidarity is a moral phenomenon, which is not amenable to exact observation and measurement, so 'we must substitute this internal datum with a visible one, with the law' (1984, p. 24). The latter often does not reflect the solidarity expressed as public interest and/or people's values. The law – although we think about it as being rational – cannot embrace neither complexity nor its variety if culture as their denominator is not present (because the first two will address a wrong content). Despite the differences between solidarity and law, they can be put into the same frame. Mary Douglas did this: 'arguing from different premises, we can never improve our understanding unless we examine and reformulate our assumptions' (1986, p. 8), so any kind of decision can exist only when individuals have the common categories of thought. Durkheim and Douglas point to public institutions that primarily formulate *assumptions* for the public (and these assumptions, as predispositions, are built into decisions). 'Ideas and values only become strongly entrenched when they are embedded in institutions' (Douglas, 2012), while the latter are embedded in a nation's culture. The PAs decisions could be more effective if they targeted our common assumptions. In cultural theory, a boundary line between legal and non-legal is not self-evident because it is *socially constructed*. This constructionism reflects the different predispositions from which people (even unintentional, known as *social fact*[6]) construct this boundary, and its position is always in dispute that arises from the social context. Classification is for social theory a creation of culture: '[t]he culturally learned intuitions guide our judgment for any of our fields of competence, [and] teach us enough probabilistic principles, but they are heavily culture bound' (Douglas, 1994, p. 57).

Complexity and variety are thus recognised in different cultural conceptions, which give direction for public reforms. Cultural theory can help us describe the complexity of modernisation (or failure/successfulness of reforms in the public sector) because it shares the common denominator. The inherited ideas, beliefs, and values bind society together and are also present in public law; the latter more or less binds us to each other through public interest and solidarity. Public opinion should not be used primarily for enhanced consultation and dialogue with citizens in search of greater legitimacy but to gain insight into people's values on a particular topic. The next chapter will show how culture reflects decisions that are also reflected in the (un) successfulness of public reforms.

THE GRID AND GROUP CULTURAL MODEL

One of the well-known typologies for the distribution of values within a population is Douglas's grid and group analysis (Douglas, 1982, 2003, 2012);[7] it shows the connections between the different kinds of social organisation and the values that support them. Her model of the distribution of values gives – under the grid and group as the basic dimensions of sociality – a fourfold typology of solidarity or four ideal types of cultural bias: individualism, hierarchy, fatalism, and egalitarianism:

Douglas's GGCT model applied Hood in the field of public management because 'a cultural theory approach has much to offer the art of the state as a framework approach for creative thinking about available forms of organization and exploring the variety of what-to-do ideas that will always surround public services and government' (1998, p. 241). To him '[t]here there is no universal agreement on what

Figure 1. Some synonyms for the four quadrants of the grid and group
(Fardon, 1999, p. 224)

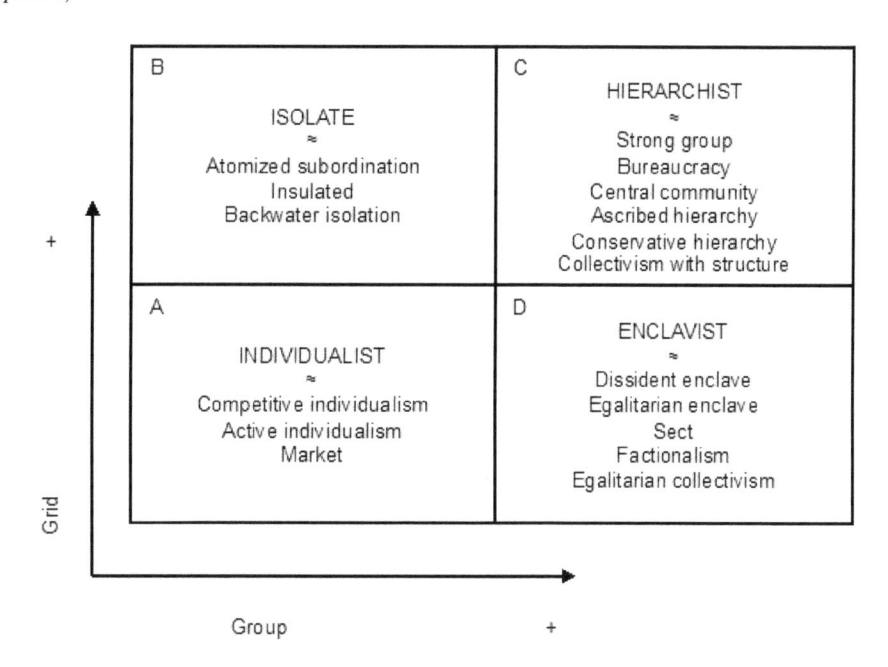

B	C
ISOLATE ≈ Atomized subordination Insulated Backwater isolation	HIERARCHIST ≈ Strong group Bureaucracy Central community Ascribed hierarchy Conservative hierarchy Collectivism with structure
A	D
INDIVIDUALIST ≈ Competitive individualism Active individualism Market	ENCLAVIST ≈ Dissident enclave Egalitarian enclave Sect Factionalism Egalitarian collectivism

Grid (vertical axis, +)
Group (horizontal axis, +)

counts as "problem" and what as "solution", or when the point is reached where the "solution" becomes worse than the "problem" (1998, pp. 24–25). For an individualist, the best approach is present in the competitive market; a hierarchic believes in expertise and authority, egalitarian in the power of groups in consensus, while an isolative fatalist does not address these topics due to the large burden of norms that hold him down. For Douglas, all cultures can be assessed and classified according to these ways of life, which constitute an exhaustive list of viable cultural possibilities. However, this cannot yet provide sufficient grounds for understanding them; countries should know what values prevail within their borders to effectively apply reforms, and a warning should be made before transferring legal institutes from other countries that do not have the same values. Nevertheless, these ideal types (that in reality display more dynamic and multiple passages from one part of the square to the other), can be helpful in arranging the tools of administrative law to be properly used in real situations.

Cultures can be assessed and classified due to their ways of life: they constitute a list of viable cultural perspectives/possibilities. Before importing foreign ideas, governments should know the values that prevail in foreign countries to have effective reforms at home. Different values will probably produce different effects. Based on the typology presented, agencies could be placed on Douglas's grid and group model that, due to their cultural differences, also have different results and ways of doing things:

Ashby's requisite variety is a method of operation (to amplify or filter), not a goal per se. We have to select the most appropriate regulative and economic tools (as amplifiers and filters) from those that are legally and materially available. Regulatory approaches require changes in behaviour by introducing negative/positive effects (penalties, higher prices/bonuses, permissions) for those who do or do not comply with regulatory provisions. Only then can the requisite variety achieve its goal. Douglas's GGCT model can be used for a better interpretation of a particular regulatory tool and its placement in a specific field within the square according to people's preferences. An analysis of people's preferences (whether they incline more towards being individualists or loners and/or whether they prefer a relationship of subordination and superiority instead of that of equality in the group or vice versa) would give better opportunities to choose the most appropriate policies and their corresponding tools. An online voting platform for people to voice their opinions and choices by filling out questionnaires or surveys on political views or similar issues important to them could provide a better means of selecting the most appropriate regulatory tool. This could be implemented by IT and, as a matter of fact, has already been done with Hofstede's cultural dimensions.

Table 1. Cultural typology of agencies (own construction)

Residual(meta) governance – agencies "enforced" from outside of the countries in development, or the countries as candidates for the EU membership ("remote steering"), decentralisation	*Hierarchy*The conventional formats for governing involving hierarchy, authority, command and control, and uniformity were once effective mechanisms but increasingly have been challenged on several grounds.
*Individualist*NPM: attention to lessons from private-sector management; the growth of hands-on "management" and of "arm's length" organizations where policy implementation was organizationally distanced from the policy-makers; a focus upon entrepreneurial leadership within public service organizations; emphasis on inputs and output control and evaluation, and upon performance management and audit; the disaggregation of public services to their most basic units and a focus on their cost management (Osborne, 2010, pp. 3–4).	*Enclave*(new) public governance that advances the plural and pluralist state, concerned with the institutional and external environmental pressures (Osborne, 2010).

ORGANISATIONAL STRATEGY, STRUCTURE, AND PROCESS

Before we turn to Hofstede's dimensions, we must mention another model that is similar to Douglas's GGCT model, namely the adaptive cycle model of Miles et al. (1978). Within this model there are three "problems" of organisational adaptation: the entrepreneurial problem (goal – strategy), the engineering problem (system – technology), and the administrative problem (structure – process). Performance depends on the adoption of strategies, systems, and processes that align with the environment of an organisation. Organisations must employ strategies for solving problems according to essentially three strategic types of organisations: Defenders, Analysers, and Prospectors,[8] while the fourth, Reactor, is residual and occurs when a business lacks insight, or if it fails to take advantage of alignment opportunities afforded by the adaptive cycle. Andrews et al. (2012), based on the work of Miles and Snow (2003), focused on the impact of strategic management on the effectiveness of public services. They have established that:

> high performance appears to be more likely for public organizations that match their decision-making structure with their strategic stance. Defending organizations with a high degree of hierarchical authority and low staff participation in decision-making, in particular, perform better, but prospecting organizations with high decision participation are also likely to do well. By contrast, hierarchy of authority and participation in decision-making make no difference to the performance of reacting organizations (Andrews et al., 2012, pp. 124–125).

They have statistically confirmed that the degree of both hierarchy of authority and participation in decision-making is unrelated to how well services perform, but on the other hand, *strategies work better if they are aligned with the organisational structure*: rational planning with hierarchy and centralisation (while centralisation is unrelated to performance with an absence of strategy), and logical incrementalism with decentralised responsibility.[9] 'Public managers should not seek the best strategy but ought to identify and accommodate the many contingencies that shape the success of different strategies: 'what counts is the combination of strategy with other influences on organizational outcomes' (2012, p. 150). If we want the right fit between the desired goals, we should be aware of the ways in which they are formed. Miles and Snow are one step ahead of Douglas because they emphasize the right fit between strategy, systems, and process, and not just the strategic typologies. The latter can be aligned with Douglas's GGCT model in the following way: Hierarchist – Defender; Individualist – Prospector; Enclavist – Analyser; Isolate – Reactor. This typology and Douglas's GGCT model will now be used in Hofstede's cultural dimensions.

CULTURAL DIMENSIONS

Geert Hofstede has examined variations in values and organisational norms over three decades in fifty countries. A cultural perspective has quite a lot to do with public management reform because 'Hofstede's measures…reflect the broad cultural climates in which management reforms will have to be announced, interpreted, promoted, and resisted in each particular country' (Pollitt & Bouckaert, 2011, p. 64). In the style of cultural relativism, Hofstede et al. claim '[w]e cannot change the way people in a country think, feel, and act by simply importing foreign institutions…Each country has to struggle through its own type of reforms, adapted to the software of its people's minds' (2010, p. 25). According to them, there are six dimensions of culture that can be measured in relation to other cultures, but here we shall use only the 1st, 2nd and 4th dimensions:[10]

1. Power Distance; it is defined as "the extent to which the less powerful members of institutions and organizations within a country expect and accept that power is distributed unequally" (ibid, p. 61). 2. Collectivism versus Individualism; "individualism pertains to societies in which the ties between individuals are loose: everyone is expected to look after him or herself and his or her immediate family. Collectivism as its opposite pertains to societies in which people from birth onward are integrated into strong, cohesive in-groups, which throughout people's lifetime continue to protect them in exchange for unquestioning loyalty" (ibid, p. 92). 4. Uncertainty Avoidance; "the extent to which the members of a culture feel threatened by ambiguous or unknown situations" (2010, p. 191).

If these dimensions and their specifics are applied to the actions of the countries, the differences between them can be more easily understood. The following sections attempt to do exactly that. Hofstede's cultural dimensions can first be compared with Douglas's GGC model: the latter is similar to Hofstede's collectivism versus power distance (first two dimensions). The power distance corresponds to the grid, while individualism versus collectivism corresponds to the group. Many countries that score high on the power distance index, PDI (the horizontal axis) score low on the individualism index, IDV (vertical axis), and vice versa. They are either hierarchical or individualistic. Countries with low PDI and IDV are enclavist, and those with high PDI and IDV are isolative. Although the first two fit very well into Hofstede's classification, the enclavist and isolative do not. It should be stressed that Douglas's model is an ideal type. It is a useful methodological device to begin comparing biases within related cultures with; however, a social reality is more complex. Her description of the isolate and egalitarian positions can hold if we are within[11] a nation's culture, but if we compare cultures, the positions exchange places: the isolate becomes egalitarian and vice versa. Countries with a high grid value and a low group value are more consensus-oriented and egalitarian; their rankings and ordering are the usual ways of controlling the social impact, they have (modest) citizen participation, problems of leadership, authority, and decision making, whereas countries with a low grid value and a high group value (from their point of view) might be more influenced by randomness, isolation, and dependence on other countries. This is shown in the next section.

BETWEEN CONCEPTIONS AND COUNTRIES

The legal and administrative framework within which individuals, companies, and governments interact determines an institutional environment that is codetermined also by socio(cultural)-economic context. Although the latter is mainly influenced by technology, place, and time, an institutional environment depends on the fit between the strategies, tools, and procedures of the implementation processes. This will be verified by analysing the global competitiveness and human development indexes. Because the focus is on PAs, the quality of institutions, and the quality of life are relevant here. Both indexes for specific countries will be transferred to Hofstede's PDI v. IDV model (Figure 1). The numbers added into his model are the rankings of the quality of institutions from The Global Competitiveness Report 2012-2013 (Schwab, 2012), and the numbers in the brackets are the Human Development Index 2011 rankings (2011):

As can be seen in the figure above, the highest-ranking institutions and the highest quality of life can be found in the Prospector (Individualist) countries (e.g. Norway, New Zealand, the Netherlands), but also in the Defender (Hierarchist) countries (e.g. Singapore, Japan). Although this confirms the analysis of Andrews et al. – that neither centralised nor decentralized decision making has an independent effect

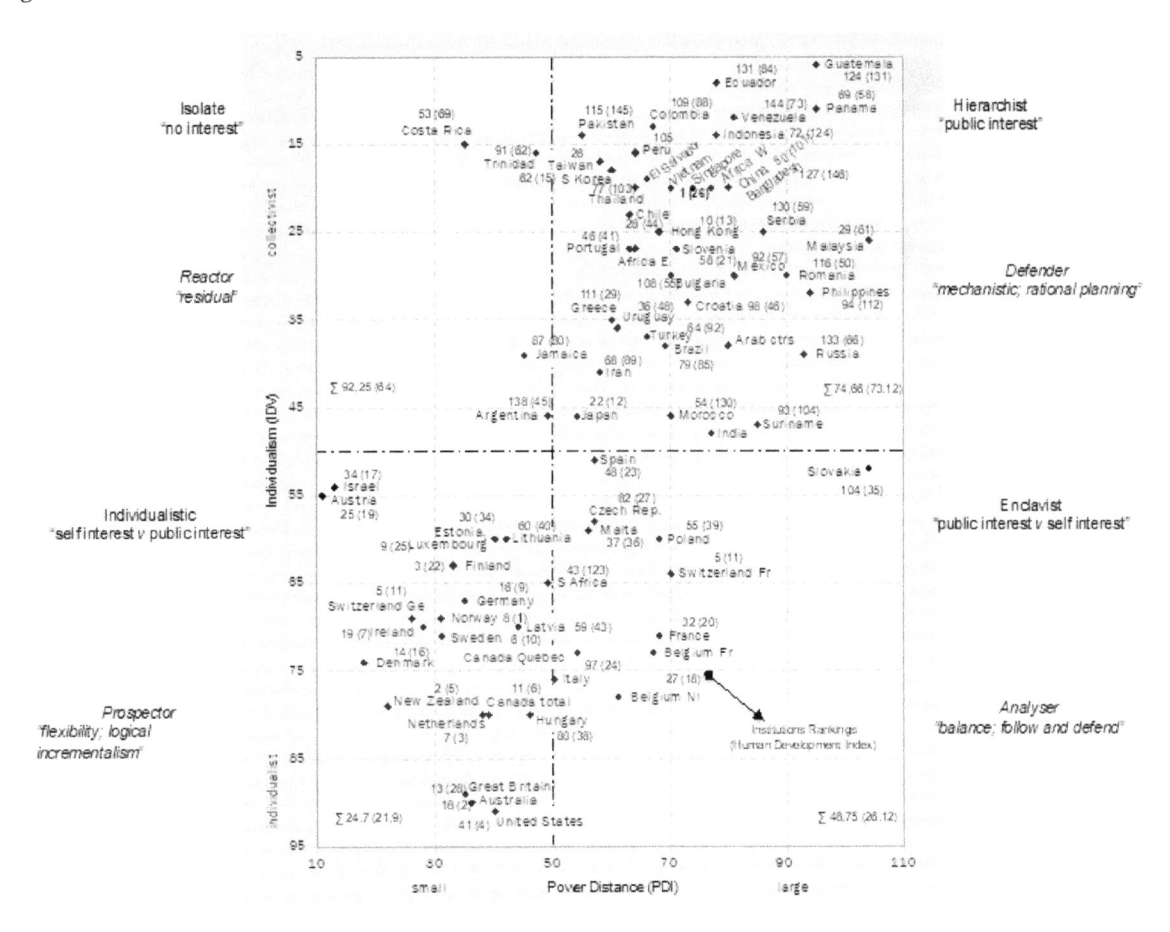

The Importance of Culture and Values in Public Reforms

Figure 2. Power distance versus individualism[12]

on public service performance – the average number of countries in each quadrant confirms even more Miles and Snow (2003) arguments that an organisation's overall strategy must fit its environment, organizational structures and management processes, while the entire organisation must continually adapt to maintain its fit over time. The top countries can be found in the lower quadrants and in the right upper quadrant, but the average numbers show that 1) the Prospector area of Prospector ($\sum$ 24,7 [21,9]) is the most favourable place for institutions and in terms of quality of life; 2) the Analyser area of Analyser ($\sum$ 48,75 [26,12]) is in the middle of those countries where the quality of institutions drops faster than the quality of life; and 3) in the Defender area of Defender ($\sum$ 74,66 [73,12]) the quality of institutions is lower than that of Analyser and higher than that of Reactor ($\sum$ 92,25 [64]), but the quality of life is the lowest. Therefore, it is inappropriate for governments to use the same approach and tools for different goals, or even for the same goals at different times or places. The Defender (Hierarchist) countries can be as good as the Analyser (Enclavist) or Prospector (Individualist) ones, while all must take care of the right fit between goals, tools, and processes. In large power-distance countries, hierarchy causes a considerable dependence of subordinates on the rulers and rules, or vice versa, on rational planning, centralisation, and information channels. Defender should use Defender tools and processes; Analyser and Prospector should use their own, while Reactor usually uses those of Defender. Collectivist countries should be careful when using individualistic methods for economic incentives, while individualistic countries could use collective methods mainly for the rule of law and basic social welfare.

The figure can also highlight a set of ideal types to manage performance. To Bouckaert and Halligan, '[t]he compatibility of performance systems and tools with the broader public administration framework is important because there is little evidence that a strong performance focus can co-exist with an inconsistent public administration context' (2007, p. 198). They chose countries of different cultural and political administration systems, with a high level of commitment to apply the results in practice (Australia, Canada, the Netherlands, Sweden, the United Kingdom, and the United States), but according to Hofstede's PDI v. IDV, these countries belong to the lower left quadrant, where the power distance is small and individualism is high (in Douglas's model they belong to the low group and the low grid section, ie, individualism). They are not as different as it seems after all. People want to decrease uncertainty. As laws and rules are, among other methods (religion, culture, technology) most convenient for reducing uncertainty, uncertainty avoidance can be presented to show differences between countries (Figure 2), first because of its similarity to the law, that is, with legal certainty and legal expectations.

In the figure above, Singapore and New Zealand are the starting points, being the countries of the first and of the second rank in terms of the quality of institutions. The arrows point from these two countries to the countries that are in their neighbourhoods, while here are placed more apart due to the uncertainty avoidance dimension. Countries within the quadrant of individualistic countries (with low PDI and high IDV) in the PDI – IDV model retained a more similar position than countries with high PDI and low IDV. Due to the added uncertainty avoidance dimension, countries with high PDI and high IDV are more similar to countries with low IDV (Portugal, Slovenia, Serbia, South Korea, and Chile with France and Belgium). Although the last two states place high value on individualism, it seems that it is not as powerful as in the countries with the same degree of individualism but with a smaller PDI (otherwise the uncertainty avoidance value would be similar as for the first cited countries). According to the Global Competitiveness Index, the inefficient government bureaucracy is among the most problematic factors for doing business (Schwab, 2012). The figures of power distance versus individualism and power distance versus uncertainty avoidance can give some explanation of why the "euphoria" of NPM cannot bring good results to NPM in the areas of reactor, protector, or analyzer (from worse to less bad): countries in these areas have other backgrounds and use different models for institutions and rules. The ideas (e.g., "let the middle managers manage' and / or 'slim down central civil service"') are not as easily achieved in countries with a high PDI and a high(er) IDV as they can be in those with a low PDI and a low (er) IDV.

Countries in the Prospector (Individualist) area, with a high IDV and low PDI, are on average the best for maintaining competitiveness and the quality of life – but only on average. The top countries in terms of these criteria are also found in the areas of Analyser (Enclavist) and Defender (Hierarchist), although they represent a minority among the countries of the same type. Creating a strategy with the right tools and processes is vital for overall success. Introducing the NPM in hierarchical countries might cause the side effect of a larger bureaucracy, more public servants, waste of money and resources, re-regulation, higher corruption,[14] etc., because they are not accustomed to the decentralised methods of organisation and individualistic mentality; individualistic countries should be cautious about introducing hierarchical elements because these diminish democracy and freedom, as well as enhance control and obedience. All of these elements are elements of centralised organisations, which from a collectivist point of view are essential for good administration. People living in hierarchical countries do not view their freedom as the people of individualistic ones; they have a different perspective, so it is not useful

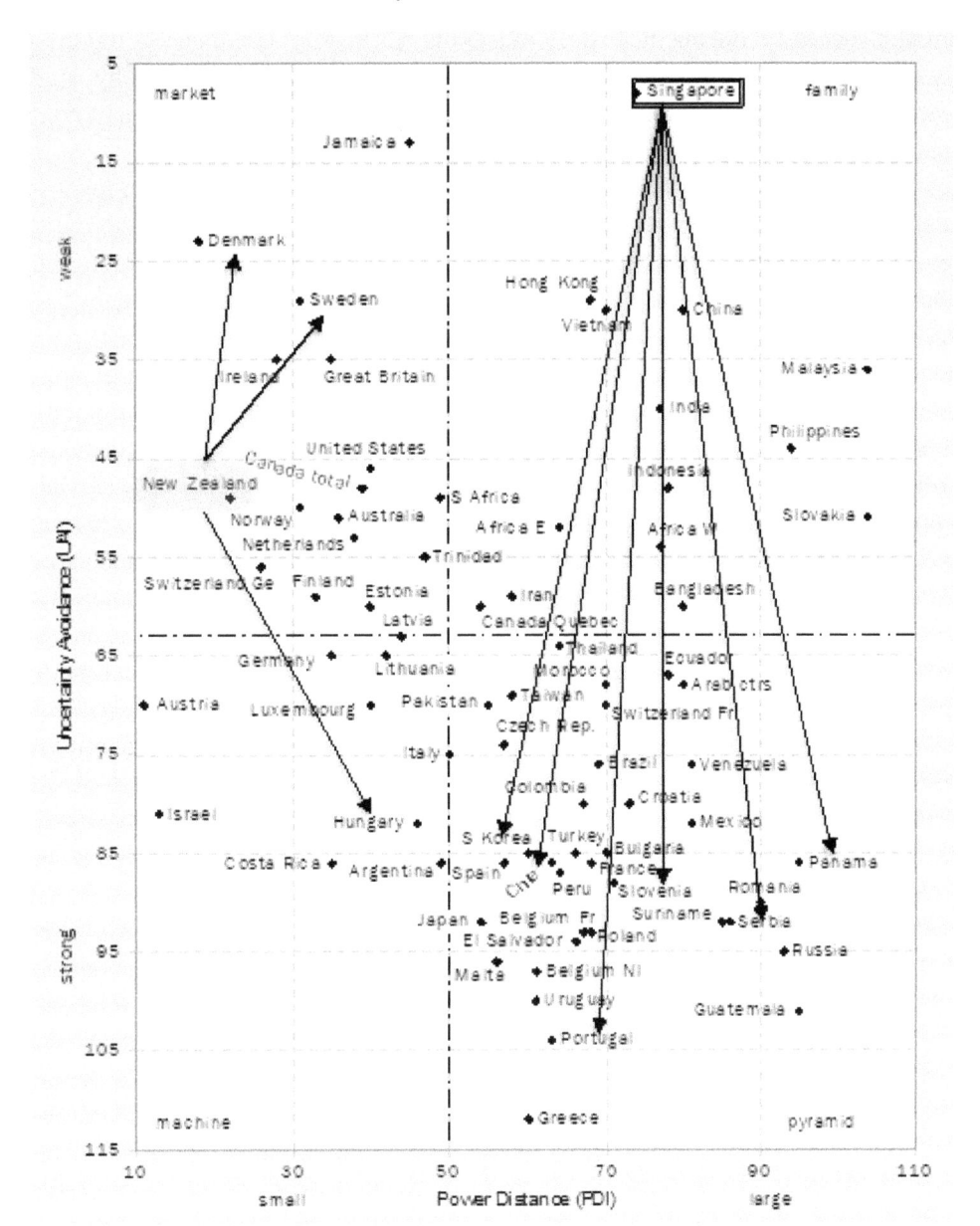

The Importance of Culture and Values in Public Reforms

Figure 3. Power distance versus uncertainty avoidance[13]

to talk about freedom from the individualistic point of view in hierarchical countries, just as it is useless to talk about the 'selfish' individualistic mentality from the hierarchical point of view. Exporting ideas to other countries without regard to their respective contexts and values into which new ideas are transferred can have limited success (although the transfer is well-intentioned). In addition to a different cultural context, there are also complexity and randomness that replace determinism and rationalism. Apart from determinism and rationalism, there are also other elements which (un)intentionally or (un)knowingly affect the behaviour of different parts that affect/change decisions. Properties are constantly changing, and we know only where they are at the time of our measurement or interaction with them, but not where they are now. Every country has its own causes for the prevalence of specific values (they have been proven successful during the history of a country's history; they have stored information that is constantly transmitted into values). Values can be changed only incrementally, by small steps. The human power to move and change physical things is, or can be, used for the efficient control over our psychological elements, which we can influence indirectly through our activities.[15]

Activities that cause failure or success are usually formed in a sequence; each level represents its distinct tendency, but together they form an interactive whole in which higher levels provide the context for the lower ones. Imitation is the most basic force known from our childhood. Through imitation, we establish practices that can prevent us from using new techniques or tools. This tendency to resist change is called the law of inertia and can be changed only by a net external force. At first, we are in denial because previous practices have proved to be successful; we are unwilling to try something new and put even more force into implementing the established practices (exaggeration). The cumulative effects of these stages ultimately manifest themselves in a paradigm shift, from "it has always been done this way" to "we are going to challenge our assumptions as often as we can". Unpredictability can be undermined by predictions and preparation. Multiminded purposeful organisations are the basic requirement for all countries (i.e. with a high or low PDI or IDV) to enable the amplifiers and filters (managing variety) to be formed at the right time and place. There is a constant need for better information in PAs, but apart from information, a commitment to evaluate it – and to change our practice if this is necessary for better results – is much appreciated. An answer to what is needed, urgent, or better can be found only in the relative (higher or lower) importance of our goals that emanate from our values. Each country or decision-maker must create its own model that will correspond not only to its (overall) ranking but to characteristics within its own cultural dimension.

The World Values Survey should not be disregarded in this context; for Inglehart and Welzel, the world cross-cultural variation is based on two dimensions: i) traditional values vs. secular-rational values and ii) survival values versus self-expression values.[16]

Therefore, decision makers must be attentive to different cultural, social, economic, and other backgrounds. They affect other decisions also; they affect what will (not) work. Reality is more complex than the legal rules or decisions of public agencies today. Taking a system apart does not reveal much about its relations and operations. Its vitality and purpose are related to other systems and relevant processes that do not always lead systems to inevitable and distinct ends. Cultural predisposition as the real purpose of action can be slowly changed by the longevity determination and modelling behaviour if appropriate strategies, tools, and processes are used. The institutional environment depends on the fit between strategies, tools, and implementation processes, while all derive their meanings and understandings from the cultural value background. Although the introductory idea and hypothesis of this paper can be confirmed, it has only methodological validity. Countries should consider dependencies between decisions and their (cultural) predispositions; a general nomothetic recipe cannot bring the same results in different countries (even technology can have different results in different countries, although differences might be smaller than in the law and/or public agencies). Countries have inevitable differences and specifics that form their specific varieties. The latter can be addressed only with opposite varieties within the mix of organisational strategies, structure, and process that corresponds to specific cultural dimensions.

Reforms can be successful, not only if they include cultural dimensions, but primarily if they serve as the starting point of reform. The latter are always, de facto, heavily burdened with values. Hood's core values in public management are the Sigma-type values (match resources to defined tasks),[17] Theta-type value (honesty, fairness, mutuality) and Lambda-type values (reliability, robustness, adaptivity) (Hood,

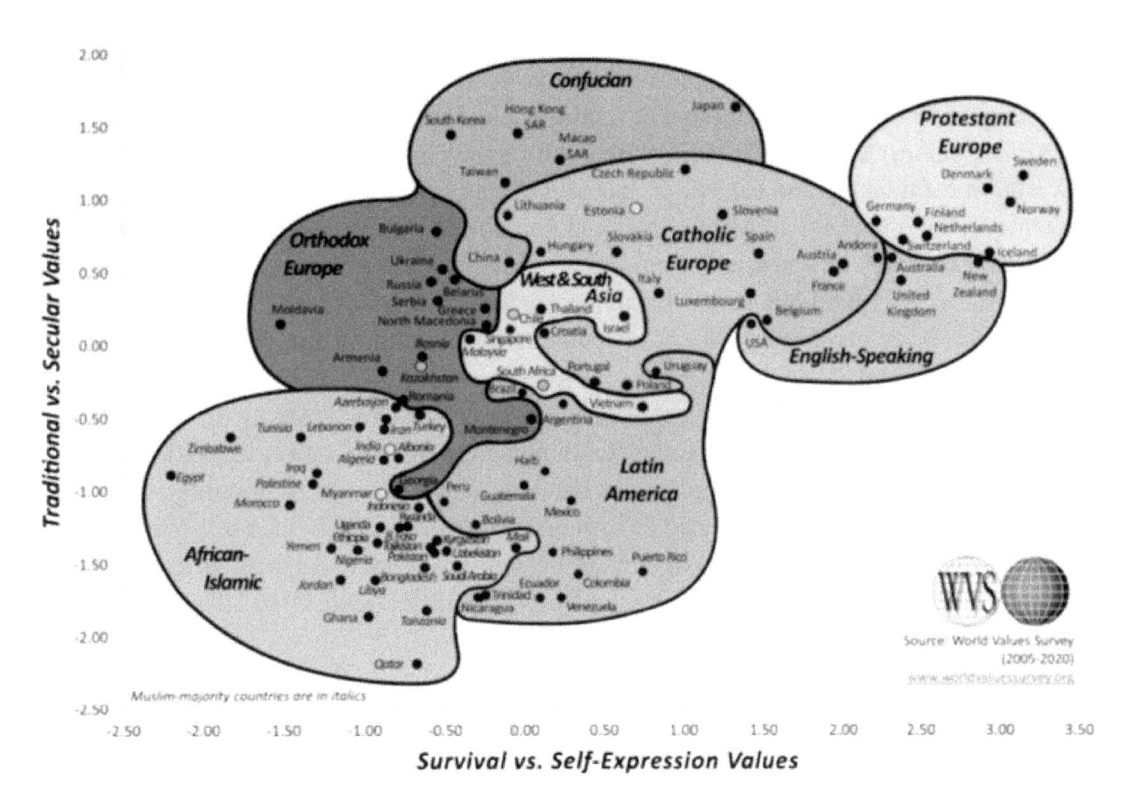

The Importance of Culture and Values in Public Reforms

Figure 4. The Inglehart-Welzel World Cultural Map (2020)
(World Values Survey Association, 2020)

1991). As the first two are traditionally present in public administration, the third is the most appealing essence of public agencies. Due to their lesser burden on the numerous laws and public employees, interest communities, big ministries, long innovation/approval paths present in the traditional (*robust-stable*) public administration, agencies could have their relevant *raison d'être* in the *flexibility* and *agility* leading towards *resilience,* along with taking into account the previous Sigma and Theta-type values. The name of Hood's values is not explained, but as mythological symbols they fit the meaning of the relevant Greek letters: sigma (a measure of volatility), theta (a symbol of death) and lambda (numerous characters): letters could inversely represent reasonableness, life, and stability specific to the context of their use.

VERSIONS OF PUBLIC AGENCIES IN DIFFERENT ENVIRONMENTS

Decision makers should first divide the processes into two large fields: *Newtonian mechanics* with simple, more certain, and uniform distributions (short-tail Gaussian distribution) where the probability (of decreasing part of the distribution is effectively short and thus) increases, and *complexity*, where dynamism, flexibility, uncertainty, diversity or variability, and ambiguity prevail (long-tail distribution), where the probability (of increasingly large numbers far from any central area of the distribution) due to power-law distribution and exponential distribution decreases. The complex environment has no solution that would be valid at all times and for all similar cases, and thus makes simple solutions ineffective. It is thus of utmost importance to know in which of those two field solutions are proposed. Administrative and any kind of other *viable* behaviour is based on the most important (human) factor of *adaptation* to its surroundings. All that is to hand in the complex environment is confidence in a *process* built up in a knowable or understandable way to gather unknowable or unpredictable data. There is a difference between the incremental or partial solving of a problem and its dissolving so that the problem as such does not exist anymore (Ackoff, 1978) and/or between single- and double-loop learning, where the latter reshapes patterns of thinking and behaviour that govern actions (Argyris, 2006). In complex situations, solutions invented in the classic, linear, stable, and non-dynamic environment are not effective. Public agencies should take this into account during their implementation of public tasks. A public agency that thinks systemically should consider this to have effective system management. In Figure 1 below, various possibilities are given with respect to problems / stimuli and solutions/responses to achieve a better reaction from public agencies.

The diagonal line is *the requisite variety* or *line of adaptation*, which starts with the straight line in a routinised regime where appropriate solutions to known problems are always found, to the curved one, where solutions are increasingly ambiguous, to the open one at the top right corner, where solutions are unknown in advance and can solely be determined *postfestum* as good/bad in a trial-and-error procedure or experimentation. Here, chaos or a black swan reigns as an event with three attributes: rarity, extreme impact, and retrospective (not prospective) predictability (Taleb, 2010). The diagonal line from

Figure 5. Reigns in the requisite variety

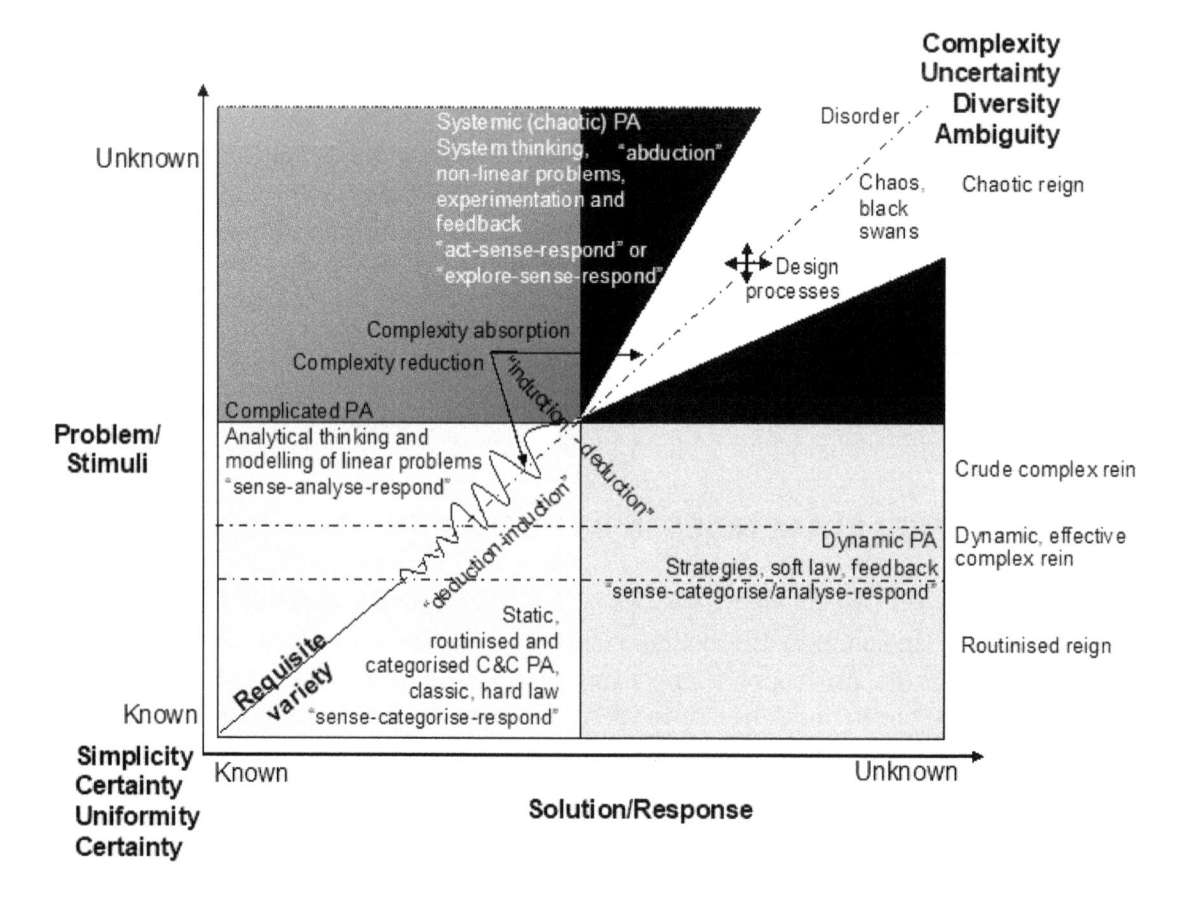

bottom left to top right can also be a change from the central, hierarchic, and homogeneous model of government with equality, proportionality, balance, and averages towards the heterarchic, decentralised, heterogenic, net model of difference, unbalances, extremes, or unique cases. In complex and chaotic regimes, a power law prevails as a relationship in which a relative change in one quantity gives rise to a disproportional change in the other quantity, independent of the initial size of those quantities (Bar-Yam, 2011) and exponential functions. A division among the (un)known problems and solutions can give different versions of PAs; the latter do not fit firmly in any one quadrant but have movable positions in this 'problem solution' space.

Classic and Dynamic Public Agency

A classical command-and-control public agency is based on static and routinised practices with high enough frequencies to achieve statistical representation, sampling, and probability. Here, the hard law is usable. A dynamic public agency is along the stable environment faced with the dynamic but still manageable (effective) and also with the unmanageable (crude) complexity. It is still based on hard law, but it also uses government strategies, programs, white and green books, guidelines, and other methods of soft law. Feedback is (more) intuitively applied here (systematically). Both types of public agency are based on the sense-categorise-respond and sense-categorise/analyse-respond methods.

Complicated Public Agency

There is a difference between 'complicated' and 'complex'. The first is present when components can be separated and dealt with in a reductionist and logical way relying on a set of static rules and algorithms (an assembly of a space shuttle is complicated but still based on order, control, known cause-effect relations, and thus predictable behaviour); the second one is present when one cannot separate parts and for which there are no rules, algorithms, or natural laws. It is based on interconnectedness that leads to characteristics such as adaptive behaviour and leaderless emergence (Nason, 2017). A complicated public agency deals with the complicated problems of education, healthcare, traffic, public utilities, elderly, pension systems, migrations, etc., which can be ultimately predictable with sufficient analysis and modelling. Here, government research units, universities, and research institutions can be helpful. The complicated public agency deals with problems that can be bound together in manageable linear relationships in which Gaussian averages prevail. Here, the sense-analyse-respond method is (mainly) applied (along with the three methods mentioned three methods).

The difference between 'complicated' and 'complex' can be established with the help of the Turing test, designed by Alan Turing (1950) as an imitation game in which an evaluator must decide whether he or she is speaking with a machine or with a human, while both are hidden behind a curtain. The same approach can be used to determine (administrative or any other) complexity: if an evaluator cannot determine which respondent (an administrative expert on one side or a machine, robot, citizen, temporary worker, or intern to the other) has replied on the question, then a state of (administrative) complexity is present. In contrast, when a difference was determined in favour of an expert, there is a complicated or even a simple state. As a general rule of thumb, Nason's framework for classifying system types can also be used:

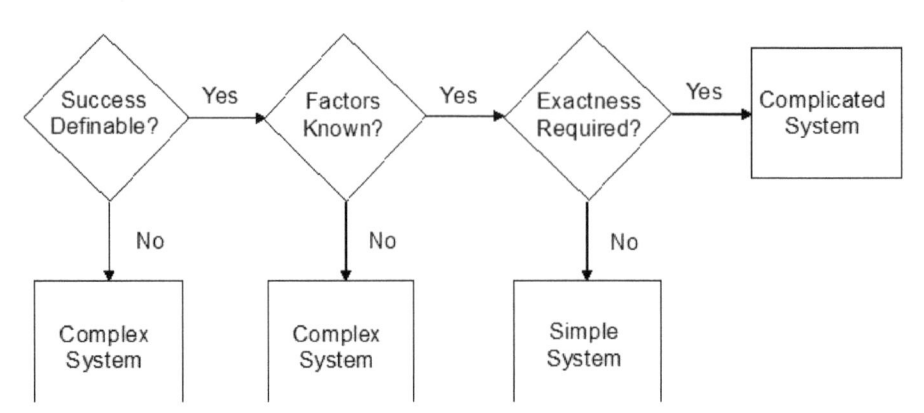

Figure 6. Decision framework for classifying system type
(Nason, 2017)

```
         Yes              Yes              Yes
Success ─────→ Factors ─────→ Exactness ─────→ Complicated
Definable?     Known?         Required?        System
   │              │               │
   │ No           │ No            │ No
   ↓              ↓               ↓
Complex        Complex         Simple
System         System          System
```

The framework is based on three easy-to-answer questions in which some elements (e.g., unpredictability, emergence, equifinality, and exponentiality) of complexity are left out of the framework because they are difficult to identify before they appear.

Lean Public Agency

Among the dynamic and complicated public administration is Seddon's *freedom from command and control*. Public agencies gain legitimacy through the trust of citizens, which is obtained when public goals are met. Organisations should be managed as systems rather than as functional hierarchies, where command and control rules are 'an organisational prison' (Deming, 2000). Seddon emphasizes lean management, which should be – as the effectiveness of the system – designed and measured in terms of customer purposes, a systematic analysis of demand, studying the flow of work or how everything works end-to-end from the customer's point of view, and how the service is redesigned to meet the customers' demands. He developed the 'Check-Plan-Do' methodology as a variation of Deming's 'Plan-Do-Check-Act' model (Deming, 2000), which starts with 'Check' (rather than "Plan") from the customer's point of view. Then successively follows the analysis of the type and frequency of customer demands on the system, the capability of the response of a system, the workflow, its value and waste, and the causes of waste located with the system: structure, measures, process design, procedures, information technology, and management roles that determine how work is carried out. Now, finally, you can see how the current thinking about the design and management of work is the root cause of suboptimal performance:[18]

With an emphasis on the purpose and effectiveness of a citizen, system thinking can also deliver efficiency improvements as a second-order result. This type of thinking (see Figure 4) demands clear answers regarding purpose, demand (the value and failure demand; the first is what an institution has been established to serve and what customers want, that is of value to them; the second is the demand that the institution cannot serve due to a lack of information or supporting operations), capability (to deliver end products against the purpose of the system), workflow (all the various steps and decision points in the flow), redesign (experiments with new methods of working in the 'Plan' part and implementation in the rest of the organisation in the 'Do' part) and the key points of new arrangements.

The Importance of Culture and Values in Public Reforms

Figure 7. Performance improvement through "check-plan-do"
(Seddon, 2005, p. 156)

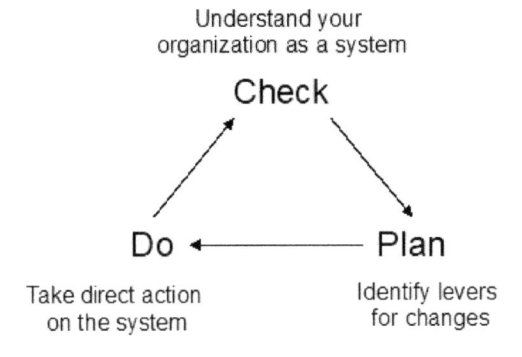

```
           Understand your
         organization as a system
                Check
               /     \
              /       \
             /         ↘
          Do  ←———————  Plan
      Take direct action    Identify levers
        on the system        for changes
```

Figure 8. Check the model of system analysis
(Seddon, 2005, p. 158)

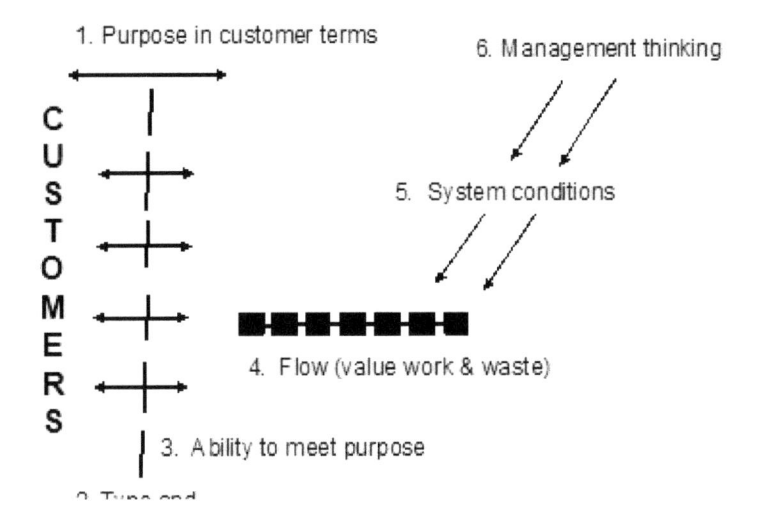

```
         1. Purpose in customer terms        6. Management thinking

     C                                         ↘ ↘
     U                                          
     S                                      5. System conditions
     T                                          ↘ ↘
     O
     M                       ■■■■■■■
     E
     R               4. Flow (value work & waste)
     S
              3. Ability to meet purpose
```

From the workflow onward, especially, there are specific institutional-type conditions and a way of thinking that can be changed by analysing data that could show an emerging problem within the *predispositions* of decision makers. The purpose of the system in the public sector is multidimensional and layered; a precise answer should be given to the question of *who* a customer is. The idea 'what matters is what matters to the customer' can be true when collected transparently and democratically from a *diverse* range of stakeholders ('requisite variety'). Although important, customer focus is also subject to customer predispositions, based on their previous experience. Therefore, the 'Check' phase should be reconfirmed or redesigned with the help of all involved on all sides. Due to the higher dynamics of the system, cybernetics, and complexity theory that go into the check model, decision makers must cope with the increased complexity. Here, systemic (based on the chaotic as its contra pole) public administration is present.

Systemic or Complex Public Agency

Classic reductionist approaches are of limited use when complex social problems are considered. A complex situation is 'a whole made up of complicated or interrelated parts' (Merriam-Webster, 2018), which is due to multiple, mixed relations and interrelated causative forces that are difficult to define; it can or may not change slightly or significantly when applied in connection with some other element. It may not have one "best" answer. It has no (or few) precedents with many stakeholders and different perspectives and is often surprise prone. Complex adaptive systems self-organise out of relations between structures and their parts that affect each other in a constant dynamic of change and adjustment. There is usually no direct cause-and-effect chain, only layers of causes that, as outputs, affect other causes and effects in a nonstop and circular way. They are governed by feedback, are resistant to change (path dependence), and are characterised by non-linear relationships. Chapman's parable of throwing a rock and a bird visually explains the difference between the mechanistic linear approach and the holistic, systemic approach to policy: '[m]echanical linear models are excellent for understanding where the rock will end up, but useless for predicting the trajectory of a bird – even though both are subject to the same laws of physics' (Chapman, 2004, p. 19). Systems theory fits into institutional versions of regulations that evolve around biological adaptation, on how living organisms self-regulate and relate to their environment. 'One of the central findings of systems theory is that systems tend to be closed, self-referential "spaces" that perpetuate their own existence by a series of operations and a system of language that is only comprehensible internally to those who speak the language of the system and understand its workings' (Morgan & Yeung, 2007, p. 69).

The systemic public agency as a 'vehicle of modernity in rational legisprudence' relies on systemic thinking, filtered data from the environment, increased experimentation with test groups, patterns based on stocks and flows, actions based on the principle of care and precautions that apply thresholds to which pre-advanced determined responses were established using a variety of different and numerous inputs. All variations of public agencies can be adaptable in their own ways; they can be defined as 'systemic public agencies' if they apply the basic elements of the system. Therefore, they must continuously adapt through a regulatory cycle and follow relations in which institutions, their structures, processes, and purposes mutually connect. Due to its focus on results, cooperation between multiple actors in the internal and external environment of the public agency is needed in all forms of public administration. To produce change, it develops a desired future goal and purpose, defines elements according to which a future system will operate, creates sensors and thresholds that can sense and react to differences (that is, information) and starts to adapt a set of interventions that can convert an existing system into a desired one.

REFERENCES

Ackoff, R. L. (1978). *The Art of Problem Solving: Accompanied by Ackoff's Fables*. John Wiley & Sons.

Andrews, R., Boyne, G., Law, J., & Walker, R. (2012). *Strategic Management and Public Service Performance*. Palgrave Macmillan. doi:10.1057/9780230349438

Argyris, C. (2006). *Reasons and Rationalizations: The Limits to Organizational Knowledge*. Oxford University Press.

Armstrong, M. (2003). A Handbook of Human Resource Management Practice (9th ed.). London and Sterling: Kogan Page Publishers.

Bar-Yam, Y. (2011). Concepts: Power Law. NECSI. http://www.necsi.edu/guide/concepts/powerlaw.html

Bouckaert, G., & Halligan, J. (2007). *Managing Performance: International Comparisons*. Routledge. doi:10.4324/9780203935958

Chapman, J. (2004). *System Failure: Why Governments Must Learn to Think Differently*. Demos.

Crozier, M. (1964). Bureaucratic Phenomenon (y First edition edition). Chicago: University of Chicago Press.

Deming, W. E. (2000). *Out of the Crisis*. MIT Press.

Douglas, M. (1982). *Essays in the Sociology of Perception*. Routledge Kegan & Paul.

Douglas, M. (1986). *How Institutions Think*. Syracuse University Press.

Douglas, M. (1994). *Risk and Blame: Essays in Cultural Theory*. Routledge.

Douglas, M. (2003). *Natural Symbols: Explorations in Cosmology* (3rd ed.). Routledge.

Douglas, M. (2012). *A History of Grid and Group Cultural Theory*. Chass. http://projects.chass.utoronto.ca/semiotics/cyber/douglas1.pdf

Durkheim, E. (1982). *The Rules of Sociological Method* (W. D. Halls, Trans.). The Free Press. doi:10.1007/978-1-349-16939-9

European Commission. (2015). *Quality of Public Administration—A Toolbox for Practitioners*. European Union. https://ec.europa.eu/digital-single-market/en/news/quality-public-administration-toolbox-practitioners

Fardon, R. (1999). *Mary Douglas: An Intellectual Biography*. Routledge.

Glasser, W. (1994). *Kontrolna teorija*. Taxus.

Hofstede, G., Hofstede, G. J., & Minkov, M. (2010). *Cultures and Organizations: Software of the Mind* (3rd ed.). McGraw-Hill.

Hood, C. (1991). A Public Management for All Seasons? *Public Administration*, *69*(1), 3–19. doi:10.1111/j.1467-9299.1991.tb00779.x

Hood, C. (1998). *The Art of the State: Culture, Rhetoric, and Public Management*. Oxford University Press.

Kuipers, S., & Boin, A. (2009). Path Dependence, Institutionalization and the Decline of Two Public Institutions. In G. Schreyögg & J. Sydow (Eds.), *The Hidden Dynamics of Path Dependence: Institutions and Organizations* (pp. 50–69). Palgrave MacMillan.

Lucretius, T. C. (1926). *Lucretius on the Nature of Things*. Clarendon Press.

Luhmann, N. (1996). *Social Systems* (J. B. Jr & D. Baecker, Trans.). Stanford University Press.

Merton, R. K. (1968). *Social Theory and Social Structure*. Free Press.

Miles, R., & Snow, C. (2003). *Organizational Strategy, Structure, and Process* (1st ed.). Stanford Business Books. doi:10.1515/9780804767170

Miles, R. E., Snow, C. C., Meyer, A. D., & Coleman, H. J. Jr. (1978). Organizational Strategy, Structure, and Process. *Academy of Management Review*, *3*(3), 546–562. doi:10.5465/amr.1978.4305755 PMID:10238389

Morgan, B., & Yeung, K. (2007). *An Introduction to Law and Regulation: Text and Materials*. Cambridge University Press. doi:10.1017/CBO9780511801112

Nason, R. (2017). *It's Not Complicated: The Art and Science of Complexity in Business*. University of Toronto Press. doi:10.3138/9781487514778

Nehl, H. P. (1999). *Principles of Administrative Procedure in EC Law*. Hart Publishing.

OECD. (1999). European Principles for Public Administration. (SIGMA Papers, No. 27). OECD. https://www.oecd-ilibrary.org/docserver/download/5kml60zwdr7h.pdf?expires=1459602912&id=id&accname=guest&checksum=AD8421691668211416DB861810C0B737

Ongaro, E. (2010). *Public Management Reform and Modernization: Trajectories of Administrative Change in Italy, France, Greece, Portugal and Spain*. Edward Elgar Pub.

Osborne, S. P. (Ed.). (2010). *The New Public Governance: Emerging Perspectives on the Theory and Practice of Public Governance*. Routledge. doi:10.4324/9780203861684

Parsons, T. (1985). *Talcott Parsons on Institutions and Social Evolution: Selected Writings*. University of Chicago Press.

Pečarič, M. (2018). Legal Principles as Extrapolated Reality. *Archiv Für Rechts- Und Sozialphilosphie*, *104*(3), 397–420.

Pollitt, C., & Bouckaert, G. (2011). *Public Management Reform: A Comparative Analysis - New Public Management, Governance, and the Neo-Weberian State* (3rd ed.). Oxford University Press.

Schwab, K. (2012). The Global Competitiveness Report 2012—2013. *17th PACI Task Force Meeting Executive Summary*. WeForum. https://reports.weforum.org/global-competitiveness-report-2012-2013/

Seddon, J. (2005). *Freedom from Command and Control: Rethinking Management for Lean Service*. Productivity Press.

Simon, H. A. (1997). *Administrative Behavior* (4th ed.). Free Press.

Skinner, B. F. (1969). *Contingencies of Reinforcement: A Theoretical Analysis*. Prentice Hall.

Taleb, N. N. (2010). The Black Swan: The Impact of the Highly Improbable Fragility (Kindle Edition). New York: Random House Publishing Group.

Turing, A. M. (1950). Computing Machinery and Intelligence. *Mind*, 49.

UNDP. (2011). *Human Development Report 2011*. UNDP. https://www.undp.org/content/undp/en/home/librarypage/hdr/human_developmentreport2011.html

Waldo, D. (1948). *The Administrative State: A Study of the Political Theory of American Public Administration*. The Ronald Press Company.

World Values Survey Association. (2020). *WVS Database—Findings and Insights*. WVSA. https://www.worldvaluessurvey.org/WVSContents.jsp

ENDNOTES

[1] Variety or relativity is known for a long time: the Roman poet Lucretius coined the expression in the first century BC, "*quod ali cibus est aliis fuat acre venenum*" (what is food to one, is to others biting poison) (Lucretius, 1926, p. 181).

[2] About Ongaro's *Public Management Reform and Modernization*, Pollitt says 'this book is another nail in the coffin of "generic" public management or "global recipes", because what we see here is some very different types of systems, which exhibit both continuity and change as they pursue distinctive trajectories of their own' (2010, p. viii). Ongaro claims (with regard to a number of important features, however) 'the basic note seems to be one of continuity: the public administration of the five countries under examination [Portugal, Greece, Spain, France and Italy] still displays many of the basic characteristics that could be found 30 or 40, or many more, years ago' (2010, p. 263). According to Pollitt and Bouckaert (2011), from the late 1990s to 2010 there is '[n]o dominant model [of public management, but rather] several key concepts, including governance, networks, partnerships, "joining up", transparency, and trust' (2011, p. 11).

[3] Although the principle of care is now established as a legal requirement, it cannot provide appropriate grounds for making decisions in the first place: principles can be more fully embraced with the help of more systematically-elaborated reality (Pečarič, 2018).

[4] Path dependence theory holds that the mechanisms that bring performance, stability, and external support "lock-in" further organizational development. It suggests that the roots of institutionalization can put an organization on a trajectory from which deviation becomes increasingly difficult over time. Path dependence may thus account for the organization's lack of adaptive capacity. The very path-dependent mechanisms that help an organization institutionalize in its early years may bring about its institutional demise years down the road (Kuipers & Boin, 2009, p. 50). The organisational "lock-in" resembles to Luhmann's operational closure of social systems (they are operationally closed but cognitively open to information) (Luhmann, 1996) or to institutionalization (an active upholding of path-dependence processes).

[5] There are ways of acting, thinking and feeling which possess the remarkable property of existing outside the consciousness of the individual. This is 'a category of facts which present very special characteristic: they consist of manners of acting, thinking and feeling, external to the individual, which are invested with a coercive power by virtue of which they exercise control over him (Durkheim, 1982, p. 52).

[6] There are ways of acting, thinking and feeling which possess the remarkable property of existing outside the consciousness of the individual. This is 'a category of facts which present very special characteristic: they consist of manners of acting, thinking and feeling, external to the individual, which are invested with a corcive power by virtue of which they exercise control over him' (Durkheim, 1982, p. 52).

[7] The group dimension taps the extent to which 'the individual's life is absorbed in and sustained by group membership', while the grid dimension is characterised by 'an explicit set of institutionalised classifications that keeps individuals apart and regulates their interactions' (Douglas, 1982, pp. 202–203).

[8] 1. Defenders are organizations which have narrow product-market domains. Top managers in this type of organization are highly expert in their organization's limited area of operation but do not tend to search outside their domain for new opportunities. These organizations seldom need to make major adjustments in their technology, structure, or methods of operation. Instead, they devote primary attention to improving the efficiency of their existing operations. 2. Prospectors are organizations which almost continually search for market opportunities, and they regularly experiment with potential responses to emerging environmental trends. However, because of their strong concern for product and market innovation, these organizations are usually not completely efficient. 3. Analysers are organizations which operate in two types of product-market domains, one relatively stable, the other changing. In their stable areas, these organizations operate routinely and efficiently through the use of formalized structures and processes. In their more turbulent areas, top managers watch their competitors closely for new ideas, and then they rapidly adopt those which appear to be the most promising. 4. Reactors are organizations in which top managers frequently perceive change and uncertainty occurring in their organizational environments but are unable to respond effectively. Because this type of organization lacks a consistent strategy-structure relationship, it seldom makes adjustments of any sort until forced to do so by environmental pressures (R. Miles & Snow, 2003, p. 29).

[9] Reactors perform better only when they are subject to regulation that complements their existing strategic orientation' (2012, p. 145). 'Prospecting will improve performance if carried out in combination with a high level of decision participation…[while] organizations that adopt a defending strategy enhance their performance if they centralize authority and reduce decision participation' (2012, p. 122).

[10] Because the 3rd, 5th, and 6th one (Femininity versus Masculinity, Long-term versus Short-term Orientation and Indulgence versus Restraint) cannot be connected with Douglas's GGCT model and Miles and Snow's strategic typology, they will all later be put in the model of ranking values in cultural dimensions.

[11] The extreme top on the left side has strong grid controls, without any group membership to sustain individuals. Anyone who arrives here is a cultural isolate…as far as public policy is concerned. Isolates attract no attention; no one asks for their opinion or takes them seriously in argument. Hence their reputation of apathy (Douglas, 2012).

[12] The basic scheme is taken from Hofstede et al. (2010, p. 103). The following has been added to the original scheme: the quality of institutions and human development indices, a grey area indicating the dominant positions of countries between the PDI and IDV, and descriptions next to individual quadrants pointing out the prevailing ideas according to Douglas's GGCT model and Miles and Snow's model of adaptive cycle.

[13] The basic scheme is taken from Hofstede et al. (2010, p. 303). The arrows added to the original figure show how some countries that are close to each other in the PDI – IDV model are here separated.

[14] From 2001 to 2011 the Corruption Perception Index mostly got worse for hierarchical countries: Slovenia (34–37), Croatia (47–62), Russia (79–133), Romania (69–66), Hong Kong (14–14), Brazil

(46–69), Turkey (54–54), Greece (42–94), Thailand (61–88), Taiwan (27–37), Malaysia (36–54). Available at: http://www.transparency.org (accessed 20 December 2018).

[15] Because we always have control over our component of behaviour, there are also simultaneously – if we significantly change our behaviour – changed components of thinking and feeling and our physiology. The more we actively engage in the active behaviour…the more we will also revise our thoughts, feelings, and listen to what our body tells us. If this gives us greater control, there will also be better feelings, more pleasant thoughts, and physical comfort (Glasser, 1994, p. 51).

[16] *Traditional values* emphasize the importance of religion, parent-child ties, deference to authority and traditional family values. People who embrace these values also reject divorce, abortion, euthanasia and suicide. These societies have high levels of national pride and a nationalistic outlook. *Secular-rational values* have the opposite preferences to the traditional values. These societies place less emphasis on religion, traditional family values and authority. Divorce, abortion, euthanasia and suicide are seen as relatively acceptable. *Survival values* place emphasis on economic and physical security. It is linked with a relatively ethnocentric outlook and low levels of trust and tolerance. *Self-expression values* give high priority to environmental protection, growing tolerance of foreigners, gays and lesbians and gender equality, and rising demands for participation in decision-making in economic and political life. Societies that have high scores in Traditional and Survival values (Zimbabwe, Morocco, Jordan, Bangladesh). Societies with high scores in Traditional and Self-expression values: the U.S., most of Latin America, Ireland. Societies with high scores in Secular-rational and Survival values: Russia, Bulgaria, Ukraine, Estonia. Societies with high scores in Secular-rational and Self-expression values: Sweden, Norway, Japan, Benelux, Germany, France, Switzerland, Czech Republic, Slovenia, and some English speaking countries (World Values Survey Association, 2020).

[17] It is no surprise (or a coincidence) that the same name of SIGMA stands as an acronym for the Support for Improvement in Governance and Management as a joint initiative of the OECD and the European Union to strengthen the foundations for improved public administration reforms.

[18] "Check" asks: What is the purpose of this system? Demand: What is the nature of customer demand? Capability: What is the system predictably achieving? Flow: How does the work function? System conditions: Why does the system behave in this way? "Plan" asks: What needs to change to improve performance against purpose? What action could be taken and what would be the predicted consequences? Against what measures should action be taken (to ensure learning)? "Do" consists of: Take the planned action and monitor the consequences versus purpose. And then you cycle back to "check" (Seddon, 2005, p. 156).

Chapter 6
A Brief History of Public Agencies

ABSTRACT

The concept of agency refers to an individual's ability to act, not just their intentions to do something. Agency concerns events that an individual is responsible for, meaning that those events would not have occurred without their intervention. The concept of public agency is derived from human agency, with the latter being the ability of an individual to act. Public agencies are usually established to carry out specific functions on behalf of the state or society. Agency theory has emerged to address the challenges of principals ensuring that agents carry out their duties as intended. This theory proposes that monitoring and setting objectives for agents can ensure that objectives are achieved. Overall, agency is an essential element of human essence, and its theories have been used to explain the relationships between individuals and organizations, including public agencies.

THE NOTION OF "AGENCY" AND ITS THEORY

The question I'm always asking myself is: are we masters or victims? Do we make history, or does history make us? Do we shape the world, or are we just shaped by it? The question of do we have agency in our lives or whether we are just passive victims of events is, I think, a great question and one that I have always tried to ask.

– Salman Rushdie

All being said about agencies, it is now time to dig deeper into them. The notion of 'agency' was first recorded in 1650–60; it emerged from medieval Latin *agentia*, equivalent to Latin *ag-* (the root of *agere* 'to do, act, manage') + *-entia* noun: the office or function of an *agent*, one that acts or exerts power; something that produces or is capable of producing an effect; a means or instrument by which a guiding intelligence achieves a result (Merriam-Webster, 2017). The notion of 'public agency' is probably derived from the older notion of a human as an 'agent' and his ability to act, *i.e.*, 'human agency'. To Giddens,

DOI: 10.4018/979-8-3693-0507-2.ch006

the agent is placed between the unacknowledged conditions and unintended consequences of action, where the latter are connected to the former with feedback. Among such conditions and consequences, the agent reflexively monitors activity as a chronic feature of everyday actions of an individual and others based on the rationalisation and motivation of action. Human agency does not refer to people's intentions to do something, but rather to their ability to do things.

Agency concerns events of which an individual is the perpetrator in the sense that the individual could, at any phase in a given sequence of conduct, have acted differently. Whatever happened would not have happened if that individual had not intervened. Action is a continuous process, a flow, in which the reflexive monitoring which the individual maintains is fundamental to the control of the body that actors ordinarily sustain throughout their day-to-day lives (Giddens, 1984, p. 9).

Human agency [is…] the temporally constructed engagement by actors of different structural environments – the temporal-relational contexts of action – which, through the interplay of habit, imagination, and judgment, both reproduces and transforms those structures in an interactive response to the problems posed by changing historical situations (Emirbayer & Mische, 1998, p. 970)

As the agent and agency refer to doings, the latter have their effects not only between the acknowledged conditions and intended consequences, but also between the unacknowledged conditions and unintended consequences of action. The scope of control is usually limited to the immediate contexts of action or interaction, while for more distant and unknowledgeable ones, a different control is needed, one that could more quickly spot the unintended consequences of intentional conduct. Here, systems theory, cybernetics, and complexity theory can be helpful in connecting agency with control of individual and more complex collective activities. The successful and legitimate administration of agencies is more important when action, that is, the agency, is directly connected with power as the latter is created only in *relations* (Arendt, 1972; Foucault, 1978, 1995, 2002, 2004; Luhmann, 2013). The location of real power is consequently – due to the dynamic element of relations – always in the course of its re-formation, the notions of agent and agency as tightly connected elements of human essence can be seen already in Aristotle, in his practical science where humans as actors or doers act in practice towards the good of things. Based on this description, the notion of agent as 'one who is authorized to act for or in the place of another' (Merriam-Webster, 2017) came later to the fore. In the law, the latter notion is usually used when an agent is meant to do something: 'one who is authorised to act for or in place of another' (Garner, 2004, p. 68).

From such a meaning of an agent is derived agency as "a fiduciary relationship created by express or implied contract or by law, in which one party (the agent) may act on behalf of another party (the principal) and bind that other party by words or actions (Garner, 2004, p. 67). The *delegated* power to act, according to the written or oral authorisation of the principal, on behalf of a principal or to represent the latter became the basic essence of an agent in the law and in the science of public administration. An agency is hence nothing but, or still is, regardless of its level of autonomy or independence from the agents of the state. From this (second) meaning of agency, also agency theory has emerged where 'principals (owners and managers) have to develop ways of monitoring and controlling the activities of their agents (staff). Agency theory suggests that principles may have problems in ensuring that agents do what they are told. It is necessary to clear up ambiguities by setting objectives and monitoring performance to ensure that objectives are achieved' (Armstrong, 2003, p. 281). Agency theory designates conditions in which one party (the agent) acts on behalf of another (the principal) (Heath, 2009; Panda & Leepsa, 2017), who delegates tasks to the agent due to a possession of certain types of information, skills, competence, or simply time the principal lacks (there can be also other various reasons for delegation, e.g., to resolve commitments promised to the people, to enhance the efficiency or even to avoid taking blame for unpopular policies). In the ideal type of principal-agent relationship, the interests of both sides and the knowledge needed to understand the policy and its implementation on both sides are aligned, so there is no agency loss. Agency theory is ironically based on the assumption of self-interested agents, rewarded by pay-performance sensitivity; such an economic interpretation is absent in cases where social forces and power (grouped in institutions) (Bruce, Buck, & Main, 2005), professional partnerships (a lawyer and his client) or even love (between the relatives, parents, and children) play an important role. In such relationships, self-interest, goal conflict, bounded rationality, information asymmetry, the preeminence of efficiency, risk aversion, and information as a commodity are so important. This self-interest can be present also in a relation between a parent ministry and a subordinate agency, because public servants are not only rent seekers, but also work unselfishly in the name of the public interest. The principal-agent relations should recognise also the importance of social, *i.e.*, the institutional context (in which such relations occur; one among the most important is the rule of law and control that both prevent egocentric agents to seek only their benefits at the expense of the principal). Social mechanisms and/or institutional context[1] impact the content, material, and formal agreements on the various roles people have, as well as how they interact with each other (Wiseman, Cuevas-Rodríguez, & Gomez-Mejia, 2012). These mechanisms entered the lexicon, under the terms institution, cognition, network, and power (Dobbin, 2004) in which the socially embedded nature of principal–agent contracts occurs. The agent's self-interest is bounded not only by bounded reason and risk aversion (Eisenhardt, 1989), but also by reciprocity and fairness norms (Bosse & Phillips, 2014). The apparent agent's self-interest can be turned into cooperation based on purely rational game theory: based with a tournament held on various strategies for the prisoner's dilemma, Axelrod found the *tit for tat* strategy as the winner. The strategy collaborates on the first move, after which it then does whatever its opponent has done on the previous move (Axelrod, 2006).[2] Agency theory should be used with complementary theories; the first presents only a partial view of the world that, that ignores a good bit of the complexity of organizations. Additional perspectives can help to capture the greater complexity (Eisenhardt, 1989). The same applies to the NPM view on public agencies.

Economic theory on the relationship between the principal and the agent can be seen in Articles 766 to 787 of the Slovenian Obligations Code (OJ, nos. 97/07 and 64/16), which refer to the order (mandate) contract (the Anglo-Saxon law speaks of "the contract of agency"). The agent undertakes to the principal to perform certain tasks for him. The agent must execute the order according to the instructions received as a good master; in doing so, he must remain within the contract's limits and pay attention to the client's interests; (this must be the agent's guideline in all things). If the agent thinks that the execution of an order according to the instructions received would be detrimental to the principal, he must warn him and request new instructions. If the principal has not given specific instructions on the business to be carried out, the agent is obliged, taking into account primarily the interests of the principal, to act as a good master or as he would in his *own* affairs under the same circumstances. The agent may deviate from the received order and instructions only with the consent of the principal; if, for a short time or for some other reason, he cannot ask for his consent, he may withdraw from the order and instructions only if, after considering the circumstances, he can reasonably think the interests of the principal so require. If the agent exceeds the limits of the order or deviates from the instructions received, although this exception is not mentioned, he is not considered an agent, but a manager without an order unless the principal later approves what he has done. Reporting - the agent must report the status of transactions to the principal at his request and give him an invoice before a certain time. Liability for the use of the principal's money - if the agent used for himself the money he received for the principal, he must pay him interest at the maximum allowed contractual interest rate, calculated from the day he started using it, while for other money owed to him that was not delivered on time, he must pay the default interest, calculated from the day on which it should have been handed over. Invoicing - the agent as the order's recipient must give an invoice for the performed transaction and hand over to the principal without delay everything he received from performing the entrusted transactions, regardless of whether what he received for the principal was owed to him or not.

When a transaction with the same contract has been entrusted to several agents to carry it out jointly, they are jointly and severally liable for the obligations arising from such an order, unless otherwise agreed. The principal must give the agent, at his request, a certain amount of money for the expected expenditure, to reimburse the agent for all necessary expenses incurred in the performance of the contract, including interest from the date on which he paid them, even if his efforts failed without his guilt. The principal must accept obligations incurred by the agent when performing the tasks entrusted to him on his behalf, or otherwise release the agent from these obligations. The principal is obliged to reimburse the agent for the damage caused to him without fault by fulfilling the order. Unless otherwise agreed, the principal must pay the agent after the transaction has been completed. If the agent, through no fault of his own, has executed the order only in part, he shall be entitled to a proportionate part of the payment. In securing payment and costs, the agent has a lien on the principal's movable property, which he received based on the order, as well as on the monetary amounts received for him (pledge). When several persons have entrusted the agent with the execution of the order, they are jointly and severally liable. The principal may withdraw from the contract. If he does so, according to the contract by which the agent is paid for his efforts, the principal must pay him the appropriate part of the payment and reimburse him for the damage caused by withdrawal from the contract, if there were no good reasons for withdrawal. The agent can cancel the order whenever he wants, just not at the wrong time. The principal must reimburse him for the damage caused by cancelling the contract at an inappropriate time, unless there are good reasons for the cancellation. Even after termination, the agent must continue with the transactions that cannot be postponed until the client can take care of them. The order terminates with the death of the agent. The agent's heirs are obliged to inform the principal as soon as possible that the agent has died and to take all necessary measures to protect his interests until he can take care of them himself. The order terminates with the death of the principal only if so agreed or if the agent has taken over the order according to his personal relationship with the principal. In this case, the ordering agent must continue the business entrusted to him, if otherwise, the damage would occur to the heirs until they can take care of it themselves. If the principal agent is a legal entity, the order terminates when that entity terminates. The order is terminated if the principal or agent goes bankrupt or if he loses all or part of his legal capacity. If the principal withdraws from the contract, as well as if he dies or goes bankrupt, or if he loses all or part of his legal capacity, the order is terminated when the agent learns of the events that led to the termination of the order. If the agent has received written authorization, he must return it after completing the order. If the order was placed so that the agent could achieve the fulfilment of some of his claims against the principal, he cannot withdraw from the contract, and the order does not end with the death or bankruptcy of the principal, nor if he loses all or part of his legal capacity.

From the above provisions, it is possible to understand the purpose of the relationship between the principal and the agent: the latter takes over the order and executes it as if he had carried it out in his *own* affairs; it is a relationship of *trust* that does *not allow any concealment* of facts or information. The financing of the order is the principal's duty, while the agent must provide all information on the costs incurred in carrying out the order. Public agencies as legal entities are not in the same role as the agent in private legal relations: agencies cannot cancel the contract because tasks are delegated to them by law. Different conditions apply when a ministry or an agency ceases to operate in private relations, but here care for mutual interests is also evident. In a classic mandate contract, one person does the business for another person at his or her expense and his or her account. A public agency also does business in a manner of performing tasks in its name and for its account (in this part it is similar to a business contract, as the agency is primarily the holder of benefits and benefits, not the ministry as the principal). The mandate is always legal; it is a bilateral legal transaction that causes both parties to commit to certain acts. The public agency is obliged not only to legal actions but also other (factual, real) actions that contribute to the implementation of the tasks delegated to it. The commitment of the public agency is to carry out tasks and of the ministry to coordinate and supervise. There is also a difference in risk, as according to the classic mandate contract, the risk is at the principal, and in the case of a public agency at the latter (there is also a similarity with a business contract). Another similarity of the business contract is in the business's purpose (lat. *causa*); the latter is at the classical mandate of a confidential nature; while the agent acts in the principal's interest, the public agency (as the entrepreneur or agent) acts within the client's (ministry's) instructions, but in its own (agency's) interest. In terms of mutual benefits, the work of a public agency is closer to a social contract *mea et tua gratia* than to a mandate, as the latter is not (as in a social contract) a joint investment and effort for the common good, but for the benefit of the principal (the agent can benefit only when this is not contrary to the benefit of the principal). As in other cases of transfers of private law institutes within the framework of public law, it is also possible here to establish that the private law institutes change and adapt to circumstances that follow the public interest.

Today, the term (public) 'agency' is an umbrella concept for different forms and names of organizations that operate at arm's length of ministries (*e.g.*, executive agencies, regulatory commissions, nongovernmental public bodies, public corporations, government corporations, local government bodies, autonomous bodies, quangos, non-departmental public bodies, extra-governmental organisations, subsidiary organisations), and has no position on its legal status except maybe the division of public-private law. They mushroomed after WWII, when governments took a larger role in social and economic activities with regulation (indirect enforcement of legislation), implementation (direct enforcement of legislation), monitoring, administration, licencing, issuing permits, granting benefits, determining eligibility to receive a service, and adjudication/inspection. Agencies are (more or less) subject to public law while private companies are subject to private law; at first, there is a discussion about the public management/administration of agencies, while at the second, the appropriate term could be "operations management".[3] The division is relevant as the government also affects private companies (beneficiaries) with various approaches: by sponsored, state-aid enterprises, funded research and development corporations, non-profit organisations and venture capital funds (private equity stakes in start-ups and small- to medium enterprises with strong growth potential). Given this very wide or general notion, it is no surprise there are many variables or different bodies named as agencies on the international (*e.g.*, International Atomic Energy Agency, World Bank[4]), EU (decentralised agencies, *e.g.*, Europol;[5] agencies under common security and defence policy; executive agencies, EURATOM agencies and bodies), private (*e.g.*, travel, employment agencies; other organisations) and the public level or sector. This work is focused solely on the latter, *i.e.*, national public agencies which are all (if this notion is not labelled a ministry itself or Type 0 agency – see below) based on one common denominator – they are more/less distant from the central organisational spine, and as such also provide public services disintegrated from the latter. In this relationship, the basic functions of delegation – enforcement, decision-making (as a

A Brief History of Public Agencies

type of enforcement), and control – are present.[6] Agencies in this regard provide alternative or additional public services that are not already provided by central units.

FIRST PUBLIC AGENCIES AND LE BON'S WARNING ON THEIR RENAMING

One of the oldest human agencies is found in Bible, where Jethro, the priest of Midian and father-in-law of Moses, gives him advice how to place judges over people,[7] while public agencies as are known today can be found a few centuries ago. In the United Kingdom, from which came the 'Next step' idea of agencies, the concept of quasi-independent organisations was not new: Henry VIII in 1546 established the Navy Board, which remained almost unchanged for 300 years (Royal Naval Museum Library, 2014),[8] the Board of Trade, also called Lords Commissioners of Trade and Plantations, was English governmental advisory body established by William III in May 1696 to replace the Lords of Trade (1675) in the supervision of colonial affairs (Encyclopædia Britannica, 2019). Blackstone in his first volume of *Commentaries on the Laws of England* of 1753 99 times mentions "commissioners".[9]

The oldest agency in Denmark (Sorø Academy – an educational institution) was formed in 1586, while the first big wave of agencification is most plausibly interpreted as a response to the increasing variation and complexity across ministries that followed the post-war expansion of the welfare state. Ministries are organized in two basic types of units: small strategic policy-oriented departments close to the minister and the political system, and large directorates with more specialized regulation or implementation of tasks somewhat disconnected from daily politics (Balle Hansen & Andersen, 2012). Agencies have been in Finland a solid and long-standing part of Finnish state administration; some of them were established in the early 17th century (Salminen, Viinamäki, & Jokisuu, 2012). The Swedish dual political (small ministries) – administrative (large agency) system exists since the 17th century (Niklasson, 2012). The purpose of the creation of agencies in Sweden was not greater efficiency or better managerial chances to manage, but to constrain the powers of the top executive branch of government, *that is,* the King to use the public administration as a means to harass individual citizens (Pierre, 2004). The first autonomous agencies in Norway were created in the 1850s within the communications sector. In the 1870s, the second wave of independent agencies followed, imitating the Swedish agency model. A third wave began in the mid-1950s, based on a more proactive attitude of the government toward reform and the use of independent agencies. The idea was to relieve ministry workload by placing technical and routine tasks in agencies (Lægreid, Roness, & Rubecksen, 2012). 'The usual distinction [NPM' between steering and rowing in public management appears to be less viable in these cases [Nordic local governments]. The interaction of the public sector and society in governance, and the importance of public values, makes steering and rowing almost synonymous' (Peters, 2011, p. 11). 'The first administrative agency in Canada was established in 1851, 16 years before the Confederation. The Board of Railway Commissioners was established under the Railway Act primarily to approve rail rates. In 1912, the British Columbia government established its first administrative agency, the Workmen's Compensation Board. The First World War, the Great Depression, and the Second World War all stimulated the federal and provincial governments to become more involved in regulating the economy and in influencing social and cultural issues' (Nastasi, Pressman, & Swaigen, 2020, p. 25). The first US administrative agency was created by Congress in 1789 to provide pensions to injured Revolutionary War soldiers, while the first permanent administrative agency was created in 1887 (the Interstate Commerce Commission, ICC), by the Interstate Commerce Act (49 USCA. § 10101 et seq. [1995]), to regulate commerce among states, particularly interstate transport of persons or goods by carriers. Probably one of the most well-known agencies in the world is the US Central Intelligence Agency (CIA) created under the National Security Act of 1947 (50 USC. 15 401), but this type of agency is not a non- or paragovernmental organisation – as this is usually thought when people speak about agencies – it is part of the federal government. Agencies have a long history, while their growth was emphasized in the 1980s NPM's liberal wave of public administration reforms.

As presented, agencies have existed long before NPM emerged, while their popularity (and/or better: faith to be less rigid and apt to change) sprang (again) from the 1980s onward. Their popular ideas of greater organizational flexibility and efficiency – as well as other notions and institutions – could be sieved through Le Bon's warning about "new words" (that can also be applied to 'new' institutions): In 1895, he knew that a new meaning given to the crowd in a moment of public upheaval is more important than the meaning words they formerly or formally have:

thus, when crowds have come, as the result of political upheavals or changes of belief, to acquire a profound antipathy for the images evoked by certain words, the first duty of the true statesman is to change the words without, of course, laying hands on the things themselves, the latter being too intimately bound up with the inherited constitution to be transformed (Bon, 2001, p. 64).

The Machiavellian line of thought for statesmen thus proposes new, popular, or indifferent words with which the crowd 'can live' instead of their old names. Many times, new words/institutions could be invented due to the old ones' ineffectiveness and inefficiency (*e.g.*, effectiveness – managing and delivering performance; regulation – good and/or smart regulation; administration – good administration; governance – good governance; policy and operation dichotomy – steer, not row; decentralisation – joint-up government and later as whole-of-government approach, and other Emperor's New Clothes' metonyms[10]). In this sense, the popularity of newly established agencies can be understood as the positive effect of the existent, negatively understood, ineffective governmental, ministerial bodies. If this is so, the problem is not with the latter *per se*, but with their management, with their inflexible system (they were established by the left and by the right-wing parties). The main message of agencification could be that 'it is better to create new institutions than to reform the old ones' (that in most cases still exist and operate with even fewer duties).

However, also structurally separated agencies and their executive tasks from parent ministries, greater autonomy of managers, and their accountability related to performance criteria, have not automatically led to improved performance. OECD in 2001, based on an accelerated pace of agency creation, warned that the agencification approach is not a 'magic bullet' to cure administrative problems. Instead of claiming the (dis)advantages of agencies, there is 'the need [not only] for transition countries to analyse their administrative problems with care and examine all options before deciding on the architecture of an agency management regime. The question should not be "where can we use agencies?" But a rather broader and more fundamental question "what are the problems with the present arrangements and how can they best be resolved?"' (SIGMA, 2001, pp. 8–9). Understanding the warning of SIGMA and Le Bon, each new institution must have clear intent, goals, functions, feedback, indicators, and other elements of the system under which the relevance of the institution under consideration can be evaluated *versus* the old one. The mentioned (here understood as primary) elements are not a complete expose of organisational analysis that would, among others, include also the values, strategies, leadership styles, culture, structures (specialization and division of work, responsibility, departmentalization, hierarchy,

[de]centralization, formalization or rules) and processes (decision making, communications, change and innovation), technology, different environments and incentives, people (as groups - cohesion and teamwork; and as individuals – motives, perception, motivation, job satisfaction, and organizational commitment). These elements could be seen as secondary, as they mostly derive their meaning – from the system and complexity perspective – from the primary ones.

REFERENCES

Arendt, H. (1972). *Crises of the Republic: Lying in Politics, Civil Disobedience on Violence, Thoughts on Politics, and Revolution*. Harcourt Brace Jovanovich.

Armstrong, M. (2003). A Handbook of Human Resource Management Practice (9th ed.). London and Sterling: Kogan Page Publishers.

Axelrod, R. (1986). An Evolutionary Approach to Norms. *The American Political Science Review*, *80*(4), 1095–1111. doi:10.2307/1960858

Axelrod, R. (2006). *The Evolution of Cooperation* (Revised edition). Basic Books.

Balle Hansen, M., & Andersen, N. (2012). Denmark. In K. Verhoest, S. V. Thiel, G. Bouckaert, & P. Lægreid (Eds.), *Government Agencies: Practices and Lessons from 30 Countries* (pp. 212–222). Palgrave Macmillan. doi:10.1057/9780230359512_20

Blackstone, W. (2011). *Commentaries on the Laws of England in Four Books, vol. 1 [1753]*. Indiana: Liberty Fund, Inc. http://files.libertyfund.org/files/2140/Blackstone_1387-01_EBk_v6.0.pdf

Bon, G. L. (2001). *The Crowd: A Study of the Popular Mind*. Batoche Books.

Bosse, D. A., & Phillips, R. A. (2014). Agency Theory and Bounded Self-Interest. *Academy of Management Review*, *41*(2), 276–297. doi:10.5465/amr.2013.0420

Bruce, A., Buck, T., & Main, B. G. M. (2005). Top Executive Remuneration: A View from Europe*. *Journal of Management Studies*, *42*(7), 1493–1506. doi:10.1111/j.1467-6486.2005.00553.x

Dobbin, F. (Ed.). (2004). *The New Economic Sociology: A Reader*. Princeton University Press. doi:10.1515/9780691229270

Eisenhardt, K. M. (1989). Agency Theory: An Assessment and Review. *Academy of Management Review*, *14*(1), 57–74. doi:10.2307/258191

Emirbayer, M., & Mische, A. (1998). What Is Agency? *American Journal of Sociology*, *103*(4), 962–1023. doi:10.1086/231294

Encyclopædia Britannica. (2019). *Board of Trade: British government*. Encyclopedia Britannica. https://www.britannica.com/topic/Board-of-Trade-British-government

Foucault, M. (1978). The History of Sexuality: Vol. 1. *An Introduction (Reissue edition)*. Vintage Books.

Foucault, M. (1995). *Discipline & Punish: The Birth of the Prison* (2nd ed.). (A. Sheridan, Trans.). Vintage Books.

Foucault, M. (2002). *The Order of Things: Archaeology of the Human Sciences* (2nd ed.). Routledge.

Foucault, M. (2004). *Naissance de la biopolitique*. Seuil.

Garner, B. A. (Ed.). (2004). *Black's Law Dictionary* (8th ed.). Thomson West.

Giddens, A. (1984). *The Constitution of Society: Outline of the Theory of Structuration*. Cambirdge: Policy Press.

Hart, H. L. A. (1994). *The Concept of Law* (2nd ed.). Clarendon Press.

Heath, J. (2009). The Uses and Abuses of Agency Theory. *Business Ethics Quarterly*, *19*(4), 497–528. doi:10.5840/beq200919430

Lægreid, P., Roness, P. G., & Rubecksen, K. (2012). Norway. In K. Verhoest, S. V. Thiel, G. Bouckaert, & P. Lægreid (Eds.), *Government Agencies: Practices and Lessons from 30 Countries* (pp. 234–244). Palgrave Macmillan. doi:10.1057/9780230359512_22

Leseure, M. (2010). *Key Concepts in Operations Management*. SAGE. doi:10.4135/9781446251720

Luhmann, N. (2013). *Oblast*. Krtina.

Nastasi, L., Pressman, D., & Swaigen, J. (2020). *Administrative Law: Principles and Advocacy* (Fourth). Torondo: Emond.

Niklasson, B. (2012). Sweden. In K. Verhoest, S. V. Thiel, G. Bouckaert, & P. Lægreid (Eds.), *Government Agencies: Practices and Lessons from 30 Countries* (pp. 245–258). Palgrave Macmillan. doi:10.1057/9780230359512_23

Panda, B., & Leepsa, N. M. (2017). Agency theory: Review of Theory and Evidence on Problems and Perspectives. *Indian Journal of Corporate Governance*, *10*(1), 74–95. doi:10.1177/0974686217701467

Peters, B. G. (2011). Steering, rowing, drifting, or sinking? Changing patterns of governance. *Urban Research & Practice*, *4*(1), 5–12. doi:10.1080/17535069.2011.550493

Pierre, J. (2004). Central agencies in Sweden: A report from Utopia. In C. Pollitt & C. Talbot (Eds.), *Unbundled Government: A Critical Analysis of the Global Trend to Agencies, Quangos and Contractualisation* (pp. 203–214). Taylor & Francis.

Royal Naval Museum Library. (2014). *A Brief History of the Royal Navy*. Royal Naval Museum Library. http://www.royalnavalmuseum.org/info_sheets_naval_history.html

Salminen, A., Viinamäki, O.-P., & Jokisuu, J. (2012). Finland. In K. Verhoest, S. V. Thiel, G. Bouckaert, & P. Lægreid (Eds.), *Government Agencies: Practices and Lessons from 30 Countries* (pp. 223–233). Palgrave Macmillan. doi:10.1057/9780230359512_21

Sutherland, J., & Canwell, D. (2004). *Key Concepts in Operations Management*. Palgrave MacMillan. doi:10.1007/978-0-230-21177-3

Wiseman, R. M., Cuevas-Rodríguez, G., & Gomez-Mejia, L. R. (2012). Towards a Social Theory of Agency. *Journal of Management Studies*, *49*(1), 202–222. doi:10.1111/j.1467-6486.2011.01016.x

ENDNOTES

[1] The institutional environment (political intervention, transparency, intermediation, labour market, country risk/turbulence), cognitive framework (instrumentality of leadership, income as value metric, belief in meritocracy), social networks (network density, social capital) and power relations (diversity of principles, ownership concentration, family influence) (Wiseman, Cuevas-Rodríguez, & Gomez-Mejia, 2012).

[2] The agent should first cooperate and then imitate the principle's previous action – if the latter is cooperative, then also the agent is; if not, also the agent is uncooperative. Similarly, norms can be examined in terms of expectations, values, and behaviour. As a norm exists in a given social environment to the extent to which individuals behave in a certain way and are often punished if they do not behave in this way, Axelrod arguments that the norm is more about a stage than the proposition in the sense of "all or nothing" (Axelrod, 1986). That allows to think of a norm's growth or decline in accordance with an individual's behaviour. As a norm exists in a given social environment to the extent to which individuals behave in a certain way and are often punished if they do not behave in this way, he puts the argument that the norm is more about a stage than the proposition in the sense of "all or nothing". Such features of a rule supports also Dworkin (see Hart, 1994). While the notions of fully actors have value, the empirical examples on changing norms suggest that people behave more on tests and errors then on detailed calculation that is based on accurate future beliefs. Axelrod in *The Evolution of Cooperation* (2006) rejected the rationalistic approach and used an evolutionary one that is still based on the principle of 'what works well for a player will likely be reused and what is bad, will probably be refuted'. In the evolutionary approach, there is no need to provide rational calculations to determine the best strategy. This approach allows the introduction of new strategies in terms of random mutations of old ones. Players observe each other and those with poor reward imitate those who are doing better. Thus, there is no (necessary) need for the presumption that an individual is rational and that he understands all strategic impact of a given situation.

[3] Operations management deals with the design of products and services, the buying of components or services from suppliers, the processing of those products and services and the selling of finished goods (Sutherland & Canwell, 2004, p. 167). Operations management is the business function dealing with the management of all the processes directly involved with the provision of goods and services to customers (Leseure, 2010, p. 5). All processes can be grouped under the notion of *holistic* management as the term that comes from system theory. It is surprising that operations management is considered as a discipline to be one of the orphans of the business world and/or as a low-brow discipline and a technical subject (Leseure, 2010; Sutherland & Canwell, 2004). On the public side of study, public agencies are considered well studied in their specifics (such as firms in the private sector through specialisation, division of labour, products, services or outputs), but not in their holistic systemic way that could give all types of agencies guidelines for better alignment to their environment (adaptation, survival, growth, values, outcomes).

4   The list of 59 international agencies is available at: https://unstats.un.org/home/international_agencies/

5   The list of 34 EU decentralised and other agencies is available at: https://europa.eu/european-union/about-eu/agencies_en

6   In the situation of a low level of decentralization, merely enforcement functions are delegated, while at a high degree of decentralization, the enforcement and decision-making, as well as a part of the control function is delegated to lower levels. However, it is not possible to transfer all three functions fully, as such a transfer would no longer mean decentralization of the system, but its disintegration and emergence of new smaller decentralized units.

7   You must be the people's representative before God and bring their disputes to him. Teach them [the people] his decrees and instructions, and show them the way they are to live and how they are to behave. But select capable men from all the people—men who fear God, trustworthy men who hate dishonest gain—and appoint them as officials over thousands, hundreds, fifties, and tens. Have them serve as judges for the people at all times but have them bring every difficult case to you; the simple cases they can decide themselves (Exodus 18:22).

8   Based on the Statute of Sewers, 23 Hy. VIII c. 5 (1531) that authorized the appointment of commissioners charged with the drainage of low-lying land that was liable to floods was decided one of still the well-known cases on discretionary decision-making, *Rooke's case* (A. D. 1598).

9   One of the most direct Blackstone's citations focused on the executive posts is 'that no persons concerned in the management of any duties or taxes created since 1692, except the commissioners of the treasury, nor any of the officers following, (viz., commissioners of prizes, transports, sick and wounded, wine licenses, navy, and victualling; secretaries or receivers of prizes; comptrollers of the army accounts; agents for regiments; governors of plantations and their deputies; officers of Minorca or Gibraltar; officers of the excise and customs; clerks or deputies in the several offices of the treasury, exchequer, navy, victualling, admiralty, pay of the army or navy, secretaries of state, salt, stamps, appeals, wine licenses, hackney coaches, hawkers, and pedlars,) nor any persons that hold any new office under the crown created since 1705, are capable of being elected or sitting as members of the house of commons' (Blackstone, 2011).

10   Metonymy or renaming is a rhetorical figure in which the name for a thing is replaced by another name that is related to the first causally or in some other way. In metonymy, "the whole bus sang" it is not the bus that sang, but the passengers on it.

Chapter 7
"Potemkin" Reason for Efficiency

ABSTRACT

Efficiency is one of the primary reasons for creating agencies, as this is thought to improve their effectiveness and efficiency. This belief was emphasized in literature and in the creation of agencies in the 1980s. However, there is little hard evidence to suggest that the agency form is more efficient than other forms of government operation. The German sociologist Max Weber believed that bureaucracy was the most efficient way to set up an organization, administration, and organizations, while Woodrow Wilson believed public administration should be geared toward maximization of effectiveness, efficiency, and economy. The criterion of efficiency is neutral as to what goals are to be attained, and this principle influences the decisions made by members of any administrative agency.

INTRODUCTION

The most general law in nature is equity-the principle of balance and symmetry which guides the growth of forms along the lines of the greatest structural efficiency.

– Herbert Read

Efficiency is one of the most prominent rational reasons for agencification. The goal of NPM's creation of '1980s agencies' was often said to be in their effectiveness and efficiency, e.g. 'governments have created arm-length bodies for two main reasons: to improve the efficiency and effectiveness of the system; and to legitimise decision-making by providing some independence from direct political intervention' (OECD, 2003, p. 7). This belief – that moving government operations away from the classical bureaucratic administration will create these operations more effective and more efficient – was emphasised also in the literature (Bouckaert & Peters, 2004; Davis & Rhodes, 2000),[1] but those two reasons were already present in the history as the main ones for the technical superiority of bureaucracy, and even more – they are, especially efficiency, a permanent partner of human development. This can be appealing especially because hard evidence for the increased efficiency of the agency form is not available (Pollitt, Talbot,

DOI: 10.4018/979-8-3693-0507-2.ch007

Caulfield, & Smullen, 2004). Agency performance seems to depend more on the 'quality of relations' between the agency and its parent ministry than just on some formal performance criteria.

The 1980s idea of agencification was to separate policy from operations; on the other hand, Rudolf Gneist emphasised the vanity of any attempt to establish/transfer representative institutions (in his case the parliamentary system of England) without considering their close connection with administrative institutions (Gneist, 1891). The parliamentary government cannot be comprehended apart from its administrative system, and/or constitutional law cannot be understood without administrative law. Goodnow also claimed that due to the great complexity of political conditions 'it is necessary not only that the will of the sovereign be formulated or expressed before it can be executed, but also that the execution of that will be intrusted in a large measure to a different organ from that which expresses it' (Goodnow, 1900, p. 10). Such statements could be seen as natural descendants of Locke's division of power into legislative and executive, where the latter also partly has legislative function (supreme power) (Locke, 2010). After 211 years, Goodnow still thought that for *efficient* administration, the parliamentary function of expressing the will of the state should be harmoniously connected with (at the same time subordinative and controlled) administrative execution of that will, and this has still not been changed. Politics should be considered together with administration, while the first should be at the same time prevented to influence (centralised) administration (accompanied by a greater permanence in the tenure of administrative officers) in its details.[2] For Goodnow there are three kinds of authorities which are engaged in the execution of the state will: judicial, executive and administrative authorities (Goodnow, 1900, p. 18), also named as the agencies of federal/state government. At the end of the nineteenth century, the German sociologist and author of *The Protestant Ethic and the Spirit of Capitalism* (1905), Max Weber, used and described the term "bureaucracy" (it is known as the bureaucratic theory of management, bureaucratic management theory, or Max Weber theory). The Weberian type of bureaucracy is mentioned because the managerial approach to public administration promotes essentially the same reason of efficiency along the lines of ideal type bureaucracy. Weber believed bureaucracy was *the most efficient way* to set up an organisation, administration, and organizations:

the technical utilization of scientific knowledge, so important for the living conditions of the mass of people, was certainly encouraged by economic considerations...[while] this encouragement was derived from...the rational structures of law and administration (Weber, 2001, pp. xxxvii–xxxviii).

State bureaucracy was thus already similar to Weber (and not only in the contemporary theories of public administration) seen in the promotion of *rational/technical efficiency*, continuity of operation, speed, precision, and calculation of results (Weber, 1946). The greater efficiency of human cooperation was based on the development of the discipline (Weber, 1994) that caused the iron cage of rationalist order. Another founding father of public administration, Woodrow Wilson, also spoke about the facile, well-ordered, and effective public administration that must be *business-like* (Wilson, 1887). He set forth three core values of public administration: 'it is the object of administrative study to discover, first, what government can properly and successfully do, and, secondly, how we can do these proper things with the utmost possible efficiency and at least possible cost either of money or energy' (Wilson, 1887, p. 481). To him, public administration should be geared toward maximisation of effectiveness, efficiency, and economy. The exercise of authority and the development of organizational loyalty to Simon *are two* principles by which the organization influences the value of the individuals. The issues that underlie decisions are determined by a principle that is present in all rational behaviour: the criterion of efficiency:

To be efficient simply means taking the shortest path, the cheapest means, toward the attainment of the desired goals. The efficiency criterion is completely neutral as to what goals are to be attained. The commandment, "Be efficient"! is a major organisational influence over the decisions of the members of any administrative agency; and a determination whether this commandment has been obeyed is a major function of the review process (Simon, 1997, p. 12).

Practical usage of efficiency is hence older, as its appeal within agencification; it can be seen as a special feature of the organic/thermodynamic/chemical principle of minimisation of energy needed to accomplish – through adaptive changes – tasks or goals (known as organic, thermodynamic, and chemical equilibrium). Life is the harnessing of chemical energy in such a way that the energy-harnessing device makes a copy of itself. No energy - no evolution (Lane, Martin, Raven, & Allen, 2013). The application of the laws of thermodynamics to open systems is known as thermodynamic potential: living systems can achieve a reduction in their entropy as they grow and develop; they create structures of greater internal energy (*i.e.* they lower entropy) out of the nutrients they absorb (Encyclopaedia Britannica, 2020). Efficiency can be in this manner seen as an equilibrium constant (the latter is a (bio)chemical reaction [among reactants *vs.* products] with values that can be used to ascertain the composition of the system at equilibrium (Khan Academy, 2020)) that equals reactions between reactants (demand to fulfil public tasks) and the product (realised public goals). A further elaboration of the relation between efficiency and the very basic elements of life and energy deserves a whole discussion, so it should be enough here to infer that it is not only human, but a general natural tendency to *spend a minimum of energy needed and save it for future tasks*. This tendency is also seen in the organisation of public administration. Efficiency can be seen because of specialisation and the latter of the division of work that produces more with the same or even less amount of energy. Effectiveness and efficiency are hence the permanent elements of all endeavours to make the government more aligned with its main goals and their execution, and the same stands for the relationship between decisions and their execution: although the primary function of agencies is the execution of political decisions, they also create rules in this process. Institutions and/or agencies that operated at an arms-length distance from policymakers, were the key operative structure of central government long before the idea of reinventing the government or NPM emerged. DiMaggio and Powell replaced the rational iron cage with *isomorphism* i.e., the claim that organisations are becoming more homogeneous, and bureaucracy remains the common organisation form not on the basis of efficiency but on procedural structuration of organisational fields; organisational changes 'occur as the result of processes that make organizations more similar without necessarily making them more efficient' (Powell & DiMaggio, 1991, p. 65). Pollitt discusses about *coercive isomorphism* (which occurs when the pressure to adopt a particular form comes from other organizations which can exercise power over the subject organization), *mimetic isomorphism* (it occurs where, under conditions of uncertainty, the safest strategy appears to be to copy whatever is in fashion with other organizations which are perceived as "modern" or "successful") and *normative isomorphism* (this type of copying results from processes of professionalization and institutionalization) (Pollitt, 2001).

Countries, despite an expected substantial level of convergence in practice, have agencies with significant differences in their prevalence, legal structure and form, control arrangements, and autonomy (Verhoest, Roness, Verschuere, Rubecksen, & MacCarthaigh, 2010). As convergence can occur at different stages or levels, Pollitt elaborated the phenomenon of convergence with respect to the extent of convergence and the reasons and motives for it. With regard to extent, there are four overlapping but not coterminous zones of convergence: type A - reforms are put into action and this produces a convergence of results or outcomes; type B - results may not converge with actual practices (actions); type C - similar external labels are used although the substantive content may vary considerably; type D - is confined just to the world of talk (Pollitt, 2001, pp. 943-944). Some pro-oriented people could claim that there is Type B (or even the pure type A) convergence going on, while contra-oriented ones can say that much of the convergence is actually of types C and D. Highly structured bureaucratic forms provide a context in which individuals strive to act reasonably within all vagueness and restrictions, but a result – seen as *the aggregate* - still leads to similarities in the organisational structure, culture, and results on higher and lower levels. In this line of thought, Thiel has made categorization of public-sector organizations just into five types of agencies (Thiel, 2012). The isomorphism supported by a neo institutional mixture of variables (see Chapter 11) is one of the explanations for the differences present in the types of agencies, their creation, and operational conditions. Other scholars also consider similarity as being equal to *institutions*, as the stable, valued, recurring patterns of behaviour (Huntington, 1968), as the persistent rules that shape, limit, and channel human behaviour (Fukuyama, 2014) or decide what looks the same or different: '[s]imilarity is institution' (Douglas, 1986, p. 55). Similarity is also seen in recursions on different levels *a la* Russian dolls.[3]

OTHER REASONS FOR THE CREATION OF AGENCIES

As it was seen in the previous section, efficiency as a principle was present in the science of public administration from its very beginnings, and has *not* become one of the guiding factors of the modern and post-modern theories of public administration; the recognition of efficiency an important *rational* value for the public administration and civil service is not of recent origin, and hence even less of independent[4] agencies. Along the *rational* elements of agencification (efficiency, public choice, or principal–agent theory, game theory) there are also the *institutional* ones. Their focus is on the context of agencification, on the existing culture, traditions, (systemic) structures, norms and values, and on the management of information. The core elements of the agency are 'structural disaggregation[5] and/or the creation of "task-specific" organisations, performance "contracting" – some form of performance target setting, monitoring and reporting and deregulation (or more properly reregulation) of controls over personnel, finance and other management matters (Talbot, 2004, p. 6). There is also another lesson from the classical emphasis on public administration efficiency: Weberian inference on the powerless diletant monarch in the face of the superior knowledge of the bureaucratic expert (Weber, 1978) could be seen as one among the institutional reasons for the creation of independent agencies as substitutes for the division of power. The creation of agencies could be seen as an attempt to regain (Parliamentarian) control above the Executive by transferring some of the latter's tasks to independent agencies, but history can repeat itself: just as the benefits of ministries' efficiency and effectiveness can correlate with the loss of (Parliamentarian) accountability, policy focus and excessive discretion that causes fear against a too powerful and unelected Executive, the same holds for agencies *in relation to* ministries. This idea emerged in the notion of the hollow state (Milward & Provan, 2000) that has not enough expertise to control agencies and the consequent rise of regulation (reregulation) (Majone, 1996; Vogel, 1998) in an attempt to regain control over them.[6] 'Agencies can only be steered by their parent ministries if the ministries have the information, the appropriately skilled staff and the authoritative levers with which to steer' (Pollitt & Talbot, 2004, p. 283), otherwise, 'castles are built on sand' in Pollitt's words. It seems some basic, underlying structural elements at work produce similar results – they should thus be identified and addressed differently than they are now. One of them is known by its very own name – the principal-agent problem (also known as the *agency problem*) happens when a superior person or entity (the agent) can decide, act, or otherwise effect on a superior person or entity (principal) (Eisenhardt, 1989).

The same problem applies also to *communication*, where the government could be left without data: under the NPM model, 'agentification and outsourcing produced a marginalisation of digital technology, as IT operations were assigned to separate, specialised agencies or contracted to global service providers. Digital expertise lay outside of government, and sources of data were fragmented' (Misuraca, 2020, p. 22). This could also lead to limited accountability and transparency of private service contractors. The relationship between the ministry and agency is always divided between the control/coordination of the first and autonomy of the second. 'In reality, the informal contacts between [Swedish] departments and agencies have proven critical to the efficiency of this institutional arrangement' (Pierre, 2004, p. 213). Unlimited autonomy is a contradiction; there must always be someone at a higher level who grants it, sets its framework, or allows it as such. Even in the most optimal relationship, the Russian adage seems to be appreciated: 'trust, but verify'. Along with three elements (structure, performance, reregulation) '[n]umerous other elements of public sector reform – efficiency, customer orientation, service standards, transparency and accountability, innovative management, revenue generation, resource (accrual) accounting, etc. – have been more or less associated with agency initiatives' (Talbot, 2004, p. 7).

On the other hand, the UK is well known for its next step agencies, so it can be valuable to see on their reasons for agency. In the UK, the Fulton Report of 1968 proposed the principle of *management by objective*:[7] executive operations should be "hived off" to independent boards with the aim of accountable and efficient management when outputs can be measured against costs or other criteria and where individuals can be held personally responsible for their performance, and when measures of achievement can be established in quantitative or financial terms.[8] When these two conditions are met accountable units should be set up.[9] The report enumerated three main obstacles that stand in the way of the effective allocation of responsibility and authority: the several departments, or several branches within a department, the number of levels in the hierarchy, and cases where administrators and specialists are jointly engaged on a common task that demands constant reference to and from the parallel hierarchy. The Pliatzky Report of 1980 outlined four reasons for the creation of these bodies:

Because the work is of an executive character which does not require ministers to take responsibility for its day-to-day management; because the work is more effectively carried out by a single purpose organisation rather than by a government department with a wide range of functions; in order to involve people from outside of government in the direction of the organisation; in order to place the performance of a function outside the party-political arena (p. 557).

Minister Thatcher's 'Efficiency Unit' in his report on *Improving Management in Government* of 1988 established that the management of government business is much better, especially where there are clear tasks to be performed and services to be provided. Based on the determined five weaknesses[10] the Report gave three main recommendations:

The work of each department must be organised in a way that focuses on the job to be done; the systems and structures must enhance the effective delivery of policies and services. The management of each department must ensure that its staff have the relevant experience and skills needed for the tasks that are essential to effective government. There must be a real and sustained pressure on and within each department for a continuous improvement in the value for money obtained in the delivery of policies and services (Jenkins, Caines, & Jackson, 1988, p. 7).

The identification of fundamental changes needed to achieve a further major step forward in the delivery of services and the management of government, the Efficiency Unit named as 'the next steps'

(Jenkins et al., 1988) or 'the executive agencies' (they conduct executive, administrative, regulatory, advisory or commercial functions). The central goal was to have a relatively small civil service with its core engaged in the function of servicing ministers and managing departments, while respondents to these departments will be a variety of agencies with their staff (with or without the status of Crown servants) concerned with the delivery of their particular service with clearly defined responsibilities between the governmental and agency levels, where both departments and their agencies should have a more open and simplified structure. The interrelated complements of the new (commonwealth) paradigm in public administration in 1995 involved the provision of high-quality services that citizens value, increased autonomy of managers from central agency controls, measurement and rewards of organisations and individuals based on performance targets, the needed human and technological resources and managers to meet performance targets, receptiveness to competition, and an open-minded attitude about which public purposes should be performed by the public sector as opposed to the private one (CAPAM, 1995). The importance of political sustenance should always be emphasised in all political reforms, as they depend on the real support from above: Next-step ideas become a reality based on just two things: one report and Mrs Thatcher's support.

Along the British or Westminster 'Next step' type of agency (headed by a chief executive who is responsible to a Ministry and not an independent board), there is also the *Nordic* type of agency with a small ministry (policy formulation and planning), and a number of larger agencies (with their own boards that take care of implementation), the US type of agency embedded within executive departments but with their more/less own status in public law (separate budget, the head appointed by the President, *eg*, the Federal Bureau of Investigation within the Department of Justice) and the (quasi)autonomous agencies that are not so tightly connected to ministries, but still by various ways subordinated to ministries, within or outside ministries, without or with legal personality, founded under the public (and responsible to the Parliament) or private law (not-for-profit organizations) providing public services and other *sui generis* (*e.g.* national banks) organisations, in which different types of autonomy are present or intertwined. The complexity of typology of all agencies can be presented with the combination calculator that shows 462 combinations and even 46.656 permutations among the six types of autonomy (or anything else). Along the dimensions mentioned, there are also variations in the activities of the agencies: They implement public policy through the delivery of services and the transfer of funds. Implementation usually means also the enactment of secondary legislation by agencies (implementation by regulation of society or economy), providing advice, development of policies, the collection and dissemination of information, research, and tribunals, and/or other public inquiries, a representation of some segments of the civil society.

Therefore, one solution to harsh criticism of government institutions in the last two decades of the 20th century was to "unbundle government", *i.e.,* to break down monolithic departments and ministries into smaller, semi-autonomous agencies (Pollitt & Talbot, 2004) based on the principle of management by objective and value for money, but many reforms have implemented 'agency type' institutions without any systematic guidance on what agencies are or what their strengths and weaknesses are (Talbot, 2004). The reason behind the growth of quasi-government 'frequently lies in the wishes of the government to have a function performed and in not wanting this function to be the direct responsibility of a minister' (Coxall, Robins, & Leach, 1998, p. 162). Ministerial responsibility also applies to agencies that operate within the field of a ministry, while the extent of this responsibility varies depending on the different types of agencies and their autonomy. As a rule of thumb, the division between general policy making and specific task implementation could be used: a minister is responsible for policy for the general framework of the agency's structure (working conditions), coordination, and control, while responsibility is lowered or minimised in the agency's adjudication or independent, specific, or individual processes and decisions,[11] when also general decisions are made at the agency's level if an agency has such delegated authority, especially when such decisions are taken by the board members consisting of various stakeholders. Ministerial focus on responsibility and coordination should be aligned with the agency's focus on performance and efficiency: if an agency is output oriented (results) and a ministry more input oriented (legality, source), and/or when both sizes emphasise different perspectives or values – drawbacks are inevitable. It is urgent that this relation be calibrated on the same values, purposes, goals, processes, and other elements that make this relation effective and efficient, although these (the same) elements are seen from different (up-down and down-up) positions. This calibration can be done by appointing a relevant agency to prepare draft rules (based on its expertise and knowledge of the field that will be then enacted as valid law by the Executive or the Legislator) individually or as a member of an *ad hoc* created commission especially for this purpose. Daily, this is done informally with tight communication between the agency and a governmental (line) official (from a "parent" ministry), who is responsible for this agency that the latter reports in time on its doings, operations, financial transactions, etc... It matters to a great extent how this ministerial official understands a relevant agency that is under his work duties, how he reports further to higher officials, state secretaries, or a minister on agency effectiveness, efficiency, or other evaluation elements. In such a way, formal coordination and control are in practice often realized informally, based on the mutual interdependency between an agency and a ministry: first, from an agency's expertise and knowledge, and the second from government resources and support.

There were probably more reasons for agency than the stated ones; according o the line of Le Bon's thinking, 'as the post-war state grew unchecked, there was an increasing sense of ungovernability and that the state was overloaded. The creation of quangos was one way of reducing the size and scope of the state. The political institutions were simply not designed and not able adequately to oversee and control the burgeoning bureaucracy' (Flinders, 1999, p. 29). For these reasons, the bad reputation of politics and bureaucracy, new, complex, and (ethically or for other reasons) sensitive issues previously absent from ministerial corridors could be added, but along the enumeration of different reasons, one step behind should be made: there should be a clear picture on the systemic nature on which agencies act. Hood already in 1981 spoke about Quango's reincarnation that follows a historical pendulum (Hood, 1981). Indeed, 'within a very short period of eliminating thirty executive bodies, the government created thirty new quangos' (Coxall et al., 1998, p. 165). The mentioned reasons for the creation and operation of agencies are based on various elements that were predominant in specific time frames and contexts. As they vary from case to case, they cannot offer systematic explanations of agencification processes, and it seems, they can serve for only the probable and ex-post explanations, when agencies were already created. Sharing this in mind, many times resemble to various cognitive biases such as fundamental attribution error, unconscious bias, priming bias, confirmation bias, belief bias, framing embodied cognition, anchoring, overconfidence etc... Along with various reasons for the creation of agencies, all can be put together by the structure of their (already mentioned) underlying systems. If within the latter is found a leverage, *i.e.,* trim-tab[12] that can affect events the most with the minimum level of energy, then agencies could exhibit a new level of efficiency and public trust. The ability to make predictions on various perspectives of agencification is in this way more likely and will be addressed in a special chapter about complexity theory and systems theory.

REFERENCES

Bouckaert, G., & Peters, B. G. (2004). What is available and what is missing in the study of quangos? In C. Pollitt & C. Talbot (Eds.), *Unbundled Government: A Critical Analysis of the Global Trend to Agencies, Quangos and Contractualisation* (pp. 22–49). Taylor & Francis.

CAPAM. (1995). *Government in Transition*. Commonwealth Secretariat. doi:10.14217/9781848595286-

Coxall, B., Robins, L., & Leach, R. (1998). *Contemporary British Politics*. Macmillan International Higher Education.

Davis, G., & Rhodes, R. W. (2000). From hierarchy to contracts and back again: Reforming the Australian public service. In M. Keating, J. Wanna, & P. Weller (Eds.), *Institutions on the edge? Capacity and Governance* (pp. 74–98). Allen & Unwin., doi:10.4324/9781003116127-4

Douglas, M. (1986). *How Institutions Think*. Syracuse University Press.

Eisenhardt, K. M. (1989). Agency Theory: An Assessment and Review. *Academy of Management Review*, *14*(1), 57–74. doi:10.2307/258191

Encyclopedia Britannica. (2020). *Thermodynamics—Open systems*. Encyclopedia Britannica. https://aws.qa.britannica.com/science/thermodynamics

Flinders, M. (1999). Quangos: Why Do Governments Love Them? In M. J. Smith & M. V. Flinders (Eds.), *Quangos, Accountability and Reform* (pp. 26–39). Palgrave Macmillan. doi:10.1007/978-1-349-27027-9_3

Fukuyama, F. (2014). *Political Order and Political Decay: From the Industrial Revolution to the Globalization of Democracy*. Farrar, Straus and Giroux.

Fulton, J. S. (1968). *Fulton Report Into the Civil Service 1968 Cmnd-3638*. https://docs.google.com/document/d/1ANxPtL_7QUg4-adwzU28uAVOVReR_VCpM7ea8ukt9ug/edit

Gill, D. (2002). *Signposting the Zoo – From Agencification to a More Principled Choice of Government Organisational Forms*. OECD Publishing.

Gneist, R. (1891). *The History of the English Constitution* (P. A. Ashworth, Trans.). William Clowes and Sons.

Goodnow, F. J. (1900). *Politics and Administration: A Study in Government*. The MacMillan Company.

Hood, C. (1981). Axeperson Spare that Quango. In C. Hood & M. Wright (Eds.), *Big Government in Hard Times* (pp. 100–122). OUP.

Huntington, S. P. (1968). *Political order in changing societies*. Yale University Press.

Jenkins, K., Caines, K., & Jackson, A. (1988). *Improving Management in Government: The Next steps: Report to the Prime Minister*. Civil Servant. https://www.civilservant.org.uk/library/1988_improving_management_in_government_the%20_next_steps.pdf

Khan Academy. (2020). *The equilibrium constant K (article)*. Khan Academy. https://www.khanacademy.org/science/chemistry/chemical-equilibrium/equilibrium-constant/a/the-equilibrium-constant-k

Lane, N., Martin, W. F., Raven, J. A., & Allen, J. F. (2013). Energy, genes and evolution: Introduction to an evolutionary synthesis. *Philosophical Transactions of the Royal Society of London. Series B, Biological Sciences*, *368*(1622), 20120253. Advance online publication. doi:10.1098/rstb.2012.0253 PMID:23754807

Locke, J. (2010). *Dve razpravi o oblasti Pismo o toleranci*. Krtina.

Majone, G. (1996). *Regulating Europe*. Routledge.

McGuire, L. (2004). Contractualism and performance measurement in Australia. In C. Pollitt & C. Talbot (Eds.), *Unbundled Government: A Critical Analysis of the Global Trend to Agencies, Quangos and Contractualisation* (pp. 113–139). Taylor & Francis.

Meadows, D. H. (2008). *Thinking in Systems: A Primer*. Chelsea Green Publishing.

Milward, H. B., & Provan, K. G. (2000). Governing the Hollow State. *Journal of Public Administration: Research and Theory*, *10*(2), 359–380. doi:10.1093/oxfordjournals.jpart.a024273

Misuraca, G. (Ed.). (2020). *Assessing the impacts of digital government transformation in the EU*. Luxemburg: Publications Office of the European Union.

OECD. (2002). *Distributed Public Governance Agencies, Authorities and other Government Bodies: Agencies, Authorities and other Government Bodies*. OECD Publishing.

OECD. (2003). *Public Sector Modernisation: Changing Organisations GOV/PUMA(2003)19*. OECD. http://www.oecd.org/officialdocuments/publicdisplaydocumentpdf/?cote=GOV/PUMA(2003)19&docLanguage=En

Pierre, J. (2004). Central agencies in Sweden: A report from Utopia. In C. Pollitt & C. Talbot (Eds.), *Unbundled Government: A Critical Analysis of the Global Trend to Agencies, Quangos and Contractualisation* (pp. 203–214). Taylor & Francis.

Pollitt, C. (2001). Convergence: The Useful Myth? *Public Administration*, *79*(4), 933–947. doi:10.1111/1467-9299.00287

Pollitt, C., & Talbot, C. (Eds.). (2004). *Unbundled Government: A Critical Analysis of the Global Trend to Agencies, Quangos and Contractualisation*. Taylor & Francis. doi:10.4324/9780203507148

Pollitt, C., Talbot, C., Caulfield, J., & Smullen, A. (2004). *Agencies: How Governments Do Things Through Semi-Autonomous Organizations*. Palgrave MacMillan.

Popova, M. (2015). *Buckminster Fuller's Brilliant Metaphor for the Greatest Key to Transformation and Growth*. Brain Pickings.

Powell, W. W., & DiMaggio, P. (Eds.). (1991). *The New institutionalism in organizational analysis*. The University of Chicago Press. doi:10.7208/chicago/9780226185941.001.0001

Simon, H. A. (1997). *Administrative Behavior* (4th ed.). Free Press.

Smullen, A. (2004). Lost in translation? Shifting interpretations of the concept of 'agency': The Dutch case. In C. Pollitt & C. Talbot (Eds.), *Unbundled Government: A Critical Analysis of the Global Trend to Agencies, Quangos and Contractualisation* (pp. 184–202). Taylor & Francis.

Talbot, C. (2004). The Agency idea: Sometimes old, sometimes new, sometimes borrowed, sometimes untrue. In C. Pollitt & C. Talbot (Eds.), *Unbundled Government: A Critical Analysis of the Global Trend to Agencies, Quangos and Contractualisation* (pp. 3–21). Taylor & Francis.

Thiel, S. V. (2012). Comparing Agencies Across Countries. In K. Verhoest, S. V. Thiel, G. Bouckaert, P. Lægreid, & S. V. Thiel (Eds.), *Government Agencies* (pp. 28–28). Palgrave Macmillan. doi:10.1057/9780230359512_2

Verhoest, K., Roness, P., Verschuere, B., Rubecksen, K., & MacCarthaigh, M. (2010). *Autonomy and Control of State Agencies: Comparing States and Agencies*. Palgrave MacMillan. doi:10.1057/9780230277274

Vogel, S. K. (1998). *Freer Markets, More Rules: Regulatory Reform in Advanced Industrial Countries*. Cornell University Press. doi:10.7591/9781501717307

Weber, M. (1946). *From Max Weber: Essays in Sociology* (H. H. Gerth & C. W. Mills, Trans.). Oxford University Press.

Weber, M. (1978). Economy and Society: An Outline of Interpretive Sociology (New Ed edition; G. Roth & C. Wittich, Eds.). Berkeley, California: University of California Press.

Weber, M. (1994). *Weber: Political Writings*. Cambridge University Press. doi:10.1017/CBO9780511841095

Weber, M. (2001). *The Protestant Ethic and the Spirit of Capitalism* (T. Parsons, Trans.). Routledge.

Wilson, W. (1887). The Study of Administration. *Political Science Quarterly*, *2*(2), 197–222. doi:10.2307/2139277 PMID:4591257

ENDNOTES

[1] In Australia the general performance indicators framework has the elements of effectiveness (assembled from the outcomes, access, equity, appropriateness and quality) and efficiency (input per output unit) (McGuire, 2004, p. 121).

[2] In 1980s agency's terminology, the question was/is how both parts can be "joined up", how politics and administration should be vertically and horizontally coordinated, how the inter-institutional communication and exchange of data take place.

[3] On this theme see section on comparative dimensions of agencies as the Russian dolls of ministries.

[4] A large or small (physical) distance or separateness between an agency and a ministry is not *sine qua non* also for political independence. An agency can be very tightly connected with the Executive and be politically dependent (intelligence agency) or independent (police, tax, customs agencies). 'It seems that separateness is most justified when the state or the government of the day, as a special stakeholder, has a particular political interest in the outcome of individual decisions, such as for many regulatory functions' (OECD, 2002, p. 21). The notion of independency of agencies

is usually aligned with political independency by banning politicians from influencing on *concrete* procedures carried out by the agencies. This distinction is based on the difference between the general (regulation) and individual (adjudication) procedures. 'The key issue for policy independence is to provide a credible assurance that there will be no political inference in the decision-making of individual cases' (Gill, 2002, p. 65). While it is understandable that policy influence is to some extent present at the general level, where everything should be regulated equally from the point of view of equality (including through the delegation of regulatory powers to agencies), such influence is prohibited in individual proceedings. An equal treatment of parties in the proceedings, who are subject to pre-established and known rules, must not be corrupted by politicians. If this is self-evident in the relation between politicians and the judiciary, this is not yet the case in relation to agencies in the case of individual decision-making and/or adjudication.

5   Under structural disaggregation can be put the task specification, task specialization, unit accountability, chief officer accountability, managerial autonomy, financial flexibility, personnel flexibility and organizational flexibility, and under performance contracting can be put achievement performance, performance reporting, performance accountability, performance audit, performance improvement, improved economy, improved efficiency, improved effectiveness, improved outputs, improved quality of service, improved outcomes, performance budgeting, improved policy making, performance management and improved strategic management (Smullen, 2004).

6   In reality – it became increasingly clear during the 1990s that management by objectives was not [for Swedish agencies] a very efficient strategy for guiding the agencies. First of all, as is the general problem in this relationship, agencies control more of the detailed know-how than the departments and know what works and what does not. As a result, departments frequently formulated objectives in concert with the agencies themselves, or…it was seldom not the agencies themselves that tended to design the objectives which they were to pursue. Second, the system lacked a corrective mechanism; there was little that the departments could do to correct agencies which did not pursue the agreed objectives…The result of all this has been that a new steering model called *verksamhetsstyrning* (steering of activities) has evolved during the past couple of years. This model draws heavily on performance indicators as a base for reviewing the agencies (Pierre, 2004, p. 211).

7   A form of a performance contract in which objectives are agreed (between individual managers and the state department) and reviewed *vis-à-vis* their achievements. Objectives are needed if units are to be held accountable: 'accountable management means holding individuals and units responsible for performance measured as objectively as possible. Its achievement depends upon identifying or establishing accountable units within government departments—units where output can be measured against costs or other criteria, and where individuals can be held personally responsible for their performance' (Fulton, 1968, p. 51). And to hold someone accountable some criteria are needed. This is known as performance management (see chapter 10).

8   The Report gave some proposals where such aims could be established: the management of the department's executive activities, many of them laid down by legislation; administrative activities, mostly of a non-executive character, concerned often with the operation and adaptation of existing policies; the day-to-day organisation of the department's staff and work and the provision of its internal services and the formulation and review of policy under political direction (Fulton, 1968, p. 51).

9   The most straightforward cases are where there is a physical output *e.g.,* in stores or supplies. But it is also possible to measure output against costs wherever many similar and defined opera-

tions are performed. For example, in the registration of applications, the payment of benefits and the handling of individual employment problems, local offices could establish standards of achievement by using the statistical data they already collect relating to transactions handled (Fulton, 1968, p. 52).

[10] A lack of clear and accountable management responsibility and the self-confidence that goes with it particularly among the higher ranks in departments; the need for a greater precision about the results expected of people end of organisations; a need to focus attention on outputs as well as inputs; the handicap of imposing a uniform system in an organisation of the size and diversity of the present Civil Service; and a need for a sustained pressure for improvement (Jenkins, Caines, & Jackson, 1988, p. 7).

[11] It seems somewhat self-evident that the agency must be independent and autonomous in individual proceedings, but the question of implementation of political promises of a winning political party to its constituents in the elections arises without being able to influence the results. The answer to this question is given in the possibility of formulating new policies (in legislation/regulation if needed) or in work programs and performance contracts in line with the promised policy goals, as long as they remain within legal (constitutional) frames. Within the latter, agencies must then pursue the policy independently and impartially in accordance with the principles of equality, non-discrimination, preestablished procedures and criteria.

[12] The idea of leverage points is not unique to systems analysis— it is embedded in legend: the silver bullet; the trimtab; the miracle cure; the secret passage; the magic password; the single hero who turns the tide of history; the nearly effortless way to cut through or leap over huge obstacles. We not only want to believe that there are leverage points, we want to know where they are and how to get our hands on them. Leverage points are points of power (Meadows, 2008, p. 145). Fuller proposed an excellent naval metaphor on the way we transmute little things into the momentous ones, as individuals and as a society. In 1972 Playboy interview, he presents the "trim tab" — a small mechanism that helps stabilize an enormous ship or aircraft — that could become a central metaphor in for the transformation and growth (Popova, 2015).

Chapter 8
Dimensions of Public Agencies

ABSTRACT

This chapter discusses various aspects of agency, autonomy, control, and decentralization in the context of different organizations and institutions, such as state bodies, semi-autonomous organizations, private law-based organizations, and commercial companies. The definition of an agency varies based on the type of organization, its legal status, and its relationship with other organizations. The chapter also explores different forms of decentralization, such as territorial decentralization and technical decentralization, and the challenges that arise with each. The concept of Latour's chain of translation is introduced to describe the transformation of ideas through intercessors. The passage concludes by discussing the importance of institutional arrangements, constitutional and legal demands, political culture, and public values in determining the meaning of agency and its relationship with other organizations.

INTRODUCTION

Everything is expressed through relationship. Colour can exist only through other colours, dimension through other dimensions, position through other positions that oppose them.

That is why I regard relationship as the principal thing.

– Piet Mondrian

In the effort to define the notion of agency and to it correlate the notions of autonomy, control, independence[1] etc. cautiousness is needed: already the Roman jurist Gaius Octavius Javolenus Priscus said 'every definition in civil law is dangerous, for rare are those that cannot be subverted' (*Omnis definitio in iure civili periculosa est; parum est enim, ut non subverti posset*; Dig. 50.17.202).[2] Indeed, "agency" can stand for state bodies, semi-autonomous organizations or next-step agencies, legally independent organizations or public establishments, private law-based organizations or commercial companies; 'autonomy' can mean managerial, institutional, functional and financial autonomy, while 'control' can be ex ante, ex post, positive, negative feedback, budget control, cost-benefit analysis or financial ratio,

DOI: 10.4018/979-8-3693-0507-2.ch008

statistical control, statistical sampling, etc. Along with different notions there are also their binary or dichotomous (what is agency can be understood only with the relation to other organisations, autonomy to control, costs to benefits, etc.) and multiple relations (relative to whom, to what, when, where, how, with what and why).

For Pollitt et al., an agency is an organization which has its status defined principally in public law, is functionally disaggregated from the core of its ministry, enjoys some degree of autonomy which is not enjoyed by the core ministry, is nevertheless linked to the ministry which permits ministers to alter the budget and main operational goals of the organization, is not statutorily fully independent of its ministry, and is not a commercial corporation (Pollitt, Talbot, Caulfield, & Smullen, 2004, p. 10).[3] This kind of *control–autonomy dimension* could be added to the known *state–market dimension* (from organizations with no to wholly immersed into commercial purposes), while there is also the *state–civil society dimension* (from wholly state-owned to voluntary organisations) (Pollit, Bathgate, Caulfield, Smullen, & Talbot, 2001). For Pollitt et al., the ideal NPM-style agency would be:

professionally managed, flexible, customer-responsive, specialized, efficient, and intensely performance-oriented. Its operations would be transparent, and, using the latest IT and accounting techniques, it would render to its democratic watchdogs a "balanced scorecard" of its achievements and weaknesses. It would learn swiftly from its rare mistakes and would always be listening to its stakeholders (Pollit et al., 2001, p. 279).

For Talbot, the agency is an organisation that should be 'at arm' (or further) from the main hierarchical 'spine' of central ministries/departments of the state; carrying out public tasks (service provision, regulation, adjudication, certification) at a national level; staffed by public servants (not necessarily "civil servants"); financed (in principle) by the state budget; and subject to at least some public/administrative law procedures. One further distinction…is that between quasi-autonomous agencies within departments or the civil service (e.g. Next Steps agencies in the UK; many federal agencies in the USA) and those outside departments or the civil service (e.g. Independent Administrative Institutions (IAIs) in Japan; Non-Departmental Public Bodies (NDPBs) in the UK; *Zelf-standige besturrsorganen* (ZBOs) in the Netherlands) (Talbot, 2004).

Due to the wide variety of forms and / or initiatives of all agencies, the notion of "agency" could be simply synonymous with the *organisation* and/or *institution* as the first does not tell anything new. The latter two notions could be (roughly – given the mix and/or presence of private organisations that implement tasks in the public interest and *vice versa*) divided in the private-public interest division: the former (organisations) are present in the private, while the latter (institutions) – due to the implementation of tasks in the public interest – in the public sector. As mentioned, conditions, predispositions, *i.e.*, a contextual frame (*e.g.*, institutional arrangements, constitutional and legal demands, political culture, public values, and/or ways of looking at things) are very important to determine what one knows, wants, can, or should do. Each word, element, or doing can be addressed from different perspectives, while this interesting part of addressing is present in persons who address perspectives. Here fits Latour's notion of a chain of *translation* that describes the transformation of a larger problem into a smaller one through a sequence of intercessors, that reshape, reinvent and adjust ideas every time they are chosen by different individuals and/or organizational "translators": 'in the translation model, there is *no transportation without transformation*–except in those miraculous cases where everybody is in total agreement' (Latour, 1996, p. 119). Different meanings are obtained in different cultural and other contexts from the same idea.[4]

Dimensions of Public Agencies

Based on the analysed Dutch agency experience, Smullen confirms the idea of translation[5] that can be described as "please choose among elements at your convenience".[6] When only some of the aspects of the agency idea are recognised as "appropriate" and selected, the meaning of chosen aspects is different as they are inserted into the unique governmental mechanism of a specific country.

Based on various approaches and experiences with agencies, SIGMA concluded that 'as even a cursory review of international experience reveals, the term public agency, when used by a national government, really carries whatever meaning that the government wishes to give to it' (SIGMA, 2001, p. 14).[7] *All actions are Janus-faced, they all have contrasting aspects, they can lead to the intended and unintended consequences.* A prevalent opinion is that agencies should be more or less independent and/or autonomous. On the other hand, both terms per se are *contradictio in adiecto* if not understood relative to something that gives independence or autonomy. The intention of downsizing and outsourcing can cause 'information vacuum' or Pollitt's sandcastles, improve service efficiency and quality can lower expertise in ministries of improving transparency can be made publicly available irrelevant or too complex data that people do not understand, decentralised management that leads to too diffuse and therefore unmanageable management, task specialization that creates tunnel visions, output focussed that can disregard inputs and processes, performance contracting that disregards other goals connected to the first. Such intentions call on the other hand for stricter coordination and control of higher ministerial levels that should harmonise the actions of different agencies with respect to higher public goals. In the rule-of-law frame, this means the enactment of more authorised rules, which lead to more rules and/or re-regulation. Beware of popular notions; unusual enthusiasm can lead to confirmation bias; various approaches that are placed under the same umbrella should be chosen carefully regarding other possibilities or alternatives from the same or different camp.

DECONCENTRATION AND DECENTRALISATION

Deconcentration and decentralisation are the starting points for the management of administration: the latter is organised in the first or the second way. If the former (also known as administrative decentralization) operates in relation to a hierarchical unit, its instructions, the possibility to annul its decisions to reorganise (introduction of reforms), and also of direct interference with the work of the subordinate unit, the second (so-called specialised institutions[8]) does not have a higher hierarchical level; as said, a parental ministry cannot give instructions, abolish, annul or replace decisions of specialised institutions. They have a greater extent of autonomous decision-making under the Constitution and laws (only in this part, a country retains a certain degree of control). If there is a two-way system (where the country implements state tasks on a local level with its own state agencies, parallel and independent to municipalities that implement its own local tasks), the deconcentrated state authorities perform the functions of the State throughout its territory; there is thus no difference among agencies on local communities in the part of (local) organisation or dispersion. However, there is a difference in ensuring coherence, as it is easier to maintain it within deconcentrated bodies (due to greater powers of the hierarchical unit over subordinated units) than in the independent and/or decentralised bodies (in the form of territorial decentralisation and technical/specialised decentralisation). Given the changing environment and needs of the population, it could be said that both deconcentration and decentralisation are never really completed, as they have to *adapt constantly*.[9]

As was said, decentralised units are not subject to the hierarchical level of higher authorities and their instructions, but merely to state control (tutela) over the constitutionality and legality of their actions. In the context of decentralisation, it is possible to distinguish between territorial units (territorial decentralisation) and those that were set up to perform specialised tasks (technical decentralisation), to which agencies fall: there are different forms of corporate-type organisation presented that ensure to the communities of persons the performance of tasks according to the speciality of that institution through the appointed representatives by the State and other stakeholders (directors, management or administrative boards). Their powers are of a more executive technical type that is directly linked to the provision of certain services in the context of greater or lesser autonomy of action. For this reason, we can also talk about different forms of conduct: territorial communities can carry out matters of local importance autonomously (the original tasks of local self-government) and are only subject to the law (not by-laws). Given the constitutionally defined position of local self-government and, in this context, municipalities, they do not need a specific statutory power for their normative activity of original tasks. Independent regulation (that includes the issuing of general acts) of local affairs is a fundamental (usually determined already by the Constitution) task of municipalities. This competence is here exercised primarily by the adoption of municipal decrees which are equal, *i.e.*, on the same by-legislative level as the state's by-laws.

Territorial communities can regulate matters of local importance independently, while special communities (agencies) can regulate matters only when they have explicit authority in the law or in the parent act. It is this special technique of administrative action that is the main reason for choosing decentralisation instead of deconcentration. In essence, the first could be seen as more or less 'disguised deconcentration' in relation to a greater or lesser degree of autonomy - the law or other legal act determines the scope and means of interference of higher hierarchical levels of agency control (i.e., regulation in terms of behavioral impact] over its formal acts, actions, and staff in terms of counselling, coordination, annulation, approbation, authorisation, or even substitution of acts). For this reason, the relationship between a hierarchical body (ministry) and the agency needs to be examined in the context of each individual agency. However, the legal and regulatory level is generally not sufficient for the successful management of this relationship. For this reason, (performance) contracts are concluded between these two bodies to ensure timely implementation of the public interest objectives (results and their indicators) given the current situation in the economy and in other areas.

The growth of government has caused the proliferation and abundance of agencies, which could lead to the over-stretched span of control and weak synchronisation of interrelated actions. The usual governmental answer for such conditions is the consolidation of single agencies into a larger agency or even into a functionally integrated ministry. NPM's version of structural disaggregation and delegated responsibilities (agencification) on the other side caused merging tendencies of various types of coordination (hierarchy, mutual cooperation through public-public interest partnerships, markets, network). They are now known under the form of whole-of-government that can encompass the integrated service delivery,[10] whole-of-government as (more informal) coordination and (more formal, with a common mission or structure) collaboration,[11] whole-of-government as integrating and rebalancing governance,[12] and whole-of-government as culture change[13] (Halligan, Buick, & O'Flynn, 2011). As with other reform programmes, the whole government agenda is a subject of focus, interest, cycle, and commitment. Based on the analysis of the four countries, Halligan, Buick and O'Flynn think that 'the prospects are both somewhat discouraging, judged by the mixed results of the experiments, and propitious in that the horizontal government continues to move into the mainstream' (Halligan et al., 2011, p. 74).

Dimensions of Public Agencies

From the system's point of view agencies are part of the larger ministerial system which is also part of the larger governmental system (which is still part of a larger subnational system). As central government should harmonise and coordinate relations among ministries to be able to most efficiently address its basic purposes, the same applies to ministries versus agencies. As relations between parents and children cannot be seen as rival ones, the same stands for the relation between a ministry and a specific agency: although they are up to some point similar to each other, they both operate on different levels with their own special goals and purposes to be able to connect on a higher level. Their various approaches should consolidate themselves into a larger meaning (of the public interest) from a different point of view: ministries from the point of political integration, consistency, and regularity, and agencies from the administrative point of independency, procedural due process, diversity adaptability, and autonomy. Despite of different historical examples, ministries and agencies are not rivalling, but just different organisational forms/approaches by which the goals are supposed to be achieved. An organisational form per se is not so important as it is its underlying structure that makes a whole difference even between the same formal organisational forms: the underlying structure could be everything that fits perfectly (that causes changes) related to order parts, inputs, main purposes, stocks and flows, feedback, indicators, patterns of outputs, decisions, leaders, professionals, and other persons, who could impact at least on some part of the system.

It hence matters how things are continually (re)connected between themselves, how they can be (re)coordinated, (dis)integrated, (de)coupled, and (dis)jointed vis-à-vis changes in their environment and vis-a-vis methods and manners by which changes were established as such: if an agency does not have some indicators of success or of its operations installed, changes are more or less intuitively and thus more arbitrarily left to decision-makers without a relevant objective basis. Between the ministry and the agency, a formal division can be made between the political and administrative lines, but only objective results (effects) can tell when the agency should be incorporated into the ministry due to its political, coordination actions (or when changes should be made in the agency to be able to remain the agency) and the contrary when some ministry's part should be created as an agency due to its mainly administrative, implementational and/or subordinative tasks. It stands is the rule of thumb that a minister should give policy guidance to agencies, while he is banned to intervene in individual administrative cases (the same stands when adjudication occurs at the ministry). He could manage citizens on a general level, but directly on the individual one.

Agencies are created or disjoined from ministries under the proposition that such autonomous, single- or few-focus units are more efficient than ministries. In a wide bowl of apparent reasons along efficiency, agencies were created due to political reasons, or to be comparable with a neighbouring country, to pass a hot problem forward, or just because to be "fashionable" or "democratic". Many times, such propositions or reasons were not tested in practice, but were nevertheless later fiercely defended by those who proposed it, who work there, or have any kind of benefit from them. One of the rules of thumb could be an answer to the simple question: 'Would I, as a public official, do the same in my own company (or from my own budget), as I do now in a public office?' Sincere answers would be a surprise to many 'organisational innovators' or agency enthusiasts and the duty, at the same time, of decision makers (to reform processes as they are such that allow unwanted and ineffective behaviour).

Organisational Division of Autonomy

The relation between deconcentration and decentralisation addresses an organisational question focused on the level of *independence* or separation from the parent ministry, that is, on the level of autonomy. Along with the known autonomy types, their organisational distribution between a ministry and an agency can be seen as a ratio between the global-level activities (policy) and the local level (the most basic primary activities) which is needed also to address properly institutional accountability and responsiveness. The disproportionate level of centralisation produces troubles like bottlenecks and the excessive, ineffective, irresponsive, and/or distant to the people bureaucracy, while such decentralization can lead to problems of control, coordination, and various executive approaches to centrally determined goals. An institution cannot be responsible for things that cannot be addressed with its resources (e.g., an agency has decision-making autonomy without the financial one; this leads to a problem of decision implementation). For Pollitt et al. (2004) independence and autonomy run together on two different dimensions: (a) how far is an agency formally separated from its parent ministry and seen as a separate entity, and (b) how far is the agency free to make its own choices on internal arrangements and/or how far are the latter externally imposed upon it. They name the first dimension as "disaggregation" and the second to "autonomization".\

The question of how far is the agency free to make its own choices basically points to autonomy or conferred discretion. That both latter notions could be synonymous can be seen from the fact that the right amount of allocated discretion also has an answer on autonomy, in the frame of organisational autonomy, on the right degree of centralisation and decentralisation. To establish an appropriate level of organisational division between the ministerial end and agency's level and/or to properly address a ratio between centralisation and decentralization of organizational resources and decision-making, the recursion/autonomy's functions table can be used. To do so, it is necessary to recall a more or less rough (because both parts are also present in both levels) difference between the centralised policy or regulatory activities and decentralised executive or implementation activities. First, relate to *purposes* that create a thoughtful system of material and procedural principles and the main systemic rules about the agency's tasks, competencies, stakeholders, their entitlements, criteria on which the latter are given, how control, coordination, transparency and performance is established to guide further the second at *procedural*[14] decision-making, regarding the people, time, place, manner, quantity or quality *vis-à-vis* the mentioned main rules. Given that autonomy is needed to support several primary tasks, what kind

Table 1. Agency-relevant administrative doctrines (Pollitt et al., 2004, p. 35)

Administrative doctrines – choice areas	'Ministries'	New style 'Agencies'	Traditional 'Boards'
Control	Control exercised principally by levers of inputs (budgets) or processes.	Control is exercised primarily through output or outcomes.	Control exercised principally by levers of inputs (budgets) or processes.
Independence	Direct control by ministers in the integrated classical bureaucracy.	Direct control by ministers through a mixture of direction and legal or quasi-legal frameworks.	Formally and legally independent 'boards' with no direct ministerial control.
Specialization	Integration of policy and operations.	Separation of policy-making and operational implementation functions.	Integration of policy and operations.
Decision-making	Decisions are made principally by rule and rote.	Mostly local discretion with some general rules.	Mostly externally imposed rules with some local discretion.

Dimensions of Public Agencies

of criteria can be applied to select centralisation or decentralisation? The essence is to understand the significance of autonomy taking into account the primary tasks that it supports. This can be considered under the following criteria of the autonomy function:

1. The autonomy of the agency is a must-have critical factor for a ministerial policy task (it is essential for the overall success, it benefits the department as a whole, it is synonymous with a high-level goal and it is linked directly to the strategy).
2. The requirement of constant autonomy for the policy task it supports is high.
3. The necessary resources to carry out autonomy are available and distributable on a central, ministerial level.
4. Agency's effectiveness and efficiency are transparently presented as a pattern (of decisions between current flow and available stocks) shown as a curve or line presented on the dependent (results) and independent (time) variables.
5. Coordination and ex-ante (input) and ex-post (results) control are present and effective at the ministerial level.

When all these conditions are met, the ministry is not "hollow" and decentralisation is probably the best choice. When just one of these conditions is not fulfilled, some form of centralisation should be considered. The ministerial level must allow variations of the agency's autonomy so that the agency can efficiently address its various tasks, while the agency must combine its resources within the budget given by the ministry and should not develop autonomy by itself. As an informal type of autonomy, this can be inevitable given the complexity of the agency's environment, but in all cases the higher level must acknowledge this type of autonomy as legit. Successful systems in general emerge from the communications or constant interactions among the policy and executive activities. It stands as *sine qua non* that the elements agencies supposed to have, can exhibit a various range of practices. Instead of the one-dimensional, there is always a better strategy for evading bias to use a *multidimensional analysis* of agency, but this approach is very complex. Already between autonomy-control relations, the combination calculator shows 462 combinations and even 46,656 permutations among six types (of anything), *sic*. Greve et al. (1999) (theoretically) established that prospects for political influence (but also ministerial responsibility) become intuitively proportionately reduced on the line away from the departmental unit, contract agencies, public body, voluntary (charity) and semi privatised towards the contracting out types of organisational forms.

AUTONOMY

If autonomy types are put under the same denominator, autonomy could mean the level of the organization's decision-making role about (human, financial, and other) resources. On the other hand, this tells us nothing about the different types of autonomy found on the central or local level. Verhoest et al. (2004) differentiate between two kinds of agency's autonomy (here presented in the high-level types): i) autonomy as the level of *decision-making competencies* of the agency (concerning management on the one hand and concerning agency policy on the other hand: managerial[15] and policy[16] autonomy) and ii) autonomy as *the exemption of constraints* on the actual use of decision-making competencies of the agency (referring to structural, financial, legal and interventional constraints on the agency's decision-making competencies – structural,[17] financial,[18] legal,[19] *and* interventional[20] autonomy). Their central hypothesis is that 'if one wants to know the level of autonomy of a public agency, they must analyse not only the decision-making competencies on managerial and policy matters of the agency but also to what extent the government can constrain the use of these competencies by structural, financial, legal and interventional means' (Koen Verhoest et al., 2004, p. 109). To compare the autonomy, control and internal management of state agencies (dependent variables) Verhoest et al. distinguished between four different theoretical perspectives[21] that are included into an integrated heuristic model with three analytical levels, which fit into each other like Russian dolls (the international level, the level of the state, and the level of the individual agency). Based on the analysis of 226 agencies among these perspectives the structural-instrumental perspective, followed by the task-specific perspective, is most important for explaining agency autonomy. Agency control is best explained by the cultural-institutional perspective, combined with factors of political salience in the task-specific perspective. The levels of managerial autonomy and result control are most important in explaining the use of management techniques, with the structural-instrumental and task-specific perspectives providing some additional explanatory power (K. Verhoest, Roness, Verschuere, Rubecksen, & MacCarthaigh, 2010, p. 262).

For agency changes to autonomy, control, and internal management, politicians and administrative officials should consider agency characteristics, because agencies [in Norway, Ireland, and Flanders] with a governing board, of a large size, or with a large budget tend to have more managerial autonomy as well as greater (result) control. Agencies which are less dependent on state funding tend to have more managerial autonomy (cf. Gains 1999, 2004). Agencies which were created in the heyday of NPM (after 1990), tend to have more HRM autonomy, but they have less policy autonomy than older agencies (cf. Carpenter 2001). Agencies in the welfare and social policy area report somewhat more managerial autonomy and more accountability, but simultaneously they have less policy autonomy. These characteristics provide agency-level pressures for conformity and similarity of agencies across states (K. Verhoest et al., 2010, p. 266).

The external and internal conditions, that is, the context in which agencies work, are hence very important, and even tougher, a determination of an appropriate ratio between autonomy and control resembles not only a moving target but also the target that also changes its numbers. Öberg and Wockelberg have – based on the mentioned six-dimensions of autonomy – statistically confirmed "the paradox of autonomization" (autonomy in managerial and operational decisions requests close control that leads to the introduction of result-control instruments): based on 182 Swedish government agencies and their 1752 observations they established that more managerial and structural autonomy (autonomisation) correlates with more external control (controlisation) (Öberg & Wockelberg, 2020).[22] This is not the paradox, as each type of autonomy is not independent *per se*: it must be always understood relative or in relation to something that enables autonomy in the first place. The importance of the already mentioned division between the (in)formal tasks and practices and regulatory cycles is seen also in the division of autonomy: 'the allocated or formal autonomy is different from the one used in practice. Therefore, [to put systemically] without an adequate time dimension to the research, there has been no investigation of the patterns of change' (Bouckaert & Peters, 2004, p. 27). It seems relations between the autonomy types are always a matter of degree or their weights *vis-à-vis* one another, tasks at hand, a relevant level of governmental control and even wider MLG styles: '[a]gency autonomy is not only the result of the interactions between agency and its political and administrative principal, but also of it operating within supra- and transnational, national, regional and sectoral networks in which they interact with other agencies, stakeholders, the public and the media' (Koen Verhoest, 2018, p. 336). The level of agency

Dimensions of Public Agencies

autonomy is a socially constructed phenomenon that emerges in the relations between different social factors and actors. The trade-off between autonomy and control can be named as 'contested autonomy', but as said, such competition continues between more numerous factors.

Elements of Independence

The independence of independent agencies might really represent 'one of the most engrossing and difficult questions [not only] in American political life' (Miller, 1988, p. 222). Independence can be expressed in *organizational* independence (no direct subordination to another state body), *functional* independence (the powers and rules of procedure are set out in the law, with no exclusive influence on the decision-making of either the founder or the users of the services),[23] *personnel* independence (along with the stated manner and criteria for appointment, there should be criteria present for dismissal of managers, which would exclude political responsibility) and *financial* independence (the possibility of [partly] self-financing through service contributions or other similar charges under well-defined criteria and rules for determining their amount). Independence is always relative; it can be increased in individual cases, but it must not nullify the influence of a democratically elected government or the users of its services. Otherwise, the rule of law and the fundamental public interest could be violated, for which independence was transferred outside the state administration in the first place. Understanding independence is crucial for understanding the tasks of agencies, their competences (policy [substantive] decisions, legal regulations and adjudication), organizational design, HRM and political/legal control (the most important governmental control on agencies is the ability to appropriate funds). Taken as a whole, the relations among these pats exhibit the agency's *underlying structure.*

The well-known statutory definition of "organisational independence" is in the US's Administrative Procedure Act (APA) that describes an independent establishment in the federal government as 'an establishment in the executive branch (other than the United States Postal Service or the Postal Regulatory Commission) that is not an executive department, military department, government corporation, or part thereof, or part of an independent establishment (5 USC. § 104 (2013)). The definition of 'personal independence' of agencies is also found in *Humphrey's Executor v. United States* (295 U.S. 602 (1935)), where a truly independent agency is the one divided from the executive[24] and headed by the multimember, non-partisan and expert body whose members serve fixed terms and are protected from removal except for the cause (295 U.S.at 629). A degree of control (or independence from the other aspect) of agencies can be estimated according to *persons* (input ex ante formalities) and their *actions* (output ex post substance): based on key qualifications for agency decision makers (multimember board or commission and a director) as persons, on their appointments and dismissals, and on their substantive results, their capacity to make policy decisions with (based on the ministerial approval before implementation) or without political interference (policy making autonomy). Based on this double division elements can be in numerated that fit into one or another frame:

After analyzing the elements of each agency on the scale from -1 to 1, the agencies can present overall scores that show the level of their independence or autonomy (higher scores – less independence):

This approach can be used for different agencies across countries. In an ideal version, the legislator could have a predetermined scale that could show in what form or type a proposed new/changed institution should be created, but there are always some specifics that should also not be disregarded. This kind of assessment of agency independence gives results in a specific period of time, while behind the mentioned elements the underlying structure of relations, systems, flows, stocks, feedbacks, values,

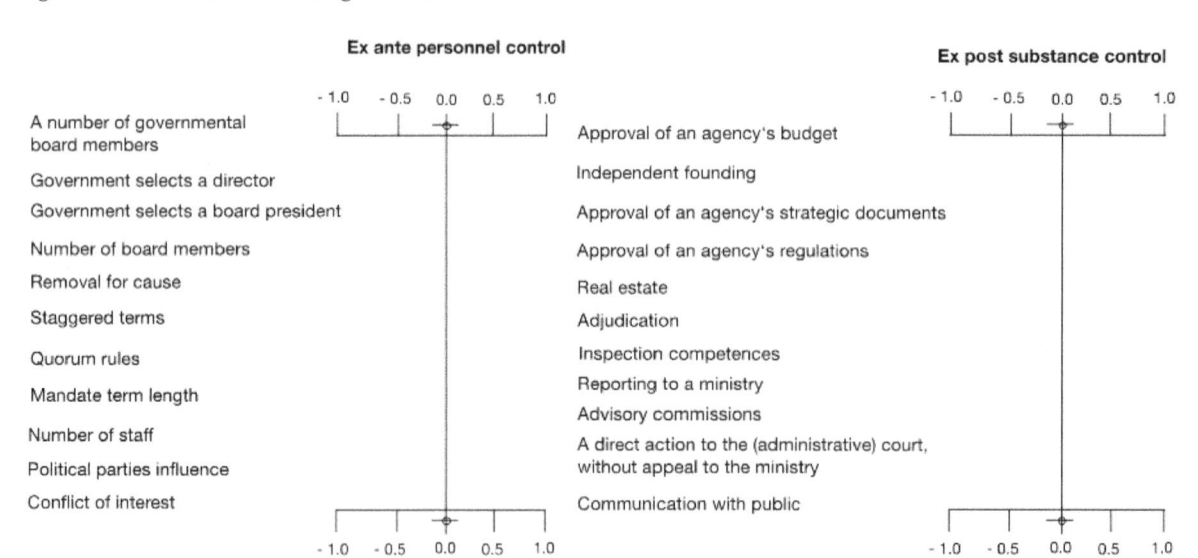

Figure 1. Personnel/actions governmental control

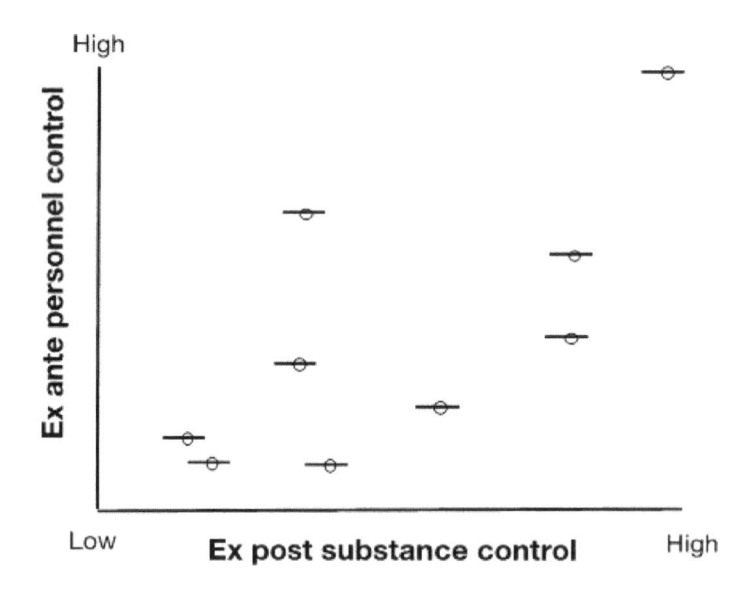

Ex ante personnel control

- A number of governmental board members
- Government selects a director
- Government selects a board president
- Number of board members
- Removal for cause
- Staggered terms
- Quorum rules
- Mandate term length
- Number of staff
- Political parties influence
- Conflict of interest

Ex post substance control

- Approval of an agency's budget
- Independent founding
- Approval of an agency's strategic documents
- Approval of an agency's regulations
- Real estate
- Adjudication
- Inspection competences
- Reporting to a ministry
- Advisory commissions
- A direct action to the (administrative) court, without appeal to the ministry
- Communication with public

Figure 2. Overall independence positions of agencies

internal and external context, results, stakeholders,, and the general public should not be overlooked as they crucially affect the level of independence. This structure[25] affects the *ex-ante* personnel and *ex-post* substantial elements mentioned and thus also changes the political influence on an agency's independence over time. Some of the stated personnel elements are similar to the High (appellate) courts (bipartisan appointment, removal for cause, multi-membership), while some substantive ones are more tightly connected with executive agencies (adjudication, inspection, reporting, budget approval) – despite of their *sui generis* form, independent agencies could be hence placed between[26] courts and executive agencies.

Dimensions of Public Agencies

Regardless of all being said, there is still a missing reason for which agencies are created as independent and not as the executive ones. The Slovenian Public Agencies Act (OL, no. 52/02) among the criteria for agency creation states (Article 4): 'A public agency is established when this enables the more efficient and optimal performance of tasks, as would be the case in performing tasks within an administrative body (especially if the performance of administrative tasks can be fully or primarily financed by administrative fees or user payments), or if depending on the nature or type of tasks, permanent direct political control over the performance of tasks is neither necessary nor appropriate. A public agency may be established when the organizational form of the body within the ministry[27] would not be possible to achieve the goal referred to in the first condition'. One reason for independence could be the view of agency as the 'arm of Congress' (Verkuil, 1988), when the Parliament does not trust the Government. In the coalition governments – where the parliamentary coalition also has its political members in the executive (ministers, state secretaries) – this could not hold. Another one could be in bad implementation of the executive, and Parliament thus designs independent agencies to be isolated from political influence to better serve the public interest. But why not hence improve the effectiveness and efficiency of the government instead of creation of new institutions? The mentioned reasons might be connected with another element of the underlying structure that is, *intention* or *purpose* for which independency is valued per se; this intention is usually the product of political compromise.[28] The latter might not be always sincere,[29] but it has its best moments when focused on matters that are valued in public. Such matters are usually the most important achievements valued in democratic societies; if the most important values are considered as criteria, then each independent agency that promotes them and in which politics should not interfere, is justified;[30] such agencies can be found on the fields that are focused on justice and human rights, public and private funds, communications, privacy, expression, thought, research, business, environment, health and energy. Their common denominator is the human *i.e.,* what is essentially important for someone to fully develop as a human person in all his glory dignity.

Specialized institutions in France fall into two categories: those of institutions which provide a public service of an administrative character, and those of institutions which exercise industrial and commercial activity, often having the more precise character of industrial and commercial public service. Specialised institutions are public enterprises, corporative institutions with administrative public (chambers of profession, unions) and other types of specialised institutions. Within the latter, Chapus argues that separation is justified solely on liberalities:

The simple reason for the separation of the budget of a special independent institution is that a beneficiary of liberalities has the guarantee that the goods or funds given will be used as he sees fit [for the implementation of obligations to perform specific services]. It is therefore interesting to set up as public establishments the services most likely to benefit from such donations: charitable and social assistance services, medical services, scientific or cultural services ... For other services, their legal personalization appears, more or less easily, as abuse of the formula of the specialized institution, because we do not see how the service will be better assured and the general interest better satisfied (Chapus, 2001, pp. 375–376).

What is essentially important, of course, depends also on the context and location of the person under question. As already mentioned, the range of values and the focus of agencies also vary. When talking about the creation of a new agency, the importance of basic values in which politics should not be interfered directly should not be disregarded, whereas when the public agency is already created, the same public agency could enhance its legitimacy when tasks are implemented in ways that emphasise also the mentioned value of human dignity. The latter is all the more important in the context of an increasingly complex, complicated, and flexible world. For some, precisely these conditions cause the creation of new independent agencies.[31] The mentioned conditions are more fully elaborated in further chapters of this work. One of the most relevant types of autonomy that could administer dignity, flexibility, and complexity is the autonomy of policymaking. Public agencies work in the principal-agent relationship; a public agency is an extended arm of the founder or service provided by public authorities to their citizens. Therefore, the policy as such is reserved to the founder, but the agency also has some options to maximize this policy. If it is successful in this doing, its importance, legitimacy, and resources would probably rise.

Policy-Making Autonomy

Policy making autonomy could be one of the most important types of autonomy, because other types basically depend on it, on good policy and such results for the people. When policy is framed and implemented successfully, it can also affect or change the levels of structural, financial, legal, and interventional autonomy. It matters how policy is made. One of the most known cases of decision or policy making autonomy of agencies in the US's administrative law is the case *Chevron U.S.A., Inc. v. Natural Resources Defense Council*, Inc., 468 U.S. 837 (1984). Here, the Supreme Court made the doctrine of judicial deference given to administrative actions by public agencies (the so-called "Chevron Deference" as the highest level of deference) *vis-à-vis* primary legislation.[32] This ruling has the following two-step process for reviewing an agency's *interpretation* of a statute: in a step one a court must determine whether Congress expressed intent in the statute and, if so, whether or not the statute's intent is ambiguous. If the intent of Congress is unambiguous or clearly stated, then the inquiry must end. Agencies must fulfill the clearly expressed intent of Congress. If, however, the intent of Congress is silent, unclear, ambiguous, that is, when the statute lacks direct language on a specific point, then a federal court must decide whether the agency interpretation is based on a *permissible* construction of the statute, one that is *not arbitrary or capricious or obviously contrary* to the statute. In step two the court must in examining the agency's reasonable construction, assess whether the decision of Congress to leave an ambiguity, or fail to include express language on a specific point, was done explicitly or implicitly. If the decision of Congress was explicit, then the agency's interpretations are binding on the federal courts unless they are *arbitrary, capricious or manifestly contrary* to the statute. If the decision of Congress was implicit, then so long as the agency's interpretation is *reasonable*,[33] a federal court cannot substitute its own statutory construction superior to the agency's construction.

The Supreme Court made the Chevron case a powerful interpretative weapon in the collection of agency regulatory techniques. If therefore Congress expressly delegates the implementation of a particular statue to a federal agency, the responsibility to interpret the statute is at the agency, or in other words, where Congress clearly intended to grant authority to an agency, the courts should defer to the agency's interpretation (so the agency's regulations are binding), unless it is not permissible, that is, when it is arbitrary, capricious or obviously contrary to the statute. With an explicit intent to delegate authority (Congress intended a particular result, but was not clear about it – this is a question of law, and must be properly resolved by the courts), an agency's interpretation should not be arbitrary, capricious, or manifestly contrary to statute (hard look review[34]), that is agency must consider all relevant facts as part of its decision-making process, while with the implicit intent (Congress had no particular intent on the subject, but meant to leave its resolution to the agency) agencies' interpretations must be reasonable (this means the conferral of discretion upon the agency, and the only question of law presented to the courts is whether the agency has acted within the scope of its discretion i.e., whether its resolution of the ambiguity is reasonable (Scalia, 1989, p. 516) that privileges deference – soft(er) look review. A judge here does not step "in an officer's shoes" and considers if he would decide the same, but considers if an officer's decision could be plausible, feasible, credible (although the judge would decide differently). The first step seems to use an arbitrary and capricious standard in form, while the second (reasonableness) uses the "arbitrary or capricious in substance".[35]

Public agencies should at the interpretation of primary legislation that is its implementation, rely on factors which Parliament has considered or intended to consider, they must analyse important aspects of a problem, offer an explanation for its decision aligned with the evidence, while their decisions should be credible and based on expertise. The regulations of public agencies must reflect a fair and considered judgment on the matter in question that is not clearly erroneous or inconsistent with the regulation. Their level of analysis should show an available knowledge of a situation at the time of an evaluated act, and not simply a post hoc rationalization simply to defend their past actions. The other documents and correspondence of the public agencies must have 'the power to persuade', established on the thoroughness evident in their consideration, the validity of their reasoning, and their consistency with earlier and later pronouncements. When such (ideal) conditions are met a public agency is almost on a way of Confucious's effortless *wu-wei* action (2003) with a perfect harmony between one's inner dispositions and external movements. This is an ideal state that is rarely achieved, but there are agencies which are even more famous (e.g., FBI, CIA, MI6, Red Cross) than their parent ministries. Therefore, the internal harmony of the agency, with its emphasis on public values, legality, and people's well-being, is very similar on the common level to a virtuous person on the individual level.

IDEAL-AGENCY MODEL AND ITS PRACTICAL CHARACTERISTICS

Ideal-type agency of NPM (K. Verhoest et al., 2010) is assembled from key dimensions such as *structural disaggregation* (the large bureaucratic and monolithic departments are disaggregated into single-purpose and client-oriented organizations with a focus on service delivery focus), *managerial freedom* (a goal is to act more or less independently of their core government departments with the aim of increased efficiency, 'let managers manage' should encourage professionalism), results control (a change of control from ex ante to results-based control, based on contractual instruments; a drop of input and process control for a firmer control of performance) and the 'policy operations' split (policy preparation as a 'political' task should be performed by democratically elected representative [and their direct subordinate core departments), while policy operations as an 'administrative' task is to be performed by agencies 'arm', more or less free of ministerial interference). When leaders would follow this ideal-type model, agencies should probably have high levels of managerial freedom/autonomy and administrative implementation (that is ex-post controlled by results) and low levels of policy autonomy. The "convergence–divergence" discussion is as the ex post emphasis on results, focused on practical similarities or differences between agencies, while it does not answer on reasons of similarities or differences. The conclusion that agencies are similar or different does not tell anything about their contexts of doing things, about their dynamics among other higher- or lower-level organizations, about their relationships with their stakeholders and other people, about the ways they obtain people's trust and legitimacy. A practical choice of agency type, be it *ad hoc* or more like a text book (general draft or form) like – although the first is more common due to various (political and other interests) – have in common that both choices disregard substantial relations and context in a specific country that would be established with a serious analysis and research. To compare the autonomy, control, and internal management of state agencies (dependent variables) Verhoest et al. distinguished between four different theoretical perspectives that are included into an integrated heuristic model with three analytical levels, which fit into each other like Russian dolls (the international level, the level of the state, and the level of the individual agency). Based on the analysis of 226 agencies among these perspectives the structural-instrumental perspective, followed by the task-specific perspective, is most important for explaining agency autonomy. Agency control is best explained by the cultural-institutional perspective, combined with factors of political salience in the task-specific perspective. The levels of managerial autonomy and result control are most important in explaining the use of management techniques, with the structural-instrumental and task-specific perspectives providing some additional explanatory power (K. Verhoest et al., 2010, p. 262).

In agency changes to autonomy, control, and internal management, politicians and administrative officials should (but in practice usually only do) consider agency characteristics, because

Agencies [in Norway, Ireland, and Flanders] with a governing board, of a large size, or with a large budget tend to have more managerial autonomy as well as greater (result) control. Agencies which are less dependent on state funding tend to have more managerial autonomy (cf. Gains 1999, 2004). Agencies which were created in the heyday of NPM (after 1990), tend to have more HRM autonomy, but they have less policy autonomy than older agencies (cf. Carpenter 2001). Agencies in the welfare and social policy area report somewhat more managerial autonomy and more accountability, but simultaneously they have less policy autonomy. These characteristics provide agency-level pressures for conformity and similarities of agencies across states (K. Verhoest et al., 2010, p. 266)

Path-dependency as an element of complexity is very much present also in agencies (this can be an additional reason for the use of complexity theory in the field of agencies). Pollitt et al. confirmed this idea on the basis of a multiple case study in four states (Pollitt et al., 2004) that was further confirmed by Verhoest et al. (K. Verhoest et al., 2010) on the basis of a multiple case study in three states: 'the autonomy of agencies, and the way they are controlled by ministers or parent departments, is strongly influenced by extensive national path dependence and politico-administrative regimes' (Pollitt et al., 2004, p. 246). 'Our evidence of agency reforms in these three small European states demonstrate that path-dependency indeed matters a great deal, as reflected in the relevance of administrative law traditions, cultural traits, the tradition regarding agencification and common norms on agency roles and positions, or even the legacy of past budgetary and financial crises. Trust, consistent behaviour, clear role divisions and consensus between politico-administrative actors with respect to reforms, the introduction of managerial autonomy and result control also seem to matter also in a positive way' (K. Verhoest et al., 2010, p. 266). Like Pollitt et al. (Pollitt et al., 2004) and other researchers (Hogwood et al. 2000), Verhoest et al. also 'found that agencies with large budgets tend to be controlled more and have less (financial) management autonomy. Moreover, agencies that have a high degree of face-to-face interaction with large groups of users, like agencies in the welfare and social policy area, tend to be controlled in a stricter way' (K. Verhoest, Roness, Verschuere, Rubecksen, & MacCarthaigh, 2010, p. 267). Control and coordination as examples of good regulation can enhance the use of these management techniques on the level of agency when backed up with the agency's managerial autonomy, boosted with the good delivery of services, a large size of agency, its own sources of income, and high public trust.

Institutions operate in the dynamic environment, and such are also their interchanges that are affected by the various natural (processes, substance, time, form, extent or dimensions, energy, their combinations and causalities) and formal contexts (procedures, rules, authorities, public institutions, officials).

Dimensions of Public Agencies

Their specifics are too complex to be analysed only with surveys or questionnaires. They have two major limitations: the answers exhibit a *too subjective* nature (based on the person's experiences, practice, education, background, values, etc.), and they can provide only *historical* or *ex-post* evidence of the state of affairs that could no longer be relevant for future occasions or even for a time in which a person wants to make a decision. Agencies, as the right hand of the country, are present in all over the world. The same stands for the people: we are everywhere, at some points similar and at the others dissimilar at the same time; our life patterns evolve and change, we are interested for different domains, purposes, goals,, and tasks, our freedom/autonomy, control, self-management and relations with others are caused and changed by different factors. The parallel between people and agencies is made because the latter, as organisations, are an extension or a tool (gr. *organon*) that serves us to achieve our goals. Because agencies are a reflection of people, they often exhibit similar characteristics as we do. It is hence not so much important to determine how we behave in individual countries (where it is always possible to find differences and similarities or generalise results, despite all specifics), but how we (*can*) behave in certain circumstances under which we try to reach common goals (that may be different from a country to a country). The established similarities and differences among people in different countries can be valuable for anthropological or sociological reasons, they can even answer on some managerial questions (how to lead the people), but they cannot provide answers on how to react in future cases, in different circumstances and contexts.[36]

State-level characteristics *with respect to agency* characteristics can be statistically generalized when different countries are considered, but differences may be their specific success factors that could not be relevant for other countries, and also statistical aggregation cannot give specific imports for an agency under question. Autonomy, control and internal management with various weights or importance in a different environment can lead to (dis)similar results. On the other hand, when only one country is considered, there is no room for comparison based on which its level of success could be improved. A solution could be done on a meta-level: all that can be advised is only general guidance that can be found within the frameworks of morality, ethics, and fundamental legal principles. The same stands for agencies: only common guidelines (based on the same morality, ethics, and the general legal principles) can be given that agencies should follow to be *adaptable* as much as possible to their environment (e.g., a human vs. agency: do not steal – not be corrupt; do not lie – be transparent; enhance trust – always act similarly in similar conditions; do not hate – be impartial; help the one in need – deliver its services; do not change your mind without due cause – respect the rule of law). Only various, but general perspectives (here given with the help of systems and complexity theory) can be thus considered when the time comes to be as much as adaptable as possible. Only in this way (higher adaptability in parallel with the successfulness of organisation) agencies be able to help people by fulfilling the tasks of agencies in the utmost possible way and level. Reasonably, the mentioned general perspectives can be shown with the combination of various types of autonomy and of organisation. The diagonal "steps of success" lead towards strategic management:

The vertical (autonomy) and horizontal (organisation) stages of agency development at their peak represent an ideal type of agency (its sign with two lying A resembles DNA structure or a spiral with its two A grouped together). This is, of course, only a picture that cannot represent reality, and the same stands for the ideal type of agency. Nevertheless, reality could be different, and here mental representations are also helpful. Each type of agency can make progress on the diagonal line towards whole-up autonomy (that groups all versions of autonomy) and self-organisation and/or self-development. This of course cannot mean absolute autonomy and organisation, as this would put public agency completely

Figure 3. Ideal-type agency

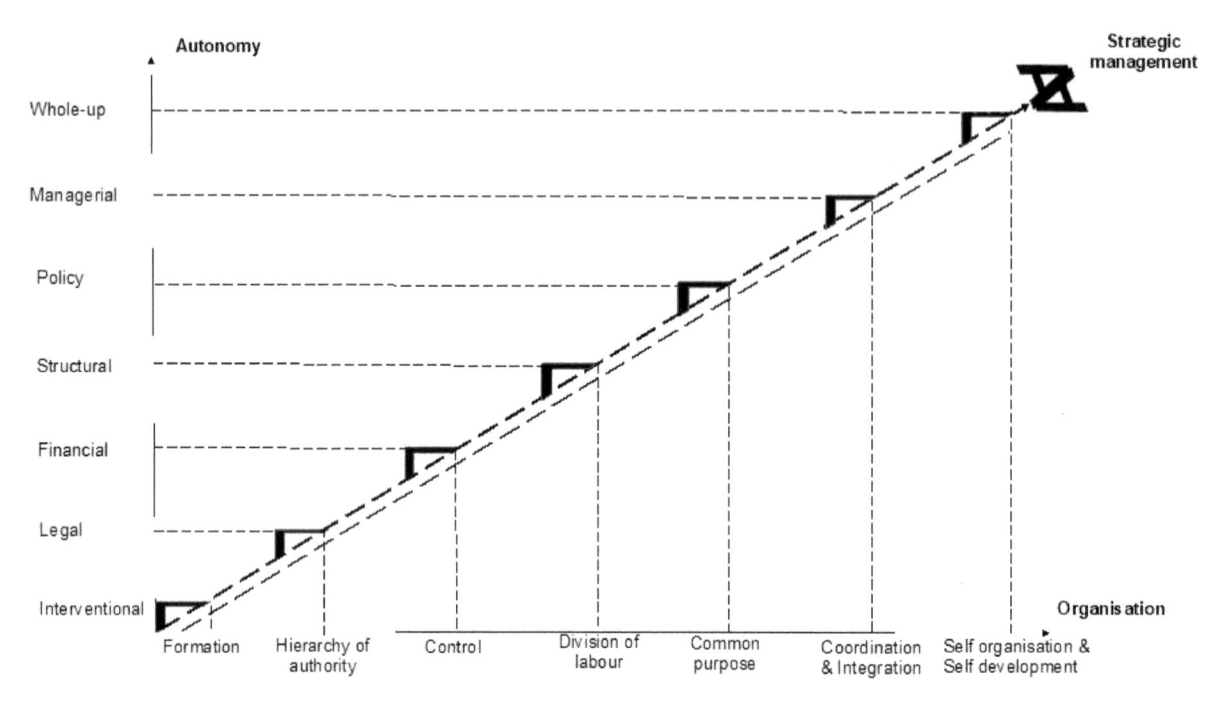

out of hierarchical subordination from the parental ministry and/or Parliament, but it can mean lower ministerial intensity of dealing with an agency as the latter not only successfully implement its tasks, but also transparently present its results to all stakeholders. This means that an agency's structure changes for good or for worse in time; this is at first sight contrary to its legal arrangements, but the latter are also made from abstract words that are subject of interpretation. Hayek claimed an evident order is not the product of designing human intelligence but the result of adaptive evolution, where 'no institution will continue to survive unless it performs some useful function...but the function which it serves at a given time may not be that for the sake of which it was originally established' (Frazer in Hayek, 2011, p. 115) or, as Sir James Mackintosh expressed by saying that 'Constitutions are not made, but grow'.

Agencies can also grow towards strategic management,[37] but there is no recipe for a specific agency what could be done written in a book without a specific analysis of an evaluated agency given its whole context. In line with Darwinism, the legal arrangement and the existent practices of public agencies can be seen as 'hereditary variation', where not everything is conditioned by randomness, but the latter (also with the help of intuition and subjectiveness) builds on layered, cumulative processes of iterations to produce the intended results, where also slight (accumulated) changes ('mutations') in the long run cause the emergent new things or processes. A degree of strategic management achieved for an agency under question can be established along the known methods also with the Integrative Propositional Analysis (IPA) that is focused not directly on empirical approaches (the correspondence between concepts and reality or its facts as this holds in correspondence theory[38]) but the *coherence between concepts*. As we live in a world of systems (physical, ecological, social, etc.) the IPA perspective suggests that such a world would be best understood and engaged by theories and models that are themselves systemic, also. IPA evaluates the conceptual structure of theories and models; the more complex and systemic they are,

Dimensions of Public Agencies

the more it can be expected that they will be suitable in a realistic application. A usual, more intuitively based and then tested hypotheses approach is not systemic enough; a more systemic perspective is needed that evaluates various theories and models for their internal coherence.[39]

Such a description emphasizes the underlying adaptive structure, different from approaches that emphasise the relevancy of leadership as *ipso facto* or a final state, without giving ways how to become such leaders. Goodsell's "mission mystique" is such example. The mentioned notion describes that 'truly exceptional public agencies possess a radiating aura of special importance and excitement that derives from the substantive nature of the work they do and how they do it' (2010). This mission could be a reference point for the concept of 'belief systems' of the agency, where interrelated properties embody powerful flows of emotional affect. For Goodsell, these two concepts can explain how public agencies reflect not only the fulfilment of legal demands and performance effectiveness, but also the institutional vitality. Public employees are to him 'turned on' by the importance of public tasks. On the other hand, there are at least three objections: i) jumping from a personal, subjective mood level in the organisational one is too big (as is does not explain how a personal feeling on the importance of the task at hand is transferred at the agency level; ii) a majority of (public) employees probably find their work important (or reasons for this importance) as their *psyche* or mental apparatus demands this from them to avoid feeling of personal redundancy or irrelevancy; iii) if the importance of public tasks is the basic element of people's cohesiveness, then officials of the most important public institutions would have by definition this mission mystic. This could be a *cum hoc ergo propter hoc conflation fallacy* ("with this, therefore because of this") conflation fallacy, as the importance of public tasks does not directly cause passion, special pride, commitment, dedication, or diligence in officials – the supreme judges, MPs, and the highest Executive's public officials do not all exhibit such mental states, neither do the highest institutions reflect a kind of magnetism or institutional-level charisma (otherwise there would be a great demand for such positions and a highly increased voter turnout). The first *could* lead to another, but it is not necessarily so; a desire to improve is the first step (that is why also this book is written), but employees must know what parts and how to improve them at first and then agencies' tasks. For this, the operative *underlying structure* on which a public agency works should be known to them; when they include it in the identification of relevant parts and manners by which they can be changed, a result could be the emergence of the already mentioned mission mystique.[40] The point is hence to make one step back and identify or recognise the basic perspectives, ways of doing things to change everything (or a specific thing under question) that emerges from them.

Goodsell's and others' works that emphasise the meaning of leadership in public administration could be put in the camp of Aristotle's final end desired for its own sake, *i.e.,* the good life, while there is a wide variety of agencies, tasks, objects, goals from which no *finis ultimus* nor *summum bonom* can be present in the singular, even when public interest or communal good is considered (as people have different meanings from what is in the public interest). Even Aristotle's happiness as the final good could be attained as the *mean relative to us*,[41] and people (neither agencies) in the presence of multiple priorities, interests, goals and purposes have no single dominant aim (task). A leader's practical wisdom or leadership is important, but a leader should also possess characteristics based on which he could spot all subtleties and details relevant for the institution – along with effective practices, values, internal and external support he should understand and be attentive to the mentioned underlying structure, presented here through system and complexity theory. The tasks, purposes, goals, values, and culture of public agencies are very important, but it should first be known how they evolve, grow, and change. Here, the mentioned structure comes to the fore. Understanding the principles of the latter gives a decisive advantage over other elements and other organizations, while understanding the embeddedness of a public agency in other agencies and systems resembles something that could be named the excellence of a public agency.

TYPES OF AGENCIES

The notion of "agency" can describe 'any body, such as a board, commission, or tribunal, established by government and subject to government control to carry out a specialized function that is not an integral part of a government ministry or department' (Nastasi, Pressman, & Swaigen, 2020, p. 16), but this kind of definition (from Canadian authors) is not precise enough. Such departmental offshoots or freestanding agencies fit within the Type 2 agency (see below) that is usually a reserved term also for agencies in Europe. Nastasi et. al. (2020) among the categories of agencies, enumerate the adjudicative agencies ("tribunals"), regulatory agencies, advisory agencies, operational enterprises, operational services agencies, Crown foundations, trust agencies, nonscheduled agencies "Watchdog" bodies and ombudsperson-like agencies bodies and ombudsperson-like agencies, commissions, and inquiries. Agencies examine, inspect, advise, recommend, decide, investigate, adjudicate, hold hearings, monitor, regulate, plan, assess, set standards, provide professional education, etc. The key condition for the actions of the agencies is to build the agency in a way that reasonably avoids any kind of unfairness in the execution of the mentioned tasks. This is usually done on an *ad hoc* basis: each agency is created individually with its specific context; this kind of creation can lead to unexpected variations of power and inconsistencies in their actions that can (un)justifiably differentiate its way of doing things from other, although similar agencies.

Given the various and numerous differences among the organizational forms of agencies and/or agents, the first problem of further research is the language or *the name problem*, because the notion of 'agency' can mean different things in different countries and even in the same country. Some scholars even do not operate with the notion of agency and include it into the notion of not-for profit organisation.[42] The lack of terminological and operational clarity hinders further development; a remedy for this could be a topography with all diversity and clarity included at the same time. Another approach could be the practice of the European Court of Justice that uses its own terminology given all the variety of names in the EU member states (*e.g.,* "services of general public interest' for national "public services"). The first approach could present agencies on a subsectional map based on their types of tasks and types of agency to present this plethora of various agencies and / or 'quangoland' (Greve et al., 1999) or a presentation of a more advanced general categorization of public sector organizations that can be made (Thiel, 2012). In 2008 and 2009, an expert survey was conducted among members of the CRIPO network (the result of COST Action IS0601, named CRIPO or Comparative Research into Current Trends in Public Sector Organization) and agency researchers from 21 countries. All respondents were experts in the field of agency research. They filled out an e-mail questionnaire with questions related to 25 executive tasks,[43] asking about whether the task in question is a government task, what kind of organization (agency) carries it out, and when that organization was established in its current legal form. Based on experts' answers, a categorization of agencies was developed to allow comparison of different (legal) types of organizations. Of the 525 possible combinations (25 tasks * 21 countries), respondents could identify 498 (95%):

In various countries, mostly agency types 0 – 2 prevail, with the most numerous Type 1:

Dimensions of Public Agencies

Table 3. *Categorization of public-sector organizations (Thiel, 2012, p. 20).*

Type	Definition	Examples	Number
0	Unit or directory of the national, central or federal government (not local, regional or state)	Ministry, department, ministerial directorate/directorate general (DG), state institution	104 (20%)
1	Semi-autonomous organization, unit or body without legal independence but with some managerial autonomy[44]	Next Steps Agencies (UK), contract/executive agencies (NL, B, AUS, IRL), state agencies (Nordic countries), Italian Agenzia, service agency (A), state institutions (EST), central bureaus (HUN), direct agencies (GER)	142 (27%)
2	Legally independent organization/ body (based on statutes) with managerial autonomy, either based on public law or private law[45]	Public establishments (IT, POR), ZBO (NL), NDPB (UK), parastatal bodies (B), statutory bodies or authorities (not corporations: A, EST, AUS, IRL, POR), indirect agencies (GER)	106 (20%)
3	Private or private-law based organization established by or on behalf of the government like a foundation or corporation, company or enterprise (the government owns majority or all stock, otherwise category)[46]	Commercial companies, state-owned companies (SOC) or enterprises (SOE), and government foundations	62 (12%)
4	Execution of tasks by regional or local bodies and/or governments (country, province, region, municipality)	Länder (GER), regions (B, I, UK), states (AUS), cantons (CH)	54 (10%)
5	Other, not listed above[47]	Contracting-out to private companies and privatization with the government owning minority or no stock	28 (5%)

Table 4. *Types of organizations in countries for 25 tasks (Thiel, 2012, p. 21).*

Country	Agency Type (N) 0	1	2	3	4	5
Scandinavia (N, DK, F, SW)	6	**39**	19	14	11	6
Central East Europe (HUN, LIT, RU, E)	9	**47**	17	12	5	6
South Europe (POR, SP, IT)	22	6	**25**	12	3	3
NW Europe (NL, B, UK, IRL)	21	**26**	19	9	14	9
Non-Europe (TAN, IS, AUS)	**31**	10	18	6	0	3
Mid Europe (A, G, CH)	15	14	8	**11**	**21**	1

According to the presented typology of agencies, the so-called *quango* (a quasi-autonomous non-governmental organisation) is a hybrid form of organization that has elements of non-government organizations (NGOs) and public sector bodies and fits into agency Types 1 – 3. Despite that quangos have less various forms than agencies their profusion is still so large that it is believed that 'if quangos did not exist, they would have to be invented' (Smith & Flinders, 1999, p. vii). Among legal entities under public law, there are some that are in terms of an organization very similar to each other (all of them or agencies in the widest sense, while in the narrower one they are having different names).

Goodnow shaped a dichotomy between politics as the sphere that "guides or influences governmental policy" and the administration that "executes that policy" (1900). If Goodnow has created a dichotomy at the highest political level, similar activities (according to systems theory) also occur at lower levels (multi-layered arrangements): at all levels it is about setting goals and enforcing them, everywhere there is a level that sets goals (doing the right things) and the level that executes them (doing the things right),

Figure 4. The Essence of All Agencies

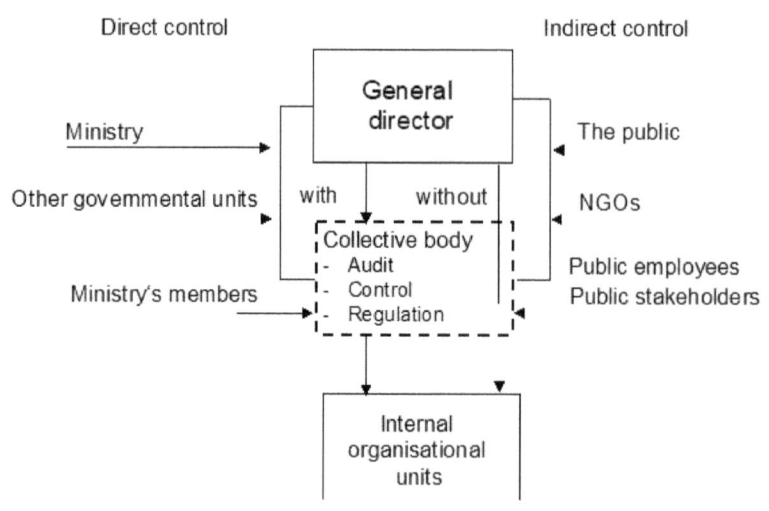

```
        Direct control                              Indirect control

                              ┌──────────────┐
                              │   General    │
          Ministry            │   director   │            The public
        ─────────────────────▶│              │◀─────────
                              └──────┬───────┘
     Other governmental units    with │   without          NGOs
        ─────────────────────▶┌ ─ ─ ─ ┴ ─ ─ ─ ┐◀─────────
                              ┊ Collective body ┊
                              ┊ - Audit         ┊       Public employees
       Ministry's members     ┊ - Control       ┊       Public stakeholders
        ─────────────────────▶┊ - Regulation    ┊◀─────────
                              └ ─ ─ ─ ┬ ─ ─ ─ ─┘
                                      ▼
                              ┌──────────────┐
                              │   Internal   │
                              │ organisational│
                              │    units     │
                              └──────────────┘
```

there is always one person (a director, a manager) connected to (or not) collective bodies (a board, a council, a committee, a commission).

Given the (lower than parliament) level of agencies, it is clear they do not carry out legislative tasks directly, but they further implement them through regulations, individual administrative procedures and other substantive actions. Although (departmental and nondepartmental public agencies) have different names (e.g., a public agency, public fund, a public institute, a commission), they have basically a similar organizational structure or dichotomy, regardless if it is between a single person or a multiperson body (i.e., directors and administrators in the broadest sense of the word). Both are under a greater or lesser intensity of control and membership (some bodies do not have a collective body, e.g., Court of Audit, Commission for the Prevention of Corruption, departmental agencies, bodies within the ministry, while others do e.g., non-departmental public agencies, public funds, public institutes). In the case of collective bodies, there are also differences in their competencies and/or functions (audit, control, regulation, and administrative functions) and their composition (representatives of the public, nongovernmental organizations, employees, ministries). The competencies and composition of the collective body vary between agencies according to their specifics, and it is not possible to clearly define in advance what content should be the first or the second present. As a general rule of thumb, the greater the autonomy of the agency, the smaller the influence of the ministry in terms of control and membership.

One of the key characteristics of public agency Type 2 is its separation from central state administration; a public agency implements various policies "on the ground", or closer to the people, but on the type of agency depends whether its tasks are directly related to the *people's needs* (executive tasks or public service) or to the more regulatory, developmental, expert-based, controlling, or monitoring tasks, focused on other *institutions and/or special fields*. In the first case, there is public service obligation present as a form of service of general (economic) interest in which a state can subsidize a specific tasks (the market itself does not deliver or is legally prohibited to deliver a level of service, continuity of service, regularity, minimum quality of service, service standards, affordability or minimum capacity to ensure access, equality for all that could be eligible under pre-given criteria, non-discrimination, user or consumer protection) and such specific agency could implement social public service (e.g., Book agency[48])

Dimensions of Public Agencies

while in the second case, as was said, tasks are more focused on fields (e.g., higher education, securities market, civil aviation, medicinal products) where public authority comes more to the fore, and thus no direct public service is involved. Otherwise named institutions, *i.e.*, a public fund, a public institute, and a public enterprise, can also be closely connected with the modus operandi of public agencies. A public fund is established to promote development in a specific field, to implement social, cultural, environmental, housing, spatial, agricultural, nature conservation, mining, or other policies of the founder, to settle long-term obligations of the founder, to manage the founder's real estate, to promote creativity in science, culture and education by awarding the prizes, scholarships, tuition fees, financing projects and other forms of (financial) incentives, and carrying out other activities specified by law.

Their fundamental feature is the use of *dedicated assets* for the aforementioned tasks and thus no public service obligation is present. Public institutes are organizations established to provide *social public services* (on the level of EU, so-called services of noneconomic general interest) in the fields of education, science, culture, sports, health, social care, child care, disability care, social insurance or other activities if the purpose of the activity is not to make a profit. A public enterprise also executes a public service, here of *economic* nature (on the level of EU, the so-called services of economic general interest). Public utility services provide material public goods as products and services whose permanent and uninterrupted production in the public interest is provided by the government or local community to meet public needs if and to the extent that they cannot be provided on the market. In the following text, the term public agency will be used for all types of legal entity under public law separated from the narrower part of the state administration. When some institution implements a public service, it is important whether its tasks express public authority (*acta iure imperii*)[49] or social public service and/or economic public service (*acta iure gestionis*), because in the first two cases the EU member states do not fall under the EU Court's jurisdiction regarding state aid (as long as they are not involved in economic activities on the market).

The Ministry

The Ministry has public authority (acta iure imperii) needed to perform various sovereignty functions among which are the classical five (defence, internal affairs, foreign affairs, justice, finances) and other ones, where due to the nature and/or importance of these tasks exist the clear need for direct ministerial responsibility and close oversight of the field. The Ministry is focused on policy issues for which different administrative and non-commercial tasks are performed in one or more administrative areas. As said, among the tasks of the ministry are cooperation in policy formulation (the preparation of draft laws, regulations and other acts and other materials and provision of other professional assistance in policy formulation), while also other (multifunctional) tasks are tightly connected with policy issues, like the executive tasks (implemented directly or through delegation to non-departmental agencies, where the focus is more on advice and control), monitoring (and care for the development of the field in accordance with adopted state policy, management, maintenance and integration of databases and records), development tasks (promotion and direction of social development) and provision of public services. The presence of the ministerial form is also anticipated where qualities intrinsic to certain activities cannot be clearly or easily specified, observed, and measured (or when ambiguous or contradictory goals exist if not considered with care), when the (rapid and unpredictable) context is highly relevant and important for sovereignty and public values, and when there is a clear need to coordinate the interconnected functions. Within the context of notions of adaptability, the ministry is appropriate for robust main purposes (that are not changed easily, while other organisational forms can be better for flexible, agile, and resilient approaches) and for cases where uncertainty is too high for them and salience is too large to be placed into the other organisational form.

Departmental Agencies

Departmental agencies or bodies within the Ministry have no separate legal status; they are the Ministry's subsidiary and part of the public administration and the civil service. A body within the Ministry is established to perform specialized professional tasks, executive and developmental administrative tasks, inspection and other control tasks, and tasks in the field of public services. Such a body may be set up to carry out those tasks on a larger scale if this ensures greater efficiency and quality in the performance of the tasks or when the nature of tasks or a work area makes it necessary to ensure a greater degree of independence in the performance of those tasks. A form of departmental agency should improve performance with a better focus on specialised, specific tasks based on cohesive and functional assemblages of administrative tasks, focused largely on measurable services. Minister has formal, indirect control here, while Director-General has operational and direction control. The Minister may request reports, data, and other documents related to the performance of the work of the agency. The agency's head must report regularly to the Minister or at his special request on the agency's work on all important issues in the agency's area of work. The departmental agency performs its duties in accordance with the law, other regulations, the work program adopted by the Minister on the proposal of the head of the agency, and the financial plan adopted in accordance with the Public Finance Act. The Minister gives guidelines to the agency and issues mandatory instructions, and instructs it to perform certain tasks or take certain measures within the limits of its competence, on which shall the agency report thereon. Before the National Assembly and the government, the agency is represented by the minister. If provided by a special regulation, the ministry or other state administration body may perform all or some of the tasks of professional assistance to the agency's head in the field of management of human, financial, information, and other resources.

Nondepartmental Public Agencies or Indirectly Controlled Bodies

Indirectly controlled bodies are detached from ministries and often have their own legal entity. They represent indirect administration, with a certain degree of autonomy in implementing public law (administrative functions) or private law (commercial, industrial or financial activities – public and/or government enterprises, state-owned enterprises, and not–for-profit government enterprises). They are called independent agencies. Independence denotes division from the executive government, although such independent agencies are still part of the public sector, have regulative and adjudicative authority, they are protected against direct presidential or executive control, and are more or less shielded against the governmental power to dismiss the agency head or member without cause. Such agencies are usually established by the legislative branch that defines the agency's goals. The Agency issues generally acts on issues within its competence. The Agency may, by a general act, regulate in more detail the issues that arise in the implementation of individual provisions of laws in the areas within its competence. Within the framework of its regulatory powers, the Agency can issue recommendations by which it nonbindingly recommends certain actions to the addressees. The Agency decides also on individual matters within the scope of its competences by a decision or resolution. The agency's statute and its

Dimensions of Public Agencies

other general acts for the exercise of public powers are usually published in the Official Gazette. The members of the agency council are appointed by the government. The President of the Agency Council is elected by the members of the Agency Council from among themselves by a majority vote (it can also be by secret ballot). The government uses the criterion of professionalism and qualification of a person when appointing candidates for members of the Agency's Council. The director of the agency is usually appointed by the government on the proposal of the council of the agency following a previously conducted public competition.[50]

Among indirectly controlled bodies, also a government enterprise is present; such form is recommended when government wants to align commercial purpose with market activities outside the public administration, when performance can be measurable, when tasks are not based on public power or authority, and can be thus transferred to the market, when there is no need for numerous regulations. Figure below shows the array of central government organisational forms; along the left axis, the different legal forms and on the right side the commercial ones. Beneath the boxes diverse horizontal arrays illustrate main features of the sorts of bodies, e.g., staffing, revenue sources, and legal jurisdiction:

Public Law Administrations (PLAs; or nondepartmental public agencies) implement administrative functions. A public agency is established to perform regulatory, developmental, or professional tasks in the public interest (unless otherwise provided by law). In performing its tasks, the public agency is independent. A public agency is established if it enables more efficient and effective performance of tasks

Figure 5. Executive central government
(Gill, 2002, p. 67)

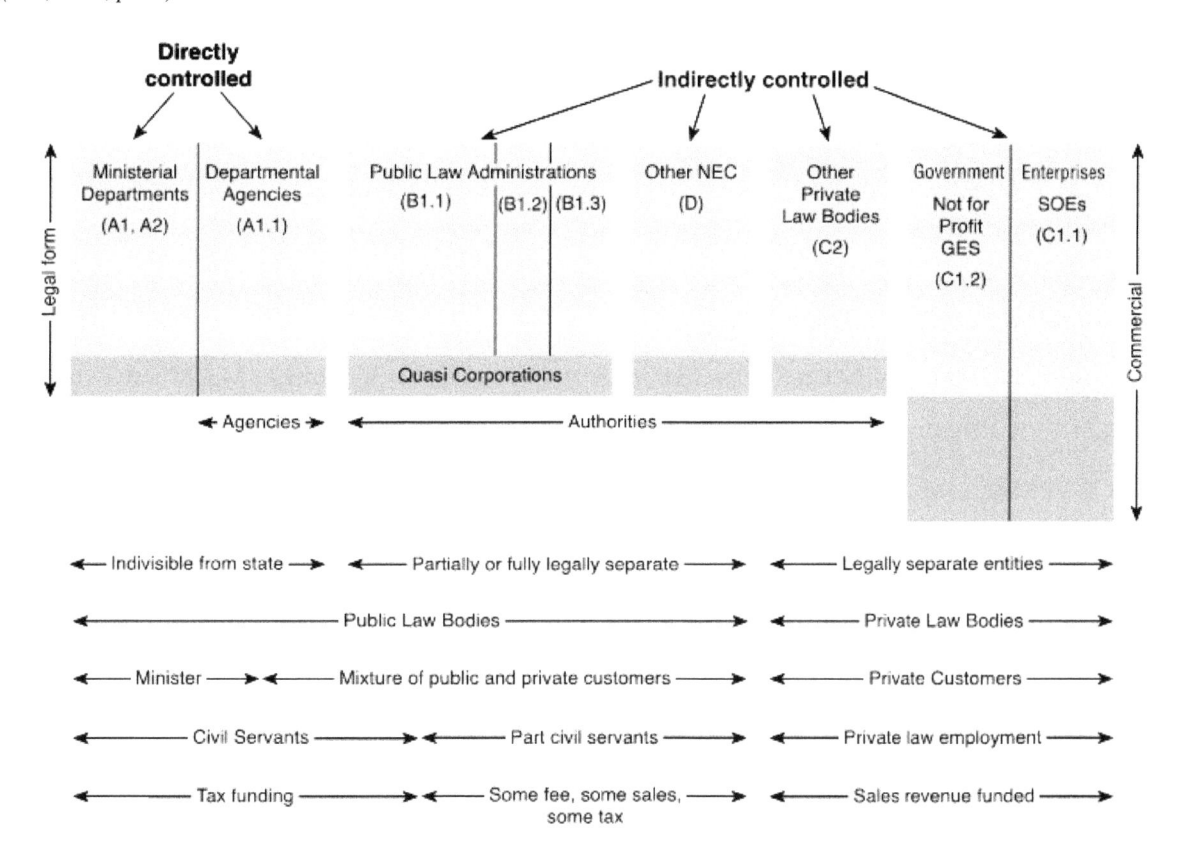

than would be the case in performing tasks in an administrative body (a public agency can be established only when with the organizational form of the body within the ministry [departmental agency] this goal could be achieved), in particular, if the performance of administrative tasks can be financed entirely or mainly by administrative fees or user payments, or if, depending on the nature or type of tasks, permanent direct political control over the performance of tasks is not necessary or appropriate. Such agencies could increase performance for the consistent and interconnected group of functions, when a governance board and a director tightly cooperate and first provide effective supervision and second tough leadership in an environment tailored to the entity's status, purpose and tasks. In addition to the independence of the agency, its legitimacy can also be enhanced when experts or civil society are involved.

REFERENCES

Aquinas, T. (1920). The "Summa Theologica" of St. Thomas Aquinas. Part I QQ I.-XXVI. (Second and revised edition, Vol. 1). London: Burns Oates and Washbourne.

Aristotle. (1992). *Eudemian Ethics Books I, II, and VIII* (M. Woods, Trans.). Clarendon Press.

Baker, D. (2007). *Strategic Change Management in Public Sector Organisations*. Chandos Publishing.

Bouckaert, G., & Peters, B. G. (2004). What is available and what is missing in the study of quangos? In C. Pollitt & C. Talbot (Eds.), *Unbundled Government: A Critical Analysis of the Global Trend to Agencies, Quangos and Contractualisation* (pp. 22–49). Taylor & Francis.

Chapus, R. (2001). *Droit administratif général* (15th ed.). Montchrestien.

Confucius. (2003). *Analects: With Selections from Traditional Commentaries* (E. Slingerland, Trans.). Hackett Publishing.

Fiorina, M. P. (1982). Legislative Choice of Regulatory Forms: Legal Process or Administrative Process? *Public Choice*, *39*(1), 33–66.

Gill, D. (2002). *Signposting the Zoo – From Agencification to a More Principled Choice of Government Organisational Forms*. OECD Publishing.

Goodnow, F. J. (1900). *Politics and Administration: A Study in Government*. The MacMillan Company.

Goodsell, C. T. (2010). *Mission Mystique: Belief Systems in Public Agencies*. CQ Press.

Greve, C., Flinders, M., & Thiel, S. V. (1999). Quangos—What's in a Name? Defining Quangos from a Comparative Perspective. *Governance: An International Journal of Policy, Administration and Institutions*, *12*(2), 129–146. doi:10.1111/0952-1895.951999095

Gulick, L. (2003). Notes On the Theory of Organisation. In K. Thompson (Ed.), *The Early Sociology of Management and Organizations: Papers on the Science of Administration* (Vol. IV, pp. 1–49). Routledge.

Halligan, J., Buick, F., & O'Flynn, J. (2011). Experiments with joined-up, horizontal and whole-of-government in Anglophone countries. In A. Massey (Ed.), *International Handbook on Civil Service Systems* (pp. 74–102). Edward Elgar Publishing.

Hayek, F. A. (2011). *The Constitution of Liberty: The Definitive Edition (The Collected Works of F. A. Hayek edition* (R. Hamowy, Ed.). University Of Chicago Press.

Hegel, G. W. F. (1991). *Elements of the Philosophy of Right (A. W. Wood* (H. B. Nisbet Ed. & Trans.). Cambridge University Press.

Justia. (2018). *Independent Agencies.* Justia. https://www.justia.com/administrative-law/independent-agencies/

Latour, B. (1996). *Aramis, or the Love of Technology.* Harvard University Press.

Miller, G. P. (1988). Introduction: The Debate over Independent Agencies in Light of Empirical Evidence. *Duke Law Journal, 1988*(2/3), 215–222. doi:10.2307/1372674

Nastasi, L., Pressman, D., & Swaigen, J. (2020). *Administrative Law: Principles and Advocacy* (Fourth). Torondo: Emond.

Öberg, S. A., & Wockelberg, H. (2020). Agency control or autonomy? Government steering of Swedish government agencies 2003–2017. *International Public Management Journal, 0*(0), 1–20. doi:10.1080/10967494.2020.1799889

OECD. (2002). *Distributed Public Governance Agencies, Authorities and other Government Bodies: Agencies, Authorities and other Government Bodies.* OECD Publishing.

Pollit, C., Bathgate, K., Caulfield, J., Smullen, A., & Talbot, C. (2001). Agency fever? Analysis of an international policy fashion. *Journal of Comparative Policy Analysis, 3*(3), 271–290. doi:10.1080/13876980108412663

Pollitt, C., Talbot, C., Caulfield, J., & Smullen, A. (2004). *Agencies: How Governments Do Things Through Semi-Autonomous Organizations.* Palgrave MacMillan.

Scalia, A. (1989). Judicial Deference to Administraitve Interpretations of Law. *Duke Law Journal, 1989*(3), 511–521.

Selin, L. J. (2015). What Makes an Agency Independent? *American Journal of Political Science, 59*(4), 971–987.

SIGMA. (2001). *Financial management and control of public agencies.* SIGMA. https://www.oecd-ilibrary.org/docserver/5kml60vk0h9x-en.pdf?expires=1603963677&id=id&accname=guest&checksum=AB63FFD9902F2673A133FDC1F219CAA0

Smith, M. J., & Flinders, M. V. (1999). *Quangos, Accountability and Reform.* Palgrave Macmillan.

Smullen, A. (2004). Lost in translation? Shifting interpretations of the concept of 'agency': The Dutch case. In C. Pollitt & C. Talbot (Eds.), *Unbundled Government: A Critical Analysis of the Global Trend to Agencies, Quangos and Contractualisation* (pp. 184–202). Taylor & Francis.

Talbot, C. (2004). The Agency idea: Sometimes old, sometimes new, sometimes borrowed, sometimes untrue. In C. Pollitt & C. Talbot (Eds.), *Unbundled Government: A Critical Analysis of the Global Trend to Agencies, Quangos and Contractualisation* (pp. 3–21). Taylor & Francis.

Thiel, S. V. (2012). Comparing Agencies Across Countries. In K. Verhoest, S. V. Thiel, G. Bouckaert, P. Lægreid, & S. V. Thiel (Eds.), *Government Agencies* (pp. 28–28). Palgrave Macmillan.

Verhoest, K., Roness, P., Verschuere, B., Rubecksen, K., & MacCarthaigh, M. (2010). *Autonomy and Control of State Agencies: Comparing States and Agencies*. Palgrave MacMillan.

Verhoest, K. (2018). Agencification in Europe. In E. Ongaro & S. V. Thiel (Eds.), *The Palgrave Handbook of Public Administration and Management in Europe* (pp. 327–346). Palgrave MacMillan.

Verhoest, K. Demuzere, S., & Rommel, J. (2012). Belgium and Its Regions. In K. Verhoest, S. V. Thiel, G. Bouckaert, & P. Lægreid (Eds.), Government Agencies: Practices and Lessons from 30 Countries (pp. 84–97). Basingstoke: Palgrave Macmillan.

Verhoest, Koen, Peters, B. G., Bouckaert, G., & Verschuere, B. (2004). The study of organisational autonomy: A conceptual review. *Public Administration and Development*, 24(2), 101–118. doi:10.1002/pad.316

Verkuil, P. (1988). The Purposes and Limits of Independent Agencies. *Duke Law Journal*, 37(2), 257–279.

Wallis, S. E. (2016). The Science of Conceptual Systems: A Progress Report. *Foundations of Science*, 21(4), 579–602. doi:10.1007/s10699-015-9425-z

ENDNOTES

[1] It seems that separateness [of an agency from a ministry to enable policy independence] is most justified when the state or the government of the day, as a special stakeholder, has a particular political interest in the outcome of individual decisions, such as for many regulatory functions (OECD, 2002, p. 21).

[2] The similar saying was repeated by Hegel in his Philosophy of Right; for him, 'definitions should contain universal determinations but in the present context these would immediately make the contradictory element' (1991, p. 26).

[3] Pollit et al have also presented their working definition of agencies 'as those bodies that have all or most of the following characteristics:

• They are at arm's length from the main hierarchical spines of ministries, i.e., there is a degree of structural disaggregation

• They carry out public tasks (service provision, regulation, adjudication, certification) at a national level

• Their core staff are public servants (not necessarily civil servants—definitions here again vary enormously between countries)

• They are financed, in principle at least, by the state budget. In practice, some agencies recover a good deal of their financial needs from charges (e.g., charging for a driving or television license). However, even in these cases, the state retains the residual financial liability

• They are subject to at least some administrative law procedures (i.e., they are not wholly or predominantly private law bodies) (Pollit, Bathgate, Caulfield, Smullen, & Talbot, 2001, pp. 274–275).

[4] Very similar approach is used the children's game named) telephone (or Chinese whispers).

Dimensions of Public Agencies

5   While NPM may have informed the categories and labels associated with the agency identity, their meaning and content are subject to wide variation across national and organizational cultures. This can give the impression of a great deal of conformity across national and international borders, while still offering a great deal of discretion in the way organizational work is understood and conducted (Smullen, 2004, p. 198).

6   The same approach is spotted in neoliberalism, where the most promotive of it, Hayek did not put his faith solely to competition, but the latter parallel with the strong rule of law (Hayek, 2011), while many countries have embraced only the first, without the second element.

7   SIGMA has nevertheless presented the list of characteristics as a working description:
- the organisation operates with some degree of autonomy from political direction by a minister or other political leader;
- the strategic direction of the body is established in a founding law, charter or contract which may be supplemented, to the extent permitted in rules, by the instructions of a minister or other political leader;
- the organisation manages its budget autonomously, but within a framework of rules set by the government;
- financing comes from some combination of own source revenues, earmarked contributions, and operating and/or investment subsidies from the state budget;
- the assets of the body are publicly owned and may not be used for private benefit;
- the nature and degree of public accountability are defined by law and tradition (SIGMA, 2001, p. 14).

8   The nature of their independence is further discussed in subchapter on elements of independence.

9   There is also the notion of devolution present which means the transfer of the centre's competences to local governments or communities (where the first retain full control on the execution of desks as it is present in locally dispersed governmental bodies) or from the first to subnational (international, EU) levels, that are largely outside the direct control of the central government.

10   The process of bringing, and fitting together government services to provide seamless services to citizens, also known as a "one-stop shop" or "single window" that aims to ensure one-stop access to services through coordination (sharing of work for mutual benefit), collaboration (coordination with sharing of power) and clustering (cluster similar government services together so citizens can access the services in one place).

11   This approach reflects both traditional coordination and new forms of organizing, structuring, and coordinating that seek to connect distinct parts of the public sector.

12   Whereas the forms mentioned above usually arise with regard to specific problems, here the agenda relates more to systemic weaknesses, in particular the rebalancing of the administrative machinery. This is multi-faceted and the dimensions involving coordination and integration are not necessarily congruent. They range from centrally driven policy and implementation processes to attempts to make horizontal interaction a routine part of agency management.

13   Organizational culture is an important factor in understanding organizational behaviour as it is a powerful, latent, and often unconscious set of forces that determine individual and collective behaviour, ways of perceiving, thought patterns and values.

14   The nature of the interrelation between departments organized on the basis of purpose and those organized on the basis of process may be illustrated best by considering the former as vertical departments, and the latter as horizontal departments (Gulick, 2003, p. 17).

[15] The agency may set the procedures for e.g. financial transactions itself within general principles concerning the use of inputs set by central government (Koen Verhoest, Peters, Bouckaert, & Verschuere, 2004, p. 108).

[16] The agency may decide upon which policy instruments to use and output norms within the objectives and effect norms set by government. The agency head may decide itself on individual applications of general regulations (Koen Verhoest et al., 2004, p. 108).

[17] The agency head is appointed and evaluated by the supervisory board in which the representatives of government have a majority vote. These representatives could be resigned by government at any time (Koen Verhoest et al., 2004, p. 108).

[18] The agency is financed primarily through income from other sources than the central government (e.g., tariffs, contributions, and prices), but a minor part of the funding stems from central government. The agency has to cover a major extent of deficits itself (e.g., by the imposition of a hard budget constraint).

[19] The agency has a legal personality under public law and is created by a parliamentary act (ibid). Here could be added that in the line of the principle of division of power, also agencies' directors or boards enact general ("legislative") decisions that are further implemented in individual cases.

[20] The agency has only limited reporting requirements on a general level to central governments and is only ad hoc subjected to evaluation or audits commissioned by central government. The norms as basis for evaluation and auditing are neither explicit nor strict. Sanctions and interventions are only possible after consultation of the agency and there is only a limited threat of sanctions or intervention by central government. Sanctions are rather soft (Koen Verhoest et al., 2004, p. 108).

[21] (1) a structural-instrumental perspective (formal organizational structure and rational choice of actors); (2) a cultural-institutional perspective (organizational culture and organizational path dependency); (3) a task-specific perspective (the characteristics of organizational tasks); (4) an environmental perspective (institutional environments and other elements of politico-administrative environment).

[22] One limitation of such an approach comes from the noninclusion of relation between the formal directive and its practice, i.e. how the first is de facto respected.

[23] The pursuit of long-term political goals is a necessary element of the operation of public agencies, as they are established for long-term provision of public interests, the definition of which is within the competence of the national authority. In this sense, it is also a factor in preventing the excessive independence of public agencies, by eliminating any possibility of influencing their operation and appropriate sanctioning of inappropriate performance of tasks. This serves primarily to protect the public interest and the interests of users, who in this way could ensure the realization of their legally protected interests, which is impossible with excessive closure of the system and the independence of public agencies.

[24] Such a body [independent agency] cannot in any proper sense be characterized as an arm or an eye of the executive. Its duties are performed without executive leave, and, in the contemplation of the statute, must be free from executive control. To the extent that it exercises any executive function – as distinguished from executive power in the constitutional sense – it does so in the discharge and effectuation of its quasi-legislative or quasi-judicial powers, or as an agency of the legislative or judicial departments of the Government. 295 U. S. at 627-628.

[25] At agency design, delegation, and political control bureaucratic structure (that is not static) and statutory restrictions should not be disregarded (Selin L., 2015).

Dimensions of Public Agencies

[26] In Humphrey's Executor v. United States, 295 U.S. 602 (1935) the court stated that the character of the Commission is 'an independent, nonpartisan body of experts, charged with duties neither political nor executive, but predominantly quasi-judicial and quasi-legislative', at 624.

[27] State Administration Act (OL, no. 113/05) in Article 21 states that 'body within the ministry may be established to perform the ministry's administrative tasks of a greater extent, provided that this ensures greater efficiency and quality in the performance of tasks, or if, due to the nature of tasks or field of work, it is necessary to ensure a higher degree of independence in performing the tasks referred'. These reasons are almost identical as ones for the creation of agency; this points at their common ground (principal-agent) relation from which both organisational forms have emerged, and on the other hand, ambiguity in the use of one form or another.

[28] What is lacking in the creation of independent agencies is any attempt in the legislative history to explain why Congress (or the President, for that matter) preferred one organizational form at over the other. New agency structures often appear to be created in a vacuum or almost by random selection' (Verkuil, 1988, p. 258).

[29] One factor that could show the level of independence of agencies is the number of "midnight regulations", that is regulations published at the very end of an outgoing Parliament's or President's term (before a new coalition takes over): more there are such regulations less agencies are independent. Politicization of agencies is well described by seeing of the ex-Secretary of the Interior, Donald Hodel, who regarded this king of legislation as "an old political ploy–if you can't force your political views on an agency, then make the agency independent" (Hodel in Verkuil, 1988, p. 277). It could be that independent agencies allowed elected officials to shift the costs of decision-making, shift blame for decisions they believe would be unpopular or to delegate tasks where uncertainty blossoms, to seek legislative rent in case of vague law, due to ideology or philosophy, but 'they are largely rationalizations which scholars are too quick to believe…where our work is only beginning' (Fiorina, 1982, p. 60).

[30] E.g., overall justice and all human rights – Ombudsman, gender equality commissioner; legitimacy – the state election commission; public funds – a national review commission, a court of audit; all funds – national banks, systemic risk boards; free communications – a communications networks and services agency, a cybersecurity agency; privacy and family life – a privacy commissioner, national post; free expression – a national press agency, public information (information commissioner; press, radio, TV – associations of journalists are the closest, but there are no independent commissioners for his field), book agency; free thought – education (universities and a national quality assurance agency) and free research (a research agency, a patent agency); free business – a securities and exchange commission, a competition protection agency, an innovation, technology and networks agency, business register; environment – environmental agency; health – agency for medicinal products and medical devices, disease prevention and control agency; safety – agency for safety and health at work, food, maritime, and aviation safety; utilities – energy, traffic agency.

[31] In most cases, legislators 'create an independent agency to supervise an area that is too complex and dynamic to be regulated by the passage of a statute or subsumed within an existing administrative agency. Independent agencies are not subject to direct control by the president or the executive branch, unlike executive agencies' (Justia, 2018).

[32] When an agency's own regulation is interpreted the so-called Auer deference applies (Auer v. Robbins, 519 U.S. 452 (1997)): this intermediate level of deference applies where an agency is interpreting its own regulation, when the latter is ambiguous and the interpretation reflects the

agency's "fair and considered judgment on the matter in question" and is not "plainly erroneous or inconsistent with the regulation" or simply a "post hoc rationalization" promoted by the agency to defend its past actions. Skidmore deference (Skidmore v. Swift & Co., 323 U.S. 134 (1944)) as the lowest level of deference applies to the agency's interpretations (opinion letters, operating manuals, guidelines) and is "entitled to be uphold only to the extent that those interpretations have the power to persuade". This deference is assessed by using various elements enumerated by the Supreme Court, including "the thoroughness evident in [the agency's] consideration, the validity of its reasoning, [or] its consistency with earlier and later pronouncements".

[33] In Graham v. Connor, 490 U.S. 386 (1989) the US's Supreme Court stated the "reasonableness" inquiry is an objective one: the question is whether the officers' actions are "objectively reasonable" in light of the facts and circumstances confronting them, without regard to their underlying intent or motivation". The Court stated the reasonableness of a particular use of force must be judged from the perspective of a reasonable officer on the scene, rather than with the 20/20 vision of hindsight. Reasonableness hence contains an objective test that invokes the position of a neutral ("reasonable") person with the background available knowledge of a situation in which parties were at the time of an evaluated act. The reasonable man is a fictional man who possesses and exercises the qualities of attention, knowledge, intelligence, and judgment that a particular action requires for the protection of its own interests and the interests of others.

[34] Normally, an agency rule would be arbitrary and capricious if the agency has relied on factors which Congress has not intended it to consider, entirely failed to consider an important aspect of the problem, offered an explanation for its decision that runs counter to the evidence before the agency, or is so implausible that it could not be ascribed to a difference in view or the product of agency expertise ... We may not supply a reasoned basis for the agency's action that the agency itself has not given. We will, however, uphold a decision of less-than-ideal clarity if the agency's path may reasonably be discerned. Motor Vehicles Manufacturers Ass'n v. State Farm Mutual Automobile Insurance Co., 463 U.S. 29 (1983), at 42-43.

[35] The case of United States v. Mead Corp., 533 U.S. 218,227 (2001) uses this phrase to describe the Chevron reasonableness assessment: 'when Congress has explicitly left a gap for an agency to fill, there is an express delegation of authority to the agency to elucidate a specific provision of the statute by regulation…and any ensuing regulation is binding in the courts unless procedurally defective, arbitrary or capricious in substance, or manifestly contrary to the statute'.

[36] Aligned with this, also feedback loops always "guarantee" slightly different situations then the started ones, as they always something add (positive feedback) or take away (negative feedback).

[37] See chapter on Performance management.

[38] A classic example of correspondence theory is the statement by Thomas Aquinas: "Veritas est adaequatio rei et intellectus" ("Truth is defined by the conformity of intellect and thing") (Aquinas, 1920 I. Q.16, A.2).

[39] The core of IPA is reached by the following six steps: 1. identify propositions within one or more conceptual systems (models, etc.); 2. Diagram those propositions with one box for each concept and arrows indicating directions of causal effects; 3. Find overlaps between causal concepts to eliminate redundancies and link concepts within and between propositions; 4. Identify the total number of concepts (to find the Complexity); 5. Identify concatenated concepts; 6. Divide the number of concatenated concepts by the total number of concepts in the model (to find the Systemicity). E.g., among three concepts (A, B, and C), the Complexity of the theory is $C = 3$. If there is among

Dimensions of Public Agencies

these, one concatenated concept (B), dividing this concatenated concept by the total concepts gives us a Systemicity of 0.33 (if there is one concatenated concept divided by five total concepts, the Systemicity of the model is S = 0.20; this means a 20% chance of successfully achieving stated goals for policy). One might say that the complexity of the conceptual system is a measure of its "breadth" while systemicity is a measure of its "depth" (Wallis, 2016). We should hence select and use roadmaps with many dots connected by many lines, not maps with few connected dots. On the above figure that represents the ideal-type agency a management of an agency under question can analyse how many parts of autonomy and organisation are connected in their case (in the ideal version, when all parts (Complexity=14) are connected systemicity= 100%). Everything more than 20% is appropriate, while each agency should strive to achieve a higher percentage in the future.

[40] One among first signs of this mystique could be present when a public employee asks himself if he would do the same tasks in his own company as he does in a public agency.

[41] For opposites rule out one another; the extremes are opposed both to one another and to the mean, because the mean is each one of the opposites in relation to the other: the equal is larger than the smaller, but smaller than the larger. So it must be the case that virtue of character is concerned with certain means and is itself a certain mean state. So we must note what sort of mean state is virtue, and what are the sorts of mean it is concerned with (Aristotle, 1992, pp. 16–17).

[43] Registration (statistics, drivers licenses, vehicle registration, meteorology, land register); Security (prosecution, prisons, police, intelligence, immigration); Education (universities, museums, broadcasting); Payments (unemployment, taxes, EU subsidies, student loans, development aid); Caretaking (housing, employment office, hospitals); Infrastructure (railway, airport, forestry, road maintenance).

[44] Type 1 Internally autonomous agencies without legal personality (departmental agencies)
– No legal personality
– Under ministerial hierarchy, but with some operational decision-making authority delegated to the agency head
– Separate budgets and/or accounts, implying some financial management freedom (mainly in terms of shifting budgets over posts and over years)
– HR managerial autonomy is nihil to limited, because general civil service statute applies fully (Koen Verhoest, Demuzere, & Rommel, 2012, p. 86).

[45] Type 2(a): Internally autonomous agencies with public law legal personality
– Public-law legal personality, separate from the state
– Under ministerial hierarchy, but with some operational decision-making authority delegated to the agency head. Ministerial oversight remains intact, since these organizations do not have a governing board
– Separate budgets and/or accounts, with varying degrees of financial management freedom
– Own assets and liabilities
– Own personnel statute which is compulsory similar to the general civil service statute (resulting in mainly operational HRM autonomy)
Type 2(b): Externally autonomous agencies with public law legal personality
– Public-law legal personality
– Restricted ministerial oversight and presence of a governing board
– Separate budgets and/or accounts, with varying degrees of financial management freedom
– Separate patrimonium

- Own personnel statute which in most cases is compulsory similar to the general civil service statute (resulting in mainly operational HRM autonomy) (Koen Verhoest et al., 2012, p. 86).

[46] Type 3: Externally autonomous agencies with hybrid or private law legal personality
– Legal personality either based on a combination of public and private law or vested fully in private law
– Restricted ministerial oversight, and top governance structures which are largely similar to private associations and companies (like General Assembly of Shareholders and Board of Directors) Organizations created by or (partially) owned by government as non-profit associations or companies with limited liability, with a legal identity mainly vested in private law
– Separate budgets and/or accounts and large degrees of financial management freedom (although in several cases this is severely restricted)
– Separate patrimonium
– Own personnel statute (resulting in strategic and operational HRM autonomy in most cases) (Koen Verhoest, Demuzere, & Rommel, 2012, p. 88).

[47] In the Type 5 agency could fit advisory bodies, which consist of groups of specialists (expert advisors) set up by ministers or by the Government.

[48] According to the Slovenian Book Agency Act (OL, no. 112/07) the Book Agency performs certain tasks in the public interest determined by this Act in order to ensure permanent conditions for the development of the book field and to make professional and independent decisions on the selection of programs and projects financed from the state budget. Despite the fact that public service obligation (as an 'obligation which the ... undertaking ... if it were considering its own commercial interests, would not assume or would not assume to the same extent or under the same conditions' see Article 2(1) of Regulation (EEC) no. 1191/69) is used for undertakings and it is not mentioned as such, this kind of activity would be (according to the EU's case law) probably public service. Contrary, according to the Slovenian Constitutional court 'public service is a normative phenomenon and not an actual one...there is no public service without its normative part (normative definition) and/or without legal regulation there is no special legal regime of an individual activity (i.e. public service), which significantly differentiates a legal position of this activity in relation to exactly the same activity under the private law regime' (decision, no. 156/08-16 of 14. 4. 2011).

[49] In Case C-47/08, European Commission v. Kingdom of Belgium [2011] the court stated that 'the concept of official authority implies the exercise of a decision-making power going beyond the ordinary law and taking the form of being able to act independently of, or even contrary to, the will of other subjects of law. Official authority manifests itself in particular, according to the Court's case-law, in the exercise of powers of constraint (Case C-114/97 Commission v Spain [1998], para. 37). In the view of the Commission and the United Kingdom, activities connected with the exercise of official authority must be distinguished from those carried out in the public interest. A number of professions are entrusted with special powers in the public interest, but are not for all that connected with the exercise of official authority'. At 40-41.

[50] The Council of the Agency usually adopts its rules of procedure, gives opinions on the work program, financial plans and annual report, gives its consent to the statute adopted by the Director of the Agency, proposes the appointment or dismissal of the Director of the Agency, proposes a temporary ban on the Director's duties, or proposes the early dismissal of the members of the Agency's Council. Members of the Agency's Council or persons authorized by the Agency's Council may inspect business books as defined in Accounting Standards and the Agency's accounting

documents. The Director must always submit to the Agency's Council, at his request, a report on the Agency's operations and other information necessary for the Agency's Council to exercise its powers. The Council of the Agency may propose to the Director improvements in the operations of the Agency, draw attention to possible irregularities in the operations of the Agency, or inform the competent authorities thereof. Agency director represents the Agency, manages its operations and organizes its work, also by appointing its deputies for individual areas; it adopts the agency's statute, work program, financial plan and annual report of the Agency, he conducts proceedings and gives the power to conduct proceedings in matters within the competence of the Agency, issues individual acts and adopt general acts and recommendations within the competence of the Agency, protects the business secrets of the Agency, cooperates with the Agency Council and the Sectoral Consultative Councils in accordance with their respective competencies. The director is liable to the agency for damages caused by his negligent or unlawful conduct.

Chapter 9
Agencies' Tasks

ABSTRACT

Governments may outsource executive tasks to agencies to improve service provision, increase efficiency, reduce conflicts of interest, and allow higher ministerial levels to focus on policy-making and strategic management. Administrative agencies are set up for various reasons, including to demonstrate independence, reduce the size and workload of departments, provide flexibility in human resources, ensure representativeness, and achieve coordination and uniformity. Agencies execute a wide range of tasks, such as providing guidance on delegated legislation, setting standards, regulating businesses and professions, administering the activities of other organizations, and providing goods and services. Delegating the day-to-day management of spending programs to specialized executive agencies has been a trend in public service reform over the last two decades. These tasks may include managing projects, adopting budget implementation instruments, and gathering and transmitting information to guide program implementation.

INTRODUCTION

The three hardest tasks in the world are neither physical feats nor intellectual achievements, but moral acts: to return love for hate, to include the excluded, and to say 'I was wrong.'

– Sydney J. Harris

The logic for outsourcing executive tasks to agencies is in an apparent better provision of service and higher efficiency gains, and to relieve higher ministerial levels, to focus primarily on policy-making and/or strategic management. The reasons why a government may choose to set up an administrative agency rather than delegate a task to a department are numerous, for example, to demonstrate independence, reduce the size, workload, or budget of a department, to reduce conflicts of interest, to provide flexibility in human resources and to reduce labour costs, to provide expertise and specialization, to ensure representativeness, to avoid permanence, to signal a new or different approach, or to achieve coordination or uniformity (Nastasi, Pressman, & Swaigen, 2020, pp. 26–27). Agencies execute a wide variety of tasks:

DOI: 10.4018/979-8-3693-0507-2.ch009

Agencies' Tasks

they offer guidance on delegated legislation, they set standards, regulate businesses and professions, administrate the activities of other organisations, and provide goods and services. 'Delegating the day-to-day management of spending programmes to specialised [executive] agencies has been a leitmotiv of public service reform at the national level over the last two decades. This had essentially two aims: improving service delivery (through reduced red tape, increased specialisation, and enhanced commitment to specific results) and enabling central authorities to concentrate on "core functions" such as policy design and supervision' (European Court of Auditors, 2009, p. 8). According to Article 6 of Council Regulation (EC) No. 58/2003 of 19 December 2002, laying down the statute for executive agencies to be entrusted with certain tasks in the management of Community programmes, states that 'the Commission may entrust an executive agency with any tasks required to implement a community programme, except for tasks requiring discretionary powers in translating political choices into action. Executive agencies may in particular be entrusted with the following tasks: (a) managing some or all phases in the lifetime of a project, in relation to specific individual projects, in the context of implementing a Community programme and carrying out the necessary checks to that end, by adopting the relevant decisions using the powers delegated to it by the Commission; (b) adopting the instruments of budget implementation for the revenue and expenditure and carrying out all activities required to implement a Community programme on the basis of the power delegated by the Commission, and in particular activities linked to the awarding of contracts and grants; (c) gathering, analysing, and transmitting to the Commission all the information needed to guide the implementation of a Community programme. The terms, criteria, parameters and procedures with which an executive agency must comply when performing the tasks and the details of the checks to be performed by the Commission departments responsible for Community programmes in the management of which an agency is involved shall be defined by the Commission in the instrument of delegation.

Since the institutional set-up of agencies at the EU level can be seen as a kind of collection of best practices at national level, the findings or provisions at the EU level can also be applied directly back to all national agencies. The EU Commission in 2014 established guidelines for the establishment and operation of executive agencies financed by the general budget of the Union C(2014)9109/F. Executive agencies may be entrusted with the following tasks: the management of some or all stages in the lifetime of projects; the provision of support in programme implementation;[1] the provision of administrative and logistical support services (the centralisation of those support services would result in additional cost-efficiency gains and economies of scale; the provision of support services may only constitute an auxiliary task for the agency (not a core task)). Among tasks reserved to the Commission are tasks involving a large measure of discretion implying political choices; decisions submitted to the comitology; and other tasks reserved to the Commission (the Commission may not delegate to the executive agencies tasks resulting from its prerogatives at institutional level pursuant to the TFEU and the Euratom Treaty and under specific powers directly conferred on it by the Treaties). Annex 1 to the guidelines enumerates factors (to be considered whether an agency should be set up or the mandate of an existing agency): the need for a high level of technical and financial expertise throughout the programme and project management cycle; the need of efficiency and flexibility in the implementation of the delegated tasks; the need to simplify the procedures used; clear division of programme management tasks between the Commission and the agencies; the need for the Commission to focus on legislative and strategic tasks in policy formation and monitoring, including those connected with Union programmes; the need to carry out certain activities with increased visibility without any intervention by third parties as intermediaries; the proximity of the delegated tasks to final beneficiaries; the need to establish a single entry point for all potential recipients of Union funds in a given field; the possibility of economies of scale and prior examination of the possibility of delegating tasks to another structure. The assessment of these factors must be addressed in the compulsory cost-benefit analysis and analysed in detail. These tasks from the different point of view address the efficiency which was addressed here in Chapter 7; managing tasks more efficiently, with lower costs compared to the ministry, and more effectively with the help of a higher degree of specialisation or rearranging similar activities within one agency to achieve economies of scale.

The scope of an agency's tasks can be divided into five major groups: i) granting authorisations, approvals, opinions, decisions and orders to the relevant organizations that work in a particular area; ii) monitoring, collecting and verifying reports and notifications by organisations and other entities that are required to submit reports and/or notify the agency of certain facts and circumstances in compliance with the legal provisions; iii) conducting examinations and audits of the operations of relevant organisations; iv) imposing supervisory measures in accordance with a relevant act; v) preparing and issuing implementing regulations pursuant to the primary legislation. The tasks of executive agencies are different from those of regulatory agencies; the latter deal with tasks of regulation where a higher level of independence is usually present. The main distinction among those two types of agencies is that executive agencies implement programmes (delegation of operational tasks) and are more dependent on the parent organisation, whereas regulatory agencies provide common rules and services and usually operate under a management board composed of various members.

To Flinders, Harden and Marquand quangos generally have three types of tasks: policy implementation (doing the job), scrutiny (supervision, regulation and auditing) and providing information or advice to government (Flinders et al., 1997). The core of the agency programme can be grouped in three ideas: structural disaggregation and/or the creation of "task-specific" organisations; performance "contracting" – some form of performance target setting, monitoring and reporting; and deregulation (or more properly reregulation) of control over personnel, finance and other management matters (Talbot, 2004, p. 6). Despite agencies implementing various tasks, they can be put on a common denominator: they are all *executives* in their character.

Along with the mentioned naming problem, an essential distinction should be also made between (in)formal tasks and their (in)formal implementation.[2] Each element can be evaluated from the formal (legal) and informal (actual) level, so *e.g.* the level of agencies autonomy can be quite low formally and high informally and contrary. The same applies to agency tasks: informality, practice, established paths, mores, tradition, etc. play very important "undetermined indicator". Such approaches come as a result of historical, contextual, economic, political, institutional, legal, and other elements that make

Table 1. Categories of organizations in charge of 25 tasks in 21 countries (Thiel, 2012, p. 24)

Task	Agency Type (N)					
	0	1	2	3	4	5
Registration (statistics, drivers licenses, vehicle registration, meteorology, land register)	13	35	15	0	5	3
Security (prosecution, prisons, police, intelligence, immigration)	35	31	6	0	3	0
Education (universities, museums, broadcasting)	0	2	16	13	5	8
Payments (unemployment, taxes, EU subsidies, student loans, development aid)	15	20	4	5	2	2
Caretaking (housing, employment office, hospitals)	1	6	8	3	21	4
Infrastructure (railway, airport, forestry, road maintenance)	1	11	5	28	7	8

all evaluations of agencies complex: 'it is not so much the type of task that is relevant to distinguish between quangos but the conditions [finance, ministerial responsibility, control mechanisms, public desk and public domain] under which they operate' (Greve, Flinders, & Thiel, 1999, p. 141). Although agencies are executive in their character, this element is more complex: a simple mathematical permutation reveals that between two parts four permutations are possible, and the same holds for rules' creation and their execution: rule-rule, rule-execution, execution-rule, and execution-execution. The second and third options are often disregarded although they carry an important message: the creation of the rule is a first part of its execution (a rule that is so clear and unambiguous that can be directly applied), and the latter can in the process of execution create rules to fill all missing, but pre-planned details (secondary legislation). From this point of view, an agency also enacts the general legal rules needed to implement primary legislation in practice. And from a legal point of view, from the point of an ordinary citizen, the hierarchy of legal rules is not so much relevant than the importance of the full respect of the rules regardless of their rank (otherwise the citizen will not receive what he applied for). It is therefore all the more important that tasks are continuously adjusted to their overall (political, economic, legal and other) context and evaluated in the view of possible future changes. There could be at the time of creation of the task determined its lifespan after which the evaluation and needed changes should be made. Closely connected with this is the early adoption of agency annual work programmes through which ministries can be acknowledged at the beginning of the year with programs and tasks' efficiency and effectiveness (this predisposes the presence of task impact indicators and their changes if needed). This also predisposes to an earlier adoption of the ministries' financing decisions that directly affect the scope of the agency's tasks.

Regardless of specific tasks, there is also one approach, similar to the word "task": it is "tasc". It represents the accountability and success checklist:

T—Who owns the task?
A—Do they have the authority to be held accountable?
S—Do we agree that they are set up for success (time, resources, clarity)?
C—Do we have a checklist of what needs to happen to accomplish the task?

(Brown, 2018).

REFERENCES

Brown, B. (2018). *Dare to Lead: Brave Work. Tough Conversations. Whole Hearts.* Random House.

European Court of Auditors. (2009). *Delegating Implementing Tasks to Executive Agencies: A Successful Option?* ECA. https://www.eca.europa.eu/lists/ecadocuments/sr09_13/sr09_13_en.pdf

Flinders, M. V., Harden, I., & Marquand, D. (Eds.). (1997). How to Make Quangos Democratic. London: Charter 88.

Greve, C., Flinders, M., & Thiel, S. V. (1999). Quangos—What's in a Name? Defining Quangos from a Comparative Perspective. *Governance: An International Journal of Policy, Administration and Institutions, 12*(2), 129–146. doi:10.1111/0952-1895.951999095

Nastasi, L., Pressman, D., & Swaigen, J. (2020). *Administrative Law: Principles and Advocacy* (Fourth). Torondo: Emond.

Talbot, C. (2004). The Agency idea: Sometimes old, sometimes new, sometimes borrowed, sometimes untrue. In C. Pollitt & C. Talbot (Eds.), *Unbundled Government: A Critical Analysis of the Global Trend to Agencies, Quangos and Contractualisation* (pp. 3–21). Taylor & Francis.

Thiel, S. V. (2012). Comparing Agencies Across Countries. In K. Verhoest, S. V. Thiel, G. Bouckaert, P. Lægreid, & S. V. Thiel (Eds.), *Government Agencies* (pp. 28–28). Palgrave Macmillan. doi:10.1057/9780230359512_2

ENDNOTES

[1] The provision of support in programme implementation may comprise in particular: (1) collecting, processing and distributing data, and in particular compiling, analysing and transmitting to the Commission all information required to guide implementation of the programme, promoting coordination with other Union programmes, Member States or international organisations; (2) contributing to evaluation of the impact of the programme and to monitoring the actual effect of its activities on the market; (3) managing and directing a network, in particular concerning the target public (recipients, projects, actors); (4) organising meetings, seminars or talks (if this is operational expenditure); organising trainings in agreement with the Commission; (5) carrying out studies, provided that the management of such service contracts can bring added value; (6) contributing to evaluations, in particular the annual and/or mid-term evaluation of implementation of the programme, and contributing to preparation and implementation of follow-up action on evaluations; (7) preparing recommendations for the Commission on implementation of the programme and its future development; (8) planning and implementing information operations; (9) producing overall control and supervision data; (10) contributing, at the request of the Commission to preparatory work on work programmes and financing decisions.

[2] Remember that between 2 parts are always 4 combinations possible: formal tasks and formal implementation, informal tasks and formal implementation, informal tasks and informal implementation, formal tasks and informal implementation.

Chapter 10
Performance Management

ABSTRACT

Performance management is a strategic and integrated approach to improving the performance of people in organizations by developing the capabilities of teams and individual contributors. It involves continuous and flexible controlling and directing processes to accomplish tasks in future-focused work, with indicators used to measure success in terms of efficiency and effectiveness. Strategic performance management encompasses the clarification, assessment, implementation, and continuous improvement of organizational strategy and its execution. However, many organizations spend too little time clarifying and agreeing on their strategies and measuring everything that is easy to measure, without turning performance data into meaningful insights and learning. The main activities in performance management include role profiling, performance contract planning, personal development planning, managing performance throughout the year, and performance review. Finally, leveraging critical success factors and using key performance indicators can help organizations achieve their outcomes.

INTRODUCTION

What we can control is our performance and our execution, and that is what we are going to focus on.

– Bill Belichick

To make the right works or actions right, *i.e.*, more efficient and successful, is the common denominator of all human action, and for organisations it is the same. People organise to be more efficient. A predisposition is to know which goals should be achieved, and a predisposition of goals is to plan well (goals are nothing but planned actions expressed as results). Therefore, performance contracting should be directly connected with ex ante performance management as 'a strategic and integrated approach to delivering sustained success to organisations by improving the performance of the people who work in them and by developing the capabilities of teams and individual contributors' (Armstrong, 2003, p. 477). The management of performance is about the continuous and flexible controlling and directing process of the accomplishment of a cooperative (where managers and employees mutually strive to accomplish

DOI: 10.4018/979-8-3693-0507-2.ch010

tasks) in future focused work, while indicators are used to measure/record the success of this endeavour in the form of closer-to-action outputs (efficiency), as well as sometimes in more distant outcomes (effectiveness). The management could also be seen as strategic performance management, that is, 'the organizational approach to clarify, assess, implement, and continuously improve the organizational strategy and its execution. It encompasses strategic frameworks, performance indicators, methodologies, and processes that help organizations with the formulation of their strategies and enable employees to gain relevant insights, which allows them to make better-informed decisions and learn' (Marr, 2009, p. 3). It deals with the recognition or identification, measurement, and management of things, people, and processes to improve the (old) effectiveness and efficiency and / or the overall performance of an organisation. In most governments, public sector, and nonprofit organizations, according to Marr (2009) the majority of organizations spend too little time clarifying and agreeing the strategy and spend too much time measuring everything that is easy to measure, while they do not spend enough effort ensuring the performance data are turned into meaningful insights and learning.

Public agencies need a serious approach to strategy formulation with the clarification of their overall aims, outcomes, outputs, and enablers (the [in]tangible resources) of performance (the mentioned words can be seen as another version or description of system theory, which here has a special chapter to enable a deeper understanding of the nature of core activities and resources required to deliver them by agencies or other public and even private organisations). Public agencies in large part implement tasks delegated to them directly by legislation or through a parent ministry. The implementation or accomplishment of work, there is nothing but the other name for performance. If someone would like to stress the importance of task implementation, he could address this topic as performance management. It is the management of numbers in a transformative way: 'measurement may use numbers, but it is not about numbers; it is about perception, understanding, and insight' (Spitzer, 2007, p. 3).[1] It is about the context of measurement, the context of not seeking examples of "the best employee of the month" or violators, but of positive motivation and empowerment – based on the effective use of measurement *as a source of information* to improve the work to be done – that makes management successful (Spitzer talks about the transformational performance measurement when is consisted of the Context, Focus [what gets measured gets managed and what gets managed gets done], Integration [the relationships among measures], and Interactivity [dialogue]). Performance management is about applying information to what is being implemented. Performance management can be seen as a broad concept, that is, a more comprehensive, continuous, inclusive, and flexible natural-like cycle or approach than the older top-down merit rating and management by objectives. The main activities in performance management are the role profile[2] and the performance contract[3] (plan), the personal development plan (act), managing performance throughout the year (monitor), and performance review (review) (Armstrong, 2003, p. 486). Because the tasks of the agencies inevitably affect the external environment, that is, stakeholders, it is urgent that the legitimacy also have their input. This is done with a system or a 360-degree feedback process in which employees receive confidential, anonymous feedback from the people who work around them. Managers use 360 feedback surveys to get a better understanding of their strengths and weaknesses to create a new development plan. 360 feedback can be valuable to support people to be more effective in their roles and to understand what areas should receive attention. Government and public agencies are always in lack of resources to satisfy all public needs; it is hence all the more important that (i) right leverages (known also as critical success factors, CSF)[4] are discovered and addressed with the (ii) right manners (balanced-scorecard perspectives[5]) and (iii) tools (key performance indicators, KPIs). Leverages are essential elements of complex adaptive systems as they 'have the property that a small input can produce a major predictable, directed change with an amplifier effect' (Holland, 1995, p. 5) *e.g.,* a vaccine *vis-à-vis* the whole immune system. Essential elements can lead the agency to achieve its outcomes (success criteria) all more likely when the latter depend on the main objectives and can be measured by KPIs. Performance measurement cannot be synonymous with better performance. On the other hand, it is essential to know that each action may inspire unintended or even unwanted behaviour. Measurement approaches are frequently patched together without awareness of the CSF of the specific agency and understanding of the *behavioural consequences of a measure* (Parmenter, 2012). Leaders should have in mind that KPIs should be based on leverages and assembled from various perspectives. Even then, its abuse can be present in cases where KPIs do not follow their main purpose or when the rights of others are violated.[6]

Performance (indicators) can be focused on outputs (the immediately seen agency's work results) or results (a degree of change in a wider environment due to the agency's outputs). Outputs are more quantitative, outcomes more qualitative; the first apply rules (e.g., finances for projects or a number of accreditations), the second affect principles (e.g., the number of innovations, patents, or quality of high education) and/or strategic goals of organisation. When outputs are not numerical, moral hazard can occur, but many times even outputs are not (easily) measured due to the lack of methods (e.g., domestic violence cannot be measured just by SOS telephone answering calls), other reasons that affect work (e.g., Covid-19 crisis) or to time delays (work is not immediately seen in the environment), while outcomes can be many times only indirectly seen through values surveys. Despite the intuitively acceptable idea of indicators, there are some caveats present[7] and there is also a lack of evidence on how agency successfulness is used for the future's allocation of funds, for the new determination of performance contracts, agency accountability, a level of ministerial control, coordination etc.[8] The answer to this is tightly connected with the determination of goals. Strategies, the external and internal rules, and practices can give some insight into how an agency acts, but from the hierarchical point of view it usually matters more if an agency fulfils its goals. This can be the right approach when the agency's goals are clear and measurable,[9] but contrary, when the agency has vague or very general goals, what these goals really mean can be seen from the situation (or the context in which officials do their jobs), workers' practises, their personal beliefs and other forces that affect their jobs (this can stand also for general guidelines or principles of good performance management[10] that only want from organizations to perform the best; at first sight this could seem as a paradox, but the basic rule of general notions is in their specific application in a relevant content of people, resources, time, place etc.). This is especially relevant in expert agencies that employ highly trained experts, where their personal, subjective elements come to the fore the most; here maybe even more than leaders' praise are relevant peer opinions on matters of the situation and on their praise: 'peer expectations not only affect how hard people work at their jobs, they can affect what they decide the job *is*' (Wilson, 1989, p. 48). Officials may have their own views on the organization's predispositions, attitudes, and other preferences that affect formal goals. Over these subjective elements, the agency can have very little control; for such reasons, performance can rely on very different approaches that can be read from the agency's formal documents. Personal attitudes (and values) can have more influence on how a job is performed when goals are more generally stated and/or dependent on personal knowledge. On the other hand, on such occasions, there is a higher probability of experts to be exposed to external pressures (agency capture).

Based on the extent to which the tasks of agencies are shaped by *external* pressures, Wilson (Wilson, 1989) presented four political environments that surround the agency: a *client* agency focuses its goals towards the single, organized group with which it deals daily. With time, such agencies could reflect the views of this group. An *entrepreneurial* agency is created as the result of entrepreneurial politics; it is born out of an attack on the interests it is now supposed to regulate; agencies born of entrepreneurial politics are at risk of capture, but capture is not inevitable. An *interest group* agency operates with contending interest-groups. Interest-group pressures set the outer limits of the agency's tasks, but within those limits the agency's personnel is able to define their tasks in accordance with professional norms. *Majoritarian* agencies, due to their good approach operate in an environment devoid of important interest groups and/or where a hostile interest group is not formed. Agencies are a typical example of nonmajoritarian institutions, defined as 'those governmental entities that (a) possess and exercise some grant of specialised public authority, separate from that of other institutions, but (b) are neither directly elected by the people, nor directly managed by elected officials' (Sweet & Thatcher, 2003, p. 2). The mentioned grant of public authority and/or delegation[11] means the transfer of public authority from representative (directly elected) organs to the Executive and further to the bureaucratic public administration or to non-majoritarian institutions, whether the public (agencies) or private NGOs (unincorporated, voluntary associations, trusts, charities, foundations, or not-for-profit companies or *lex specialis* bodies created under special NGO or non-profit laws). The topic of delegation to non-majoritarian institutions is usually presented with agency theory and/or principal-agent (P-A) relations. Despite its age, its relevancy, especially in the EU frame (the EU as the principal and member states as agents) should not be disregarded.

Parliamentarism is a particular agency delegation regime (delegation from the people to the Parliament) that can be understood with the help of the concept of agency theory. There are four major measures by which principals can hold agents to account: (1) contract design, (2) screening and selection mechanisms, (3) monitoring and reporting requirements, and (4) institutional checks (Kiewiet & McCubbins, 1991). The first two are the more numerous ex ante mechanisms, and the second two are the less numerous ex post mechanisms. If a principal in the main (legal) act defines, e.g., big, wide, popular, complicated, or professional goals, in areas of higher uncertainty, there is a higher probability that an agent will have more power (wider discretion) and a larger budget. In such conditions, it is expected the principal will more often use control mechanisms, but with the delegation of such tasks comes also the appropriate level or zone of discretion (a freedom to decide within the pre-given outer frames in which decision is expected to be done). If the principal wants such tasks to be implemented, it must usually understand that its ex-post control will not be as intensive as it can be in the case of clearly specified tasks, while its ex-ante control (with regards to discretion) is almost null. On the other hand, when the agency successfully delivers its outputs and outcomes (without the violation of the rule of law, human rights or other rights and obligations), its legitimacy rises, and with that also its power *vis-à-vis* the principal and/or a possibility to demand a larger budget, wider or new competences regarding implementation or even, not only to propose, but also to substantially contribute to policy by proposals to amend primary or to enact secondary legislation. Despite such mechanisms, the value of a principal-agent relationship is usually not fully optimized since both sides have usually at least slightly different interests, amplified by more or less asymmetric (not equal) information and opportunistic behaviour; all together create a larger possibility of emergent unanticipated, unwanted consequences. Within this transfer always emerge discrepancies between a principal's desires and an agent's affect.[12] Having these limitations in mind, there may be a long *sequential* (or a singular[13]) chain of delegation as it is present in parliamentarism (from voters to elected representatives, to the executive branch [specifically to the prime minister], to the heads of different executive departments and then to civil servants), or *parallel* as it is present in presidentialism, where the more complex, grid-like relations of delegation and accountability (to the president, Congress and courts) exist (Strøm, 2000). In the classical parliamentary system of government, the 'singularity principle' prevails where in each step there is a single and non-competing principal for each agent, while in the presidential system, agencies can apparently be controlled by more numerous political principals (the president, the legislator and the courts) that compete with each other to increase or retain control over public agencies. Here, there is hence no restricted, binary relationship between agencies and their political principals. Following the singularity principle in the classic parliamentary model of government, the binary models of political delegation and control *vis-à-vis* the bureaucratic autonomy of agencies prevail. Along with such classic model of government, there are also the notions of holistic governance (Dunsire, 1990), the system of governance (Hood & Lodge, 2006), network governance (Sørensen & Triantafillou, 2016), models (Larmour, 1996) and modes of governance (Jessop, 2010) present. Besides them, the structuration of government in the meaning of agencification has caused the networks of accountability to various political principals. Agencies are supposed to answer for their actions additionally also to various (outside the government) stakeholders (citizens, syndicates, interest groups, public opinion, media).

The structure and location of the agency in the administrative hierarchy do not always predict its (perceived) level of autonomy (Yesilkagit & van Thiel, 2012) or its elements. Having this limitation in mind, Yesilkagit and van Thiel (2012) based their survey on a sample of 219 Dutch agencies, which showed that 'agency leaders perceive influence of the minister of the parent ministry as identifiably distinct from the influence of other governmental as well as nongovernmental principals and stakeholders…in line with the constitution of parliamentary democracy, ministers ultimately have the most central say in the affairs of the public administration even when executive agencies operate at a distance' (Yesilkagit & van Thiel, 2012, p. 115). Yesilkagit and van Thiel (2012) in none of their analyses found any association between governmental and nongovernmental actors that could hint at the existence of networks of governmental and nongovernmental stakeholders that share similar beliefs and interests. Conclusions based on questionnaires filled out by agency employees, who can subjectively answer 'what they want' or 'their truth' can be misleading. A small number of them would probably admit also other influences on their work; they could be present on a friendly level, on a level of mutual benefit, political, friend, personal (politically or otherwise influenced) views or even unconscious, cognitive levels. By 'leaving out of the equation', relations with citizens agencies refute their democratic element.

With due respect to all researchers and their findings on the responsibility of agencies, it is not so important whether the agency can(not) resist to politicians, the executive, a parent minister or to him subordinate leaders, whether the agency can be detailly controlled or subdued to the former's will or what level or type of autonomy the agency has etc. because the first are only the ex post results (without considering the input context and different perspectives) and the second are only ex ante formal frames (without considering the output contexts and different perspectives). Indeed, 'a broad range of outcomes are impossible to predict from the initial conditions of delegation, but are instead produced by the dynamics of interactions between NMIs [Non-Majoritarian Institutions] and other multiple actors' (Sweet & Thatcher, 2003, p. 16). In this line of thought, 'different countries' patterns of corporate governance in general, and executive pay in particular, cannot be explained by conventional principal-agent theory alone' (Bruce, Buck, & Main, 2005, p. 1504). Without considering the history, national values, informal practices and rules, mores, and other (local/national) conditions and ways of looking at things, results will always be limited, while the evaluation of such a large number of elements is too complex to really be done in practice. In practice there is probably a denser network of accountability among agencies and other stakeholders than questionnaires can show; there may be other horizontal, diagonal and other kinds of influence and 'tit-for-tat accountability' to informal coalitions of national and international 'friends or friendly institutions'. In such networks, agencies – similarly as in the case of other interested persons or stakeholders – form close bonds based on joint patterns of beliefs concerning a similar problem of policy, implementation, or something else. Based on common interests and joint understandings, these actors synchronise their actions and diligently collaborate within the context of a problem. Such behaviours can be understood and imagined, but they cannot be never fully illuminated. They constantly adapt to changes, and they must do so. As a result, findings are always incomplete; only certain orientations, perspectives on looking at agencies, or other complex adaptive systems can be thus given. Only when such perspectives are given analysis of a specific agency could be done beyond the simple logic of its tasks, various interests and the modes of policy and implementation.

Even agencies with the same organisational form do not behave equally or have the same problems. Some problems can be attributed to a formal arrangement of management, but this is just one perspective. When an agency's management is placed under one person (director) rather than a multimember corporative group,[14] the vulnerability to various interests can be reduced, while a management board is more suitable due to its democratic and balancing elements. Such direction can be appropriate, but it can be also the other way around: various interests more easily submit a one director, while a management board can lead to the surreptitious actions of board members, to »check mate« or deadlock positions. When both statement or point of view seems equally probable, there is the need to apply a different method of argumentation, methodology or perspective. The legislator can through the agency' formal arrangement, predict how an agency can do its work (it allows an impact of different interest groups, by giving discretionary power to officials, it allows them a wider space of actions, a relation between citizens or client fixes with material and procedural rules, etc.), but there are also many other, complex and unpredictable elements (the environment, context, personal characteristics of employees and clients or citizens, *esprit de corps*, public values and personal virtues, reflected also through organisational culture or through many competing cultures inside and outside of organisation) that make prediction of agencies operations almost impossible. In such conditions, indicators can be appropriate as they show the current state of affairs. On the other hand, two large focus or emphasis on one or just a few indicators can blur the picture; a solution could be in (stochastic) indicators that randomly change based on a random number generator. The introduction (and consequent use) of performance indicators can be hampered by the antagonism and distrust of public employees, who do not want to be measured, along with the apparently incompatible struggle between those who demand value for money (efficiency or doing things right), those who demand effectiveness (doing the right things), and the government that balances between the efficiency and effectiveness. This chapter can be closed with the still genuine quote from Jowett and Rothwell:

On the positive side, what the government's assault has done is to stimulate those concerned into reappraising their reason for being: public sector organisations have … been forced to examine their consciences and determine whether or not (and to what extent) they are actually providing value for money and fulfilling the needs of their customers. Attitudes and managerial techniques must change, but this is a long and lengthy process. Rome was not built in a day, and similarly … a new, vigorous, commercially-minded and effective public sector will not overnight rise phoenix-like out of the dying embers of the inefficient … model (Jowett & Rothwell, 1988, p. 100).

REFERENCES

Armstrong, M. (2003). *A Handbook of Human Resource Management Practice* (9th ed.). London and Sterling: Kogan Page Publishers.

Bruce, A., Buck, T., & Main, B. G. M. (2005). Top Executive Remuneration: A View from Europe*. *Journal of Management Studies*, *42*(7), 1493–1506. doi:10.1111/j.1467-6486.2005.00553.x

Campbell, D. T. (1979). Assessing the impact of planned social change. *Evaluation and Program Planning*, *2*(1), 67–90. doi:10.1016/0149-7189(79)90048-X

Dunsire, A. (1990). Holistic Governance. *Public Policy and Administration*, *5*(1), 4–19. doi:10.1177/095207679000500102

Goodhart, C. (1981). Problems of Monetary Management: The U.K. Experience. In A. S. Courakis (Ed.), Inflation, Depression, and Economic Policy in the West (pp. 111–116). Totowa, New Yersey: Barnes and Noble Books.

Holland, J. H. (1995). *Hidden order: How adaptation builds complexity*. Addison-Wesley.

Hood, C., & Lodge, M. (2006). *The politics of public service bargains: Reward, competency, loyalty and blame*. Oxford University Press. doi:10.1093/019926967X.001.0001

Jessop, B. (2010). Metagovernance. In M. Bevir (Ed.), *The SAGE Handbook of Governance* (pp. 106–123). SAGE.

Jowett, P., & Rothwell, M. (1988). *Performance Indicators in the Public Sector*. McMillan. doi:10.1007/978-1-349-08987-1

Kiewiet, D. R., & McCubbins, M. D. (1991). *The Logic of Delegation*. University of Chicago Press.

Larmour, P. (1996). *Models of Governance and Development Administration*. Bell School. https://dpa.bellschool.anu.edu.au/experts-publications/publications/1586/models-governance-and-development-administration

Marr, B. (2009). *Managing and Delivering Performance*. Butterworth-Heinemann. doi:10.4324/9780080943015

Parmenter, D. (2012). *Key Performance Indicators for Government and Non Profit Agencies: Implementing Winning KPIs*. John Wiley & Sons. doi:10.1002/9781119201038

Sørensen, E., & Triantafillou, P. (2016). *The Politics of Self-Governance*. Routledge. doi:10.4324/9781315554259

Spitzer, D. (2007). *Transforming Performance Measurement: Rethinking the Way We Measure and Drive Organizational Success*. AMACOM.

Strøm, K. (2000). Delegation and accountability in parliamentary democracies. *European Journal of Political Research*, *37*(3), 261–289. doi:10.1111/1475-6765.00513

Sweet, A. S., & Thatcher, M. (2003). *The Politics of Delegation*. Frank Cas.

The Law Dictionary. (2020). *Board, Council, Commission, Committee, Tribunal*. https://thelawdictionary.org

Toshniwal, S. (2019). *What is the difference between Board, Council, Committee, Commission and Tribunal in India?* Quora. https://www.quora.com/What-is-the-difference-between-Board-Council-Committee-Commission-and-Tribunal-in-India

Wilson, J. Q. (1989). *Bureaucracy: What Government Agencies Do and why They Do it*. Basic Books.

Yesilkagit, K., & van Thiel, S. (2012). Autonomous Agencies and Perceptions of Stakeholder Influence in Parliamentary Democracies. *Journal of Public Administration: Research and Theory, 22*(1), 101–119. doi:10.1093/jopart/mur001

ENDNOTES

[1] The major functions of performance management are: *measurement* directs behaviour, increases the visibility of performance, focuses attention, clarifies expectations, enables accountability, increases objectivity, provides the basis for goal-setting, improves execution, promotes consistency, facilitates feedback, increases alignment, improves decision making, improves problem-solving, provides early warning signals, enhances understanding, enables prediction and motivates (Spitzer, 2007, pp. 16–20)

[2] The role profile describes a role holder's tasks, a role's overall purpose, and the needed key competencies of the role holder.

[3] Performance contract address objectives and standards of performance, performance measures and indicators, competency assessment and core values or operational requirements.

[4] Leverage is one of the most important concepts that was ever discovered. The concept was most famously expressed by ancient Greek mathematician Archimedes when he said, "Give me a lever and a place to stand, and I will move the world" (Spitzer, 2007, p. 79).

[5] Along Kaplan and Norton's original four perspectives (financial, customer, internal process, and learning and growth) Parmenter adds also *staff satisfaction* and *environment and community* (Parmenter, 2012).

[6] Dysfunctional performance is caused when abuse of KPIs purpose is done: the actual state of abuse of KPI arises when an implementer derives from an admissible (abstract) KPI, which is concretized and materialized in a way that his conduct exceeds the KPI's limits or purpose; additionally, such unilateral conduct constitutes a conflict of two KPIs (one KPI prevents the other), which are not mutually exclusive, but one is exercised in a way that prevents the real exercise of the other; the subject derives from an abstract KPI, but exercises it by interfering with other KPI that is implemented by another implementer. E.g.: older, more skilled officials work on the easiest cases and transfer the difficult ones to the inexpert staff (trainees, beginners), because success is measured with the number of closed cases. Abuse of the closed cases indicator is based on biasedly assigned or transferred cases; the closure of the case must not affect the lawfulness of the conduct (exceeding the limit of justification or abuse of KPI's purpose) or the rights of others to equal treatment. In the presented example the latter was present (the inequal treatment of younger officials).

7   Goodhart's law states that 'any observed statistical regularity will tend to collapse once pressure is placed upon it for control purposes' (Goodhart, 1981, p. 116), while more explainable Campbell's law states that 'the more any quantitative social indicator is used for social decision-making, the more subject it will be to corruption pressures and the more apt it will be to distort and corrupt the social processes it is intended to monitor' (Campbell, 1979).

8   A past successfulness of an agency's performance contract could be compared with the allocation of resources in the new performance contract, but there are also many other contingent factors that should be considered.

9   Even when goals are clearly stated, the pragmatic, contextual situation can outline tasks differently, especially when a different way of doing the job appears simpler or more appealing. One of the first serious indices of how much some institution may be serious on performance measurement may be an insight into its strategy from which it is possible (or not) to see and understand its orientation to main (outcomes) and specific goals (outputs), KPIs, the time plan, responsible persons, reporting, the openness of data, etc.

10 E.g. organizations that perform best are those which are able to (1) create clarity and agreement about the strategic aims, (2) collect meaningful and relevant performance indicators, (3) use these indicators to extract relevant insights, (4) create a positive culture of learning from performance information, (5) gain cross-organizational buy-in, (6) align other organizational activities with the strategic aims outlined in the performance management system, (7) keep the strategic objectives and performance indicators fresh and up-to-date, (8) report and communicate performance information well, (9) use the appropriate IT infrastructure to support their performance management activities and (10) give people enough time and resources to manage performance strategically (Marr, 2009, p. 272).

11 Along delegation of tasks to (non-representative) agencies, the latter also gained their space in questions of policy. The classical or even theoretical division between policy and implementation (if ever really existed) broke down with delegation. In the EU, the number of agencies has grown – first in the field of utilities or infrastructure, and then also to other areas (fundamental rights, border and coast guard, medicines, etc.) – in the real network of almost 50 agencies.

12 Gaps can emerge due to the poor understanding of actual situations, inappropriate delegation of competencies or tasks by the former or due to the poor performance, erroneous use of discretion, incomplete presentation of factual state of affairs by the latter, etc.

13 Sequential phases could be also named as the singularity principle (however, due to the gradual and multiple transitions from one level to another, the first naming could be more appropriate): parliamentary democracy is a single chain of delegation with multiple links. In each link, a single principal delegates to a single or to multiple non-competing agents. In a similar fashion, under parliamentary democracy agents are accountable to a single (though not necessarily individual or unique) principal (Strøm, 2000).

14 A corporative group of the agency's members can be assembled as the board, council, commission, committee, or tribunal. Among them are differences that affect the leadership style: '**Board** is a committee of persons organized under the authority of the law to exercise certain authorities, have oversight or control of certain matters, or discharge certain functions of a magisterial, representative, or fiduciary character. **Council** is an assembly of persons for concerting measures of state or municipal policy. **Committee** is an individual or body to whom others have delegated or committed a particular duty, or who have taken on themselves to perform it in the expectation of

their act being confirmed by the body they profess to represent or act for. **Commission** is a warrant or authority or letters patent, issuing from the government, or one of its departments, or a court, empowering a person or person named to do certain acts, or to exercise jurisdiction, or to perform the duties and exercise the authority of an office. **Tribunal** is the seat of a judge; the place where he administers justice; a judicial court: the bench of judges' (The Law Dictionary, 2020).

'**Board** is a group of people who have the power to decide and control the working of a body. They are usually at the apex of the organization. The members of the board are appointed by the real owners of the organization. **Council** is a body, generally large in size than other types of groups mentioned here. The members of the council are elected by the members. They act as representatives of the people. Thus, elections are conducted for forming the council. Councils are formed when there is a large body of people who have come together for a purpose. **Committees** are subgroups of the original body. They are formed for a specific purpose. The members of the committees are generally selected on merit or some other criteria. **Commission** is similar to Committees except for the fact that Commissions are formed by government bodies or Statutory bodies. The members of the commission are either selected or nominated by the interested groups. Commissions can be permanent or temporary depending upon the purpose of such commission. **Tribunal** is very different from the above types of groups. The members of the tribunal are current or retired judges. Sometimes, people having relevant experience and knowledge in the field are also appointed. The Tribunals are adjudicating authority' (Toshniwal, 2019).

Chapter 11
New Institutional Analysis

ABSTRACT

New institutionalism emerged in the 1980s as an alternative to old functional institutionalism. It focuses on the importance of informal actions on the persistence of institutions through time, discovering institutional underlying patterns and processes. The new institutionalism tends to reduce variety, operating across organizations to override diversity in local environments. The mentioned elements derive legitimacy from more symbolic elements, sensible to cultural forms and cognitive models rather than from the discursive reason. The concept of agency emerged as the answer to the question of how to improve public institutions with the emphasis on larger autonomy, flexibility, performance, and more direct contact with the environment and citizen's needs. The agency's apparent hybrid nature based on private-sector methods could gain some advantage when formal goals would be not only quasi but de facto optimised with practice when the agency's autonomy and independence are balanced with control and accountability.

INTRODUCTION

Students of administration have long sought a single principle of effective departmentalization just as alchemists sought the philosophers' stone. But they have sought in vain. There is apparently no one most effective system of departmentalism (Gulick, 2003, p. 33).

Renewed interest in institutions began in the 1980s, especially when March and Olsen offered the notion of new institutionalism that insists on a more autonomous role for political institutions, because "the organization of political life makes a difference", distant from the formal wording of laws and of formal organisation. Institutions express also institutional coherence (institutions as decision-makers) and autonomy (institutions are more than simple mirrors of social forces). The order can be imposed by *reason* and by *competition* and *coercion,* while new institutionalism gives additional notions or order: *historical* (the efficiency of historical processes), *temporal* (linkages among means and ends are less consequential, but also affected by time allocation or arrival), *endogenous* (order is imposed not only by the external environment but also by internal institutional processes), *normative* (order is not static, the

DOI: 10.4018/979-8-3693-0507-2.ch011

relations among norms, the significance of ambiguity and inconsistency in norms, and the time path of the transformation of normative structures), *demographic* (the ways organizations adapt through turnover, institutions are driven by their cohort structures, and the pursuit of careers and professional standards dictates the flow of events) and *symbolic* (the processes by which symbols shape the behaviour of the society as a whole) (March & Olsen, 1984, pp. 743–744). The idea was to look afar the formal rules and admit the importance of various *informal* actions on the persistence of institutions through time to discover institutional underlying patterns and processes. Indeed, even the 'Next Steps' concept was "the product of compromise and accommodation":

Developed institutional arrangements [surrounding the concept of Next Steps] illustrate the path dependency of policy change. Both the agency concept and how this concept was adopted in departments, depended upon the existing formal and informal institutional arrangements. The agency policy carried a mix of old and new 'rules of the game', the introduction of arms-length control alongside maintenance of the doctrine of ministerial responsibility (Gains, 2004, p. 71).

The new institutionalism stresses the ways in which *cognitive* dimensions of *practical* (and semiautomatic, non-calculative) action are structured and order is made by the systems of rules that constrain a capacity to optimize as well as privilege some groups by prevalent rewards and sanctions. In the frame of "old functional institutionalism" (Selznick, Parsons, Spencer) interests are a result of political trade-offs and alliances, while the new stresses i) a relationship between stability and legitimacy and the power of common understandings that are seldom explicitly articulated; ii) locates irrationality in the formal structure itself, and not in the "shadowland of informal interaction"; iii) rather than being co-opted by organizations, environments penetrate the organization, generating lenses through which actors see the world and the categories of structure, action, and thought; iv) organizational forms, structural components, and rules, not specific organizations, are institutionalized; v) tends to reduce variety, operating across organizations to override diversity in local environments; vi) the rejection of the unreflective, routine, taken-for-granted nature of most human behaviour and views interests and actors as themselves constituted by institutions; vii) not norms and values but taken-for-granted scripts, rules, and classifications are the stuff of which institutions are made (Powell & DiMaggio, 1991). The mentioned elements derive legitimacy from more symbolic elements, sensible to cultural forms and cognitive models rather from the discursive reason, internalization, sanctions, norms, values, and roles. These were replaced by cognitive theory, practical reason, imitation, *ad hoc* scripts and schemas, accounts, loose coupling and routines. These new perspectives of the "new institutionalism" are nevertheless still focused on organizations in their various "rainbow" environments than on "the specific dynamics of the institutional systems" (Turner, 2003). For Turner 'one way to overcome this mesolevel bias in institutional analysis is to conceptualize the levels at which human societies unfold as they grow and develop. Each level ... is driven by its own distinct set of forces, creating structural and cultural forms that are unique to a given level of reality' (Turner, 2003, p. 2). Each level of reality intertwines and affects other lower or higher levels (face-to-face interactions at the microlevel affect organisational units at the macrolevel, and the latter affects social institutions at the macrolevel, and contrary. They, all of their net of communicative actions, contribute to the increased/lowered legitimacy that offers better/worse contact with resources, and further enhances/reduces possibilities for a survival of organization. These elements resemble two elements of complexity theory that are elaborated later in the special section.

Comparative studies reveal considerable diversity between and within countries (OECD, 1997; Pollitt & Bouckaert, 2017). Ministerial background and/or path dependencies on the prevailing arrangements of values, decision-making, organizational narration and approaches, bureaucratic resistance, political, constitutional, and legal views or positions exhibit variances in (in)formal roadblocks, even in most pro-stance countries like in the United States and Canada, where reforms were incremental and did not lead to radical changes in governance structures (Graham & Roberts, 2004). For quangos in Dutch government case study evidence suggests there is neither immediate nor overall improvement of performance in terms of cost efficiency and effectiveness (Ter Bogt 1997, 1999; Van Berkum and Van Dijkem 1997; Van Thiel 2001a), while in other areas, the quality of products or customer service, some improvements have been obtained, at least in the newly acquired, more business-like style and market awareness (van Thiel, 2004). There is no reliable, objective explanation for the international convergence towards "agencification"; there are just many various perspectives that could explain agencies' growth from political (re-election, legitimacy), economic (free economic initiative, efficiency), international (stable, from the rule-of law-based country) point of view. SIGMA in 2001 determined that 'since the 1980s there has been an explosion of interest in the agency model in many countries, driven largely by pressures to restrain spending and make service to citizens more responsive' (SIGMA, 2001, p. 8).[1] Despite numerous approaches towards "agencification", agencies per se did not prevent the rise of socioeconomic inequality since 1980 (Piketty, 2020).

New (in)formal procedures and positions always emerge and co-exist parallel with the existing cultures and opinions. This features the vague, vibrant and often institutional specific understanding: a reality of agency arrangements show variable perspectives, intonations and inclinations. Their common denominator was the effort to establish a more effective strategy for achieving management goals. The concept of agency occurred in the right time as the answer to the question of how to improve public institutions with the emphasis on larger autonomy, flexibility, performance, and more direct contact with the environment and citizens' needs. Despite such very attractive ideas, "agencification" denotes a very complex package of ideas that "land on the specific soil of each country". Similarly stands also for other ideas, e.g., new governance (Osborne, 2010), digital era governance (Dunleavy, Margetts, Tinkler, & Bastow, 2006).

Are agencies just another name for governmental bodies despite their – at arm's length – formal distance? If agencies implement tasks similarly as the public administration – are there any rational grounds for their existence at all? The agencies of Types 2 and 3 and/or quangos should not only be distanced from the public administration, but they should also be different in their *modus operandi* – to gain public confidence, and legitimacy in their work they should exhibit proactive transparency, accountability and close relations with civil society in the sense of responsiveness, flexibility, agility and public participation. The agency's apparent hybrid nature (based on private-sector methods to achieve public aims in the most optimal manner possible) could nevertheless gain some advantage when formal goals would be not only quasi but *de facto* optimised with practice[2] when the agency's autonomy and independence are balanced with control and accountability. Both parts are very important for agencies because they reflect the element of "immortality" (their abolition is seldom on the political agenda). The complexity of various views on agency is nothing new, as parts always produce their relations and combinations that are incomprehensible for one view or one mind. Their common denominator could be the system, and/or their underlying structure on which agencies operate. Along with the theoretical (especially NPM's) ideas of efficiency, effectiveness, manager's autonomy, impartiality, and apolitical nature of agencies, practice shows a more blurred picture; despite political *de rigueur* (*i.e.* prescribed or required by fashion, etiquette, or custom) *pro* stance for agencies, it seems that various attempts of institutional reforms and agencies' forms could not prevent the rise of burgeoning economic inequality (Joseph, 2017; Piketty, 2014, 2020). It seems that along with different institutions and their formal rules, there are also different (in)formal practices (dis)similar ways of doing, sublime and inferior elements present that produce institutional results/patterns, caused *by the underlying system structure* (Meadows, 2008). Behaviour is latent in the *interaction* of parts (Bertalanffy, 1968), influenced by the structure (Senge, 2010). Actions and results are hence not caused primarily by the external environment *per se*, but by multiple *interrelationships* (Ackoff, 1978) that cause new emergent things.

For each institution and/or agency hence the *system*, through its (in)formal "sensors", documents information only if the latter's structure is *similar* to the system's structure. It thus matters how systems and/or circumstances or working conditions are arranged, aligned, and adjusted with the external environment and other stakeholders. Institutions direct decisions on what is similar, different, complex and chaotic.

Institutions do not merely reflect the preferences and power of the units constituting them; the institutions themselves shape those preferences and that power. Institutions are therefore constitutive of actors as well as vice versa. It is therefore not sufficient in this view to treat the preferences of individuals as given exogenously: they are affected by institutional arrangements, by prevailing norms, and by historically contingent discourse among people seeking to pursue their purposes and solve their self-defined problems (Keohane, 1988, p. 382).

Institutions are assembled with people and their roles; both parts constitute each other and constrain it at the same time and contrary. Neo-institutionalism claims that actors and their interests are institutionally constructed (Powell & DiMaggio, 1991). Formalities and interest emerge within particular institutional and subjective contexts. When the notion of "institution" is mentioned, it is usually taken for granted without being defined at all. Maybe 'the only idea common to all usages of the term "institution" is that of some sort of establishment of relative permanence of a distinctly social sort' (Hughes, 1936:180, quoted in Zucker, 1977, p. 726) in which fits a complex social form that reproduces itself, be it the government, region, church, family, language, university, military, school, business corporation, etc. Institution may also 'refer to a general pattern or categorization of an activity or to a particular human-constructed arrangement, formally or informally organized' (Keohane, 1988, p. 383). And when there are generalisations, there is the law. The law thus comes to life in institutions (Waldron, 2011), not only in the general legislation, regulation, and adjudication, but every day in relations between public servants and citizens. Their ways of doing things, established routines, and procedures impact formal goals, and with no varying changes in their underlying structure, institutions thus continue with their usual practices regardless of their formal names. A recipe for institutionalization consists of people's roles, their constant or durable relationships that evolve around prescribed or anticipated behaviours with respect to some general goals, purposes or interests (expectations).

As institutions can be seen as systems, the first should also act as the second. Due to the various contexts in which agencies operate, one of the elements of the system is of specific importance: *equifinality*. It refers to the ability of open systems to reach their goals with different means and processes and from different places. Bertalanffy describes it as the 'very characteristic aspect of the dynamic order in organismic processes...[which can be contrary to machine-like structures that follow a fixed pathway] reach the same final state ... from different initial conditions and in different pathways' (Bertalanffy, 1968, p. 132). In legal science, equifinality is the closest to responsive regulation (Ayres & Braithwaite, 1995), while in an organisational manner of agencies, they should be robust and at the same time flexible, agile, and resilient.[3] Equifinality is tightly connected with the notion of emergence that is 'the appearance of a level of complexity more advanced than the existing components of a system' (Feltz, Crommelinck, & Goujon, 2006, p. 341). Emergence is a state of affairs that occurs as a result of dynamic nonlinear systems, i.e., their *interactions:* 'an emergent property is a global behaviour or structure which appears through the interactions of a collection of elements, with no global controller responsible for

New Institutional Analysis

the behaviour or organization of these elements. The idea of emergence is that it is not reducible to the properties of the elements' (Feltz et al., 2006, p. 341). All is not only more than the sum of its parts, but what is or could be more cannot be known in advance, until shown or tried in practice. Another characteristic of emergent property is its 'complex behaviour [that emerges] from simple rules. Those rules imply general regularity, but the working out of an individual case exhibits special regularities in addition' (Gell-Mann, 2002, p. 313).

On a more general level, each agency is assembled from the parts, connections among them, purpose, flows, and stocks, patterns as results or flows and stocks or their ratio, indicators of performance, positive and negative feedbacks, decision(s) that affect the mentioned ratio between stocks and flows, emergence based on interrelationships among parts, and equifinality (as the possibility to enact such decisions to reach intended goals despite changes). These elements are present in each type of agency, so to change its performance the mentioned elements should be addressed. They could be more data-driven, context-aware, and context-smart when decision-makers/managers are aware of the power of system thinking backed up by IT. This brings the idea of agency into the realm of governance, and the latter back to systems as self-organising entities of various stakeholders that manage their goals based on goals and interaction of all elements/parts. The organizational structure should hence address its specific environment; it should adapt/respond to it and not to other institutional forms per se that lead to institutional similarity and/or homogeneity of the structure (institutional isomorphism). The state of urgency (e.g., the epidemic situations, earthquakes, floods) or other situations in which a purpose must be achieved in the shortest time possible, in the »hostile« environment and with limited resources are one of the best testing grounds not only for people but also for organisations. As no one wants such conditions in reality, there are stress tests available that can show how a person/organisation works during physical/organisation's activities.

COMPARATIVE DIMENSIONS OF AGENCIES AS THE RUSSIAN DOLLS OF MINISTRIES

From a comparative perspective, there should be some common elements that exist in agencies to be able to make a typology and/or ranking of agencies. Structure within public institutions cannot just be detached from external structures that are an intrinsic part of the government, or, in other words, 'the internal structures of public agencies reflect, in part, the jurisdictional structures of the government body under which they operate' (Rainey, 2009, p. 230). In Goodnow's manner, 'it is believed that the real political institutions of different peoples at the same stage of intelligence and morality will show a great similarity, even where the external forms of government appear very different…after all, a a man is man everywhere and at all times, and all political organizations of men must therefore have ultimately the same ends, and must adopt in a general way the same methods for their satisfaction' (Goodnow, 1900, p. 7).[4] This approach is in general systems theory described as *a hierarchy* as an essential feature of complex systems, not in the sense of vertical power differences and subordination, but as a mechanism of *clustering*: systems are comprised of multiple subsystems, and the first themselves are also contained within larger systems.

The bourgeois revolution established the unitary or federal nation-states that are a powerful instrument of security and equality of all citizens.[5] Along the public services,[6] a national state has been also a powerful creator and – through public law, state aids, taxes, etc. – enforcer of competitive markets. The

18-19th century bourgeois revolution abolished intermediary levels (villains, knights, barons, or lords) that were present between the people and central state authority (the king). They ended feudal social formations that obtained significant privileges by serving the sovereign in some capacity or another, and transformed them more to "associative" forms based on contractual bonds. The sovereign state, especially when seen as the unitary state (if international levels are put aside), seems as the only formation within its borders, but there are also other residual levels that had transformed their antient roots into modern ones (medieval communes into local municipalities or local self-government) and new deconcentrated, subsidiary levels[7] that burst especially after the WWII, with the emergence of the citizens' rights and welfare state. With the additional development of technology and the increasing complexity of the environment, accordingly, questions about the approximation of services for citizens begin to appear, which are always inevitably connected with the development of new institutions and their organizational forms. Relations between the centralised state and society are filled with many intermediary levels that address various public needs. The pluralist and monist concepts of politics, bottom-up and top-down rationalisations, can be traced back at least to Aristotle's politics, but the emergence of the international community, the supranational European Community, now known as the EU, its member states and their institutional arrangements across their territories lead to new practices (and/or new structures put in place by the Maastricht Treaty of 1992) that connected the structural funds of the EU (funding weaker regions) not only with their member states, but also their regional institutions directly with the EU, where member states responded with the desire to control these direct supranational-subnational processes. Such practises[8] were described as "multi-level governance" (MLG)[9] that seek to explain 'the dispersion of central government authority both vertically, to actors located at other territorial levels, and horizontally, to non-state actors' (Bache & Flinders, 2005, p. 4) and/or 'a diverse set of arrangements, a panoply of systems of coordination and negotiation among formally independent but functionally interdependent entities that stand in complex relations to one another and that, through coordination and negotiation, keep redefining these relations' (Piattoni, 2010, p. 26). MLG pictures the world of governance not as a simple binary black or white entity, but as a rainbow, as a rich multi-coloured ensemble, where each part contributes to an intricate, interrelated and multidimensional whole. MLG describes the ways of vertical dispersion of power between many levels of government and horizontal dispersion across multiple quasi-government and non-governmental organizations and actors (Cairney, Heikkila, & Wood, 2019). MLG focuses on many ways in which functions can be executed by agencies or other differently named institutions located outside of the central government. MLG is a concept that groups together unity and fragmentation; it is focused on the central government and other levels at the same time, with many actors, including the non-state ones, as well as on the various ways in which public tasks can be done by agencies other than the central government itself. Such a multilayered system is due to its multiple jurisdictions that are at the same time intertwined, overlapped, and coordinated, contrary to a simple hierarchic arrangement. Here the policy and implementation can be mixed and grouped in one, over a private-public vision of whole. Governance turns out to be structured through multiple jurisdictions and cannot be understood any more as a central-state monopoly.

"Multi-level" refers to the interdependence of governments functioning at different territorial levels, whereas "governance"[10] refers to the interdependence between governments and non-governmental actors at different levels. The relation between these two notions opens a space of possibilities where different ways of work and their levels function on multiplying stages and fields with various organizations, and where politics is made and implemented. Here are at work various general and specific tools combined and present in different operational units that act and are connected horizontally and vertically. The

New Institutional Analysis

overall question is how these multilayered arrangements affect citizens, democracy, and legitimacy, *i.e.*, how MLG is organized. Marks and Hooghe (2005) present two contrasting visions of MLG: Type I and Type II. The first resonances federalist system, with the general-purpose jurisdictions, nonintersecting memberships, jurisdictions at a limited number of levels, and system-wide and durable architecture, while the second is more complex, with task-specific jurisdictions, intersecting memberships, no limit to the number of jurisdictional levels, and with a flexible design related to demands of needed changes in governance. Flexibility is rooted in Tiebout's argument that the mobility of citizens among rival authorities provides a functional counterpart to market competition (Tiebout, 1956), where the public goods and services and organisations that provide them accommodate to citizens' preferences. Type I is usual in conventional territorial government up to the national level, with the intrinsic community that has democratic voice and systems of conflict articulation, while Type II is inserted in legal frameworks determined by Type I jurisdictions, with the extrinsic community that has a possibility of exit when Type II jurisdiction no longer serves its needs, and where energy is focused on improving efficiency and conflict avoidance. The effect is a large(r) number of functionally distinguished Type II jurisdictions vis-à-vis a smaller number of general-purpose, Type I jurisdictions. In general, Type I jurisdictions are suited to political deliberation about basic choices in a society: who gets what, when, and how. Type II jurisdictions, in contrast, emphasize problem solving' (Marks & Hooghe, 2005, p. 29).[11] The distinction between Type I and Type II MLG can show us the vertical and horizontal placement of various bodies in the (supra)national matrix, but except flexibility there are no other elements that could serve or explain why such arrangements occur.

Practical examples show that Type II jurisdictions are usually embedded in Type I jurisdictions. The latter give a general frame in which the former can more freely move, *i.e.*, apply the basic principles on a more flexible manner. Within Type II jurisdictions various public and private organisations and/or agencies can be found. From this various and multiple numbers can be inferred, there are many parts that work within a larger system. When multiple parts are indirect, this inevitably leads towards complexity. One of the first principles of cybernetics is that only *a variety can destroy (i.e. manage another) variety* (Ashby, 1957). Therefore, a complex (assembled) problem can only be administrated with the same or a similar measure of complexity (known as Ashby's *requisite variety*), so (Ashby, 1957)(William Ross Ashby, 1957) a regulator must be a model of a regulated area/thing (Conant-Ashby theorem) (Beer, 1994). People have always intuitively followed this rule and so do governments: the latter changed their structures to respond to new urgencies, and significances in a changing environment and society (underlying social trends of better, government, democratisation, rule of law, accountability, transparency, trust, confidence) to impact or to improve the management of existing ones.

Although generalisations on the perspectives from which agencies can be assessed are possible, these generalisations are only or more or less "statistically determined denominators that cannot reflect an actual state of affairs in a specific agency. To be successful in dealing with complex environments, an agency should have at least the same number of tools or approaches as the regulated environment. This requires knowledge on the administration of variety: the multidimensional analysis combined with systems theory demands that agencies consider *a quid pro quo* resemblance with ministries: if one step is made into the field of cybernetics, one of its first principles is that only *a variety can destroy (i.e., manage another) variety* (Ashby, 1957). This means a *contingency* perspective: the manner by which an organization is structured should depend on the nature of the environment to which it relates. Therefore, a complex (assembled) problem can be administrated only with the same or a similar measure of complexity (known as Ashby's *requisite variety*), so (Ashby, 1957)a regulator must be a model of a regulated area/thing (Conant-Ashby theorem) (Beer, 1994). Any decision is hence on overall, good/ bad as its decision-maker. Systems theory additionally emphasises the *parallelism and/or mirroring* of systems on a whole level: the smaller ones are (like Russian dolls) embedded in the larger ones being their smaller copies (self-similarity and recursion on other nested upper- or sub-levels). The same holds for institutions as systems: hierarchically subordinate institutions (more or less) reflect hierarchically superior ones and *vice versa*. In this line of thought agencies reflect (up to a point) bigger governmental institutions like ministries; the traditional linear (bureaucratic) model of public administration – even when we speak about the unbounded government – conflicts with the more open, heuristic, complex, net or DNA replication-based style of administration that can with their multiple and intertwined relations more realistically capture the reality of governance. Therefore, there is 'a need to be more attuned to the multiple dimensions of public organization' (Bouckaert & Peters, 2004, p. 28).

Complexity represents things with many parts that interact with each other in multiple relations, while variety is the measure for defining the number of these possible relations. To obtain the number of complexities or binomial coefficients, Pascal's triangle is used as the nth power of 2 (2n) (Mlodinow, 2008). Complexity cannot be addressed by the public administration's existing solutions (from a simple example it can be demonstrated how numbers exponentially rise[12]). Ashby proposed variety as a measure of complexity in the 1950s. For him '[a]n essential feature of the good regulator is that it blocks the flow of variety from disturbances to essential variables' (Ashby, 1957, p. 201). If the variety in outcomes is to be reduced to some assigned number, then the variety of tools a regulator has with respect to the environment 'must be increased…to at least the appropriate minimum' (Ashby, 1957, p. 206). Only Variety$_1$ can force down Variety$_2$ and vice versa: *only variety can destroy variety.* Ashby's variety balances the system from a control point of view between the regulator and the outer environment. For effective administration, a homeostatic loop of the regulator amplifiers (from the regulator to the system) and filters (from the system to the regulator) should be inserted to deal only with an interested part of the environment (the latter is otherwise too complex to deal with it as a whole). The larger the variety of actions controllers embrace, the larger the variety of perturbations that must be compensated for. There should be as many elements on the one side as there are on the other side, if one wants to establish variety in their relations (requisite variety).[13] This idea is taken into account in Margetts et al. (2012). They built modernisation reforms on Ashby's law of requisite variety and Douglas's grid group cultural theory (GGCT). For them, a success in modernisation depends on the requisite variety on

Balance between the three modernization strategies of modernization – Integration (interconnectedness, standardization, central control and formal rules), Economic Rationalism (incentivization, economic efficiency), and Specialization (scientific advancement, expert knowledge, technological development and quantification) and a counterbalance from the elementary forms of social organization – the hierarchy and individualism that both sustain the three modernization strategies and that they in turn tend to cultivate, but also enclaved and isolated orderings (Margetts et al., 2012, pp. 224–227).

Requisite variety is a tool that can give an appropriate modus operandi with which decision-makers can be closer to their goals (just like there should be at least eleven players in each football team at the start) – in order to deal effectively with diverse problems, there must be multiple responses that should be as nuanced as the problems at hand. This idea of requisite variety is presented also in Conant-Ashby theorem by which 'every good regulator of a system must be a model of that system' (Conant & Ashby, 1970). This nuanced approach is *a sine qua for* managing variety, but it cannot explain why one alternative is chosen instead of another. This can be explained with *values* – they can give us an answer to why a hierarchist would never choose an isolationist stance and *vice versa*. Values are not only present in our decisions, but form their pre-decisional (cultural) point.

The creation of a separately managed or quasi-independent body should be distinguished from autonomy and/or regulation, because '[s]eparation does not necessarily mean autonomy – many formally independent public organisations are tightly regulated in matters of personnel, finance, procurement, and a host of other issues, which severely limit managerial autonomy' (Talbot, 2004, p. 9). Such cases are Slovenian administration units or police stations that are separated but highly regulated; structural separation should not be directly equated with autonomy or decentralization, where only higher control and reduced deconcentrated operations are carried out, which is just brought closer to the living areas of citizens. On the other hand, structural separation could mean in a relevant context a lower level of regulation with the aim of more liberal management and thus greater freedom of action. As a rule of thumb, it could be said that the higher level of autonomy could be proportionately present with the higher level of expertise needed for the implementation of tasks of expertise of technical, more or less static, unmovable nature. Taleb describes the difference between the (embrained) "know-how" and (embedded) "know-what". The first is connected with life skills knowledge, the second with knowledge. The Greeks made a distinction between *technē* (craft skills) and *episteme* (knowledge science). There are (dynamic) matters in which people know even more than experts (P. E. Tetlock, 2006; P. Tetlock & Gardner, 2015), and *vice versa*.[14] Autonomy is also not directly related to static nature, but with performance indicators (performance contracts)[15] that show the overall agency's effectiveness and efficiency. Contracting is the NPM's organising principle, so 'great faith is placed in performance monitoring as a mechanism for improving accountability, policy coordination and responsiveness of service providers to clients' (McGuire, 2004, p. 117). In this line of thought, Behn speaks on "earned autonomy", about higher autonomy and deregulation as a reward for the agency's good performance (Behn, 2001).

If Twain's quote is paraphrased, history does not repeat itself exactly, but many similar patterns nevertheless repeat themselves – due to their similar or even the same *structural backgrounds:* if tasks are done in the same way as in ministries, by almost the same people in their status and their salary (public employees), etc. Then it is irrelevant whether this is done by a formally independent institution. The independency of agencies could lift their legitimacy, but it can, on the other hand, raise concerns on accountability and control. It is hence important to have answers about agencies: what they do (tasks), for whom were they established (clientele), how and why they do their tasks (modus operandi, intent), and for how long they were meant to operate (sunset). Despite national differences, there are common denominators that could be used to evaluate the performance of agencies. Many times, governments and scholars use dichotomies, Boolean yes-or-no (0 or 1) truth values rather than a more-or-less type of opinion (somewhere between 0 and 1).[16] The first is based on traditional dual logic, where a statement is true or false and nothing in between, while e.g., in fuzzy set theory[17] (and even more in quantum theory), an element is based on potentiality and can even either belong to a set or not. The fuzziness and/or uncertainty, imprecision, and vagueness are present in human language, as well as in the human judgment, evaluation, and (legal) decisions (a person takes a more certain decision, *i.e.,* more probable). While legal science formally bases general legal rules on determinism, agencies in practice operate on a $(0-1$ or $1-100)$ scale of certainty, monotony, inability, ignorance towards uncertainty, potentiality, predictability, and anticipation. Things change,, and hence also agencies' properties; most systems are too complex to be put on a binary (or even numerical – if numbers are seen just as weights of higher / lower importance) scale as they cannot represent the whole system. The fuzzy logic approach does not demand detailed knowledge of the system as its properties are determined by linguistic rules and shown on a scaling line.[18] The fuzzy approach can be more robust because fuzzy logic is more general linguistic controllers can embrace more variability in the inputs and hence can avoid the problem of overspecialization. The known cases of biological extinction have been caused by overspecialization, whose concentration of only selected genes sacrifices general adaptability (Fuller & Applewhite, 1997). Thus, it is important to have an agency that is robust, flexible, agile, and resilient at the same time.

Taylorism or management by science emphasises a clear description of tasks and purposes based on *data* obtained in (experimental) practice. Political independence and other forms of autonomy (managerial, financial, etc.) and other elements of agencies can be given to the latter only when the obtained and evaluated data show a specific type of agency as the most appropriate given its purpose, goals, and other predispositions that should already prior establish clear relations between systemic elements that should be then posteriorly controlled in practice. Only in such manner the division of work, functionalism and specialisation of agency can be really attuned with ministerial coordination and control. This is especially relevant because all public agencies are, as saints, in close relation with immortality: they seldomly die.[19] Provided that agencies' effectiveness was ex-ante clearly established (right goals), they should be very efficient (the right manner of achieving goals) at implementing services. This should be so not only for economic reasons but also for the political ones: good performance or implementation of services, *depoliticises agencies* and gives them the practical amount of independence. Only a careful assessment (of the relevant field, citizens' needs, a distance between a ministry and citizens, nature, or a type of service, agency type) can ensure that all dependent and related situations are addressed satisfactorily; this assessment is many times only one presented by the authorities regardless of the objectivity of the proposal. From this point of view, it is especially desirable to have a system that allows the widest possible set of information, in accordance with the cybernetic principle of redundancy of a potential command that runs contrarily with the importance of top-level hierarchy:[20]

The concept of hierarchy is good for some formal purposes, but it is an almost useless model for understanding the actual regulation of institutions. Command in living systems is potentially extended across the entire system. Different people are able to make small decisions, which in the end are reflected in the main one. The potential of command is relevant only because of the distribution of information across the entire system at a given time. The role of hierarchies is nothing more than that the formal organizational structure corrects the distribution of information (Beer & Eno, 2009, p. 26).

The principle of redundancy of a potential command has a great democratic charge: the more information there is, the more arguments in favour of a certain decision show, the more justified the latter is per se, and the less chance there is for political games that run counter to objective data. If the latter are provided, there is no need for some higher authority to tell the people what is right or wrong. On the contrary, when data show that services could be more effectively provided by departments, the cycle of reforms should go in this direction. When this path is taken solely because departments cannot effectively coordinate and control agencies, the wrong presumption is repeated as it was before for some agencies: when there are real possibilities to correct mistakes within an organisation, there is no reason to transfer its competences to another organisation.[21] When these mistakes (ways of doing things) are not properly addressed, there is real probability they will be present also on another level.[22] A usual division between a ministry and an agency is division between policy and its implementation through services. The majority of work in the ministry should be given to questions of policy and in the agency to questions of services. However, the reality is more complex. According to the World Bank, 'there is no hard evidence available that "single-roof" agencies (multi-purpose bodies retaining both policy and service delivery responsibilities) perform less well or are less readily held to account than their single-purpose counterparts' (Gill, 2002, p. 65). A decision on division should be made based on the context analysis (pros and cons), availability of data, and ability of data measurement (*e.g.*, customs and taxes vs. security, education, foreign affairs).

When services can be delivered effectively and independently (and unselfishly given the private interest of officials) delivered also at the ministerial level, there is no reason to create a new agency. The problem of information asymmetry within a ministry and vis-a-vis agencies and backwards is not in information per se, but in ways of non-provision of data or silence of nontransparent procedures and manners by which information could be hidden, redesigned, embellished, or adapted to show its possessors in the best possible light. Management of performance and performance indicators which results can be in real-time seen to both, coordinating and implementing institutions at the same time, of utmost importance.

A decision to delegate some public tasks to agencies or to redelegate them back to ministries should follow the strategic and systemic review of governmental institutions on the delivery of services. This scrutiny of public programmes could be focused on issues like the scope to which they served the public interest, the time needed to deliver services, their costs per employee and citizens, gains and loss of alternative organisational and procedural arrangements on quality, affordability, trust, etc.

As with principles also at service stands excesses lead to unwanted consequences and side effects. For each element, it is evident that the more we investigate it, the more other questions are opened (this is similar to the coastline paradox that prolongs the length of a coastline proportionally to the more detailed measurement) – and consequentially differently answered due to different (national, economic, etc.) contexts. There is no point in suggesting some ideal model of agency due to the variety and complexity of the environment in which organisations implement their tasks. The questions of better or worse approach are always weighted with various other elements, and these weights cannot be given here but also in the practice of an evaluated pragmatic relation between some public goal and its implementation *vis-à-vis* the most appropriate organisational form in which this relation should be the best addressed. Contrary to the impossibility of giving some ideal of the agency's form there is clear responsibility present at the ministerial level to provide the best possible mean of service delivery. The ministerial responsibility to evaluate conditions in real-time frames given the context, processes, citizens' needs, and criteria used that would serve for a specific case of agency creation or abolishment is evidently present.

SEVEN GOLDEN QUESTIONS

"We trained hard—but it seemed that every time we were beginning to form up into teams we were reorganized. I was to learn later in life that we tend to meet any new situation by reorganizing, and what a wonderful method it can be for creating the illusion of progress while actually producing confusion, inefficiency, and demoralization."

— *Petronius Arbiter*

Agencies could be described with the help of seven golden questions:

Who?
What?
When?

Where?
Why?
How?
With what?

Rhetoric Hermagoras from Temnos, as it is indicated in the pseudo-Augustine's *De Rhetorica*, has defined seven circumstances as a locus of matter: *quis, quid, quando, ubi, cur, quem ad modum, quibus adminiculis* (who, what, when, where, why, how, with what) (Robertson, 1946). Canon number 21 of the Fourth Lateran Council (1215 A.D.) states that the confessor should carefully investigate the circumstances in which sinners made their sins *et peccatoris circurnstantias et peccati*. This approach has been used to guide confessors in their consideration of the circumstances in which the sin was committed (Robertson, 1946, p. 7). At each hearing on the committed sin, the circumstances of sin and sinners had to be carefully investigated, as says the canon. In any action or person connected with it, they do not stop with the proceeding until all answers were given. It is the rule of five (six, seven) questions, which was formulated in ancient times in the Mediterranean region and in legal rhetoric. Today, it serves as the basis for the collection and reporting of the collection and reporting of criminal and journalistic information.

EQUAL AGENCY'S TYPES AND DIFFERENT RESULTS

Government agencies can be seen from the top down and from the bottom up. The first view is the political one, where the agencies are told exactly *what to do*. Here a presumption is that when rules and structures are changed, the results are improved. This approach is appropriate only when goals can be precisely specified in advance, and when they can be measured with highly reliable methods. Otherwise, reforming strives will be in vain (and equally repeated towards the next failure). The focus on the goals, relationships, resources, and structures of the agency is not always the best way to know or predict what the agency will de facto do. The second view is focused on *how to do*. This is especially important when there are many similar organisations, with the same structure, type, processes, finances, and other elements, but still with different performance results. When the basic two conditions for the top-down approach are not present (clear, objective goals and reliable measurement), a higher level of politics should determine tasks, but leave and/or delegate discretion on how tasks could be achieved (mission-oriented system, tactical consideration[23] or freedom of action). Therefore, clear goals, but various, wide, or numerous alternatives on their implementation. This results in a flexible and agile organisation. The crucial distinction between more and less successful agencies has less to do with formal arrangements (budget, competences, goals, and other arrangements) than with the underlying *organizational structure*, based on the awareness of purposes, parts, their connections, tactics, patterns of outputs, and outcomes, feedback, in short, on the awareness about the functioning of systems. The enumerated elements do not lead directly towards success; they must be understood as such and put in the right spot in the first place, and this is mainly achieved through the highly system-aware people who work in a specific agency. Such awareness is two-way: people affect organisation and the latter affect the former.

Is the rationalization of agencies the right way to rationalize society? At the end of the line, the architects of bureaucracy and the agencies within it are legislators, but in the majority cases drafts of reorganisation are prepared by the executive, *that is,* by public servants who work in the ministries. When legislators blame agencies for the red tape, it could be up to a point similar to an architect complaining how really bad a house is constructed. However, many cases of red tape emerge later based on officials' interpretations *in* the context of a rule / decision application that is contrary to the intent of a legislator. Given all that has been written so far it is clear that the management of agencies depends on many various factors. In theory, it could be that 'organization development is a plant systematic process in which applied behavioural science principles and practices are introduced into an ongoing organization toward the goals of effecting organization improvement, greater organizational competence and greater organisational effectiveness. The focus is on organisations and their improvement…on *total system change*. The orientation is on action–achieving desired results as a consequence of planful activities. The setting is real organizations in the real world' (French & Bell, 1978, p. 3). Practice shows that the totality of the (open) system cannot be reached; the essence of organisation development is to energise and revitalize *all* resources to be flexible and adaptive *with respect to* the main purposes (the results), the goals (the results), the internal and external (in) formal environment (iceberg principle) environment, but there are so many (also apparent, imaginary) relations, correlations, causations, and combinations present that development could be done only with a focus on a smaller number of things, and even then success cannot be guaranteed (an apparently very good football team can also lose a match). The emphasis could be on groups (work teams) and processes, on human and social relations, on the collaborative management of the total, on-going system of actions based on research and feedback, but with a focus on a smaller number of things, perspectives or a starting point from which former could be addressed or administrated.

REFERENCES

Ashby, W. R. (1957). *An Introduction to Cybernetics*. Chapman and Hall.

Ayres, I., & Braithwaite, J. (1995). *Responsive Regulation: Transcending the Deregulation Debate*. Oxford University Press.

Bache, I., & Flinders, M. V. (Eds.). (2005). *Multi-level Governance*. Oxford University Press.

Beer, S. (1994). *Beyond Dispute: The Invention of Team Syntegrity*. Wiley.

Beer, S., & Eno, B. (2009). *Think Before You Think: Social Complexity and Knowledge of Knowing*. Wavestone Press.

Behn, R. D. (2001). *Rethinking Democratic Accountability*. Brookings Institution Press.

Bouckaert, G., & Peters, B. G. (2004). What is available and what is missing in the study of quangos? In C. Pollitt & C. Talbot (Eds.), *Unbundled Government: A Critical Analysis of the Global Trend to Agencies, Quangos and Contractualisation* (pp. 22–49). Taylor & Francis.

Cairney, P., Heikkila, T., & Wood, M. (2019). *Making Policy in a Complex World*. Cambridge University Press., doi:10.1017/9781108679053

Conant, R. C., & Ashby, W. R. (1970). Every Good Regulator of a System Must be a Model of that System. *International Journal of Systems Science*, *1*(2), 89–97. doi:10.1080/00207727008920220

Dunleavy, P., Margetts, H., Tinkler, J., & Bastow, S. (2006). *Digital era governance: IT corporations, the state, and e-government*. Oxford University Press. doi:10.1093/acprof:oso/9780199296194.001.0001

Feltz, B., Crommelinck, M., & Goujon, P. (2006). *Self-organization and Emergence in Life Sciences.* Springer Science & Business Media. doi:10.1007/1-4020-3917-4

French, W. L., & Bell, C. (1978). *Organization Development: Behavioral Science Interventions for Organization Improvement.* Prentice Hall.

Fuller, R. B., & Applewhite, E. J. (1997). *Synergetics: Explorations in the Geometry of Thinking.* MacMillan.

Gains, F. (2004). Adapting the agency concept: Variations within 'Next Steps. In C. Pollitt & C. Talbot (Eds.), *Unbundled Government: A Critical Analysis of the Global Trend to Agencies, Quangos and Contractualisation* (pp. 53–74). Taylor & Francis.

Gell-Mann, M. (2002). The Quark and the Jaguar (VIII edition). New York: W.H. Freeman & Company.

Gill, D. (2002). *Signposting the Zoo – From Agencification to a More Principled Choice of Government Organisational Forms.* OECD Publishing.

Goodnow, F. J. (1900). *Politics and Administration: A Study in Government.* The MacMillan Company.

Graham, A., & Roberts, A. S. (2004). The agency concept in North America: Failure, adaptation and incremental change. In C. Pollitt & C. Talbot (Eds.), *Unbundled Government: A Critical Analysis of the Global Trend to Agencies, Quangos and Contractualisation* (pp. 140–164). Taylor & Francis.

Gulick, L. (2003). Notes On the Theory of Organisation. In K. Thompson (Ed.), *The Early Sociology of Management and Organizations: Papers on the Science of Administration* (Vol. IV, pp. 1–49). Routledge.

Joseph, P. (2017). *The New Human Rights Movement.* BenBella Books.

Kemp, P. (1990). Can the civil service adapt to managing by contract? *Public Money & Management, 10*(3), 25–31. doi:10.1080/09540969009387612

Keohane, R. O. (1988). International Institutions: Two Approaches. *International Studies Quarterly, 32*(4), 379–396. doi:10.2307/2600589

March, J. G., & Olsen, J. P. (1984). The New Institutionalism: Organizational Factors in Political Life. *The American Political Science Review, 78*(3), 734–749. doi:10.2307/1961840

Margetts, H. 6, P., & Hood, C. (2012). Paradoxes of Modernization: Unintended Consequences of Public Policy Reform. Oxford: Oxford University Press.

Marks, G. (1992). Structural Policy in the European Community. In A. Sbragia (Ed.), *Euro-Politics: Institutions and Policy-making in New European Community* (pp. 191–224). Brookings Institution.

Marks, G., & Hooghe, L. (2005). Contrasting Visions of Multi-level Governance. In I. Bache & M. V. Flinders (Eds.), *Multi-level Governance* (pp. 15–30). Oxford University Press.

McGuire, L. (2004). Contractualism and performance measurement in Australia. In C. Pollitt & C. Talbot (Eds.), *Unbundled Government: A Critical Analysis of the Global Trend to Agencies, Quangos and Contractualisation* (pp. 113–139). Taylor & Francis.

Mlodinow, L. (2008). *The Drunkard's Walk: How Randomness Rules Our Lives.* Pantheon Books.

OECD. (1997). *In Search of Results: Performance Management Practices*. OECD Publishing.

Osborne, S. P. (Ed.). (2010). *The New Public Governance: Emerging Perspectives on the Theory and Practice of Public Governance*. Routledge. doi:10.4324/9780203861684

Piattoni, S. (2010). *The Theory of Multi-level Governance:Conceptual, Empirical, and Normative Challenges: Conceptual, Empirical, and Normative Challenges*. Oxford University Press. doi:10.1093/acprof:oso/9780199562923.001.0001

Piketty, T. (2014). *Capital in the Twenty-First Century* (T. Goldhammer, Trans.). Harvard University Press. doi:10.4159/9780674369542

Piketty, T. (2020). *Capital and Ideology*. Harvard University Press.

Pollitt, C., & Bouckaert, G. (2017). *Public Management Reform: A Comparative Analysis Into the Age of Austerity* (4th ed.). Oxford University Press.

Powell, W. W., & DiMaggio, P. (Eds.). (1991). *The New institutionalism in organizational analysis*. The University of Chicago Press. doi:10.7208/chicago/9780226185941.001.0001

Rainey, H. G. (2009). *Understanding and Managing Public Organizations* (4th ed.). Jossey-Bass.

Robertson, D. W. (1946). A Note on the Classical Origin of 'Circumstances' in the Medieval Confessional. *Studies in Philology, 43*(1), 6–14.

SIGMA. (2001). *Financial management and control of public agencies*. SIGMA. https://www.oecd-ilibrary.org/docserver/5kml60vk0h9x-en.pdf?expires=1603963677&id=id&accname=guest&checksum=AB63FFD9902F2673A133FDC1F219CAA0

Talbot, C. (2004). The Agency idea: Sometimes old, sometimes new, sometimes borrowed, sometimes untrue. In C. Pollitt & C. Talbot (Eds.), *Unbundled Government: A Critical Analysis of the Global Trend to Agencies, Quangos and Contractualisation* (pp. 3–21). Taylor & Francis.

Taleb, N. N. (2010). The Black Swan: The Impact of the Highly Improbable Fragility (Kindle Edition). New York: Random House Publishing Group.

Tetlock, P., & Gardner, D. (2015). Superforecasting: The Art and Science of Prediction (Kindle edition). London: Random House.

Tetlock, P. E. (2006). Expert Political Judgment: How Good Is It? How Can We Know? New Yersey: Princeton University Press.

Tiebout, C. M. (1956). A Pure Theory of Local Expenditures. *Journal of Political Economy, 64*(5), 416–424. doi:10.1086/257839

Turner, J. H. (2003). *Human Institutions: A Theory of Societal Evolution*. Rowman & Littlefield.

van Thiel, S. (2004). Quangos in Dutch government. In C. Pollitt & C. Talbot (Eds.), *Unbundled Government: A Critical Analysis of the Global Trend to Agencies, Quangos and Contractualisation* (pp. 167–183). Taylor & Francis.

von Bertalanffy, L. (1968). *General system theory: Foundations, development, applications*. George Braziller.

Wilson, J. Q. (1989). *Bureaucracy: What Government Agencies Do and why They Do it*. Basic Books.

Wollmann, H., & Marcou, G. (Eds.). (2010). *The Provision of Public Services in Europe: Between State, Local Government and Market*. Edward Elgar Publishing. doi:10.4337/9781849807227

Zucker, L. G. (1977). The Role of Institutionalization in Cultural Persistence. *American Sociological Review, 42*(5), 726–743. doi:10.2307/2094862

ENDNOTES

[1] When deciding about creation of agencies reformers should carefully analyse the specific objectives, tools methods, procedures and other contextually important elements when the right choice and classification of agency models, is made, when the appropriate degree of autonomy is determined, when the legal status, real property assets, borrowing, agency revenue policies, cash programs administered on behalf of the government, earmarked contributions, budget review and control for agencies financed by their own revenues and operating close to commercial markets, budget review and control for agencies significantly dependent on state budget support to their operations, selling private goods in competition with the private sector accounting and reporting is clearly determined (SIGMA, 2001, pp. 9-12).

[2] In the parable, we could compare hybrid agencies with hybrid cars that go increasingly in the direction of electrified ones.

[3] The last part of the sentence is at odds with the classical understanding of agencies, where the latter are supposed to resist innovation (the performance of new tasks or a significant alteration in the way in which existing tasks are performed): 'the reason an organization is created is in large part to replace the uncertain expectations and haphazard activities of voluntary endeavors with the stability and routine of organized relationships. The standard operating procedure is not the enemy of organization; it is the essence of organization. Stability and routine are especially important in government agencies where demands for equity (or at least the appearance of equity) are easily enforced' (Wilson, 1989, p. 221).

[4] Just as we would be unable to conceive of a horse in the abstract, if concrete horses did not resemble each other, so would we be unable to think of the state apart from the concrete examples of the states we know, were there not great similarity between these concrete states (Goodnow, 1900, pp. 7–8).

[5] The principles of liberty, equality, fraternity, and the rule of law were prima facie contrary to the "communal" feudal system that gave various privileges only to feudal lords based on their kinship, loyalty, personal ties, and merits for the defence of a country or other (matrimonial, connubial) reasons.

[6] 'Public service' exists, and can be identified in one way or another, as soon as government acknowledges that it has to achieve a certain level of coverage of collective needs considered as essential, and that that level cannot be attained merely by matching supply and demand on a market (Wollmann & Marcou, 2010, p. 3).

7   E.g., the US Postal Inspection Service of 1775 (the Post Office Department was created in 1792), the Interstate Commerce Commission of 1887.
8   Instead of the advent of some new political order, however distant, one finds an emerging political disorder; instead of a neat, two-sided process involving member-states and Community institutions, one finds a complex multi- layered, decision-making process stretching beneath the state, as well as above it; instead of a consistent pattern of policymaking across policy areas, one finds extremely wide and persistent variations. In short, the European Community seems to be part of a new political (dis)order that is multi-layered, constitutionally open-ended, and programmatically diverse (Marks, 1992, p. 221).
9   Notions known as multi-tiered, polycentric, multi-perspective governance, FOJC (functional, overlapping, competing jurisdictions), fragmentation, and SOAs (spheres of authority) have also been employed to capture these trends.
10 Governance can be understood simply 'as binding decision making in the public sphere' (Marks & Hooghe, 2005, p. 15).
11 As each two pairs form four combinations the same stands for this case: there is also the combination of Type I – Type II present and contrary. There are also chances of flexibility present in Type I (e.g., joint intermunicipal administration and police) and also rigid structures in Type II (e.g., the pay and promotion system based on civil service system).
12 Complexity can be shown by a very simple case of a statute that would have only four measures of achieving a goal. The number of their states n (n-1) is 12, and the number of connections between means n (n-1) / 2 is 6; the input variety (2^n) would already enable 16 possibilities ($2^4=16$), while the output variety ($2^{n \times 2n}$) would enable 2^{64} or exactly 18446744073709551616 possibilities. We cannot avoid this, but we can put more variety (more transparency, data, mutual connections, and control) into a more balanced implementation of the law.
13 If it is almost self-evident that two sports teams should have a same number of players, this self-evident condition is somehow lost in more important things...
14 The presence/absence of knowledge depends on the stabile/dynamic environment: experts who tend to be experts: livestock judges, astronomers, test pilots, soil judges, chess masters, physicists, mathematicians (when they deal with mathematical problems, not empirical ones), accountants, grain inspectors, photo interpreters, insurance analysts (dealing with bell curve–style statistics)… [and] experts who tend to be…not experts: stockbrokers, clinical psychologists, psychiatrists, college admissions officers, court judges, councillors, personnel selectors, intelligence analysts, economists, financial forecasters, finance professors, political scientists, risk experts… and personal financial advisers. Simply, things that move, and therefore require knowledge, do not usually have experts, while things that don't move seem to have some experts. In other words, professions that deal with the future and base their studies on the non-repeatable past have an expert problem. The problem with experts is that they do not know what they do not know. Lack of knowledge and delusion about the quality of your knowledge come together—the same process that makes you know less also makes you satisfied with your knowledge (Taleb, 2010, p. 79).
15 The advantage of certain performance criteria over traditional work in ministries is that agencies have at least determined clear goals that are verified in a shorter period of time, while these goals at the ministry level are most often written in job classifications (sometimes also in strategies and work programs) while they are (more or less) checked mainly at the promotion of individual civil servants. Sir Peter Kemp, the first head of the central "Next Steps" Unit in the UK, described this

new procedure as the 'move from management by command to one of management by contract' (Kemp, 1990, p. 28).

[16] There are more numerous cases when water is somewhere between 0 and at 100 degrees Celsius than just 0 or 100.

[17] Zadeh, the founder of the theory of fuzzy (uncertain) logic (that resembles human reasoning that "computes" words not numbers), described the principle of incompatibility between precision and complexity: 'as the complexity of a system increases, our ability to make precise and yet significant statements about its behavior diminishes until a threshold is reached beyond which precision and significance (or relevance) become almost mutually exclusive characteristics' (Zadeh, 1973).

[18] Similar approach is a Likert scale, where respondents specify their level of agreement or disagreement on a symmetric agree-disagree scale for a series of statements. Results then emerge from collective responses to a set of usually eight or more items.

[19] Agencies were many times promoted by the international community just because governmental departments (especially in the third world countries) were seen as ineffective or corrupt. This path of ineffectiveness extends further towards the civil society (NGO's) and business firms (charities, foundations).

[20] Master and slave, squire and servant boss and employee, ruling classes and proletariat… the notion of hierarchy is endemic to the human experience of social system. And yet it seems never to suffice as an organising principle. We are always found to supplement, indeed to enrich, they simply autocratic chain of command (Beer, 1994, p. 3)

[21] In this manner, when a department can improve its coordination and control elements there is no reason to create a new agency. And the contrary, when data show services could be enhanced through agency, its creation is appropriate. And again contrary, when an agency deals primarily with questions of policy instead of services there is a time for its abolishment.

[22] When services are not effectively provided at the level of ministry, the same mistakes could be repeated given the inappropriate ministerial coordination and control of services at the level of agencies.

[23] The Slovenian Police Tasks and Powers Act (OJ, No. 15/13) in Article 7 determines tactical considerations: '[w]hen performing police duties, police officers assess what decisions, police powers or official actions they will take to effectively prevent and eliminate dangers, based on the facts and circumstances known to them at the time of the assessment'.

Chapter 12
Systems Theory and Agencies

ABSTRACT

A system is not just a collection of individual parts or ministries without any links or purpose between them. It is a set of elements that interact to achieve goals, and this requires a whole picture framework. Public administration must be effectively managed to change the pattern of results in a planned way. When classical rules cannot cope with complex environment, it not only creates a problem of efficiency, but also a major problem of legitimacy. Bureaucratic power is not only unelected, but its frameworks of public authority do not reflect the reality in which people live and are, therefore, mismanaged. A partial centralised approach can be more effective than a holistic one when a collective one must be used, and humans are complex adaptive systems, so diverse people should be involved in decision-making. The underlying structure of a system goes beyond individual political mandates, which they usually do not want to change.

INTRODUCTION

If a factory is torn down but the rationality which produced it is left standing, then that rationality will simply produce another factory. If a revolution destroys a systematic government, but the systematic patterns of thought that produced that government are left intact, then those patterns will repeat themselves in the succeeding government. There's so much talk about the system. And so little understanding - Pirsig, 2009, p. 102.

If you cannot guarantee the integrity of the system, then there is no system at all.

–Terry McCaleb, Blood Work (Clint Eastwood)

In our desire to be as free as possible, we are constantly looking for structure. The latter is a fundamental element of the system. In the public discourse of politicians and experts, it is often claimed that a certain area should be approached in a "systemic" way, that an area will be regulated in a "systematic way" or that something is being "regulated in a systemic way" for the first time, but the very subject

DOI: 10.4018/979-8-3693-0507-2.ch012

(apart from the word "system") contains little or nothing that resembles the workings of a system. This is what von Bertalanffy pointed out (1968), and if this was justified then because of the development of a new field, it is no longer the case today. Conversely, when we start talking about or acknowledging interconnectedness and interdependence, we are already talking in the language of the system, we are talking about cooperation, about a way of working that does not know unilateralism (nor the failed unilateral actions of the state), but parallelism, interconnectedness, multiculturalism, inclusion, political correctness, sustainability, environmental education, symbiosis, participation, and hierarchy as coordination. Anyone who is 'trapped' in thinking that something may not be directly a problem, but only a symptom of 'something deeper', something that (itself) produces similar results, despite change in people, is on the threshold of system thinking. On the threshold of putting aside ministers and other officials and examining the homogeneous, infinitely small, and large, but connected elements that affect people through certain, similar patterns of (co)action. Only in this way can one discover the *underlying structure* (i.e. the key relationships that influence behaviour over time, but not of people, but of key elements that aggregate to represent the population, economic conditions, rule of law, etc.) on which (as a platform) (personal and collective) events unfold. If, despite all efforts, a situation does not change, this is an indication that a structural feedback loop is operating in the background to prevent change.... It may be that 'solutions to modern social problems are less about the moral aptitude of society and more about how society is definitely organised' (Joseph, 2017, p. xvii). The idea of structuralism and/or larger-order relationships based on which social affairs evolve is tightly connected also with the system of public administration. One of the major pitfalls of any institutional organisation of public institutions is that it can lead to bad outcomes, which are not intentionally by public servants, but result from the very structure of the links that shape such an institution as an institution, which additionally creates links with other institutions and the wider environment. If it is understandable that it is "in the nature of the fox to hunt its prey", it is less understandable/understood that institutions also have their own nature, which is admittedly easier to change than people's individual characters. The key rational question or element of good administration is hence not how public administration influences or causes collective patterns of behaviour, but how systemically and/or structurally various public agencies intersect their processes and cause chain/aggregate reactions/results in more or less distant fields.

If 'a system s approach is one of the foundations of organization development' (French & Bell, 1978, p. 78) a big question is how come this approach is still not used in practice. Agencies can also be addressed with systems theory. Systems are not only a collection of things or people that relate to each other, but '[i]n fact, most systems of interest in decision making may often consist of abstract things and their relationships' (Daellenbach, 1996, p. 28). A system *per se* cannot be divided into independent parts without the loss of its essential functions, and by its default should be attentive to the whole vis-à-vis its parts. In the system, the rules of interaction collectively have a given purpose or are purposeful, i.e., 'strive towards some state of balance' (Daellenbach, 1996, p. 5) – that is the same as equilibrium in complexity – and/or 'can select both means and ends in two or more environments' (Ackoff, 1999, p. 21). Decision-makers must not blind their eyes to the fact that such concepts are not present in the organisation of public agencies. Public agencies are not only suitable to be studied as a system, but they are supposed to be a system (a coherent collection of dynamically connected parts, representing a network of relationships with a certain function/purpose); the dividing line between a good and a bad system is *control*, but not in the sense of coercion, as the ascertainment of the conformity of an activity with certain rules, regulations; control, supervision, but as the ascertainment of the actual state, position of something; inspection, examination. The essence of control in a systemic sense is the interconnectedness (everything is connected in a system, which can only be understood when we are aware of this interconnectedness and when it becomes our object of study) of the parts which (self-)regulate each other towards the achievement of a fundamental purpose. Failure to understand the systemic approach results in the public administration being a "prisoner of its own system" or, conversely, a generator and executor of new ideas. Seen from that point of view, system and systems thinking can be seen as a generalising tendency towards fairness (Schmidt-Aßmann, 2006).

The assumption is that knowledge of systems theory is essential for good public administration and *vice versa*, ignorance leads to "automatic" operation of the system, often to our detriment. The power of the system is well described by the psychologist Zimbardo: 'the greater power to create evil out of the good [comes from] the system, [as] a complex of powerful forces that create the Situation. Much evidence from social psychology supports the concept that situational power triumphs over individual power in given circumstances' (Zimbardo, 2008, p. x). An integrated, holistic view, combining knowledge in and across different fields, implies interdisciplinarity, something that should be a fundamental reflection of public administration. Since the beginnings of general systems theory in the middle of the last century (Ludwig von Bertalanffy,[1] Kenneth Boulding, Ralph Gerard, James Grier Miller and Anatol Rapoport) to its later development (Ross Ashby, Heinz von Foerster, Stafford Beer, Russell Ackoff, and West Churchman, Ervin Laszlo, Erich Jantsch, Jay Forrester, Ralph Abraham, Stuart Kauffman, Robert Rosen, Louis Kauffman, and Humberto Maturana), to the present day (Fritjof Capra, Peter Senge, Allan Savory, David Korten, Paul Hawken, Amory in Hunter Lovinski, Donella Meadows), has brought together a wide range of disciplines (organic biology, Gestalt psychology, engineering, management, cybernetics, information theory, ecology and social theory) that reflect autonomy, subsidiarity, but also integrity, wholeness and synthesis. Nevertheless, there is still a gap not only of misunderstanding, but above all a lack of practical application of systems theory - which was the basis for cybernetics (Ashby, 1957), information theory (Shannon & Weaver, 1964), complexity theory (Waldrop, 1993) and/or complex adaptive systems theory (Gell-Mann, 2002), gestalt psychology (Köhler, 1969), organic biology (Berryman, 1992), ecology (Hutchinson, 1965), management (Grösser & Zeier, 2012) and social theory (Parsons, 1991) it is time to (re)revitalise it also in the field of public administration (Meyer, 1973).

In public administration as a whole, the use of the word "system" or "systemic" (as in the phrase "public interest") is still more about rhetoric as an art of persuasion, rather than a scientific-empirical mapping of the workings and verification of the different parts of the system on a particular issue. Although the systemic approach was already pointed out by Woodrow Wilson as the father of administrative science,[2] Henry Fayol as the father of scientific management,[3] and Luther Gulick[4] as a management expert, it seems that it will have to be rediscovered, that the importance of connectedness, which is essentially our fundamental, intrinsic characteristic, needs to be re-emphasised: our perceptions often do not control behaviour, as individuals change it, i.e. administrate it (sic) as necessary to control our perceptions, to enjoy the desired results and to avoid undesirable ones (e.g. do not dream of going to the cinema, but do it in the Roman style of *acta non verba* - actions, not words), and therefore an awareness of connectedness is also necessary in the public system of goal attainment or public administration: it is not only the perception that controls our behaviour, but also the perception controls it. Information is thus not (in)correct per se, but the accuracy of its prediction according to a set model (of information gathering).[5] Thus, from the outset, systems theory is closely linked to the rule of law principle of clarity and certainty by setting criteria or benchmarks. A system is not a "thing", but a list of selected criteria (Ashby, 1957), against which we judge the same system. Information gathering is different in a mechanical, reductionist style than in a holistic, systemic, or dynamic one: local perceptions are directly acquired through the senses (from which we draw conclusions), whereas systemic perception is primarily about understanding interlocking processes and chain reactions. A system is 'a collection of things, units, or people that relate to each other in certain ways, are organised, i.e., follow certain rules of interaction, and have a certain common purpose, i.e. strive towards a certain state of equilibrium' (Daellenbach, 1996, p. 5).

A system is a group of interconnected, interdependent devices, preparations forming a functional whole; a planned, rationally arranged set of units, principles, procedures determining how an activity is to be carried out, especially in relation to the achievement of a specific goal; a totality of social units, components, and relationships based on interconnected principles, rules, and regulating social events. A system can therefore be understood as a collection of things, units, or people that relate to each other in certain ways, follow certain rules of interaction, and have a certain common purpose (system = elements, connections, purpose). A mere collection of individual parts (which can also be ministries) without any links or purpose between them is not a system. It is, however, a set of elements that interact to achieve goals, provided that the "whole picture/framework", i.e., the system per se, is (at all) visible to the one who "looks", i.e. who has pre-prepared criteria or thresholds by which to recognise the emerging pattern. Thus, also in public administration;[6] the latter is effectively managed when it can change the pattern of final results in a planned way.

A complex, dynamic environment influences static rules, regardless of their democratic core. If classical rules cannot cope with such an environment, there is not only a problem of efficiency, but also a major problem of legitimacy: bureaucratic power is not only unelected, but its frameworks of public authority do not reflect the reality in which people live and are, therefore, mismanaged. Existing public (decision-making) structures may be transparent per se, but they still have (or "hide"[7]) its dependence on the path caused by the underlying basic structure (Meadows, 2008). Since all structures work differently to some extent than formally stated (seen as bureaucratisation, delays, unintended consequences, etc.), a partial centralised approach can be more effective than a holistic one (when a collective one has to be used, when the whole community is considered); humans are complex adaptive systems, so reality is "more real" when diverse people are involved in decision-making. They use their brains and have relationships with others, regardless of formal options, so it would be useful for them to use their homo mensura element for the benefit of the whole community. From a systems point of view, perception per se does not control behaviour because people can adapt/influence their behaviour/systems by perceiving according to their method of questioning (Capra & Luisi, 2014; Feynman, Leighton, & Sands, 1965; Lanza & Berman, 2013; Maturana & Varela, 2012), in terms of its meaning and purpose, or simply by its mere presence; our method of questioning here is systemic, and thus focused on the underlying structures that give rise to collective patterns of behaviour - the underlying structure goes beyond individual political mandates, which they usually do not want to change (which is why they got them, other material benefits, etc.), which is why the major achievements of human society have usually been achieved through various forms of social unrest, protests, revolutions, and other movements of people in the streets...This is also why it is important to know the workings of the system, and the elements that make it work.

SYSTEM ELEMENTS

System (gr. *systēma*, "whole compounded of several parts«, from *synhistanai* "to cause to stand" (Merriam-Webster, 2017) is a collection or combination of related things or parts forming a complex or unified whole. 'A system is an interconnected set of elements that is coherently organized in a way that achieves something...a system must consist of three kinds of things: elements, interconnections, and a function or purpose' (Meadows, 2008, p. 11). A system is a grouping of parts working together for a common purpose (Forrester, 1968, p. 1). Systems are seen as feedback processes with a specific and ordered structure. If in private life everyone bears his/her own consequences, in public life we all feel them; it is therefore important to know the basic elements of how the system works and how to monitor/change the results. The five principles of the system, i.e. 'openness, intentionality, multidimensionality, emergent properties and counter-intuitive behaviour, working together as an interactive whole, define the essential characteristics and assumptions of an organisation's behaviour, viewed as an intentional, multi-layered system' (Gharajedaghi, 2007, p. 52). The nature of (any) system should be consistent with the Conant-Ashby theorem, according to which any good regulator of a system must itself be a model of that system, or, as Sir Geoffrey Vickers put it: 'the trap is a function of the nature of the trapped' (Beer, 1994, p. 253). The key is an (open) system, capable of adapting (externally and internally) and learning from experience. Therefore, how the systems are set up is important. The system records information and responds as/if its structure allows it to do so.[8]

Individual Parts of the System

A system is a system; whether it is good or bad is judged by the parts, links, and purposes or by the information we have about it. The basic element of a system is its parts, which per se do not yet constitute a system, but are necessary for its existence. Although it is the basic element, it is also the most interchangeable, as the parts have the least impact on the functioning of the whole system: if they are replaced (so also the Minister, the Director), the system will still exist in a similar form as before, without significantly affecting the links and the purpose of the system (which remain the same - unless the change of the part also changes the links or the purpose). A system has components. The system is the organised whole, consisting of the interconnected and interdependent parts, components, and subsystems. The general scheme of an open system is made up of the following parts: 1. input, matter, energy, and information; 2. a transformation process as the process by which input quantities change into the output of the system; 3. output is the result of the transformation process; 4. the environment - an open system is surrounded by an environment from which it receives input resources and into which it gives back outputs; 5. feedback - to maintain a current situation, a constant feedback flow from the output to the input is needed; the feedback is the necessary communication channel for the control mechanism; 6. the control mechanism compares the values of the actual output with goal values and gives an initiative for necessary changes to maintain the system in a stable and/or more preferable state; 7. a boundary of the system is determined by frames that separate it from the environment.

Relationships, Relationships, and Interrelations Between Parts

In contrast to the physical sciences, organic studies study not only parts and processes in isolation, but also the organisation and order that unites them, starting from the dynamic interaction of the parts, which makes the behaviour of the parts different when they are studied separately or as a whole. Even if we knew all the properties of the individual parts in detail, we could not yet say anything definite about their interaction, about the relations between them on that basis. A change in the relationships (as opposed to a change in parts) thus has a significant impact on the system. Bertalanffy (the founder of systems theory) believed that systems are governed by the dynamic interaction of their parts (Bertalanffy, 1968). Numerous links between the individual parts, which can be calculated using the equation $n(n-1)$ (Beer, 1959) – do not allow classical causality or causal relationships to be established. Carnap argued as early as 1966 that causality is not a thing that causes an event, but a process ... [in which] some processes or events cause other processes or events' (Carnap, 1966, p. 190). The relationships between the individual elements and their effects, as well as the links between the system and its environment, are still neglected in public administration, even though they are a key factor in achieving the objectives,[9] and something that would also allow a better understanding of the authority itself..[10]

The idea of an integrated state was born out of an awareness of the interconnections within systems (holistic government, which is a system in itself, that is, an integrated whole, gr. synhistanai, "to join together"), which is a fundamental milestone of the reforms of public administration in the 21st century, like the new public governance in the closing decades of the last century. Integrated government emphasises (among other things) horizontal integration and integration between areas and functions, integration of information systems, focusing on results rather than functions, and a preprepared state that moves from prevention (audit, early warning systems and scenario-based risk management with safeguards), to anticipation, to negative targets, to reducing or eliminating risks, to positive behaviour and strategic governance (Perri, 1997). 'True holistic government emerges where government agencies and their partners share reinforcing objectives and can identify a shared commitment to a range of mutually supportive tools to achieve that objective... Te key challenge is how to give recognition to the need for a division of labour in any bureaucracy and its beneficial contribution of expertise while wedding out those roots of fragmented governance that undermine the system's capacity to get things done' (Perri, Leat, Seltzer, & Stoker, 2002, p. 2). Joint commitment, horizontal and vertical integration are just some of the elements, and other elements of the system should also be mentioned.

New Emergence, New Value

A system is not just an assemblage of interconnected parts, but their interconnections create new values that the individual parts (before) do not have, even if we know them (analytically) well. Interconnections create a new value, a new emergence, which the parts do not have: the collective as a whole is more than the sum of its parts; it is a phenomenon that is not and cannot be (simply) the average of (still only) the sum of individuals or their actions. General Systems Theory is the general science of the whole: the meaning of the somewhat mystical expression "The whole is greater than the sum of its parts" is simple, since the constituent characteristics cannot be explained from the characteristics of the isolated parts. The characteristics of the complex therefore appear as new or emergent' (Bertalanffy, 1968, p. 55). Emergence (combined with the impossibility of fully identifying the causal link) is the one that requires the operator to constantly monitor the situation - where things change, new things happen, again and again. The same is true of rules: when combined, or in conjunction with each other, or in combination, they create a new value that the rules do not have at the beginning of their implementation, or without combinations[11] - they also require constant monitoring of the system and its surroundings.[12] The functional concept of emergence represents an autonomously higher level of abstraction than the reductionist decomposition of the fundamental forces of nature into smaller parts. 'The resulting property is the global behaviour of the structure, occurring through the interactions of a collection of elements, without a controller responsible for the behaviour or organisation of these elements. The idea of emergence is that, it cannot be reduced to properties of elements [...] we can only say that the sum is more than the sum of their parts' (Feltz, Crommelinck, & Goujon, 2006, p. 241).13 It can also be said that the problem cannot be fully solved unless we change the links that created it.

Connections, the (dis)embeddedness in the context of many intertwining events that create new value, so characteristic of systems, can also be an outlet for avoiding classical accountability. The ancient Romans were already familiar with the intertwined web of relationships which, in isolation, have no weight, but in their common (if unintentional) connections take on a new appearance, a new result that cannot be attributed to anyone individually. A saying attributed to Cicero says that senators are good men, while the Senate is a real beast (lat. senatores boni viri, *senatus autem mala bestia*) – the difference between individual behaviour (which is usually friendly) and group behaviour (as a monster) is in the group dynamics, where the group's interest can go beyond human rights. Hannah Arendt described such a phenomenon as "nobody's rule", as perhaps one of the most powerful forms of man's lordship over man, which goes by the name of bureaucracy: it is a 'legally complex system of offices in which no one, not one, not the best, not a few, not many, cannot be held accountable' (Arendt, 1972, p. 137). Arendt's reminder of the banality of evil, attributed not only to the convicted Nazi "criminal" Eichmann but to all those who simply - don't - think, is timeless, and at the same time one of the best justifications for not imposing responsibility on an individual who, in a web of relationships, can hardly be blamed for the ultimate negative outcome. Acting in a multitude of relationships and connections, where each contributes only a piece of the mosaic to the whole picture, without the behaviour in itself having any value connotation, can lead (by creating a new emergence through relationships) to an outcome that no one actually wants, yet everyone has contributed to. In such circumstances, it is difficult to hold anyone accountable in the classical sense. Einstein thought that 'groups are guided to a lesser extent by conscience and a sense of responsibility [but on the other hand] nothing can be achieved without the participation of many people of goodwill. The latter are no happier than when a community project is carried out, even at the expense of many sacrifices, with the united aim of promoting life and culture' (Einstein, 1960, p. 54). Because 'we have learned through painful experience that rational thinking is not sufficient for the problems of social life...institutions [are] also morally impotent unless they are backed by a sense of responsibility on the part of living individuals' (Einstein, 1960, pp. 148, 27). It is true that the ability to reason and to distinguish between good and evil are fundamental tools at one's disposal, but their (in) functioning is also shaped by the circumstances, i.e. the context, in which one finds oneself (Milgram, 2009; Zimbardo, 2008). In view of the above, one cannot expect or rely on Kant's "starry sky above me and the moral law within me" (Kant, 2003), but it is all the more important to understand how systems work and to "create the conditions" in which legitimate public objectives can be identified and pursued. Therefore, while being aware of the many relationships, the primary responsibility always lies with the (decision maker) who fails to ensure that the system is structured in such a way as to detect thresholds, changes/ deviations in performance in relation to the set target, and consequently, to correct the performance of the system itself accordingly.

These various relations or connections can be managed solely by the *limitation of the flow of diverse data*. According to Ashby, a complex (assembled) problem can be administrated only with the same or a similar measure of complexity known as the requisite variety (Ashby, 1957). A decision that addresses numerous people can be manageable only with the cooperation of all people. This is usually not possible in the reality of complex life, so Ashby's idea of requisite variety needs 'regulation that blocks the flow of variety...an essential feature of the good regulator is that it blocks the flow of variety from disturbances to essential variables' (Ashby, 1957, pp. 199, 201). A homeostatic loop of the amplifiers (from a regulator to a system) and filters (from the system to the regulator) is inserted to deal with an interesting part of the environment. If this is not done, the system self-regulates towards its own equilibrium. Reality is too complex to be fully addressed; combinations exponentially increase when new parts are added, new interconnections, and new patterns emerge, so it is essential that representativeness (a sample size) is established. To prevent disruptions, a good regulator limits the flow of diverse data to only some, essential, manageable criteria that address the observed surroundings. To Nonaka, strategy, propelled by knowledge creation, is a process of managing flow (Nonaka & Zhu, 2012, p. 98), and the management of flow is also a crucial element of system theory. The system is flexible when it changes its actions (when it switches to other alternatives) in the face of detected changes through indicators/sensors. The system is agile when it can detect changes and quickly organise appropriate actions/responses to these changes. An example of such system is pragmatic organisation with its pragmatic strategy that is further elaborated in section on strategy.

The Function or Purpose of the System

The function is used for technical systems, not social systems. A change of purpose also has a profound effect on the whole system and can change it beyond recognition (e.g. the purpose of a public administration is different if it is seen as an employer providing jobs or as a system looking after the public interest). The system can change completely, even though the links between the parts remain the same when the purpose changes. Since the purpose of a system is always only what it actually does, its true purpose can only be ascertained by observing what it actually does, not what would be formally defined as its purpose. Systems can be located within broader and narrower systems (e.g. a pupil in a primary school as part of primary education, primary schools embedded in the whole national and wider education system), so there can also be purposes within purposes.

Fundamental, Supporting Structure: Stocks, Flows, Feedbacks, Indicators, Patterns, and Decision-Making

Relationships are the result of the underlying structure that makes them possible;14 it is about the relationship between structure and behaviour. A system is made up of its elements, its links and its formal purpose, and its real purpose is only what it actually does (not how it is addressed, but what consequences it produces).15 Purpose becomes the result of behaviour, not of formal rhetoric, not of rules per se, but of their structure. Thus, it does not matter who implements the rules, i.e. who exercises power: it is the structure that creates the (im)balance. It is only through understanding the various interactions and influences that we can begin to address/change systems embedded and multiplied in other systems: just as a system is embedded in another system (e.g. scissors in the hands of a hairdresser as part of the beauty industry), we can speak of the embeddedness of purpose in purpose. Each part is connected to the other, and only in this way can it be understood (usually we speak of context). The importance of feedback (or ex-post analysis) only becomes apparent in a new perspective: a person in a system who makes a decision based on feedback cannot change the behaviour of the system that triggered the current feedback, but only the future behaviour of the system will be influenced by the decisions he makes. The

Systems Theory and Agencies

relations between parts represent the flow of information. This flow depends on the underlying stocks and current consumption. The simplest example of a system is a sink into which water flows from collected/measurable supplies (tank, storage16), which change according to the (greater or lesser) flow of water (i.e. accumulation and outflow of water, or deaths and births, growth and declines, investments and losses, saving and spending, successes and failures), creating a dynamic between stocks and (current) consumption. The outcome of the system is thus not just a single event, but emerging and changing trends (patterns as a form of the dependent variable) over time, which give intermediate results on the relationship between stocks and consumption. Since systems are always embedded in other systems, their purpose is to be a fundamental discriminating unit that allows the observation of a single event over time (e.g. the feedback could be the height of the water in the sink [flowing in and out] or in the glass into which the water is poured) and the regulation or control of the stock-consumption relationship, for which the feedback between current consumption and the underlying stock is essential. This information allows consumption to be varied in relation to stocks, which is achieved by taking decisions (or physical actions).17 Feedback is one of the most powerful control principles.

Feedback loops. Things self-regulate if a regulator does not regulate them (Vickers, 1995). Even when the regulator does this, all things do not converge into a desired state; the regulator's goal is to estimate a region in which things / motions / actions converge a lot and to find the proper nudges to push them toward a desired position (reinforced learning). This is done with the help of a feedback loop as the nonlinear or non-stationary system element. 'Control of a machine on the basis of its *actual* performance rather than its *expected* performance is known as *feedback,* and…when 'the information which proceeds backward from the performance is able to change the general method and pattern of performance, we have a process called learning' (Wiener, 1989, pp. 24, 61). The feedback loop should respond and accommodate values automatically; its internal autonomy is not jeopardised because the system reproduces itself through its own operations (the combinations and values of internal parameters change if this change is based on pre-written codes or scripts (i.e., rules) as alternative scenarios in the face of changed values). In this way, 'the *expectation of disappointment*, which is the core reason for communicating expectations in a normative style' (Luhmann, 2004, p. 241) could also be smaller. Feedback is the most important element of the system since it allows the latter to adapt to a desired position by making concrete decisions; dynamic balance exists with the continuous input data and the acceptability of outputs (results) for the environment (humans). Maintaining the state and adjusting activities through feedback and decision-making according to the final goals of the system represent a *sine qua non* of each adaptation in nonlinear systems (the cyclicality of events is present due to the growth and expansion, regression, and recession). Controlling the tendency toward disorganisation and/or the process by which living beings resist the general stream of decay is known as homeostasis. If a homeostatic system is constructed, there is no need for strong legal enforcement to realign the input-output relations. There would be less need to maintain a 'manually' feedback loop through public administration or court adjudications or through general legislation when a situation requires so. This commitment should be engraved *on* the system.

One of the most important functions of feedback becomes homeostatic or (self-)regulation, which keeps a given variable within desired limits - a system can be self- or auto-regulated (e.g. we take off our jacket when we are hot, we would not think, the functioning of internal organs), or regulated by a higher entity (e.g. a human being directly or indirectly[,18] similarly, a public authority) in the light of the information it receives via the feedback loop19 what illustrates the Watt regulator. :

Figure 1. Operator and throttle valve
(Routledge, 1900, p. 6)

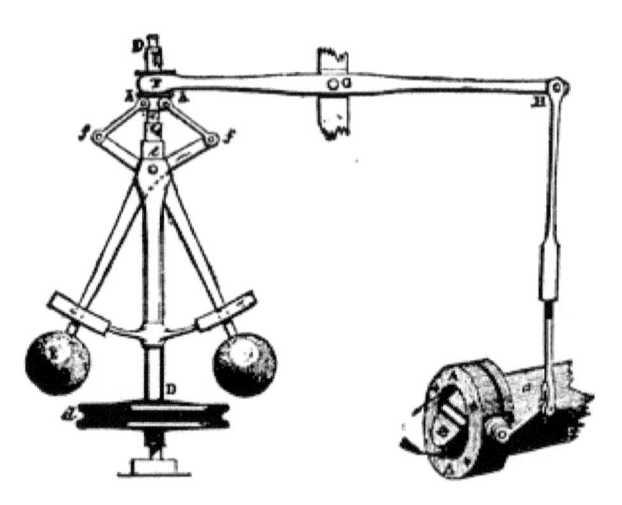

The above figure shows the control centrifugal rotating balls: they rise or fall as the speed increases or decreases, as the valve closes or opens, until a balance is reached between the requirements and the relative benefit between the connection and the valve.[20] To form a system, there should be 'closed boundaries around the system, feedback loops within those boundaries, level (stock) variables representing the accumulation within the feedback loops, velocity (flow) variables as the activities within the feedback loops, and a target, observed state, detection and action based on the discrepancy as the [four] components of the velocity variable' (Forrester, 1961, p. 12). The detection of a discrepancy (between the desired results and the observed output pattern) and the consequent action within the current flows (current consumption) vis-à-vis the underlying stocks (assets, equipment) is synonymous with a decision that controls the relationship between stocks and flows, which is usually the result of a hierarchy or decision-maker so set up, who also sets milestones or individual indicators in order to achieve or verify the achievement of the set objective (as an element of future creation). In this sense, it can also be said to be a matter of creation, of creating an order based on iterations or the emergence of new[21] not just for predicting the future. Like systems, human beings have the ability to start anew, to create new categories, and to form new standards of judgement for events that have happened, as well as for those that may occur in the future. People learn from experience and feedback, which is the basis for a dynamic and adaptive behavioural system. To model the latter, there should be 'closed boundaries around the system, feedback loops within these boundaries, level (stock) variables representing the accumulation within the feedback loops, rate (flow) variables as the activities within the feedback loops, and goal, observed state, detection and action based on discrepancy as the [four] components of the rate variable' (Forrester, 1961, p. 12). The detection of a discrepancy and the consequent action within the current flows (current consumption) vis-à-vis the underlying stocks (assets, equipment) is synonymous with a decision that changes the relationship between stocks and flows. Feedback is 'a mechanism (rule, information flow or signal) that enables [the knowledge to] change stocks according to the flow into or out of those stocks' (Meadows, 2008, p. 187), or in other words, it is information on the relationship between stocks (underlying objectives, resources) and current consumption (their achievement).

It is information on the relationship between stocks (underlying objectives, resources) and current spending (their achievement), which generates a certain pattern of actions or results depending on the decision taken and its actual execution. It is only the decision that attempts to correct deviations from the desired path, and this is where the value of the indicators that indicate the failure/success of the decision comes into play (in fact, in the real, complex world, there are rarely linear relationships where one action has a corresponding effect in another). Decision failure is always linked to bad/good results. The main idea is nicely summarised by the statement that the (real) purpose of a system is what it actually does (Beer, 2002, p. 2). The idea is also consistent with "light action" (*wu-wei*), which represents the perfect human harmony between inner dispositions and outer movements (Confucius, 2003). It is also often wrong to equate the very existence of feedback with the system: (negative-inhibitory or positive-reinforcing) feedback only communicates a good or bad state; the state depends on set thresholds (if the perception mechanisms are correct, adequate), always comes with a certain delay, is often incomplete, or can be understood in several ways (good, bad, side, unexpected, undesired consequences). Since we have said that relations create new emergence, we can say that the system creates its own behaviour. Systems theory, with its fundamental elements, has contributed significantly to the emergence of artificial intelligence systems (which are still primarily systems, but ported to the programming environment of computers), which reveal patterns of action from unstructured data and provide decision support. The following are some orientations for the future, more "systems-based" functioning of public administration.

ESSENTIAL ELEMENTS OF SYSTEMIC AGENCIES

Systems are all around us; systems thinking starts with observing data and events, looking for patterns over time, discovering the structures that drive behaviour, examining and changing structures that are no longer helpful, being open to different solutions to a problem, and having the courage to choose the best possible long-term solution, not just the easy one or the one that is the most popular. Systems theory applies not only directly to systems, but to all the things that connect systems into a whole. It can also be applied even (only) to theory, which, through a systematic view (linking concepts), also gives hope for better empirical results. The fundamental shortcomings of public administration in relation to systems theory, which should be given more emphasis in the future, are: i) data that are not just data, but what has been obtained on the basis of set criteria or personal assumptions; ii) the relationship between formal and actual intent; iii) the lack of perceptual mechanisms; iv) too much static thinking; v) the lack of perceived interconnections and effects. iii) the lack of perceptual mechanisms; iv) too much static thinking; v) the lack of perceived interrelationships and effects; (vi) the gap between the actual situation and that in the documents; (vii) unclear, conflicting objectives; (viii) the objectification and openness of criteria; (ix) the lack of clarity in determining the impact of actions; (x) (too) many bodies and ineffective coordination; (xi) the role of responsible persons and civil servants; and (xii) coordination as a role of the central managing authority.

Quid pro quo resemblance. The decision maker should consider that: a) only diversity can address diversity; a complex (assembled) problem can be administrated only with the same or a similar measure of complexity (Ashby's requisite variety) (Ashby, 1957); b) the regulator must be a model of a regulated area/thing (Conant-Ashby theorem) (Beer, 1994); c) any decision is as good as its regulator. The administration of development requires the continuous monitoring, control, and evaluation of effects because the main purpose of the first is to ensure the effectiveness and efficiency of implemented measures in a managed field. For the purpose of good governance, planning, monitoring, and impact assessment, timely responses to deviations are needed, which means that the fundamental elements of the system are present in decision making.

A probable future. As in the case of complexity of an environment, reality is replaced by a simpler representation; in the legal field, reality is represented by a legal model. The usual way in science is to find the properties, capabilities, and limitations of a model, while in the second case, a proposed legal rule – after its enactment – is usually directly applied *without* testing, despite the fact that rules regulate *pro futuro* cases where at the time of enactment there are no causal relations known; they are difficult to establish even for past or present states (Carnap, 1966; Cziko, 2000). Statistical models can be used for the past (adjudication, the testing of hypotheses, explanation) that indicate the strength of the relationship (in-sample strength-of-fit) or for the future (prediction) in which the accuracy of out-of-measurable-sample predictive power can be estimated. For the first methods, regression analysis (the coefficient of determination or R^2) and structural equation models (Chi-Squared, Akaike information criterion) can be used, while for the second predictive analytic tools can be used (all statistical models, machine learning and data mining algorithms that can produce predictions, like the k-nearest neighbour algorithm, random forest, decision tree learning (CART), Monte Carlo method or Bayesian networks) (Nielsen & Jensen, 2007; Pearl, 2009; Shmueli, Bruce, Stephens, & Patel, 2017). A further step from sampling towards better future decisions is the so-called field of business analytics or data mining. The study of these questions is the task of systems theory that uses mathematical and other tools that give predictive power to a model, so the merits of various model alternatives may be ranked before investing resources to build the most successful or highly predictive alternative. And the same also applies for the legal field, for which a system's elements should be given and interconnected in the first place (the communications, model, system, feedback, adaptation, black box, stability, responsiveness, autopoiesis,[22] input-output relations, predictions, homeostasis) to represent the legal system as responsive, without adjusting it manually i.e. by implementing rules one by one, usually after a violation has occurred.

Agencies and probability. At first sight, the principle of legal certainty based on which agencies must act contravenes probability. Among lawyers, Kelsen made a clear distinction between the principle of causality ("If *a* is, then *b* is or will be") (*sein*) and the principle of imputation ("If *a* is, then *b* ought to be") (*sollen*), the first being part of natural (descriptive) science while the second of normative science (the normative connection between two facts) that addresses conditioned human behaviour dependent on 'a legal authority (that is, by a legal norm created by an act of will)' (Kelsen, 2005, p. 77). On the other hand, a simple mathematical rule shows that two parts (2^n) always have four combinations, so there must be something more than sole authority. The normative element of ought also includes uncertainty – and with that also the applicability of probabilistic methods to tasks that require reasoning under uncertainty (Pearl, 2014) – because legal actions are conditioned on the actions of other facts (be they persons or things). In *Philosophical Foundations of Physics*, Carnap has, even for the natural sciences, demonstrated causality 'is not a thing that causes an event, but a process…[in which] certain processes or events cause other processes or events' (Carnap, 1966, p. 192). A state where each consequence is also a cause that together with other causes contributes to the later multilevel and intertwined consequences is more and more complex, in which all relevant facts cannot be known, so causal relation means solely potential predictability. Legal accountability is possible only in cases where sufficient regularity in causal relations can be established to be able on this basis to predict consequences with high probability. A model's value increases proportionately with a higher level of prediction, and the stands for the legal principle of certainty.

Interactions. A solution to a problem should not be treated independently from other aspects of the problem, or a system's performance cannot be evaluated from the standpoint of its part: it is the product of the interactions of *all* parts. Among the additional elements are the administration of uncertain information and quantitative methods that address the former. They both address intuition's shortcomings; their content is separated from the cybernetic elements because they can be studied clearly (in the view of the more adaptive and reliable regulatory model, they are additional elements that must be built into the model).

Quantitative methods. In past decades, there was significant interest in the assessment of probability, risk analysis and related similar methods that address uncertainty. Decision makers should prefer quantitative methods because '[t]he major advantage [*vis-à-vis* qualitative language]...is that quantitative concepts allow us to formulate quantitative laws. Such laws are enormously more powerful, both as ways to explain phenomena and as means for predicting new phenomena' (Carnap, 1966, p. 106). A legal system to predict optimal general rules and/or decisions should, therefore, have its origin in the quantitatively assessed probability that deals with uncertainties (a classical way is to use intuition based on experiences) in a more objective manner. By this way, it could be inferred with a higher probability whether a proposed legal rule is effective.

Systems theory is not based on a rigid, totalitarian, and controlled totality; it is a holistic model of a dynamic, creative, inclusive, self-renewing, and self-propagating community that embraces unity in diversity. It is "*in varietate concordia*", *united in diversity* – the official motto of the European Union). A good, systemic regulatory framework and its systemic functioning are a prerequisite for good public service delivery. Since the internal consistency of a theory can have a "hypnotic effect of satisfaction", its value must always be tested in practice. Despite the use of "systemic" or "holistic", it is worth noting that public administration is only one system, embedded in other systems (citizens' groups, interest groups, NGOs, political parties, etc.) and vice versa, networks within other networks. This "democratic" element allows for the ability to switch attention back and forth between system levels and to know that the system (self-)regulates itself from within, without, and in combinations thereof. Despite the importance of single reporting, it cannot be successful if it focuses (only) on the implementation of actions in sectors, without (real, not just textual) systemic governance of the whole framework and the links beyond it. The first condition for good public service delivery is a good systemic regulatory framework and its systemic functioning. Systems thinking is a mental outlook on the effects of the world around us, rather than a directly applicable method. If, in the future, the fundamental flaws in the functioning of public administration are addressed from a systems-theory perspective, we will be able to speak of a systemic public administration. The rest are just a bunch of books and articles, including the one you have just read. Systems theory can only be helpful here if we want to understand it - and apply it. Let us not forget - structure influences behaviour...

The mentioned feedback, feedback loop or feedback is indispensable but, due to cognitive errors, it does not always provide objective information: feedback does not provide complete information because it is based on probability only (there is no certain overall one-to-one correspondence between an action and its outcome [the latter may have been influenced by several factors unknown to us]), because it is incomplete (people often do not and cannot know/know the results of potential alternative actions that could have been taken), hidden (in terms of good/bad consequences that cannot be directly inferred from an action. e.g. bad behaviour at an event influences nonattendance at another distant event), ambiguous (it is difficult to determine what exactly led to the benefits or losses of an action), absent, and biased (telling only those things that fit with assumptions, usually positive, about oneself; people do not want to communicate unpleasant information to other people). In addition to these faults, there are also personality trait deficiencies in monitoring feedback: people focus only on positive events, make self-fulfilling prophecies (the expectation comes true because they believe it and act on it), do not recognise their own mistakes in feedback (they do not recognise that they have made a mistake), disproportionately seek feedback in line with their own self-image, accept positive and accurately sift negative feedback, understand positive actions broadly and negative actions narrowly, attribute positive results to themselves and negative results to others, or forget about (parts of) the feedback which are therefore wrongly taken into account (Dunning, 2012, pp. 65–78). These shortcomings are compounded by hindsight bias (tendency to understand that "we knew all along"), sampling bias (people pay less attention than they should even to things that did not materialise), post hoc bias (the temptation to infer cause and effect when all we see is a sequence of events), confirmation bias (people seek, interpret, and recall only data that confirm their prior beliefs or hypotheses) and other biases that are all the more expressive the more intuition is used instead of rigorous scientific methodology. The latter is also (too) often used in the drafting of regulations, despite the known biases and other psychological flaws of mental reasoning. Another approach that could adress these shortcomings or at least to be more aware of them, is complexity theory.

REFERENCES

Ackoff, R. L. (1999). *Re-creating the Corporation: A Design of Organizations for the 21st Century*. Oxford University Press. doi:10.1093/oso/9780195123876.001.0001

Ashby, W. R. (1957). *An Introduction to Cybernetics*. Chapman and Hall.

Beer, S. (1994). *Beyond Dispute: The Invention of Team Syntegrity*. Wiley.

Carnap, R. (1966). *Philosophical Foundation of Physics: An Introduction to the Philosophy of Science* (M. Gardner, Ed.). Basic Books.

Cziko, G. (2000). *The Things We Do: Using the Lessons of Bernard and Darwin to Understand the What, How, and why of Our Behavior*. MIT Press.

Daellenbach, H. G. (1996). *Systems and Decision Making: A Management Science Approach* (1st ed.). Wiley.

Dunning, D. (2012). *Self-Insight: Roadblocks and Detours on the Path to Knowing Thyself*. Psychology Press. doi:10.4324/9780203337998

Forrester, J. W. (1961). *Industrial Dynamics*. MIT Press.

French, W. L., & Bell, C. (1978). *Organization Development: Behavioral Science Interventions for Organization Improvement*. Prentice Hall.

Joseph, P. (2017). *The New Human Rights Movement*. BenBella Books.

Kelsen, H. (2005). *Pure Theory of Law*. The Lawbook Exchange, Ltd.

Luhmann, N. (2004). *Law as a Social System* (F. Kastner, R. Nobles, D. Schiff, & R. Ziegert, Eds., ZiegertK. A., Trans.). Oxford University Press. doi:10.1093/oso/9780198262381.001.0001

Meadows, D. H. (2008). *Thinking in Systems: A Primer*. Chelsea Green Publishing.

Nielsen, T. D., & Jensen, F. (2007). *Bayesian Networks and Decision Graphs* (2nd ed.). Springer.

Nonaka, I., & Zhu, Z. (2012). Pragmatic Strategy: Eastern Wisdom, Global Success. Cambirdge: Cambridge University Press. doi:10.1017/CBO9780511736568

Pearl, J. (2009). *Causality: Models, Reasoning and Inference* (2nd ed.). Cambridge University Press. doi:10.1017/CBO9780511803161

Pearl, J. (2014). *Probabilistic Reasoning in Intelligent Systems: Networks of Plausible Inference*. Morgan Kaufmann.

Shmueli, G., Bruce, P. C., Stephens, M. L., & Patel, N. R. (2017). *Data Mining for Business Analytics: Concepts, Techniques, and Applications with JMP Pro*. John Wiley & Sons.

Vickers, G. (1995). *The Art of Judgment: A Study of Policy Making*. SAGE Publications, Inc.

Wiener, N. (1989). *The Human Use of Human Beings: Cybernetics and Society*. Free Associations Books.

Zimbardo, P. G. (2008). *The Lucifer Effect: Understanding How Good People Turn Evil*. Random House Trade Paperbacks.

ENDNOTES

[1] Ludwig von Bertalanffy is widely considered as the father of general systems theory...The concept of open systems, inspired by his work in developmental biology, is his most important contribution to the field. It is essentially based on the proposition that living organisms cannot be understood as equilibrium systems. Instead, they are able to maintain themselves in a constant state of disequilibrium and maintain a complex level of organisation by importing substances and energy from the environment and exporting their entropy. Although he did not speak in terms of the "spontaneous emergence of order" that characterises more recent developments in chaos theory, similar insights are reflected in his emphasis on the autonomy, creativity and spontaneity of living organisms and the gradual emergence of increasingly complex self-organising systems (Hammond, 2011, p. 18).

[2] For him, 'public administration is the detailed and systematic implementation of public law' (Wilson, 1887, p. 212). Difficulties of governmental action are ... the reason why administrative tasks have nowadays to be so studiously and systematically adjusted to carefully tested standards of policy, the reason why we are having now what we never had before, a science of administration' (Wilson, 1887, p. 200).

[3] The best method [for a view on the organisation] is a study of what I have described as the administrative apparatus...It is a system of recording which includes the present, the past and the future; in which the contributions made by senior members of the staff, together with information from outside sources, ensure for the Directors the best possible means of appreciating the probable consequences of their decisions. It must comprise: The Survey, The Plan, Reports and Statistics, Minutes of Meetings, and The Organization Chart' (Fayol, 1954, p. x).

4   It is axiomatic that the whole is equal to the sum of its parts. But in dividing up any "whole," one must be certain that every part, including unseen elements and relationships, is accounted for. The marble sand to which the Venus de Milo may be reduced by a vandal does not equal the statue, though every last grain be preserved... a piece of work to be done cannot be subdivided into the obvious component parts without great danger that the central design, the operating relationships, the imprisoned idea, will be lost....It is self-evident that the more the work is subdivided, the greater is the danger of confusion, and the greater is the need of overall supervision and co-ordination. Co-ordination is not something that develops by accident. It must be won by intelligent, vigorous, persistent, and organized effort (Gulick, 2003, pp. 4-5).

5   For administrative law science, such a starting point means that we cannot build public law systems and their decisions only on the basis of the data we have, because only our system of setting up detectors/sensors/criteria and detecting the data (similarly to the way in which the installation of sensors in an airplane only allows it to fly properly or to react to its surroundings in a timely manner) allows us to draw conclusions about the (in)appropriateness of a particular regulation. It is not a question of making the best decisions on the basis of the factual situation, but rather that the reality detection system is designed to detect data from which recurring patterns of behaviour can only be discerned.

6   Given the time when systems theory was first developed, the idea was soon transferred to the field of public administration, but unfortunately it remained unheard. Thus, as early as 1944, Renwick proposed a method by which the laws of public administration can be discovered, referring to the source relationships, e.g.: (1) Proposition: That where thinking is centralised and action decentralised, efficient administration tends to be ensured. (2) Definitions required: Of "thinking," "centralised" and "decentralised," "efficient administration." (3) We need a series of cases showing how, when and where such results have or have not been obtained, and why. (4) These can be obtained from contemporary and historical survey, from which our raw material is sifted out, finally giving us: (5) The conclusion, stating under what conditions the proposition is found true' (Renwick & Cyril, 1944, p. 82).

7   We often rely on "common sense" and "systemic regulation". Both can be misleading - the former when applied to new dynamic situations and experiences, i.e. all complex situations different from the everyday situations under which it has emerged ('the paradox of common sense is that it can give us some sense of the world, but on the other hand it actively undermines our ability to make sense of it' (Watts, 2011, p. xviii)), and the other is when, over time, we no longer see, verify or understand the existing, underlying structure of the system, taking its assumptions for granted (Dr Martin Luther King called such a situation "poverty of spirit"). Unrecognised situations that lead to unintended, negative side-effects caused by the system itself constitute structural violence (if we actively defend it, we also speak of cultural violence, of cultural aspects that normalise structural violence and its mechanisms). (Joseph, 2017). One example of structural violence is that the enduring structural links between political and property regimes have led to a concentration of wealth in France on the eve of the First World War and for more than a century after the abolition of feudal privilege, even greater than at the time of the Revolution, or that inequality has been rising on all continents since the 1980s, irrespective of political systems (Piketty, 2020).

8   The supporting structure of the system allows it to function in a certain way, so it is often irrelevant to replace only individual parts (e.g., the same/similar functioning of the civil service regardless of a change in power, individual employees in new or old offices, etc.) without being aware of the

Systems Theory and Agencies

way the whole system works. If we only replace individual parts and put the system outside its "comfort zone" (established ways of working), it will sooner or later return there. In this context, it is common to talk about resilience to change, but in fact often it is not even about real change, i.e., change aimed at changes in relations, new criteria, ways of perceiving and changing the situation.

9   The dichotomy between politics and administration thus becomes a *contradictio in adiecto*: the two poles are indispensable elements that interrelate and not only complement each other, but also build on each other (so it is not a question of a dichotomy between politics and administration at all, but of a new content that arises only in the relationship between the two poles).

10   If the relationship is to be essential for understanding power, we can assume that those who understand the system also "understand" power. Luhmann gave one of the most sophisticated theories of society, usually labelled "systems theory" as a medium of communication. He understood power as the establishment of a situation in which the subordinate party wishes to avoid a negative consequence more than the superior wishes to enforce it: 'the code of power must ensure the possibility of a relationship between the relations. On this assumption, there is the possibility of a conditional association of undesirable alternatives with a less negatively valued combination of alternatives... Power is therefore based on being given options, the realisation of which is avoided (Luhmann, 2013, p. 29). Foucault also thought that power is a relation, not a property: power is not a property or a power; it is always a *relation* that can only be studied in relation to the links between which it is established (Foucault, 2015).

11   For example, a good football team is not one that has good players, but one where there are good links between them.

12   The bureaucratic saying "that's the way it's done here" should be replaced by "there's always something new here".

13   So we could draw an equivalence between a system and a relationship. In systems, the principle of emergence prevails, so that the environment and information per se are not (only) a matter of our cognition, but of the relations that only make information possible: relations participate in the renewal of the system, maintaining or reestablishing it, while cognition, as patterns that have already emerged, only detects them post festum. It is up to us, then, to set up the structure on the basis of which an occurrence can "emerge", i.e. to make the connections possible.

14   A boomerang returns because of its structure, not because of the hand that throws it; a shock absorber can absorb shocks as far as its springs allow; cats chase mice because their nature is written as such in the DNA of the structure; a public administration is as responsive, flexible and efficient (and what other adjectives there are) as its underlying, supportive structure of operation (the established, well-established ways of working) allows it to be.

15   In a non-democratic country, the rules may be written in a democratic way, but that does not change the fact that it is nondemocratic.

16   The stock (base rate) can also be of a more abstract nature, e.g. the number of previous coin tosses, a person's past behaviour/performance.

17   A good example of how the system works is driving a car: we have a fuel reserve and its current consumption (we will drive faster if we want to get to our destination sooner or slower if we want to conserve as much fuel as possible), individual parts interacting with others to cause the car to move according to a specific purpose or direction using individual indicators, giving the current state of the vehicle as well as the environment in which it is located (sensors in the car, human senses and the external environment) as feedback to the destination, the driving destination and

the necessary decisions such as (contextually appropriate) driving on the road towards the desired destination. This integrated structure of action is then reflected in the behaviour (steady driving, braking, and accelerating, changing direction) of the vehicle on the road. Given a predefined goal, each system must be equipped with sensors to detect the actual situation on the one hand, and with retarders (preventive filters to prevent certain phenomena from entering or curative penalties) in the case of moving away, and action boosters (incentives) in the case of accelerating towards the final goal.

[18] The first real feedback system was the Watt Regulator, invented in 1788 by the British engineer James Watt. The Watt Regulator marks the beginning of the Industrial Revolution, of surplus energy and of the development of public utilities as one element of the later established principle of the welfare state. For this reason, the Watt regulator could be used as a symbol of governance.

[19] E.g. people can adapt to the new legislation by reaching their destination in different ways (a neutral measure is to avoid a traffic accident or find another route, a negative one is that higher taxation of wealth causes it to "migrate" to other countries, by avoiding it or by abusing its purpose (e.g. transferring property to straw men), and public authorities can try to correct such behaviour (e.g. 'the concept of self-organisation is fundamental to general systems theory and emerged initially from theoretical work in developmental biology; it provides a biological framework for the understanding of social organisation that could support participatory and inclusive forms of social organisation. In contrast to the classical mechanistic view, which tends to reinforce a deterministic understanding of human behaviour, many in the general systems group emphasise the importance of creativity and spontaneity, which encourages individuals to participate more actively in the process of determining their own reality' (Hammond, 2011, p. 23).

[20] For a full description of how it works see (Routledge, 1900, p. 6).

[21] Iteration is the essence of a holistic approach and a fundamental element of design methodology. In the case of attractors, it is iteration that allows order to emerge from chaos. Nature automatically creates an iteration, while social beings can only return to the beginning by choosing to start a new iteration. Design from the beginning is a reflection of this imperative (Gharajedaghi, 2007, p. 52).

[22] The concept [of autopoiesis] merely states that the elements and structures of a system exist only as long as it manages to maintain its autopoiesis. The concept does not say anything about the kind of structures that are developed in cooperation with the structural couplings between system and environment...Differentiations become conditions for further differentiations and systems become, if further differentiations are evolutionarily successful, environments for further systems. All this is achievable—and this is what autopoiesis tells us—only through the system's own operatively closed efforts and not through a decomposition of a whole into parts (Luhmann, 2004, pp. 87, 467).

Chapter 13
Complexity Theory and Agencies

ABSTRACT

Complex problems are characterized by uncertainty, complexity, exponentiality, divergent values, self-organization, emergence, interdependent processes, structures, and actors. To address such problems, a solution is to reflect real-life complexity using complex adaptive systems (CAS). Complexity theory emphasizes the benefits of CAS, which is attentive to the heterogeneity in the various subsystems, how parts at a sub-level in a complex system affect the emergent behaviour, and outcome of the system. The main aim of complexity theory is to explain counterintuitive order creation out of local simple rules, distant from the second law of thermodynamics that point at the increasing, irreversible entropy of the system and its surroundings. Public agencies can also be understood using the CAS model, with their levels of autonomy and independence from politics, the element of self-organization is roughly similar in CAS vis-à-vis public agencies.

INTRODUCTION

The way to build a complex system that works is to build it from very simple systems that work.

–Kevin Kelly

'Different as commercial enterprises, hospitals, universities and administrative agencies are, what they all have in common is that they are complex, dynamic, nonlinear, probabilistic, networked systems. Their respective environments – complex systems themselves – form an interlaced and interwoven, dynamic, non-linear system ecology … complex systems have their own laws, qualities and behavioural patterns which are fundamentally different from those of simple systems' (Malik, 2011, p. 25). Public problems are becoming so complex that they are called 'wicked' (again, it is about a new name instead or as a replacement of the old, unsolved one; complex - wicked). The term denotes an issue highly resistant to resolution; it shares a range of characteristics that go beyond the capacity of any organisation to understand

DOI: 10.4018/979-8-3693-0507-2.ch013

and respond to. Along with this, there is often disagreement about the causes of problems and the best way to tackle them. Causality-based research in complex systems is fruitless; wicked problems require thinking that is capable of grasping the big picture, including the interrelationships among the full range of causal factors underlying them (Australian Public Service Commission, 2018). The boundaries of rational construction of unchangeable and all-encompassing general rules focused in the future are torn down; the presence of complex/wicked problems makes the rules of action, practice, flexibility, agility, adaptation and their institutional (re)organization the more important beside the endeavours to coordinate, lead, and control actions towards common goals. 'In order to adapt to change, organizations must become even more complex—and the more complex they become, the more difficult it is for them to be managed. And the more complexity and change there is, the more crucial measurement is' (Spitzer, 2007, p. 13). Wicked troubles (i.e., problems characterized by the uncertainty, complexity, exponentiality, divergent values, self-organisation, emergence, interdependent processes, structures and actors) call for constant adjustments throughout a policy/implementation cycle, and the same stands for complex problems. Based on the rule of requisite variety, decision makers could solve complex problems in the frame of uncertain and complex challenges (whose scale and nature go beyond the existent ineffective methods in the presence of wicked problems only with the similar level of complexity).

A possible answer to the question 'how to adjust' is the enhanced systemic approach based on the complex one. This approach requires multiple and collaborative actors, but also various actors within, across, and outside the government. Although public administrations address 'systems' (Frederickson, Smith, Larimer, & Licari, 2012; Peters & Pierre, 2012; Rosenbloom, Kravchuk, & Clerkin, 2014), they do not address them from the point of view of interactions and / or systems. The external and internal interactions of open systems do not address only the classical structural features of organizations, but they essentially *substitute substantial content with processes; they are focused more on material functionalistic elements than on the formal ones*. 'The distinctive stance taken by complex systems theory is that it is concerned with systems that exhibit: (i) a large number of elements comprising the system; (ii) significant interactions among these elements; and (iii) organisation in the system. This system anatomy generates three highly related characteristics of a complex system: nonlinearity, emergence, and self-organisation' (McCarthy & Gillies, 2003, p. 72).

Public agencies are one of the largest institutional clusters in the country that introduce, implement and manage public processes. Their focus is (among others) on basic effectiveness and efficiency (from which other approaches or principles can be derived), but there is much more: a deeper insight into agencies could be done from a natural science point of view – that addresses the biological and natural systems. Public administration as a social organization is rooted in biology (Fukuyama, 2012, 2014), and the same goes for institutions that assemble first; they all should *adapt* to new circumstances and/or information to *survive*. A human is an example of the biological *complex adaptive system* (CAS; it is also, *for example,* the environment, language, bacteria, ecology, and economy). CASs consist of 'many interacting components, which undergo constant change, both autonomously and in interaction with their environment. The behaviour of such complex systems is typically unpredictable, yet exhibits various forms of adaptation and self-organization' (Heylighen, 1999, p. 1). Such states have been researched from different viewpoints, known as systems theory, complexity theory, complex adaptive systems, dissipative structures, autopoiesis, or chaos theory. Agencies are also a system, they are also complex ones, but it remains to be open for analysis up to what point are they also adaptable. A solution to manage wicked problems is to reflect 'real-life complexity' with the help of complex adaptive systems (CAS) as an outline to understand such complex systems.

Complexity Theory and Agencies

Complexity theory emphasizes the benefits of CAS by being attentive to additional general aspects that were not fully elaborated in system theory, like the emergence, bifurcation, adaptation, and new order far from equilibrium. The specific priority of CAS is its ability to represent a system by portraying the conduct of parts (agents, officials) when they cooperate, intermingle, and produce new emergent resulting patterns of performance at the level of the results and outputs of the system. While systems theory focuses on the structure, relations, and interdependencies between parts of the system, complexity theory also refers to the heterogeneity in the various subsystems and how parts at a sublevel in a complex system affect the emergent behaviour and outcome of the system (Amagoh, 2016). If system theory emphasizes the relations among parts and their interconnectedness, complexity theory expands this reductionistic framework not only by accepting the parts of the system that contribute to the whole but also by understanding the relations of parts that cause the emergence of a new entity. A more comprehensive and complete understanding of the whole is here achieved by new perspectives that can further explain the system's complex behaviour.

The main aim of complexity theory is to explain contraintuitive order creation out of local (simple) rules, distant from the second law of thermodynamics that point at the increasing, irreversible entropy of the system and its surroundings. Although dynamical and thus complex systems (a state of parts or ensemble of them varies over time, like the life itself) are mostly unstable (fluctuations, instability, and bifurcation are here very common), they contradict this view, as they point to a world where the level of order increases. Such systems are not only described as systems comprised of several interconnected parts that interact (mostly) in a nonlinear manner, but can reveal the elements of self-organisation and emergence. Such systems are also open systems, where interactions, changes or transformations take place in far from equilibrium conditions. Agencies always up to some point self-organise and/or exhibit new properties that were not pre-planned in a formal frame of rules. It matters that the leader understands the main elements of complex systems to be able to effectively address the management of an agency. Public bodies have usually been analysed from a reductionistic point of view (it assumes that the analysis of individual parts could predict the behaviour of a whole system), while the inevitable part of any kind of aggregation is some new entity that parts *per se* do not and cannot have. The evidence of this can be evolution and biology: development is not based on the assemblage of things, but in new emergent properties that are absent in parts, and thus cannot be reduced to them. Emergence can thus be seen as a main sign of self-organisation, or adaptation, of order. Order can hence arise "spontaneously" (out of disorder or chaos through a process of self-organisation) when the system experiences far-from-equilibrium conditions, where nonlinear relationships prevail (Prigogine & Stengers, 1984). Under such conditions, systems are very sensitive to external influences. In time, fluctuations can become very powerful (remember on the Butterfly effect) which can, as a result of positive feedback, change a preexisting structure. This is a bifurcation point that leads to disintegration (chaos), or it may develop a new meta-level of order and/or a 'dissipative' (energy-consuming) structure (for dissipative systems it is essential that a continual stream of energy flows through them to maintain their internal structure). This new order is of course not legal, but an order as a different state or condition of a structure that still exists, but is nevertheless changed or improved. It is hence relevant what kind of conditions can push agencies in the state out-of-equilibrium to be prepared to overturn them (when seen as negative) or to adapt to them (when seen as useful). The quality of public agencies are very important for the well-being of its citizens; agency basically addresses and reflects *behaviour* (Ridder, 2007) as a derivate of the adaptability of living organisms. Agencies nowadays work in a dynamic and complex environment, while the latter is often (usually or at least without specific attention) not included in their work. Ashby addressed complexity with the notion of variety (William Ross Ashby, 1957) defined as the "number of possible states of a situation". As the combinations of numbers increase exponentially increase ($2^2=4$, $2^4=16$, $2^{16}=65536,...$) the growing number of multiple relationships between parts inevitably leads to complexity and also to a lower level of predictability, but, on the other hand, complexity theory claims that order can emerge from a few simple rules.

Complexity theory despite numerous works that emphasized the benefits of complex adaptive systems (CAS) for the behaviour of the law and society system (Ruhl, 1996), organizations (Anderson, 1999), public service (Haynes, 2015), public administration (Kiel, 2014; C. J. Koliba, Meek, Zia, & Mills, 2010; Snellen & Klijn, 2009), public administration research (Klijn, 2008), public decision-making (Gerrits, 2012), political science and public policy (Cairney, 2012; Morçöl, 2012), public institutions/public policies (Room, 2011, 2016) and governance systems (G. Teisman, Buuren, & Gerrits, 2009) is still absent in the practice of public agencies. Rhodes and her colleagues (Eppel & Rhodes, 2018a, 2018b; C. Koliba, Gerrits, Rhodes, & Meek, 2016; M. L. Rhodes, 2008; Mary Lee Rhodes & MacKechnie, 2003; Mary Lee Rhodes, Murphy, Muir & Murray, 2010; Mary Lee Rhodes & Murray, 2007) along with other authors (Bovaird, 2008; Haynes, 2008; Klijn, 2008; G. R. Teisman & Klijn, 2008) stress how little attention has been paid to how complexity theory can be translated in the practise of public administration (Eppel & Rhodes, 2018b, p. 1) despite claims on the relevancy of systems/cybernetic approaches for public institutions (European Commission, 2017; Gharajedaghi, 2007; Morgan & Yeung, 2007; OECD, 2017). Complexity can be seen as the system's ability to *switch* between different ways of behaviour according to different conditions in the environment (Nicolis & Prigogine, 1989); this is also called 'development' as the ability to choose (Gharajedaghi, 2007).

Based on the relationship between the system and the agents which act within it, CAS are distinguished as the ordered and chaotic systems (Berreby, 1996). In the first, all agent behaviour is limited to the system rules, while in the second, agents are unrestricted and prone to various examinations. 'Agents [the same term as at public agents and agencies] are the decision-making entities (e.g., operators, control systems, managers, designers, etc.) that receive and process local information to create the events, outputs and internal dynamics of the system' (McCarthy & Gillies, 2003, p. 73). In CAS, a system and its agents co-relate and co-evolve: the first up to a point restrains agent behaviour, while on the other hand agents can modify the system by their interaction with it. This co-evolving nature of CAS is its intrinsic characteristic that exhibits its ability to *self-organise*, adapt, and be distinguish from other (self-organizing) systems. CAS self-organise out of the relations between parts and their relations that form structures; parts interact in a constant dynamic of change and adjustment. There is usually no direct cause and effect chain, only layers of causes that, such as outputs and outcomes, affect other causes and effects in a nonstop and circular way. They are governed by feedback, are resistant to (easy) change (path-dependency[1]) and characterised by non-linear relationships. Chapman's parable of throwing a rock and a bird visually explains the difference between the mechanistic linear approach and the holistic (all-encompassing) systemic approach to policy: '[m]echanical linear models are excellent for understanding where the rock will end up, but useless for predicting the trajectory of a bird – even though both are subject to the same laws of physics' (Chapman, 2004, p. 19). Systems theory fits into institutional versions of regulations that evolve around biological adaptation, on how living organisms self-regulate, and relate to their environment. Already these few statements open a deeper view into the behaviour of public agencies that do not work only under the legal rules.

One of the main elements of CAS is their *self-organisation*, which does not need a central hierarchical control. However, how can this be understood with the numerous and various public agencies present in the public management systems as parts of the larger central government? From the systemic point of view, public agencies are just parts of the larger system, and as all parts combined together form a complex whole. The notion of "complex" means 'a whole made up of complicated or interrelated parts', something that is 'hard to separate, analyse, or solve' (Merriam-Webster, 2018). These parts interact with each other in many ways, where the *richness* of interactions allows the system to undergo and exhibit spontaneous self-organisation (Waldrop, 1993). The model of CAS can be applied for public agencies with their levels of *autonomy and independence from politics*; the element of self-organisation is roughly similar in CAS *vis-à-vis* public agencies: also CAS has some inevitable parts that produce an adaptive system as such, like public agencies have formal legal outer frames (policy) within which they autonomously implement their tasks; adaptability comes to the fore also when other organisational forms of agencies are used that go toward private ones, a feature that is essential for understanding public service provision in various models of (network) governance, on the line from public organizations to increasingly private forms, the ones very much emphasised in the NPM's ideas on privatisation. CAS is not only a system (Greek *systēma*, an arrangement system, from *synistanai* to combine, from *syn-* together and *histanai* cause to stand (Merriam-Webster, 2017)) as the assemblage or combination of correlated parts forming a complex or unitary whole, but it can also *adapt*, change and self-organise. Systems theory corresponds to biological adaptation, how living organisms learn, self-regulate, and relate to their environment. Designing the socially adaptive-legal-and-administrative system that at the same time reflects the basic insights of CAS is difficult, but there is a solution: in studying CASs, an observer 'follows what happens to the information' (Gell-Mann, 2002, p. 23). As the law comes to life in institutions (Waldron, 2011), it is important how they manage information, organize actions, and communicate knowledge to simplify their processes. The adaptability of CASs is of utmost importance in the increasingly changing environment.

A system is not a loose conflux of events, but a tight and knowable network of communications, consisting of numerous information that presents reality as a network (Beer, 1986; Luhmann, 2013). Complexity is based on the same logic as creativity: taking ideas from one place and applying them as a new value in another one.[2] And the same can stand for agencies: any agency should be evaluated and/or compared with other agencies to gain some valuable information on its efficiency and other comparative criteria to gain new value. Ministries have several divisions and tasks, while agencies have a smaller number of tasks and a simple(r) organisational structure. The first promote incorporation, consistency, and a uniform, rule-driven behaviour, while agencies endorse self-governance, diversity, and adaptability. Along such "simple" descriptions of elements, they are into same time the basic ingredients of complexity theory.[3] It is valuable for the efficient management of agencies to know how the mentioned elements interact and evolve (along the human resource management processes, organisational behaviour, the nature of work and employment, organisation jobs and roles, employee resourcing, performance management, human resource development, rewards and sanctions, employee relations and practices etc.) as they are no "self-sufficient and lonely islands". To be more fully acknowledged, the rule of law principle that is very important (and obviously for the law *per se*) for the public agencies is to know how order in the meaning of mutually affecting relations between parts emerges.

Complexity lies between totally ordered and totally random. It exponentially rises with every new part, with every new relation: 'when the range of size is great, what is true at one end of the scale may be false at the other…in a large system there is no a priori necessity for the properties of the whole to be a simple copy of those of the parts' (William Ross Ashby, 1957, p. 112). In such conditions similar systems could be analysed on how they behave. Already Heinz von Foerster (1960) formulated the principle of "order from noise". He noted that the larger the random perturbations that affect a system, the more quickly it will *self-organize*. Perturbations have something to do with complexity; the latter is based on iterations of simple rules or actions governed by anticipations accompanied by learning and adaptation. CAS is supposed to be present at the edge of chaos, between order and chaos; this can be seen as a splendid bargain between structure and surprise. One of the appreciated modus operandi management styles is to have some key variables based on which predictions are made and control is maintained over all of them. As much as this intuitively seems to be the good approach, it is nevertheless a bad presentation of reality (as some would like to represent a mountain with a mathematical form of cone). Such an approach would, when seen from above, on the colony of ants, pedestrians, traffic, or taxis on city streets, demand a central coordinator or transmitter that sends all these 'moving parts' where they should be. This is notoriously not true.

Complexity theory follows a different tactic that explains such situation with the help of few simple *local* rules that cause results in their interactions. They are a form of collective action that arises when a larger number (of people or other things) work (comes into contact) independently on a single (whole or modular) issue and produces a collective result. The emergence as one of the elements of CAS, is at the level of social insects known as stigmergy, as a form of self-organization by insects, termits (Grassé, 1959) and bees (Camazine & Sneyd, 1991) that achieve intelligent behaviour. Basic components of stigmergy are goal-directed action and coordination, while both can be part of self-organisation; provided the latter is the basic rule for all complex systems (W. Ross Ashby, 1960; William Ross Ashby, 1957) also a person or agencies can be addressed from this point of view. Stigmergy is as a mechanism of indirect coordination of insects, based on a few simple rules: a trace left by one stimulates a subsequent action/route of another etc., or for a consumer "buy qualitative but cheap goods" and "compare prices", or for a taxi driver "stop anyone who waves" and "drive to his wanted destination". The tactic of following a few simple rules seen from a distance is seen as a complex behaviour, but its patterns are not made by some central controller. Their actions/patterns advance spontaneously, but when seen as a whole, they reflect a very good approximation of the best dissemination of things according to their purposes and a few local rules. Understanding how emergence emanates/appears also presents a major challenge for the management of agencies. Seen from the complexity theory, their autonomy (local rules *vis-à-vis* purposes) is very much appreciated; as full control from above not only resembles Orwell's 1984 work or the socialist and totalitarian states of eastern Europe, it is not appreciated if we want good results.

PAs are networks and as such are 'the ensemble of direct and indirect linkages defined by mutual relationships of dependencies' (Scharpf, 1978, p. 362). These connections could be determined with structural *perception*, with the help of CAS. Complexity is the most elaborate concept in complexity theory. A particular strand of it is complex adaptive systems (CAS) theory that can be applied also to public administration, public organisations, and public service systems. Since outputs are seldom fully predictable in public administration (this stands even more for outcomes), they nevertheless many times deliver services, which points to their element of self-organisation and emergent order distant from the central government. Along the multiple, more or less predictable, intense, and usually nonlinear interactions between the central government and its agencies the latter exhibit similar characteristics as are present in CAS that have one especially important additional characteristic for agencies, that is, adaptability. The latter is absent many times not only in central government but also in public agencies, not only because legal arrangements would not allow it, but due to the unsuitable systems on which agencies and the people in it operate. Therefore, the use of CAS in the case of public agencies seems reasonable. Instead of full control from above, coordination should focus more on new, emerging things that arise from the self-organisation of the system and dedicate energy to perpetuating conditions in which the best solutions develop and grow. With the division of problems into their parts and/or policies into multiple autonomous agencies, a comparison between them will probably show the fittest player, but not necessarily the best solution. If Kauffman's fitness landscape metaphor is used, the best condition is achieved when a tested area merges with its more efficient neighbourhood area until there are no more efficient areas. Agencies similarly should cooperate with each other until the best solution is found on a line between the more reductionistic, smaller agencies and more holistic, grouped agencies. By the way of their local interaction a more global/central emergent order appears that through feedback affects agencies, their connections, and their clusters in a constant dance (similar as in the field of university autonomy, culture, or art); their local results reflect higher order (the rule of law) as an emergent property of dynamical systems.

The aspects of CAS could be integrated into the knowledge of agencies, especially on data-flows, on the ways *how* information is recognized, how results are interpreted, analysed and how they were gathered in the first place. Information as 'communicated knowledge' is *per se* based on *activity:* information means grouping things (animals, humans) that move in formation in a particular order or pattern. The more or less static regulation and implementation cannot be successful when CASs are addressed. This logical inference shows that there are problems present on the practical and cognitive levels. The arrangement of 'real-world models' suggests an impact on the institutionalised structured pattern of behaviour that should be flexible flexible enough (responsive to change), complex (consisting of vertical and horizontal parts), autonomous (independent of major or minor external influences) and consistent (consistency of parts toward a common goal) set of information. CASs form endless amazements; they always add, take of or do differently than in the previous cases; they, out of microinteractions, self-produce new results in exponential combinations, are able to adapt, to exhibit agility and are because of this also resilient and robust against malfunctioning. The dynamic models of reality are similar to a process human use on a daily basis*: learning*. Learning is the basic element of humans as CAS, and it means a process of acquiring knowledge and skill by prediction-based internal feedback (John H. Holland, Holyoak, Nisbett, & Thagard, 1989). Learning is by its definition (through the use of multiple feedbacks) a system per se. 'Learning by doing' is connected with the feedback loop to obtain information on the effectiveness of actions (OECD, 2017), but learning is not a system approach per se. It needs Senge's "metanoia" (2010), *a shift of mind* because the existing structure influences what can be experienced/learned in it. In PA, this is known as the path dependency, as 'a sequence of events narrowing the scope of action eventually resulting in a state of persistence or inertia' (Schreyögg & Sydow, 2009, p. 4). It is the embodied knowledge of an organisation, founded on its human and other resources, their relations and results. Thus, it is important how learning evolves and thrives, in this case, how data and information flow through MLG interactions. If looked even more precisely, actions are not based on information, but on our *attention* that collects the former. Learning is an ability not only to identify constraints but to remove them, not only to (re)solve a problem but to eliminate (dissolve) it. A presumption is that learning uses (invisible, intuitive, and rational) indicators or anchors upon which content is attached and processed in the surrounding of other anchors. In cognitive science, this is known as a schema and/or a pattern of thought that organises categories of information and the relationships among them (DiMaggio, 1997).

The process of learning develops ways of behaving that are not only internally or externally caused and determined: as an example of CAS, men come to conclusions through the mixture of (un)conscious relations, interconnections, and combinations of different parts. Final results cannot be known in the beginning, because they – due to emerging combinations – always show more variety than at the beginning. Learning should understand the complex environment in which is based. This can be done with the help of new perspectives and stochastic indicators/sensors: they show a system's pattern and minimise system delays. The cause of "time-gap" is in different positions between the time of their evaluation and the time when they were in a time of action (in the evaluation time, they are already different in content or in place, and connected with different things). To manage such state, there must be real-time sensors by which a controller could gain insight into a current state of affairs in the shortest time possible. Indicators should be taken stochastically from a larger list to prevent subjectivity and to open horizons. This mode (of creative thinking) requires a different approach to the adoption and execution of decisions: different perspectives, shared experiences, used, different skills, brainstorming. Understanding the nature of a decision and the connections between the types of knowledge and the institutional units headed by experts or citizens is incomplete without a conceptual framework that could dynamically integrate individual-group activities with institutional forms and the latter with societal institutions. Actions cannot be successfully managed in the more or less static regulation and implementation when they address CASs. A good model of CAS could identify the most important elements in the system, elements that represent the underlying system structure elements that interact vis-à-vis systems purpose, its parts and their relations, elements that can change a relation between systems flows and stocks based on results seen as patterns given the systems feedback and indicators of success (performance). CAS is nothing but an open and adaptable system, and a good model or approach of CAS can spot the most important parts that can affect the whole structure. CAS is not a type of mechanical structure or machine; it works as a concept, and the place for concepts is in the human mind. Agencies therefore operate good or bad based on decision-makers' perceptions on their effectiveness and efficiency, on their knowledge on internal ways through which parts interact and affect each other related to the external environment, which leads to (un)wanted consequences labelled as public goals.

The description and characterization of public agencies as systems (maybe also as 'artificial beings' that act and react to different changes in their environment) can be investigated when seen as CAS: how can their complexity and adaptability be examined. Rhodes et al. (Mary Lee Rhodes et al., 2010) for their goal (the characterization of the public sector projects) created a researchable "6+4" analytical framework, from the six core elements of the CAS framework (system, environmental factors, environmental rules, agents, processes, and outcomes) plus the four unique CAS dynamics (path-dependency, adaptation, bifurcation and emergence) (Mary Lee Rhodes et al., 2010, p. 201). In terms of how a manager's practice might be affected, we believe that the implications of the four CAS dynamics are the most important. They challenge the professional to engage in prior and real-time analysis that is not always central to the traditional process methods and assumptions of either the classical bureaucratic model or the rational-analytic, rational choice models that underpin much of the new public management tradition. The great importance of path dependency and its creation of initial conditions indicates that the 'start' date of a project should be viewed as a continuum that stretches back into time, rather than as present time. As with all systems and human phenomena, setting time boundaries is a challenge: when does history begin and end for any management project or undertaking? A clear message from the research is that ignoring history is likely to be a recipe for ineffective action, or even disaster. As public service systems become more diversified in the numbers and types of agents involved, this is a matter of concern. In a more networked world, many of the agents are highly specialized and have little interest, or capacity, to understand, the path dependencies that set the initial conditions. That some of the agents should undertake to understand the path dependencies is vital, and this seems to fall to core agents in policy-making and implementation roles (Rhodes, Murphy, Muir, & Murray, 2010, p. 205).

Figure 1. CAS model: The '6+4' analytical framework
(Mary Lee Rhodes et al., 2010, p. 202)

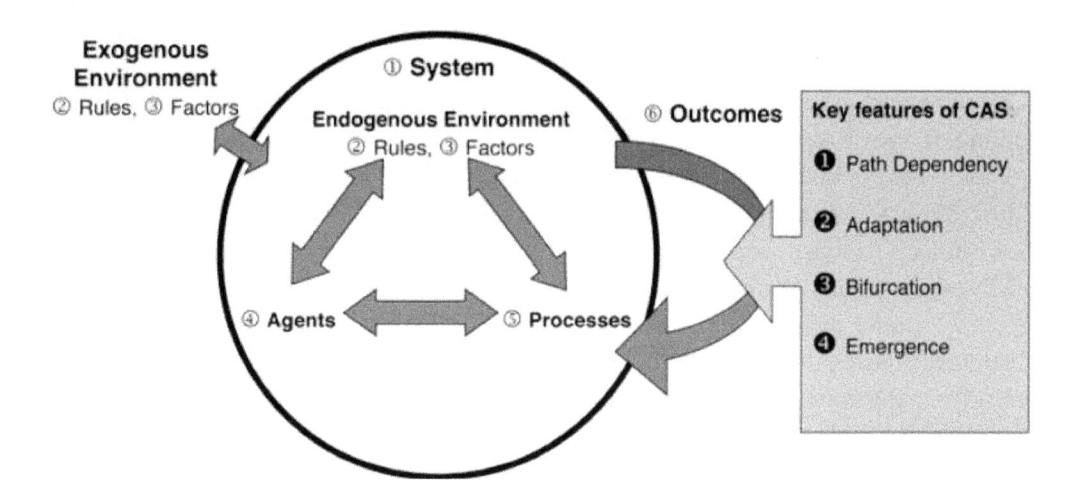

CAS can also be used for a social system as a typical product of multiple interactions between individuals, and not from individuals themselves.[4] The theory of CAS can be used in organisations (and thus also agencies as organisations) because also here parts (people, processes, data, information, technology) interact and therefore can produce a new order through self-adaptation (self-organisation); the awareness of a new (emergent) order or other things based on interaction that cause emergence should prepare organisations to be more attentive to their surroundings, based on which their operations can be more attuned to the organisations' purposes and goals. Negative trends can prepare organisations for the effective contractions, while the positive ones can be seen as new opportunities for the enhancement of their success and overall legitimacy (reactions to both trends are examples of organisational adaptation). One of the most important things that understanding CAS can give decision-makers is the awareness of self-realisation, self-regulation, or the production of a new order that emerges from interactions among various parts. These interactions can be described as an active exploration of the space of possibilities in the frame of external environment, the people or the external stakeholders, the central and coordinating hierarchical units, legal rules and the internal environment of leaders, employees, resources and internal acts. The principle of self-organisation or equilibrium between competing combinations from evolutionary biology can be used in social systems:

In collective decision making, fitness can be defined as 'the probability of an actor achieving its problem and solution definitions, that is, the actor's desired goal(s) as defined in its PSD [problem and solution definition]. An actor's ability to get closer to its goal depends on its position relative to other actors, not just on its own intentions or deliberate planning but also on what others connected to that actor do' (Gerrits & Marks, 2017, p. 75).

Agencies always up to some point, even not intentionally "deviate" from formal legal rules, because rules are always applied in the context of other things, which combinations produce different results than those imagined by the central government (that did not include them at the time of preparation, or because other perspectives or things emerged post-festum, when rules were already enacted). Even when agencies are highly regulated, this paradoxically can easily be circumvented due to numerous combinations among rules that were not considered (and even cannot be considered due to their multiplicity) at the time of their enactment. Rules can be imposed top-down, but they will be implemented down-top. For this reason, it is of utmost importance that central government has established coordination and control systems that should be tightly connected in the real time and space in which agencies operate, to manage their interconnectedness and knowledge and actions creating a network of relations. To do so, some common characteristics of CAS should be known to be able to perceive them in the first place (remember on Berkeley's immaterialism) – if they are unknown to decision makers, they cannot even be considered. Only new or changed perspectives can enable to see new relations among things and their patterns, different ways of acting and working. An altered way of thinking about organisations could change the visionary, strategic, and tactic thinking on styles of creation, management, coordination, and control of new organisational forms, that is, of their structures, values, people, and technology. This stands also for agencies and/or different organisational forms and their relations. CAS based on interactions and their combinations exhibit the mentioned elements and other elements that are enumerated below to be more fully understood in understanding the formation, activities, and implementation of public agencies. In collective doings various agents and their relations always up to some level autonomously (due to the information asymmetry and impossibility of constant control from the higher level) do their work, where new things emerge, where formal competences are dispersed, where they intermingle among different stakeholders (distributed functioning); such elements affect central control, pre-programming, and centralization.

COMMON CHARACTERISTICS OF COMPLEX ADAPTIVE SYSTEMS

Understanding and including elements of complex systems in agency management offers a different approach to the adoption and execution of (public) decisions. Different perspectives based on the general characteristics of the CAS lead to new experiences, different skills and competences, which can further lead to the different organizational arrangements of the agencies, their management, coordination and control. Such perspectives can be seen as an attempt to avoid blind spots as *"not seeing that one is not seeing"* (Lodge, 2018). Each challenge up to a point confronts the established ways of doing things and affects the operative actions of organizations, but it has to be remembered that changes or exceptions should always be taken *cum grano salis*, with caution, as they could cause new blind spots. Mitleton-Kelly et al. (2003) begin to develop a theory of complex social systems and its application on organisations. The latter are CAS and accepting them as such provides a way to create settings that could help organisations to coevolve in the constantly changing economic and market environment. Their approach is based on the generic characteristics of complex adaptive systems: 'self-organisation, emergence, connectivity and interdependence, feedback, far-from-equilibrium, exploration-of-the-space-of-possibilities, co-evolution, historicity, path dependence and the creation of new orders' (Mitleton-Kelly, 2003, p. 5).

Before some of the general characteristics are described, a disclaimer should be put on them similarly as it stands for principles: they are always only common, give only frames or lenses and ways of possible interpretations, while specific results should be always obtained in a specific context and/or environment. This stands also for the transfer of natural science characteristics to the social one: they all should be carefully tested in a specific social environment.

Interdependence (or one but many, and not vice versa). Connectivity between individual elements is the basic cause and the root of complexity and is also known in systems theory. Complex theory to the connectivity of elements, to their relations adds also interdependence. Traditional thinking/learning

Figure 2. Five areas of research and characteristics of complex systems (Mitleton-Kelly, 2003, p. 24)

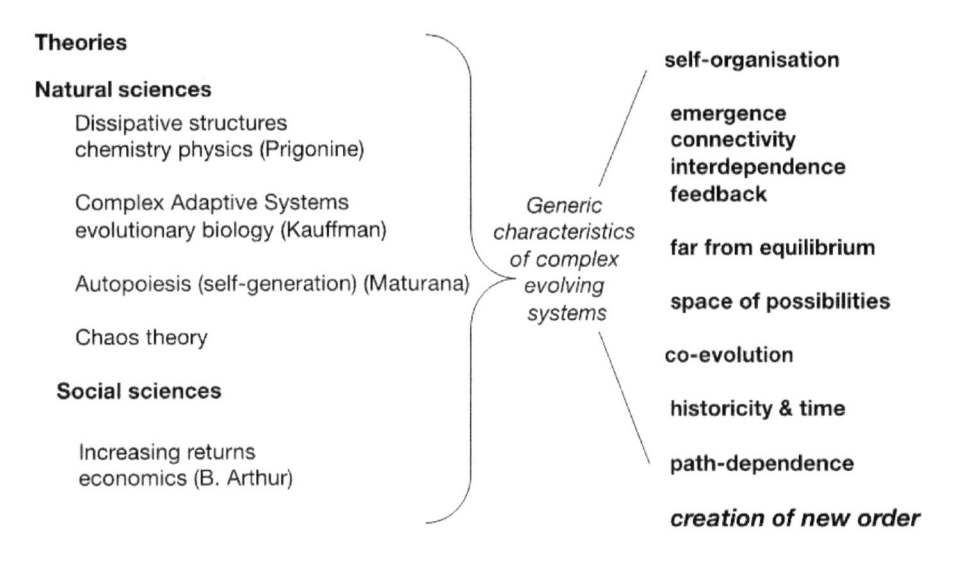

Theories

Natural sciences

Dissipative structures
chemistry physics (Prigonine)

Complex Adaptive Systems
evolutionary biology (Kauffman)

Autopoiesis (self-generation) (Maturana)

Chaos theory

Social sciences

Increasing returns
economics (B. Arthur)

Generic characteristics of complex evolving systems:

- self-organisation
- emergence
- connectivity
- interdependence
- feedback
- far from equilibrium
- space of possibilities
- co-evolution
- historicity & time
- path-dependence
- creation of new order

neglects the system's *interconnections;* it only looks at final goals and assumes a single (or few) cause(s) rather than multiple interrelated connections; the latter lead to multiple causations that affect interrelated parts (individuals, things, organisations, systems, or technologies). If one system part is taken out or when its performance is changed, the whole system changes. By focusing on one part, the experience is based only on that part, although from this standpoint later conclusions are usually erroneously deduced on larger entities (without considering their connections and relations). A whole system will not be more effective if the focus is given only on one part – the whole system and especially its connections should be considered. Many times, only the initial conditions are (apparently) known under which final results are (prematurely) predicted. Rules regulate *pro futuro* cases wherein the time of enactment there are also unknown causal relations; they are hard to establish even for past or present states because causality 'is not a thing that causes an event, but a process…[in which] certain processes or events cause other processes or events' (Carnap, 1966, p. 190). This element of "one but many, and not vice versa" warns against conclusions that are only feedback into the regulatory cycle or other forms of decision-making in PA: such conclusions are based on connections and relations that evaluated solid rules/decisions do not have (any more) post festum. From this standpoint, so numerously emphasized ex-post regulatory impact assessment is shown as more complex: every experience enacted and implemented changes the one who acts and implements, while this modification affects, the quality of all consecutive experiences. Interdependence is present not only among individual parts, but is further reflected in the relations between groups of things, clusters, further to the social and natural (eco)system. In the same way, an agency's employee is grouped with his coworkers in a working team and with the management, they are connected with other agencies and stakeholders, further with other public bodies and the central government and the latter further with the international and supranational community of states, where connections are not only present in sequential connections, but also parallel vertical and horizontal lines that form a network of connections that also bypass, skip or jump through other connections (MLG). In time such dense connections resemble a spider net where a whole net moves when one part of it is moved. In each highly interdependent state system-wide changes may occur due to changes in any of its subsystems. Therefore, it matters how the relations are present in each case individually and specifically as they co-create, co-evolve, co-operate, and further transfer their (and other's) results. Relations (re) form not only their connections but also their results – they can adapt or self-organise, sometimes even in the absence of causal relations between them.[5]

Self-organization (or adaptation) means 'the appearance of a structure or pattern without an external agent imposing it' (Heylighen, 1999, p. 253). It addresses the spontaneous emergence of order (seen in, for example, the ice structure or in the snowflake) that is also a crucial element in chaos theory.[6] The British cybernetician Ashby introduced the principle of self-organization through which a dynamic system, independently of its type or composition, tends to evolve towards a state of equilibrium, when 'the system is complex enough, or large enough, to show: (1) a high intensity of selection by running to equilibrium, and also (2) that this selected set of states, though only a small fraction of the whole, is still large enough in itself to give room for a wide range of dynamic activities' (W. Ross Ashby, 1960, p. 231). In the same year as Ashby, von Foerster formulated the principle of order from noise: 'in the long run, only those components of the noise were selected which contributed to the increase of order in the system' (Foester, 1960, p. 48). The greater the number of random perturbations that affect a system, the faster the system will self-organize. Self-organization should not be equated with simple regime order – 'it tends towards "complex order" spontaneously by adaptation (when all parts are in equilibrium, they stop, become inflexible, and order tends to disappear) in a complex environment' (S. A. Kauffman, 1993, p. xv). A result of self-organisation is autopoiesis and/or a system's ability to reproduce itself.[7] Kauffman has demonstrated the spontaneous (natural) order exhibits itself as a consequence of autocatalytic reactions or the collective dynamics network.[8] A crucial feature of CAS is their capacity to generate *new order:* they produce something different, inventive and new. Self-organisation is the capability of systems to spontaneously produce order from the interaction of parts that based on their rules respond to feedback from other parts and their environment. British cybernetician Ashby introduced "the principle of self-organisation" through which a dynamic system, independently of its type or composition, tends to evolve towards a state of equilibrium, when

The system is complex enough, or large enough, to show: (1) a high intensity of selection by running to equilibrium, and also (2) that this selected set of states, though only a small fraction of the whole, is still large enough in itself to give room for a wide range of dynamic activities. Thus, selection for complex equilibria, within which the observer can trace the phenomenon of adaptation, must not be regarded as an exceptional and remarkable event: **it is the rule** (W. Ross Ashby, 1960, p. 231).

Spontaneous order. Order spontaneously emerges without the intervention of a central controller. Self-organisation as the principle should not be equated with simple regime of formal legal order – 'it tends towards "complex order" spontaneously by adaptation (when all parts are in equilibrium they stop, become inflexible, and order tends to disappear) in a complex environment' (S. A. Kauffman, 1993, p. xv). In the same year as Ashby, von Foerster formulated the principle of "order from noise": 'in the long run, only those components of the noise were selected which contributed to the increase of order in the system' (Foester, 1960, p. 48). The greater the random perturbations that affect a system, the more quickly the system will self-organise. A decision-maker should not only be prepared (to stop the new order of things) at the time of a proposal to do something new, but during the whole time in which proposal obtain content in mutual cooperation and later implementation with different stakeholders. Emergence and adaptation (or self-regulation) are the inevitable facts of life, so it is worthwhile to see how they are shown in agencies. From this point of view, (public) actions can be viewed as an element

Complexity Theory and Agencies

within the larger space of possibilities and different combinations. All cases are to some extent self-regulating until they reach the point in the perception of citizens or decision-makers that needs to be regulated on a different level. When actions and reactions are left alone, they *will* regulate *themselves*. It should not be disregarded that agencies are always embedded in other systems with their own rules (morals, values, habits, and practice) that will codetermine the first in complex equilibria. There are always parallel arrangements present along with the enacted ones. The challenge of spontaneous self-organization compels decision-makers to focus on the real-time, nonstop interactions that form their patterns (if not otherwise managed by them). Self-organization (originally developed in the context of physics and chemistry) hence describes the emergence of patterns of processes and interactions; complex collective behaviour can hence emerge from interactions among individual parts (be it a molecule, a swarm or a person) s that exhibit simple behaviour.

Emergence. Self-organization is closely connected with a puzzle as regards how new things or processes adapt to changing contexts. The order of chaos (Odell, 2003; Prigogine & Stengers, 1984) presented by self-organization 'is often associated with emergence, which means the appearance of a level of complexity more advanced than the existing components of a system' (Feltz, Crommelinck, & Goujon, 2006, p. 341). Emergence is not reducible to the properties of the elements (Feltz et al., 2006). The Nobel Prize-winning chemist Ilya Prigogine established all sufficiently complex systems can develop unpredictable emergent behaviour ('the interaction of a system with the outside world, its embedding in non-equilibrium conditions, may become in this way the starting point for the formation of new dynamic states of matter - dissipative structures' (Prigogine & Stengers, 1984, p. 143)) far from equilibrium (very small perturbations or fluctuations can become amplified into gigantic, structure-breaking waves). Under such conditions, dissipative structures and/or a system can reorganise itself (self-reorganisation) in new order through fluctuations (Nicolis & Prigogine, 1977).[9] The traditional thinking on the management of agencies neglects the predisposition of interconnections of this basic system - it looks only towards final goals (irrespective of how they are assembled) and assumes a single (of few) cause(s) rather than the multiple interrelated causations[10] or at least correlations that must to be checked. 'When the organism has to adapt (to get its essential variables within physiological limits) by working through an environment that is of the nature of a Black Box, then the process of trial and error is necessary, for only such a process can elicit the required information' (Ashby, 1960, p. 83). Having this in mind, Ashby built an adapter and/or the Homeostat, a device built to know its exact nature and to observe what will happen in various conditions. In all equality-at-the-start cases, stability is then upset by the environmental randomness, so to cope with it, variety should be put in by the installed "pointers" (step-functions) as intermediate targets that show a path towards main goals. Ashby named this ultrastability when second-order feedbacks[11] veto all states of equilibrium except those that leave each essential variable within its proper limits. All is not only more than the sum of its parts, but what is or could be 'all' *cannot* be known in advance; it emerges only expost through interactions.[12] With the emergence tightly connected characteristic is bifurcation: things emerge not only in a whole new way but they also split from the existing ones. The analysis of initial conditions is important, but decision makers should also consider that along the process things emerge and bifurcate. This calls for the continuation of the system's modification. A further characteristic of emergent property is its complex behaviour that emerges from simple rules. The challenge of emergence obliges public servants to be watchful and prompt in identifying and responding to changing patterns in administrated environments.

Collectivity. Rationality and rules emerge in some complex combinatory forms of collectivity (a result of emergence). It emerges through the mutual tensions of different parts in different combinations that produce a new result in some moment without the possibility to predict which factor was the prevailing one and what the next result will be. Collectivity puts public accountability and integrity of public bodies and their employees in a new light: to demand accountability, the consequences must be attributed to a specific action of a public agency or of an individual, while a result in the complex, nonlinear and adaptable system is always (at least somewhat) later different from the planned one, and thus unknowable. The challenge of collectivity can be put into the frame of accountability only when different scenarios are given upfront and reacted to them in the real-time dimension.

Self-catalytic reactions. Kauffman introduced a mechanism that could explain the emergence of hierarchical ordered levels with the help of catalysis: a set of chemical reactions becomes self-catalytic in the vicinity of a *sufficient variety* of other molecules. The basis for life lies in catalysis: chemical reactions start in the presence of at least two molecules, where one acts as a catalyst, which starts the reaction (as the lock and key that fits together, or metabolism). 'If a sufficiently diverse mix of molecules accumulates somewhere, the chances that an autocatalytic system—a self-maintaining and self-reproducing metabolism—will spring forth becomes a near certainty' (S. A. Kauffman, 1993, p. 27). Collectively, autocatalytic sets are the example of self-organisation, not reducible to parts, but irreducible from their connections and processes. Changes occur in sufficiently complex non-equilibrium systems, that address each other in the key-lock metaphor: 'at a certain point, when the when the diversity of molecules is high enough and the ratio of reactions to molecules is high enough, it becomes expected that each molecule has at least one reaction leading to its formation catalyzed by at least one member of the reaction system. At this point the emergence of collectively autocatalytic systems becomes a near certainty' (S. A. Kauffman, 2010, p. 60).

Practice. In this manner to reductionism is added life, and the agency that arises with life produces Kauffman values, meaning, and action into the universe. The existence of agency takes us beyond reductionism to a broader scientific worldview, the existence of actions as subsets of events that occur among a wider set of events and possibilities surrounding the action. A mutually defining circle of concepts, jointly needed for one another, is what Wittgenstein meant by a language game. He has rejected the paradox of following and breaking the rule by treating the action in accordance with the rule as its *practice*: 'there is a way of grasping a rule which is not an interpretation, but which is exhibited in what we call "obeying the rule" and "going against it" in actual cases... And hence also "obeying a rule" is a practice' (Wittgenstein, 1986, p. 81). That complexity can be addressed/revealed solely through *practice* confirms also the cybernetic idea that *the (real) purpose of the system is what it does* (Beer, 2002). A crucial unity of knowledge, variety, and action, the latter being the natural disclosure of the first two, is also reflected in the arrangement of agencies. They are mainly what the real-world experience shows; they are not what they should formally be. The probability of cooperative changing behaviour (a phase transition) thus rises proportionately with the higher degree of frequency of exchanges or contacts.

Robustness, Resilience, Flexibility, and Agility (Exploration-of-the-Space-of-Possibilities). Darwin envisioned that evolution occurs by mutation or the adaptive incremental accumulation of useful variants, while Kauffman told us what kinds of systems can evolve successfully by random variation and selection for fitter variants (fitness landscape).[13] The relation between selection and self-organization, Kauffman presented as the structure of fitness landscapes as 'any well-defined property and its distribution across an ensemble' (S. A. Kauffman, 1993, p. 37)[14] to demonstrate the spontaneous emergence of order, *i.e.* the occurrence of self-organisation, while the latter is based on adaptability. Evolution or selection depends on the moves of an adapting population to arbitrary regions of the landscape where the fit is higher. Adaptation normally progresses through small changes involving a local search in the space of possibilities (Jacob, 1977); progress occurs by adaptive processes that gradually accumulate advantages *vis-à-vis* their competitors in the selected context-dependent environment. The similar logic applies with agencies: if changing contexts are not appropriately addressed, situations will spontaneously – due to the very richness of interactions (Waldrop, 1993) – regulate themselves towards their equilibrium (S. Kauffman, 1996; Prigogine & Stengers, 1984). The fitness landscape is in organisational terms more known or similar to the notions of robustness, resilience, flexibility and agility; they can be seen as the results of the exploration of the space of possibilities[15] that has various alternatives at hand to operate successfully. The 'adaptive evolution' of an agency in a given context can be viewed as its 'fitness landscape' or a hill climb process:

The rational robustness applies to accountability. Reason and knowledge cannot be monopolized and are distributed and represented at multiple places in the system. If one part is taken down, the others are still present; there will be no essential loss of rationality or knowledge in other parts because of this. Although the system could be changed as a whole, it remains robust in case of damage (or the abuse of power). Formal decision-makers are usually as intelligent as other people are (the first have only formal powers to decide). A new decision can emerge only from numerous and diverse interactions. This is the argument for public participation in the form of collective intelligence.

Impossibility to grasp the basic elements of CAS by changing challenges into solutions. It would be a mistake to simply change the above-mentioned challenges into solutions. New results will still be due

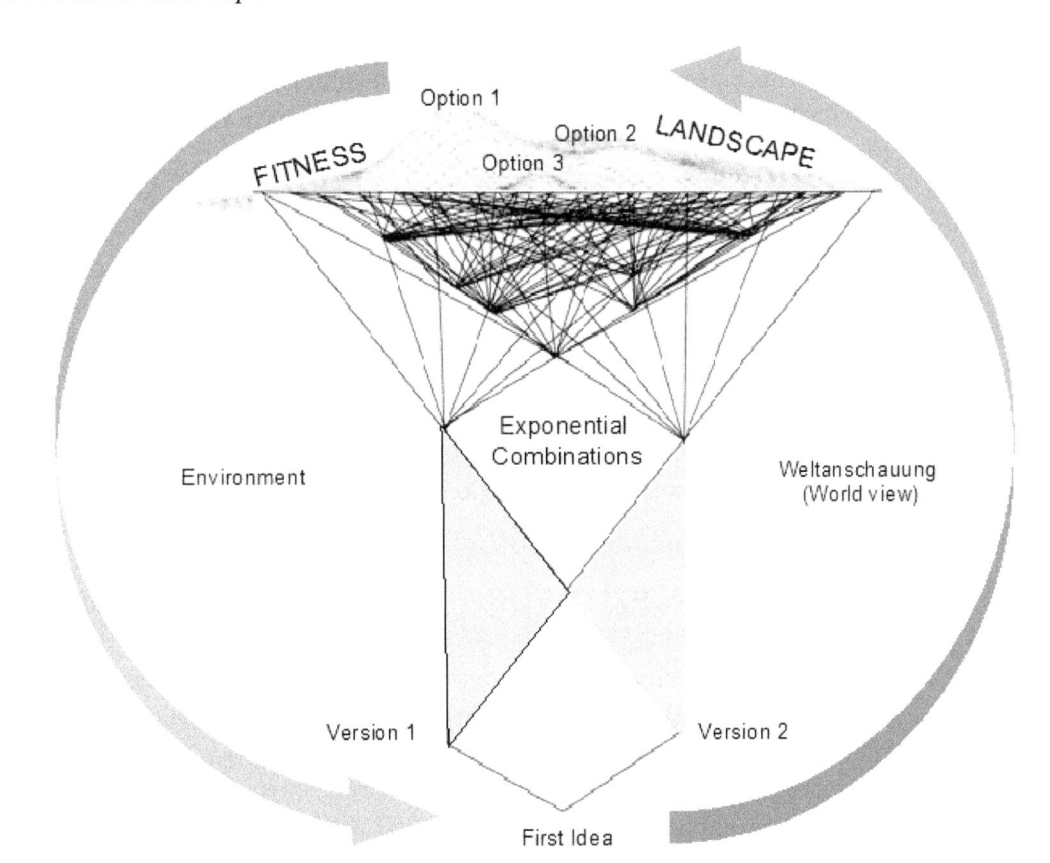

Figure 3. Fitness landscape

to self-organisation and emergence, the irreversibility of time, complexity, interdependent processes, among structures and actors – unknown. The same argument shows that the ex-ante and ex-post RIA methods are unsuccessful, despite their popularity even in the document that favours systems approaches (OECD, 2017). Actions of CASs can be explained and followed/changed in a short period of time but never fully predicted. Combinations emerge, rearrange, diminish, grow, or stop. In CASs, there is only a possible solution: it could be in a self-corrected learning model of decision-making that must be, due to different versions of rationality, at first communicated in cognitively open domains, to convince also the structurally closed ones. *Interactions change the intentions, tools, and goals of the act.* Interactions among parts when the system runs (when a legal act is valid vis-à-vis other valid acts and the environment) can change daily; a factual state of affairs hence becomes different from the one envisaged in a preparatory phase. A solution for this can be stochastic indicators and their relevant sensors: such indicators cannot not only spot changes, but also impartially determine relevant connections (e.g. randomised algorithms compare nearby neighbours and switch to one with the highest efficiency, known as stochastic local search), because 'groups whose members represent disparate points of view or special interest populations may err by focusing on their shared perspectives and thereby negating any advantage that accrues from multiple sources of diverse input' (Stasser & Titus, 1985, p. 1477).

The stochastic indicators/sensors are a tool for the more successful management of the above-mentioned challenges. A network can be put together, but it instantly produces more or less unmanageable unpredictable processes. Actions are not based on information but on our *attention* that collects the former. Decision-action adjustments can be improved with the focus on *relations* in the real-time dimension. The cause of the 'time gap' is in different positions between the time of their evaluation and the time when they were in a time of action. In the evaluation time, they are already different in content or in place, connected with different things than before. To manage such positions, there must be real-time sensors by which a controller could gain insight into a current state of affairs in the shortest time possible. Indicators are randomization elements[16] and should be stochastically taken from a larger list to prevent subjectivity. The mentioned challenges can only be systematically monitored, while decisions and/or adjustments should be in the meantime based on several stochastic indicators that can go over the current state of affairs, over the conventional, accepted wisdom in a relevant field. The ongoing evaluation and monitoring system should be an integral component of all viable systems that address CAS. Evaluation and monitoring provide the information necessary to refine and improve the functioning of the system over time. The true choice is usually not to follow a rule per se, because it is rarely given in isolation. A true choice is rather between the different but always interconnected rules/parts and various authorities/stakeholders that enact/implement them. The common characteristics mentioned above of CASs can be valuable perspectives for the evaluation of agencies' actions or future doings.

THE ADDED VALUE OF COMPLEXITY FOR THE MANAGEMENT OF AGENCIES

The importance of complexity for decision makers or leaders is in their recognition that agencies' problems are difficult to grasp due to complex system behaviour that emerges from individual parts toward collective behaviours. They should understand that most public systems nowadays are the complex ones that reveal the characteristics of complex systems like the adaptability or self-organisation and emergence. By knowing such elements, agencies (public systems) could be modelled differently to be able to address them effectively, and thus overcome the limitations of reductionistic tactics. They should understand also that the utmost number of contacts and connections between legal actors/agencies evolve outside the formal canals established by the law, between areas that spread beyond the legal boundaries, where essential actions are also performed, and additional by individuals or communities of stakeholder that, though influenced by, are not the part of the legal frame in which agencies operate. 'Organizations themselves exist only as a complex set of social processes, some of which reproduce existing modes of behavior and others that serve to challenge, undermine, contradict, and transform current routines' (Scott & Davis, 2016, p. 20). As CAS spontaneously self-organise and adapt for public agencies the complete absence of hierarchic coordination and control and/or the absence of a controlling entity, self-adaptiveness and learning from experience can be misleading, because in such cases public agencies akt as policy-makers, not implementers. A controlling entity a) starts the system, coordinates and controls it (with the control thresholds and to them accustomed (re)actions) and b) it ends it when goals are achieved or when the system's results increasingly move away from the desired goals. Within a) also the classical – statistical, descriptive and other research – methods of evaluation and logical thinking can be helpful if grouped with the understanding of inevitable bifurcations, new emerged states can in the process due to changes provided (ex-ante determined) new rules for successful goal attainment. Understanding the elements of complexity can give a better understanding of public management in the dynamic environment.

A system does not 'start in vacuum'; the current state of affairs emerged outside the system decision makers just want to start, and a later evaluation of conditions will be different as planned because it cannot consider all the present conditions (outside the system) and their possibilities (in connection with a system). The concepts of emergence, adaptation, or self-organisation in the system are challenging in terms of the classic legal principle of certainty and predictability. The classical legal reactions are without tools for unintended, unplanned, or unprogrammed actions, driven not by command and control but by chance, adaptation, and emergence. In the flexible, dynamic environment, an approach is needed that is based on the flexible management of policies and their implementation, rather than on the classic policy planning and mechanical implementation. The need to have flexible tools that can address unanticipated, emergent changes, and changes within changes with appropriate adaptations puts decision-makers in a position where the flexibility, delegation, and discretion are urgent for desired outcomes. In such a position, only a desired goal is firmly left to decision makers, while for other states, intermediate targets or system conditions must be met.

The implications of such an approach to public management are significant in terms of governance, since so much of the present governance and accountability frameworks are based on assumptions of predictability, the elimination of uncertainty by planning and analysis methodologies, and control by compliance. An approach that might be described as 'flexible navigation' demands considerable change in the common assumptions and principles concerning governance, accountability and compliance (Rhodes, Murphy, Muir, & Murray, 2010, p. 206).

The characteristics of the exploration-of-the-space-of-possibilities show the need to have various alternatives at hand to operate successfully. Somehow or even by chance, Mintzberg's division of strategies resembles along the mentioned characteristics also to the characteristic of emergence. Strategies as ex post facto results of decisional behaviour and as strategies as a priori guidelines to decision making. A priori strategy is *intended* strategy, in a realised part it is a *deliberate* strategy, in the nonrealized one it is an *unrealised* strategy. The ex post facto strategy is *the realised* strategy; it was never intended or got changed along the way; in this part, it is understood as the *emergent* strategy (Mintzberg, 1979). 'The fundamental difference between deliberate and emergent strategies is that whereas the former focuses on direction and control-getting desired things done-the latter opens up this notion of "strategic learning".

Defining strategy as intended…effectively precludes the notion of strategic learning. Once the intentions have been set, attention is riveted on realizing them, not on adapting them…The emergent strategy itself implies learning what works, taking one action at a time in search of that viable pattern or consistency. It is important to remember that emergent strategy means, not chaos, but, in essence, unintended order' (Mintzberg & Waters, 1985, pp. 270–271). In both cases, 'actively monitoring, understanding, and controlling the criteria by which daily resource allocation decisions are made at all levels of the organization are among the highest impact challenges a manager can tackle in the strategy development process' (Christensen & Raynor, 2013). In real life, there is an ideal type, neither of intended nor of emergent strategy, but a combination of both, where the strategy is implemented on the one hand under the original intentions and the other (still within the framework of the basic postulates of an institution) with currently changing conditions. Such differentiation of strategies also allows for a fundamental understanding on the implementation of regulations, which, due to changing conditions in a complex environment, must necessarily contain elements of adaptation (which often lacks in regulation).

Agencies… are complex, dynamic, non-linear, probabilistic, networked systems. Their respective environments – complex systems themselves – form and interlaced and interwoven, dynamic, non-linear system ecology [such] … systems … form a network of complex systems which are essentially fuzzy, opaque, and absolutely inscrutable to conventional reason. Complex systems care their own rules, qualities and behavioural patterns which are fundamentally different from those of simple systems (Malik, 2011, p. 25). This is the reason why institutions' results are always somehow different from the original human intent or purpose. They "live their own life" and/or generate their own ways (of doing things); from the first point of view, this could be the awkward conclusion, but when someone begins, e.g., with only four intentional elements, complexity, that is, combinations cause 256 permutations and 35 combinations. Therefore, the actual 'personality' of the agencies is never determined by them, but how they administer numerous processes in their internal and external environment. And decision-makers should at least roughly know where they stand in the real time frames. Instead of investing large resources on accurate future predictions, regulators could refine and enhance their ability to detect and measure changes and act accordingly, *i.e.*, to learn what is effective and efficient as a reaction to unexpected opportunities and challenges. Protagoras saying that "man is the measure of all things" could be thus changed into "the measure of all things is the measure (and reaction)".[17] The illusion of certainty could be therefore dispelled with the measure-and-react (emergent) strategy: '[r]ather than predicting how people will behave and attempting to design ways to make consumers respond in a particular way…we can instead measure directly how they respond to a whole range of possibilities, and react accordingly. In other words, the shift from "predict and control" to "measure and react" is not just technological… but psychological. Only once we concede that we cannot depend on our ability to predict the future are we open to a process that discovers it' (Watts, 2011, p. 196). The measure-and-react (emergent) strategy can be seen as a consequence of 'behavior of integral, aggregate, whole systems unpredicted by behaviours of any of their components or subassemblies of their components taken separately from the whole' (Fuller & Applewhite, 1997). Buckminster Fuller called this synergy and/or *synergetics*. Such a strategy opens new possibilities to experiment with new things, approaches, or methods. The mentioned strategy can be seen as nothing more than the other word for performance management. Although science is in large part based on experiments, legal science uses them very rarely. Although science is essentially based on experiments, legal science rarely uses them, which to a certain extent represents the paradox of legal "science." Relying only on past experiences of existing regulations is tantamount to carrying out a particular experiment without reconfirming it. History does not repeat itself, so it is not a completely reliable element to rely on completely (sometimes a slight change could lead to a completely different historical event or result).

There is an obvious need to be flexible and on the other hand still to be certain, predictable, and accountable, as they are not only the classic demands of legal states, but also of a human condition of being. The Europeanization, globalisation, decentralization of power, territorial and institutional decentralization, transformation of various legal systems according to the same EU goals or directions, or the increased legal complexity in vertical and horizontal networks fit into the first need, while a demand to be certain and accountable after all should also be considered. System theory can offer solutions for both parts by forming a "flexible system" (taken by itself this is a contradiction, because each system is flexible, otherwise there is no system). With this emphasis on context or contingencies, it is evident – due to many combinations and permutations – that a full administration of such a complex field is not possible. Before giving up attempts to anticipate what will happen and how, there is a possibility of the so-called *measure-and-react strategy* (Watts, 2011). Planners should rely less on making predictions about long-term tendencies and more on quick reactions to changes on the ground (Mintzberg, 1979). This *measure-and-react approach* gives an emphasis on *performance indicators*, but also here precautions are needed; decision-makers should give proportionate emphasis on multiple (stochastic) criteria. The latter are nothing but *norms* derived from human aspirations and values that should always be considered as *intentional* rather than conditional elements of human action (Parsons, 1985). Criteria as norms are always up to a point subject to human interpretation and/or manipulation. It is crucial to have not only means through which decisions or answers can be made but also different (systemic, complex and other) perspectives by which outcomes are only inputs for other outcomes. The conceptual framework that integrates individual-group activities with institutional forms and the latter with societal institutions is the first step, but not the last. Practice, evaluation, and corrections are always needed. They all are part of adaptation that along the dynamic elements of reality represent the *sine qua non* of our lives.

RESPONSIVENESS, ADAPTABILITY, AGILITY, ROBUSTNESS, AND PRISTINE RELATIONS

The Nobel Prize-winning chemist Ilya Prigogine established that all sufficiently complex systems (and agencies as organisations are such as well) can develop unpredictable emergent behaviour ('the interaction of a system with the outside world, it's embedding in nonequilibrium conditions, may become in this way the starting point for the formation of new dynamic states of matter - dissipative structures' (Prigogine & Stengers, 1984, p. 143)) far from equilibrium (very small perturbations or fluctuations can become amplified into gigantic, structure-breaking waves). In such conditions, dissipative structures and/or a system may reorganise itself (self-reorganisation) in new order through fluctuations (Nicolis & Prigogine, 1977) (an example is chemical changes in ice by supplying heat towards the boiling water, vapour, and steam). As *ipso facto* social systems (social [in]formal institutions) are also dynamic and complex, they should be equipped with the appropriate dynamic, adaptable, robust and responsive tools by which the environment can be addressed (the social system will otherwise "regulate itself", seen as the emergence of new behaviour, fashion, customs, popular songs, movies and/or a spontaneous detour of traffic due to traffic accident).

By giving up the illusion of certainty, this enables us to enjoy and explore the complexity of the world in which we live by exploring ways of recognising types and the estimation of degrees of uncertainty and experimentation with representations to find the most transparent way to communicate and explain risks. 'There is a consensus today that the public has a right to information; but there is not yet a consensus the public also has a right to get this information in a clear and not misleading way' (Gigerenzer, 2003). Like taxation, also information needs informed representation: 'while right-to-know policies required simply that existing government reports and other documents be made available to the public, targeted transparency policies require that government agencies, companies, and other private-sector organisations collect, standardise, and release factual information to inform public choices' (Fung, Graham, & Weil, 2007, p. 28).

Even the most democratic approaches are of little value if people do not understand and use them accordingly. To survive, institutions need to retain and improve their *alignment with the external world* (as for drivers to be agile on the road), and this should be similar to the law: be certain and at the same time agile, adaptable *vis-à-vis* context in which it is used. Robustness is the ability to cope with unforeseen and foreseen changes in the environment without adapting. Flexibility is the ability to react to foreseen and unforeseen changes in the environment in a preplanned manner (predictable risk).[18] Agility is the ability to react to unforeseen changes in the environment in an unforeseen and unplanned manner (unpredictable uncertainty).[19] Resilience is the ability to survive foreseen and unforeseen changes in the environment that have a severe and enduring impact (Husdal, 2010).[20] A successful organisation should prepare alternatives to cope with different planned scenarios (flexibility), and should have a capacity of quick formation of responses to unanticipated situations (agility). A result of this is resilience (an ability to quickly return to its normal/previous condition after a stressful situation) or even robustness, when such a critical situation cannot affect organisation practices. Intuitively, robustness can be seen as the best for organisation, but it does not enable learning (an organisation is not a boxer). The organisational structure needs confrontation of its established values, norms, and practices in order to increase its capability of adaptation. An agency needs to change to 'stay the same', it needs to maintain its relations at a sufficiently high level to retain its unique identity. An agency reflects a sustainable institutional system when it cultivates the capacity to plan, create, regulate, implement, and check its results according to its purposes, tasks, and goals. Through this, the agency self-replicates and self-constructs its new missions, within the constraints of external and internal structures. If it is successful at this, the agency can set and push its own milestones of autonomy (if political interests or inconsistencies are put aside). The "good" side of the Covid-19 crisis was that it allowed at least approximate daily monitoring of the state of affairs (the number of tested, infected and deceased people) and responding appropriately to changed conditions — this situation very plastically shows how responsiveness, adaptability, agility and robustness are needed in the law due to inevitability of dynamic changes.

Complexity is not enough considered in the public administration, although its elements of interaction, emergence, self-organisation, or adaptability are directly reflected in the notion of public interest. It is more than the sum of its parts, it binds together particularities with a new, emerged content, that is not present in the parts themselves. The same stands for other common notions among people that group them together, that make from the people community that maintain/conserve relations among them and establishes them as a social group. *Such a group emerges only from people's interactions, and not from individuals themselves.* For agencies, the same holds: they form social bonds (and results) based on interactions and not on employees or agencies *per se*. These interactions are very complex and all are unknowable to people. The so-called Newton dream began with the publication of his *Principia;* his work gave an integrated mathematical handling of motion on earth and other objects in outer space. Newton's laws of motion and gravitation were very impressive for hundreds of years, as they carried a promise: 'to understand all of nature, in the way that he was able to understand the solar system, through principles of physics that could be expressed mathematically' (Weinberg in Sweet Stayer & Ravindra, 1990, p. 285). The method of mechanism was the combination of experiment and mathematical analysis, that has been outmoded by the special relativity, quantum mechanics, complexity, wave mechanics, uncertainty principle, etc. Today, Newton's dream can become more real with the existence and calculation of large and various data sets (that hide/show patterns and correlations) based on computing power and different software applications to make informed decisions based on algorithms. To manage CASs their changing patterns (results in time periods) should be understood. The same applies to the agency. Interrelations among CAS can be based also on their seven basics and/or the properties of aggregation, nonlinearity, flow, and diversity on the mechanisms of tags, internal models, and building blocks (John Henry Holland, 1995). Along these and other interrelations, more attention can also be paid to the behaviour of agencies, the emergence of new connections and things, their adaptability, and/or self-organisation. Algorithms based on large databases can extract patterns that could also be useful for the management of agencies.

Detection of (non)compliance or (un)desirable behaviour and aligning them with agencies purposes and tasks is not based on the simple rule of thumb, intuition, and common sense. When to them the basic elements of system theory are added, agencies and employees are on a good path towards success. Successes are usually 'the result of skilled executives who correctly identified the critical tasks of their organizations, distributed authority in a way appropriate to those tasks, infused their subordinates with a sense of mission, and acquired sufficient autonomy to permit them to get on with the job' (Wilson, 1989, p. 365). If an agency is to have a sense of mission, if constraints are to be minimized, if authority is to be decentralized, and if officials are to be judged on the basis of the outputs, they produce rather than the inputs they consume, then legislators, judges, and lobbyists will have to act against their own interests. They will have to say "no" to influential constituents, forgo the opportunity to expand their own influence, and take seriously the task of judging the organizational feasibility as well as the political popularity of the proposed new program (J. Q. Wilson, 1989, p. 376). The system and complexity theory will be elaborated later as at first the "mind should be open" to them. The same holds for the Weberian, self-sufficient concept of in-house operations in a government organization ("machine bureaucracies") that is no longer seems adequate: 'via their IT needs (as well as in political and other ways) government organizations are increasingly defined and constituted also by their external relationships, partners, and dependencies' (Dunleavy, Margetts, Tinkler, & Bastow, 2006, p. 15). Technical progress is indeed far ahead of the human one. A metaphor of "standing on the shoulders of giants" is more present in the first part than in the second part, but personal choices are all people must have to have their goals flourish, and they are such when their *relationships* improve. It is no coincidence that the notion of (personal) "relationships" comes from "relations", which are also the constituent parts of system theory. In his study of a government agency, the Tennessee Valley Authority, Selznick found that formal organisation can be along the rationally ordered structure and stated goals seen as an *adaptive social structure* that exhibits (in)formal co-optation as a proces of (in)formal absorbance of new elements into the leadership structure as a means of survival, stability or existence (1949). An organisation has a life of its own; as a system it resists complete outside control, but it is forced to adapt to other centres of interest and power to remain "alive". Selznick in 1951 claimed that any kind of institutional structure should be treated as an autonomous system, with its inner potentialities and weaknesses, even though this autonomy is limited and behaviour is a resultant of many interacting forces (2014). Selznick's "organizational weapon" is to search for *latent* structures, a unique set of commitments, and/or an emergent pattern of adherence and control, of self-perpetuating, interlocking commitments. Organisations, agencies as adaptive social structures should thus evolve under *responsive* law (Nonet & Selznick, 2001) as a reasoned effort to realize an ideal of polity that is achieved by periodical studies of agencies and their redesign to improve their ability to fulfil public expectations. This is done using a responsive form of governance mix between sociology, law, philosophy, and politics. It was already mentioned in this work that problem solving is based on the principles through which problems in their context are elaborated. This is similar to the responsive law that Selznick describes as principles-based and problem-centred rather than rule-centred, less interested in rule-compliance than in pursuing the reasons behind the rule and energies mobilising for the achievement of public purposes, which requires respect for the needs of the enterprise (Selznick, 1994, p. 470).

Baldwin and Black claim that 'to be "really responsive", regulators have to respond not merely to firms' compliance responses but also to their attitudinal settings; to the broader institutional environment of the regulatory regime; to the different logics of regulatory tools and strategies; to the regime's own performance; and finally to changes in each of these elements' (2007, p. 17). These settings are aligned with the enforcement functions of detection, response, enforcement, assessment, and modification:

This kind of a regulatory responsive framework after which follows the development of rules and tools that are fit for purpose can be good for good discussion while in the practice of public agencies are usually not found. At first, every service, every system behaves in a way that *its structure allows it*; a system encounters problem whenever its structure cannot adapt to different conditions. If such, the above-given frameworks, would be enough to solve an adaptability problem, there would be no problems with responsiveness. Differences in conditions or constant changes are the *sine qua non* of life, and a successfulness of agency is conditioned with its level of responsiveness and mutual adaptability. This cannot be done by agencies *per se*: their *employees should do this* – they are systems as well. Here an old distinction can be used between mechanical and organic solidarity to show also the difference between retributive and distributive justice on which working guidelines can be made for public agencies.

For Durkheim 'social harmony derives essentially from the division of labour…it consists of a co-operation that is automatically produced by the fact that each person follows his own interest' (1984, p. 149). He distinguishes between mechanical and organic solidarity. The first represents the social unity of small, homogenous societies and the second societies distinguished by a relatively complex division of labour. The first socially integrates members of a society with common values and beliefs that constitute an internal "collective conscience" among individual members which leads them to cooperate. The second emerges out of the demand of individuals for one another's skills; due to a greater division of labour, individuals specialize and are thus more interdependent, although distinguished parts of a larger, living body. In the first group identity is confirmed by punishing violators who infringe what is sacred to the group, in the second social harmony derives from the division of labour (due to its spontaneity, there is no need for a coercive apparatus to create it or to sustain it).[21] Based on the mentioned Durkheim's distinction Selznick (1969) distinguishes two types of law: in the first, to impose and reaffirm the common conscience, the group resorts to *punitive law, constraint and repressive sanctions* among equal persons, while in the second *restitutive* law prevails among different persons. This is the law of *cooperation;* its purpose is to re-establish social equilibrium by making a man whole again *i.e.*, compensating him for losses incurred when someone fails to fulfil his legal responsibilities. Durkheim's very interesting claim

Table 1. A really responsive enforcement framework (Baldwin & Black, 2007, pp. 26–27)

	Detection	**Response**	**Enforcement**	**Assessment**	**Modification**
Compliance Response	1. Are objectives clear? 2. Do regulatees supply accurate data on their activities? 3. Do detection processes reveal the extent of undesirable as well as noncompliant activity?	1. Does the regulator have the tools to deal with the full variety of compliance responses?	1. Are objectives clear? 2. Do enforcement strategies deal with 'off screen' activities? 3. Are strategies optimally targeted?	1. Are objectives clear? 2. Can compliance records be measured and related to outcome objectives?	1. Can changes be made when achieving objectives will require new tools/strategies?
Attitudinal Setting	1. Are there ideas/ cultures/ traditions - within the regulated population or the regulatory body – that impact on effective detection?	1. Do ideas/ cultures traditions affect the potential use of certain tools?	1. Do ideas/ cultures/ traditions affect the potential use of certain strategies?	1. Is assessment undermined by ideas/ cultures/ traditions (e.g. that may corrupt data supply/ quality)?	1. Are cultures consistent with a capacity and inclination to modify when necessary? 2. Is there awareness of the need to change tools/strategies in the policymaking culture?
Logics of Tools and Strategies	1. Do different tools/ strategies operate harmoniously to facilitate detection?	1. Are tools consistent or at tension?	1. Are strategies consistent or at tension? 2. Are positive combinations of strategy exploited? 3. Are known weaknesses of strategies dealt with?	1. Do the various assessment procedures operate consistently?	1. When modifications are carried out are interactions of logics taken into account?
Regime Performance	1. Are objectives clear? 2. Is the regulator confident about the accuracy of the detection system?	1. Does the system allow the performance of particular tools to be measured?	1. Are objectives clear? 2. Does the system allow the performance of particular strategies to be measured? 3. Can needs to adjust strategy be assessed?	1. Are objectives clear? 2. Do assessment methods link closely to objectives?	1. Are modifications based on evidence from assessments?
Change	1. Are objectives clear? 2. Can the detection regime cope with changes in objectives/operational arrangements/ resourcing/ regulate response?	1. Can new tools be resourced/ legislated for?	1. Can strategies be adjusted to cope with new risks and risk creators?	1. Can assessment methods be adjusted to cope with new risks risk creators/ objectives etc.?	1. Can modifications be introduced quickly enough to cope with changes in risk/ objectives etc.?

is that contracts are not the foundation of a social order, because they could be applied when social order already exists.[22] Contracts presume social order and cannot serve for its basis. Society here relies less on imposing uniform rules on everyone and more on regulating relations between different groups and persons, often through the greater use of contracts or similar regulatory tools.

From this follows two interesting inferences: as public agencies work in the complex environment and with various stakeholders, and a greater division of labour their solidarity is organic. This presupposes *restitutive law*, autonomy as it facilitates *the morality of cooperation* and an already established *social order*. If the contract is the supreme legal expression of cooperation (as the normal form of exchange) as Durkheim claimed, then contractual parties have a real need of one another. Different public agencies as complex entities, their work and funding should hence also be based on the expressed contractual corporation, not on the governmental or ministerial non-contractual constraint or repression. For Durkheim the object of administrative law 'is to fix how social functions should co-operate' (Durkheim, 1984, p.

166), when the intrinsic morality of cooperation is not developed enough or when there is no corporation at all. Here caution is needed because in the complex environment regulation cannot be very detailed; if it is such, it misses its aims already at the start and opens a room for inventive individual initiatives. Administrative law should – when social order is not developed enough – provide a frame and basic conditions on which corporation could evolve and further act, while in developed societies cooperation should prevail over repression, or distributive over retributive justice. This is similar to Piaget's stages of a child's moral development (1932)[23] where first imperatives, submission to older people (authority) and their rules (externality of rules) are present, while later became more alert to reciprocity, equality, and mutual respect.

During the first stage, justice is not distinguished from the authority of law: just is what is commanded by the adult. It is naturally during this first stage that retributive justice … proves stronger than equality … During a second stage, equalitarianism grows in strength and comes to outweigh any other consideration. In cases of conflict, therefore, distributive justice is opposed to obedience, to punishment, and very often even to those more subtle reasons that come to the fore in the third period.

Finally, during a third stage, mere equalitarianism makes way for a more subtle conception of justice which we may call "equity" and which consists in never defining equality without taking account of the way in which each individual is situated (Piaget, 1932, pp. 283–284).

Only in well-doing for others in a way of negative Golden rule can be found reciprocity over antagonism, autonomy over heteronomy, equality over inequality, respect over condemnation and cooperation over dissociation. By this way we came to the point Confucius named as *wu-wei,* or ruling through the power of virtue rather than force.[24] In such frames and/or where the effective division of labour prevails, contract precedes any kind of detailed or enforced legislation or regulation. This kind of regulatory approach is more appropriate to cope with the dynamic, flexible and complex environment that rigid rules. For the American psychiatrist William Glasser, pristine relations[25] are not built on power and competences, but on dialogue and negotiation. These could be Selznick's latent structures. In *polity i.e.,* institutional or organisational structure and context debate the mentioned administration of personal relations fits into the actor-based option of institutionalism that emphasises the impact which the decisions, interests, skills and competencies (through reason, but also empathy, emotions and values) of the relevant stakeholders (political, economic, non-governmental, the public) can use over the course of institutional development. It could be that an external control should be replaced with the internal one, with "choices that [not only] determine the course of our lives" (Glasser, 2010) but also of our institutions, it could be better to replace the punishment and similar styles a parent ministry *vis-à-vis* its subordinate public agency uses with the golden rule and negotiation on differences instead of force and retaliation. Such stance is not always possible (due to path dependencies, legal demands or unwilling people) but this does not relieve us from trying so.

REFERENCES

Amagoh, F. (2016). Systems and Complexity Theories of Organizations. In A. Farazmand (Ed.), *Global Encyclopedia of Public Administration, Public Policy, and Governance* (pp. 1–7). Springer International Publishing., doi:10.1007/978-3-319-31816-5_73-1

Anderson, P. (1999). Perspective: Complexity Theory and Organization Science. [world]. *Organization Science*, *10*(3), 216–232. doi:10.1287/orsc.10.3.216

Ashby, W. R. (1957). *An Introduction to Cybernetics*. Chapman and Hall.

Ashby, W. R. (1960). *Design for a Brain: The Origin of Adaptive Behavior*. Chapman and Hall.

Australian Public Service Commission. (2018). *Tackling wicked problems: A public policy perspective [Text]*. APSC. https://www.apsc.gov.au/tackling-wicked-problems-public-policy-perspective

Bach, T., & Wegrich, K. (Eds.). (2018). *The Blind Spots of Public Bureaucracy and the Politics of Non-Coordination*. Palgrave MacMillan.

Bache, I., & Flinders, M. V. (Eds.). (2005). *Multi-level Governance*. Oxford University Press.

Baldwin, R., & Black, J. (2007). Really Responsive Regulation. *The Modern Law Review*, (71), 59–94.

Beer, S. (1986). Recursions of Power. In R. Trappl (Ed.), *Power, Autonomy, Utopia: New Approaches Toward Complex Systems* (pp. 3–18). Plenum Press. doi:10.1007/978-1-4613-2225-2_1

Beer, S. (2002). What is cybernetics? *Kybernetes*, *31*(2), 209–219. doi:10.1108/03684920210417283

Berreby, D. (n.d.). Between Chaos and Order: What Complexity Theory Can Teach Business. *Strategy Business*. https://www.strategy-business.com/article/15099?gko=73fbc

Bovaird, T. (2008). Emergent Strategic Management and Planning Mechanisms in Complex Adaptive Systems. *Public Management Review*, *10*(3), 319–340. doi:10.1080/14719030802002741

Brown, D. R., & Harvey, D. F. (2006). *An Experiential Approach to Organization Development*. Pearson Prentice Hall.

Cairney, P. (2012). Complexity Theory in Political Science and Public Policy. *Political Studies Review*, *10*(3), 346–358. doi:10.1111/j.1478-9302.2012.00270.x

Camazine, S., & Sneyd, J. (1991). A model of collective nectar source selection by honey bees: Self-organization through simple rules. *Journal of Theoretical Biology*, *149*(4), 547–571. doi:10.1016/S0022-5193(05)80098-0 PMID:1943133

Carnap, R. (1966). *Philosophical Foundation of Physics: An Introduction to the Philosophy of Science* (M. Gardner, Ed.). Basic Books.

Chapman, J. (2004). *System Failure: Why Governments Must Learn to Think Differently*. Demos.

Christensen, C., & Raynor, M. (2013). *The innovator's solution: Creating and sustaining successful growth*. Harvard Business Review Press.

Confucius. (2003). *Confucius Analects: With Selections from Traditional Commentaries* (E. Slingerland, Trans.). Hackett Publishing Company.

DiMaggio, P. (1997). Culture and Cognition. *Annual Review of Sociology*, *23*(1), 263–287. doi:10.1146/annurev.soc.23.1.263

Dunleavy, P., Margetts, H., Tinkler, J., & Bastow, S. (2006). *Digital era governance: IT corporations, the state, and e-government.* Oxford University Press. doi:10.1093/acprof:oso/9780199296194.001.0001

Durkheim, E. (1984). *The Division of Labor in Society* (W. D. Halls, Trans.). Palgrave Macmillan. doi:10.1007/978-1-349-17729-5

Eagleman, D., & Brandt, A. (2017). *The Runaway Species: How Human Creativity Remakes the World.* Canongate Books.

Eckhart, R. (1987). Stan Ulam, John von Neumann, and the Monte Carlo Method. *Los Alamos Science, Special Issue*, (15), 131–137.

Eppel, E. A., & Rhodes, M. L. (2018a). Complexity theory and public management: A 'becoming' field. *Public Management Review*, 20(7), 949–959. doi:10.1080/14719037.2017.1364414

Eppel, E. A., & Rhodes, M. L. (2018b). Public Administration & Complexity—How to teach things we cannot predict? *Complexity. Governance & Networks*, 4(1), 1–9. doi:10.20377/cgn-61

European Commission. (2017). *European Semester: Thematic factsheet – Quality of public administration – 2017.* EC. https://ec.europa.eu/info/sites/info/files/file_import/european-semester_thematic-factsheet_quality-public-administration_en_0.pdf

Feltz, B., Crommelinck, M., & Goujon, P. (2006). *Self-organization and Emergence in Life Sciences.* Springer Science & Business Media. doi:10.1007/1-4020-3917-4

Foester, H. (1960). On Self-Organizing Systems and Their Environment. In M. C. Yovits & S. Cameron (Eds.), *Self-Organizing Systems* (pp. 31–50). Pergamon Press.

Frederickson, H. G., Smith, K. B., Larimer, C. W., & Licari, M. J. (2012). *The Public Administration Theory Primer.* Westview Press.

Fukuyama, F. (2012). *The Origins of Political Order: From Prehuman Times to the French Revolution.* Farrar, Straus and Giroux.

Fukuyama, F. (2014). *Political Order and Political Decay: From the Industrial Revolution to the Globalization of Democracy.* Farrar, Straus and Giroux.

Fuller, R. B., & Applewhite, E. J. (1997). *Synergetics: Explorations in the Geometry of Thinking.* MacMillan.

Fung, A., Graham, M., & Weil, D. (2007). *Full Disclosure.* Cambridge University Press. doi:10.1017/9780521699617

Gell-Mann, M. (2002). The Quark and the Jaguar (VIII edition). New York: W.H. Freeman & Company.

Gerrits, L. (2012). *Punching Clouds: An Introduction to the Complexity of Public Decision-Making.* ISCE PUB.

Gerrits, L., & Marks, P. (2017). *Understanding Collective Decision Making: A Fitness Landscape Model Approach.* Edward Elgar Publishing. doi:10.4337/9781783473151

Gharajedaghi, J. (2007). Systems Thinking, Third Edition: Managing Chaos and Complexity: A Platform for Designing Business Architecture (3 edition). Burlington, MA: Morgan Kaufmann.

Gigerenzer, G. (2003). Reckoning with Risk: Learning to Live with Uncertainty (Kindle version). London: Penguin UK.

Glasser, W. (2010). *Choice Theory: A New Psychology of Personal Freedom.* New York: Harper Collins e-books.

Grassé, P. P. (1959). La reconstruction du nid et les coordinations inter-individuelles chez Belicositermes natalensis et Cubitermes sp. La théorie de la Stigmergie: Essai d'interprétation du comportement des termites constructeurs. *Insectes Sociaux*, *6*(6), 41–80. doi:10.1007/BF02223791

Haynes, P. (2008). Complexity Theory and Evaluation in Public Management. *Public Management Review*, *10*(3), 401–419. doi:10.1080/14719030802002766

Haynes, P. (2015). *Managing Complexity in the Public Services.* Routledge. doi:10.4324/9781315816777

Heylighen, F. (1999). The Science Of Self-Organization And Adaptivity. In: Knowledge Management, Organizational Intelligence and Learning, and Complexity, in: The Encyclopedia of Life Support Systems, EOLSS, 253–280. Publishers Co. Ltd.

Holland, J. H. Holyoak, K. J., Nisbett, R. E., & Thagard, P. R. (1989). Induction: Processes of Inference, Learning, and Discovery. Cambridge: MIT Press.

Holland, J. H. (1995). *Hidden order: How adaptation builds complexity.* Addison-Wesley.

Husdal, J. (2010). A Conceptual Framework for Risk and Vulnerability in Virtual Enterprise Networks. In P. Stavros (Ed.), *Managing Risk in Virtual Enterprise Networks: Implementing Supply Chain Principles* (pp. 1–27). IGI Global. doi:10.4018/978-1-61520-607-0.ch001

Jacob, F. (1977). Evolution and tinkering. *Science*, *196*(4295), 1161–1166. doi:10.1126/science.860134 PMID:860134

Kauffman, S. (1996). At Home in the Universe: The Search for the Laws of Self-Organization and Complexity (Reprint edition). New York: Oxford University Press.

Kauffman, S. A. (1993). *The Origins of Order.* Oxford University Press. doi:10.1093/oso/9780195079517.001.0001

Kauffman, S. A. (2010). *Reinventing the Sacred: A New View of Science, Reason, and Religion.* Basic Books.

Kiel, L. D. (2014). Complexity Theory and Its Evolution in Public Administration and Policy Studies. *Complexity. Governance & Networks*, *1*(1), 71–78. doi:10.7564/14-CGN9

Klijn, E.-H. (2008). Complexity Theory and Public Administration: What's New? *Public Management Review*, *10*(3), 299–317. doi:10.1080/14719030802002675

Koliba, C., Gerrits, L., Rhodes, M. L., & Meek, J. W. (2016). Complexity theory, Networks and Systems Analysis. In C. Ansell & J. Torfing (Eds.), *Handbook on Theories of Governance* (pp. 364–379). Edward Elgar Publishing. doi:10.4337/9781782548508.00041

Koliba, C. J., Meek, J. W., Zia, A., & Mills, R. W. (2010). *Governance Networks in Public Administration and Public Policy*. Routledge.

Lodge, M. (2018). Accounting for Blind Spots. In T. Bach & K. Wegrich (Eds.), *The Blind Spots of Public Bureaucracy and the Politics of Non-Coordination* (pp. 29–48). Palgrave MacMillan.

Luhmann, N. (2013). *Introduction to Systems Theory* (P. Gilgen, Trans.). Polity Press.

Malik, F. (2011). *Corporate Policy and Governance: How Organizations Self-Organize*. Campus Verlag.

Maturana, H. R., & Varela, F. J. (1980). *Autopoiesis and Cognition: The Realization of the Living*. D. Reidel Publishing Company. doi:10.1007/978-94-009-8947-4

McCarthy, I., & Gillies, J. (2003). Organisational Diversity, Configurations and Evolution. In E. Mitleton-Kelly (Ed.), *Complex Systems and Evolutionary Perspectives on Organisations* (pp. 71–98). Emerald Group Publishing Limited.

Mintzberg, H. (1979). Patterns in Strategy Formation. [JSTOR. Retrieved from JSTOR.]. *International Studies of Management & Organization*, *9*(3), 67–86. doi:10.1080/00208825.1979.11656272

Mintzberg, H., & Waters, J. A. (1985). Of strategies, deliberate and emergent. *Strategic Management Journal*, *6*(3), 257–272. doi:10.1002/smj.4250060306

Mitleton-Kelly, E. (Ed.). (2003). *Complex Systems and Evolutionary Perspectives on Organisations*. Emerald Group Publishing Limited.

Morçöl, G. (2012). *A Complexity Theory for Public Policy*. Routledge.

Morgan, B., & Yeung, K. (2007). *An Introduction to Law and Regulation: Text and Materials*. Cambridge University Press. doi:10.1017/CBO9780511801112

Nicolis, G., & Prigogine, I. (1977). *Self-organization in nonequilibrium systems: From dissipative structures to order through fluctuations*. Wiley.

Nicolis, G., & Prigogine, I. (1989). *Exploring Complexity: An Introduction*. W.H. Freeman.

Nonet, P., & Selznick, P. (2001). *Law and Society in Transition: Toward Responsive Law*. Transaction Publishers.

Odell, J. (2003). Between Order and Chaos. *Journal of Object Technology*, *2*(6), 45–50. doi:10.5381/jot.2003.2.6.c4

OECD. (2017). *Systems Approaches to Public Sector Challenges: Working with Change*. OECD Publishing.

Parsons, T. (1985). *Talcott Parsons on Institutions and Social Evolution: Selected Writings*. University of Chicago Press.

Peters, B. G., & Pierre, J. (2012). *The SAGE Handbook of Public Administration*. SAGE. doi:10.4135/9781446200506

Piaget, J. (1932). *The Moral Judgement of the Child*. The Free Press.

Pollitt, C., Talbot, C., Caulfield, J., & Smullen, A. (2004). *Agencies: How Governments Do Things Through Semi-Autonomous Organizations*. Palgrave MacMillan.

Prigogine, I., & Stengers, I. (1984). *Order Out of Chaos*. Bantam Books.

Rhodes, M. L. (2008). Complexity and Emergence in Public Management. *Public Management Review*, *10*(3), 361–379. doi:10.1080/14719030802002717

Rhodes, M. L. Murphy, J., Muir, J., & Murray, J. A. (2010). *Public Management and Complexity Theory: Richer Decision-Making in Public Services*. New York: Routledge.

Rhodes, M. L., & MacKechnie, G. (2003). Understanding Public Service Systems: Is There a Role for Complex Adaptive Systems Theory? *Emergence*, *5*(4), 57–85. doi:10.1207/s15327000em0504_6

Rhodes, M. L., & Murray, J. (2007). Collaborative Decision Making in Urban Regeneration: A Complex Adaptive Systems Perspective. *International Public Management Journal*, *10*(1), 79–101. doi:10.1080/10967490601185740

Ridder, J. (2007). Factors for legal quality of administrative decision-making. In K. J. Graaf, J. H. Jans, A. T. Marseille, & J. Ridder (Eds.), *Quality of Decision-making in Public Law: Studies in Administrative Decision-making in the Netherlands* (pp. 31–51). Europa Law Publishing.

Room, G. (2011). *Complexity, Institutions and Public Policy: Agile Decision-making in a Turbulent World*. Edward Elgar Pub. doi:10.4337/9780857932648

Room, G. (2016). *Agile Actors on Complex Terrains: Transformative Realism and Public Policy*. Routledge. doi:10.4324/9781315660769

Rosenbloom, D., Kravchuk, R., & Clerkin, R. (2014). *Public Administration: Understanding Management, Politics, and Law in the Public Sector* (8th ed.). McGraw-Hill Education.

Rossi, P. H., Lipsey, M. W., & Freeman, H. E. (1999). *Evaluation: A Systematic Approach* (6th ed.). SAGE Publications.

Ruhl, J. B. (1996). Complexity Theory as a Paradigm for the Dynamical Law-and-Society System: A Wake-Up Call for Legal Reductionism and the Modern Administrative State. *Duke Law Journal*, *45*(5), 851–928. doi:10.2307/1372975

Scharpf, F. W. (1978). Inter-organisational policy studies:issues, concepts and perspectives. In K. Hanf & F. W. Scharpf (Eds.), *Interorganizational Policy Making: Limits to Coordination and Central Control* (pp. 345–370). SAGE Publications.

Schreyögg, G., & Sydow, J. (2009). *The Hidden Dynamics of Path Dependence: Institutions and Organizations*. Palgrave MacMillan.

Scott, W. R., & Davis, G. F. (2016). *Organizations and Organizing: Rational, Natural and Open Systems Perspectives*. Routledge.

Selznick, P. (1949). *TVA and the Grass Roots: A Study in the Sociology of Formal Organization*. University of California Press.

Selznick, P. (1969). *Law, Society, and Industrial Justice*. Russell Sage Foundation.

Selznick, P. (1994). *The Moral Commonwealth: Social Theory and the Promise of Community*. University of California Press. doi:10.1525/9780520354753

Selznick, P. (2014). *The Organizational Weapon: A Study of Bolshevik Strategy and Tactics*. Quid Pro Books.

Senge, P. M. (2010). *The Fifth Discipline: The Art & Practice of The Learning Organization*. Crown Publishing Group.

Snellen, I., & Klijn, E.-H. (2009). Complexity Theory and Public Administration: A Critical Appraisal. In G. Teisman, A. van Buuren, & L. M. Gerrits (Eds.), *Managing Complex Governance Systems* (pp. 17–36). Routledge.

Spitzer, D. (2007). *Transforming Performance Measurement: Rethinking the Way We Measure and Drive Organizational Success*. AMACOM.

Sweet Stayer, M., & Ravindra, R. (1990). Newton's Dream. *American Journal of Physics*, *58*(3), 285–286. doi:10.1119/1.16203

Teisman, G., van Buuren, A., & Gerrits, L. M. (2009). *Managing Complex Governance Systems*. Routledge. doi:10.4324/9780203866160

Teisman, G. R., & Klijn, E.-H. (2008). Complexity Theory and Public Management. *Public Management Review*, *10*(3), 287–297. doi:10.1080/14719030802002451

Verhoest, K., Roness, P., Verschuere, B., Rubecksen, K., & MacCarthaigh, M. (2010). *Autonomy and Control of State Agencies: Comparing States and Agencies*. Palgrave MacMillan. doi:10.1057/9780230277274

Waldron, J. (2011). The Rule of Law and the Importance of Procedure. In J. E. Fleming (Ed.), *Getting to the Rule of Law* (pp. 3–31). NYU Press.

Waldrop, M. M. (1993). *Complexity: The Emerging Science at the Edge of Order and Chaos*. Simon and Schuster.

Watts, D. J. (2011). *Everything Is Obvious: *Once You Know the Answer*. Crown Publishing Group.

Wilson, J. Q. (1989). *Bureaucracy: What Government Agencies Do and why They Do it*. Basic Books.

Wittgenstein, L. (1986). *Philosophical Investigations* (G. E. M. Anscombe, Trans.). Basil Blackwell.

Wright, S. (1931). Evolution in Mendelian Populations. *Genetics*, *16*(2), 97–159. doi:10.1093/genetics/16.2.97 PMID:17246615

ENDNOTES

1. Path-dependency as an element of complexity is firmly present also in agencies (this can be an additional reason for the use of complexity theory in the field of agencies). Pollitt et. al. confirmed this idea on the basis of a multiple case study in four states (Pollitt, Talbot, Caulfield, & Smullen, 2004) that was further confirmed by Verhoest et al. (Verhoest, Roness, Verschuere, Rubecksen, & MacCarthaigh, 2010) on the basis of a multiple case study in three states and/or 226 agencies.

2. Public officials who work in agencies exhibit all elements of CAS; already from the types of learning and their basic corresponding actions taken from Bloom's taxonomy can be seen that the static or Weberian bureaucratic point of view fits mainly to (from the most fit to the least): *knowledge* (recalling facts), comprehension (capacity to see and understand relationships), *application* (use of knowledge), analysis (deconstruction and investigation of knowledge), synthesis (combining information into a new connected unit of knowledge) and evaluation (judging the value or appropriateness). The classic view on public agencies can be equated with "knowledge", less with "skills" and even less with "competencies". If we all want effective and efficient public agencies, they should also be creative at their doings. The existent legal order is only one element among others that surround public and private institutions. To be creative various options should be allowed and proliferated, risk-tolerance enabled and wrong answers creatively dissolved through experience. For Brandt and Eagleman spark of creativity comes from taking ideas from one place and applying them in another one; a trick is to surround oneself with many different inputs and influences, where new information is combined with the old one. Inputs are constantly being smashed with other inputs. These are constantly re-configured in the brain. Inputs are recombined with what is already in the brain's memory. The brain takes in inputs and then it twists those to make something new. Creativity is about refashioning what already exists. The human brain constantly works over the sensory data it receives – and the fruit of that mental labour is new versions of the world. People learn facts and generate fictions, we master what is, and envisage what-ifs (Eagleman & Brandt, 2017). Public agencies (as the examples of human collective doings) alter what is already known and "bend, break and blend" them with new inputs to create something new. Each public agency exhibits more complex relations as they were predicted or determined in a legal act that created it. Lawyers should know this, as also the law is only one part of human interactions. There is a context of surrounding things, relations, and matters that affects/alters the mentioned interactions, always on the edge or balance between the repetition of known acts and prediction of new ones.

3. Multi-level governance as an analytical model assesses how it captures the changing nature of decision making, and as a normative model assesses a mode of allocating authority – both, in the context of complexity (Bache & Flinders, 2005).

4. This effect of newly invented things among individuals can be used also as a distinction between public institutions and public organisations: only the first can produce new things and are able to adapt what is best for the public (interest), while the second can be seen just as a group of individuals, a collective.

5. This is known as "structural coupling" (conservation of adaptation): 'in the history of interactions of a composite unity in its medium, both unity and medium operate in each interaction as independent systems that, by triggering in each other a structural change, select in each other a structural change' (Maturana & Varela, 1980, p. xxi). Pairing or coupling between a system and its environment affects only structures of the first and of the second that is relevant to these structures. Structural

6   coupling is present in the nature (e.g., a crab that lives in a sea snail shell) or in the society (e.g., a horse and its rider, parliamentarian coalition). Such entities are not glued together, so decoupling is always possible.

6   Chaos theory is based on the Prigonine's notion (Prigogine & Stengers, 1984) that order and organization can arise "spontaneously" out of disorder and chaos through a process of "self-organization" (lat. *ordo ab chao*).

7   Autopoiesis is the idea that different parts of the system interact in a way to create and re-create the parts of the system; through its parts the system reproduces itself (e.g. a living cell) (Maturana & Varela, 1980).

8   In 1965, he programmed the $N = 100$ gene network (now known as the Kauffman/Boolean network), with each gene receiving $K = 2$ randomly chosen inputs from among 100. Such a network has 2^{100} states. 'It turned out from numerical evidence that the median number of states on a state cycle was *the square root of N*...Self-organisation that confines patterns of model gene activities to tiny regions of the network's state space arises spontaneously in these networks. There is order for free' (S. A. Kauffman, 2010, p. 110).

9   Dissipative structures 'are ways in which open systems exchange energy, matter, or information with their environment and which when pushed 'far-from-equilibrium' create new structures and order. The Bénard cell is an example of a physico-chemical dissipative structure' (Mitleton-Kelly, 2003, p. 32).

10 The traps of non-systems thinking lie in two simple dimensions; firstly, avoiding the inevitable interconnectivity between variables – the trap of reductionism, and secondly, working on the basis of a single unquestioning perspective – the trap of dogmatism (Reynolds & Holwell, 2010, p. 6).

11 The organism that can adapt has a motor output to the environment and two feedback loops. The first gives the organism non-affective information about the world around it, and the second carries information about whether the essential variables are (not) driven outside normal limits and it acts on (external) parameters. The first feedback plays its part within each reaction; the second determines which reaction shall occur (Ashby, 1960, pp. 82-84).

12 In this line of thought the answer to the representation of institutions that reflect preferences of individuals or collective outcomes (that are not the simple sum of individual interests) is for the latter: institutions should reflect collective outcomes; while they in practice also reflect individual preferences, this could be a sign of male adaptation to institutional goals and purposes.

13 Such landscape emerged from Wright's shifting balance theory that has presented the occurrence of genetic flow in small populations in accordance with environmental factors in order to understand evolution as a process of cumulative change that depends on a balance of conditions (Wright, 1931).

14 In coevolutionary processes, the fitness of one organism or species depends upon the characteristics of the other organisms or species with which it interacts, while all simultaneously adapt and change. A critical difference between evolution on a fixed landscape and coevolution is that the former can be roughly characterized as if it were an adaptive search on a "potential surface" or "fitness surface", whose peaks are the positions sought (S. A. Kauffman, 1993, p. 33). Kauffman gave an example of protein space: 'an adaptive walk might begin with any peptide. The walk will "move" to a one-mutant neighbour only if the second peptide is fitter than the first. Then any adaptive walk starts at a peptide and passes via fitter one-mutant neighbours which improve fitness until a peptide is reached which is fitter than all its one-mutant neighbours. Any such peptide is a local

optimum in peptide space' (S. A. Kauffman, 1993, p. 39). Fitness landscape is very similar to the Monte Carlo methodMonte Carlo method (Eckhart, 1987).

15   Complexity suggests that to survive and thrive an entity needs to explore its space of possibilities and to generate variety. Complexity also suggests that the search for a single 'optimum' strategy may neither be possible nor desirable. Any strategy can only be optimum under certain conditions, and when those conditions change, the strategy may no longer be optimal. To survive, an organisation needs to be constantly scanning the landscape and trying different strategies. An organisation may need to have in place several micro-strategies that are allowed to evolve before major resources are committed to a single strategy (Mitleton-Kelly, 2003, p. 35).

16   It is important not to confuse randomization (random assignment) with random sampling. Whereas the first means taking a set of units and assigning each unit to an experimental or control group by means of some randomizing procedure, the second consists of selecting units in an unbiased manner to form a representative sample from a population. Thus, random sampling might be used to select a representative group for study from a target population and then use random assignment to allocate each member of the sample to experimental or control conditions. 'Although the use of random samples to form a set of targets that is then randomized to form experimental and control groups is a highly recommended procedure, many randomized experiments are conducted using sets of targets that have not been selected by random sampling (i.e., that do not necessarily represent a given population)' (Rossi, Lipsey, & Freeman, 1999, p. 284). The desirable feature of randomization is that it is a sure way of achieving unbiased allocation of eligible targets to the experimental and control groups. Unbiased allocation requires that the probability of ending up in either the experimental or control group is identical for all participants in the study. Correspondingly, biased assignment occurs when individuals with certain characteristics have a higher probability than others of being selected for either group. In constituting experimental and control groups from a population with equal proportions of men and women, for example, an assignment procedure would be biased if members of one sex or the other were more likely to be in either the experimental or the control group (Rossi et al., 1999, p. 290).

17   Without relevant measurable approaches towards the more objective determination of factual state of affairs, agency cannot be managed properly. Bach and Wegrich warn of blind spots, rooted in the institutional nature of organizations: 'blind spots are characterized by an organization's unawareness of its incomplete information processing, or "not seeing that one is not seeing"… Accordingly, the distinct nature of a blind spot entails an organization's inability to detect and categorize (potentially important) information, without being aware of this inability' (Bach & Wegrich, 2018, p. 19). Blind spot occurs when an agency does not possess an information (but it could – a reason is a lack of measurement/tools), when it has it, but does not see it as such, or when it cannot extract or determine problems' causes even when there is information at hand. The interesting thing with blind spots and/or attention bias is in its apparently *intentionally rational* organizational behaviour (if seen as irrational, it could be more easily fixed). The problem of blind spots can last for years before it is resolved, sometimes even with the change of generations, or through scandals or other cases that caused (internal or external) attention. An agency's organizational attention is more partial than it could be holistic, so a central structure is needed to integrate those partial views.

18   This is called also as the renewing/transformational management (hyper turbulent environment, high adaptation) that refers to introducing change to deal with future conditions before these conditions actually occur. 'Organizations that exist in a hyper turbulent environment must not

only respond to change, they must proactively take advantage of new opportunity and innovation. These organizations tend to fit the renewal/transformational orientation and to be champions of innovation; they are faster at developing new ideas, more responsive to competitive changes (a more sensitive thermostat), and more participative in getting the commitment and involvement of organization members in the renewal process. Organizations with a high level of adaptation existing in a rapidly changing environment tend to utilize the renewing managerial style' (Brown & Harvey, 2006, p. 39).

[19] This is known also as the reactive Management (hyper turbulent environment, low adaptation). 'Organizations that have a low level of adaptation but exist in a rapidly changing environment tend to deal with problems on a short-run, crisis basis. Reactive management refers to the style of reacting to a stimulus after conditions in the environment have changed. It is a short-term, crisis type of adaptation, often involving replacement of key people, hasty reorganization, and drastic cutting of personnel and product lines' (Brown & Harvey, 2006, p. 38).

[20] This is known also as the satisficing management (stable environment, high adaptation): 'satisficing management, a term related to the word "satisfactory," is management that is adequate and average. It is a style of managing that emphasizes a more centralized decision-making structure with problems referred to the top. Because of the stable environment, there tend to be more levels of management, with coordination done by for- mal committees. Planning and decision-making are usually concentrated at the top, with high clarity of procedures and roles. Change is accomplished at a rate that is "good enough" to keep up with the industry, but certainly well behind the state of the art' (Brown & Harvey, 2006, p. 38).

[21] Since the rules where sanctions are restitutory do not involve the common consciousness, the relationships that they determine are not of the sort that affect everyone indiscriminately. This means that they are instituted directly, not between the individual and society, but between limited and particular elements in society, which they link to one another. Yet on the other hand, since society is not absent it must necessarily indeed be concerned to some extent, and feel some repercussions. Then, depending upon the intensity with which it feels them, it intervenes at a greater or lesser distance, and more or less actively, through the mediation of special bodies whose task it is to represent it. These relationships are therefore very different from those regulated by repressive law, for the latter join directly, without any intermediary, the individual consciousness to that of society, that is, the individual himself to society (Durkheim, 1984, p. 71).

[22] The contract is not sufficient by itself, but is only possible because of the regulation of contracts, which is of social origin (Durkheim, 1984, p. 162).

[23] Piaget discovered that children's concepts about rules, moral judgements and punishment change with their age. In the phase of heteronomous morality (moral realism 5-9 years) morality is enforced externally. Children submit to other people's rules and laws that cannot be changed. In the phase of autonomous morality (moral relativism 9-10 years) morality is based on a child's own rules. He recognizes the flexibility of rules, that there is no absolute right or wrong and that morality depends on intentions, not results. Piaget delineated the morality of cooperation as the stage reached after the age of ten. Rules are here changed based on mutual consent and agreement with others. At this age, children realize people should work jointly to achieve coherence in the community, i.e., to aim for the common good. Motivation, intent, personal capabilities, and situational context are all factors that must be taken into account. As children enter adolescence, their meaning of fairness

extends further from strict reciprocity and take into account the interests of other persons (ideal reciprocity, similar to the old Golden Rule).

[24] If you try to guide the common people with coercive regulations (zheng) and keep them in line with punishments, the common people will become evasive and will have no sense of shame. If, however, you guide them with Virtue, and keep them in line by means of ritual, the people will have a sense of shame and will rectify themselves (Confucius, 2003, p. 8).

[25] To achieve and maintain the relationships we need, we must stop choosing to coerce, force, compel, punish, reward, manipulate, boss, motivate, criticize, blame, complain, nag, badger, rank, rate, and withdraw. We must replace these destructive behaviors with choosing to care, listen, support, negotiate, encourage, love, befriend, trust, accept, welcome, and esteem. These words define the difference between external control psychology and choice theory (Glasser, 2010).

Chapter 14
Strategies and Scenario Planning

ABSTRACT

The function of public agencies is to provide expectations, which are often unfulfilled in an increasingly complex environment. However, consistency and coherence usually presuppose a static environment, whereas the relationship between means and ends is dynamic, multi-layered, interdependent, and thus complex. The new approach aims to address and respond to a dynamic environment in relation to the content of rules and proposes solutions that can adapt to change in line with the principle of proportionality. The concept of emergence can be useful to describe the end of a decision-making process where the final decision is the result of many intertwined combinations that influence arguments and parts that were not included in the initial idea. To cope with this, legal norms should be more adapted to the elements of the future than is possible with classical law. This could be done with sunset clauses, legal experiments, flexible legal rules, decision-making algorithms, and simulations that could serve as inputs without legal force for the subsequent adoption of general legal rules.

REASONS FOR NEW APPROACHES

Let our advance worrying become advance thinking and planning.

– Winston Churchill

The function of public agencies is the same as that of law: it is to provide expectations (Luhmann, 2004), which are often unfulfilled in an increasingly complex environment. Today, they increasingly require decisions that go beyond procedural correctness towards the duty to make rational and consistent decisions. Rationality as a universal promise of modernity also applies to public agency, and thus the notions of consistency and coherence can also be understood as manifestations of "systemic" rationality. But here problems can arise: consistency and coherence usually presuppose a static environment, whereas the relationship between means and ends is not only static, linear, but also dynamic, multi-layered, in-

DOI: 10.4018/979-8-3693-0507-2.ch014

Strategies and Scenario Planning

terdependent and thus complex, where one mode is replaced by many interactions, where the latter are interdependent and non-linear, where there are time lags between means and ends, and where several iterations also change the means, processes and ends themselves, towards the creation of a new entity that is not the same as the one at the beginning. The key assumption here is that the dynamic elements are not sufficiently embedded in the work of public agencies as a dedicated system for achieving formal objectives. Any purpose-driven system must be fundamentally flexible, and the implementation of rules is still largely carried out with the classical legal tools familiar to public administrations, inspections, administrative and administrative-judicial procedures. These tools adapt too slowly to the rapidly changing conditions of the environment. The new approach therefore aims to address and respond to a dynamic environment in relation to the content of the rules and to propose solutions that can adapt to change (in line with the principle of proportionality) i.e., flexible approaches that change according to perceived situations. When a system is adaptive (when its environment is used according to its objectives), the ability to maintain expectations is built into the system as an element (one way to do this is to enact different rules, adopt strategies or scenarios adapted to different conditions/thresholds/thresholds for the same situation).

Goals never only reflect beginnings, but also new content that is not known at the outset; all forms of complex adaptive systems as 'systems involving many components that adapt or learn in interaction with each other' (Holland, 2006, p. 1) have a characteristic known as emergence: 'the emergence characteristic is a global behaviour or structure that emerges through the interaction of a set of elements, without a global controller responsible for the behaviour or organisation of those elements' (Feltz, Crommelinck, & Goujon, 2006, p. 241). Everything is not only more than the sum of its parts, but the end (because of the many combinations) cannot be known in advance. It comes out of the interaction through combinations that increase exponentially with additional parts or relations: 2 elements produce 4 combinations (as in any other combination or 2^2), 4 produce 16 combinations, etc. This is also known as the butterfly effect, where small causes can have large effects (Lorenz, 1963). If the idea of emergence is generally accepted and understood, it is still not embedded in the legal system, and thus not in the system of functioning of public agencies. In complex, compound cases, the final solutions are different from the initial ones, with the spontaneous and simultaneous emergence of new states of affairs among the several relationships that arise during problem solving. The concept of emergence can be useful to describe the end of a decision-making process: the final decision is usually the result of many intertwined combinations that influence arguments and parts that were not included in the initial idea. The beginning and the end are only indirectly linked to the exposure of the problem and the final solution; the latter reflects the different arguments of several stakeholders who have adapted to the environment of other arguments and who have changed their content in their "conflicts with each other". Each solution is the result of several combinations, each solution has more than a beginning, and each solution represents the exponential result of the best outcome, which we do not know until it happens. All others are, from the point of view of the future, just (good/bad) predictions. The decision maker should choose to continuously correct mistakes or adapt to changes in the environment, according to predefined thresholds that would require different reactions.

Reality is neither deterministic, precise, nor certain. It is complex, made up of many parts and their relationships; it is rarely directly conditioned by a specific consequence and more often than not exponential. That the properties of systems cannot be reconstructed from knowledge of its parts may be counter-intuitive, yet a system cannot be truly understood even if its relevant legal, financial, economic, political, psychological, ecological and other relevant subsystems are fully known (Klir & Elias, 2003).

Along with the known parts, there are also relationships between them; flows/processes (current consumption) flow through them, according to (integrated) stocks, external system boundaries, thresholds, sensors, measuring instruments, patterns and feedback. They can be known from our point of interest because the system is not a thing but a list of (selected) variables (Ashby, 1957). No subsystem per se has sufficient information to allow an accurate understanding of the larger system (society, nature), since the latter gives meaning to the former: statements can therefore be "true" if they are not derived from themselves, but only from other, higher systems (Beer, 1994; McCulloch, 1945).

The duality between naming and actual life, between form and content or theory and practice, is always present; actions, effects can "speak" in a different way than their (however beautifully written) ideas. The same applies to rules and their enforcement.[1] Through enforcement, a set of rules designed to influence human and institutional behaviour is translated into social reality. Although enforcement measures are necessary in all regulatory regimes, regardless of the way in which the control is implemented, the literature on enforcement and compliance focuses primarily on the enforcement carried out in the traditional command and control system, which is only a partial picture of the whole picture. Many problems and resolutions also stem from informal, or a combination of formal and informal practices, which are ultimately attributed in one way or another to the (in)precise and (in)certain parts of human communication. Although the latter causes many problems, it is also a creative potential to overcome the limitations of rule-based control. The importance of exploring, understanding and explaining how public agencies ensure compliance is not negligible. At the heart of studies of regulatory enforcement is the breadth of discretion (in the hands of both public and private actors), which provides opportunities for human agency, error, manipulation and creativity. Although the objectives of public agencies may have been clearly identified (the right thing to do - performance), they have yet to be executed in the right (effective) way. Legal science – and thus also administrative science as far as the enforcement of rules by public agencies is concerned – still formally uses a binary (if-then) approach, where values are given as "yes" or "no" types of legal rules based on traditional binary logic, where a statement is true or false - and nothing in between. The principle of legal certainty presupposes knowledge of the structure and parameters of rules, where there is no doubt about their value or their occurrence, where the actual presence of an unforeseeable future is treated as a kind of "open secret" (where everyone knows about an unknown future regulated by known rules); legal science is still (at least formally) based on general rules of law, starting from determinism rather than from potentiality, foreseeability or predictability, although the last three concepts are present in non-determined legal concepts. The latter are also found in the legal concepts of public interest or public security, in standards of proof (e.g. probability, suspicion, grounds for suspicion, sufficient proof) or in the well-known legal principle of proportionality (legitimate aim, reasonableness, necessity and proportionality *stricto sensu*) where its elements are defined in terms of degrees and linguistic rules, rather than in numerical values.

Probability theory and statistics have been the dominant theories and tools for modelling uncertainty and are usually missing from legal drafts. Anticipative general rules are future-oriented; to cope with this, legal norms should be more adapted to the elements of the future than is possible with classical law. This could be done with the well-known sunset clause and legal experiments (which are incorporated in legal rules); this can also be done with flexible legal rules (different action options/scenarios applied at different thresholds previously adopted by Parliament), but also with newly developed (adapted to changes in the environment) strategies, negative scenarios, decision-making algorithms and simulations that could serve as inputs without legal force for the subsequent adoption of general legal rules. The latter could be equipped with the power of computational data processing, allowing (practical) experiments

Strategies and Scenario Planning

with less cost, less time, and less negative consequences. Belgian chemist and Nobel Prize winner Ilya Prigogine found that all systems that are complex enough can develop unpredictable new behaviours. These are dissipative structures,[2] arising from nonlinear processes in systems out of equilibrium (very small disturbances or fluctuations can turn into large waves through amplification - the so-called butterfly wing effect). This also includes social systems (the reason is positive, amplifying feedback built into the system), with implications for policy makers in the public sector. Unstable dynamic systems operate on the basis of diversity, nonlinearity, chance, and irreversibility, leading to dissipative structures. Under such conditions, dissipative structures or systems can reorganise (self-organise) into a new order/state based on fluctuations (Nicolis & Prigogine, 1977). As *ipso facto* dynamic social systems are involved, it is inevitable to have appropriate dynamic tools/approaches to deal with the environment in a legitimate way - otherwise the social system will self-regulate (e.g. the emergence of new rules of behaviour, fashion, customs, popular songs, films). Adaptation reflects a combination of speed and the ability to cope with complexity, based on Ashby's Law of requisite variety (Ashby, 1957): the only way to manage diversity (complexity) is to have the same amount of diversity (flexibility, resilience). The latter results in robustness as 'the potential to succeed in a variety of future circumstances or scenarios', while the former is responsiveness as the ability to 'quickly 1) detect changes in the environment; 2) formulate a response to that change; and 3) reallocate resources to execute the response' (Bettis & Hitt, 1995). Peter Drucker once said that "the best way to predict the future is to create it". One way to do is to use strategy.

STRATEGY

"Agency" can be seen also as the position of strategic action. In addition to existing legislation, public administrations operate on the basis of different strategies which they try to apply to their work. In doing so, it is often the case that they serve only as a form, as a "must have", but not "must live by it" document. Enforcement always relates not only to the design/preparation/implementation of rules, but also to a range of strategies relating to the collection of information on the "reality on the ground" and on compliance and behavioural change in the event of identified breaches. Strategy refers to the procedures, planning and management of major (at first, of military) operations, or the means to achieve an objective. Any discussion on enforcement and thus also strategy should be considered as a "living system" that adapts. Enforcement cannot be automated in most cases/contexts; it usually involves decisions between alternatives in terms of perceiving information and finding ways to change behaviour or its doings in the face of changed conditions. Decisions have to be made according to the motivations and capacities of the regulated subjects. Enforcement is thus far from being a machine where we can observe the intended effects based on the choice of certain settings. The main objective of strategic planning is to create a reasonable path to short- and long-term growth. A number of variables need to be analysed using traditional methods, SWOT, ABCDE, or some other method of analysis. The information is then used to better inform the decision-making process.

Given the above-mentioned emergence there should be also search strategy that could successfully address it. Among various authors Mintzberg calls into attention also the emergent strategy. A strategy is for him 'a pattern in a series of decisions. When a certain sequence of decisions in a given area shows consistency over time, a strategy is considered to have been formulated' (Mintzberg, 1979, p. 935).[3] The strategies that public agencies could use also relate to finding this "pattern", where an agency is considered in control when it can purposefully influence the formation of this pattern. The issue here is one of "double compliance" as a match between the appropriateness of the regulatory instrument and the context of the problem/area and as a control over compliance, i.e. the achievement of results. On the one hand, activities are aimed at detecting infringements, graduated (see responsive regulation) accountability and punishment of offenders, and on the other hand at persuasion, emphasising cooperation and advice over coercion, both at the individual level (protection of customers' rights, preventive work by administrative authorities) and at the collective level (e.g. law enforcement). The two strategies are hypothetical situations which are rarely found in their pure form. Which strategy will achieve the best results depends on evidence-based analysis.[4] A large part of the "action-behaviour" problem stems from the fact that many decision-makers (who are often not professionally qualified to do so) make decisions and take actions with little regard for the knowledge base that could shed light on their decisions. To help understand the approach to the use of different strategies, we can use Mintzberg's basic classification of strategies (Mintzberg & Waters, 1985, p. 258):

Mintzberg divided strategies into ex post facto results of decision-making actions (realised strategy) and strategies as a priori guidelines for decision-making (intended strategy); the comparison between the intended and realised strategy allows to distinguish between a deliberate strategy, partly realised as intended and partly as an emergent strategy, realised in spite of or in the absence of the original intentions. If the strategy is not realised, it is an unrealised strategy. 'The fundamental difference between reflective and emergent strategies is that the former focuses on directing and controlling the implementation of what is desired, while the latter opens up space for "strategic learning". Defining the strategy as intended ... excludes the notion of strategic learning [and hence the capacity to adapt]. Once intentions are set, the focus is on implementing them, not adapting to them...Emergent strategy involves learning about what works as an action in search of an adaptive pattern or consistency. Emergent strategy is not about chaos, but about unintentional order' (Mintzberg & Waters, 1985, pp. 270–271). The intended strategy is deliberate, analytical, data-driven and top-down. Such a strategy only succeeds in stable environments that address all relevant elements, that manage to maximise the consensus of all those involved in the strategy and that are not subject to major external influences (policy, markets, technology, etc.).

Given the state of flux of our every day's environment the emergent strategy could be probably the most relevant for public agencies. The complex environment, with its diversity of structures, actions, and processes, offers only limited possibilities to effectively manage dynamic, exponential, new and therefore largely unpredictable issues. Here, regulators cannot rely on precise intentions or long-term forecasts, but on rapid reactions to change. Instead of investing heavily in accurate forecasts, they should improve their ability to detect change and act accordingly, i.e., learn what is effective in response to unexpected opportunities and challenges. In such circumstances, it is not so much a question of designing strategies as of how they are implemented, incorporating new relevant developments as the strategy is executed and

Figure 1. Types of strategies

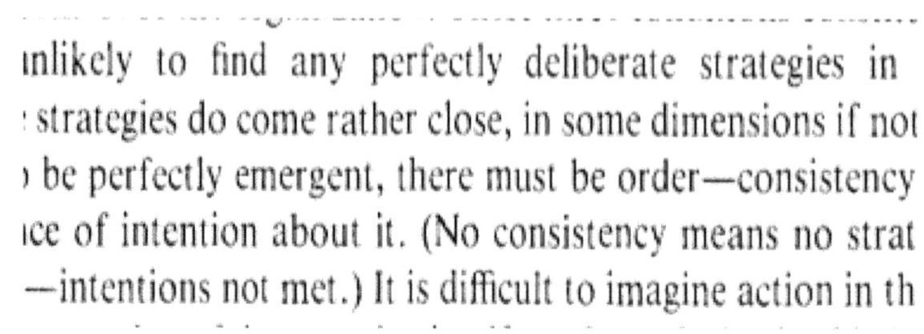
ınlikely to find any perfectly deliberate strategies in
: strategies do come rather close, in some dimensions if not
› be perfectly emergent, there must be order—consistency
ıce of intention about it. (No consistency means no strat
—intentions not met.) It is difficult to imagine action in th

integrated into the strategy itself. The effects of a strategy are always somewhat different from what was intended; unintended consequences and side-effects are inadvertently (due to complexity, ambiguity and uncertainty) "built into" the strategy alongside the intended ones, resulting from ignorance of the whole environment and the nature in which the public agency operates. In such cases, one can only speak of the emergent strategy. The latter occurs as a bubbling result within the organisation and represents the cumulative effect of the day-to-day prioritisation and decision-making on certain behaviours by middle managers, engineers, sales and finance staff. These are usually tactical, day-to-day operational decisions made by people who are not in a visionary, futuristic or strategic state of mind. The emergence processes should prevail in circumstances where the future is difficult to discern and where it is not clear what the right strategy should be in the first place. Actively monitoring, understanding and controlling the criteria on which day-to-day resource allocation decisions are made at all levels of the organisation are among the most important challenges a leader can face in the process of strategy development (Christensen & Raynor, 2013).

In real life, there is no ideal type of either purposeful or purely emergent strategy, but various combinations of these two, where the strategy is implemented, on the one hand, in accordance with the original intentions and, on the other, adapted (within the framework of the root causes of the creation of an institution) to changing situations. This distinction between these types of strategies also provides a fundamental understanding of the implementation of regulations, which must necessarily contain elements of adaptation (often absent from regulations) in order to cope with changing circumstances in the complex environment. The fundamental elements of any good strategy are the identification of the problem, the ways and means of solving it, and the coordination of these ways and means with a view to responding to the problem as quickly and optimally as possible. Rumelt in this regard speaks about the kernel of a strategy that contains three (similar) elements,[5] while in the third element (coordination) should be emphasised also the importance of adressing non-stop emerging various changes in the environment that can change the problem's content or even its essence, and hence the previously established problem may be no (or not so important) problem at all. The acute problem in strategy formation is thus how to associate specific emergent things and processes *vis-à-vis* the public interest? This question shifts the approach of prediction and control towards a practice of perception and improvisation. The Protagorean dictum that "man is the measure of all things" could thus be modified: "The measure of all things is the measure (and the reaction to it)". The illusion of certainty could be removed by an (incidence-based) action-response strategy: 'instead of predicting how people will behave and trying to design specific ways for consumers to respond... we can instead directly measure how they react to a range of options and react accordingly. In other words, the shift from "predict and control" to "measure and react" [the measure-and-respond approach] is not just technological...it is psychological. It is only when we recognise that we cannot depend on our ability to predict the future that we are open to the process of discovering it' (Watts, 2011, p. 196).

An answer could be an agile organisation/strategy that can find an answer to changing conditions. Nonaka and Zhu in this regard propose a pragmatic strategy, which core is action-oriented: it emphasises prevalence of practice in which knowledge (as the people's capacity to act – action and knowledge are the same) is authenticated. The pragmatic strategy is based on 'knowledge creation, not knowledge *per se*, that fuels winning strategy. To know is not to stockpile knowledge, but to continuously renew it through experimental activities' (Nonaka & Zhu, 2012, p. 42); a synergistic link among rational ideas or human minds on one side and the world of human action, experiment, and experience, on the other is the pragmatism's core. For Nonaka and Zhu *knowledge is* the *capacity to act* through six faces of strategy:

contingent (be cautious about one-size-fits-all best practice), consequential (path-dependent), continuous (strategy as a hypothesis about things that are in constant lux); courageous (intent and commitment), collective (the involvement of all people) and co-creative (everything relates to everything else) and/or practical, processual, creative, holistic, ethical and communal.

Strategy is about adjusting and coordinating personal goods into a shared common good appropriate to particular situations. Since situations are ever-changing in unrepeated and unpredictable ways, the more diverse a community's capacities to act, the more chances it will have to sense, seize and realise emerging opportunities (Nonaka & Zhu, 2012, p. 66). To pragmatism, a practically wise strategy is based on technical competence, situated judgement, moral sensibility, communal justification, openness to diversity and on-the-spot experimentation (Nonaka & Zhu, 2012, p. 74).

The pragmatic strategy uses rationality, routine, imagination, values, interests, emotions, social ties, power, politics, skills, and events as inputs that may in the process of action execution be a part of deliberate design, incremental improvisation, trial and error, and ex-post synthesis (and their combination) that as results go (as consequence-based learning) back to inputs. This type of strategy shows that the organisation's system is not just an "objective machine", distant or separate from human beings, but that the latter are a fundamental component of the system. Strategy is the mirror of a specific organisation. The environment around it is multidimensional, unstable, and fluid, so organisational tools and employees' minds should express similar variety of adaptable actions and their alternatives. In Cybernetics, this is known as the rule of requisite variety.

In an increasingly complex world, it is time for higher level reasoning, at the level of scientific research, cybernetic or systems approaches. Regulatory techniques need to be "breathed life" into the enforcement process if the underlying purpose is to be achieved (with the exception of "code architecture", where rules are self-enforcing). Regulatory strategies are about understanding the different challenges associated with using rules as a mechanism to guide behaviour; by focusing on enforcement and compliance, we focus on the dynamic, complex and socio-contextual nature of the regulatory process. In the context of compliance and enforcement, a strong emphasis is placed on formal, as well as widely shared informal, informal practices. Rules are interpreted and implemented by people. Compliance and enforcement research is therefore based on the "human face" of regulation. Central to the study of enforcement is the (wide/official) discretion within regulatory systems (in the hands of public and private actors), which allows for a wide range of human actions, errors, manipulations and creativity. These allow for different responses to underlying intentions, which during implementation take on different prefigurative (planned, [un]realised or emergent) strategies.

Any strategy must first and foremost be a plan of behaviour that responds to the behaviour of others. A strategy sets out the procedures or means to achieve an objective; regulatory strategies show the coherence between the achievement of regulatory objectives and the instruments to achieve them, they show and respond to a "pattern of behaviour towards desired outcomes". Choosing the right strategy can be a choice between success and failure, optimal use and waste, non/efficiency and non/legality. Any strategy must not only be effective and efficient, but also based on a reasoned choice. Awareness of the (cultural) situation of society and the shaping of its values, an investigation of the reasons for market failures, their equivalents in society that do not stem directly from economic inefficiency (communitarian reasons), and a consideration of alternatives to regulatory failures can give us a basis for choosing the most appropriate regulatory instrument in relation to the desired objectives.

SCENARIO PLANNING – ANTICIPATING POSSIBLE FUTURES

There's nothing quite as practical as a good theory (Lewin, 1951, p. 169)

Our brains are always imagining, creating scenarios, interpreting signals from the environment, transforming them into meaningful images of wants and needs, and creating picture guidelines for future behaviour. If it is a matter of wish/dreams, we talk about a vision (where we know, at least roughly, the trends of future development), if it is a matter of putting the vision into more concrete terms (what is to be done and why it is to be done), we talk about a mission, if we set short- and long-term goals and determine how they will be achieved (how, how much, when, in what way), we talk about a strategy, and if we wonder what can objectively happen in the future, we talk about a scenario. It is about anticipating future possibilities of events based on an assessment of probability (which is not as pronounced in a vision or mission and strategy), based on historical collected, evaluated data, thereby reducing uncertainty. 'Scenario planning helps us sharpen strategies, plan for the unexpected, keep looking in the right direction and answer the right questions; it helps us strategize, learn new skills, evaluate old ones and invent new processes. Scenario planning differs from classical (more simple, static, deterministic, quantitative, clear) planning (where the past explains the present) mainly in its greater degree of dynamism, flexibility, uncertainty, presence of many possible realities (where the future is the reason for the existence of the present). Scenarios should be used as a strategic planning tool when there is a sufficiently high degree of uncertainty, non-linearity' (Lindgren & Bandhold, 2009), emergence exponentiation, i.e. complexity. In such a situation, there is a proportionally growing need for scenario planning (new assumptions), which serve as a basis for planning more robust strategies (existing assumptions).

Scenario planning *explores an unknown future*, actively seeks answers to uncertainty,[6] and charts a vision for a favourable course. It is not difficult to know what a "good" future is, because we imagine it almost every day. For institutions, it means achieving their fundamental objectives – given the variations of unownable future – and different ways in which objectives can be achieved (different scenarios). There are basically three main types of scenarios, based on trends, their alternatives and norms: they are therefore related to probable, possible and desired/undesired futures. A scenario can be prepared by an individual expert, a group (through participation), or an organisation. The roles of presenting the results, responsibility for carrying out the tasks, and control of the activities carried out are then usually divided between these three actors. The strategy framework is composed of different approaches, all of which contain elements of detection, observing changes in the environment that may affect the organisation's core objectives, analysing these consequences, imagining the possibilities of future events, deciding on the weight of the information arrived at in this way, identifying choices and taking action through the setting of short- and long-term objectives, and tracking the action itself.

Personal imagery can also be transferred to institutions; scenario planning helps strategists and policy makers to better understand the context in which they find themselves. It is about the observation about making sense of experiences and greater possibilities to improve the situation by considering alternative frameworks to realise new learning opportunities with different futures, in order to create a self-determined path. 'The focus is shifted to re-examining assumptions and asking better questions through a process of discovery, interactive and integrated learning and inventing in [uncertain] "TUNA"' [Turbulence, uncertainty, novelty and ambiguity] environment' (Ramirez &

Wilkinson, 2016). A "scenario" generally refers to an imaginary or planned sequence of events, a large number of detailed plans or possibilities; in this context, it is not surprising that the concepts of planning, thinking, anticipating, analysing and learning are associated with a scenario. The concept of scenarios predates the concept itself; people were interested in the future from a very early stage and used descriptions of possible future events as a tool to explore the future of society and its institutions indirectly. In this context, scenarios are found in the form of treatises on utopias (gr. *ou* and *topos* = no place, no place, nowhere) and dystopias (negative utopia; fiction with a touch of horror), such as Plato's description of the ideal state or the visionary writings of Thomas More (*Utopia*, 1516), Francisa Bacona (*The New Atlantis*, 1626) and Georgea Orwella (*1984*). As a strategic planning tool, scenario techniques are firmly rooted in the military, where they have been used by military strategists throughout history, usually in the form of wargame simulations. (Sun Tzu, Niccolò Machiavelli). Despite a long military history, the first documented outlines of what today could be considered scenarios appeared only in the 19th century in the writings of von Clausewitz and von Moltke, two Prussian military strategists who formulated the principles of strategic planning (Reibnitz, 1989). Modern scenario techniques emerged initially as a response to the demands of World War II, but expanded especially in the 1960s, with the development of two geographical centres in the USA and France. After the Second World War, the US Department of Defence was faced with the task of selecting projects to finance the development of new weapon systems. Decision-making in this situation gave rise to two specific needs, namely, the need for a methodology that would ensure a reliable consensus among a large and diverse group of experts, and the need to develop simulation models of future environments that would allow the exploration of different policy alternatives and their implications. The need to elicit and synthesise expert opinion has driven the development of the Delphi technique, and the need for simulation models has led to the development of an approach called "systems analysis", from which the explicit use of scenario techniques has emerged (Raubitschek in Bradfield, Wright, Burt, Cairns, & Van Der Heijden, 2005, p. 798). Both of these techniques were developed in the 1950s by the Rand Corporation (short for Research and Development), a research group that evolved out of a joint project between the US Air Force and Douglas Aircraft in 1946, and which until the 1960s was almost exclusively concerned with studies of the defence management of US aviation (Cooke, 1991). The combination of computer development (which provided the data processing capability needed to simulate solutions), game theory (which provided the theoretical structure for exploring social interaction), and the U.S. military's need for military game simulation models, provided the platform for the emergence of Rand corporation scenario techniques (Schoemaker, 1993).[7] A big increase in the number of scenarios came after Shell's use of a series of stories by Frenchman Pierre Wack in 1972, which included the possibility of unexpected disruptions to the oil supply.[8] Scenario planning only became widely used in Europe after the first oil crises in 1973 (Malaska, Malmivirta, Meristö, & Hansén, 1984), a technique that also uses the EU.[9] Scenario planning is now used in a wide range of increasingly interconnected fields, and interest in this type of technique has increased since 9/11 and the 2008 financial crisis. Scenario planning is a methodology that uses the innate human ability to imagine the future to better understand the current situation and identify options for a new strategy. It is used primarily in institutional planning contexts such as businesses, government and intergovernmental bodies, as well as in non-profit organisations and other communities (Ramirez & Wilkinson, 2016).

There are in short seven criteria for a good scenario set for strategy purposes:

Strategies and Scenario Planning

- Decision-making power. Each scenario in the set, and the set as a whole, must provide insights useful for the question being considered. Most generic industry or general scenario sets lack this power and need to be complemented for decision purposes.
- Plausibility. The developed scenarios must fall within the limits of what future events that are realistically possible.
- Alternatives. Each scenario should be at least to some extent probable, although it is not necessary to define the probabilities explicitly. The ideal is that the scenarios are all more or less equally probable, so that the widest possible range of uncertainty is covered by the scenario set. If for instance only one of three or four scenarios is probable, you only have one scenario in reality.
- Consistency. Each scenario must be internally consistent. Without internal consistency the scenarios will not be credible. The logic of the scenario is critical.
- Differentiation. The scenarios should be structurally or qualitatively different. Thus, it is not enough for them to be different in terms of magnitude, and therefore only variations of a base scenario.
- Memorability. The scenarios should be easy to remember and to differentiate, even after a presentation. Therefore, it is advisable to reduce the number to between three and five, although in theory we could remember and differentiate up to seven or eight scenarios. Vivid scenario names help.
- Challenge. The final criterion is that the scenarios really challenge the organization's received wisdom about the future (Lindgren & Bandhold, 2009, pp. 32–33).

The information needed to develop good scenarios can be obtained through different communication channels: media (internet, social networks, online groups of people addressing a similar problem, keyword and content analysis of articles and books), interview (Delphi method, structured interview, opinion polls, focus groups, expert panels, prominent personalities, independent reviewers' opinions and professional networks), Intuition (brainstorming, pictures of the future), statistical, probabilistic analysis, analogies, trends, systems theory, systems modelling, analysis of (including cross-cutting, combinatorial) effects,[10] event simulation and other approaches that are able to provide new knowledge or a new perspective on existing or imagined situations. Having said all this, scenario planning cannot be a well-defined field. It is a multitude of perspectives and methods that could be applied in different contexts, in different ways and for different purposes. This is not to forget the active monitoring of scenarios and reacting accordingly, because without good implementation of the strategy, it is just an intellectual training of our brains. Scenario planning is therefore one of the techniques for better decision-making. The test of good scenario planning is not whether it accurately predicts the future, but whether it predicts several good futures, whether we have made better decisions by considering possible futures.

DIFFERENCES BETWEEN STRATEGY AND SCENARIO

Direct enforcement and/or strategy implementation do not involve explaining the causes of rule-breaking, the motivations and capacity of regulated entities, the types of sanctions likely to ensure sustained voluntary compliance, but such elements are at the heart of the study of enforcement, which cannot be answered in a quick/complete way. While strategic planning usually starts with agreeing on the vision of the company, scenario planning ends with it. Strategy addresses the future achievement of *known* goals (and thus involves setting measurable goals, their indicators, implementors, and deadlines), while scenario planning can lay the foundations for strategy development. The main objective here is to define what could lie ahead. The strategic planning process usually focuses on specific variables: strengths, weaknesses, threats, and opportunities that are in scenario planning not expressed in a more detailed level as they are in strategy. One way to develop future scenarios is to assess the trends that are most likely to emerge and those that are most important to the success of the organisation. These trends become the core of the planning process. The initial trend analysis is the basis for deciding which scenarios require the most in-depth planning. A vision is then created (or confirmed), which is balanced (adapted) to the scenarios most likely to occur. The real output of the strategic planning process is a detailed implementation plan, while the output of scenario planning is slightly different: although it can provide more information for the strategic plan, its main output is the creation of a broader picture of the future possible situations, and with them also possible reactions. Strategic planning usually focuses on a timeframe of three to five years; scenario planning is more useful for long-term planning, perhaps even 10 years or more (Taken from Cohen, 2016). Strategic planning includes vision, mission, principles, key success indicators (quality, cost, existing and future programmes, employee satisfaction), analysis of the external environment (relationship between the institution's products/processes and the market/field in which they are used, customer satisfaction, competition, technological developments, impact of policy, regulation and other factors), internal and external constraints and strengths resulting from the analysis of the external environment, objectives, measures, and ways to achieve measures and monitoring, follow-up of the implementation of the strategy. Scenario planning includes the identification of the issue and the decisions to be taken, the key (mini, micro, macro) factors, their ranking in terms of importance and uncertainty, the logic of the scenario, the identification of the implications of the scenarios on the decisions, the identification of the key indicators and the peripheral points/times of their verification. Strategic planning and scenario planning try to anticipate the myriad of variables that could hinder the growth of an individual or an organisation. Strategy and scenarios can are adaptation tools; another is collective wisdom.

REFERENCES

Ashby, W. R. (1957). *An Introduction to Cybernetics*. Chapman and Hall.

Bettis, R. A., & Hitt, M. A. (1995). The new competitive landscape. *Strategic Management Journal*, *16*(S1), 7–19. doi:10.1002/smj.4250160915

Bradfield, R., Wright, G., Burt, G., Cairns, G., & Van Der Heijden, K. (2005). The origins and evolution of scenario techniques in long range business planning. *Futures*, *37*(8), 795–812. doi:10.1016/j.futures.2005.01.003

Christensen, C., & Raynor, M. (2013). *The Innovator's Solution: Creating and Sustaining Successful Growth*. Harvard Business Review Press.

Cohen, S. (2016). *Growing Talent Management Firms: Scenario vs. Strategic Planning*. TD. https://www.td.org/insights/growing-talent-management-firms-scenario-vs-strategic-planning

Cooke, R. M. (1991). *Experts in Uncertainty: Opinion and Subjective Probability in Science*. Oxford University Press. doi:10.1093/oso/9780195064650.001.0001

Feltz, B., Crommelinck, M., & Goujon, P. (2006). *Self-organization and Emergence in Life Sciences.* Springer Science & Business Media. doi:10.1007/1-4020-3917-4

Fowles, R. B. (1978). *Handbook of Futures Research.* Greenwood Press.

Holland, J. H. (2006). Studying Complex Adaptive Systems. *Journal of Systems Science and Complexity*, *19*(1), 1–8. doi:10.1007/s11424-006-0001-z

Lewin, K. (1951). *Field Theory in Social Science: Selected Theoretical Papers* (D. Cartwright, Ed.). Harper & Row.

Lindgren, M., & Bandhold, H. (2009). *Scenario Planning: The Link Between Future and Strategy.* MacMillan.

Lorenz, E. N. (1963). Deterministic Nonperiodic Flow. *Journal of the Atmospheric Sciences*, *20*(2), 130–141. doi:10.1175/1520-0469(1963)020<0130:DNF>2.0.CO;2

Luhmann, N. (2004). *Law as a Social System* (F. Kastner, R. Nobles, D. Schiff, & R. Ziegert, Eds., ZiegertK. A., Trans.). Oxford University Press. doi:10.1093/oso/9780198262381.001.0001

Malaska, P., Malmivirta, M., Meristö, T., & Hansén, S.-O. (1984). Scenarios in Europe—Who uses them and why? *Long Range Planning*, *17*(5), 45–49. doi:10.1016/0024-6301(84)90036-0

Mintzberg, H. (1979). Patterns in Strategy Formation. [JSTOR. Retrieved from JSTOR.]. *International Studies of Management & Organization*, *9*(3), 67–86. doi:10.1080/00208825.1979.11656272

Mintzberg, H., & Waters, J. A. (1985). Of strategies, deliberate and emergent. *Strategic Management Journal*, *6*(3), 257–272. doi:10.1002/smj.4250060306

Nicolis, G., & Prigogine, I. (1977). *Self-organization in nonequilibrium systems: From dissipative structures to order through fluctuations.* Wiley.

Nonaka, I., & Zhu, Z. (2012). Pragmatic Strategy: Eastern Wisdom, Global Success. Cambirdge: Cambridge University Press. doi:10.1017/CBO9780511736568

Prigogine, I., & Stengers, I. (1984). *Order Out of Chaos.* Bantam Books.

Ramirez, R., & Wilkinson, A. (2016). *Strategic Reframing: The Oxford Scenario Planning Approach.* Oxford University Press. doi:10.1093/acprof:oso/9780198745693.001.0001

Reibnitz, U. V. (1989). *Scenario Techniques.* McGraw-Hill.

Rumelt, R. (2011). *Good Strategy Bad Strategy: The Difference and Why It Matters.* Crown Business.

Schoemaker, P. J. H. (1993). Multiple scenario development: Its conceptual and behavioral foundation. *Strategic Management Journal*, *14*(3), 193–213. doi:10.1002/smj.4250140304

Schwenker, B., & Wulf, T. (2013). *Scenario-based Strategic Planning: Developing Strategies in an Uncertain World.* Springer Science & Business Media. doi:10.1007/978-3-658-02875-6

van Vught, F. A. (1987). Pitfalls of forecasting: Fundamental problems for the methodology of forecasting from the philosophy of science. *Futures*, *19*(2), 184–196. doi:10.1016/0016-3287(87)90050-4

Watts, D. J. (2011). *Everything Is Obvious: *Once You Know the Answer*. Crown Publishing Group.

ENDNOTES

[1] In fact, there are not two poles but four combinations: a regulation can be just a regulation, a dead letter on paper, a bad regulation is poorly implemented, a good regulation is well implemented (that's what we all want), or practice itself takes care of the effects without a regulation, or practice influences the regulation in a substantive, contextual way.

[2] The interaction of the system with the outside world, its placement in conditions of non-uniformity, can thus become the starting point for the emergence of new dynamic states of matter - dissipative structure (Prigogine & Stengers, 1984, p. 143).

[3] A pattern is one of the building blocks of systems theory, showing results on a specific time line. When a certain sequence of decisions over time reflects the underlying intentions through the results, this is consistency; we can say that the outlined strategy is actually working in the observed area.

[4] The basic idea of evidence-based decision-making is that good, quality decisions should be based on a combination of critical thinking and the best available evidence. Although decision-makers usually use (some) evidence, many pay little attention to the quality of that evidence. It is therefore more a matter of scientifically-informed decision-making practice in determining the nature, content and processes of decision-making. This type of practice reduces the costs of free, unguided judgement and (unconscious) biased decisions. It helps professionals to overcome these barriers by using decision aids, practices and frameworks to support better quality decisions. This will usually be the kind of substantive evidence that a reasonable person could accept as relevant (to justify a decision that cannot be overturned in the absence of other evidence that directly or indirectly i.e., by reasonable inference, supports or contradicts some other material fact).

[5] 1. A diagnosis that defines or explains the nature of the challenge. A good diagnosis simplifies the often-overwhelming complexity of reality by identifying certain aspects of the situation as critical.

2. A guiding policy for dealing with the challenge. This is an overall approach chosen to cope with or overcome the obstacles identified in the diagnosis.

3. A set of coherent actions that are designed to carry out the guiding policy. These are steps that are coordinated with one another to work together in accomplishing the guiding policy (Rumelt, 2011).

[6] Underestimating uncertainty can be dangerous. At worst, it leads to strategies that cannot protect companies from threats. At best, it leads to strategies that ignore the potential opportunities that uncertainty brings. For example, in 1876, the financial company Western Union believed that the telephone would never replace the telegraph. An internal memo of that year stated that "the telephone has too many drawbacks to be seriously considered as a means of communication". In 1977, Kenneth H. Olsen, then President of the US information technology company Digital Equipment Corporation, reportedly announced that "there is no reason for an individual to have a computer in his home". Darryl Zanuck, a film producer at 20th Century Fox, stated in 1946 that "television will not last, because people will soon get tired of looking at a box of plywood every night." In 1911, in the final year of the First World War, the French Marshall Ferdinand Foch, the famous military theorist and Supreme Allied Commander, said, "Aeroplanes are interesting

Strategies and Scenario Planning

7   toys, but of no military value". Similarly, the last German Emperor Wilhelm II failed to grasp the enormous potential of the automobile when he declared in 1905: "I believe in horses. Cars are an out-of-bounds phenomenon". The list of such quotes could go on and on. Nevertheless, these few examples illustrate the point: if you stick strictly to your dogmas and doctrines, you will never find the right answers in a world of uncertainty, where big and dynamic changes are at stake (Schwenker & Wulf, 2013, p. 23).

7   With this platform, Herman Kahn, head of civil protection and strategic planning at the Rand Corporation in the 1950s, began to develop scenarios for air defence as a large-scale protective warning system. Kahn is credited with coining the phrase "thinking the unthinkable"; he used a combination of facts and logic to prove that military planning is based on wishful thinking, not on reasonable expectations. In Europe, the French were the first to systematically study the "scientific and political foundations of the future" using scenario techniques; as in the US, the pioneering work was almost exclusively related to public policy and planning. While Khan was developing scenarios for the military in the 1950s, the French philosopher Gaston Berger founded the *Centre d'Etudes Prospectives*, where he developed a scenario-based approach to long-term planning that he called prospective thinking, or *La Prospective* (Bradfield et al., 2005: 798, 802). Berger was concerned with the long-term political and social future of France, his fundamental philosophical assumption being that the future is not part of a "pre-determined continuity of time", but something that has to be created and can be "consciously modelled for the benefit of man". The main objective of his centre was to develop an acceptable scenario-based methodology for developing positive images or "normative scenarios" of the future, translating these images into the political arena, where they would serve as a guiding vision and basis for action for policy-makers and the state itself (Fowles, 1978; van Vught, 1987).

8   When the 1973 oil crisis actually happened, the company's rapid recognition of and response to this industry-changing event helped Shell emerge as one of the strongest of the weakest of the 'seven sisters' of the international oil industry. Shell's scenario department continued to develop this methodology and in the following years helped the company to anticipate and adapt to the second oil crisis in 1979, the collapse of the oil markets in 1986, the fall of the Soviet Union, the rise of Islamic radicalism and the increasing pressure on companies to take account of environmental and other social pressures.

9   In the report "Scenarios for Europe 2010 - Five possible futures for Europe", the European Commission's research unit uses the scenario technique to develop a set of future images of Europe, such as "Winning Markets" (the dominance of neoliberal models), "A Hundred Flowers" (the retreat of the state, the loss of touch with reality, greater importance of bottom-up initiatives, local communities, neighbourhoods and municipalities) and "Turbulent Neighbourhoods" (political instability, threat of terrorism, regional conflicts, organised crime, greater social inequality) which she described on the basis of factors such as the political system, technology and culture/values (https://www.ab.gov.tr/files/ardb/evt/1_avrupa_birligi/1_6_raporlar/1_3_diger/scenarios_europe_2010.pdf). In March 2017, the European Commission published a White Paper on the future of Europe (Reflections and scenarios for the EU-27 to 2025), in which it envisaged five scenarios (Business as usual; Single market only; Those who want more, do more; Doing less, but more effectively; Doing much more together) (https://ec.europa.eu/commission/sites/beta-political/files/bela_knjiga_o_prihodnosti_evrope_sl.pdf).

[10] A conventional simulation exercise involves events that are more predictable, while a scenario allows for the simulation of events that have not yet occurred or are not occurring. In the 1980s, a nationwide Yugoslav campaign ("nothing should surprise us") was held in which the Yugoslav authorities prepared people for the worst: how to deal with natural disasters, wars, nuclear, biological and chemical attacks. It was a mass participation of working people and citizens with all the structures in the then system of popular defence and social self-defence. The main objective was to plan, coordinate, train and test the ability of working people and citizens, units and bodies of services and leaderships to act in situations of war or natural disasters.

Chapter 15
Preconditions of Collective Wisdom Within Agencies and the Move From Experts to the People and Databases

ABSTRACT

When people join groups, their personal biases and cognitive biases can lead to extreme herd behaviour, group polarization, and groupthink. Social systems can evolve to better adapt to environmental pressures by developing specialized organizations with legitimate authority. Traditional public deliberation may be less efficient as individuals tend to conform their interpretations to match those of others, rather than their actions, and they may not be aware of alternative possibilities. Evolutionary changes require diversity and independent thinking to adapt based on new information. Regulators need to consider diverse and unshared information to avoid unintended consequences. The degree of collective intelligence is linked to an individual's social sensitivity and ability to think about the mental states of other individuals. Superforecasters, who are open-minded, diverse, and analytical with developed social abilities, can beat individual experts and prediction markets.

INTRODUCTION

While much of our discussion will focus on science and scholarship and the role of experts, we must bear in mind that in the long run attempts to impose solutions on human societies from above often have destructive consequences. Only through education, participation, a measure of consensus, and the widespread perception by individual people that they have a personal stake in the outcome can lasting and satisfying change be accomplished (Gell-Mann, 2002, p. 330).

Spitzer underscores the significance of integrating and interacting measurements effectively, wherein 'the most important aspect of measurement is the dialogue that should occur at every stage in the mea-

DOI: 10.4018/979-8-3693-0507-2.ch015

surement process' (Spitzer, 2007, p. 105). In one part, he has the point various people should provide information, but the latter could be even more successfully elaborated then through the dialogue. Collective wisdom is the deepest level of understanding (starting with data, information and knowledge). Firstly, it is necessary to eliminate the dilemma regarding the superiority of experts compared to ordinary citizens in certain situations. Simply listing conditions for citizen wisdom (CW) after the fact or relying on biased choices to justify its use would not be appropriate if the results did not confirm its benefits. However, the advantages of CW have been confirmed. To navigate a complicated environment, one can strive to collect information with exceptional precision (Ayres, 2007; Dawes, 1979, 1979; Galton, 1889; Malone, 2018; Meehl, 2013). For Le Bon the characteristics of group mentality include tendencies towards impulsiveness, volatility, irritability, vulnerability to persuasion, gullibility, exaggeration, naivety, intolerance, authoritarianism, resistance to change, and a lack of moral judgement (Bon, 2001). While people may have noble reasons for joining groups, their ability to think critically and form opinions may be negatively impacted by individual shortcomings such as bias, lack of knowledge, susceptibility to influence, aversion to risk, over or underestimation of confidence, concern for reputation, hindsight bias, and other cognitive biases. These flaws may arise due to the collective behaviour of group mentality, social pressure to conform, and groupthink (Janis, 1980); the situations described may be exacerbated by group polarization and cascade effects, which can lead to the intensification or amplification of these conditions (Sunstein, 2006, 2009). Even if they are intelligent, quieter members of a group are often overlooked in favour of louder members who are more emotionally appealing, despite being to a lesser extent intelligent. Therefore, it is essential a thorough investigation of important issues is conducted to ensure that information that contradicts the existing beliefs of the group is also considered. This information may not be shared by members who are more vocal, but is nevertheless important to explore (Stasser & Titus, 1985). Experimental evidence suggests that even a slight social influence can weaken the cognitive dissonance effect (Lorenz, Rauhut, Schweitzer, & Helbing, 2011). It is thus crucial to recognize the elements that contribute to cognitive dissonance, starting with evolution as the primary factor.

Over time, small changes have occurred through the process of evolution, which Darwin considered alongside Adam Smith (Ridley, 2017), and it is possible that Darwin was influenced by the concept of the "invisible hand", which suggests that personal self-interest may lead to indirect benefits for society that surpass the effects of straight, public actions. Similarly, Parsons adopted also an evolutionary perspective, theorizing that social systems can evolve to better cope with environmental pressures by enhancing their capacity to adapt (Parsons, 1991); through increasing professional diversity, specialized organizations may emerge and gain "legitimate authority" within a normative order (1985). For Parsons (1985) a system of action includes integration, goal-attainment, pattern-maintenance, and adaptation, and serves as a bridge among the system's structural and dynamic aspects. Just as humans and other systems have evolved over time, these functions have also evolved to allow for greater efficiency and effectiveness within the system, where 'collective decision-making processes are *par excellence* of evolutionary processes in the social realm…[that] develop because of the selection pressures exerted on it' (Gerrits & Marks, 2017, p. 6). Challenges in adapting to changing circumstances are often faced by decision-makers that should nevertheless effectively address more and more complex systems. Traditional public deliberation may not be effective in this regard, as people tend to conform to the opinions of others without critically evaluating alternative options. However, all components of a system are interconnected and have an impact on each other, and it is therefore important to involve the entire community in decision-making rather than just a select few. This is particularly relevant from an evolutionary perspective.

Preconditions of Wisdom and Move From Experts to People, Databases

Evolutionary changes reflect a diversity in the degree of critical and independent thinking that is applied to re-evaluate actions. 'In the presence of change it [the absence of diversity] reduces the robustness of the system' (Johnson, 2002). When too many inflexible units are integrated into a collective, the system's ability to communicate and coordinate with the external environment may be compromised, which can threaten its overall robustness. According to Surowiecki (2005), diversity and independence are crucial conditions for achieving collective wisdom and avoiding problems related to cognition, coordination, and cooperation. To create the necessary conditions for collective intelligence, a structured system is required to connect all individuals in a manner that doesn't limit high-ability individuals because of the presence of low-ability individuals, and vice versa. This can be achieved by methods such as negative correlation or statistical regression. Additionally, the system should have the capability to rapidly collect new data and implement or modify decisions and actions, while also integrating feedback loops to adjust its behavioral patterns.

It has been observed that single communications can result in nonlinear effects, which leads to the conclusion that dispersed public information is inherently diverse. Hayek believed that the ability to adapt to this diverse information is crucial: 'civilization rests on the fact that we all benefit from knowledge which we do not possess. And one of the ways in which civilization helps us to overcome that limitation ... is by the utilization of knowledge which is and remains widely dispersed among individuals' (Hayek, 1998, p. 15). Professionals, despite their expertise, are bound to miss numerous pieces of small and diverse information possessed by the general public. A potential solution to this is the implementation of "regulatory due process," which includes public feedback as a safeguard against errors. However, relying solely on this process cannot prevent groupthink, as further processing is required. Formal political legitimacy alone is not enough to avoid groupthink, as mistakes can still occur. Active citizenship from a bottom-up approach can create more pressure for enhanced provision than top-down inspection and control; it is nevertheless not enough. To create a meaningful whole, the system needs to process all diverse information and incorporate everyone's opinions into the final decision. Legal rules can facilitate this by transitioning from being static to dynamic.

To make effective decisions, a system must intentionally examine and reconcile the different factors and perspectives of its members. Merely adopting or holding onto ideas based on the agreement or sway of others without considering a variety of different and opposing viewpoints, even if based on factual evidence, can lead to mistakes despite the most convincing logical arguments. Therefore, impartial diversity should be the fundamental standard for the acceptance of any decision. Page identifies four procedural requirements (the problem must be challenging, the members must be intelligent and varied, the group must exceed a few individuals and be selected from a vast population) that enable groups to exceed the capabilities of individual professional (Page, 2008, p. 162).[1] In social science, experts are often not better at making predictions than regular people. This is explained in the next subsection, but the main idea is that individual predictions may contain both true and false elements, which cancel each other out when combined with others' predictions. The more diverse opinions that are included, the truer elements can be united. The essence of the law of large numbers is that collective prediction, typically measured as an average or median, is more accurate than any individual's prediction.

Opposing views can nullify each other. It is essential for regulators to comprehend the thought processes and responses of individuals in relation to regulated issues; otherwise, regulations will reflect only the limited perspectives of experts, leading to similar outcomes and potential unintended consequences. Participation in decision-making is not valuable solely for democratic reasons but also, under the conditions of collective wisdom, for a more accurate estimation of reality. While Rousseau is primarily associated with direct democracy, it is not as widely recognized that he also spoke about the importance of collective judgment in decision-making; he discussed on the "extrapolated democracy"[2] (Aristotle did the same about the virtue of character),[3] which relates to the phenomenon of mutual cancelling regression analysis, where opposing forces nullify each other. They noted that groups can display this phenomenon under certain conditions. They observed that in certain circumstances, groups could exhibit greater intelligence than individuals because the mix of correct and incorrect responses tends to result in the cancellation of erroneous answers, leaving only accurate ones (O'Reilly, 2010).[4] This could also apply to cognitive biases, as these biases are also likely to be balanced out during the decision-making procedure.

Woolley et al. presented two studies (with 699 people paired in groups) from which they discovered indications of a CW factor that is connected with 'the average social sensitivity of group members [as measured by the Reading the Mind in the Eyes test], the equality in distribution of conversational turn-taking, and the proportion of females in the group' (Woolley, Chabris, Pentland, Hashmi, & Malone, 2010, p. 686), and not with the average or highest individual intelligence of group members. Such deductions oppose the cascade effects and group polarisation. Engel et al. (2014) discovered that CW correlates with the individual group members' capacity to think on the mental states of others (this social ability is termed 'Theory of Mind'[5]) that works also in online environments. The CW factor is crucial in inducing group functioning, both in online settings and face-to-face. Effective comprehension and consideration of others' mental states – that falls under the umbrella of emotional intelligence (Engel et al., 2014) or wider social intelligence[6] – can make text-based online communication adequate. To achieve diversity, it is important to avoid forcing everyone to agree on the same thing. Instead, we should encourage individuals to form their own opinions and then work to find connections between them. This way, diverse and independent perspectives can exist in people who are open-minded and impartial, similar to a large database that uses negative correlation to reduce biases. Choosing between relying on data or values depends on what information is available and how uncertain the situation is. Developing social skills, as well as independence and diversity, is crucial for creating CW. Individuals who possess social skills, are careful, modest, do not rely on absolute predictions, are receptive to new ideas, reflective, skilled in analysing data, have a variety of perspectives, understand probabilities, consistently review and correct their biases, and think critically are referred to as superforecasters (Tetlock & Gardner, 2015) (these individuals could also be placed within Rawls' concept of the "veil of ignorance", where they are unaware of their personal characteristics, social and historical context, and must rely solely on their intellectual abilities to solve a drawback). Tetlock and Gardner (2015) verified that when these individuals work together, not merely outperform specific experts but also outperformed prediction markets as a type of collective wisdom.

FORMULA VS. PROFICIENCY

The widely recognized truth that a collective of people can produce more precise forecasts than single experts is often overlooked by those making decisions. Experts as individuals cannot store or process a large amount of information in their minds. Galton showed that the group's median estimate can be more precise than the estimates provided by individual specialists (Galton, 1907). This alternate tactic is founded on the scientifically confirmed idea of a shared origin and mathematical formulas (Dawes, 1979; Galton, 1907; Grove & Meehl, 1996; Meehl, 2013; Page, 2008; Woolley et al., 2010). Correlation analysis, which discloses only the connection between two variables is like the conventional majority voting style. On the other hand, regression analysis in CW lets us comprehend the effect of a single or multiple variables on the dependent one. In the model of CW democracy, people function as independent variables, submitting their votes privately without awareness of other people's decisions. These votes are subsequently examined to uncover the average viewpoint of the community. 'In sharp contrast to traditional experts, statistical procedures not only predict, they also tell you the quality of the prediction. Experts either don't tell you the quality of their predictions or are systematically overconfident in describing their accuracy' (Ayres, 2007, p. 116). This distinction marks the shift from depending on specialists to making choices based on evidence, which clearly highlights the amount of data, significance, prediction, and its quality. The "expert camp" utilizes artificial intelligence through a "rule-based" approach (if X, then Y) that fails when multiple or new options arise. On the other hand, the "neural networks" camp does not teach computers human-designed rules but instead recreates the human brain. By analysing numerous samples of a specific occurrence, neural networks (a combination of algorithms and power to compute) can recognise arrangements within the vast data quantities (Lee, 2018). Gulick has In *Notes on the theory of organization* introduced the widely recognized POSDCORB abbreviation (Planning, Organizing, Staffing, Directing, Coordinating, Reporting, and Budgeting) to designate the functions of a chief executive. Additionally, he cautioned about the potential pitfalls of relying too heavily on experts (*caveamus expertum*) who have 'tendency to assume knowledge and authority in fields in which he has no competence. In this particular, educators, lawyers, priests, admirals, doctors, scientists, engineers, accountants, merchants and bankers are all the same—having achieved technical competence or "success" in one field, they come to think this competence is a general quality detachable from the field and inherent in themselves. They do not remember that the robes of authority of one kingdom confer no sovereignty in another; but that there they are merely a masquerade' (Gulick, 2003, p. 11).

Theory of expert competence (Shanteau, 1992) distinguishes among the dynamic and static domains; cognitive decision-making researchers should focus on both aspects. This difference can be applied as a rule of thumb solution for the expert versus the non-expert dilemma (Taleb, 2010); the latter is based on a distinction between what moves (and hence needs knowledge, *episteme*) and what does not (and requires only craft, not knowledge). Only apparent experts are thus for Taleb 'stockbrokers, clinical psychologists, psychiatrists, college admissions officers, court judges, councillors, personnel selectors, intelligence analysts ... economists, financial forecasters, finance professors, political scientists, risk experts ... and personal financial advisers' (Taleb, 2010).[7] In the ever-changing public area, those making decisions may not be viewed as experts when they fail to integrate dynamical elements in their decisions. In situations which are in continuous development, data is essential; therefore, experts who are not conscious of these transformations cannot precisely forecast results based only on their previous experiences. Science should capture the complexity of nature and gather information through diverse disciplinary perspectives, enabling it to support and be indistinguishable from various competing political positions driven by values (Sarewitz, 2004). These perspectives should connect science and potential paths of action (Pielke Jr, 2007).

Also for Slovic (1987) 'the common man is a better judge of his own needs in the long run than any cult of experts' (Gulick, 2003, p. 11), because ordinary individuals possess a more complex understanding of risk compared to specialists. Particularly when confronted with differing values and significant uncertainty, experts should serve as impartial facilitators of various policy options (Pielke Jr, 2007). The suggested plan includes offering various options and enabling decision-makers to refine their selections according to their priorities and principles. In situations with significant risks, it is crucial to involve not only specialists but also diverse individuals who can contribute a broader scope of knowledge. Decision-making that relies on extensive, quantitative data and frequent events generally yields more precise predictions than relying solely on experts along their experience.

Independent individuals with diverse perspectives may be more accurate predictors than experts, who may suffer from overconfidence, confirmation bias, a disregard for base rates, narrow thinking, inflexibility, an inability to consider personal or opposing opinions, a failure to update beliefs considering new evidence, and an insistence on using logic and experience when common sense may not be sufficient in new circumstances. Due to these factors, experts can sometimes perform worse than chimpanzees who guess randomly (Rosling, Rönnlund, & Rosling, 2018; Tetlock & Gardner, 2015).

In addition to collective intelligence derived from one or multiple groups, there is also the concept of "big data wisdom". By utilizing deep learning algorithms, it is possible to uncover new insights and correlations within large sets of data (Christian & Griffiths, 2016; Lee, 2018). Regression models are not affected by emotions and can update their beliefs when presented with new, disconfirming information. Unlike experts, who may be influenced by their own biases and convictions, regression models can impartially weigh various factors to arrive at a prediction. Experts may benefit from using statistical predictions as a guide, but they may still ignore them and rely on their own judgement. To determine when to rely on statistical models instead of expert opinion, it is important to track how often experts ignore predictions. Ideally, a combination of expert evaluation and statistical modelling could be used, where the potential biases of experts cancel out each other, and the weight of expert opinion increases in proportion to the importance of the problem at hand.

VIABLE AGENCY

Without going into details, agencies across countries do a lion's share of public service compared to their parent ministries. So many words and works about agencies that demonstrate their importance, but so little firm guidelines. Even the one made, resemble more to Simon's principles as mere proverbs. How come? For Simon (1997), administrative theory should focus on weights applied to relevant criteria; their importance in any concrete situation is always relative, contingent. Maybe an approach based on agencies full description, mutual comparison and generalisation was/is not the right one? Is it even possible to infer future actions from the past ones if they depend to a significant extent on variable, changeable events? Agencies are complex systems embedded in larger systems and consist subsystems in a complex web of relations vis-à-vis other elements and environments. For complex systems is not so much important with what someone starts but with what ends up, the latter being really the only point in time-space conditions. The aim is to understand, to see a maybe a slightly larger picture (of how and when one moves on the way) than just to enumerate large amounts of data and facts. The main reason for this is *interactions* among parts that cause not only unpredicted but also faster and exponential changes, which makes things hard to plan ahead. This is valid for the nature, society and its subsystems, organisations, and people. The rate of change is faster than in the past, but still, there is some kind of system present which usually prevents things to go straight towards infinity or extinction, but to resemble the sinusoidal curve that illustrates the progression and depression of a situation.[8] The need to adapt to the speed of change (by which changes happen) is higher than changes themselves; for the problem of planning/adaptation the rate of change is more important than the change *per se*. The same stands for the administration of organisations and/or agencies, where dynamism has an increasingly leading role instead of stability. A goal is not just to have a larger amount of data, but to design a system that could show where an agency stands in a real context of time and the other for the agency relevant elements. A goal is hence in (cybernetic) control *vis-à-vis* the technological, substantial procedural and personal changes that affect a main purpose and goals. A goal is in the effective and efficient administration and management of data flows that serve for optimal decision-making.

The most important principles of control are that the controller should be part of the system under control,[9] with the present feedback (Beer, 1981). Stability is achieved when the system is acknowledged with the internal and external tendencies to abandon stability given stimulus, when there is a transducer that transports the former from sensorial units to other parts and output, and that is further been through feedback assessed in the light of inputs and the main system's purposes and goals. The input, output, and the way that connects the previous two are the main elements of control. Agencies cannot be managed or dominated by forward lines (which makes agency just as a transducer or a conductor between policy and citizens' needs), but by feedback lines that make an agency as an independent and relevant partner of politics and citizens only when the variety of agency outputs is similar to the variety of situation that must be controlled. Variety as the number of distinguishable elements is usually more known as uncertainty that can be minimised only with the actions that its decision-making (its basic form is simply "yes" and "no") on which actions are based. Organisations are tools by which human actions can be amplified. That is why their management is so important. From the classical point of view, based on stability it could be contra intuitively to see agencies and their administration only as approximations to ideal type of agency, because legal goals are known, but their fulfilment given the time, sources, manner is not. That is why they are managed by general rules and not by the particular ones, that is why also learning, training, researching, experimenting, and correcting are so important as they discover not only new ways of adaptation, but also prevent to settle down and be overspecialised that is not useful in the presence of changeable and flexible environment.

Beer in *Brain of the Firm (1981)* created a model of organisation based on physiology of the human brain as the most intimate and internal human control system. The control echelons from 1 (least) to 5 (most developed) or spinal vertebral level, spinal cord, mesencephalon, diencephalon, and cerebral cortex. Based on this five-part division, Beer designed a five-part model of the organisational structure of any living or autonomous system (Beer, 1972: 129) that is able to survive (VSM - viable system model). The model is based on the connectivity, interaction, or communication among five elements, which represent implementation, coordination, control, intelligence, and decision-making:

System 1 contains several primary activities in charge of producing services or products. In any System 1, a primary activity is able to survive itself due to the recursive nature of the systems. It refers to the performance of a function performed as a major part of the organisation's operations. System 1 are (public) employees who work in the lowest (administrative) production units.

System 2 represents the coordination or information channels and bodies that allow the primary activities in System 1 to communicate with each other and that allow for System 3 to monitor and coordinate activities within System 1. System 2 represents the allocation function of common resources used by System 1. Coordination does not mean "top-down" direction and control, but rather mutual, horizontal adjustments between autonomous units and support functions. Leaders of System 1 reflect System 2.

System 3 represents the control structure and activities whose task is to establish the rules, resources, rights, and responsibilities of System 1 and to provide an interface for System 4 and System 5. It represents a "big picture" of the processes within System 1; although the efficient use of communication channels can significantly reduce the need for higher control, two-way communication between subunits and higher units is a prerequisite for viability. System 3 is the channel through which resources are negotiated, instructions from management are set, and supervisory reports go up to the management, thus keeping in touch with what is happening. Just as IT technology is a good tool for facilitating channels within System 2, reporting systems are one form of reducing direct commands here. Within this part of the system, a monitoring channel is also installed, through which it is ensured that the monitoring reports are complied with and that the latter reflect the actual situation. System 3 controls (audit) leaders of System 2.

System 4 is the body responsible for looking outwards, into the changing environment, for monitoring and proposing ways in which the organisation should adapt to stay alive (a change agent, or catalyst). The intelligence (research) department represents here a two-way connection between primary activities and the external environment (determining the market situation, changes in technology, operating trends, in short, all trends that are added in the environment and vice versa - communicating the environment about the organisation's activities). In System 4, there are "leaders in disguise" - not so much about the facts as about how facts are presented, as the presentation can decisively influence the final decision. System 4 is/research unit(s); they basically represent a system's feedback loop, where actions follow research, and after execution, research follows actions.

System 5 is responsible for major decisions within the organisation as a whole, for balancing requirements from different parts of the organisation, and for managing the organisation as a whole. It thus connects the autonomous parts into a cohesive whole on the basis of received and "cleaned" information from systems 4 and 3. The main role is to ensure clarity and direction of the future operation of the entire organisation. System 5 is a director or board as the main decision-making unit that is concerned with an organisation's overall pattern. Beer's five-part viable structure of organisation can be transferred easily also two other kinds of institutions, from higher (on a state level, from citizens [1], to public institutions [2], government [3], academia [4] and Parliament [5]) to the lower (on an agency level from public servants [1], organisational units [2], council [3], R&D [4] and director [5]) ones. VSM, connected with its five systems, could be used also for the organisation of agencies. Such an organisation, institution or agency is here called *viable* as these five connected and mutually (more or less) affected systems resemble the very essence of human life.

Viable Agency and Its Autonomy

Contrary to many works that equate autonomy with the whole organisation, for Beer autonomy is needed to maintain a stable internal environment in decentralised Systems 1, 2 and 3. Here, based on receptors, effectors, and feedback structure, more than the vertical and hierarchical command and control, the horizontal informational (peripheral) control or exchange of information takes place (twin centres of different tendency):

If a division of the firm were really and truly autonomous it would not be part of the firm at all... If the heart of the liver were really autonomous, they might decide to renegue on the body. On the other hand, if the heart and liver were not more or less autonomous, we would have to remember to tell them what to do all the time - and we would be dead in ten minutes. In the same way, if a division of the firm is not more or less autonomous, the main board has to run it directly - which is equally impossible. The body has understood this dilemma for several hundred thousand years, and we can learn from it. It solution is called the autonomous nervous system (Beer, 1981, p. 100).

Preconditions of Wisdom and Move From Experts to People, Databases

The expression of autonomy in an organisation is in the *mutual help of the group members* who assist each other in effective leadership and their personal and official behaviours, because a formal leader cannot perform all leadership in all circumstances at all times. A system becomes autonomous when its three control systems work in such a coordinated way (the successful regulation of internal stability) that higher instances do not detect discrepancies and problems. System 4 and 5 are oriented towards the external environment where adjustments are needed, so they cannot be fully autonomous; System 4 links volitional and open autonomic control by alerting System 5 of discrepancies between plans and the external environment. System 5 makes decisions but it must respect higher levels (a parent ministry, government, rule of law). As systems are embedded in other systems System 1 to 5 are part in other systems. This is known also as the recursive system theorem: 'if a viable system contains a viable system, then the organisational structure must be recursive' (Beer, 1981, p. 287). System 1 - 5 are present in a human and other systems, their subsystems, and higher systems which they are part:

The viable agency consists of Systems 1 – 5; it is an autonomous system based on the principle of subsidiarity that can (re)produce itself. Such an agency is not only organised, but it works in a way that can successfully meet the demands of its stakeholders in the constantly changing environment. Its qualities are based on the main one: *adaptability;* this one is the result of effective and efficient relations among Systems 1 – 5 that should not be only seen as formal units, but are present in all places, where actions

Figure 1. The automatic system of a firm having subsidiaries A, B, C and D
(Beer, 1981, p. 130)

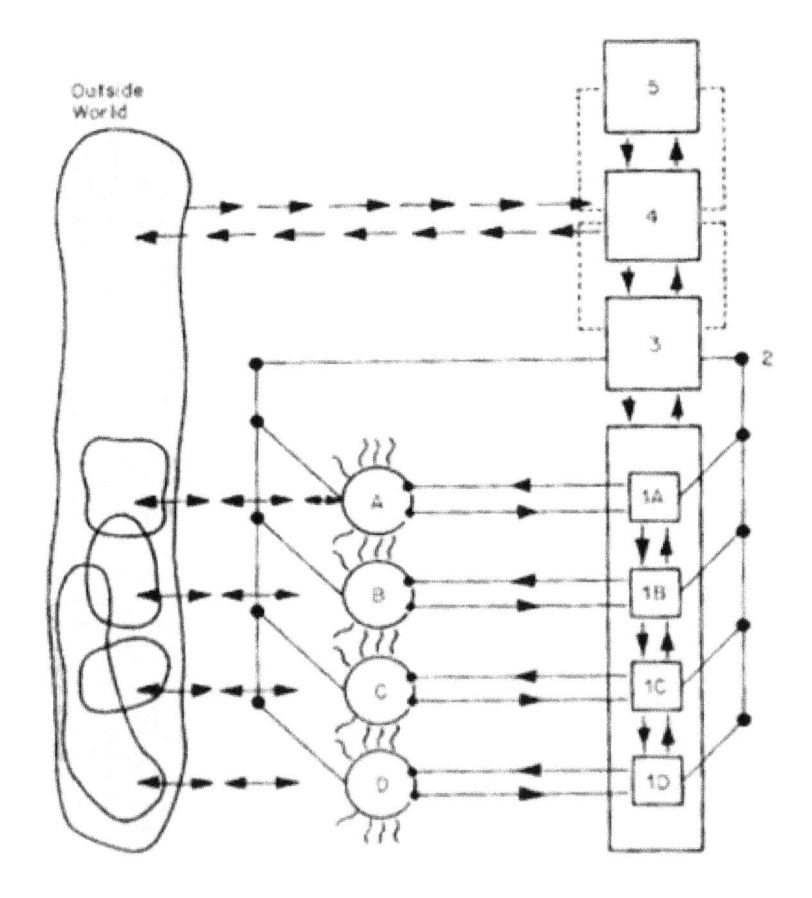

Figure 2. Two dimensions of neuropsychological control: the main vertical control system (somatic) and the sympathetic and para-sympathetic system (automatic)
(Beer, 1981, p. 130)

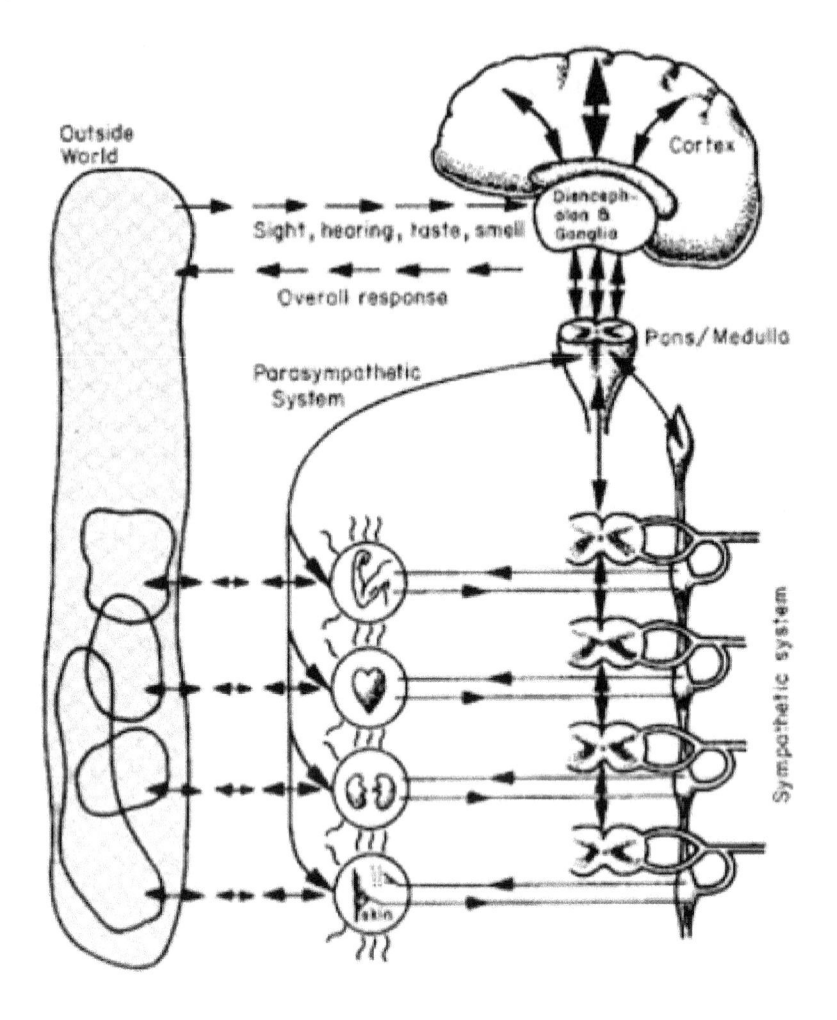

of Systems 1 – 5 take place. These parts are systems when they consist the essential parts of all systems (inputs, outputs, flows, stocks, feedback, indicators, patterns, and to them relevant decision-making), when they fulfil and/or go towards their main goals. Regardless that the latter are in the law more firmly put as in other environments, successful public agencies (based on their reputation or importance for the public goals or the public interest) can in time also change them (through reasonable proposals towards the parent ministries, stakeholders or the public as a whole.

The concept of the viable agency could be – through its five-part organisation, its vertical and horizontal connections – the answer for cooperation problems.[10] The idea is that control systems of the firm can be more successful when they resemble systems of the human body. A view on Slovenian public institutions can show a slight resemblance to the mentioned five-part structure:

In the above given structure public agencies usually have no System 4 (the executive has Secretariat, but it does not perform R&D task); individual bodies lack System 3, and all collective bodies have System 3. Even when all of them have a formally five-part organisational structure, the latter should be

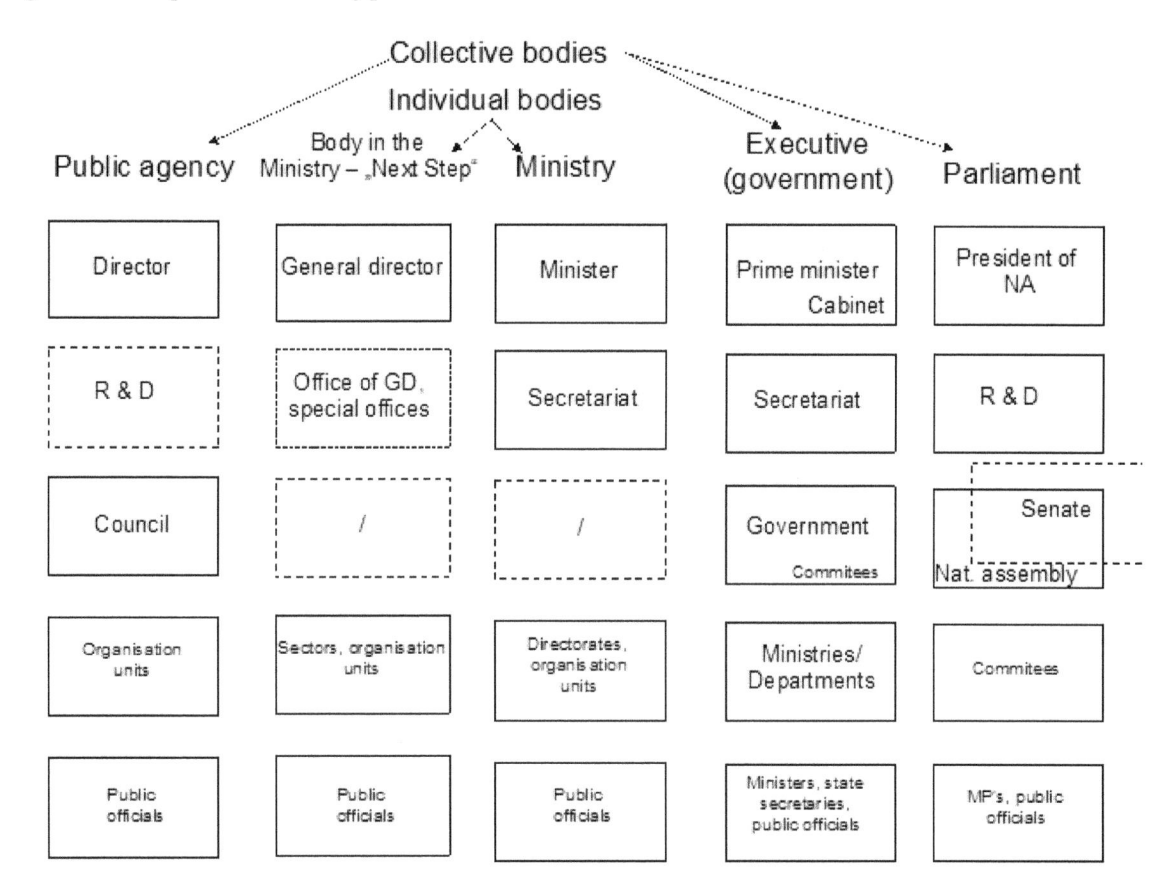

Figure 3. Five-part structure of public institutions

	Collective bodies			
	Individual bodies			
Public agency	Body in the Ministry – "Next Step" / Ministry		Executive (government)	Parliament
Director	General director / Minister		Prime minister Cabinet	President of NA
R & D	Office of GD, special offices / Secretariat		Secretariat	R & D
Council	/ / /		Government Committees	Senate / Nat. assembly
Organisation units	Sectors, organisation units / Directorates, organisation units		Ministries/ Departments	Commitees
Public officials	Public officials / Public officials		Ministers, state secretaries, public officials	MP's, public officials

as such present and active in reality, in mutual communications and/or connections, where each system may affect the other ones. Parts should be linked with multiple connections to be viable.[11] 'Organisations are collections of decision elements and channels by which they are connected. A constructive employment of apparently superfluous numbers of nodes and channels provides protection against error, when everything about the system stands a finite chance of being wrong' (Beer, 1972, p. 291). This is known as the redundancy of a potential command: a command centre shifts from time to time, from an occasion to another occasion based on the available information and/or information flow that determines which series of information matters vis-a-vis goals. When a decision is relevant for System 1, the decision is taken there (and this is valid for System 1), and when it is relevant for System 5 decision is taken there (and is valid for all subsystems).

Given the not so marvellous ranking of Slovenia on various international indexes, it is evident that an agency cannot be successful even when it has formally established Systems 1 – 5. The secret is in their *connections* and *mutual influences*. The agency should therefore have vertical and horizontal information lines and connections to be able to prevent taking inappropriate decisions at an appropriate level. It happens many times that important decisions are formally taken by leaders in System 5 (who pretend to understand or are easily manipulated by those who know the facts), but are substantially prepared at lower levels, by public servants, interest groups or the so-called "experts". This can be improved by a different kind of decision-making or information-gathering system, known as collective wisdom. This could be one way to institutionally impose more connections and relationships, to raise management awareness of the importance of the views of agency civil servants and other citizens. Probably the greatest advantage of this form of viable agency is its universal applicability, irrespective of the otherwise formally differently named public institutions: a ministry, a body attached to a ministry, a public institute, a public agency, a public fund, etc. It is a different name for otherwise very similar forms of action, where institutions are always at least somewhat different, even if they have the same formal form. Thus, a public institution could function in the same way even if it were called a public institute, a public agency, or a public fund, and vice versa: whatever the differences between the individual situations in terms of their competences, tasks, and fundamental objectives, they are all similar in terms of the internal and external relations, the interactions between the institution's bodies and external stakeholders.

COLLECTIVE WISDOM APPROACH TOWARDS NOMO-DYNAMICS

No one is able to attain the truth adequately, while, on the other hand, we do not collectively fail, but everyone says something true about the nature of things, and while individually we contribute little or nothing to the truth, by the union of all a considerable amount is amassed (Aristotle, 2015 Book II).

Isaac Newton in his reworking of Bernard de Chartres' quotation famously stated, '[i]f I have seen a little further it is by standing on the shoulders of giants' (Newton, 1675). The scientific community has progressed numerous times by building on previous discoveries, but this is not evident neither in the majoritarian nor in the proportional electoral systems. Representative democracy emerged in the 18-19th century due to various reasons (among them were/are lack of time, expertise, large distance, disinterest, a lack of motivation, etc.), but in the era of information technology (IT) at least the lack of time and distance can be left out of consideration. If election systems could be seen as a "hot chestnut" when talking about changes the latter can be more easily implemented in public agencies. The importance of adaptation to changing conditions and/or environment cannot be emphasised enough; this stands also for the performance of a collective of people or an organisation that is nowadays faced with increasingly complex tasks. The latter can be solved more successfully when a sufficient degree of members' cognitive variety[12] is present; this variety can be managed with cooperation and communication through which also their common abilities can be expressed: 'more complex, multi-faceted tasks that require each member of the team to perform a subtask and then combine inputs into a team product are the most influenced by the average ability of team members, because higher average cognitive ability is associated with greater propensity to adapt to a changing environment, as well as to learn from new information discovered during work' (Engel et al., 2014, p. 11). A group's collective intelligence is connected with the average social perceptiveness of the group members,[13] with the degree to which group members participate about equally in conversation, and with the proportion of women in the group (Woolley et al., 2010). Adaptation can be the other word for 'general intelligence (the ability to achieve a wide range of different goals effectively in different environments) that requires an intelligent actor to be not just good at a specific kind of task but also good at learning how to do a wide range of tasks. In short, this definition of intelligence means roughly the same thing as "versatility" or "adaptability"' (Malone, 2018, p. 25).

Collective intelligence or wisdom (CW) can be used also in public agencies; the citizens' perspectives, choices, incorporating beliefs and cultural backgrounds should be included in public decision-making

Preconditions of Wisdom and Move From Experts to People, Databases

and implementation, especially when this is not so hard to do, when there are no big coordination problems (the help of IT is here self-evident). Although individually each person has diverse knowledge or differing beliefs, their CW provides more accurate data. This could be *sine qua non* of the new "smart legitimacy". When authority and openness walk hand in hand, mechanisms can be created to extract CW from diverse participants. The complexity of relations makes things complicated, so a smart assembly of parts to form the manageable (able to change), systemic is needed. Even if the elaboration of relations cannot be known with full mathematical precision (like all details of the plane's operations are not known) their overall understanding can be. Based on the mentioned elements of complexity, diversity and variety in the environment, only the similar conditions in the society can address them – through some system. Here (see the below Figure), people and their data come to the fore in various ways:

There are a) simple, b) complicated and c) more complicated ways to harness CW: a) and b) can be made from the *unconnected* individuals, who (independently and without knowing each other's answers) provide data for other purposes (in the open databases) or to solve a specific problem, while the more complicated ways can be made with the *connected* individuals, who act with a certain degree of mutual dependency (from the most loose connection, where results of others are seen [which can

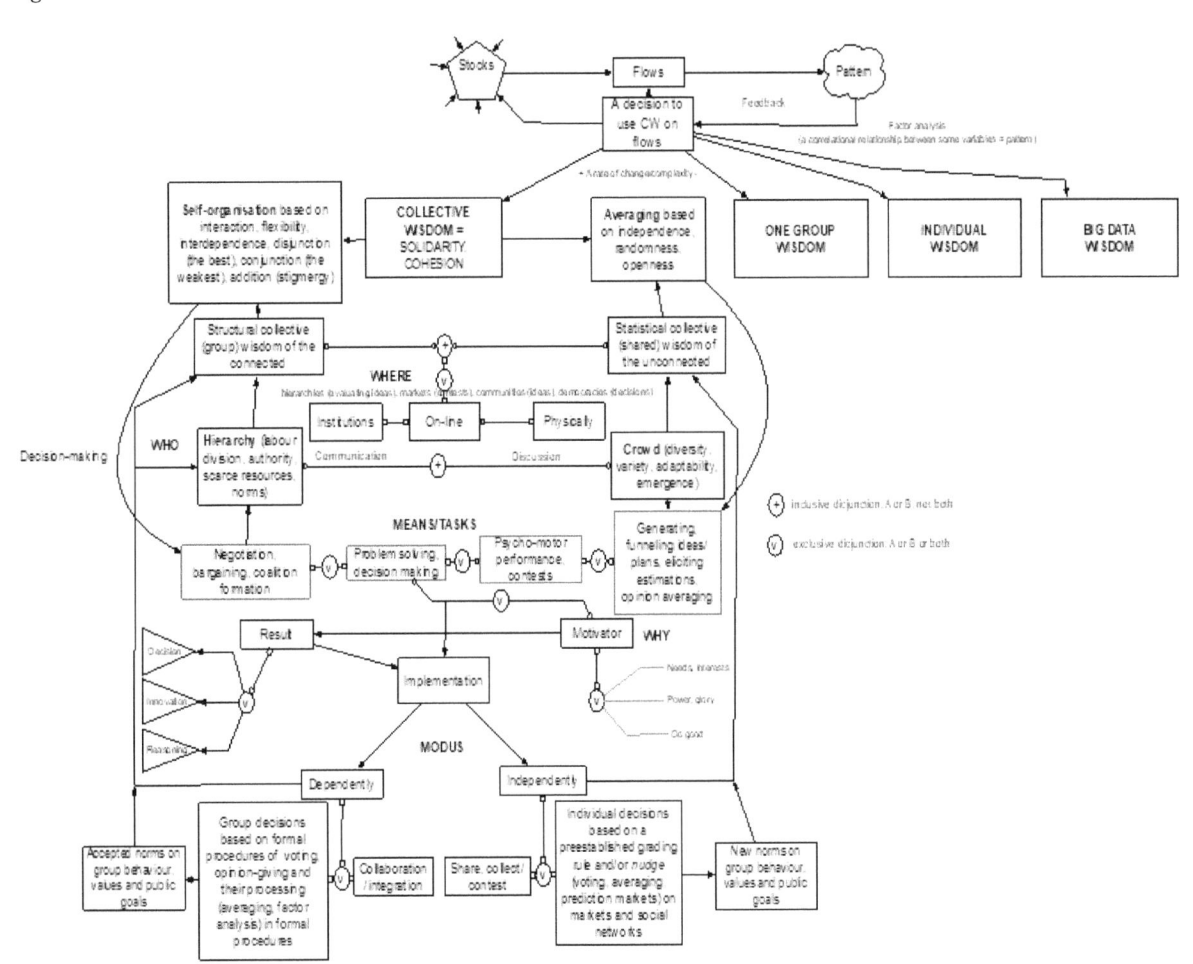

Figure 4. Collective wisdom and its alternatives

affect decisions of the later opinion-givers], to the more connected (where social ability comes to the fore) and the most connected, where the later opinion-givers mimic the previous ones. The options a) and b) are based on data aggregation and statistical analysis, while c) results in self-organisation processes. The examples of a/b/c are the open data (portals)/public forums/communication (*via* pheromones of mimicking insects) that gives and changes weights of given alternatives. These options circulate the notions of 'social machines', 'social computing' as a crowdsourced media reports on public problems (Shadbolt, O'Hara, Roure, & Hall, 2019) or "social collective intelligence" as a mix of CW and social informatics (Miorandi, Maltese, Rovatsos, Nijholt, & Stewart, 2014) that includes the ideas of hybrid computing (people and machines working together to create new types of problem-solving ability, from peoples' everyday use of their mobile connection to data, algorithms and social networks), adaptivity and learning (gaining knowledge of how the system responds to different circumstances and using that to readapt). One of such examples is the Smart Society project (Smart Society Project, 2017) as a socio-technical ecosystem, in which the physical and virtual dimensions of life are intertwined and where people interact. All alternatives of CW could serve as an input for flows that together with the stocks, patterns and feedback represent the system (the upper part in Figure 1). CW could be the answer on the question on '[h]ow much energy and creativity might be unlocked if all people in an organization feel in control' (Malone, 2003, p. 63)? Regarding the implementation steps, the government could establish different public platforms on which the people could provide their opinions on public matters. This citizen-centred approach could reframe discussion between autonomy and paternalism towards the *shared* decision making, collaboration or the *calibration* of public interest according to the citizen's inputs, towards partnerships among the public institutions, citizens and communities. Such an approach could promote practices that will more likely nurture CW than simply proclaim the principle of autonomy.

One of the most obvious ways IT can help 'is by helping groups remember and share the lessons that individuals have learned separately' (Malone, 2018, p. 233). CW can better adapt than the classical static rules due to its mimicking of complex adaptive systems. Among the usual (more mechanically-connected) ways of reaching CW and/or collective decisions are the charrette, focus groups, future search, the Samoa circle or the Delphi method, while the IT (especially Internet) - based (unconnected people as individuals, but statistically [just] aggregated) ways are many forms of crowdsourcing that integrate the creative energies of online communities into day-to-day operations (to rate or design product or solve problems) of many organizations (Brabham, 2013; Grier, 2013), like the prediction markets (e.g. the University of Iowa's Iowa Electronic Markets, the Hollywood Stock Exchange, FantasyScotus, Amazon Product Review Tool, customers' [books, films, photos] ratings) supported with the various decision-making software based on more the collaborative decision-making, big data and machine learning (e.g. Decision Lens, LexPredict, Foldit, Climate CoLab). From the systemic (and formal, institutional) point of view, self-interest could not be at odds with the greater good, if a public model of "CW decision-making" (CWDM) is organised. One of the first was examples was participatory budgeting that started in Porto Alegre, Brazil, in 1989, as an anti-poverty measure that helped reduce child mortality by nearly 20%. Since then PB has spread to over 3,000 cities around the world (Oliveira, 2017). Based on the mentioned examples a political organization based on the CWDM can be a new way to address complexity. How much time *Homo politicus* has left to realise this (especially in the more and more connected, intertwined problems that are more and more present on the global level)?

Preconditions of Wisdom and Move From Experts to People, Databases

In the meantime, along the experts and MPs (public assemblies), other ways can express a larger diversity than the first two; this can be done with the committees or groups of experts, with an individual that enables/builds diversity into his decisions (by using Bayes theorem or Bayes nets, a Markov chain or other stochastic models) (Carrier, 2012; Edwards, Jr, & Winterfeldt, 2007; Gamerman, 1997; Nielsen & Jensen, 2007), while CW (through the aggregation and statistical analysis of independent, individual opinions) probably bits them all. CWDM emphasizes consensus-building; it does this not by the 'winner-takes-all' dynamic of majoritarian decision-making, but by the independent, diverse and analysed citizens' inputs. In the majoritarian case, a minority will probably do everything in its power to undermine the majoritarian decision (for the important cases, the classical legal theory provides solutions in a higher majority or in negotiation), while in the second all are represented in it. This way can be named as *synomy* (*syn*, together and *nomos*, laws) or the wisdom of collective decision-making. This kind of collective decision-making does not disregard an opposing part: it is included in a decision. CWDM should thus be able to i) process data obtained from the real world (based on [stochastic] indicators); here a citizen scientist as a volunteer comes to the fore who collects and/or processes data as part of a scientific enquiry (e.g. the Christmas Bird Count as a major source of scientific data on trends in the status of bird species in North America, the Evolution MegaLab and OPen Air Laboratories – citizen science projects invite the public to take part in scientific investigations by contributing data, processing data or both (Silvertown, 2009; Worthington et al., 2012); ii) record measurements that uncover patterns between interactions; iii) enable/change different and independent input values and follow how patterns change; iv) compare results of patterns vis-à-vis predictable scenarios based on the average or median result and/or various (publicly-known) algorithms and v) adapt new decisions/scenarios. If citizens' inputs are included in such (or similar) way in decision-making, CWDM is present (Brabham, 2013; Briskin, Erickson, Ott, & Callanan, 2009; Landemore & Elster, 2012; Surowiecki, 2005; Tovey, 2008) provided that in search for optimal decisions includes the patterns, network, connections, diversity, aggregation and averaging (instead of singular decision–makers, deliberation, division, disconnection and sameness). The power of CW can due to mutual cancelling remove the behavioural and other biases (Ariely, 2008; Kahneman, 2013); due to the higher calculation power over brains' limits of processing power (Marois & Ivanoff, 2005) CW can be a better answer for the complex environment, with its numerous combinations.

The environment evolves in its own (systemically-interconnected) ways, and it does not consider formal (democratic) decisions automatically. The latter must hence address the first accordingly with the similar level of complexity: simple rules for the known environment, dynamic or adaptable norms for the dynamic environment, systemic rules for the complicated environment for CW for the complex environment.

CW is the capacity for a group of individuals to envision a future and reach it in a complex context. By using the nervous system metaphor CW is the ability to identify patterns in the world, encode these patterns in some medium, and utilize this patterned medium to make useful, non-random decisions. CW is a form of choice architecture that could be installed into democratic general rulemaking (at least for more complex, dynamic problems). The emphasis is on the citizens' knowledge who, together with authorities' pattern policies. The more and more increasing complexity of regulation of society prevents the classical idea of society's management to be fully apprehended in legal norms. Since this is not possible, an increasing gap opens between the formal determination of rights and obligations and their actual implementation. The theory of complex systems could with an analysis of complexity that looks for patterns in a simple behaviour from a data set with the concept of emergence give a new perspective on a rule's understanding: an essential difference from the present understanding is not only that the collective as a whole represents more than just the sum of its parts. Only appropriately sized (numerically) dominated diversity can tame opposing diversity: only diversity$_1$ can break diversity$_2$ and *vice versa*. Stability of a dynamical system is, therefore, the property of the system (and not of the people as individuals) as a whole; stability means the coordination of measures between the system's parts.

CW is about the inclusion of all diverse information, where the essential creator is the people, our evolutionary skills of selection that look for relevant information but grouped in a common pattern. This paper claims that events cannot be satisfactorily regulated if diversity is not similar on the side of regulator and the side of regulated; emergence is the cause that complex systems cannot be precisely predicted in advance; an awareness (of self and others) is the basis of every management; the implementation of awareness is possible through sensors that measure previously given criteria that allow the fact-finding and adapting to new circumstances. These inferences show that public systems and their decisions cannot be built solely based on the information we have, because it is the system of different sensors in different places with the detection of data (similar as the installation of sensors in the plane allows you to fly properly or promptly to respond to the surroundings) that enables deduction on appropriateness of some sort of regulation. It is not about to be able based on facts to make the best decisions and *ex-post* enforce also subjective responsibility for mistakes, but to have also the *ex-ante* system of facts perception that is designed to allow the detection of a wide range of data from which patterns can be seen. First, it is necessary to have relevant data (which we recognise/understand as such), and only then it can be analysed and placed in mutual relations. Mechanical – by the hand of one or some experts – rules can cope neither with dynamic nor with the complex environment. If this is common sense, it is not so common in the present parliamentarian and bureaucratic procedures. Decreased costs of IT should change the public decision-making processes, but further efforts are needed to undermine the Motorhead lyrics that "everything changes, [but] all stays the same".

REFERENCES

Aggarwal, I., Woolley, A. W., Chabris, C. F., & Malone, T. W. (2019). The impact of cognitive style diversity on implicit learning in teams. *Frontiers in Psychology*, *10*, 112. doi:10.3389/fpsyg.2019.00112 PMID:30792672

Ariely, D. (2008). *Predictably Irrational: The Hidden Forces That Shape Our Decisions*. HarperCollins.

Aristotle. (1992). *Eudemian Ethics Books I, II, and VIII* (M. Woods, Trans.). Clarendon Press.

Aristotle. (2015). *Metaphysics*. Aeterna Press.

Ayres, I. (2007). *Super Crunchers: Why Thinking-By-Numbers is the New Way to Be Smart*. Bantam Books.

Beer, S. (1981). *Brain of the Firm: A Development in Management Cybernetics* (2nd ed.). Herder and Herder.

Bon, G. L. (2001). *The Crowd: A Study of the Popular Mind*. Batoche Books.

Brabham, D. C. (2013). *Crowdsourcing*. MIT Press. doi:10.7551/mitpress/9693.001.0001

Briskin, A., Erickson, S., Ott, J., & Callanan, T. (2009). *The Power of Collective Wisdom and the Trap of Collective Folly*. Berrett-Koehler Publishers.

Carrier, R. (2012). *Proving History: Bayes's Theorem and the Quest for the Historical Jesus*. Prometheus Books.

Christian, B., & Griffiths, T. (2016). *Algorithms to Live By: The Computer Science of Human Decisions*. Henry Holt and Co.

Dawes, R. M. (1979). The robust beauty of improper linear models in decision making. *The American Psychologist*, *34*(7), 571–582. doi:10.1037/0003-066X.34.7.571

de Oliveira, O. P. (2017). *International Policy Diffusion and Participatory Budgeting: Ambassadors of Participation, International Institutions and Transnational Networks*. Springer. doi:10.1007/978-3-319-43337-0

Edwards, W., Jr. R. F. M., & Winterfeldt, D. von. (2007). Advances in Decision Analysis: From Foundations to Applications. New York: Cambridge University Press.

Engel, D., Woolley, A. W., Jing, L. X., Chabris, C. F., & Malone, T. W. (2014). Reading the Mind in the Eyes or Reading between the Lines? Theory of Mind Predicts Collective Intelligence Equally Well Online and Face-To-Face. *PLoS One*, *9*(12), e115212. doi:10.1371/journal.pone.0115212 PMID:25514387

Galton, F. (1889). *Natural inheritance*. MacMillan and Co.

Galton, F. (1907). Vox Populi. *Nature*, *75*(1949), 450–451. doi:10.1038/075450a0

Gamerman, D. (1997). *Markov Chain Monte Carlo*. Chapman and Hall/CRC.

Gell-Mann, M. (2002). The Quark and the Jaguar (VIII edition). New York: W.H. Freeman & Company.

Gerrits, L., & Marks, P. (2017). *Understanding Collective Decision Making: A Fitness Landscape Model Approach*. Edward Elgar Publishing. doi:10.4337/9781783473151

Goleman, D. (2007). *Social Intelligence: The New Science of Human Relationships*. Bantam.

Grier, D. A. (2013). *Crowdsourcing For Dummies*. John Wiley & Sons.

Grove, W. M., & Meehl, P. E. (1996). Comparative Efficiency of Informal (Subjective, Impressionistic) and Formal (Mechanical, Algorithmic) Prediction Procedures. *The Clinical–Statistical Controversy.*, *2*(2), 293–323.

Gulick, L. (2003). Notes On the Theory of Organisation. In K. Thompson (Ed.), *The Early Sociology of Management and Organizations: Papers on the Science of Administration* (Vol. IV, pp. 1–49). Routledge.

Hayek, F. A. (1998). *Law, Legislation and Liberty: A New Statement of the Liberal Principles of Justice and Political Economy*. Routledge.

Janis, I. L. (1980). Groupthinking. In H. J. Leavitt, L. R. Pondy, & D. M. Boje (Eds.), *Readings in Managerial Psychology*. University of Chicago Press.

Johnson, N. L. (2002). *The Development of Collective Structure and Its Response to Environmental Change* (SSRN Scholarly Paper No. ID 2232154). Rochester, NY: Social Science Research Network. https://papers.ssrn.com/abstract=2232154

Kahneman, D. (2013). Thinking, Fast and Slow (Reprint edition). New York: Farrar, Straus and Giroux.

Landemore, H., & Elster, J. (Eds.). (2012). *Collective Wisdom: Principles and Mechanisms*. Cambridge University Press. doi:10.1017/CBO9780511846427

Lee, K.-F. (2018). *AI Superpowers: China, Silicon Valley, and the New World Order*. Houghton Mifflin Harcourt.

Lorenz, J., Rauhut, H., Schweitzer, F., & Helbing, D. (2011). How social influence can undermine the wisdom of crowd effect. *Proceedings of the National Academy of Sciences of the United States of America*, *108*(22), 9020–9025. doi:10.1073/pnas.1008636108 PMID:21576485

Malone, T. W. (2003). Is Empowerment Just a Fad? Control, Decision Making, and IT. In T. W. Malone, R. Laubacher, & M. S. S. Morton (Eds.), *Inventing the Organizations of the 21st Century*. The MIT Press.

Malone, T. W. (2018). *Superminds: How Hyperconnectivity is Changing the Way We Solve Problems*. Oneworld Publications.

Marois, R., & Ivanoff, J. (2005). Capacity limits of information processing in the brain. *Trends in Cognitive Sciences*, *9*(6), 296–305. doi:10.1016/j.tics.2005.04.010 PMID:15925809

Meehl, P. E. (2013). *Clinical Versus Statistical Prediction: A Theoretical Analysis and a Review of the Evidence*. Echo Point Books & Media.

Mintzberg, H. (1983). *Structure in Fives: Designing Effective Organizations*. Prentice Hall PTR.

Miorandi, D., Maltese, V., Rovatsos, M., Nijholt, A., & Stewart, J. (2014). *Social Collective Intelligence: Combining the Powers of Humans and Machines to Build a Smarter Society*. Springer. doi:10.1007/978-3-319-08681-1

Newton, I. (1675). *Isaac Newton letter to Robert Hooke, 1675*. HSP. https://discover.hsp.org/Record/dc-9792/

Nielsen, T. D., & Jensen, F. (2007). *Bayesian Networks and Decision Graphs* (2nd ed.). Springer.

O'Reilly, T. (2010). Government as a Platform. In D. Lathrop & L. Ruma (Eds.), *Open Government: Collaboration, Transparency, and Participation in Practice*. O'Reilly Media, Inc.

Page, S. E. (2008). The Difference: How the Power of Diversity Creates Better Groups, Firms, Schools, and Societies. Princeton, N.J.; Woodstock: Princeton University Press. doi:10.1515/9781400830282

Parsons, T. (1985). *Talcott Parsons on Institutions and Social Evolution: Selected Writings*. University of Chicago Press.

Parsons, T. (1991). The Social System (New edition). London: Routledge.

Pielke, R. A. Jr. (2007). *The Honest Broker: Making Sense of Science in Policy and Politics*. Cambridge University Press. doi:10.1017/CBO9780511818110

Premack, D., & Woodruff, G. (1978). Does the chimpanzee have a theory of mind? *Behavioral and Brain Sciences*, *1*(4), 515–526. doi:10.1017/S0140525X00076512

Ridley, M. (2017). *What Charles Darwin owes Adam Smith*. Learn Liberty. https://www.learnliberty.org/blog/what-charles-darwin-owes-adam-smith/

Rosling, H., Rönnlund, A. R., & Rosling, O. (2018). *Factfulness: Ten Reasons We're Wrong About the World—and Why Things Are Better Than You Think*. Hodder & Stoughton Ltd.

Rousseau, J.-J. (2002). *The Social Contract and The First and Second Discourses* (S. Dunn, Ed.). Yale University Press.

Sarewitz, D. (2004). How science makes environmental controversies worse. *Environmental Science & Policy*, *7*(5), 385–403. doi:10.1016/j.envsci.2004.06.001

Shadbolt, N., O'Hara, K., Roure, D. D., & Hall, W. (2019). *The Theory and Practice of Social Machines*. Springer. doi:10.1007/978-3-030-10889-2

Shanteau, J. (1992). Competence in experts: The role of task characteristics. *Organizational Behavior and Human Decision Processes*, *53*(2), 252–266. doi:10.1016/0749-5978(92)90064-E

Silvertown, J. (2009). A new dawn for citizen science. *Trends in Ecology & Evolution*, *24*(9), 467–471. doi:10.1016/j.tree.2009.03.017 PMID:19586682

Simon, H. A. (1997). *Administrative Behavior* (4th ed.). Free Press.

Slovic, P. (1987). Perception of Risk. *Science*, *236*(4799), 280–285. doi:10.1126/science.3563507 PMID:3563507

Spitzer, D. (2007). *Transforming Performance Measurement: Rethinking the Way We Measure and Drive Organizational Success*. AMACOM.

Stasser, G., & Titus, W. (1985). Pooling of unshared information in group decision making: Biased information sampling during discussion. *Journal of Personality and Social Psychology*, *48*(6), 1476–1478. doi:10.1037/0022-3514.48.6.1467

Sunstein, C. R. (2006). *Infotopia: How Many Minds Produce Knowledge*. Oxford University Press. doi:10.1093/oso/9780195189285.001.0001

Sunstein, C. R. (2009). *Going to Extremes: How Like Minds Unite and Divide*. Oxford University Press. doi:10.1093/oso/9780195378016.001.0001

Surowiecki, J. (2005). The Wisdom of Crowds (Reprint edition). New York, NY: Anchor.

Taleb, N. N. (2010). The Black Swan: The Impact of the Highly Improbable Fragility (Kindle Edition). New York: Random House Publishing Group.

Tetlock, P., & Gardner, D. (2015). Superforecasting: The Art and Science of Prediction (Kindle edition). London: Random House.

Tovey, M. (Ed.). (2008). *Collective Intelligence: Creating a Prosperous World at Peace*. Earth Intelligence Network.

Woolley, A. W., Chabris, C. F., Pentland, A., Hashmi, N., & Malone, T. W. (2010). Evidence for a Collective Intelligence Factor in the Performance of Human Groups. *Science*, *330*(6004), 686–688. doi:10.1126/science.1193147 PMID:20929725

Worthington, J. P., Silvertown, J., Cook, L., Cameron, R., Dodd, M., Greenwood, R. M., McConway, K., & Skelton, P. (2012). Evolution MegaLab: A case study in citizen science methods. *Methods in Ecology and Evolution*, *3*(2), 303–309. doi:10.1111/j.2041-210X.2011.00164.x

ENDNOTE

[1] Surowiecki identifies four characteristics that are typical of intelligent crowds: "diversity of opinion," "independence," "decentralization", "aggregation"(Surowiecki, 2005, p. 10).

[2] 'There is often a great deal of difference between the will of all and the general will; the latter regards only the common interest, while the former has regard to private interests, and is merely a sum of particular wills; but take away from these same wills the pluses and minuses which cancel one another, and the general will remains as the sum of the differences' (Rousseau, 2002, p. 142).

[3] 'In all cases, the mean relative to us is best; for that is as knowledge and rational principle prescribe. And in all cases that also produces the best state. And this is evident from induction and argument. For opposites rule out one another; the extremes are opposed both to one another and the mean because the mean is each one of the opposites concerning the other: the equal is larger than the smaller but smaller than the larger. So it must be the case that virtue of character is concerned with certain 35 means and is itself a certain mean state' (Aristotle, 1992, p. 16).

[4] For example, Michaela and Juliana made predictions about the upcoming performance of three children named Maggie (6), Cole (5), and Brody (1). Michaela predicted they would achieve 6th, 3rd, and 5th place, respectively, while Juliana predicted they would achieve 10th, 7th, and 1st place, respectively. To calculate the accuracy of their predictions, the errors are squared to avoid the cancellation of positive and negative errors. Michaela's error is calculated as $(6-6)^2 + (3-5)^2 + (5-1)^2 = 0 + 4 + 16 = 20$, while Juliana's error is calculated as $(10-6)^2 + (7-5)^2 + (1-1)^2 = 16 + 4 + 0 = 20$. The average error between them is 20, but their collective prediction for Maggie, Cole, and Brody's places (8th, 5th, and 3rd) had a lower error of $(8-6)^2 + (5-5)^2 + (3-1)^2 = 8$. This suggests that their collective prediction was more accurate than either of their individual predictions. If more people were to make predictions, the accuracy of the collective prediction would increase further. For more information on prediction diversity, please refer to the source (Page, 2008, pp. 197–235).

[5] 'When an individual ascribes mental states to themselves and others, such as beliefs, intentions, desires, and feelings, they are said to possess a theory of mind. This type of inference system is considered a theory because mental states cannot be directly observed, and the system can be used to predict how others will behave based on their internal states' (Premack & Woodruff, 1978).

[6] Social sensitivity refers to the ability to understand and navigate social situations effectively. It can be broken down into two components: social awareness, which encompasses our perception of others and their emotions, and social facility, which refers to our ability to respond appropriately to those perceptions (Goleman, 2007).

[7] The process of enumeration is comparable to the types of experts described by Gulick above.

8   This could be also presented as the law of diminishing returns where the decrease of the output in a production process cannot be improved just by enforcing new resources or energy, but by the new perspectives, approaches, tools and methods. E.g., Covid-19 situation can not only be improved with ever new or tougher protection measures, but with a vaccine (in the short term) or natural resistance (in the long term).

9   In living systems, an innate control function is their inevitable part, spread through their whole organism under which the system determines its overall position. A purpose of control is hence not to sanction but to know and be adaptable to the internal and external conditions.

10 Mintzberg's five coordinating mechanisms (1983) as the apparent fundamental ways in which an organization coordinates its work, are in viable agency reflected (only) through its System 1 – 3 parts (System 1 = mutual [informal] adjustment; System 2 = direct supervision; System 3 = standardisation of work; standardisation of outputs; standardisation of skills and knowledge processes), while the System 4 (the body responsible for looking outwards intelligence and/or research department) and System 5 (major decisions) are missing. When organizational work becomes more complicated, the favoured means of coordination in Mintzberg shift from the lowest to the highest and then finally revert back to mutual adjustment, while complicated and complex tasks all the more require the input of Systems 4 and 5.

11 Even then public institutions will vary a great deal from one another, as their tasks, clientele, processes etc., are different.

12 Cognitive style diversity impacts team learning indirectly through its influence on the team's collective intelligence: 'having cognitive style diversity is likely to ensure that the team has access to different ways of approaching the problem at hand. It can also reduce the chances that the team will fall into confirmation bias traps where members confirm each other's beliefs as a result of viewing information similarly. Cognitively diverse teams may more easily catch each other's blind spots, which would facilitate performance across domains. While having the maximum amount of perspectives possible is likely to give the team the best set of resources to approach an array of problems, it is important to take coordination processes into account, which may be influenced by how team inputs are configured in the team … a moderate level of diversity appears to provide the requisite level of cognitive resource without being completely offset by the associated process losses, and influences the team's collective intelligence (Aggarwal, Woolley, Chabris, & Malone, 2019, pp. 6–7).

13 Social perceptiveness can be in systems ensured with indicators.

Chapter 16
Base-Rate Questions for Present Agencies

ABSTRACT

The chapter discusses the concept of holistic agencies (HAs) and their potential role in public administration. Successful public agencies reflect some of the holistic elements, making them more adaptable and intelligent. HAs are seen as a part of overall institutional design and must be perceived as legitimate by society while also relating to norms, values, and culture. The demand for better institutions is necessary to achieve public goals optimally. The scholars or reformists should be pointing the way for future institutional development if there is a lack of demand from the people. Fukuyama's four aspects of stateness—organizational design and management, political system design, basis of legitimization, and cultural and structural factors—are essential for HA's success. The chapter concludes that establishing the reality on the ground is crucial to achieving HA's success, and while there may not be an optimal form of organization, HA is more about a manner of acting than a form.

INTRODUCTION

Judge a man by his questions rather than his answers.

– Voltaire

Already the second chapter describes some of the most important elements of HA, and shows a direction of AI in which HA will probably go. An assumption is that HAs are not yet present in the practice of public administration, although the more successful agencies reflect some of the holistic elements – the more they resemble human conscious beings with their intelligent capacity to adapt, the more successful they are. On the *supply* side of institutional capacity Fukuyama places four aspects of stateness: (1) organizational design and management, (2) political system design, (3) basis of legitimization, and (4) cultural and structural factors (Fukuyama, 2004). At first sight, HA clearly fits into the first aspect of stateness, but regarding of what was already written above, it is more than clear a successful public

DOI: 10.4018/979-8-3693-0507-2.ch016

Base-Rate Questions for Present Agencies

agency and/or HA, fits at the same time in three other aspects: it has to be seen as a part of overall state's institutional design rather than the individual agency (already mentioned governmental platform), it has to be perceived as being legitimate by the underlying society, and it also relates to norms, values, and culture (social capital).

The demand side of institutional capacity depends on the people's expectations or better demands for institutions that can successfully and the most optimally achieve public goals. In the absence of demands for better institutions from the people, it is the scholars or reformists who should be pointing the way for the future development of institutions. There really may not be no optimal form of organisation, as Fukuyama says, but HA is more about a manner of acting that of form. People have also some equal properties despite a myriad of other differences; that is why HA only wants to mimic human performance in its robustness, adaptability, flexibility and agility. On the road to HA, reformers could at first establish the reality on the ground, which is the basis for further change. In addition to other ways of establishing the reality and the degree of realisation of the HA idea, the questions below can serve for this purpose. A reform of the field of agencies should have answers to the below given Talbot's questions to establish the base rate from which HA could be further developed.

- 'Up to what point are agencies separate entities within national public administrations?
- Are some of the news agencies' de facto new organisations, or are they simply the re-labelling of existing structures with minor tweaks?
- Up to what degree agencies de facto along merely formal rules, change how things are done?
- Has the changed (or existing) semi-autonomous status of agencies gives agencies' managers the 'freedom to manage'?
- What are the consequential effects on the structure of "parent" state department from which state department agency functions were detached?
- Have the relevant state departments become truly "strategic" or do they still seek to "micro-manage" that would be the task of agency?
- Do large agencies and small ministries, or conversely small agencies in large ministries, create substantial power and information asymmetries?
- Does "agency" status necessarily mean that these organisations escape from the clutches of system-wide regulation within government and if they do, is it a good thing?
- Why does a government, or why should a government, adopt the AQUA (the autonomous and quasi-autonomous) style of delivering a service to the public, rather than more conventional means through ministerial hierarchies? On what bases can such choices be reasonably made?
- Has the burden of auditing, inspecting and monitoring on organisations which are "agencified" been eradicated, merely reduced, perhaps shifted into other forms or maybe even increased?
- Have the state organs charged with scrutinising agencies proved capable and willing to do so?
- Has been the result of increased transparency of agencified functions a loss of traditional forms of public accountability?
- What – if any – forms of "performance contracting" have been introduced for agencies? Are agencies required to produce any performance information at all about their activities? If so, what does this information focus on Inputs? Processes? Efficiency? Outcomes? Equity? Equality? Or some combination of these?

- Do agencies have targets for performance and, if so, who sets the targets? The agencies themselves? Their 'parent' bodies? A process of negotiation (and, if so, who is the dominant partner in the bargaining)?
- Who enforces any "contract" or who is responsible for taking action if an agency is seen to be "failing"? Similarly, what happens if an agency is "successful", who decides, and what actions are taken?
- Is performance information publicly available and, if so, how accessible, understandable and credible is it?
- Is performance information audited?
- Do parliamentary or other democratic institutions take an active part in the "performance regime" in setting targets, monitoring results and rewarding/punishing the poor/good performers?' (Talbot, 2004, pp. 18–19).

To these questions, some additional, controlling questions could be added that emphasise the systemic approach, based also on values:

- Who, where, when, and by what method was the factual state of affairs determined?
- How you will know this state is changed?
- For whom this state is good, who benefits the most?
- How many databases are connected with each other within the agency, with what kind of rules (algorithms), and what they can reveal as a whole?
- How do you know the real-time condition of an agency's action?
- Where and how do the feedback loops operate?
- What is an agency's function as a whole?
- What are its essential parts?
- How these parts (should and could) relate or connect?
- What are functions of these parts individually and taken in different combinations?
- Would a specific action be operative if some parts and relations were removed?
- Can the parts be assembled differently to reach the same goals?
- What (thresholds) determine(s) an agency's effectiveness and efficiency?
- Do you have scenarios (a space of possibilities) for different conditions and what triggers the first?
- From which point and with what tools can the same goals be achieved?
- Can the agency force a parameter's variable to take a prescribed value and/or can this be triggered in the changing environment?
- How can a specific action be abused and how can this be recognised and prevented?
- How do we know these actions work? (Adapted from Pečarič, 2020, pp. 16–17).
- How do you know when the result is based on the agencies' action, on other causes, and when the result co-evolves from the latter two?
- How time and space affect actions, resources, and results?
- How values affect actions, resources, and results?
- How the agency's adaptability can be achieved?
- What types of path-dependency affect the agency's tasks and results?
- How can be established that a new emergent thing (order) is present?
- With what resources or actions can be this new order the most successfully managed?

After the analysis of national public agencies based on the above-given questions and with the help of research methodology each country (or a manager for his agency) can know better up to what point agencies or a specific agency differentiates from the concept of HA. A result can be the additional reason along others (political, economic, historical, etc.) that can serve for agencies' further benefits,[1] divisions, or transformations. Given the great diversity and complexity of the composition of agencies in different countries, it would be entirely pretentious or even rude to suggest a single appropriate approach to the governance of a specific agency. Rather, it is the idea of systemic adaptation, which respectfully needs to be mastered according to the context of the specific situation in which a particular agency or country finds itself. The idea of HA can be seen as a new perspective, a new look on things that could be otherwise disregarded.

REFERENCES

Fukuyama, F. (2004). *State Building: Governance and World Order in the 21st Century*. Cornell University Press.

Pečarič, M. (2020). Systemic legislation: By what right are distinctions made? *Cogent Social Sciences*, 6(1), 1837424. doi:10.1080/23311886.2020.1837424

Talbot, C. (2004). The Agency idea: Sometimes old, sometimes new, sometimes borrowed, sometimes untrue. In C. Pollitt & C. Talbot (Eds.), *Unbundled Government: A Critical Analysis of the Global Trend to Agencies, Quangos and Contractualisation* (pp. 3–21). Taylor & Francis.

ENDNOTE

[1] Benefits of bringing together several regulators into one public agency: a lean public administration; transparent, unified and integrated goal-setting, development planning, policies and programmes; reorganisation and rationalisation of general services and reorientation of staff towards substantive areas, lower operating costs; rationalisation of information systems, creation of a single business information system, transfer of records, registers to a single information system, creation of a single portal or website; greater efficiency and flexibility in planning and organising work, organising project work on concrete cases, easier removal of bottlenecks, establishing more uniform working protocols; strengthened supervision, more effective planning and targeting of supervision, possibility of joint supervision of market participants in specific activities; increased visibility for users, market participants; compliance with European rules dictating cooperation between regulators in the market; achieving positive synergies through the substantive integration of areas, in particular through the flow of information from different subject areas, the cooperation of experts from different subject areas and the transfer of knowledge, skills and experience between staff; a clearer autonomous governance structure (e.g. two governing bodies, a Council and a Management Board); uniform procedures for the collection of applications (open competition), selection and choice (committee or council) and appointment (by the National Assembly on a proposal from the Government); transparent financing: two sources of revenue (budget, market revenues); pursuit of

substantive, organisational and financial independence and autonomy: autonomous and independent adoption of general acts governing various aspects (internal organisation, operations), independent substantive decision-making (judicial review in specific cases), and the possibility of setting up an economic analysis unit to support professional decisions.

Chapter 17
Conclusion

ABSTRACT

In the natural sciences, accurate testing of hypotheses using observed, collected, and comparable data can lead to new theories or guidelines for action. However, in social sciences, such as public agencies, recognizing patterns, forming categories, measuring, and comparing phenomena vis-a-vis the human will, make it difficult to reach similar levels of accuracy. Social science theory involves editing and studying factual material, where evidence is largely presented with definitions, concepts, and metaphors. The meaning of theories in social science is normative, explaining what should be, in addition to the actual sein or what is. However, the description of past events and inference on conclusions, causes, or events may be subject to cognitive biases such as confirmation bias or post hoc ergo propter hoc. Comparisons of past events and their placement on common denominators may not be a true description of the current state of affairs, as reasons, contingencies, and intentions behind similar occurrences may differ.

INTRODUCTION

A country normally has an administrative apparatus no worse than it deserves

(Meier, 2000).

Science in the natural or physical field represents the accurate testing of theorems and hypotheses using the observed, collected, and comparable data. If hypotheses successfully pass repetitions with similar results tested by measurement, they could serve for new theories or as guidelines for action. In the social sciences (of which public agencies are the institutional part), there is a bigger (more complex) problem of recognizing patterns, forming categories, measuring and comparing phenomena vis-a-vis the human will, so goals are here different (expectations are lower) than in natural science. Social science theory means the editing and study of factual material (history, events, examples, stories), where evidence is largely »proven« (more likely just presented) with definitions, concepts, and metaphors that make easier understanding. The latter is always at least partially subjective, both on the side of a theorist and on the side of a reader/user. In addition to the actual (*sein*), the meaning of theories in social science

DOI: 10.4018/979-8-3693-0507-2.ch017

is always also normative (*sollen*), when they explain what it "should be". The description of apparent laws of behaviour or conduct is the basis for the assessment of normative consequences of behaviour (as it should be - *sollen*); thus, *sein* and *sollen* are the necessarily connected members of the mentioned transition that has also a virus of (mis)understanding: a description of an event that can be rationally followed because of its logical elaboration and argumentation based on concepts, connections, metaphors or parables is still *a mere description*. The latter falls under a number of cognitive errors, among which are *e.g.* confirmation bias or a tendency to seek or favour selected information that further supports previous beliefs or values; there is also the error "after that, therefore because of it" or *post hoc ergo propter hoc* (ex-post-facto error or reasoning) as an error of reasoning, where we assume a relationship between current events and past events as a causal one. The description of past events and inference on conclusions, causes, or events are a popular way of understanding that psychologically can calm us down or contrary reinforce it – by an amplification of opinions with similar opinions (*a la* »Twitter bubble« style), but there is not necessarily a connection with reality. Here the cognitive bias of Maslow's (or golden) hammer can be given (it includes excessive reliance only on a known tool and/or "it is always a temptation to treat everything as if it were a nail if the hammer is the only tool we have") that is similar to the paradox of success (the capability to adapt can be subverted by the very successes of the institution that does not change its "winning formula" and/or a vicious cycle of regression).

The comparison of past events and their placement on common denominators is logically possible and permissible, but such doings are not necessarily a true description of the state of affairs. The same approach is usually taken at elaboration of agencies on various levels – comparative approach between different states and their agencies could discover some similarities and similarities that could be put on equal denominators, but such comparison could have little connection with reality, with "here and now". Comparisons are ipso facto focused in the history and not in the changeable future. Reasons, contingencies, starting points, intentions behind the similarly established occurrences/results of agencies could be very different – the fact, e.g. that autonomy is more emphasised across multiple countries could result from very different causes; additionally, the fact that a whole country and its relation to its agencies described only by one author (as it is usually the case in papers or monographs) can be misleading also – another author will for sure, up to a point, differently describe the same agencies within the same country, so slightly different conclusions will emerge compared to other countries; this state of affairs could be improved with the same methodology used, but even then will people with the different cultural and other backgrounds and traditions reply differently on equal questionnaires. If comparison as such between countries could be enough, there would be no problems present after the analysis is made, but this is not so in practice. There are no cheap solutions; considering the number of books written on agencies, there would be no problem present at all when only comparisons and some statistics between them would be enough. This is not workable. Solutions are usually more complex.

In addition to facts, public administration (and the public agencies within it) also includes a number of purposes, interests, public, (in)formal) authority (power) that natural science does not. The former could be called the "classic approach" that considers science, as well as other aspects. To a greater extent than natural science, it is based on subjective reason and intuition, which can deceive us in matters that change rapidly, combine with each other, and exponentially multiply, but it can also open new possibilities in the form of new hypotheses or different questions. As public agencies group together many interests (and thus also various views) on the question of public interest it is sometimes difficult to answer, let alone measure and classify what this interest is. Many elements are all the more subjective when the public interest is understood as the public interest by only one individual or a handful of civil

Conclusion

servants, who prepare and propose public drafts/measures. In this, still classical way of doing things can include also the behavioural one, where collective human behaviour could show sufficient legitimacy to justify strict research, measurement, classification and presentation of this order (two notions, which are well-known here are collective intelligence and collective wisdom). If we observe the subjective interests, morals, or ethics of the individual, as well as other obscure concepts as an aggregate or a middle between two extremes, such variables can become empirically achievable and verifiable theories. Agents and agencies are curved out from various economic, social, legal, and political brawls. There is *no final organisational design* for these autonomous forms of administration; there is only flexibility, dynamism along with rigidness, resilience and adaptation present. This represents the concept and/or the notion of *holistic agency*. Agencies are here seen as chameleons due to their diverse practice in various contextual elements; there is no single homogenous agency; there is only a variety of roles and activities which differ from one agency to another. This difference many times causes not only coordination problems but also self-centred practices. Present agencies have emerged from various pathways and exist because they successfully cope with various tensions in their environments. This led to the emergence of even formal, equal but different and specific agencies in practice with varying degrees of autonomy; what the majority of agencies have in common is the lack of consistency of approaches that could serve them to cope with different struggles in their environment. And this consistency is in the inconsistency of specific approaches and in the consistency of general, holistic ones. Holism cannot mean that unity (or agency as such) is unchangeable; it means that its units, as its fundamental components, exhibit (emerging) existence that is more than the mere sum of their parts. Holism resembles or really represents adaptive changes in their relations according to internal purposes and goals and the external environment. After the agency creation – even if more of them are formally/legally equal or similar – there are so many factors that affect their operations on a daily basis that cannot be upfront determined as their real affects: it is really more bird-like when left out of the hands than rock-thrown, regardless that both act within the same laws of physics. In such frames, the effectiveness, efficiency, accountability, responsibility and other leading principles (legitimacy) become embroiled in complex networks; here such principles can be evaluated only with elements that describe complexity per se. Otherwise, the principles, although formally stated, cannot be materially used in practice. Practical results often have little to do with the original formal creation and the original claims of optimal design. Agencies exhibit coherence in the complex environment only with complex perspectives.

Nature's coordinate system – and the holistic agency within it – can be understood as synergetics – synergy means the behaviour of whole systems unpredicted by any part of the system as considered only separately (Fuller & Applewhite, 1997). Synergy means the behaviour of integral, aggregate, whole systems unpredicted by the behaviours of any of their components or subassemblies of their components taken separately from the whole. The same is basically valid for agencies as autonomous, but still intertwined units, embedded in higher and present in lower units. Observing the world through formalisms and individual activities of each agency, for which competent authorities consider they have an ultimate truth and correctness, changes a man – a client/ consumer/ citizen into an object of their activities. Notwithstanding the recognition that public authorities are expanding and increasing in power with each new jurisdiction, such processes say nothing about the manner of solving problems. Democracy is not a simple opportunity to select people that will govern above other people, but still less that employees in agencies (who were not selected by voters) rule unquestionably above the people.

Democracy does not mean only a mandate of command and control. It means also that both reflect the people's basic needs. Politics usually does not settle for comprehensive solutions as this could lead to a loss of political support, or because it simply does not know how to solve problems, because the administration does not present them (this could result in "cosmetic corrections" in cases where a real "surgical operation" would be more needed). The rule of the people is filled with content mainly through public institutions. The selection, which is done by an agency (or someone else), retroactively closes the notion of choice, the opportunity to be able to act otherwise. Only by not following the established paths, a closed circle of determinism can be resolved and an open a new moment of freedom initiated, and one option for this could be also the concept of holistic agency. Man always searches for an order for common properties of things (abstraction as a process of creating the law) that things per se do not have. The mysterious formula of order is constantly present and absent at the same time; it is about the idea that we continually implement that formula without really seeing it. It is about a combination of our innate, instinctive desire to see and refine order through specific circumstances that point at them only in shadows. The infinite possibility of limited units nevertheless points at the open space of potentiality, free space and freedom. Chaos shows there is always a hidden agenda, which automatically appears regardless on the behaviour of humans. The global changes, warming, energy, migration – all works alone, but in accordance with other order(s), that is/are, for some visible, and for others not. Regardless of whether an order is present in the nature, or we just see it as such from the nature, in both cases, this shows the ongoing efforts for order are always present but conditioned by concrete situations and their interpretations from the higher, meta-frames. The only rule of order, which can be read in history and which has a high degree of probability is that the person writes his verdict alone, without a full knowledge of its operative part. That knowledge can be gained only through careful logical reasoning and practical observation; from this point of view also chaos has its simple rules that with repetition goes into complexity. The latter one can or should be in the field of human behaviour equated with management. The latter is also based on some simple rules that can create marvellous results and that can change according to different situations. The same stands for the management of agencies. They are still managed mainly in statical frames regardless of exponential flexibility and dynamism; they are therefore just a pale approximation of new (more complex but still simple) orders. Regardless of all theories, there are always just the systems and people in them.

The holistic agency exhibits some teachings that are present or are very similar to the two universal truths of Buddhism: *Karma* and/or causation (law of cause and effect) is built on the *interconnectedness of all things*; the second is a *permanent change*, where nothing is fixed, permanent or immovable. Due to greed and ignorance of the law of Karma suffering (*saṃsāra*) emerges; people create a world of suffering, but it can be also the opposite: the way of life that reduces suffering and leads to liberation is called the Middle Way (right view, thought, speech, action, livelihood, effort, mindfulness, and concentration). When holistic agency demonstrates this eightfold path, its employees i) act with wisdom and compassion for others, ii) have clear and kind thoughts, iii) speak kind and with helpful words, iv) see themselves first before criticise others, v) do not harm other people, vi) do their best at all times and have goodwill toward others, vii) are aware of their thoughts, words, and deeds and viii) focus on one thought or object at a time. When this path is practised, also the third universal law (nothing is lost in the universe) can be seen at the work of the holistic agency, as its doings have an impact on many other (again – interconnected) things. Regardless of the centuries, there are some universal, common denominators to which research or thinking can reach regardless of the tools and paths used. 'It is almost redundant to stress holism, or the relational spirit, in Confucianism. As in other Eastern philosophies, there is a tacit emphasis on the relatedness of everything ... The holistic spirit inspires us to see that strategic issues tend to be multifaceted, reciprocal and mutually determined (Nonaka & Zhu, 2012, pp. 48, 49). From a holistic perspective, human conduct is contextual; according to process thinking, contexts are always changing. Accordingly, ethical conduct cannot be captured in fixed, universal codes (Nonaka & Zhu, 2012, p. 56).

Some of ancient civilisations were much bigger that most of today states; they all have believed in God or in a king as the God (theocracy) and did not have theories about public administration. They did not have much of a technology but they succeeded in many great things. They have had some high-calibre, motivated and conscious individuals, determined in their causes. And that matters the most. They act and as unity as a holistic agency. Such people also live today, and many of them work in agencies. Let this work be of help for them and for other people to see agencies as autonomous units, but still connected and embedded in the higher frames of institutions and the environment of many other things. The collaborative management of agencies could be a proper phrase of holistic agencies where collaboration and management act hand-in-hand. To collaborate is to labour together as the etymology of the word suggests, while to manage means to direct and control, to be in command of something; the management of agencies should be based on collaboration, cooperation and coordination and control in the same time, so: *trust but verify*. The concept of holistic agency is not about the best organisational form, but about the shifting, adaptive assemblage of people, resources and actions in the view of environmental context and final goals. This could be useful for many small things, but also for the national (e.g., migrations, health, education, water scarcity) and global ones (e.g. global warming, biodiversity loss, ocean conservation). This book is based on the ideas of adaptiveness, systems, complexity, strategic management, scenario planning, and collective wisdom to see at least slightly similar what was seen centuries ago. This similarity gives weight to our suppositions and new energy to search forward on this path.

REFERENCES

Fuller, R. B., & Applewhite, E. J. (1997). *Synergetics: Explorations in the Geometry of Thinking*. MacMillan.

Meier, K. J. (2000). *Politics and the Bureaucracy* (4th ed.). Harcourt College Publishers.

Nonaka, I., & Zhu, Z. (2012). Pragmatic Strategy: Eastern Wisdom, Global Success. Cambirdge: Cambridge University Press. doi:10.1017/CBO9780511736568

Compilation of References

Ackoff, R. L. (1978). *The Art of Problem Solving: Accompanied by Ackoff's Fables*. John Wiley & Sons.

Ackoff, R. L. (1994). *The Democratic Corporation: A Radical Prescription for Recreating Corporate America and Rediscovering Success*. Oxford University Press. doi:10.1093/oso/9780195087277.001.0001

Ackoff, R. L. (1999). *Re-creating the Corporation: A Design of Organizations for the 21st Century*. Oxford University Press. doi:10.1093/oso/9780195123876.001.0001

Adams, D. (2014). *Dirk Gently's Holistic Detective Agency*. Gallery Books.

Aggarwal, I., Woolley, A. W., Chabris, C. F., & Malone, T. W. (2019). The impact of cognitive style diversity on implicit learning in teams. *Frontiers in Psychology*, *10*, 112. doi:10.3389/fpsyg.2019.00112 PMID:30792672

Amagoh, F. (2016). Systems and Complexity Theories of Organizations. In A. Farazmand (Ed.), *Global Encyclopedia of Public Administration, Public Policy, and Governance* (pp. 1–7). Springer International Publishing., doi:10.1007/978-3-319-31816-5_73-1

Anderson, P. (1999). Perspective: Complexity Theory and Organization Science. [world]. *Organization Science*, *10*(3), 216–232. doi:10.1287/orsc.10.3.216

Andrews, R., Boyne, G., Law, J., & Walker, R. (2012). *Strategic Management and Public Service Performance*. Palgrave Macmillan. doi:10.1057/9780230349438

Aquinas, T. (1920). The "Summa Theologica" of St. Thomas Aquinas. Part I QQ I.-XXVI. (Second and revised edition, Vol. 1). London: Burns Oates and Washbourne.

Arendt, H. (1972). *Crises of the Republic: Lying in Politics, Civil Disobedience on Violence, Thoughts on Politics, and Revolution*. Harcourt Brace Jovanovich.

Arendt, H. (1981). *The Life of the Mind*. Harcourt Brace Jovanovich.

Argyris, C. (2006). *Reasons and Rationalizations: The Limits to Organizational Knowledge*. Oxford University Press.

Ariely, D. (2008). *Predictably Irrational: The Hidden Forces That Shape Our Decisions*. HarperCollins.

Aristotle. (1992). *Eudemian Ethics Books I, II, and VIII* (M. Woods, Trans.). Clarendon Press.

Aristotle. (2015). *Metaphysics*. Aeterna Press.

Armstrong, M. (2003). A Handbook of Human Resource Management Practice (9th ed.). London and Sterling: Kogan Page Publishers.

Compilation of References

Arnauld, A., & Nicole, P. (1996). *Logic Or the Art of Thinking* (J. V. Buroker, Trans.). Cambridge University Press. doi:10.1017/CBO9781139166768

Aronson, M. (2009). The Great Depression, this Depression, and Administrative Law—Federal Law Review—ANU. *Federal Law Review*, *37*(2), 165–203. doi:10.22145/flr.37.2.1

Arya V. Bellamy R. K. E. Chen P.-Y. Dhurandhar A. Hind M. Hoffman S. C. Zhang Y. (2019). One Explanation Does Not Fit All: A Toolkit and Taxonomy of AI Explainability Techniques. *ArXiv:1909.03012 [Cs, Stat]*. http://arxiv.org/abs/1909.03012

Asch, S. E. (1955). Opinions and Social Pressure. *Scientific American*, *193*(5), 31–35. doi:10.1038/scientificamerican1155-31

Ashby, W. R. (1957). *An Introduction to Cybernetics*. Chapman and Hall.

Ashby, W. R. (1960). *Design for a Brain: The Origin of Adaptive Behavior*. Chapman and Hall.

Auby, J.-B. (2017). The Transformation of the Administrative State and Administrative Law. In A. von Bogdandy, P. M. Huber, & S. Cassese (Eds.), *The Max Planck Handbooks in European Public Law: The Administrative State* (pp. 601–630). Oxford University Press.

Australian Public Service Commission. (2018). *Tackling wicked problems: A public policy perspective [Text]*. APSC. https://www.apsc.gov.au/tackling-wicked-problems-public-policy-perspective

Axelrod, R. (1986). An Evolutionary Approach to Norms. *The American Political Science Review*, *80*(4), 1095–1111. doi:10.2307/1960858

Axelrod, R. (2006). *The Evolution of Cooperation* (Revised edition). Basic Books.

Ayres, I. (2007). *Super Crunchers: Why Thinking-By-Numbers is the New Way to Be Smart*. Bantam Books.

Ayres, I., & Braithwaite, J. (1995). *Responsive Regulation: Transcending the Deregulation Debate*. Oxford University Press.

Ayres, I., & Nalebuff, B. (2015). The rule of probabilities: A practical approach for applying Bayes' rule to the analysis of DNA evidence. *Stanford Law Review*, *67*(6), 1447–1503.

Bache, I., & Flinders, M. V. (Eds.). (2005). *Multi-level Governance*. Oxford University Press.

Bach, T., & Wegrich, K. (Eds.). (2018). *The Blind Spots of Public Bureaucracy and the Politics of Non-Coordination*. Palgrave MacMillan.

Baker, D. (2007). *Strategic Change Management in Public Sector Organisations*. Chandos Publishing.

Baldwin, R., Cave, M., & Lodge, M. (2012). The Oxford Handbook of Regulation (Reprint edition). Oxford; New York: Oxford University Press.

Baldwin, R., & Black, J. (2007). Really Responsive Regulation. *The Modern Law Review*, (71), 59–94.

Baldwin, R., Cave, M., & Lodge, M. (2013). *Understanding Regulation: Theory, Strategy, and Practice* (2nd ed.). Oxford University Press.

Balle Hansen, M., & Andersen, N. (2012). Denmark. In K. Verhoest, S. V. Thiel, G. Bouckaert, & P. Lægreid (Eds.), *Government Agencies: Practices and Lessons from 30 Countries* (pp. 212–222). Palgrave Macmillan. doi:10.1057/9780230359512_20

Barnard, C. I. (1968). The Functions of the Executive. Cambirdge: Harvard University Press.

Barnard, C. I. (1968). *The Functions of the Executive*. Harvard University Press.

Bar-Yam, Y. (2011). Concepts: Power Law. NECSI. http://www.necsi.edu/guide/concepts/powerlaw.html

Bauman, Z. (2011). *Collateral Damage: Social Inequalities in a Global Age*. Polity.

Beauvois, J.-L. (2000). *Razprava o liberalni sužnosti: Analiza podrejanja*. Ljubljana: Krt.

Beck, U. (1992). *Risk Society: Towards a New Modernity*. SAGE Publications Ltd.

Beer, S. (1981). *Brain of the Firm: A Development in Management Cybernetics* (2nd ed.). Herder and Herder.

Beer, S. (1986). Recursions of Power. In R. Trappl (Ed.), *Power, Autonomy, Utopia: New Approaches Toward Complex Systems* (pp. 3–18). Plenum Press. doi:10.1007/978-1-4613-2225-2_1

Beer, S. (1994). *Beyond Dispute: The Invention of Team Syntegrity*. Wiley.

Beer, S. (2002). What is cybernetics? *Kybernetes*, *31*(2), 209–219. doi:10.1108/03684920210417283

Beer, S., & Eno, B. (2009). *Think Before You Think: Social Complexity and Knowledge of Knowing*. Wavestone Press.

Behn, R. D. (2001). *Rethinking Democratic Accountability*. Brookings Institution Press.

Bell, J., Elliott, M., Varuhas, J. N., & Murray, P. (Eds.). (2016). *Public Law Adjudication in Common Law Systems: Process and Substance*. Hart Publishing.

Berkeley, G. (2003). *A Treatise Concerning the Principles of Human Knowledge* (T. J. McCormack, Ed.). Dover Publications, Inc.

Berreby, D. (n.d.). Between Chaos and Order: What Complexity Theory Can Teach Business. *Strategy Business*. https://www.strategy-business.com/article/15099?gko=73fbc

Bettis, R. A., & Hitt, M. A. (1995). The new competitive landscape. *Strategic Management Journal*, *16*(S1), 7–19. doi:10.1002/smj.4250160915

Bevir, M. (Ed.). (2010). *The SAGE Handbook of Governance*. SAGE.

Bignami, F., & Zaring, D. (Eds.). (2016). *Comparative Law and Regulation: Understanding the Global Regulatory Process*. Edward Elgar Publishing. doi:10.4337/9781782545613

Black, J. (2012). The Role of Risk in Regulatory Processes. In R. Baldwin, M. Cave, & M. Lodge (Eds.), The Oxford Handbook of Regulation (Reprint edition, pp. 302–348). Oxford; New York: Oxford University Press.

Blackstone, W. (2011). *Commentaries on the Laws of England in Four Books, vol. 1 [1753]*. Indiana: Liberty Fund, Inc. http://files.libertyfund.org/files/2140/Blackstone_1387-01_EBk_v6.0.pdf

Bobek, M. (2017). Europeanization of Public Law. In A. von Bogdandy, P. M. Huber, & S. Cassese (Eds.), *The Max Planck Handbooks in European Public Law: The Administrative State* (pp. 631–674). Oxford University Press.

Boin, A., Fahy, L. A., & 't Hart, P. (Eds.). (2020). *Guardians of Public Value: How Public Organisations Become and Remain Institutions*. Springer Nature.

Boisot, M., & McKelvey, B. (2011). Connectivity, Extremes, and Adaptation: A Power-Law Perspective of Organizational Effectiveness. *Journal of Management Inquiry*, *20*(2), 119–133. doi:10.1177/1056492610385564

Boltanski, L., & Thévenot, L. (2006). *On Justification*. Princeton and Oxford: Princeton University Press.

Compilation of References

Bon, G. L. (2001). *The Crowd: A Study of the Popular Mind*. Batoche Books.

Bosse, D. A., & Phillips, R. A. (2014). Agency Theory and Bounded Self-Interest. *Academy of Management Review*, *41*(2), 276–297. doi:10.5465/amr.2013.0420

Boston, J. (2000). The Challenge of Evaluating Systemic Change: The Case of Public Management Reform in New Zealand. *International Public Management Journal*, *3*(3), 23–46. doi:10.1016/S1096-7494(00)00033-7

Bouckaert, G., & Halligan, J. (2007). *Managing Performance: International Comparisons*. Routledge. doi:10.4324/9780203935958

Bouckaert, G., & Peters, B. G. (2004). What is available and what is missing in the study of quangos? In C. Pollitt & C. Talbot (Eds.), *Unbundled Government: A Critical Analysis of the Global Trend to Agencies, Quangos and Contractualisation* (pp. 22–49). Taylor & Francis.

Bouckaert, G., Peters, B. G., & Verhoest, K. (2010). *The Coordination of Public Sector Organizations: Shifting Patterns of Public Management*. Palgrave MacMillan. doi:10.1057/9780230275256

Bourdieu, P. (1977). *Towards a Theory of Practice*. Cambridge University Press.

Bovaird, T. (2008). Emergent Strategic Management and Planning Mechanisms in Complex Adaptive Systems. *Public Management Review*, *10*(3), 319–340. doi:10.1080/14719030802002741

Brabham, D. C. (2013). *Crowdsourcing*. MIT Press. doi:10.7551/mitpress/9693.001.0001

Bradfield, R., Wright, G., Burt, G., Cairns, G., & Van Der Heijden, K. (2005). The origins and evolution of scenario techniques in long range business planning. *Futures*, *37*(8), 795–812. doi:10.1016/j.futures.2005.01.003

Breyer, S. G., Stewart, R. B., Sunstein, C. R., & Vermeule, A. (2006). *Administrative Law and Regulatory Policy: Problems, Text, and Cases* (6th ed.). Aspen Publishers.

Briskin, A., Erickson, S., Ott, J., & Callanan, T. (2009). *The Power of Collective Wisdom and the Trap of Collective Folly*. Berrett-Koehler Publishers.

Broussard, M. (2019). Artificial Unintelligence: How Computers Misunderstand the World (Kindle). London: MIT Press.

Brown, B. (2018). *Dare to Lead: Brave Work. Tough Conversations. Whole Hearts*. Random House.

Brown, D. R., & Harvey, D. F. (2006). *An Experiential Approach to Organization Development*. Pearson Prentice Hall.

Bruce, A., Buck, T., & Main, B. G. M. (2005). Top Executive Remuneration: A View from Europe*. *Journal of Management Studies*, *42*(7), 1493–1506. doi:10.1111/j.1467-6486.2005.00553.x

Burstein, F., Brézillon, P., & Zaslavsky, A. (2010). *Supporting Real Time Decision-Making*. Springer Science & Business Media.

Caiden, G. E. (1991). What Really is Public Maladministration? *Public Administration Review*, *3751*(6), 486–493. doi:10.2307/976599

Cairney, P. (2012). Complexity Theory in Political Science and Public Policy. *Political Studies Review*, *10*(3), 346–358. doi:10.1111/j.1478-9302.2012.00270.x

Cairney, P., Heikkila, T., & Wood, M. (2019). *Making Policy in a Complex World*. Cambridge University Press., doi:10.1017/9781108679053

Camazine, S., & Sneyd, J. (1991). A model of collective nectar source selection by honey bees: Self-organization through simple rules. *Journal of Theoretical Biology, 149*(4), 547–571. doi:10.1016/S0022-5193(05)80098-0 PMID:1943133

Campbell, D. T. (1979). Assessing the impact of planned social change. *Evaluation and Program Planning, 2*(1), 67–90. doi:10.1016/0149-7189(79)90048-X

Cane, P. (2011). *Administrative Law*. Oxford University Press.

CAPAM. (1995). *Government in Transition*. Commonwealth Secretariat. doi:10.14217/9781848595286-

Carnap, R. (1966). *Philosophical Foundation of Physics: An Introduction to the Philosophy of Science* (M. Gardner, Ed.). Basic Books.

Carrier, R. (2012). *Proving History: Bayes's Theorem and the Quest for the Historical Jesus*. Prometheus Books.

Cass, R. A., Diver, C. S., Beermann, J. M., & Freeman, J. (2011). *Administrative Law: Cases and Materials* (6th ed.). Aspen Publishers.

Chapman, J. (2004). *System Failure: Why Governments Must Learn to Think Differently*. Demos.

Chapus, R. (2001). *Droit administratif général* (15th ed.). Montchrestien.

Checkland, P. (1981). *Systems Thinking, Systems Practice*. J. Wiley.

Christensen, T., & Laegred, P. (2005). Regulatory Reforms and Agentification. *Unifob AS, Working Paper 6. Stein Rokkan Centre for Social Studies*.

Christensen, C., & Raynor, M. (2013). *The innovator's solution: Creating and sustaining successful growth*. Harvard Business Review Press.

Christensen, C., & Raynor, M. (2013). *The Innovator's Solution: Creating and Sustaining Successful Growth*. Harvard Business Review Press.

Christensen, T., & Lægreid, P. (2007). The Whole-of-Government Approach to Public Sector Reform. *Public Administration Review, 67*(6), 1059–1066. doi:10.1111/j.1540-6210.2007.00797.x

Christian, B., & Griffiths, T. (2016). *Algorithms to Live By: The Computer Science of Human Decisions*. Henry Holt and Co.

Cohen, S. (2016). *Growing Talent Management Firms: Scenario vs. Strategic Planning*. TD. https://www.td.org/insights/growing-talent-management-firms-scenario-vs-strategic-planning

Cole, A., & Eymeri-Douzans, J.-M. (2010). Introduction: Administrative reforms and mergers in Europe - research questions and empirical challenges. *International Review of Administrative Sciences, 76*(3), 395–406. doi:10.1177/0020852310373881

Comte, A. (1998). *Comte: Early Political Writings* (H. S. Jones, Ed.). Cambridge University Press. doi:10.1017/CBO9781139170833

Comte, A. (2009). *A General View of Positivism*. Cambridge University Press. doi:10.1017/CBO9780511692888

Conant, R. C., & Ashby, W. R. (1970). Every Good Regulator of a System Must be a Model of that System. *International Journal of Systems Science, 1*(2), 89–97. doi:10.1080/00207727008920220

Confucius. (2003). *Analects: With Selections from Traditional Commentaries* (E. Slingerland, Trans.). Hackett Publishing.

Compilation of References

Confucius. (2003). *Confucius Analects: With Selections from Traditional Commentaries* (E. Slingerland, Trans.). Hackett Publishing Company.

Cooke, R. M. (1991). *Experts in Uncertainty: Opinion and Subjective Probability in Science*. Oxford University Press. doi:10.1093/oso/9780195064650.001.0001

Coxall, B., Robins, L., & Leach, R. (1998). *Contemporary British Politics*. Macmillan International Higher Education.

Crawford, A. (2006). Networked governance and the post-regulatory state? Steering, rowing and anchoring the provision of policing and security. *Theoretical Criminology*, *10*(4), 449–479. doi:10.1177/1362480606068874

Crowder, G. (2004). Isaiah Berlin: Liberty, Pluralism and Liberalism. *Polity*.

Crozier, M. (1964). Bureaucratic Phenomenon (y First edition edition). Chicago: University of Chicago Press.

Crozier, M. (1964). Bureaucratic Phenomenon. Chicago: University of Chicago Press.

Cziko, G. (2000). *The Things We Do: Using the Lessons of Bernard and Darwin to Understand the What, How, and why of Our Behavior*. MIT Press.

Daellenbach, H. G. (1996). *Systems and Decision Making: A Management Science Approach* (1st ed.). Wiley.

Darwin, C. (1871). *The Descent of Man, and Selection in Relation to Sex*. J. Murray.

Davis, K. C. (1979). Discretionary Justice: A Preliminary Inquiry (Fifth printing). Urbana, Chicago, London: University of Illinois Press.

Davis, G., & Rhodes, R. W. (2000). From hierarchy to contracts and back again: Reforming the Australian public service. In M. Keating, J. Wanna, & P. Weller (Eds.), *Institutions on the edge? Capacity and Governance* (pp. 74–98). Allen & Unwin., doi:10.4324/9781003116127-4

Dawes, R. M. (1979). The robust beauty of improper linear models in decision making. *The American Psychologist*, *34*(7), 571–582. doi:10.1037/0003-066X.34.7.571

Dawkins, R. (2006). *The Blind Watchmaker*. Penguin.

de Oliveira, O. P. (2017). *International Policy Diffusion and Participatory Budgeting: Ambassadors of Participation, International Institutions and Transnational Networks*. Springer. doi:10.1007/978-3-319-43337-0

Deming, W. E. (2000). *Out of the Crisis*. MIT Press.

Denhardt, J. V., & Denhardt, R. B. (2011). *The New Public Service: Serving, Not Steering* (3rd ed.). Routledge.

Denhardt, R. B., Denhardt, J. V., & Blanc, T. A. (2013). *Public Administration* (7th ed.). Wadsworth Publishing.

Descartes, R., de Spinoza, B., & Leibniz, G. W. V. (1974). *The Rationalists: Descartes: Discourse on Method & Meditations; Spinoza: Ethics; Leibniz: Monadolo gy & Discourse on Metaphysics*. Anchor Books.

Diefenbach, T. (2009). New public management in public sector organisations: The dark sides of managerialistic 'enlightenment'. *Public Administration*, *87*(4), 892–909. doi:10.1111/j.1467-9299.2009.01766.x

Dijkstra, G. (2013). *Paradoxes around good governance, Inaugural Lecture*. University of Rotterdam. https://repub.eur.nl/pub/39219/metis_186511.pdf

DiMaggio, P. (1997). Culture and Cognition. *Annual Review of Sociology*, *23*(1), 263–287. doi:10.1146/annurev.soc.23.1.263

Dobbin, F. (Ed.). (2004). *The New Economic Sociology: A Reader*. Princeton University Press. doi:10.1515/9780691229270

Dodge, H. F., & Romig, H. G. (1959). *Sampling inspection tables: Single and double sampling.* Wiley.

Douglas, M. (2012). *A History of Grid and Group Cultural Theory.* Chass. http://projects.chass.utoronto.ca/semiotics/cyber/douglas1.pdf

Douglas, M. (1982). *Essays in the Sociology of Perception.* Routledge Kegan & Paul.

Douglas, M. (1986). *How Institutions Think.* Syracuse University Press.

Douglas, M. (1994). *Risk and Blame: Essays in Cultural Theory.* Routledge.

Douglas, M. (2003). *Natural Symbols: Explorations in Cosmology* (3rd ed.). Routledge.

Drucker, P. F. (1980). The Deadly Sins in Public Administration. *Public Administration Review, 40*(2), 103–106. doi:10.2307/975619

Dunleavy, P., Margetts, H., Bastow, S., & Tinkler, J. (2005). New Public Management Is Dead—Long Live Digital-Era Governance. *Journal of Public Administration: Research and Theory, 16*(3), 467–494. doi:10.1093/jopart/mui057

Dunleavy, P., Margetts, H., Tinkler, J., & Bastow, S. (2006). *Digital era governance: IT corporations, the state, and e-government.* Oxford University Press. doi:10.1093/acprof:oso/9780199296194.001.0001

Dunning, D. (2012). *Self-Insight: Roadblocks and Detours on the Path to Knowing Thyself.* Psychology Press. doi:10.4324/9780203337998

Dunsire, A. (1990). Holistic Governance. *Public Policy and Administration, 5*(1), 4–19. doi:10.1177/095207679000500102

Durkheim, E. (1982). *The Rules of Sociological Method* (W. D. Halls, Trans.). The Free Press. doi:10.1007/978-1-349-16939-9

Durkheim, E. (1984). *The Division of Labor in Society* (W. D. Halls, Trans.). Palgrave Macmillan. doi:10.1007/978-1-349-17729-5

Durkheim, E. (1992). *Professional Ethics and Civic Morals* (2nd ed.). Routledge.

Durkheim, E. (1995). *The Elementary Forms of Religious Life* (K. E. Fields, Trans.). The Free Press.

Dworkin, R. (1986). *Law's Empire.* Belknap Press of Harvard University Press.

Eagleman, D., & Brandt, A. (2017). *The Runaway Species: How Human Creativity Remakes the World.* Canongate Books.

Eaglestone, R. (2017). *The Broken Voice: Reading Post-Holocaust Literature.* Oxford University Press. doi:10.1093/oso/9780198778363.001.0001

Eckhart, R. (1987). Stan Ulam, John von Neumann, and the Monte Carlo Method. *Los Alamos Science, Special Issue,* (15), 131–137.

Edwards, W., Jr. R. F. M., & Winterfeldt, D. (2007). Advances in Decision Analysis: From Foundations to Applications. New York: Cambridge University Press.

Edwards, W., Jr. R. F. M., & Winterfeldt, D. von. (2007). Advances in Decision Analysis: From Foundations to Applications. New York: Cambridge University Press.

Edwards, W. (1999). *Decision Science and Technology: Reflections on the Contributions of Ward Edwards.* Springer Science & Business Media.

Compilation of References

Eisenhardt, K. M. (1989). Agency Theory: An Assessment and Review. *Academy of Management Review*, *14*(1), 57–74. doi:10.2307/258191

Emirbayer, M., & Mische, A. (1998). What Is Agency? *American Journal of Sociology*, *103*(4), 962–1023. doi:10.1086/231294

Encyclopædia Britannica. (2019). *Board of Trade: British government*. Encyclopedia Britannica. https://www.britannica.com/topic/Board-of-Trade-British-government

Encyclopedia Britannica. (2020). *Thermodynamics—Open systems*. Encyclopedia Britannica. https://aws.qa.britannica.com/science/thermodynamics

Engel, D., Woolley, A. W., Jing, L. X., Chabris, C. F., & Malone, T. W. (2014). Reading the Mind in the Eyes or Reading between the Lines? Theory of Mind Predicts Collective Intelligence Equally Well Online and Face-To-Face. *PLoS One*, *9*(12), e115212. doi:10.1371/journal.pone.0115212 PMID:25514387

Eppel, E. A., & Rhodes, M. L. (2018a). Complexity theory and public management: A 'becoming' field. *Public Management Review*, *20*(7), 949–959. doi:10.1080/14719037.2017.1364414

Eppel, E. A., & Rhodes, M. L. (2018b). Public Administration & Complexity—How to teach things we cannot predict? *Complexity. Governance & Networks*, *4*(1), 1–9. doi:10.20377/cgn-61

Eskridge, W. N. Jr, Frickey, P. P., Garrett, E., & Brudney, J. J. (2014). *Cases and Materials on Legislation and Regulation: Statutes and the Creation of Public*. West Academic Publishing.

Espejo, R. (2003). Social Systems and the Embodiment of Organisational Learning. In E. Mitleton-Kelly (Ed.), *Complex Systems and Evolutionary Perspectives on Organisations* (pp. 53–70). Emerald Group Publishing Limited.

Espejo, R., & Reyes, A. (2011). *Organizational Systems: Managing Complexity with the Viable System Model* (2011 edition). Springer. doi:10.1007/978-3-642-19109-1

Eubanks, V. (2017). *Automating Inequality: How High-Tech Tools Profile, Police, and Punish the Poor*. St. Martin's Press.

European Commission. (2015). *Quality of Public Administration—A Toolbox for Practitioners*. European Union. https://ec.europa.eu/digital-single-market/en/news/quality-public-administration-toolbox-practitioners

European Commission. (2017). *European Semester: Thematic factsheet – Quality of public administration – 2017*. EC. https://ec.europa.eu/info/sites/info/files/file_import/european-semester_thematic-factsheet_quality-public-administration_en_0.pdf

European Court of Auditors. (2009). *Delegating Implementing Tasks to Executive Agencies: A Successful Option?* ECA. https://www.eca.europa.eu/lists/ecadocuments/sr09_13/sr09_13_en.pdf

Farazmand, A. (2004). *Sound Governance: Policy and Administrative Innovations*. Praeger.

Fardon, R. (1999). *Mary Douglas: An Intellectual Biography*. Routledge.

Fayol, H. (1954). *General and Industrial Management* (Reprinted edition). (C. Storrs, Trans.). Sir Isaac Pitman & Sons, Ltd.

Fayol, H. (2003). The Administrative Theory in the State. In L. Gulick & L. Urwick (Eds.), *Papers on the Science of Administration* (Vol. IV, pp. 109–124). Routlege.

Feltz, B., Crommelinck, M., & Goujon, P. (2006). *Self-organization and Emergence in Life Sciences*. Springer Science & Business Media. doi:10.1007/1-4020-3917-4

Feynman, R. P., Leighton, R. B., & Sands, M. (1965). The Feynman Lectures on Physics, Vol. (Later Printing edition). Reading, Mass.: Addison Wesley. doi:10.1119/1.1972241

Fiedler, K., & Juslin, P. (Eds.). (2006). *Information Sampling and Adaptive Cognition*. Cambridge University Press.

Finkelstein, M. O., & Fairley, W. B. (1970). A Bayesian Approach to Identification Evidence. *Harvard Law Review*, *83*(3), 489–517. doi:10.2307/1339656

Fiorina, M. P. (1982). Legislative Choice of Regulatory Forms: Legal Process or Administrative Process? *Public Choice*, *39*(1), 33–66.

Flinders, M. V., Harden, I., & Marquand, D. (Eds.). (1997). How to Make Quangos Democratic. London: Charter 88.

Flinders, M. (1999). Quangos: Why Do Governments Love Them? In M. J. Smith & M. V. Flinders (Eds.), *Quangos, Accountability and Reform* (pp. 26–39). Palgrave Macmillan. doi:10.1007/978-1-349-27027-9_3

Foester, H. (1960). On Self-Organizing Systems and Their Environment. In M. C. Yovits & S. Cameron (Eds.), *Self-Organizing Systems* (pp. 31–50). Pergamon Press.

Forrester, J. W. (1961). *Industrial Dynamics*. MIT Press.

Foucault, M. (1978). The History of Sexuality: Vol. 1. *An Introduction (Reissue edition)*. Vintage Books.

Foucault, M. (1995). *Discipline & Punish: The Birth of the Prison* (2nd ed.). (A. Sheridan, Trans.). Vintage Books.

Foucault, M. (2001). *Power (The Essential Works of Foucault, 1954-1984) (J. D. Faubion* (R. Hurley Ed. & Trans.). The New Press.

Foucault, M. (2002). *The Order of Things: Archaeology of the Human Sciences* (2nd ed.). Routledge.

Foucault, M. (2004). *Naissance de la biopolitique*. Seuil.

Foucault, M. (2007). *Življenje in prakse svobode*. Založba ZRC.

Foucault, M. (2015). *Družbo je treba braniti: Predavanja na College de France 1975-1976* (A. M. Habjan, Trans.). Studia Humanitatis.

Fowles, R. B. (1978). *Handbook of Futures Research*. Greenwood Press.

Franklin, J. (Ed.). (1998). *The Politics of Risk Society*. Polity Press.

Frederickson, H. G. (1996). Comparing the Reinventing Government Movement with the New Public Administration. *Public Administration Review*, *56*(3), 263–270. doi:10.2307/976450

Frederickson, H. G., Smith, K. B., Larimer, C. W., & Licari, M. J. (2012). *The Public Administration Theory Primer*. Westview Press.

French, W. L., & Bell, C. (1978). *Organization Development: Behavioral Science Interventions for Organization Improvement*. Prentice Hall.

Friedländer, B., Schaefer, C., & Röber, M. (2021). Institutional Differentiation of Public Service Provision in Germany: Corporatisation, Privatisation and Re-Municipalisation. In S. Kuhlmann, I. Proeller, D. Schimanke, & J. Ziekow (Eds.), *Public Administration in Germany* (pp. 291–310). IIAS, Palgrave MacMillan. doi:10.1007/978-3-030-53697-8_17

Fukuyama, F. (2004). *State Building: Governance and World Order in the 21st Century*. Cornell University Press.

Fukuyama, F. (2012). *The Origins of Political Order: From Prehuman Times to the French Revolution*. Farrar, Straus and Giroux.

Compilation of References

Fukuyama, F. (2014). *Political Order and Political Decay: From the Industrial Revolution to the Globalization of Democracy*. Farrar, Straus and Giroux.

Fuller, R. B., & Applewhite, E. J. (1997). *Synergetics: Explorations in the Geometry of Thinking*. MacMillan.

Fulton, J. S. (1968). *Fulton Report Into the Civil Service 1968 Cmnd-3638*. https://docs.google.com/document/d/1ANxPtL_7QUg4-adwzU28uAVOVReR_VCpM7ea8ukt9ug/edit

Fung, A., Graham, M., & Weil, D. (2007). *Full Disclosure*. Cambridge University Press. doi:10.1017/9780521699617

Gains, F. (2004). Adapting the agency concept: Variations within 'Next Steps. In C. Pollitt & C. Talbot (Eds.), *Unbundled Government: A Critical Analysis of the Global Trend to Agencies, Quangos and Contractualisation* (pp. 53–74). Taylor & Francis.

Galton, F. (1889). *Natural inheritance*. MacMillan and Co.

Galton, F. (1907). Vox Populi. *Nature*, *75*(1949), 450–451. doi:10.1038/075450a0

Gamerman, D. (1997). *Markov Chain Monte Carlo*. Chapman and Hall/CRC.

Garner, B. A. (Ed.). (2004). *Black's Law Dictionary* (8th ed.). Thomson West.

Gell-Mann, M. (2002). The Quark and the Jaguar (VIII edition). New York: W.H. Freeman & Company.

Gell-Mann, M. (2002). The Quark and the Jaguar (VIll edition). New York: W.H. Freeman & Company.

Gell-Mann, M. (2002a). The Quark and the Jaguar (VIII edition). New York: W.H. Freeman & Company.

Gell-Mann, M. (2012). What Is Complexity? In A. Q. Curzio & M. Fortis (Eds.), *Complexity and Industrial Clusters: Dynamics and Models in Theory and Practice* (pp. 13–24). Springer Science & Business Media.

Gerrits, L. (2012). *Punching Clouds: An Introduction to the Complexity of Public Decision-Making*. ISCE PUB.

Gerrits, L., & Marks, P. (2017). *Understanding Collective Decision Making: A Fitness Landscape Model Approach*. Edward Elgar Publishing. doi:10.4337/9781783473151

Gharajedaghi, J. (2007). Systems Thinking, Third Edition: Managing Chaos and Complexity: A Platform for Designing Business Architecture (3 edition). Burlington, MA: Morgan Kaufmann.

Giddens, A. (1984). *The Constitution of Society: Outline of the Theory of Structuration*. Cambirdge: Policy Press.

Gigerenzer, G. (2003). Reckoning with Risk: Learning to Live with Uncertainty (Kindle version). London: Penguin UK.

Gill, D. (2002). *Signposting the Zoo – From Agencification to a More Principled Choice of Government Organisational Forms*. OECD Publishing.

Glasser, W. (2010). *Choice Theory: A New Psychology of Personal Freedom*. New York: Harper Collins e-books.

Glasser, W. (1994). *Kontrolna teorija*. Taxus.

Gneist, R. (1891). *The History of the English Constitution* (P. A. Ashworth, Trans.). William Clowes and Sons.

Goleman, D. (2007). *Social Intelligence: The New Science of Human Relationships*. Bantam.

Goodhart, C. (1981). Problems of Monetary Management: The U.K. Experience. In A. S. Courakis (Ed.), *Inflation, Depression, and Economic Policy in the West* (pp. 111–116). Totowa, New Yersey: Barnes and Noble Books.

Goodnow, F. J. (1900). *Politics and Administration: A Study in Government*. The MacMillan Company.

Goodsell, C. T. (2010). *Mission Mystique: Belief Systems in Public Agencies*. CQ Press.

Graaf, K. J., Jans, J. H., Marseille, A. T., & Ridder, J. (Eds.). (2007). *Quality of Decision-making in Public Law: Studies in Administrative Decision-making in the Netherlands*. Europa Law Publishing.

Graham, A., & Roberts, A. S. (2004). The agency concept in North America: Failure, adaptation and incremental change. In C. Pollitt & C. Talbot (Eds.), *Unbundled Government: A Critical Analysis of the Global Trend to Agencies, Quangos and Contractualisation* (pp. 140–164). Taylor & Francis.

Grassé, P. P. (1959). La reconstruction du nid et les coordinations inter-individuelles chez Belicositermes natalensis et Cubitermes sp. La théorie de la Stigmergie: Essai d'interprétation du comportement des termites constructeurs. *Insectes Sociaux*, *6*(6), 41–80. doi:10.1007/BF02223791

Greve, C., Flinders, M., & Thiel, S. V. (1999). Quangos—What's in a Name? Defining Quangos from a Comparative Perspective. *Governance: An International Journal of Policy, Administration and Institutions*, *12*(2), 129–146. doi:10.1111/0952-1895.951999095

Grier, D. A. (2013). *Crowdsourcing For Dummies*. John Wiley & Sons.

Grove, W. M., & Meehl, P. E. (1996). Comparative Efficiency of Informal (Subjective, Impressionistic) and Formal (Mechanical, Algorithmic) Prediction Procedures. *The Clinical–Statistical Controversy.*, *2*(2), 293–323.

Gulick, L. (2003). Notes On the Theory of Organisation. In K. Thompson (Ed.), *The Early Sociology of Management and Organizations: Papers on the Science of Administration* (Vol. IV, pp. 1–49). Routledge.

Guy-Ecabert, C. (2018). The Pre-parliamentary Phase in Lawmaking: The Power Issues at Stake. In A. Ladner, N. Soguel, Y. Emery, S. Weerts, & S. Nahrath (Eds.), *Swiss Public Administration—Making the State Work Successfully* (pp. 87–104). Palgrave Macmillan.

Hacking, I. (2001). *An Introduction to Probability and Inductive Logic*. Cambridge University Press. doi:10.1017/CBO9780511801297

Haidt, J. (2012). *The Righteous Mind: Why Good People are Divided by Politics and Religion*. Pantheon Books.

Halligan, J., Buick, F., & O'Flynn, J. (2011). Experiments with joined-up, horizontal and whole-of-government in Anglophone countries. In A. Massey (Ed.), *International Handbook on Civil Service Systems* (pp. 74–102). Edward Elgar Publishing.

Hammerschmid, G., de Walle, S. V., Andrews, R., & Bezes, P. (2016). *Public Administration Reforms in Europe: The View from the Top*. Edward Elgar Publishing. doi:10.4337/9781783475407

Hart, H. L. A. (1994). *The Concept of Law* (2nd ed.). Clarendon Press.

Hayek, F. A. (1998). *Law, Legislation and Liberty: A New Statement of the Liberal Principles of Justice and Political Economy*. Routledge.

Hayek, F. A. (2011). *The Constitution of Liberty: The Definitive Edition (The Collected Works of F. A. Hayek edition* (R. Hamowy, Ed.). University Of Chicago Press.

Haynes, P. (2008). Complexity Theory and Evaluation in Public Management. *Public Management Review*, *10*(3), 401–419. doi:10.1080/14719030802002766

Haynes, P. (2015). *Managing Complexity in the Public Services*. Routledge. doi:10.4324/9781315816777

Compilation of References

Heath, J. (2009). The Uses and Abuses of Agency Theory. *Business Ethics Quarterly*, *19*(4), 497–528. doi:10.5840/beq200919430

Hegel, G. W. F. (1991). *Elements of the Philosophy of Right (A. W. Wood* (H. B. Nisbet Ed. & Trans.). Cambridge University Press.

Heylighen, F. (1999). The Science Of Self-Organization And Adaptivity. In: Knowledge Management, Organizational Intelligence and Learning, and Complexity, in: The Encyclopedia of Life Support Systems, EOLSS, 253–280. Publishers Co. Ltd.

Heylighen, F. (1999). The Science Of Self-Organization And Adaptivity. Knowledge Management, Organizational Intelligence and Learning, and Complexity, in: The Encyclopedia of Life Support Systems, EOLSS, 253–280. Publishers Co. Ltd.

Hofstede, G., Hofstede, G. J., & Minkov, M. (2010). *Cultures and Organizations: Software of the Mind* (3rd ed.). McGraw-Hill.

Holland, J. H. Holyoak, K. J., Nisbett, R. E., & Thagard, P. R. (1989). Induction: Processes of Inference, Learning, and Discovery. Cambridge: MIT Press.

Holland, J. H. (1995). *Hidden order: How adaptation builds complexity*. Addison-Wesley.

Holland, J. H. (2006). Studying Complex Adaptive Systems. *Journal of Systems Science and Complexity*, *19*(1), 1–8. doi:10.1007/s11424-006-0001-z

Holmberg, S., & Rothstein, B. (2012). *Good Government: The Relevance of Political Science*. Edward Elgar Publishing. doi:10.4337/9780857934932

Hood, C. (1981). Axeperson Spare that Quango. In C. Hood & M. Wright (Eds.), *Big Government in Hard Times* (pp. 100–122). OUP.

Hood, C. (1991). A Public Management for All Seasons? *Public Administration*, *69*(1), 3–19. doi:10.1111/j.1467-9299.1991.tb00779.x

Hood, C. (1998). *The Art of the State: Culture, Rhetoric, and Public Management*. Oxford University Press.

Hood, C., & Dixon, R. (2015). *A Government that Worked Better and Cost Less?: Evaluating Three Decades of Reform and Change in UK Central Government*. OUP Oxford. doi:10.1093/acprof:oso/9780199687022.001.0001

Hood, C., & Lodge, M. (2006). *The politics of public service bargains: Reward, competency, loyalty and blame*. Oxford University Press. doi:10.1093/019926967X.001.0001

Hood, C., & Peters, G. (2004). The Middle Aging of New Public Management: Into the Age of Paradox? *Journal of Public Administration: Research and Theory*, *14*(3), 267–282. doi:10.1093/jopart/muh019

Hood, C., Rothstein, H., & Baldwin, R. (2001). *The Government of Risk: Understanding Risk Regulation Regimes*. Oxford University Press. doi:10.1093/0199243638.001.0001

Hubbard, D. W. (2007). *How to Measure Anything: Finding the Value of 'Intangibles' in Business*. Wiley.

Hubbard, D. W. (2009). *The Failure of Risk Management: Why It's Broken and How to Fix It*. Wiley.

Huntington, S. P. (1968). *Political order in changing societies*. Yale University Press.

Husdal, J. (2010). A Conceptual Framework for Risk and Vulnerability in Virtual Enterprise Networks. In P. Stavros (Ed.), *Managing Risk in Virtual Enterprise Networks: Implementing Supply Chain Principles* (pp. 1–27). IGI Global. doi:10.4018/978-1-61520-607-0.ch001

Ipsos MORI. (2019). *Trust the Truth?* IPSOS. https://www.ipsos.com/sites/default/files/ct/publication/documents/2019-09/ipsos-thinks-trust-the-truth.pdf

Jacob, F. (1977). Evolution and tinkering. *Science*, *196*(4295), 1161–1166. doi:10.1126/science.860134 PMID:860134

Janis, I. L. (1980). Groupthinking. In H. J. Leavitt, L. R. Pondy, & D. M. Boje (Eds.), *Readings in Managerial Psychology*. University of Chicago Press.

Jao, C. (2012). *Decision Support Systems*. Olajnica: IntechOpen.

Jenkins, K., Caines, K., & Jackson, A. (1988). *Improving Management in Government: The Next steps: Report to the Prime Minister*. Civil Servant. https://www.civilservant.org.uk/library/1988_improving_management_in_government_the%20_next_steps.pdf

Jessop, B. (2010). Metagovernance. In M. Bevir (Ed.), *The SAGE Handbook of Governance* (pp. 106–123). SAGE.

Johnson, N. L. (2002). *The Development of Collective Structure and Its Response to Environmental Change* (SSRN Scholarly Paper No. ID 2232154). Rochester, NY: Social Science Research Network. https://papers.ssrn.com/abstract=2232154

Joseph, P. (2017). *The New Human Rights Movement*. BenBella Books.

Jowett, P., & Rothwell, M. (1988). *Performance Indicators in the Public Sector*. McMillan. doi:10.1007/978-1-349-08987-1

Justia. (2018). *Independent Agencies*. Justia. https://www.justia.com/administrative-law/independent-agencies/

Kahneman, D. (2013). Thinking, Fast and Slow (Reprint edition). New York: Farrar, Straus and Giroux.

Kahneman, D., Sibony, O., & Sunstein, C. R. (2021). *Noise: A Flaw in Human Judgment*. Little, Brown.

Karpen, U., & Xanthaki, H. (Eds.). (2017). *Legislation in Europe: A Comprehensive Guide For Scholars and Practitioners*. Bloomsbury Publishing.

Kauffman, S. (1996). At Home in the Universe: The Search for the Laws of Self-Organization and Complexity (Reprint edition). New York: Oxford University Press.

Kauffman, S. A. (1993). *The Origins of Order*. Oxford University Press. doi:10.1093/oso/9780195079517.001.0001

Kauffman, S. A. (2010). *Reinventing the Sacred: A New View of Science, Reason, and Religion*. Basic Books.

Kaufmann, D., Kraay, A., & Mastruzzi, M. (2010). *The Worldwide Governance Indicators: Methodology and Analytical Issues*. SSRN. https://papers.ssrn.com/abstract=1682130

Kearney, R. C., & Hays, S. W. (2016). Reinventing Government, The New Public Management and Civil Service Systems in International Perspective: The Danger of Throwing the Baby Out with the Bathwater. *Review of Public Personnel Administration*. (Sage CA: Thousand Oaks, CA). doi:10.1177/0734371X9801800404

Keeney, R. L., & Raiffa, H. (1993). *Decisions with Multiple Objectives: Preferences and Value Trade-Offs*. Cambridge University Press. doi:10.1017/CBO9781139174084

Kelsen, H. (2005). *Pure Theory of Law*. The Lawbook Exchange, Ltd.

Kemp, P. (1990). Can the civil service adapt to managing by contract? *Public Money & Management*, *10*(3), 25–31. doi:10.1080/09540969009387612

Compilation of References

Keohane, R. O. (1988). International Institutions: Two Approaches. *International Studies Quarterly*, *32*(4), 379–396. doi:10.2307/2600589

Khan Academy. (2020). *The equilibrium constant K (article)*. Khan Academy. https://www.khanacademy.org/science/chemistry/chemical-equilibrium/equilibrium-constant/a/the-equilibrium-constant-k

Kiel, L. D. (2014). Complexity Theory and Its Evolution in Public Administration and Policy Studies. *Complexity. Governance & Networks*, *1*(1), 71–78. doi:10.7564/14-CGN9

Kiewiet, D. R., & McCubbins, M. D. (1991). *The Logic of Delegation*. University of Chicago Press.

Klijn, E.-H. (2008). Complexity Theory and Public Administration: What's New? *Public Management Review*, *10*(3), 299–317. doi:10.1080/14719030802002675

Koliba, C. J., Meek, J. W., Zia, A., & Mills, R. W. (2010). *Governance Networks in Public Administration and Public Policy*. Routledge.

Koliba, C., Gerrits, L., Rhodes, M. L., & Meek, J. W. (2016). Complexity theory, Networks and Systems Analysis. In C. Ansell & J. Torfing (Eds.), *Handbook on Theories of Governance* (pp. 364–379). Edward Elgar Publishing. doi:10.4337/9781782548508.00041

Kose, A. M., Sugawara, N., & Terrones, M. E. (2000). *Global Recessions: Policy Research Working Paper 9172*. World Bank Group. https://documents1.worldbank.org/curated/en/185391583249079464/pdf/Global-Recessions.pdf

KramerJ.MeunierJ. (2016). Kin and multilevel selection in social evolution: A never-ending controversy? *F1000Research*, *5*(776), F1000 Faculty Rev-776. doi:10.12688/f1000research.8018.1

Kuipers, S., & Boin, A. (2009). Path Dependence, Institutionalization and the Decline of Two Public Institutions. In G. Schreyögg & J. Sydow (Eds.), *The Hidden Dynamics of Path Dependence: Institutions and Organizations* (pp. 50–69). Palgrave MacMillan.

Lægreid, P., Roness, P. G., & Rubecksen, K. (2012). Norway. In K. Verhoest, S. V. Thiel, G. Bouckaert, & P. Lægreid (Eds.), *Government Agencies: Practices and Lessons from 30 Countries* (pp. 234–244). Palgrave Macmillan. doi:10.1057/9780230359512_22

Landemore, H., & Elster, J. (Eds.). (2012). *Collective Wisdom: Principles and Mechanisms*. Cambridge University Press. doi:10.1017/CBO9780511846427

Lane, N., Martin, W. F., Raven, J. A., & Allen, J. F. (2013). Energy, genes and evolution: Introduction to an evolutionary synthesis. *Philosophical Transactions of the Royal Society of London. Series B, Biological Sciences*, *368*(1622), 20120253. Advance online publication. doi:10.1098/rstb.2012.0253 PMID:23754807

Lanza, R., & Berman, B. (2013). *Biocentrism: How Life and Consciousness are the Keys to Understanding the True Nature of the Universe*. BenBella Books, Inc.

Larmour, P. (1996). *Models of Governance and Development Administration*. Bell School. https://dpa.bellschool.anu.edu.au/experts-publications/publications/1586/models-governance-and-development-administration

Latour, B. (1996). *Aramis, or the Love of Technology*. Harvard University Press.

Lee, K.-F. (2018). *AI Superpowers: China, Silicon Valley, and the New World Order*. Houghton Mifflin Harcourt.

Lefort, C. (1999). *Prigode demokracije*. Ljubljana: Liberalna akademija.

Leseure, M. (2010). *Key Concepts in Operations Management*. SAGE. doi:10.4135/9781446251720

Lewin, K. (1951). *Field Theory in Social Science: Selected Theoretical Papers* (D. Cartwright, Ed.). Harper & Row.

Lindgren, M., & Bandhold, H. (2009). *Scenario Planning: The Link Between Future and Strategy*. MacMillan.

Lipsky, M. (2010). Street-Level Bureaucracy: Dilemmas of the Individual in Public Service. New York: Russell Sage Foundation.

Locke, J. (2010). *Dve razpravi o oblasti Pismo o toleranci*. Krtina.

Lodge, M. (2018). Accounting for Blind Spots. In T. Bach & K. Wegrich (Eds.), *The Blind Spots of Public Bureaucracy and the Politics of Non-Coordination* (pp. 29–48). Palgrave MacMillan.

Lorenz, E. N. (1963). Deterministic Nonperiodic Flow. *Journal of the Atmospheric Sciences*, *20*(2), 130–141. doi:10.1175/1520-0469(1963)020<0130:DNF>2.0.CO;2

Lorenz, J., Rauhut, H., Schweitzer, F., & Helbing, D. (2011). How social influence can undermine the wisdom of crowd effect. *Proceedings of the National Academy of Sciences of the United States of America*, *108*(22), 9020–9025. doi:10.1073/pnas.1008636108 PMID:21576485

Lowi, T. J. (2009). *The End of Liberalism: The Second Republic of the United States*. W. W. Norton, Incorporated.

Lucretius, T. C. (1926). *Lucretius on the Nature of Things*. Clarendon Press.

Luhmann, N. (1996). *Social Systems* (J. B. Jr & D. Baecker, Trans.). Stanford University Press.

Luhmann, N. (2004). *Law as a Social System* (F. Kastner, R. Nobles, D. Schiff, & R. Ziegert, Eds., ZiegertK. A., Trans.). Oxford University Press. doi:10.1093/oso/9780198262381.001.0001

Luhmann, N. (2013). *Introduction to Systems Theory* (P. Gilgen, Trans.). Polity Press.

Luhmann, N. (2013). *Oblast*. Krtina.

Lynch, G. S. (2009). *Single Point of Failure: The 10 Essential Laws of Supply Chain Risk Management*. John Wiley and Sons.

Maine, H. S. (1936). *Ancient Law*. J. M. Dent & Sons Limited.

Majone, G. (1996). *Regulating Europe*. Routledge.

Malaska, P., Malmivirta, M., Meristö, T., & Hansén, S.-O. (1984). Scenarios in Europe—Who uses them and why? *Long Range Planning*, *17*(5), 45–49. doi:10.1016/0024-6301(84)90036-0

Malik, F. (2011). *Corporate Policy and Governance: How Organizations Self-Organize*. Campus Verlag.

Malik, F. (2012). *The Right Corporate Governance: Effective Top Management for Mastering Complexity*. Campus Verlag.

Malik, F. (2016). *Navigating Into the Unknown: A New Way for Management, Governance and Leadership*. Campus Verlag.

Malik, F. (2016). *Strategy: Navigating the Complexity of the New World*. Campus Verlag.

Malone, T. W. (2003). Is Empowerment Just a Fad? Control, Decision Making, and IT. In T. W. Malone, R. Laubacher, & M. S. S. Morton (Eds.), *Inventing the Organizations of the 21st Century*. The MIT Press.

Malone, T. W. (2018). *Superminds: How Hyperconnectivity is Changing the Way We Solve Problems*. Oneworld Publications.

March, J. G., & Olsen, J. P. (1984). The New Institutionalism: Organizational Factors in Political Life. *The American Political Science Review*, *78*(3), 734–749. doi:10.2307/1961840

Compilation of References

Margetts, H. 6, P., & Hood, C. (2012). *Paradoxes of Modernization: Unintended Consequences of Public Policy Reform.* Oxford: Oxford University Press.

Marks, G. (1992). Structural Policy in the European Community. In A. Sbragia (Ed.), *Euro-Politics: Institutions and Policy-making in New European Community* (pp. 191–224). Brookings Institution.

Marks, G., & Hooghe, L. (2005). Contrasting Visions of Multi-level Governance. In I. Bache & M. V. Flinders (Eds.), *Multi-level Governance* (pp. 15–30). Oxford University Press.

Marois, R., & Ivanoff, J. (2005). Capacity limits of information processing in the brain. *Trends in Cognitive Sciences*, *9*(6), 296–305. doi:10.1016/j.tics.2005.04.010 PMID:15925809

Marr, B. (2009). *Managing and Delivering Performance*. Butterworth-Heinemann. doi:10.4324/9780080943015

Maturana, H. R., & Varela, F. J. (1980). *Autopoiesis and Cognition: The Realization of the Living*. D. Reidel Publishing Company. doi:10.1007/978-94-009-8947-4

McCarthy, I., & Gillies, J. (2003). Organisational Diversity, Configurations and Evolution. In E. Mitleton-Kelly (Ed.), *Complex Systems and Evolutionary Perspectives on Organisations* (pp. 71–98). Emerald Group Publishing Limited.

McGuire, L. (2004). Contractualism and performance measurement in Australia. In C. Pollitt & C. Talbot (Eds.), *Unbundled Government: A Critical Analysis of the Global Trend to Agencies, Quangos and Contractualisation* (pp. 113–139). Taylor & Francis.

Meadows, D. H. (2008). *Thinking in Systems: A Primer*. Chelsea Green Publishing.

Meehl, P. E. (2013). *Clinical Versus Statistical Prediction: A Theoretical Analysis and a Review of the Evidence*. Echo Point Books & Media.

Meier, K. J. (2000). *Politics and the Bureaucracy* (4th ed.). Harcourt College Publishers.

Merton, R. K. (1936). The Unanticipated Consequences of Purposive Social Action. *American Sociological Review*, *1*(6), 894–904. doi:10.2307/2084615

Merton, R. K. (1961). Social problems and sociological theory. In R. K. Merton & R. K. Merton (Eds.), *Contemporary Social Problems* (pp. 697–737). Harcourt, Brace & World.

Merton, R. K. (1968). *Social Theory and Social Structure*. Free Press.

Meßerschmidt, K., & Oliver-Lalana, A. D. (Eds.). (2016). *Rational Lawmaking under Review: Legisprudence According to the German Federal Constitutional Court*. Springer. doi:10.1007/978-3-319-33217-8

Miles, R. E., Snow, C. C., Meyer, A. D., & Coleman, H. J. Jr. (1978). Organizational Strategy, Structure, and Process. *Academy of Management Review*, *3*(3), 546–562. doi:10.5465/amr.1978.4305755 PMID:10238389

Miles, R., & Snow, C. (2003). *Organizational Strategy, Structure, and Process* (1st ed.). Stanford Business Books. doi:10.1515/9780804767170

Milgram, S. (2009). Obedience to Authority: An Experimental View (Reprint edition). New York: Harper Perennial Modern Classics.

Miller, G. P. (1988). Introduction: The Debate over Independent Agencies in Light of Empirical Evidence. *Duke Law Journal*, *1988*(2/3), 215–222. doi:10.2307/1372674

Mill, J. S. (1865). *Auguste Comte and Positivism*. N. Trübner & Co. Paternoster.

Mills, C. W. (2000). *The Power Elite: New Edition.* Oxford University Press.

Milward, H. B., & Provan, K. G. (2000). Governing the Hollow State. *Journal of Public Administration: Research and Theory, 10*(2), 359–380. doi:10.1093/oxfordjournals.jpart.a024273

Mintzberg, H. (1979). Patterns in Strategy Formation. [JSTOR. Retrieved from JSTOR.]. *International Studies of Management & Organization, 9*(3), 67–86. doi:10.1080/00208825.1979.11656272

Mintzberg, H. (1983). *Structure in Fives: Designing Effective Organizations.* Prentice Hall PTR.

Mintzberg, H., & Waters, J. A. (1985). Of strategies, deliberate and emergent. *Strategic Management Journal, 6*(3), 257–272. doi:10.1002/smj.4250060306

Miorandi, D., Maltese, V., Rovatsos, M., Nijholt, A., & Stewart, J. (2014). *Social Collective Intelligence: Combining the Powers of Humans and Machines to Build a Smarter Society.* Springer. doi:10.1007/978-3-319-08681-1

Misuraca, G. (Ed.). (2020). Assessing the impacts of digital government transformation in the EU. Luxemburg: Publications Office of the European Union.

Mitleton-Kelly, E. (Ed.). (2003). *Complex Systems and Evolutionary Perspectives on Organisations.* Emerald Group Publishing Limited.

Mlodinow, L. (2008). *The Drunkard's Walk: How Randomness Rules Our Lives.* Pantheon Books.

Molak, V. (1996). *Fundamentals of Risk Analysis and Risk Management.* CRC-Press.

Mooney, J. D., & Reiley, A. C. (1931). *Onward Industry: The Principles of Organization and Their Significance to Modern Industry.* Harper & Brothers.

Morçöl, G. (2012). *A Complexity Theory for Public Policy.* Routledge.

Morgan, B., & Yeung, K. (2007). *An Introduction to Law and Regulation: Text and Materials.* Cambridge University Press. doi:10.1017/CBO9780511801112

Moss, D. A., & Cisternino, J. (2009). *New Perspectives on Regulation.* The Tobin Project.

Nason, R. (2017). *It's Not Complicated: The Art and Science of Complexity in Business.* University of Toronto Press. doi:10.3138/9781487514778

Nastasi, L., Pressman, D., & Swaigen, J. (2020). *Administrative Law: Principles and Advocacy* (Fourth). Torondo: Emond.

Nehl, H. P. (1999). *Principles of Administrative Procedure in EC Law.* Hart Publishing.

Newton, I. (1675). *Isaac Newton letter to Robert Hooke, 1675.* HSP. https://discover.hsp.org/Record/dc-9792/

Newton. (1947). *Sir Isaac Newton's Mathematical Principles of Natural Philosophy and His System of the World* (A. Motte & F. Cajori, Eds.). Oakland: University of California Press.

Nicolis, G., & Prigogine, I. (1977). *Self-organization in nonequilibrium systems: From dissipative structures to order through fluctuations.* Wiley.

Nicolis, G., & Prigogine, I. (1989). *Exploring Complexity: An Introduction.* W.H. Freeman.

Nielsen, T. D., & Jensen, F. (2007). *Bayesian Networks and Decision Graphs* (2nd ed.). Springer.

Niklasson, B. (2012). Sweden. In K. Verhoest, S. V. Thiel, G. Bouckaert, & P. Lægreid (Eds.), *Government Agencies: Practices and Lessons from 30 Countries* (pp. 245–258). Palgrave Macmillan. doi:10.1057/9780230359512_23

Compilation of References

Noble, S. U. (2018). *Algorithms of Oppression: How Search Engines Reinforce Racism*. NYU Press. doi:10.18574/nyu/9781479833641.001.0001

Nonaka, I., & Zhu, Z. (2012). Pragmatic Strategy: Eastern Wisdom, Global Success. Cambirdge: Cambridge University Press. doi:10.1017/CBO9780511736568

Nonet, P., & Selznick, P. (2001). *Law and Society in Transition: Toward Responsive Law*. Transaction Publishers.

Noore Alam, S., & Mohd. Zin, M. (2007). Paradox of Public Sector Reforms in Malaysia: A Good Governance Perspective. *Public Administration Quarterly*, *31*(3/4), 284–312.

Nozick, R. (1993). *The Nature of Rationality*. Princeton University Press. doi:10.1515/9781400820832

O'Neil, C. (2017). *Weapons of Math Destruction: How Big Data Increases Inequality and Threatens Democracy*. Penguin Books.

O'Reilly, T. (2010). Government as a Platform. In D. Lathrop & L. Ruma (Eds.), *Open Government: Collaboration, Transparency, and Participation in Practice*. O'Reilly Media, Inc.

Öberg, S. A., & Wockelberg, H. (2020). Agency control or autonomy? Government steering of Swedish government agencies 2003–2017. *International Public Management Journal*, *0*(0), 1–20. doi:10.1080/10967494.2020.1799889

Odell, J. (2003). Between Order and Chaos. *Journal of Object Technology*, *2*(6), 45–50. doi:10.5381/jot.2003.2.6.c4

OECD. (1996). *Public Management Occasional Papers Pay Reform in the Public Service Initial Impact on Pay Dispersion in Australia, Sweden and the United Kingdom No. 10: Initial Impact on Pay Dispersion in Australia, Sweden and the United Kingdom*. OECD Publishing.

OECD. (1997). *In Search of Results: Performance Management Practices*. OECD Publishing.

OECD. (1999). European Principles for Public Administration. (SIGMA Papers, No. 27). OECD. https://www.oecd-ilibrary.org/docserver/download/5kml60zwdr7h.pdf?expires=1459602912&id=id&accname=guest&checksum=AD8421691668211416DB861810C0B737

OECD. (1999). European Principles for Public Administration. *SIGMA Papers, No. 27*. https://www.oecd-ilibrary.org/docserver/download/5kml60zwdr7h.pdf?expires=1459602912&id=id&accname=guest&checksum=AD8421691668211416DB861810C0B737

OECD. (2002). *Distributed Public Governance Agencies, Authorities and other Government Bodies: Agencies, Authorities and other Government Bodies*. OECD Publishing.

OECD. (2003). *Public Sector Modernisation: Changing Organisations GOV/PUMA(2003)19*. OECD. http://www.oecd.org/officialdocuments/publicdisplaydocumentpdf/?cote=GOV/PUMA(2003)19&docLanguage=En

OECD. (2011). *Regulatory Policy and Governance: Supporting Economic Growth and Serving the Public Interest*. OECD Publishing.

OECD. (2012). *Recommendation of the Council on Regulatory Policy and Governance*. OECD.

OECD. (2012). *The Public Sector Salary System in Slovenia*. OECD Publishing.

OECD. (2017). *Systems Approaches to Public Sector Challenges: Working with Change*. OECD Publishing.

OMB. (2021). *About OMB*. OMB. https://www.whitehouse.gov/omb/freedom-of-information-act-foia/#q1

Ongaro, E. (2010). *Public Management Reform and Modernization: Trajectories of Administrative Change in Italy, France, Greece, Portugal and Spain*. Edward Elgar Pub.

Osborne, D., & Gaebler, T. (1993). *Reinventing Government: How the Entrepreneurial Spirit is Transforming the Public Sector*. Plume.

Osborne, S. P. (Ed.). (2010). *The New Public Governance: Emerging Perspectives on the Theory and Practice of Public Governance*. Routledge. doi:10.4324/9780203861684

Page, S. E. (2008). The Difference: How the Power of Diversity Creates Better Groups, Firms, Schools, and Societies. Princeton, N.J.; Woodstock: Princeton University Press. doi:10.1515/9781400830282

Page, S. E. (2018). *The Model Thinker: What You Need to Know to Make Data Work for You*. Basic Books.

Panda, B., & Leepsa, N. M. (2017). Agency theory: Review of Theory and Evidence on Problems and Perspectives. *Indian Journal of Corporate Governance*, *10*(1), 74–95. doi:10.1177/0974686217701467

Parker Follett, M. (2003). The Process of Control. In L. Gulick & L. Urwick (Eds.), *Papers on the Science of Administration* (Vol. IV, pp. 170–180). Routlege.

Parliamentary and Health Service Ombudsman. (2017). *Principles of Good Administration*. Ombudsman. https://www.ombudsman.org.uk/about-us/our-principles/principles-good-administration

Parmenter, D. (2012). *Key Performance Indicators for Government and Non Profit Agencies: Implementing Winning KPIs*. John Wiley & Sons. doi:10.1002/9781119201038

Parrillo, V. N. (2005). *Contemporary Social Problems* (6th ed.). Pearson/Allyn and Bacon.

Parsons, T. (1991). The Social System (New edition). London: Routledge.

Parsons, T. (1985). *Talcott Parsons on Institutions and Social Evolution: Selected Writings*. University of Chicago Press.

Pasquier, M. (2018). Communication and Transparency. In A. Ladner, N. Soguel, Y. Emery, S. Weerts, & S. Nahrath (Eds.), *Swiss Public Administration—Making the State Work Successfully* (pp. 221–240). Palgrave Macmillan.

Pearl, J. (2009). *Causality: Models, Reasoning and Inference* (2nd ed.). Cambridge University Press. doi:10.1017/CBO9780511803161

Pearl, J. (2014). *Probabilistic Reasoning in Intelligent Systems: Networks of Plausible Inference*. Morgan Kaufmann.

Pečarič, M. (2018). Legal Principles as Extrapolated Reality. *Archiv Für Rechts- Und Sozialphilosphie*, *104*(3), 397–420.

Pečarič, M. (2020). Systemic legislation: By what right are distinctions made? *Cogent Social Sciences*, *6*(1), 1837424. doi:10.1080/23311886.2020.1837424

Pečarič, M. (2020). Understanding Differences between Equal Public Governance Models. *Central European Public Administration Review*, *18*(1), 69–88. doi:10.17573/cepar.2020.1.04

Peirce, C. S. (1931). *The Collected Papers of Charles Sanders Peirce (electronic edition* (C. Hartshorne & P. Weiss, Eds.). Harvard University Press.

Peng, T. C. P. (2005). *Strategies to Build Up Holistic Governance*. EA. https://www.ea.sinica.edu.tw/file/Image/Strategies%20to%20Build%20Up%20Holistic%20Governance.pdf

Perri, 6, Leat, D., Seltzer, K., & Stoker, G. (2002). *Towards Holistic Governance: The New Reform Agenda*. London: Macmillan Education UK.

Compilation of References

Perri, 6. (1997). *Holistic Government*. London: Demos.

Peters, B. G. (2011). Steering, rowing, drifting, or sinking? Changing patterns of governance. *Urban Research & Practice*, *4*(1), 5–12. doi:10.1080/17535069.2011.550493

Peters, B. G. (2020). The Politics of Bureaucracy: A Continuing Saga. *NISPAcee Journal of Public Administration and Policy*, *13*(2), 213–220. doi:10.2478/nispa-2020-0021

Peters, B. G., & Pierre, J. (2012). *The SAGE Handbook of Public Administration*. SAGE. doi:10.4135/9781446200506

Peterson, J. B. (2021). *Beyond Order: 12 More Rules for Life*. Penguin Publishing Group.

Pew Research Center. (2020). Public Trust in Government Remains Near Historic Lows as Partisan Attitudes Shift. Pew Research Center—U.S. Politics & Policy. https://www.pewresearch.org/politics/2017/05/03/public-trust-in-government-remains-near-historic-lows-as-partisan-attitudes-shift/

Piaget, J. (1932). *The Moral Judgement of the Child*. The Free Press.

Piattoni, S. (2010). *The Theory of Multi-level Governance:Conceptual, Empirical, and Normative Challenges: Conceptual, Empirical, and Normative Challenges*. Oxford University Press. doi:10.1093/acprof:oso/9780199562923.001.0001

Pielke, R. A. Jr. (2007). *The Honest Broker: Making Sense of Science in Policy and Politics*. Cambridge University Press. doi:10.1017/CBO9780511818110

Pierre, J. (2004). Central agencies in Sweden: A report from Utopia. In C. Pollitt & C. Talbot (Eds.), *Unbundled Government: A Critical Analysis of the Global Trend to Agencies, Quangos and Contractualisation* (pp. 203–214). Taylor & Francis.

Pierre, J., & Peters, B. G. (2000). *Governance, Politics and the State*. Palgrave Macmillan.

Piketty, T. (2014). *Capital in the Twenty-First Century* (T. Goldhammer, Trans.). Harvard University Press. doi:10.4159/9780674369542

Piketty, T. (2020). *Capital and Ideology*. Harvard University Press.

Plutarch. (1936). Plutarch: Moralia: Vol. V. *Isis and Osiris. The E at Delphi. The Oracles at Delphi No Longer Given in Verse. The Obsolescence of Oracles* (F. C. Babbitt, Trans.). Harvard University Press.

Pollit, C., Bathgate, K., Caulfield, J., Smullen, A., & Talbot, C. (2001). Agency fever? Analysis of an international policy fashion. *Journal of Comparative Policy Analysis*, *3*(3), 271–290. doi:10.1080/13876980108412663

Pollitt, C., Bouckaert, G., & Löffler, E. (2006). *Making Quality Sustainable: Co-Design, Co-Decide, Co-Produce, and Co-Evaluate*. Report of The 4QC Conference, Tampere. https://circabc.europa.eu/webdav/CircaBC/eupan/dgadmintest/Library/6/1/2/meetings_presidency/meeting_26-27_october/4QCREPORT_final_version_October_2006.pdf

Pollitt, C. (2000). How do we know how good public services are? In G. Peters & D. J. Savoie (Eds.), *Governance in the Twenty-first Century: Revitalizing the Public Service* (pp. 119–154). McGill-Queen's Press - MQUP. doi:10.1515/9780773568884-006

Pollitt, C. (2001). Convergence: The Useful Myth? *Public Administration*, *79*(4), 933–947. doi:10.1111/1467-9299.00287

Pollitt, C. (2003). *The Essential Public Manager*. McGraw-Hill International.

Pollitt, C., & Bouckaert, G. (2011). *Public Management Reform: A Comparative Analysis - New Public Management, Governance, and the Neo-Weberian State* (3rd ed.). Oxford University Press.

Pollitt, C., & Bouckaert, G. (2017). *Public Management Reform: A Comparative Analysis Into the Age of Austerity* (4th ed.). Oxford University Press.

Pollitt, C., & Talbot, C. (Eds.). (2004). *Unbundled Government: A Critical Analysis of the Global Trend to Agencies, Quangos and Contractualisation*. Taylor & Francis. doi:10.4324/9780203507148

Pollitt, C., Talbot, C., Caulfield, J., & Smullen, A. (2004). *Agencies: How Governments Do Things Through Semi-Autonomous Organizations*. Palgrave MacMillan.

Popova, M. (2015). *Buckminster Fuller's Brilliant Metaphor for the Greatest Key to Transformation and Growth*. Brain Pickings.

Popper, K. (2002). *The Logic of Scientific Discovery*. Routledge.

Powell, W. W., & DiMaggio, P. (Eds.). (1991). *The New institutionalism in organizational analysis*. The University of Chicago Press. doi:10.7208/chicago/9780226185941.001.0001

Premack, D., & Woodruff, G. (1978). Does the chimpanzee have a theory of mind? *Behavioral and Brain Sciences*, *1*(4), 515–526. doi:10.1017/S0140525X00076512

Prigogine, I., & Stengers, I. (1984). *Order Out of Chaos*. Bantam Books.

Raiffa, H. (1994). The Prescriptive Orientation of Decision Making: A Synthesis of Decision Analysis, Behavioral Decision Making, and Game Theory. In S. Ríos (Ed.), *Decision Theory and Decision Analysis: Trends and Challenges* (pp. 3–13). Springer Science & Business Media. doi:10.1007/978-94-011-1372-4_1

Rainey, H. G. (2009). *Understanding and Managing Public Organizations* (4th ed.). Jossey-Bass.

Ramirez, R., & Wilkinson, A. (2016). *Strategic Reframing: The Oxford Scenario Planning Approach*. Oxford University Press. doi:10.1093/acprof:oso/9780198745693.001.0001

Reibnitz, U. V. (1989). *Scenario Techniques*. McGraw-Hill.

Rhodes, M. L. Murphy, J., Muir, J., & Murray, J. A. (2010). Public Management and Complexity Theory: Richer Decision-Making in Public Services. New York: Routledge.

Rhodes, M. L. (2008). Complexity and Emergence in Public Management. *Public Management Review*, *10*(3), 361–379. doi:10.1080/14719030802002717

Rhodes, M. L., & MacKechnie, G. (2003). Understanding Public Service Systems: Is There a Role for Complex Adaptive Systems Theory? *Emergence*, *5*(4), 57–85. doi:10.1207/s15327000em0504_6

Rhodes, M. L., & Murray, J. (2007). Collaborative Decision Making in Urban Regeneration: A Complex Adaptive Systems Perspective. *International Public Management Journal*, *10*(1), 79–101. doi:10.1080/10967490601185740

Ridder, J. (2007). Factors for legal quality of administrative decision-making. In K. J. Graaf, J. H. Jans, A. T. Marseille, & J. Ridder (Eds.), *Quality of Decision-making in Public Law: Studies in Administrative Decision-making in the Netherlands* (pp. 31–51). Europa Law Publishing.

Ridley, M. (2017). *What Charles Darwin owes Adam Smith*. Learn Liberty. https://www.learnliberty.org/blog/what-charles-darwin-owes-adam-smith/

Rifkin, E., & Bouwer, E. (2007). *The Illusion of Certainty: Health Benefits and Risks* (2007 edition). Springer. doi:10.1007/978-0-387-48572-0

Compilation of References

Rigg, C., & Richards, S. (2006). *Action Learning, Leadership and Organizational Development in Public Services*. Routledge. doi:10.4324/9780203966198

Robertson, D. W. (1946). A Note on the Classical Origin of 'Circumstances' in the Medieval Confessional. *Studies in Philology*, *43*(1), 6–14.

Room, G. (2011). *Complexity, Institutions and Public Policy: Agile Decision-making in a Turbulent World*. Edward Elgar Pub. doi:10.4337/9780857932648

Room, G. (2016). *Agile Actors on Complex Terrains: Transformative Realism and Public Policy*. Routledge. doi:10.4324/9781315660769

Roosevelt, T. (1910). *Man in the Arena Speech*. World Future Fund. http://www.worldfuturefund.org/Documents/mani-narena.htm

Rose-Ackerman, S., & Lindseth, P. L. (2011). *Comparative Administrative Law*. Edward Elgar Pub.

Rosenbloom, D., Kravchuk, R., & Clerkin, R. (2014). *Public Administration: Understanding Management, Politics, and Law in the Public Sector* (8th ed.). McGraw-Hill Education.

Rosling, H., Rönnlund, A. R., & Rosling, O. (2018). *Factfulness: Ten Reasons We're Wrong About the World—and Why Things Are Better Than You Think*. Hodder & Stoughton Ltd.

Rossi, P. H., Lipsey, M. W., & Freeman, H. E. (1999). *Evaluation: A Systematic Approach* (6th ed.). SAGE Publications.

Rothwell, W. J., & Sullivan, R. L. (Eds.). (2005). *Practicing Organization Development: A Guide for Consultants*. John Wiley & Sons.

Rousseau, D. M. (Ed.). (2013). *The Oxford Handbook of Evidence-Based Management*. Oxford University Press.

Rousseau, J.-J. (2002). *The Social Contract and The First and Second Discourses* (S. Dunn, Ed.). Yale University Press.

Royal Naval Museum Library. (2014). *A Brief History of the Royal Navy*. Royal Naval Museum Library. http://www.royalnavalmuseum.org/info_sheets_naval_history.html

Ruhl, J. B. (1996). Complexity Theory as a Paradigm for the Dynamical Law-and-Society System: A Wake-Up Call for Legal Reductionism and the Modern Administrative State. *Duke Law Journal*, *45*(5), 851–928. doi:10.2307/1372975

Rumelt, R. (2011). *Good Strategy Bad Strategy: The Difference and Why It Matters*. Crown Business.

Salminen, A., Viinamäki, O.-P., & Jokisuu, J. (2012). Finland. In K. Verhoest, S. V. Thiel, G. Bouckaert, & P. Lægreid (Eds.), *Government Agencies: Practices and Lessons from 30 Countries* (pp. 223–233). Palgrave Macmillan. doi:10.1057/9780230359512_21

Sarewitz, D. (2004). How science makes environmental controversies worse. *Environmental Science & Policy*, *7*(5), 385–403. doi:10.1016/j.envsci.2004.06.001

Sartre, J.-P. (2001). *Jean-Paul Sartre: Basic Writings* (S. Priest, Ed.). Psychology Press.

Scalia, A. (1989). Judicial Deference to Administraitve Interpretations of Law. *Duke Law Journal*, *1989*(3), 511–521.

Scharpf, F. W. (1978). Inter-organisational policy studies:issues, concepts and perspectives. In K. Hanf & F. W. Scharpf (Eds.), *Interorganizational Policy Making: Limits to Coordination and Central Control* (pp. 345–370). SAGE Publications.

Schilling, E. G., & Neubauer, D. V. (2009). *Acceptance Sampling in Quality Control* (2nd ed.). CRC Press. doi:10.1201/9781584889533

Schmitt, C. (1985). *Political Theology: Four Chapters on the Concept of Sovereignty* (1st ed.). (G. Schwab, Trans.). MIT Press.

Schoemaker, P. J. H. (1993). Multiple scenario development: Its conceptual and behavioral foundation. *Strategic Management Journal*, *14*(3), 193–213. doi:10.1002/smj.4250140304

Schreyögg, G., & Sydow, J. (2009). *The Hidden Dynamics of Path Dependence: Institutions and Organizations*. Palgrave MacMillan.

Schwab, K. (2012). The Global Competitiveness Report 2012—2013. *17th PACI Task Force Meeting Executive Summary*. WeForum. https://reports.weforum.org/global-competitiveness-report-2012-2013/

Schwenker, B., & Wulf, T. (2013). *Scenario-based Strategic Planning: Developing Strategies in an Uncertain World*. Springer Science & Business Media. doi:10.1007/978-3-658-02875-6

Scott, W. R., & Davis, G. F. (2016). *Organizations and Organizing: Rational, Natural and Open Systems Perspectives*. Routledge.

Seddon, J. (2005). *Freedom from Command and Control: Rethinking Management for Lean Service*. Productivity Press.

Seidman, H. (1996). *Politics, position, and power: The dynamics of federal organisation*. Oxford University Press.

Selin, L. J. (2015). What Makes an Agency Independent? *American Journal of Political Science*, *59*(4), 971–987.

Selznick, P. (1949). *TVA and the Grass Roots: A Study in the Sociology of Formal Organization*. University of California Press.

Selznick, P. (1969). *Law, Society, and Industrial Justice*. Russell Sage Foundation.

Selznick, P. (1994). *The Moral Commonwealth: Social Theory and the Promise of Community*. University of California Press. doi:10.1525/9780520354753

Selznick, P. (2011). *Leadership in Administration: A Sociological Interpretation*. Quid Pro Books.

Selznick, P. (2014). *The Organizational Weapon: A Study of Bolshevik Strategy and Tactics*. Quid Pro Books.

Senge, P. M. (2010). *The Fifth Discipline: The Art & Practice of The Learning Organization*. Crown Publishing Group.

Shadbolt, N., O'Hara, K., Roure, D. D., & Hall, W. (2019). *The Theory and Practice of Social Machines*. Springer. doi:10.1007/978-3-030-10889-2

Shanteau, J. (1992). Competence in experts: The role of task characteristics. *Organizational Behavior and Human Decision Processes*, *53*(2), 252–266. doi:10.1016/0749-5978(92)90064-E

Shick, A. (2002). Agencies* in Search of Principles. In OECD (Ed.), *Distributed Public Governance Agencies, Authorities and other Government Bodies: Agencies, Authorities and other Government Bodies* (pp. 33–52). OECD Publishing.

Shmueli, G., Bruce, P. C., Stephens, M. L., & Patel, N. R. (2017). *Data Mining for Business Analytics: Concepts, Techniques, and Applications with JMP Pro*. John Wiley & Sons.

Sieber, S. (1981). *Fatal Remedies: The Ironies of Social Intervention*. Plenum Press. doi:10.1007/978-1-4684-7456-5

SIGMA. (2001). *Financial management and control of public agencies*. SIGMA. https://www.oecd-ilibrary.org/docserver/5kml60vk0h9x-en.pdf?expires=1603963677&id=id&accname=guest&checksum=AB63FFD9902F2673A133FDC1F219CAA0

Compilation of References

SIGMA. (2012). *Good Administration through a Better System of Administrative Procedures.* SIGMA. https://www.sigmaweb.org/publications/Comments_LawAdminProceduresKosovo_JN_Oct2012_Eng%20%20.pdf

SIGMA. (2014). *Principles of Public Administration.* OECD Publishing.

Silvertown, J. (2009). A new dawn for citizen science. *Trends in Ecology & Evolution, 24*(9), 467–471. doi:10.1016/j.tree.2009.03.017 PMID:19586682

Simon, H. A. (1997). *Administrative Behavior* (4th ed.). Free Press.

Skinner, B. F. (1969). *Contingencies of Reinforcement: A Theoretical Analysis.* Prentice Hall.

Slovic, P. (1996). Risk Perception and Trust. In V. Molak (Ed.), Fundamentals of Risk Analysis and Risk Management (p. Chapter III.1). New York: CRC-Press. doi:10.1201/9781439821978.sec3

Slovic, P. (1987). Perception of Risk. *Science, 236*(4799), 280–285. doi:10.1126/science.3563507 PMID:3563507

Slyke, D. M. (2003). The Mythology of Privatization in Contracting for Social Services. *Public Administration Review, 63*(3), 296–315. doi:10.1111/1540-6210.00291

Smith, A. (1977). *And Inquiry into the Nature and Causes of the Wealth of Nations.* University Of Chicago Press. doi:10.7208/chicago/9780226763750.001.0001

Smith, M. J., & Flinders, M. V. (1999). *Quangos, Accountability and Reform.* Palgrave Macmillan.

Smullen, A. (2004). Lost in translation? Shifting interpretations of the concept of 'agency': The Dutch case. In C. Pollitt & C. Talbot (Eds.), *Unbundled Government: A Critical Analysis of the Global Trend to Agencies, Quangos and Contractualisation* (pp. 184–202). Taylor & Francis.

Snellen, I., & Klijn, E.-H. (2009). Complexity Theory and Public Administration: A Critical Appraisal. In G. Teisman, A. van Buuren, & L. M. Gerrits (Eds.), *Managing Complex Governance Systems* (pp. 17–36). Routledge.

Snowden, D. J., & Boone, M. E. (2007, November 1). A Leader's Framework for Decision Making. *Harvard Business Review.* https://hbr.org/2007/11/a-leaders-framework-for-decision-making

Sørensen, E., & Triantafillou, P. (2016). *The Politics of Self-Governance.* Routledge. doi:10.4324/9781315554259

Spencer, H. (1898). *The Principles of Sociology* (Vol. 1). D. Appleton and Company.

Spitzer, D. (2007). *Transforming Performance Measurement: Rethinking the Way We Measure and Drive Organizational Success.* AMACOM.

Stasser, G., & Titus, W. (1985). Pooling of unshared information in group decision making: Biased information sampling during discussion. *Journal of Personality and Social Psychology, 48*(6), 1476–1478. doi:10.1037/0022-3514.48.6.1467

Strauss, P. L., Rakoff, T. D., Metzger, G. E., Barron, D. J., & O'Connell, A. J. (2018). *Administrative Law, Cases and Comments* (12th ed.). Foundation Press.

Strøm, K. (2000). Delegation and accountability in parliamentary democracies. *European Journal of Political Research, 37*(3), 261–289. doi:10.1111/1475-6765.00513

Sunstein, C. R. (2006). *Infotopia: How Many Minds Produce Knowledge.* Oxford University Press. doi:10.1093/oso/9780195189285.001.0001

Sunstein, C. R. (2009). *Going to Extremes: How Like Minds Unite and Divide.* Oxford University Press. doi:10.1093/oso/9780195378016.001.0001

Surowiecki, J. (2005). *The Wisdom of Crowds* (Reprint edition). New York, NY: Anchor.

Surowiecki, J. (2005). *The Wisdom of Crowds*. New York, NY: Anchor.

Sweet Stayer, M., & Ravindra, R. (1990). Newton's Dream. *American Journal of Physics*, *58*(3), 285–286. doi:10.1119/1.16203

Sweet, A. S., & Thatcher, M. (2003). *The Politics of Delegation*. Frank Cas.

Talbot, C. (2004). The Agency idea: Sometimes old, sometimes new, sometimes borrowed, sometimes untrue. In C. Pollitt & C. Talbot (Eds.), *Unbundled Government: A Critical Analysis of the Global Trend to Agencies, Quangos and Contractualisation* (pp. 3–21). Taylor & Francis.

Taleb, N. N. (2010). *The Black Swan: The Impact of the Highly Improbable Fragility* (Kindle Edition). New York: Random House Publishing Group.

Taleb, N. N. (2010). *The Black Swan: The Impact of the Highly Improbable Fragility*. New York: Random House Publishing Group.

Taylor, F. W. (1974). *Scientific Management*. Greenwood Press.

Teisman, G. R., & Klijn, E.-H. (2008). Complexity Theory and Public Management. *Public Management Review*, *10*(3), 287–297. doi:10.1080/14719030802002451

Teisman, G., van Buuren, A., & Gerrits, L. M. (2009). *Managing Complex Governance Systems*. Routledge. doi:10.4324/9780203866160

Terje, A. (2003). *Foundations of Risk Analysis: A Knowledge and Decision-Oriented Perspective*. John Wiley & Sons.

Tetlock, P. E. (2006). *Expert Political Judgment: How Good Is It? How Can We Know?* New Yersey: Princeton University Press.

Tetlock, P., & Gardner, D. (2015). *Superforecasting: The Art and Science of Prediction* (Kindle edition). London: Random House.

Thacher, D., & Rein, M. (2004). Managing Value Conflict in Public Policy. *Governance: An International Journal of Policy, Administration and Institutions*, *17*(4), 457–486. doi:10.1111/j.0952-1895.2004.00254.x

The Law Dictionary. (2020). *Board, Council, Commission, Committee, Tribunal*. https://thelawdictionary.org

The Parliamentary and Health Service Ombudsman. (2009). *Principles of Good Administration*. The Parliamentary and Health Service Ombudsman.

Thiel, S. V. (2012). Comparing Agencies Across Countries. In K. Verhoest, S. V. Thiel, G. Bouckaert, P. Lægreid, & S. V. Thiel (Eds.), *Government Agencies* (pp. 28–28). Palgrave Macmillan. doi:10.1057/9780230359512_2

Tiebout, C. M. (1956). A Pure Theory of Local Expenditures. *Journal of Political Economy*, *64*(5), 416–424. doi:10.1086/257839

Toshniwal, S. (2019). *What is the difference between Board, Council, Committee, Commission and Tribunal in India?* Quora. https://www.quora.com/What-is-the-difference-between-Board-Council-Committee-Commission-and-Tribunal-in-India

Tovey, M. (Ed.). (2008). *Collective Intelligence: Creating a Prosperous World at Peace*. Earth Intelligence Network.

Trevisani, D. (2007). *Regie di cambiamento. Approcci integrati alle risorse umane, allo sviluppo personale e organizzativo e al coaghing*. Franco Angeli Publisher.

Compilation of References

Turing, A. M. (1950). Computing Machinery and Intelligence. *Mind*, 49.

Turner, J. H. (1997). *The Institutional Order: Economy, Kinship, Religion, Polity, Law, and Education in Evolutionary and Comparative Perspective*. Longman.

Turner, J. H. (2003). *Human Institutions: A Theory of Societal Evolution*. Rowman & Littlefield.

Tversky, A., & Kahneman, D. (1974). Judgment under Uncertainty: Heuristics and Biases. *Science*, *185*(4157), 1124–1131. doi:10.1126/science.185.4157.1124 PMID:17835457

UNDP. (2011). *Governance Principles, Institutional Capacity and Quality*. UNDP. https://www.undp.org/content/dam/undp/library/Poverty%20Reduction/Inclusive%20development/Towards%20Human%20Resilience/Towards_SustainingMDGProgress_Ch8.pdf

UNDP. (2011). *Human Development Report 2011*. UNDP. https://www.undp.org/content/undp/en/home/librarypage/hdr/human_developmentreport2011.html

Unescap. (2009). *What is Good Governance?* Retrieved from https://www.unescap.org/resources/what-good-governance

Valdés, C. B. (2011). *Political Struggles and the Forging of Autonomous Government Agencies*. Palgrave MacMillan. doi:10.1057/9780230307957

van Thiel, S. (2004). Quangos in Dutch government. In C. Pollitt & C. Talbot (Eds.), *Unbundled Government: A Critical Analysis of the Global Trend to Agencies, Quangos and Contractualisation* (pp. 167–183). Taylor & Francis.

van Vught, F. A. (1987). Pitfalls of forecasting: Fundamental problems for the methodology of forecasting from the philosophy of science. *Futures*, *19*(2), 184–196. doi:10.1016/0016-3287(87)90050-4

Veblen, T. (1918). *The Instinct of Workmanship and the State of the Industrial Arts*. B. W. Huebsch.

Velluti, S. (2009). *Experimental Forms of New Governance and the Paradoxes of European Legal Integration*. University of Lincoln. Retrieved from https://cor.europa.eu/en/activities/governance/documents/7ad863ed-fb54-46b3-adf6-babcc0366c3e.pdf

Verhoest, K. Demuzere, S., & Rommel, J. (2012). Belgium and Its Regions. In K. Verhoest, S. V. Thiel, G. Bouckaert, & P. Lægreid (Eds.), Government Agencies: Practices and Lessons from 30 Countries (pp. 84–97). Basingstoke: Palgrave Macmillan.

Verhoest, K. (2018). Agencification in Europe. In E. Ongaro & S. V. Thiel (Eds.), *The Palgrave Handbook of Public Administration and Management in Europe* (pp. 327–346). Palgrave MacMillan.

Verhoest, K., Roness, P., Verschuere, B., Rubecksen, K., & MacCarthaigh, M. (2010). *Autonomy and Control of State Agencies: Comparing States and Agencies*. Palgrave MacMillan. doi:10.1057/9780230277274

Verhoest, K., Thiel, S. V., Bouckaert, G., & Lægreid, P. (Eds.). (2012). *Government Agencies: Practices and Lessons from 30 Countries*. Palgrave Macmillan. doi:10.1057/9780230359512

Verhoest, Koen, Peters, B. G., Bouckaert, G., & Verschuere, B. (2004). The study of organisational autonomy: A conceptual review. *Public Administration and Development*, *24*(2), 101–118. doi:10.1002/pad.316

Verkuil, P. (1988). The Purposes and Limits of Independent Agencies. *Duke Law Journal*, *37*(2), 257–279.

Vickers, G. (1995). *The Art of Judgment: A Study of Policy Making*. SAGE Publications, Inc.

Vogel, S. K. (1998). *Freer Markets, More Rules: Regulatory Reform in Advanced Industrial Countries*. Cornell University Press. doi:10.7591/9781501717307

von Bertalanffy, L. (1968). *General system theory: Foundations, development, applications*. George Braziller.

von Bogdandy, A., Huber, P. M., & Cassese, S. (Eds.). (2017). *The Max Planck Handbooks in European Public Law: The Administrative State*. Oxford University Press.

von Clausewitz, C. (2007). *On War* (M. Howard & P. Paret, Trans.). Oxford University Press.

Waldo, D. (1948). *The Administrative State: A Study of the Political Theory of American Public Administration*. The Ronald Press Company.

Waldron, J. (2011). The Rule of Law and the Importance of Procedure. In J. E. Fleming (Ed.), *Getting to the Rule of Law* (pp. 3–31). NYU Press.

Waldrop, M. M. (1993). *Complexity: The Emerging Science at the Edge of Order and Chaos*. Simon and Schuster.

Wallis, S. E. (2016). The Science of Conceptual Systems: A Progress Report. *Foundations of Science*, *21*(4), 579–602. doi:10.1007/s10699-015-9425-z

Watts, D. J. (2011). *Everything Is Obvious: *Once You Know the Answer*. Crown Publishing Group.

Weber, M. (1978). Economy and Society: An Outline of Interpretive Sociology (New Ed edition; G. Roth & C. Wittich, Eds.). Berkeley, California: University of California Press.

Weber, M. (1946). *From Max Weber: Essays in Sociology* (H. H. Gerth & C. W. Mills, Trans.). Oxford University Press.

Weber, M. (1994). *Weber: Political Writings*. Cambridge University Press. doi:10.1017/CBO9780511841095

Weber, M. (2001). *The Protestant Ethic and the Spirit of Capitalism* (T. Parsons, Trans.). Routledge.

Wetherill, G. B. (2013). Sampling Inspection and Quality Control. Verlag: Springer.

Wiener, N. (1989). *The Human Use of Human Beings: Cybernetics and Society*. Free Associations Books.

Wilén, N. (2007). *Paradoxes or Strategies in International Governance? The Case of Kosovo*. Regimen Conference. Retrieved from https://repository.uantwerpen.be/docman/irua/cbf2d4/1a86b087.pdf

Wilson, J. Q. (1989). *Bureaucracy: What Government Agencies Do and why They Do it*. Basic Books.

Wilson, W. (1887). The Study of Administration. *Political Science Quarterly*, *2*(2), 197–222. doi:10.2307/2139277 PMID:4591257

Wintgens, L., & Thion, P. (Eds.). (2007). *Legislation in Context: Essays in Legisprudence*. Ashgate Publishing, Ltd.

Wiseman, R. M., Cuevas-Rodríguez, G., & Gomez-Mejia, L. R. (2012). Towards a Social Theory of Agency. *Journal of Management Studies*, *49*(1), 202–222. doi:10.1111/j.1467-6486.2011.01016.x

Witte, E. E. (1942). Administrative Agencies and Statute Lawmaking. *Public Administration Review*, *2*(2), 116–125. doi:10.2307/972284

Wittgenstein, L. (1986). *Philosophical Investigations* (G. E. M. Anscombe, Trans.). Basil Blackwell.

Wollmann, H., & Marcou, G. (Eds.). (2010). *The Provision of Public Services in Europe: Between State, Local Government and Market*. Edward Elgar Publishing. doi:10.4337/9781849807227

Woolley, A. W., Chabris, C. F., Pentland, A., Hashmi, N., & Malone, T. W. (2010). Evidence for a Collective Intelligence Factor in the Performance of Human Groups. *Science*, *330*(6004), 686–688. doi:10.1126/science.1193147 PMID:20929725

World Values Survey Association. (2020). *WVS Database—Findings and Insights*. WVSA. https://www.worldvaluessurvey.org/WVSContents.jsp

Worthington, J. P., Silvertown, J., Cook, L., Cameron, R., Dodd, M., Greenwood, R. M., McConway, K., & Skelton, P. (2012). Evolution MegaLab: A case study in citizen science methods. *Methods in Ecology and Evolution*, *3*(2), 303–309. doi:10.1111/j.2041-210X.2011.00164.x

Wright, S. (1931). Evolution in Mendelian Populations. *Genetics*, *16*(2), 97–159. doi:10.1093/genetics/16.2.97 PMID:17246615

Yesilkagit, K., & van Thiel, S. (2012). Autonomous Agencies and Perceptions of Stakeholder Influence in Parliamentary Democracies. *Journal of Public Administration: Research and Theory*, *22*(1), 101–119. doi:10.1093/jopart/mur001

Zimbardo, P. G. (2008). *The Lucifer Effect: Understanding How Good People Turn Evil*. Random House Trade Paperbacks.

Žižek, S. (2010). *Living in the End Times*. Verso.

Zucker, L. G. (1977). The Role of Institutionalization in Cultural Persistence. *American Sociological Review*, *42*(5), 726–743. doi:10.2307/2094862

About the Author

Mirko Pečarič graduated from the College of the Interior in Ljubljana in 1995 after finishing high school. He obtained a Master of Science and a PhD from the Faculty of Law at the University of Ljubljana in 1998 and passed the national law exam in 2002. In 1998, he began his internship at the Office for Administrative and Home Affairs within the Ministry of the Interior. From 1999 to 2004, he worked as an independent criminal investigation inspector at the Department for Organised Crime in the Ljubljana Police. From 2004 to 2007, he was employed at the National Council of the Republic of Slovenia as the Commission for State Affairs' secretary and then as the Head of the Legal Department within the National Council. While serving as the General Secretary of the University of Ljubljana, he became more involved in the field of higher education. In 2009, he was appointed as an Assistant Professor in the field of administrative law and public administration. In 2013, the Government of the Republic of Slovenia appointed him as the State Secretary at the Ministry of Education, Science and Sport. So far, he has taught courses in Administrative Law, Public Services, Introduction to Law, and the Theory of Public Administration. Since 2021, he has been serving as the dean of the Faculty of Public Administration. He has written a series of legal opinions and requirements for assessing the constitutionality of laws. He is also the author of six monographs and numerous scientific articles.

Index

A

Agency Capture 167
Artificial Intelligence (AI) 13
Autonomous Bodies 108
Autonomy Dimension 128

B

Bureaucracy 18-19, 26, 28, 46, 54, 71, 90, 115-117, 121, 132, 172, 186, 190, 198-199, 235, 238, 240, 291

C

Citizen Wisdom (CW) 262
Coercion 2, 9, 54, 57, 175, 194, 250
Command-and-Control Thinking 55
Competition 28, 40, 120, 135, 149, 153, 155, 175, 181, 190, 256, 285
Complex Adaptive Systems (CAS) 41, 211-212, 214, 216
Complexity Theory 1, 3-4, 13, 15, 37, 52, 97, 105, 121, 140-141, 143, 176, 195, 206, 211-216, 231, 235-241
Cybernetically 37, 52
Cybernetics 31, 67-68, 73, 97, 105, 181, 187, 195, 206-207, 235, 252, 256, 276

D

Dynamic Institutions 22

E

Effectiveness 28, 33-34, 40-41, 60, 66, 68, 83, 87, 96, 110, 115-118, 121, 124-125, 133, 137, 143, 163, 165-166, 170, 177, 183-184, 187, 203, 212, 217-218, 262, 284, 289
Efficiency 5, 9, 23, 25, 33-34, 36, 38-41, 50, 53, 62, 66, 79, 83, 96, 102, 106, 109-110, 115-119, 121, 124-125, 129, 131, 133, 137, 139, 148, 155, 160-163, 165-166, 170, 175, 177, 181-183, 193, 196, 203, 212, 215, 218, 226, 252, 262, 277, 283-285, 289
Endogenous 175
Executive Agencies 40, 43, 50, 108, 120, 136, 155, 160-163, 169
Extra-Governmental Organisations 108

F

Formula 36, 49, 137, 264, 288, 290

G

GA 2, 4
GG 2, 4
Government Corporations 108

H

Holistic Agencies (HAs) 282
Human Essence 104-105

L

Local Government Bodies 108

N

New Public Management (NPM) 83
Non-Departmental Public Bodies 108, 128
Nongovernmental Public Bodies 108

P

Proficiency 264
Public Corporations 108
Public Interest 4, 18, 25, 27, 31, 39-40, 53, 65-66, 71, 76, 84-85, 106, 108, 128, 130-131, 135, 137,

143-144, 147, 149, 154, 158, 185, 195, 200, 230, 248, 251, 270, 274, 288

Q

Quangos 108, 112, 121-124, 145, 150-151, 162-164, 177, 187-189, 285

R

Regulatory Commissions 108

S

Subsidiary Organisations 108
Superforecasters 261, 264
System 1, 3-4, 6-7, 9-16, 18-19, 21, 23, 25-26, 30-32, 34-35, 37-38, 40, 43, 45-48, 53, 55-56, 59-68, 74-76, 78, 84, 87, 92, 94-99, 103, 109-111, 113-117, 125-126, 129, 131-132, 143, 154, 157, 166-169, 173, 175, 177-184, 186-187, 190-219, 221-232, 235, 239, 241-242, 247-249, 252, 257-260, 262-263, 266-276, 278, 280-282, 285, 289
Systemic 1-2, 4-6, 8, 10, 12, 15, 25, 32, 36, 56, 59-66, 68, 74, 81, 97-98, 113, 118, 121, 132, 142-143, 153, 155, 184-185, 193, 195-196, 203, 205, 208, 212, 214-215, 229, 246, 273-275, 284-285
Systems Theory 6, 13, 31-32, 37, 56, 58-60, 62, 66, 98, 105, 121, 145, 179, 181-182, 193-195, 198, 203-205, 207-210, 212-215, 220, 238-239, 255, 258
Systems Thinking 2, 42, 54-55, 66-67, 81, 195, 203, 205, 237

T

Technically 52
Temporal 50, 175
The Contract of Agency 106
Theory of Mind 264, 277, 279-280

U

Unshared Information 261, 279

Publishing Tomorrow's Research Today

Uncover Current Insights and Future Trends in Business & Management
with IGI Global's Cutting-Edge Recommended Books

Print Only, E-Book Only, or Print + E-Book.
Order direct through IGI Global's Online Bookstore at **www.igi-global.com** or through your preferred provider.

Developmental Language Disorders in Childhood and Adolescence
ISBN: 9798369306444
© 2023; 436 pp.
List Price: US$ **230**

The Sustainable Fintech Revolution: Building a Greener Future for Finance
ISBN: 9798369300084
© 2023; 358 pp.
List Price: US$ **250**

Cases on Enhancing Business Sustainability Through Knowledge Management Systems
ISBN: 9781668458594
© 2023; 366 pp.
List Price: US$ **240**

5G, Artificial Intelligence, and Next Generation Internet of Things: Digital Innovation For Green and Sustainable Economies
ISBN: 9781668486344
© 2023; 256 pp.
List Price: US$ **280**

The Use of Artificial Intelligence in Digital Marketing: Competitive Strategies and Tactics
ISBN: 9781668493243
© 2024; 318 pp.
List Price: US$ **250**

AI and Emotional Intelligence for Modern Business Management: Bridging the Gap and Nurturing Success
ISBN: 9798369304181
© 2023; 415 pp.
List Price: US$ **250**

Do you want to stay current on the latest research trends, product announcements, news, and special offers?
Join IGI Global's mailing list to receive customized recommendations, exclusive discounts, and more.
Sign up at: **www.igi-global.com/newsletters.**

Scan the QR Code here to view more related titles in Business & Management.

www.igi-global.com | Sign up at www.igi-global.com/newsletters | facebook.com/igiglobal | twitter.com/igiglobal | linkedin.com/igiglobal

Ensure Quality Research is Introduced to the Academic Community

Become a Reviewer for IGI Global Authored Book Projects

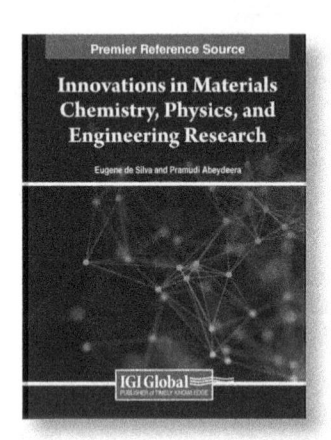

The overall success of an authored book project is dependent on quality and timely manuscript evaluations.

Applications and Inquiries may be sent to:
development@igi-global.com

Applicants must have a doctorate (or equivalent degree) as well as publishing, research, and reviewing experience. Authored Book Evaluators are appointed for one-year terms and are expected to complete at least three evaluations per term. Upon successful completion of this term, evaluators can be considered for an additional term.

If you have a colleague that may be interested in this opportunity, we encourage you to share this information with them.

IGI Global
Publishing Tomorrow's Research Today
www.igi-global.com

IGI Global Open Access Journal Program

Publishing Tomorrow's Research Today
IGI Global's Open Access Journal Program
Including Nearly 200 Peer-Reviewed, Gold (Full) Open Access Journals across IGI Global's Three Academic Subject Areas: Business & Management; Scientific, Technical, and Medical (STM); and Education

Consider Submitting Your Manuscript to One of These Nearly 200 Open Access Journals for to Increase Their Discoverability & Citation Impact

| Web of Science Impact Factor | 6.5 | Web of Science Impact Factor | 4.7 | Web of Science Impact Factor | 3.2 | Web of Science Impact Factor | 2.6 |

JOURNAL OF Organizational and End User Computing

JOURNAL OF Global Information Management

INTERNATIONAL JOURNAL ON Semantic Web and Information Systems

JOURNAL OF Database Management

Choosing IGI Global's Open Access Journal Program Can Greatly Increase the Reach of Your Research

Higher Usage
Open access papers are 2-3 times more likely to be read than non-open access papers.

Higher Download Rates
Open access papers benefit from 89% higher download rates than non-open access papers.

Higher Citation Rates
Open access papers are 47% more likely to be cited than non-open access papers.

Submitting an article to a journal offers an invaluable opportunity for you to share your work with the broader academic community, fostering knowledge dissemination and constructive feedback.

Submit an Article and Browse the IGI Global Call for Papers Pages

We can work with you to find the journal most well-suited for your next research manuscript. For open access publishing support, contact: journaleditor@igi-global.com

Publishing Tomorrow's Research Today
IGI Global e-Book Collection

Including Essential Reference Books Within Three Fundamental Academic Areas

Business & Management
Scientific, Technical, & Medical (STM)
Education

- Acquisition options include Perpetual, Subscription, and Read & Publish
- No Additional Charge for Multi-User Licensing
- No Maintenance, Hosting, or Archiving Fees
- Continually Enhanced Accessibility Compliance Features (WCAG)

| Over 150,000+ Chapters | Contributions From 200,000+ Scholars Worldwide | More Than 1,000,000+ Citations | Majority of e-Books Indexed in Web of Science & Scopus | Consists of Tomorrow's Research Available Today! |

Recommended Titles from our e-Book Collection

Innovation Capabilities and Entrepreneurial Opportunities of Smart Working
ISBN: 9781799887973

Advanced Applications of Generative AI and Natural Language Processing Models
ISBN: 9798369305027

Using Influencer Marketing as a Digital Business Strategy
ISBN: 9798369305515

Human-Centered Approaches in Industry 5.0
ISBN: 9798369326473

Modeling and Monitoring Extreme Hydrometeorological Events
ISBN: 9781668487716

Data-Driven Intelligent Business Sustainability
ISBN: 9798369300497

Information Logistics for Organizational Empowerment and Effective Supply Chain Management
ISBN: 9798369301593

Data Envelopment Analysis (DEA) Methods for Maximizing Efficiency
ISBN: 9798369302552

Request More Information, or Recommend the IGI Global e-Book Collection to Your Institution's Librarian

For More Information or to Request a Free Trial, Contact IGI Global's e-Collections Team: eresources@igi-global.com | 1-866-342-6657 ext. 100 | 717-533-8845 ext. 100